Music Education in the Caribbean and Latin America

Music Education in the Caribbean and Latin America

A Comprehensive Guide

Edited by Raymond Torres-Santos

Published in partnership with the
National Association for Music Education

ROWMAN & LITTLEFIELD
Lanham • Boulder • New York • London

Published in partnership with the National Association for Music Education

Published by Rowman & Littlefield
A wholly owned subsidiary of The Rowman & Littlefield Publishing Group, Inc.
4501 Forbes Boulevard, Suite 200, Lanham, Maryland 20706
www.rowman.com

Unit A, Whitacre Mews, 26-34 Stannary Street, London SE11 4AB

British Library Cataloguing in Publication Information Available

Library of Congress Cataloging-in-Publication Data

Names: Torres-Santos, Raymond, 1958-
Title: Music education in the Caribbean and Latin America : a comprehensive guide / edited by Raymond Torres-Santos.
Description: Lanham : Rowman & Littlefield, [2017] | Includes index.
Identifiers: LCCN 2016040823 (print) | LCCN 2016041377 (ebook) | ISBN 9781475833171 (cloth : alk. paper) | ISBN 9781475833188 (pbk. : alk. paper) | ISBN 9781475833195 (Electronic)
Subjects: LCSH: Music–Instruction and study–Latin America. | Music–Instruction and study–Caribbean Area.
Classification: LCC MT3.L37 M87 2017 (print) | LCC MT3.L37 (ebook) | DDC 780.71/08–dc23 LC record available at https://lccn.loc.gov/2016040823

Printed in the United States of America

To my wife Madelyn and my sons Jamil and Xavier

Contents

Introduction

Raymond Torres-Santos

Music is at the cultural heart of the different countries in the Caribbean and Latin America.

These countries enjoy a rich natural environment that includes the rhythmic streams of rivers and the unending flow of the ocean, the musical sounds orchestrated by its spectacular array of birds and animals, and the seductive sounds of the forests. This enriched ecological magnificence was captured by its original inhabitants way before 1492.

For the past five centuries, Caribbean and Latin American music and its different variations have thrived! Its uniqueness comes, of course, from influences of the pre-Columbian, European, and African cultures, which in turn made possible the development of new music techniques, approaches, instruments, and materials. The musical offerings in the Caribbean Islands and Latin American countries are so varied that although they may share some similar musical characteristics, there are also many styles, musical systems, instruments, and forms unique to each individual island and country.

The same is true in the music education field in the Caribbean and Latin America. Music education systems, whether formal or informal, are unique from place to place. Those educational systems have also evolved since the time of the Amerindians to our times; transformations that have been subject to racial, cultural, social, and technological changes throughout the years.

As music trends are still evolving, it must be noted that by the nineteenth century the music that represented the group of islands and countries that comprise the region had reached a defined level of uniqueness. Thus, each country had a defined music perspective.

During the past centuries, and particularly in the twentieth and the beginning of the twenty-first centuries, music education has been successful in developing a strong legacy of musicians, composers, conductors, and educators who have contributed to the world of music in general. In fact, at the end of the twentieth century much attention was given to the music education system in Venezuela. This attention propelled the idea to present the development of the music education of the Caribbean and Latin America to music educators, learners, and practitioners around the world.

Venezuela's *El Sistema*—a special training program focused on narrowing the gap between music and social justice—has been praised by distinguished musicians such as Plácido Domingo and Simon Rattle, among many others, as the most important program in classical music, and many distinguished young musicians had emerged from it, such as distinguished Venezuelan conductor Gustavo Dudamel. It is no coincidence that many countries, from Scotland to Singapore, have emulated, in some form, the Venezuelan system. Yet it represents just one perspective on music education systems in the region.

After reviewing the available literature on music education in the Caribbean and Latin America, it was evident that although there were books on material and genres as well as lessons and activities, music education journals or publications had not fully addressed the richness, uniqueness, and depth of the development of music education in the Caribbean and Latin America. It was apparent that there was a need for a book that could make this information available to music educators in the United States and around the world.

I am pleased that the National Association of Music Education (NAfME) embraced my proposal to produce such a book. I am grateful to the original NAfME director of publications, Frances Polnick, and her assistant Caroline Arlington for their support in producing this publication.

As this was a challenging but yet an exciting endeavor, the initial step was to identify scholars with enough experience and knowledge on the different subjects and invite them to write a chapter representing each island and country. My first source of contacts was the International Society of Music Education as well as colleagues from around the world who helped spread the word. After a call for chapters was distributed, I received many remarkable proposals. It is an honor that twenty-two respected authors from the most important Caribbean islands and Latin American countries accepted the task.

The islands represented in our publication include Cuba, Dominican Republic, Puerto Rico, Jamaica, Trinidad and Tobago; as for Central American countries, we include chapters on Mexico, El Salvador, Costa Rica, Guatemala, Nicaragua, and Panama. There are also chapters on the music education in the South American countries of Argentina, Brazil, Chile, Colombia, Ecuador, Peru, Uruguay, and Venezuela.

Thus, we present *Music Education in the Caribbean and Latin America* as a comprehensive guide on the music education of these countries within a historical, social, and cultural approach. Topics addressed in each chapter include: the early days; music education in Roman Catholic education systems and convents; Protestant education systems; public school music programs; cultural life; music in the community; teacher training; private teaching; conservatories and other music education institutions; music in the higher education curriculum; instrumental and vocal music; festivals and competitions; teacher education and curriculum development; and professional organizations.

The book is geared to meet the following goals and objectives as outlined by the NAfME: to advance music education by promoting the understanding and making of music by all; to build strength and promote diversity in the profession by representing a wide spectrum of people and cultures, abilities, economic backgrounds, and gender identities; and to provide music education and education leaders with engaging professional development opportunities, dynamic and effective resources, materials, publications, and learning opportunities to support best practices and serve the need of students.

The target audience for this book includes educators, scholars, students, and practitioners of music education around the world. It will be marketed to academic libraries, multicultural educators and centers, music education departments and societies in the United States, as well as similar organizations in South America, the Caribbean, and throughout the world. A book of this nature will certainly be a contribution to the educational enterprise worldwide.

But the real purpose is to celebrate music! Music celebration is not only for scholars. Mankind celebrates music! We live music, we cherish music, and by sharing the thoughts and knowledge of twenty-two distinguished authors, we hope that any reader will become acquainted with the marvelous and varied Caribbean and Latin American musical world.

I am grateful to Dr. Ruth E. Lugo and Dr. Anisia B. Quiñones for their assistance during the initial research and translation of the chapters of this book. I also wish to express my appreciation to Carlie Wall and Thomas F. Koerner of Rowman & Littlefield for their support, help, and patience as this work progressed.

Raymond Torres-Santos, PhD
General Editor

Part I

Caribbean

Chapter One

Cuba

Ricardo N. López León and Oswaldo Lorenzo Quiles

INTRODUCTION

From the geopolitical perspective, the Caribbean is divided in the Greater and Lesser Antilles. Among Puerto Rico, Dominican Republic, and Jamaica, Cuba is the largest of the Greater Antilles for its territorial extension. All of these islands have received, in more or less degree, immigrants from different ethnic groups who have contributed to the development of their identities. Nevertheless, each one has its own cultural characteristics that distinguish them.

In the case of Cuba, special attention needs to be given to the particular social interchange affecting its society and culture throughout the evolution of becoming a nation. Allende (1992) reminds us that it is not feasible to separate the cultural development of a society from social processes when the intention is to investigate its arts manifestations. Thus, music should not be seen as a product isolated from society.

Cuban music has received many influences and, instead of blindly accepting them from their neighboring countries, those influences have been transformed into autochthonous entities, *lo cubano*, becoming a seal of authenticity. Therefore, it is necessary to examine education as a vehicle to perpetuate culture as well as music as a subject of study and practice. Cuba has solidified its music education, utilizing the autochthonous music without undermining other foreign influences, which continues to strengthen its musical institutions and manifestations (Fernandez-Cueto, 2008).

Undoubtedly, the cultural exchanges influence the development of music listening and learning. Nevertheless, it is naive to assume that music education is acquired by formal educational venues only. Some scholars such as Vila (1998) believe that informal approaches can also promote music education. While formal education rests on planned, regulated, and didactic structures guided by objectives in the teaching and learning process, informal education relies on teaching and learning outside of the formality of the classroom without a sense of planning and intention, using experiences and events of the nature of sports, work, leisure, and more (Lorenzo & Rodríguez, 2005). In reference to music, the process of teaching music education during the beginning of the Antillean civilization was informal given its tradition of transmitting music by imitation or in an oral tradition (Betancur, 1999).

The Cuban contribution to the international musical scenery is a product of the cultural cohesion of its society. Since the beginning of the nineteenth century, music education in Cuba had its own identity (Carpentier, 1988). This is evident by the early concept of native music, the creation of a planning methodology of exercises according to the characteristics of the Cuban music style *son*, the publications of Cuban children songs of the past century, and the use of Cuban music for introducing musical skills in music education (Barceló, 2007).

Music can have various functions, which may include aesthetic pleasure, entertainment, communication, symbolic representation, and physical response; imposing conformity and social norms; validating institutions and religious rituals; contributing to the continuity, stability, and integration of society; and emotional expression.

Wilson (1981) points out that if one wants music education to be effective and relevant, the cultural context at which it is developed and the society it serves needs to be taken seriously. To this end, the significance of describing the history of its educational practices has acquired significant value. In the case of music in Cuba and its teaching at different phases in history, this writing attempts to give justice to the works of Cuban musicians and educators, by birth or adopted, who have influenced and marked their norms in this Caribbean region.

PRE-HISPANIC INFLUENCE

Human presence in Cuba dates to approximately six thousand years ago. The origin of its first natives is unsure, although the majority of theories indicate that natives arrived to the northern coasts of South America through the Antilles. There were three indigenous groups: *Guanajatabeyes*, *Siboneyes*, and *Taínos*. The first group belonged to a primitive culture of hunters, fishermen, and harvesters. They dealt with the arrival of another indigenous group, the *Siboneyes*, who were more advanced and were skillful in craftsmanship. Both groups settled on the island until the fifth century AD, when a group from the Orinoco River, the Taínos, invaded the region. These were superior for their cultural development, and they settled in Cuba.

Before the conquest and colonization of Cuba by Spaniards, the indigenous population had not reached a comparable development like other similar pre-Columbine cultures such as the Mayans, Aztecs, and the Incas. On the contrary, these native cultures present typical characteristics of the Paleolithic Era. However, the Taíno culture, considered the most socially advanced of the three groups, left most of the majority of their musical signs on Cuban soil (Le Riverend, 1989). On the other hand, authors such as Neira (2005) and Sánchez (2007) believe that the Taíno legacy did not cover much given the rapid disappearance of this native group after the beginning of the Spanish colonization.

When searching for early music and teaching in Cuba, all that can be affirmed is subject to the perspectives of the chronicles according to Gonzalo Fernandez de Oviedo, Fray Bartolomé de las Casas, and López de Gomara (Thompson, 1993). According to them, one of the most popular musical manifestations for the Taínos was their religious rituals known as *areyto*. In the center square of the village, the Taínos danced and sang accompanied by the rhythm of drums, during long hours, and under the direction of a master of ceremonies or *tequina*, who according to chroniclers was not the *cacique* (chief of the tribe) or the *bohique* (witch). This term has been translated as *teacher* and could have been a respected man or a woman within the tribe. This person would set up the rhythm and establish the choir during the ritual.

The themes of their songs and dances were about the *cacique*'s ancestry, their heroic stories, and their history. Its purpose was to transmit their historical knowledge to the new generations. The best methodology for learning and reaffirming their heritage to the tribe was communicating it verbally. According to Santiago (2008), one of the best-kept records about Taíno music appeared in the *General and Natural History of the Indias* (*Historia general y natural de Indias*), which best narrates the ritual objectively from Gonzalo Fernandez de Oviedo's perspective. Oviedo was a Spanish historian and chronicler of Indias, who, after the discovery, recorded as an observer the *areyto* of the Taíno of the Dominican Republic. He described it as follows: "These people had a fine way to remember the good things from the past; in their singing and dancing, which they called *Areyto*, they demonstrated their happiness. They would dance holding their hands and sometimes they would connect using their elbows and moving together, one leading and the others moving back and forth with rhythm."

According to Fernández (2001) the chronicler Fernandez de Oviedo affirmed that the natives were great dancers and sang together without dissonance or drastic changes in the rhythm during the *areyto* rituals. In reference to the Taíno instruments, Oviedo—quoted by Santiago (2008)—explained: "Sometimes with the singing, they mixed an *atambor*, a wooden round drum, hollow and concave, and as wide as a man, more or less; sounding like the deaf drums made by the Africans; without a leather cover but with small holes and rays that slid in the hollow area. The drum stands on the ground because it is difficult to be played in the air."

Bartolomé de las Casas also referred to the rough wooden *atabales* as instruments representative of the Taínos. He added that the instruments had some smooth bells, made of fragile wood, with some small stones inside.

On the other hand, Cristobal Díaz Ayala (1930–) in "Cuba Music, from the Areyto to the New Trova" (1981), demonstrated that natives already had among their instruments, in addition to the *Mayohuacan*—that is, the hollow drum without cover that Oviedo makes reference to—some *olivas sonoras* (sonorous olives), *guamos* or *trompas de caracol* (snail horns) called *Cobo* (Strombus Gigans), and the trumpets, *guamos*, or *botutos*, which have transcended to our time, which is acoustically similar to the horns used in the Old World and Asia.

Some of the research demonstrates the variety of sounds that these produced. For example, Rodríguez and Lorenzo (2005) describe a trumpet elaborated with the shell *Cassis tuberose*. According to these scholars, this shell can produce musical notes C1 and D-flat 1. This instrument, elaborated with *Charonia tritonis nobilis*, will produce notes in E-flat 1, B-flat first octave, C1, and D-flat 1. Other types used for its elaboration were the *Strombus sp*, *Xancus angulatus*, and *Charonia variegate y Cassis*.

However, according to Alejo Carpentier (1988), "We have not encountered an instrument that can produce a scale that we could establish a reveling relation with native music." Moreover, Alvar Nuñez Cabeza de Vaca, at the time of narrating the terrible hurricane he lived through in a town in Trinidad during 1527, indicated that while the storm wind sounds were heard, the Indians would make "noise with bells, flutes and tambourines" until the storm stopped.

For Vizcaino (2003), the most important of all the musical instruments used by these groups were, without a doubt, the *maraca*, made of squash or gourd, and, quoting from Díaz Ayala (1981), "the only native instrument, in addition to the human voice, that accompanied us for almost five hundred years." In addition, the Cuban *criollos* (Europeans born in Cuba) began using one maraca in each hand, complementing its rhythm and contrasting with the Taínos' tradition of using one maraca only.

DISCOVERY AND COLONIZATION

The island of Cuba was discovered by Christopher Columbus in 1492 on his first trip to the New World. It was not until 1509 that Diego Velázquez was in charge of the colonization of Cuba. He disembarked with a group of men under his command on the east side region of the island (Le Riverend, 1989). Among the *conquistadores* (conquerors), under his command there were three musicians by the names of Alonso Morón (vihuela player), Bartolomé Porras (singer), and Juan Ortíz, better known as Ortíz the Musician (viola and vihuela player). Ortíz was also considered a dance teacher. He later relocated to Mexico, where he founded a school of music (Hernández and Izquierdo, 2003). These musicians, along with others from the military, were the first performers of Spanish music in Cuba.

Spaniards brought with them a heterogeneous culture, which came from different towns that constituted Spain at that time, a nation rich with many cultures such as the Muslims, Egyptians, Jews, and Europeans (Leyva, 2002). In addition, the rhythm and dances from all regions of Spain were present in popular festivities and musical manifestations. Other artistic expressions such as theater, poetry, and literature were becoming known through the consolidation of Castilian Spanish as the official national language. The process of Spanish colonization into Cuba lasted four centuries, between the sixteenth and nineteenth, and explains some of the key elements in understanding the current situation concerning music education in this country.

Since the conquest of Cuba in 1520, the Catholic Church was responsible for educating the population. The first educational programs were parochial and covered the basic notion of reading, writing, and arithmetic, in addition to the teachings of Catholicism (Ferraz and Calero, 2007). This situation was prolonged until the end of the nineteenth century. Díaz Ayala (2006) suggests that the first document of importance regarding music education in Cuba is the constitutional decree for the chapel's music of the Santiago de Cuba Cathedral, founded in 1682. This officially recognized, for the first time, the importance of organizing and promoting music education, and appointed Domingo Flores as the first organ and voice teacher for the clergy and children.

Since its first encounter with the natives, the Catholic Church recognized the power of music as an effective method in the acculturation and socialization of the conquered towns in the New World. Bartolomé de las

Casas, one of the chroniclers of the Indias, proposed in 1531 the use of the *areyto* to facilitate the evangelization of the aborigines. Certainly the effort to spread out the Catholic faith in the New World brought the proliferation and diffusion of music education as the sacred festivities were enriched, and at the time, facilitated the evangelization of the Indians (De Couve and Dal Pino, 2006).

Among the religious orders that taught the indigenous to sing and play musical instruments were the Franciscan, Jesuit, Dominican, Augustinian, and the Carmelite missionaries. Subsequently a reduction in the clergy opened up the possibility to allow laymen to carry out musical duties. By this time the majority of the musicians on the island were of African ancestry. Therefore, this opportunity allowed the entry of Afro-Cuban music elements to the existing European music paradigm and marked the beginning of a national music education in Cuba (Díaz Ayala, 2006). Claro (1970) states that the musical activity during the second half of the eighteenth century shows an intensity in interpretation and music creativity when the Cathedral in La Habana, the Real Pontifical University of San Cristobal, San Basilio the Great Seminary, and the music chapel of the Cathedral of Santiago of Cuba were founded.

The educational process of the Catholic clergy, without any doubt, was responsible between the seventeenth and eighteenth centuries to train good musicians and prepare better human beings. This was the case of Esteban Salas y Castro (1725–1803), who began his educational journey with much interest in 1764 at the Cathedral of Santiago. For Carpentier (1988), with the musical and pedagogical work of Salas, this cathedral became a real conservatory from which many musicians were formed in the nineteenth century. This Cuban musician, a violin virtuoso, in addition to realizing various functions first as a singer and organist in the *Parroquia Mayor* and then in the Cathedral of La Habana, also taught music to the altar boys and directed chorus and different instrumental groups during various times. Claro (1970) reminds us that, in addition to the Cathedral of La Habana, his musical activity during the period was shared among the Real Pontifical University of San Cristobal, the Seminary of San Basilio the Great, and the music chapel of the Cathedral of Santiago, Cuba.

Maestro Salas was a great composer of Christmas carols, masses, and services. According to Vega (2008) his musical knowledge was superior to others in the Caribbean for his mastery in the art of the fugue and counterpoint. Unfortunately, a portion of his works was destroyed as a result of a fire during an English attack in 1762. On the other hand, his musical legacy can be found in musical catalogs in the country. The humility and modesty of this great figure of the music in Cuba is revealed in his multifaceted role as professor of music, philosophy, and morality at the San Basilio Magno Seminar *ad honorem* (without pay) (Cartaya, 1995). Salas introduced serious music in Cuba and established a demarcation between coexisting popular music without overlooking the evolution of both trends (Carpentier, 1988). Soon the musical-cultural influence from the groups of African slaves arriving in Cuba intertwined its rhythms with sacred music and profane music, which in those days was gaining popular acceptance.

ARRIVAL OF AFRICAN SLAVES

The African presence has left its contribution and strong influence on the cultures of Latin America. Most of the popular genres listened, sung, and danced in America have their roots in the traditions of the African communities that arrived to the continent on and before the sixteenth century. Through numerous processes of mixing, appropriation, and marketing, various rhythms have converted into national symbols, such as the Cuban *batá*, the Brazilian *samba*, or the Puerto Rican *bomba*, among other more contemporaneous musical manifestations. All of these rhythms were testimony of the daily life and illusions and feelings of diverse groups and generations of Afro-Caribbeans (Allende, 2008).

Prior to the discovery of the Americas, there already existed black slaves in Europe, taken by Portuguese, Spaniards, and other slave-trafficking nations. It is apparent that the cultural influence of Africa into the New World began before the conception of the new global map. Even for the African ethnic groups, which preserved primary forms of their vision and world conceptualities, significant cultural changes were unavoidable (Neira, 2005).

The swing from the endogamous and exogamous between Africans and Caribbeans was official in 1512, when the entrance of black slaves into Cuba was legally allowed. According to Betancur (1999) the contribution of the African ethnic groups was decisive in the formation of Cuban nationality. More specifically, for the Bantu and the Yoruba, for being cultures without knowledge of writing, their musical tradition was the principal venue for cultural preservation.

The rich oral African traditions are perpetuated in America, and in the same manner the promontory of its ancestral mythology are immortalized with the polytheist pantheon of black goddesses, and the ceremonials where songs and dances as well as the sacred language of the drum are channels of communications, which when exposed to the Western civilization created a syncretism evident even in our time. The strength of African music manifests from how important this artistic manifestation is for their religion. In the case of the spirituality of the Yoruba religion, music by itself is the central axis of the cult.

The longevity of these religious practices is not comparable to the Christian repertoire. The Yoruba had a complex array of sung liturgies, dances, or chants for all their *Orichas* (deities). The variety of rhythmic patterns with African influence adapted to occidental music paradigms were determinant in many of the musical conceptions already present in the Caribbean geographical region.

The conscious perspective of music education of this culture was conceived in its practice from a vocal and organological perspective. Basically, the execution of percussion instruments represented the way of acquiring the musical contexts and contents in a social and educational manner. Examples of the conservation of songs and existing rituals in countries such as Cuba and Brazil owe their importance to the cultural preservation by means of the teaching of future generations (Neira, 2005). As a complement of this legacy, the skills of corporal expression, deeply rooted in the culture, would be acquired by traditional means and as an immediate natural reaction (Quintero, 2009).

The construction of musical instruments also formed an intrinsic part of the rituals; many times emerging from the tree itself, which would serve as raw material particularly for the *bata* drums. The teaching of the interpretation of the playing of those drums as an example of the methodological characteristics of music education organilogically tied to the African culture and the folk-popular domain is worth mentioning. Given the interpretation of the *okonkolo* drum as the most simple, it is the easiest to be learned. This is followed by the *itotele* and then the *iya*, which is the most complex. One of the ways to learn is that the pupil places the drum on his legs and the teacher stands next to him/her and beats the *enu* and the *cha cha* pattern over the shoulder of the pupil.

These *toques* (rhythmic patterns) ought to be imitated by the drumming apprentice. This technique is applied to the three different drums. In addition, the use of the *nemotécnica* (mnemonics) technique contributes to the learning process of the drumming rhythmic patterns from a rhythmic-timbre perspective with the repetition of certain syllables such as jin-ka, kin-kan, kin-ta, kin-ki-ta, ki-la (Eli, 2002). It is through the combination of these patterns that the different levels of timbral registry are conveyed to the future drummer, which contribute to the memorization and eventual performance as a vehicle of expression.

The arrival of black immigrants into the island of Cuba as a measure to substitute as slaves the ephemeral indigenous working-class force was in place since the beginning of colonization. On the other hand, at the end of the eighteenth century, free black men and women from Haiti, who obtained its independence from France in 1789, arrived in Cuba bringing with them the French influence and libertarian experiences. This situation, in addition to the arrival of immigrant groups from China, which joined the working-class force, provided the ground for a new acculturation experimented in Cuba during the nineteenth century, and which is represented by the *conga* line dance so intrinsic to Cubans today (Hernández and Izquierdo, 2003).

According to Díaz Ayala (2006), due to the vigorous sugarcane industry, another slave modality developed when 150,000 Chinese arrived between 1848 and 1874 as a result of the prohibition of the black slave trade because of their abolition.

A working contract was provided to this new immigrant group, and once they completed their contract, they would be free to do as they pleased. The contribution of the Chinese population to Cuban society and culture was such that they also participated in the wars for independence, founded theaters for their music, and worked extensively in the culinary markets. The so-called *trompeta china* (Chinese trumpet), used in the *conga* line dance, was probably brought by them.

FIRST PART OF THE NINETEENTH CENTURY

In the seventeenth century, reputable musicians, who offered their services as performers and teachers, began to settle in Cuba. Music education was taking place informally during this period. Moreover, the proliferation of musical newspapers began with the first issue of *El filarmónico musical*, published in La Habana in 1812. It had a didactic purpose and was used to promote music. Hundreds of these journals existed between 1812 and 1902 (Díaz Ayala, 2006). Nevertheless, it was not until the end of the nineteenth century that music education began to emerge within more structured and organized institutions.

An event described by Carpentier (1988) highlights the arrival in Santiago of a forte piano in 1810 and the foundation of the first music academy in 1814. This institution provided services to anyone interested in developing as an instrumentalist or singer, the piano being the instrument of preference. Later in 1816 music studies on the island became evident with the foundation of the Music Academy of Santa Cecilia under the direction of French musician Juan Federico Edelmann Jr. (1795–1848), who after a prominent career as a soloist settled in Cuba (Fernández-Cueto, 2008). As a significant contribution to the cultural musical life of the country, Maestro Edelmann founded, in 1836, the first editorial with the purpose of disseminating and publishing works of Cuban composers.

Fernández-Cueto (2008) points out that during the beginning of the nineteenth century, pianists of Italian and Spanish descent lived on the island too and, even though they were not working as professionals, dedicated themselves to teaching in music institutions and in their own residences. Among some of those teachers educated in Europe before coming to Cuba to teach are Juan París, Dolores Espadero, José Miró y Maragliano, and Marescotti.

Some of Edelmann's most prominent students included Manuel Saumell, Pablo Desvernine, and Fernando Aritzi, whose educational careers began under the guidance of their distinguished maestro. At the end of the nineteenth century, the education of future pianists and music educators was the responsibility of Maestro Edelmann and his mentees who founded two similar piano schools. It is a known fact that before Ignacio Cervantes and Manuel Saumell no one had any knowledge of Cuban pianists. These opened the path to many others leading to the figure and sublime work of Ernesto Lecuona in the next century (Fernández-Cueto, 2008).

Thirty-seven years after the death of Maestro Edelmann, another foreigner continued his work in music education in Cuba: Dutch pianist and composer Hubert de Blanck (Holland, 1856 to Cuba, 1932). After establishing in La Habana, he founded in 1885 a Conservatory of Music and Declaim, the first one of its type in terms of methodology and organization, skills he acquired during his prior experiences abroad as a piano professor at the New York College of Music. A circle of music intellectuals collaborated with de Blanck on this endeavor. Figures such as Luis Casas Romero (1882–1950) taught flute, and pianist Jose Echaniz Sr. (1860–1926), and other renowned professors of different instruments and technical specialties, continued their vocation in developing music education (Cruz, 2008). Another professor recruited as part of the new conservatory was Dr. Guillermo Tomás (1856–1933), who founded in 1899 and directed the Municipal Band of La Habana for three years.

The scope of military bands provided the opportunity for the gestation of musicians, especially the underserved and poor, who received modest funds for their performance. Many of the members of these bands, after they completed their services, occupied themselves as music educators in their respective communities (Díaz Ayala, 2006). They were versatile with their rifles as well as their instruments. A good example was Luis Casas Romero (1882–1950), a soldier-musician who fought in the independence war with José Martí in 1895. Once he completed his services for his country, he founded and directed the children's band of forty-five members under the age of fourteen in Camagüey.

Apparently during the conflicts Cuban society experienced at the end of the nineteenth century (1895 and 1898), musical productions and concerts were put on hold. Nevertheless, authors such as Mena (1999) describe the musical environment as very active during this period, highlighted by the production of masterpieces of different genres and the presentation of many public concerts.

In this manner the nineteenth century comes to an end and presents the beginning of the twentieth century with drums signaling the Spanish-American War of 1898 and announcing a change of sovereignty that lasted a short time. At this moment a new educational policy, gestated in the United States, permeated throughout all Cuban institutions.

TWENTIETH CENTURY

Within the school context, in 1901 music education was divided into the six grades of elementary school. The program included basic knowledge and simplified concepts of *solfège* and music theory, in addition to singing as soloist and various voices as designed by musicians and educators Guillermo Tomás (1856–1933), Emilio Agramante (1844–1916), and Hubert de Blank (1856–1932) (Sánchez, 2004). Subsequently, in 1902 the program was abolished, but other institutions of music education contributed to the increase of other spaces dedicated to music (Barceló, 2007). The inauguration of the Municipal Conservatory of La Habana—today known as the Amadeo Roldán Conservatory—the first institution that provided free tuition and was devoted to the teaching of music, attests to the direction music education was moving toward. Other private institutions of higher education were gaining prestige during the first decades of the nineteenth century. The conservatories Ramona Sicardó, Alberto Falcón, Carlos Alfredo Peyrellade, Benjamín Orbon, Fernando Carnier, and María Jones de Castro generally had academies in other parts of the country.

In Calero, quoted by Díaz Ayala (2006), the author mentions a systematic description of the structures in place for music education in Cuba in 1929 and allocates 161 conservatories and music academies in addition to seven academies of bel canto.

The teaching and artistic offerings at the María Jones de Castro Conservatory were distinguished for the dynamic and advanced academic courses taught by a distinguished international and local faculty (Fernández-Cueto, 2008). Of great interest was the anatomy of the arm for piano students. The study of the biomechanical function of the arm, based on orthopedic concepts of the time, represented a milestone, not only for the novel vision of piano techniques but also for the serious reflection upon pedagogical methods for other musical instruments. Another one of professor Jones de Castro's successes was the commission awarded to prominent composer Carlos Berbolla to create a repertoire of Cuban music for piano didactic purposes. The culmination of Berbolla's work would be known as *Mis primeras síncopas* and the *Rítmicas cubanas*.

In 1922, a government school with a new plan of study emerged. It included singing within physical education. A new plan of studies in 1926 maintained the same focus. It is important to mention that the Ministry of Education institutionalized the position of music education at the end of the third decade of the twentieth century, and it was in force until 1960. Teachers occupied in these positions were educated in conservatories and music academies. Usually they studied as teachers in Normal Schools (liberal arts institutions), from kindergarten and so on, in parallel with their music formation (Sanchez, personal communication, La Habana, Cuba, July 2009).

During the first half of the twentieth century, methodologies came from Europe and the United States, countries that dominated music education in Cuba. According to Chavez and Rodríguez, cited by Barceló (2007), there were two pedagogical trends: the first refers to educators who adopted the artistic methodology from abroad; and the second, those who supported a national pedagogy based on the Cuban tradition. Nevertheless, it was not until 1939 that the existence of a systematic application of music education in the public schools could be affirmed, specifically in elementary schools that adopted the model from the United States called the New School, which was student centered.

During this period the figures of Joaquín Rodríguez Lanza and César Pérez Sentenat emerged. They developed two music programs to be implemented in the public schools. Rodríguez Lanza stressed his educational proposal for singing via the creation of choral groups aimed at the development of the popular culture. On the other hand, Pérez Sentenat included, in addition to singing, the playing of musical instruments, ear development, rhythm, and reading music utilizing strategies for the instruction of theory and practice within the subject areas of music history and rhythmic band, among others (Barceló, 2007).

The term *music education* became popular during the decades of the 1940s and 1950s. The designation of specialized educators and the implementation of their thematic curriculum in singing (hymn and marches), exercises, and rhythmic groups, basic elements of theory, *solfège*, and music appreciation secured the difference between conceptual and musical instruction during this period. However, it did not happen in all public schools. Urban schools were more prominent and had more access to these types of programs.

Any historical review of Cuba cannot overlook the fact that, until 1959, this country underwent very active political changes. Since the Hispanic-American War to the earliest days of the twentieth century, Cuban government experimented some instability because of the conflicts with Spain at the beginning and later with the United States. After the installation of the first republic in 1911, the changes of commanders in the government affected the progress made in music education on the island. The last of these governments was under the leadership of President Fulgencio Batista, who lost to Fidel Castro. Castro's revolution received the support from the Cuban population and abroad. Once Batista was deported from the country, Castro accepted the presidency of Cuba and implemented a socialist government.

After assuming his presidency, one of the priorities of Castro's government was to develop educational projects. Different sectors of the Cuban society implemented, at a national level, a project to combat illiteracy. Educators did not necessarily coordinate this project. Popular music composers of the stature of Silvio Rodríguez (1946–) were part of the *Brigadas de alfabetización* (literacy brigades).

The new revolutionary government systematized education at all schools in the country. Nevertheless, since 1880 classrooms had been available for teaching children from four to five years old. North American teachers who promoted child development prior to primary school founded the majority of these schools. Subsequently in the decade of the 1940s, pre-primary schools were created within the official educational system. However, the poor availability of well-prepared teachers for primary grades permitted that some teaching personnel be allowed to teach this population of students after just having a degree from a Normal School (liberal arts institution).

In addition, and as part of this effort from the country, in December of 1959 ten thousand classrooms were built in the rural areas, mobile libraries were created, and all parochial schools were nationalized. There is no doubt that during the decade of the 1960s transcendental changes in the educational Cuban system took place (Viciedo, 2005).

In 1960 specialties in the arts were eliminated, and 1965 began the experimentation with courses in music education by radio to reinforce the teacher's delivery in the classroom. The program was compulsory for the whole island in 1975 and was sustained at all provinces until 1989; in some provinces it lasted until the middle of the 1990s (Sanchez, personal communication, La Habana, Cuba, July 2009).

One of the successes, not too common, in the education renewal of the postrevolutionary stage was the interest in music education at very early ages, which proved to have scientific results in the near future. Also, childcare centers were created in response to the demand of women workers who needed places to leave their children. To fulfill this demand, childhood education as a career was created, and the formal and informal education was professionalized. In the curricula of music education, pedagogical studies were part of the education process (Mulet Artigas, 1999).

The contribution of Rosa Delgado Caraballo (1911–2008) needs to be recognized as a symbol of commitment to music education given her role as a pioneer and teacher of childhood education before the revolution. This distinguished teacher, from a rural upbringing born in San Juan and Martínez, needed to deal with adversity in order to create institutions such as the Conservatory of Montegú in the city of Pinar del Río. Her perseverance and will enabled her to become a piano teacher at the center where she learned her first notes at the age of fifteen. In addition, she composed children songs, achieving one hundred school songs and demonstrating her music skills and her vocation for teaching.

Her reputation was so known that parents entrusted her to the education of their children at kindergarten. Her childhood education institution aimed to awaken the interest and taste for music using innovative teaching methods. Rosa Delgado earned her degree in piano, theory, and *solfège* in 1931. Her trademark of working with children employed a methodology whereby they learned music before they learned to read and write. That way she gave fame and recognition to the musical kindergarten of San Juan and Martínez.

This methodology consisted of matching each note with a symbol. After children would associate the note with the symbol they were able to read the scores by using the analogies of the symbols. In order to accomplish this goal, professor Delgado used a cards system, which by visual association and audio perception students identified musical notes. For example, she would use a card with a drawing of a cat to identify pitch E, a street lamp for pitch F, a sun for pitch G, a clock for pitch D, and so on for all notes. Through young children she applied the knowledge of the new pedagogical European reforms of the eighteenth century, in particular that of Juan A. Comenio (1592–1670) and Juan Enrique Pestalozzi (1746–1827), as well as the educational thought of the nineteenth century of José de la Luz y Caballero (1880–1862) and José Martí (1853–1895).

For Delgado, the child was the center of the music learning process. This music educator composed the hymn of Pinal del Río in 1942, her first grand march. She also composed the march for the graduating class of 1946 and the hymn of San Juan y Martínez, for which she composed the lyrics and music on the same day and premiered it on February 21, 1949, commemorating the fire of San Juan y Martínez. These compositions and the ones for children were the most significant production of composer and educator Rosa Delgado. Nonetheless, it was not until 1948 that she was recognized publicly by the president of the Pinar del Río Committee, Efraín Andreu, and also by its vice president Abel Prieto Morales for her creative works and her educational contribution to education.

There was another music educator, from Pinar del Río, that stood out and is worth mentioning: Olga Charbonier Garcia (1925–). Her vibrant intelligence and talent was evident. At eight years old she began her studies in music with the piano teacher Amparo Saenz and later on she fulfilled the requirements as a piano professor at the Conservatory of the Milagrosa in La Habana. In 1938 she attended the Normal School to become a childhood education teacher and completed her degree in 1942. She also became a substitute professor until 1948 where she obtained a position in public school 5B next to the Normal School.

With the victory of the revolution in January 1959, Olga Charbonier Garcia dedicated her time with passion as the Cuban society was experiencing its own transformation given the new government. Certainly, the development of Cuban music education built up during this time. This process took place in four stages: the first (1959–1969), the establishment of the new educational system and the implementation of a primary education; the second (1970–1979), the implementation of basic secondary education and the development of adult education; third (1980–1989), the phase for the fine-tuning and educational quality of the educational system; and fourth (1990–), the phase of the educational development of a special period.

During these years using her musical knowledge and experience, Charbonier composed some hymns, among them the one for the *Brigada de Patria* (native country) or *Muerte* (death), on November 30, and one dedicated to Frank País. Her patriotic sentiment and her love to the revolution were evident. As director of the Center Conrado Benítez, she put into practice an innovative pedagogical experience, consisting of organizing class teams from third until sixth grade, which would act as mentors of earlier grades. The number of the classroom depended on the enrollment class, but each group would be integrated by a minimum of six students.

Each student from each team had the responsibility to carry out a job; for example in education, emulation, culture, health, saving, or volunteer work. This system fostered the active participation of children in the school while it built up a sense of responsibility, love for work, and committment to the community. This new experience was one of the elements that contributed to the development of a model school (*Escuela modelo*) at a national level. The Minister of Education, Armando Hart Davalos, embraced the need to implement this model in the country. This need was echoed by the national press during the revolution and the magazines *Bohemia* and *Militante Comunista* in 1965.

The first licensed teachers in music education (formerly Normal School education) began to appear in 1985, with a national character, at the Universidad Pedagógica Enrique José Varona and other educational centers in the country, such as Félix Varela in Santa Clara, Frank País in Santiago, and the universities of Pinar del Rio, Matanzas, and Holguin, all founded in 1990.

At the end of the decade of the 1980s, specifically in 1989, the extension of music education in the seventh grade and the strengthening of a radial class for the primary grades was legislated. In order to improve music education, the preprofessional practice was restated in all secondary schools in the country. During the last decades, music education in the secondary basic has stabilized given the licensed teaching faculty (Sánchez, 2004).

For some time, vocal training dominated the content of music education over corporal movement, improvisation, audio-perspective, and music reading/writing. Nevertheless, the didactic offerings optimized the integration of the practical aspect of music with all its expressions.

Other outstanding teachers in music education in Cuba were: Joaquín Nin, María Muñoz, María Jones de Castro, Cesar Pérez Sentenat, Diego Bonilla, and José Ardevol, who integrated into the faculty of the most prestigious conservatories. The teaching of disciplines such as the history of music, harmony, form and analysis, and piano performance still followed Eurocentric precepts. The only progressive trace during the time was that of the Hubert de Blanck Conservatory, which included the history of Cuban music up to the contemporary composer Amadeo Roldán (1900–1939).

Composer and teacher Carlos Borbolla (1902–1990) deserves special attention for emphasizing the concept of a national methodology of teaching music. His ideas regarding music education in Cuba, written in 1934, refer to the need for a method for the study of the interpretation of Cuban music, classified by the academy as unreachable (Ruiz, 2003). This reflection of what music education should be based on the authentic *Cubano* spirit was refined toward the 1950s when he found a receptive environment to pursue his role as a composer-educator in response to the Eurocentric trends prevailing in music education in the country.

The musical creation of Carlos Borbolla, which consisted of approximately 450 pieces, showed an ascending line between 1954 and 1983 with specific didactic objectives: *Ejercicios con ritmos cubanos* (Exercises in Cuban Rhythm) No. 179 (1954 and 1955); *Cinco cuadernos seriados* (five numbered notebooks): *Pre-ritmica cubana* (Cuban Pre-Rhythm); *Rítmica Cubana* (Cuban Rhythm) Vol. I; *Mis primeras síncopas, Rítmica* Cubana (Cuban Rhythm) Vol. II; *Música de mi Guateque* (Music of My Private Party) (1955); *Rítmica Cubana* (Cuban Rhythm) Vol. III; *Rítmo en tus dedos* (Rhythm with the Fingers) (1956); *Rítmica Cubana* (Cuban Rhythm) Vol. IV; Sonatinas (1957); *Juguetería Cuabana* (Cuban Toy Shop) (1973); and *24 estudios cubanos* (Twenty-Four Cuban Studies) (1945–1983). Since its conception, this bulk of works became part of the composer's educational tools.

Given the context of these works, Borbolla was able to systematize the didactic principles and arrange the technical-interpretative difficulties of Cuban music and the occidental piano school to make the musical legacy of the country accessible. These notebooks contained methodological indications such as: objectives, explanations on time signature, duration, equivalencies, rhythm, tempo, technique, outlines, and preliminary exercises; presenting a gradual order of difficulty. The notebooks were full of didactic content within a universal language, which included polyphonic resources and romantic harmony combined with the rhythmic motifs characteristic of the Cuban music where the *tresillo* (triplet), *cinquillo* (quintuplet), and syncopation were constant. All of the above, with a gradual introduction on peculiarities found in the intonation of native's melodic examples, contributed to the musical ambiance of the Cuban sound (Ruiz, 2003).

In the opinion of Ruiz (2003), the musical treatment that Borbolla imposed to traditional music, skillfully combined with Cuban music, gives the sensation of a succession of melodic and rhythmic motifs woven within a semantic structure that expands with the enrichment of the classic sonata without losing its primary identity. Carlos Borbolla is definitely considered the precursor of the national identity processes throughout music education. The legacy of this visionary Cuban music educator—from the first half of the last century—is considered a model of consistently including Cuban themes to the teaching of music into study plans of general education and specialized disciplines.

The inclusion of the *cubano* in music education was slow and centered in the courses of rhythmic band, chorus, history, and musical appreciation. Although the relationship between the content in each of them is not clear, the fact is that working with Cuban themes constituted a daring proposal and put them ahead of what the conservatories had accomplished. The teaching with an orientation toward what was considered Cuban in the conservatories had a late burst, given, among other causes, the lack of adequate printed materials for this purpose at the higher education level. With the rise of elaborated texts for piano instruction with popular themes approached from different perspectives (melodic, rhythmic, melodic-rhythmic treatments), musicians began to incorporate these experiences in some conservatories.

Music education with an orientation toward the popular music genre was centered in the teaching of piano, without complementing it with other subjects of general orientation. Its inclusion depended on the methodology guided by the practice in each one of them (Barceló, 2007).

It was evident that the exchange of musicians and composers from different regions, with or without any formal education, elevated music education as an important and fundamental part of the curriculum. During the decade of the 1970s, Cuban music had reached a pinnacle in the international music scene. The government used this as an important promotional tool all over the world. Thus, recognizing the massive efforts of promoting music education, it reached the broad recognition no other country in Latin America had ever reached (Díaz Ayala, 2006).

TWENTY-FIRST CENTURY

Currently, education at all levels is free in Cuba. The public education system is divided into preschool, for students up to five years of age, which includes nurseries; the elementary level, for students from six years old, which could be rural or urban and is compulsory; the secondary level (middle school), for students from thirteen years of age, which is subdivided into two cycles (*inferior* and *superior*) and could be general or technical; the high school; and university level. In the formation of adults, there is a 95 percent literacy rate. According to Lorenzino (2005), for the public educational system on the island, music education is considered compulsory at the primary level of general education, from preschool to sixth grade. The teachers of general education were trained either at the School for Arts Instruction or the Institute Enrique José Varona, University of Santiago, or Universidad of Santa Clara.

Postgraduate studies in music education are among the multiple educational opportunities for the professional development of music educators. Obtaining a master's or doctoral degree in Cuba is possible only after fulfilling the requirements and being at the same level of the graduate offerings provided by institutions such as the already mentioned Institute Enrique José Varona.

Also, music education research is in the forefront if compared with the other Latin American countries. The contribution of scholars such as Dr. Paula Sanchez offers an example of a career committed to the diffusion of research through her numerous articles, her role as director of the postgraduate program in music education, and her direction of musical education on television.

Music education in Cuba is managed through various venues. In public schools, there are institutions devoted to general education and other specialized offerings. All students registered in primary schools are exposed to a very diverse music experience, where the basic skills of audio-perspective, vocal education, and the performance of small percussion instruments are taught. Specialists in music education, art instructors, or any other trained teacher led music education at this stage. Television music education programming operated since 2001 at the primary and secondary levels, respectively, supports these personnel. The televised programs, transmitted to the public and the curricular materials used for these programs, are available to all teachers and are produced and supervised by the country's Ministry of Education.

After the first six years of basic general education, some of the students with special musical skills may be allowed to enter the specialized schools in music instruction after approving some rigorous diagnostic tests in music. The family of string instruments, including the harp, is considered instruments of long training; therefore, children with an aptitude for playing these are admitted before they finish primary school. From the intermediate level, music education of Cuban students is aimed to either build up new audiences or prepare professional musicians. Both groups satisfy their musical studies in the known *Casas de Arte* (art houses). These institutions offer courses for playing instruments and provide the necessary instruction for mastering the musical language, but not necessarily at a professional level. Those who pursue occupations related to music, such as broadcasters, disk jockeys, producers, art instructors, and others, benefit from this systematic and organized curriculum in music education to further develop their knowledge. For the professional musician, employment opportunities are diverse. Currently, thanks to the Development Plan of the Cuban Music Institute (ICM), graduates are placed according to the demands of all the provinces in the country.

Musicians become part of the symphonic orchestras, bands, chamber music groups, and popular music groups, among many others. Some musicians are given a permanent assignment, but these are few. There are numerous musical groups, theater companies, and general performances on the island. Others receive offers from other parts of the world.

The projection of the *Instituto Cubano de Música* (CIC) (Cuban Music Institute) has decreased because of the reduction in professional or preprofessional specialization. It is evident that the demands are linked to the identification of new talents from elementary schools. In the past, the students were the ones who chose their instrument of interest, and now the school places students once they match their talents to their needs. For example: clarinet, saxophone, oboe, contrabass, violin, and viola could be instruments of high needs. String instruments are important but respond to the development plan of the symphonic orchestras of the country. It seems that Cuba has a competent system when it comes to a formal music education program. According to Lorenzino (2005), it would be a good contribution to the field of music education to engage in a thorough study of the impact of music education in Cuba given the existence of a large quantity of well-educated and qualified Cuban musicians around the world.

Acknowledgments: Ministry of Education of Cuba and the director of the Music Education Program for the Schools and Television, Dr. Paula Sanchez.

REFERENCES

Allende, N. (1992). *Por la encendida calle antillana: Cultura musical y discurso histórico en la sociedad puertorriqueña en la década del treinta (1929–1939)*. Tesis de maestría inédita. Universidad de Puerto Rico.

Allende, N. (2008). Africanía de la música puertorriqueña. *Enciclopedia de Puerto Rico*. Recuperado el 18 de agosto de 2009. http://www.enciclopediapr.org

Barceló, N. (2007). "Lo cubano" en la Educación Musical del Siglo XX. Revista IPLAC Publicación Latinoamericana y Caribeña de Educación, 3.

Betancur, F. (1999). *Sin clave y bongó no hay son: Confluencias musicales de Colombia y Cuba*, 2nd Edición. Colombia: Editorial Universidad de Antioquia.

Carpentier, A. (1988). *La música en Cuba*. La Habana, Cuba: Editorial Letras cubanas.

Carpentier, A. (1999). *Ese músico que llevo dentro*. Cuba: Editorial Siglo XXI.

Cartaya, P. (1995). *Figuras relevantes de nuestra nacionalidad*. Esteban Salas. Glosas Cubanas.

Claro, S. (1970). La música virreinal en el nuevo mundo. *Revista Musical Chilena* 110, 7–31.

Cruz, I. (2008). Hubert de Blanck y la enseñanza de la música de Cuba. Educación. Disponible en: http://www.cmbfradio.cu/index.htm

De Couve, A. & Dal Pino, C. (2006). La investigación histórica en educación musical. *Revista Electrónica Complutense de Investigación en Educación Musical, 3*(1).

Díaz Ayala, C. (1981). *Música cubana, del areyto a la nueva trova*. San Juan, P.R. Editorial Cubanacán.

Díaz Ayala, C. (2006). *Los contrapuntos de la música cubana*. San Juan, P.R. Ediciones Callejón.

Eli, V. (2002). Instrumentos de música y religiosidad popular en Cuba:Los tambores batá. *Revista Transcultural de Música Transcultural Music Review 6.*

Fernández, J. (2001). *La cultura cubana crisol de culturas y credos* (Esbozo cultural. Guía de instituciones y sitios de culto). La Habana, Cuba: Editorial de Ciencias Sociales.

Fernández-Cueto, L. (2008). Orígenes y evolución de la enseñanza del piano en Cuba. *La Retreta 1*(5), 1–7.

Ferraz, M. & Calero, A. C. (2007). La política educativa española en Puerto Rico a finales del siglo XIX: Un factor más de contención en las aspiraciones independentistas. *Revista Iberoamericana de Educación 43*, 147–70.

Gardner, H. (1990). *Art Education and Human Development*. Los Angeles: The Getty Center for Education in the Arts.

Hernández, G. & Izquierdo, G. (2003). Transculturación e identidad en la cancionística cubana. *Islas 45*(138), 136–44.

Lawler, V. (1945). Music education in fourteen Latin-American republics. *Music Education Journal 31*(4), 20–23+30.

Le Riverend, J. (1989). Historia de Cuba. Tomos 1y II. La Habana, Cuba: Editorial Pueblo y Educación.

Leyva, M. (2002). El asalto de los márgenes a la cubanidad. Revista Istmo. Recuperado el día 11 de septiembre de 2009 en: http://collaborations.denison.edu/istmo/no5/index.html

Lorenzino, L. (2005). An ethnographic study of secondary music education in Santiago de Cuba: Insights for Canadian music educator. Doctoral dissertation, University of Alberta. (UMI No. 1155562701).

Lorenzo, O. & Rodríguez, C. (2005). Educación no formal y educación mediática de la sociedad. En Actas de las I Jornadas de Psicopedagogía: Evaluación e Intervención en Contextos Educativos. Publicación electrónica en CD.

Mulet Artigas, J. (1999). La formación inicial de la educación preescolar en Cuba. Revista Interuniversitaria de Formación Profesional, 35, 59–94. Cuba. Disponible en: dialnet.unirioja.es/servlet/fichero_articulo?codigo=118032&orden=59860.

Mena, A. (1999). La guerra hispano-norteamericana de 1898 y su música. *Militaria, Revista de Cultura Militar 13*, 133–42.

Neira, L. (2005). *La percusión en la música cubana*. La Habana: Editorial Letras cubanas.

Ortiz, F. (1948). *La música y los areítos de los indios de Cuba*. La Habana: Editorial Lex.

Quintero, A. (2009). *Cuerpo y cultura. Las músicas "mulatas" y la subversión del baile*. Madrid: Iberoamericana.

Rodríguez, A. & Lorenzo, R. (2005). La música y la danza en las comunidades aborígenes cubanas. *Periódico Domine* (3).

Ruiz, M. (2003). *Carlos Borgolla: De los órganos de baile a la escuela de piano cubana, un precursor*. Revista La Jiribilla, Letras Solfa: La Habana, Cuba.

Sánchez, P. (1992). *Algunas consideraciones acerca de la educación musical en Cuba*. La Habana: Editorial Pueblo y Educación.

Sánchez, P. (2004). La musicalización ciudadana, un reto de la educación musical en el contexto latinoamericano y caribeño. Disponible en: http://portal.unesco.org/culture/en/files/19565/10813483653sanchez.pdf/sanchez.pdf

Sánchez, P. & Morales, X. (2008). *Educación musical y expresión corporal*. La Habana: Editorial Pueblo y Educación.

Santiago, G. (2008). *Historia, premisas falsas, despojos y fabulaciones*. Diario Digital RD. Disponible en: http://www.diariodigital.com.do/?module=displaystory&story_id=5929&format=html

Thompson, D. (1993). *The Cronistas* de Indias Revisited. *Latin American Music Review 14*(2), 181–201.

Vega, J. (2008). Salas de la oscuridad a la gloria. Revista Voz Católica. Periódico de la Arquidiócesis de Miami. http://www.vozcatolica.org/85/esteban-salas.htm

Viciedo, M. (2005). Campañas de alfabetización: La experiencia de Cuba en el contexto de las bibliotecas públicas. *Acimed, Revista Cubana de los Profesionales de la Información y de la Comunicación en Salud 13.*

Vila, I. (1998). *Familia, escuela y comunidad.* Barcelona: ICE/ Horsori.

Vizcaino, María Argelia. (2003). Reseña sobre los instrumentos musicales creados en Cuba. Revista Electrónica Conexión Cubana. Disponible en: http://archivocubano.utils.com.ar/

Wilson, T. D. (1981). On user studies and information needs. *Journal of Documentation, 37*(1), 3–15.

Chapter Two

Dominican Republic

Susana Acra-Brache

INTRODUCTION

The Dominican Republic is a nation on the island of *La Hispaniola*, which is part of the Greater Antilles in the Caribbean and is located between Cuba and Puerto Rico. The Dominican Republic occupies two-thirds of the east end of the island consisting of 18,704 square miles with an estimated population of ten million inhabitants. Haiti occupies the west third end of the island. The Dominican Republic is the second-largest nation of the Caribbean.

The name of *La Hispaniola* was originally given to the island when Christopher Columbus landed on Guanahaní on October 12, 1492. In letters written soon after his first voyage, Columbus described the island, saying, "La Hispaniola is marvelous: the hills and mountains . . . and the lands are beautiful and thick for planting and cultivating food, for raising stock and for building villages" (Henríquez-Ureña, 1977, 332). On his second voyage to the island in 1493 he founded the first Christian city of the New World, naming it *La Isabela* in honor of Spanish Queen Isabel. In 1502, the city's name was changed to Santo Domingo de Guzmán, and the current name of the country's capital is Santo Domingo. Santo Domingo is the eldest city of America, and during the late 1400s and early 1500s it was the most important colony and center for expeditions for conquest and colonization of other neighboring islands (Henríquez-Ureña, 1977, 332). It was known as the "Crib of the New World" (Lebrón, 1981).

PRE-HISPANIC INFLUENCE

When the Spanish conquistadores arrived to the island they found a large community of two groups of indigenous Indians, the Caribes and the Arahuacos. The Caribes were inhabitants of the Lesser Antilles who engaged in excursions to the Greater Antilles. The Arahuacos migrated from South America from territories now known as Venezuela, the Guayanas, and Brasil. The Taíno Indians, descendent from the Arahuacos, were the most influential indigenous group on the island. They were peaceful, and their lifestyle, characteristic of the Stone Age, seemed rudimentary to the Europeans (Lebrón, 1981, 48).

According to Gonzálo Fernández de Oviedo in his book *Historia General y Natural de las Indias*, the Indians would pass information about their ancestral past orally by means of their *areyto* tradition. The *areyto* tradition consisted of singing and dancing at the same time as a form of preserving the history, knowledge, and stories of their past and present. It was also an important social way to interact, honor leaders, prepare for battles, celebrate victories, and commemorate the dead. In regards to the *areyto*, Oviedo described "while during the singing and dancing, other Indians provide drinks to those who are dancing who in turn drink while continuing to move their feet . . . these drinks are prepared by them for their use and when the festivities conclude, many of them end up drunk and unconscious lying on the ground for hours. Those who fall down drunk are removed from the dancing and the rest continue, until the drunkenness gives end to the *areyto*" (Lebrón, 1981, 48).

The *areyto* could be performed by men alone, by women alone, or by members of both sexes together. They would intertwine their arms and move in unison according to the model presented by the leader (could be male or female), who would step forward or backward while singing. Usually the melodic rhythm would match the movement of the feet. Whatever the leader performed, the rest of the group imitated in a call-and-response manner. The melodies sung by the leader usually told a story, and this ritual could last for hours and even from one day to the next until the story had been finished (Pérez, 2010, 199).

According the Friar Barolomé de las Casas, who arrived in Santo Domingo on June 29, 1503, and who wrote extensively about the history and destruction of the Indies, "The Indians of Santo Domingo were very inclined and used to much dancing, and, to accompany the songs they danced to, they would make use of jingle bells made of wood with little rocks inside that sounded soft and hoarse . . . they would sing and dance for long periods of time . . . sometimes they lasted all night" (Nolasco, 1948, 16).

The Indians would sometimes accompany their *areyto* song dances with a *Baiohabao*, which is a hollow tree trunk that is struck with a stick. Other instruments that were used during *areyto* celebration were wooden flutes, conch sea shells (used as trumpets for alerting from afar), and gourds (Demorizi, 1971, 145).

Very little information was documented regarding the musical structure, tonality, rhythmic characteristics, and musical instruments of the Taíno Indians of the Dominican Republic given their rapid extermination soon after the Spanish arrival at the island. Friar Bartolomé de las Casas wrote that during the eight years (1501–1509) that Nicolás de Ovando was governor of the island, nine-tenths of the Indian population had perished under the hand of the Spanish colonizers (Luna, 1973, 219).

In April 1952, an important archeological discovery was made in the town of La Caleta (a coast town twenty kilometers east of Santo Domingo). Many fragments of Taíno pottery made of clay were found, and among them five flutes of the same kind. These flutes are small, pear-shaped whistles made of cooked clay; they have an embouchure, two circular holes, another hole where the air exits, and a small perforation that indicates they were hung from the neck. It is possible that these flutes produced three- to four-tone melodies, but little is known regarding their use. These flutes belong to the archeological collection of Dominicans Emile de Boyrie Moya, García Arevalo, and Rafael Esteva (Luna, 1973).

AFRICAN INFLUENCE

Given that the indigenous tribes were quickly becoming extinct, the Spaniards saw a need to import people to do labor work as slaves. On September 3, 1500, a Royal Decree authorized Nicolás de Ovando to import black slaves of Christian property (Coopersmith, 1949, 70). Africans slaves were brought from the regions of Senegambia and Guinea and from the Congo-Angola. Some of the many ethnic groups that were brought to the island were the *ladinos*, *mandingas*, *lucumíes*, *carabalíes*, or *malembas*. Hugo Tolentino, a Dominican historian, explains that the African slaves adopted the habits, traditions, and ways of communication of the Spaniards as a means to survive (Jorge, 1982).

The repression and prohibition of African cultural and religious traditions led the Africans to maintain their culture in secrecy and to mask it with Christian practices, such as naming African gods with the names of Catholic saints. The Africans engaged in *cofradias* (congregations of religious persons that practice Christian devotion) as a way to preserve their rituals and ancestral beliefs without the fear of being persecuted (Jorge, 1982).

African musical influences had an impact on Dominican music, and this is evidenced by the use of instruments such as the *atabales* or *palos* (long, tubular drums made of hollow single tree trunks with a membrane stretched out across the top end and with an open end at the bottom), *marimba* (plucked-metal bass), and the *guiro* (a gourd scraped by a stick—though it is not clear whether it was originally Indian or African). Also, the use of pentatonic scales and polyrhythmic combinations along with a call-and-response style of singing are among the Africans' contributions.

SPANISH COLONIZATION

The first European educators and musicians were brought to the island from the Order of St. Francis soon after 1502 following the Spanish colonization. Music education was an important component of the religious formation of monks. Among the 2,500 colonists in the fleet of thirty ships that Nicolás de Ovando brought to *La Hispaniola* were the first three trumpet players and instrumentalists in the New World: Sebastian Ximénez, Fernando Paz, and Diego Hortís (Luna, 1973).

In that same year also came four monks, and among them Diego de Nicuesa, a recognized *vihuela* (a twelve-string guitar-like string instrument) player (Nolasco, 1948, 24). A Roman Catholic friar, Bartolomé de la Casas, was the first to perform a religious musical work in the New World. In 1510, he celebrated a mass with a choir in the church of the town of La Vega (Lebrón, 1981, 120). During that time, music-making and teaching in the western European tradition was available mostly in monasteries and convents, with the objective of training musicians for the Church for sacred purposes.

Cristóbal de Llerena, born in 1540, was the first musician born in the New World in Santo Domingo. He was canon, music director, and organist at the Cathedral of Santo Domingo as well as rector of the Gorjon University for over four decades. He was a teacher of organ and voice and is regarded as the first playwright and composer born in the Americas. Archbishop López de Avila in a 1588 letter written to Felipe II described Cristóbal Llerena as a man with rare abilities who in spite of being self-taught was extremely well versed in Latin and music (Demorizi, 1971, 13).

The Cathedral of Santo Domingo, consecrated in 1540, became the first cathedral of the New World, and had a *chantre*, organist, and choir. The holy liturgy was offered with the participation of organ and choir. Although for three centuries the Cathedral of Santo Domingo was the most active artistic center of the island, the Cathedral of La Vega and other churches throughout the island had a *chantre* and choirs as well (Lebrón, 1981, 120).

It is assumed that the organs must have been brought into the island at least by the early sixteenth century, but documented information make reference to them only after 1586 when British pirate Francis Drake attacked the island and sacked the city of Santo Domingo. Llerena, Quiñones y Morales informed "because the altars, altarpieces, crucifixes, images, choruses and organs . . . were burned," and Friar Juan Rodríguez Viana wrote on June 1586 "they went to the Convent of Mercedarios and burned and destroyed the choir and the organ" (Nolasco, 1948, 36).

The *Universidad de Santo Tomas de Aquino*, the first university of the New World and active since 1538, offered courses in music and singing, following the medieval tradition of Spanish universities (Henríquez Ureña 1960, 341). The solid colonial cultural development in Santo Domingo, which included musical performance, continued to evolve between the 1500s to the 1800s, and during that time many Dominican church musicians who had been trained in monasteries, churches, and convents in the precepts of Western European music had become music teachers themselves. According to Pedro Henríquez Ureña, it was Dominican Dr. Bartolomé Segura y Mieses who took to Cuba the first piano in the early 1800s (Demorizi, 1971, 14).

During the seventeenth and eighteenth centuries, there were many popular musicians who performed popular dance music such as the *fandango, jarana, cuadrilla española, contradanza*, French minuet, polkas, waltzes, and finally the *merengue* (a ballroom sliding step dance of Dominican origin performed in duple time with syncopated rhythm combining African and Spanish musical elements), which appeared around the 1850s (Luna, 1973). During the beginnings of the nineteenth century, popular orchestras included instruments such as the violin, *cuatro* (a small guitar with four or five strings or pairs of strings, used in Latin American and Caribbean music), mandolin, *tiple, tambora* (two-headed drum of African music frequently used in Dominican folkloric music), and *guiro* (handheld percussion instrument). By midcentury, popular dances were performed by sophisticated guitar-like chordophones (the cuatro, tiple, and tres), as well as percussion instruments such as the guiro and a small double-headed drum called the *balsié*, while in the dancing salons the popular orchestras had violin, flute, guitar, tambora, tambourine, and guiro (Demorizi, 1971, 151).

On August 1, 1862, archbishop Bienvenido Monzón arrived in Santo Domingo, accompanied by organist and chapel master Miguel Herrera. They formed the first classical orchestra of the country. The orchestra was composed of an organist, three violins, one flute, one clarinet, two trumpets, one cello, and one bass. It was accompanied vocally by one bass, one baritone, two tenors, and four boys. All but three of these musicians were Dominicans. Later in 1863, three more musicians (violinist, bass player, and flautist) were brought from Spain to reinforce the orchestra and performed at the church and for religious purposes alone (Luna, 1973, 234).

THE BEGINNINGS OF MUSIC TEACHING AND PERFORMANCE

By the early 1800s the capital and a few other urban centers had teachers of piano, string, and wind instruments (Guzmán, 1999). Most of these teachers had been trained by Church musicians, and by the beginning of the nineteenth century they were becoming actively involved in secular music-performing activities.

In February 27, 1844, the Dominican Republic sought its independence from Haitian domination and became an independent state. A national decree on July 15, 1845, mandated that every military regime must have a musical counterpart (Demorizi, 1971). These military regiments were usually accompanied by a drum, *pífano* (small, high-pitched fife used in Spanish military bands), and flute. By 1846, there were two military bands in the country: one in Santo Domingo and one in Santiago (Luna, 1973).

Coronel Juan Bautista Alfonseca (1810–1875), who was the first Dominican composer, conducted the band in Santo Domingo. He composed the first *danzas criollas*, which he named *merengue*. He annotated the first *merengue* songs. In 1852, Coronel Alfonseca and his military band performed regularly at town plazas. These performances were usually composed of four popular pieces such as *danzas*, *pasodobles*, *mazurkas*, *valses*, and *merengues*. These public open-air concerts, known as *retretas*, performed by municipal or military bands, promoted the social exchange and stimulated musicians to compose music for the occasions (Pérez, 1993, 498).

The existence of these military and municipal bands motivated the creation of private music academies to prepare new musicians for these bands, but also for the church and for the *orquestas de baile* (dance orchestras), which performed waltzes, polkas, mazurkas, *cuadrillas*, and popular music during social dancing events.

On July 15, 1855, José Francisco Quero and Fermín Bastidas opened the first private music school in Santo Domingo on Mercedes Street. They taught *solfège*, voice, violin, viola, cello, guitar, and flute. Father Francisco Xavier Billini directed the second music school on September 1, 1869, under the name of *Academia de Música y el Coro del Colegio San Luis Gonzaga*. On March 18, 1872, the *Orfeon del Ateneo Dominicano* was created and provided theory, instrumental, and vocal lessons. On March 1, 1885, under the initiative of Monsignor Fernando Arturo de Meriño, another music school was created in Santo Domingo under the directorship of Spanish priest Andrés Requena (Pérez, 1993, 501).

Other important musicians who provided music training in the country during the late nineteenth through early twentieth centuries were Máximo Soler, Francisco Soñé, and José Ovidio García.

Máximo Soler (1859–1922) was the founding member of the Municipal Band of Santo Domingo and taught baritone horn, clarinet, theory, and *solfège*. He was a well-known music teacher, and some of his students included Flérida de Nolasco, Luis Mena, and Esteban Peña Morell. Soler composed two-steps, polkas, mazurkas, and pieces in other styles (Pérez, 1993, 502).

Francisco Soñé (1869–1949) contributed greatly to the music development of the town of La Vega. He played various instruments but was most proficient in the clarinet. He was responsible for the formation of bands and municipal music academies in La Vega. Gabriel del Orbe and Juan Bautista Espínola were among his many students. Francisco Soñé and his wife gave free lessons to students of limited economic resources. The "Francísco Soñé" school of fine arts of La Vega was named after him (Pérez, 1993).

On September 1855 the *Sociedad Filarmónica* was inaugurated, and that year it presented a concert with repertoire from Strauss, Rossini, and Beriot (Coopersmith, 1949, 84). The concept of a symphonic orchestra began to further develop in 1904 with the creation of the *Octeto del Casino de la Juventud* (Octet of the Youth Casino) under the directorship of José de Jesús Ravelo. In 1932 it was renamed *Sociedad de Conciertos bajo el patrocinio del Ateneo Dominicano* (Society of Concerts Sponsored by the Dominican Athenaeum).

A small orchestra of Dominican musicians who would gather every Friday for "artistic sessions" and would perform a concert every month comprised this group. Twelve members of the Ravelo family were the majority of the musicians in this group. The Ravelos are considered to be the "first musical Dominican family" (Luna,

1973, 235). José de Jesús Ravelo, also known as Chuchú (1876–1951), was the father of this family and became a highly recognized musician, composer, and the first teacher of choral singing in the country.

In 1906, two years after the Octet was formed in the capital, the *Centro Lírico Rafael Ildefonso Arte* was formed in Santiago, which is the second-largest city of the Dominican Republic. Its director was Jose Oviedo García (1862–1920), who was also the director of the band and the Municipal Academy of Santiago. He was a clarinetist, composer, and teacher of theory, *solfège*, harmony, and various wind instruments.

The *Centro Lírico* performed the first important symphonic works to be heard in the country, such as Schubert's Unfinished Symphony, Haydn's Military Symphony, Beethoven's Overtures and Fifth Symphony, among others, and became the most important musical group of the *Cibao* (name for the northern part of the island). Among José Ovidio García's students were Juan Francísco García, Ramon Díaz, and Pedro Echavarría Lazala.

Ovidio had two sons: José Ovidio, who was a virtuoso pianist and became an organ and piano teacher (Dominican composer Julio Alberto Hernández studied with him); and Carlos Manuel, who was a violinist and concert master of the *Centro Lírico* and first violin of the *Eslava* Quintet (Luis Rivera was among his students) (Pérez, 1993, 502).

By the early 1900s almost every town or province had a band and a music academy. However, access to classical musical performances and private music lessons had only been available to a small, privileged group of upper-class citizens, mainly in the capital and in a few other towns, who usually had a piano in their home. Thus, José de Jesús Ravelo saw a need to create a public music school so that many people from all economic backgrounds could have access to music training, and he consequently convinced the government authorities under President Ramón Cáceres to create such a school.

Hence, the *Liceo Musical*, under the directorship of Ravelo, was founded in the capital city of Santo Domingo in 1908 following the model of the Madrid Conservatory in Spain and become the first official music school in the country. At the *Liceo Musical* students received theory and *solfège*, piano, and voice, and training in some string and woodwind instruments (Guzmán, 1999, 24).

Students from private schools and municipal academies from all around the country were examined for level proficiency at this official school. Although it was an official school, it received little support from government authorities. Despite this, the *Liceo Musical* trained the musicians that became the forefathers of music in the country. Among them are Luis Mena, Elila Mena, Mary Siragusa, and Gracita Senior y Manuel Rueda (Secretaría de Estado de Cultura, 2000, 30).

In Puerto Plata in 1916, Puerto Rican musician José María Rodríguez Arresón and Leopoldo María Mañón founded the *Sociedad Artística Centro Musical* with an orchestra and choir conducted by maestro Rodríguez Arresón. This orchestra provided performing opportunities for both foreign musicians and Dominican musicians who had received initial training in the country and later studied in conservatories in Paris and Germany (Pérez, 1993, 504).

In San Francisco de Macorís, three chamber music groups emerged: *El Octeto Santa Cecilia* (1916) conducted by Oguis Negrette and Manuel Puello with twenty musicians; the *Orquesta Filarmónica Beethoven* conducted by Luis Adolfo Betánces with sixteen musicians; and the *Orquesta Filarmónica Verdi* (1927) conducted by Lebanese Aris Azar with twenty-two musicians (Pérez, 1993, 505).

Between the years 1936 and 1946, music teacher Manuela Jiménez created a private music school named *Estudio José Manuel Jiménez* to provide private, formal piano teaching independent from the *Liceo Musical*. Aida Bonelly and René Rodríguez studied at this school (Secretaría de Estado de Cultura, 2000, 30).

In 1937, Julio Alberto Hernández conducted the newly formed *Orquesta de Conciertos* composed of musicians Pancho García, Luis Alberti, Pedro Echavarría Lazala, and Machilo Guzmán, among others, who would air weekly concerts through the H19B Radio Station (Pérez, 1993, 504).

Through the 1930s, 1940s, and 1950s, the Dominican Republic was ruled by dictator Rafael Leónidas Trujillo Molina—better known simply as "Trujillo." Trujillo was a ruthless man who throughout three decades afflicted Dominicans with brutal oppression. However, under his dictatorship, many initiatives were taken toward the development of music and musicians in the country. During the regime four official music institutions were created: *Orquesta Sinfónica Nacional* (National Symphony Orchestra) in 1941, *Conservatorio Nacional de Música* (National Conservatory of Music) in 1942, *Escuela Elemental de Música* (Elemental

School of Music) in 1947, and *Coro Nacional* (National Choir) in 1955. The *Palacio de Bellas Artes* (Fine Arts Palace) was inaugurated in 1956 (Pérez, 1993).

Trujillo was known for his open-door policy, accepting exiles from Europe after the Spanish Civil War and later World War II. As a result of this policy, there were many European musician refugees who migrated to the country and broadened the musical culture of the Dominican Republic.

Those musicians were Edward Fendler (conductor and harmony professor), Paula Marx de Abraham (pianist), Dora Merten (voice), Alfredo Matilla (music history), and Enrique Casal Chapi (orchestra conductor). Other musicians were pianists Mario Cecarelli, Enrico Cabiatti, and Pedro Lerma; cellists Ennio Orazi, Marcel Collet, and Francois Bahuaud (still active in the country); string players Francesco Montelli, Piera Costantino, Giovanni Costantino, Mario Carta, and Vito Castorina; and woodwind players Jean Jourdin (oboe), Hubert Vicent (bassoon), Jacques Rocheblade (flute), and Lorenzo Ticchioni (French horn) (Pérez, 1993, 507).

In 1952, Trujillo's brother Rafael Arismendi Trujillo directed *La Voz Dominicana* (The Dominican Voice), a radio television program that became an important school for many artists, such as lyrical singers Rafael Sánchez Cestero, Olga Azar, Fausto Cepeda, Violeta Stephen, Armando Recio, Napoleon Dhimes, Guarionex Aquino, and Gerónimo Pellerano; pop singers José Manuel López "Lope" Balaguer, Casandra Damirón "La Soberana," Joseíto Mateo "El Rey del Merengue," Elenita Santos "Rayito de Sol," and orchestra conductors Tavito Vásquez, Rafael Solano, and Ramón Antonio "Papá" Molina (Pérez, 1993).

Trujillo's regime ended with his death in May 30, 1961, and since then, music development continued through both public and private institutions and initiatives. The greatest growth has been evident in the capital city of Santo Domingo. However, music education and performance did not advance in greater measures due to low budget funding from the government. Hence, many musicians took the initiative to open their own private academies.

THE PIONEERS IN DOMINICAN COMPOSITION

Catana Pérez's book titled *El Universo de la Música* (1993, 527–74) presents a wide perspective on the education and production of the Dominican composers. It reminds us that the majority of Dominican musicians began to compose after the 1850s. These musicians had taken some classes in theory, harmony, and had learned to play various band instruments, but most of them were self-taught in terms of composition techniques. Some of the earlier compositions have been lost, but the ones that are available illustrate the musical development and foreign influence in Dominican music culture.

Clarinetist Juan Bautista Alfonseca (Santo Domingo; 1810–1875) composed military and religious works, but his innovative folkloric compositions had an important impact on Dominican culture in that these attractive arrangements of national popular music began to supplant some of the European dances.

Violinist Jose Reyes (1835–1905) composed popular and religious music, including the first Dominican requiem and the melody to the Dominican national anthem for the text written by Emilio Prud'Homme. Chapel master Jose María Arredondo (Santo Domingo; 1840–1924) composed satiric and nationalistic popular pieces, six zarzuelas, and some 135 masses (many of which have been lost). Clarinetist Pablo Claudio (Santo Domingo; 1855–1899) traveled to Rio de Janeiro hired by an opera company, and upon his return to the country he wrote the first two Dominican operas: *Maria de Cuellar* (1882) and *América* (premiered in Santiago on 1969). He is the great-grandfather of distinguished Dominican musician Luis Alberti.

José de Jesús "Chuchú" Ravelo (Santo Domingo; 1876–1951) was a clarinetist and the first Dominican teacher of school choral singing. He had been greatly influenced by the compositions of European Romantic composers of the time, and his compositions reflect such influence, in particular, that of Verdi, Tchaikovsky, Debussy, and the Russian Five. He wrote 253 works, which include two oratorios (*La Muerte de Cristo* in 1939 and *La Resurreción de Cristo* in 1942), a requiem, masses, quartets, school songs, and compositions for piano, band and orchestra.

Other musicians oriented their compositions toward the development of folkloric symphonic music. Juan Francisco "Pancho" García (1892–1974), who was born in Santiago and studied with José Ovidio García, was the first to compose European traditional forms with melodic, harmonic, and rhythmic nuances that were clearly folkloric. He was the first Dominican to compose a string quartet in sonata form and the first to write a symphony (*Quisqueyana*). He wrote a number of symphonies, orchestral works, piano pieces, quartets, songs, and others.

Esteban Peña Morel (1897–1939), born in Santo Domingo, was a clarinet and bassoon player who traveled abroad to Haiti, Puerto Rico, and Cuba and other Latin American countries. He had such good musical calligraphy that he was hired to work as copyist for George Gershwin in New York for some time. Later on he went to reside in Barcelona where he was director of the *Banda Municipal de Barcelona* and died in battle during the Spanish Civil War. Among some of his important works are *Una Marcha Funebre, My Puerto Rican Country Little Sweetheart* (for orchestra with West Indian foxtrot rhythm), *Del Cucurucho a Sosua o De Sosua al Cucurucho,* and his lyric comedy *Embrujo Antillano,* which is considered his most famous creation.

Rafael "Fello" Ignacio was born in San Francisco de Macorís (1897–1984) and was a bass player at the National Symphony Orchestra. He composed popular dances including waltzes, *danzones* (official music of Cuba, and derives from a European-influenced ballroom dance played by Cuban *charangas*), foxtrots, tangos, *habaneras* (slow Cuban dance in duple meter), and *merengues* (*El Vironay*). For orchestra he composed *Suite Folclórica, Fantasía Sinfónica en Do Mayor, Cosas Añejas, Dialogo Campesino,* and *Rondo Popular.*

Pianist and conductor Julio Alberto Hernández, born in Santiago (1900–1999), became very interested in folkloric music investigation and published *Álbum Musical No. 1 and No. 2, Música Folclórica y Popular de la Republica Dominicana, Música Tradicional Dominicana,* and *Música para Masas Corales.* He composed six symphonic works and many popular songs such as *Dulce Recuerdo* (1921) and *Amor Profundo,* for which he is very well known. His compositions and contributions to the development of music are many. His grandaugher, Maridalia Hernández, is currently a recognized singer.

Violinist Luis Rivera (1907–1986), son of José de Jesús Rivera, was born in Montecristi and studied with his father and later with Carlos Manuel García Vila in Santiago. He lived in Cuba for a while where he worked as an arranger and musical director for Ernesto Lecuona. While in Cuba, he also took composition lessons with Amadeo Roldán. He composed pieces for voice, piano, orchestra, violin, and some choral pieces. Among his works are *Rapsodia Borinqueña, Sierra del Bahoruco, La Soberana, Merengueando, Danza en Merengue,* and *Rapsodia Dominicana No. 1.*

Bienvenido Bustamante (1923–2001), born in San Pedro de Macorís, began his clarinet studies with his father, José María Bustamante, and later performed in many bands where he learned to play other instruments. He is the author of many popular pieces such as ballads, *criollas,* marches, waltzes, *merengues,* and *mangulinas* (related to merengues). His orchestral works (*Fantasía Criolla* and *Poema Sinfónico No. 1*) have received awards.

Trumpet player and conductor Ramón Antonio "Papá" Molina (b. 1925) was born in Moca and is well known for his compositions. During the Trujillo regime, he took composition lessons with Panamanian Avelino Muñoz and Italian Mario Carta. He was the first musician to use the folkloric styles of *mangulina* and *carabiné* (folkloric dance) in compositions for dancing orchestra music. He composed mambo, bolero, danzon, and other pieces that bring about Dominican folkloric roots. He received an award for his symphonic composition *Tres Imagenes Folclóricas* and wrote two pieces for piano, one of which, *Para José,* was dedicated to his son José Antonio Molina, who is a pianist, arranger, composer, and the actual conductor of the National Symphony Orchestra.

Luis E. Mena (1895–1964), born in Santo Domingo, graduated with a degree in flute performance from the *Liceo Musical* but also played many other instruments. He was director of the music school *La Voz Dominicana* and wrote almost three hundred compositions including mazurkas, works for chamber orchestra, piano, organ, band, and orchestra. His symphonic compositions include *Sinfonia Giocosa, Intermedio Andaluz y Zapateando, Ecos de la Libertad, Vals Diabolico, Tchaikovskiana,* and *Tres Preguntas.* He was the father of Elila Mena and grandfather of Oscar Luis Valdéz Mena.

José Dolores "Lolo" Cerón studied with José de Jesús Ravelo and studied bass at the *Liceo Musical.* He became the music director of the band of the National Army in 1930, for which he composed many works and was artistic director of *La Voz Dominicana.* He is known for his song *Como Me Besabas Tu,* and among his most notable symphonic works are *A la Caida de la Tarde, Las Virgenes de Galindo, Iguaniona, Suite Enriquillo, Flores del Patio,* and *Tríptico Sinfónico.*

Ramón Diaz, born in Puerto Plata (1901–1976), studied with José Ovidio García. He was a bassoon player at the Symphony Orchestra, director of bands and music academies, and church organist in Salcedo and San Cristobal. He composed waltzes, *criollas*, marches, hymns, and his three symphonic works (*Elegia, Minuetto,* and *Dos Marchas Heroicas*), which were premiered by the National Symphony Orchestra in 1941. He was among the first Dominicans to cultivate the lied with works such as *La Niña que Amo, Ansias,* and *Lo Inocultable*. His wife, Spanish Mercedes Ariza, is still an active violinist. They are the parents of pianist Ramón Díaz.

Enrique Mejia Arredondo (Santo Domingo, 1901–1951) studied with his father, José María Arredondo, and with José de Jesús Ravelo. He received guidance on composition from Enrique Casal Chapí. His compositions include *Reverie, Pequeña Suite, Renacimiento, Dos Evocaciones, En el Templo de Yocarí,* and *Cuentos Nocturnos y Pagodas,* some of which make allusion to indigenous music.

Female Dominican pianist Ninon Lapeireta (1907–1989) was born in Santo Domingo and studied composition with maestro Enrique Casal Chapí. She was attracted to twentieth-century composers such as Bartok, Stravinsky, and Hindemith and composed modern works for voice, piano, woodwinds, and orchestra that include *Suite Arcaica, Abominacin de la Espera, Suite de Danzas,* and *Romanza*.

Enrique de Marchena (Santo Domingo; 1908–1988) studied piano with Flerida de Nolasco (Dominican musicologist and folklorist) and Olivia Pichardo. He also studied at the *Liceo Musical,* and took composition lessons with Esteban Peña Morel and Casal Chapí and harmony with Luis Mena. He taught himself to play the horn because the Symphony Orchestra did not have a horn player and needed one. He was awarded numerous times for his compositions, which include orchestral works (*Arcoíris, Concertino, Canto 15, Suite Imágenes,* and *Suite Concertante Hebaricum*), piano works (*Debussyenne, Reverie, Claro de Luna, Sonata en Fa,* among others), chamber works, and a collection of ten vocal songs titled *Canciones de Amor.*

Rafael "Bullumba" Landestoy (1924–) was born in La Romana and studied piano with Mary Siragusa at the National Conservatory of Music. He also studied at the Music Conservatory of Mexico and took some courses at Julliard School of Music in New York where he currently resides. He is known for his focus on piano compositions, which include *Vals de las Ninfas, Vals de Santo Domingo, Criollo en Do,* and *Minivals,* among others.

Manuel Marino Miniño (1930) was born in Baní and studied harmony with Roberto Caggiano and took private counterpoint and fugue lessons with Alfredo Ninno in Rome. He has been the first composer to focus on the fusion of African and European religious music. He composed in an extensive variety of genres that include many works for orchestra, choir, ballets, masses, piano, chamber orchestra, and lieders. Besides his musical compositions, he is the author of three theatrical plays and two published books (*Nociones Elementales de Música, Teoría y Práctica de la Música,* and *Los Merengues de Luis Alberti*).

Manuel Simó (San Francisco de Macorís; 1916–1988) studied harmony with José Dolores Cerón, with Puerto Rican teacher Manuel Berassain, and with Enrique Casal Chapí. He obtained a scholarship from the government to study at the Conservatorio Kolisher de Montevideo in Uruguay, where in 1951 he graduated from Composition and became the first Dominican musician with a degree in Composition. Upon his return to the country he became director of the National Symphony Orchestra and of the National Conservatory of Music where he was actively involved in teaching. His compositions include works for orchestra (with soloists and choir), chamber groups, piano, experimental pieces, voice, and others.

Manuel Simó was the teacher of the first students to graduate from composition from the Conservatory and who in turn have composed many works as well. Others are Margarita Luna and Miguel Pichardo (1969), Aura Marina del Rosario, Fausto Vizcaino and Leila Pérez y Pérez (1972), Ana Silfa (1980), and Beckyrene Perez and Dante Cucurullo (1981). All these musicians have been recognized music teachers at the National Conservatory of Music and other music institutions. Three years before his death, Italian composer Antonio Braga reorganized the composition department of the Conservatory and continued the work that Simó had initiated.

Pianist, composer, and musicologist Ana Margarita Luna was born in Santiago in 1921 and currently resides in Canada. She studied with Juan Francisco García, Manuel Rueda, Manuel Simó, Juan Urteaga, and Hall Overton. She was director of various prestigious music institutions including the National Conservatory of Music and was also a teacher of harmony, analysis, and music history of many Dominican students. Among her compositions are works for orchestra, chamber ensembles, piano, voice, and chorus. Her works have been performed internationally. She translated into Spanish *What to Listen for in Music* by Aaron Copland and *The Twentieth Century Harmony* by Persichetti. She is the author of *Por el Mundo de la Orchesta* (Through the World of the Orchestra), which is frequently cited in this chapter.

In the field of popular and folkloric music there have been important musicians worthy of being mentioned for their contributions to the dissemination and development of music in this field; in particular, of the folkloric *merengue*. Some of them are Rafael Solano, Luis Alberti, Juan Francisco García, Julio Alberto Hernández, Juan Espínola, Rafael Ignacio, Ñico Lora, Toño Abreu, Isidro Flores, Dionisio Mejía, Salvador Sturla, Machilo Guzmán, Juan Lockward, Manuel Troncoso, Leonor Porcella, Manuel Sánchez, Antonio Cruz, and Cuto Estevez. Dominican musicologist and folklorist Fradique Lizardo is recognized for his publications and writings on Dominican folkloric music and instruments.

The folkloric *merengue* transformed over time into popular commercial music that is known worldwide and is directly associated with the Dominican Republic. Perhaps the contemporary recording artist that has been most responsible for exposing *merengue* to the other countries has been Dominican musician Juan Luis Guerra (Santo Domingo, b. 1957), who studied guitar and harmony at the National Conservatory of Music and later graduated in 1982 from Berklee College of Music at Boston with a degree in jazz composition. Many contemporary Dominican musicians have followed his steps by studying at Berklee, and upon their return to the country they too contributed to modernizing music-making in general.

Dominican composers of this generation have also continued to create important repertoire for orchestra, voice, and instruments. Their contributions extend beyond the realm of composition, as most of them are professors at the conservatory, recognized performing artists, or conductors. Most of them also studied at the National Conservatory of Music. Among them are: Miguel Pichardo Vicioso (Santo Domingo, b. 1939), Aura Marina del Rosario (La Romana, b. 1927), Fausto Vizcaíno (Santo Domingo, b. 1930), Ana Margarita Silfa (Puerto Plata, b. 1949), Manuel Rueda (Montecristi, b. 1921), Rafael de Jesús Campos (Santiago, b. 1939–), Nelson Lugo Camarena (La Romana, b. 1941), Luis José Mella (Santo Domingo, b. 1946), and Michel Camilo (Santo Domingo, b. 1954). Other contemporary academic composers born after 1955 include: José Antonio Molina, Amaury Sánchez, Darwin Aquino, Dante Cucurullo, Alejandro José Moya, Samuel Herrera, Josué Santana, Hector Martínez Cabruja, Jonatan Piña, José Puello, and Liova Bueno.

THE INCLUSION OF SINGING IN SCHOOLS

Throughout the colonial period, education in general had been a responsibility of the Roman Catholic Church and followed the precepts and purposes of the Church, within the canon of Spanish culture. By the late 1880s a reform had taken place under the influence of General Gregorio Luperón, where education became a shared obligation of the state with the objective to provide and supervise education for the people, creating a public education system that included secular schools (Guzmán, 1999).

General Gregorio Luperón was a military state leader and restoration hero who later became the twentieth president of the Dominican Republic for a short period between 1879 and 1880. Luperón had strong ideas at the time about public liberties, progress, and education all being part of his desire to move toward civilization. During his short time in office, he met Puerto Rican visionary educator Eugenio María de Hostos, who had been living in the Dominican Republic and who had new philosophical ideas about education and its role in the development of a nation. Soon after, Luperón entrusted Eugenio María de Hostos with the organization of a nationwide public education system (Henriquez-Ureña, 1960, 129).

The birth of school music education can be traced back to Hostos's education reform. In 1880, Hostos founded the *Escuela Normal*, a vocational school for men to provide training that would enable them to contribute in a capitalistic society. Soon after, other secular institutions began to emerge, among them in 1881 the *Instituto de Señoritas*, which was the first higher education institution for Dominican women founded by Dominican poet and educator Salomé Ureña de Henríquez.

The secular program that Hostos was advocating for in his plan for general education provided for the inclusion of singing in schools. He believed that singing would promote patriotism, help citizens develop a sense of national identity, and contribute to the educational growth of children (Guzmán, 1999, 23). However, by the turn of the century the inclusion of singing in schools had been difficult to implement given the lack of school song repertoire.

Dominican poet Ramon Emilio Jimenez had written a compilation of patriotic poems called *El Patriotismo en la Escuela* (Patriotism in the School) to be used as school text, and in 1915 with the help of Dominican musicians such as Jose de Jesús Ravelo it was turned into the first Dominican songbook. It was later published in 1933 as *La Patria en la Canción* (The Homeland in Song). Some of the Dominican musicians whose compositions are included in this songbook are José de Jesús Ravelo, Julio Alberto Hernández, Luis E. Mena, Ramón Echavarría, and Juan Francisco García. This songbook is the cornerstone of Dominican school singing and served as a model for future compositions (Guzmán, 1999, 24).

THE BEGINNINGS OF MUSIC EDUCATION TRAINING

By the late 1960s there was a growing interest in school music, but the shortage of trained music teachers limited all possibilities for development in this field. In the spirit of collaboration, the Art Faculty of the University of Chile, Inter-American Institute of Music Education (INTEM), and the Organization of American Studies (OEA) offered scholarships to a selected group of Dominican musicians so that they could travel to Chile and study at the INTEM (Acra-Brache, January 2010).

Through this agreement, a number of musicians traveled to Chile to receive training in music and music education. Some of them took courses in philosophy, education, conducting, and applied instrument, but those who studied music education were trained in the methodologies of Orff, Kodály, and Jacques-Dalcroze.

The initial group that obtained scholarships to receive training was composed of Florencia Pierret (1967), Briseida Corletto (1967), José Manuel Joa (1967), Samia Abkarian (1969), Leila J. Pérez y Pérez (1969), Griselida Taveras (1974), Ana Silfa (1975), Genarina Rodríguez (1976), Josefina Beltre (1978), Thania Alba (1983), and Mayra Peguero (1984) (SEEBAC, 1987).

From 1987 to 1989, the INTEM, in conjunction with the Secretary of State for Education, Fine Arts and Culture (SEEBAC), offered in Santo Domingo a course titled "Curso de Formación y Capacitación Musical para Docentes de Música en Ejercicio" (Course in Formation and Training for Music Teachers in Service). Some of the Dominican musicians who enrolled in this course were Sonia Peralta, Laurina Vázquez, Pascal Denise, Samuel Herrera, and María Del Pilar Dominguez, among others (Acra-Brache, January 2010).

During that same time, another group of musicians traveled abroad to receive music training in other countries. Bernarda Jorge, Mussetta Simó, and Iluminada Jimenez traveled to Argentina; Dominica Eloy and Monserrat Playa traveled to Spain; and Cesar Hilario to Italy (Acra-Brache, January 2010).

Upon their return to the Dominican Republic, these Dominican musicians and those who had enrolled in the local INTEM course began to incorporate new concepts of music education into both their private and public practice and raised the standards of music teaching and learning. Many of them enriched music education in the country through the implementation of new teaching techniques, research, publications, lectures, and teaching seminars. Most of them currently hold important teaching or administrative positions and continue to advocate for the development of music education, especially for the training of music educators.

THE INTRODUCTION OF MUSIC EDUCATION IN ELEMENTARY SCHOOLS

In the late 1960s, under the new currents in education, the Secretary of State for Education recognized the role of art in child development and recommended the inclusion of artistic activities in schools (Guzmán, 1999, 25). In 1970 the *Plan de la Reforma de Educacion Media* (Elementary School Reform Plan) took place under Ordinance No. 1-70 with the objective to better educate and empower students with personalities and skills that would enable them to function in a fast-changing social and economic society (SEEBAC, 1995).

During the reform plan, music became part of the curriculum following the precepts of modern pedagogy and a strong movement to incorporate music in schools mostly through singing activities (Guzmán, 1999). Instrumental music education was not able to be offered at the time, and the shortage of trained music educators and musically trained classroom teachers was still an impediment (Acra-Brache, January 2010).

In order promote the inclusion of music in schools, the government created the *Departamento de Educación Musical Integral* (DEMI) [Department of Integral Music Education] on April 27, 1976, through Decree 8-76. The DEMI had to (1) train and supervise choral directors, (2) train classroom teachers to include musical activities in the elementary schools, (3) prepare and disseminate teaching lesson plans in music, (4) compile, create, and disseminate musical repertoire and educational resources, (5) organize choral music festivals, and (6) organize competitions of school song compositions (Pérez, 1993, 513).

The first appointed director of the DEMI was pianist Florencia Pierret. She requested state officials to provide twenty additional musicians to work alongside with her so that the objectives of the department could be met, but only two musicians were officially named: Leila Pérez y Pérez and José Manuel Joa Castillo along with Edmundo A. Morel as copyist. The following year, Leila J. Pérez y Pérez was appointed new director and since then has become an active promoter of the importance of music education in the lives of children.

Under the directorship of Leila Pérez y Pérez, the DEMI created many songbooks, teaching guides, lesson plans, textbooks, seminars, and organized choral festivals. Between 1976 until 1997, a number of musicians collaborated with the DEMI in the creation of these materials and activities. They were Grisélida Taveras, Rafael Infante, Rafael Rodríguez Chalas, Adamilka Victoria, Juana Reyes, José Manuel Joa, Florencia Pierret, Iluminada Jiménez, Ana Silfa, Ana Luisa Arias, Briseida Corletto, Iris Diaz, Juan-Tony Guzmán, and Josué Santana. Their major objective was that through these materials and activities classroom teachers would be capable of implementing the music curriculum that the DEMI had devised.

The DEMI became very proactive and achieved an increase in classroom and choral singing. However, given the fact that the DEMI had less than a handful of appointed music educators who could provide training, department officials decided to redirect their efforts from training classroom teachers in music education to training choral specialists who would in turn conduct auditioned choirs in selected schools. By 1978 they had trained the first 130 choral conductors, and these conductors were supposed to conduct the choirs of 304 selected elementary schools (Acra-Brache, January 2010).

Thanks to the efforts of the DEMI, on July 28, 1975, the Executive Branch dictated Decree No. 1141, declaring October *El Mes de la Canción Escolar* (The Month of the School Song) and made the SEEBAC responsible for organizing a promotional campaign for education and the preservation of school values through singing (SEEBAC, 1976). Every October since then, the *Festival de Coro José de Jesús Ravelo* (José de Jesús Ravelo Choral Festival), named after the first Dominican choral conductor, is held for choirs nationwide.

On September 12, 1975, Florencia Pierret led a number of musicians, who like her had traveled to Chile to study music education during the decades of the 1960s to the 1980s, into the creation of the *Asociación de Especialistas en Educación Musical* (AEEM) [Association of Music Education Specialists] with the intent to develop ways to introduce music education in schools that reflected modern practices in music education. Another main objective was to develop an understanding among the community and its leaders about the importance of music education (Acra-Brache, January 2010).

Members of the Association conducted both a radio program and a television program called *Educación por la Música* (Education through Music). The radio program aired every Saturday from 6 p.m. to 7 p.m. on *Radio Televisión Dominicana* (Dominican Radio Television). Topics discussed were related to the importance of music education in child development and the role of the classroom teacher in the implementation of the new music education program designed by the DEMI. The television program was aired the last Sunday of every month in a simulated classroom setting with fifty students. The objective was to train classroom teachers through demonstrations of the musical activities and teaching approaches proposed by the DEMI. Both the radio and television program functioned only between 1976 and 1978 (Acra-Brache, January 2010).

The DEMI had to face many challenges: the fact that music was not valued by the community as an important academic subject, the fact that the government allocated reduced funding for music education, and the fact that there were very few trained music educators. Nonetheless, their contributions to music education had a substantial impact on the development of music education in the twentieth century.

ARTS EDUCATION IN SCHOOLS

In 1994, the government devised a national curricular transformation to elevate the quality of education. This transformation, also known as the Decennial Plan of Education, developed a program for arts education. Music, theater, applied arts, and visual arts were integrated into one subject called *Educación Artística* (arts education). All four disciplines are integrated and interrelated within that subject. Artistic education has become a mandatory subject at all school levels. At the elementary level, artistic education is taught by the classroom teacher, and at the secondary level, each art is supposed to be taught by a specialist in that particular art.

The term *Educación Artística Especializada* (Specialized Arts Education) is used to refer to artistic education that is offered outside of the formal school setting to students who exhibit clear artistic aptitudes and skills with the objective of providing them with training that is more specialized, with the hope that some of these students will grow interested in becoming artistic teachers themselves (Ministerio de Cultura, 2010, 65).

In the *Plan Decenal de Educación 2008–2018* (Decennial Plan of Education, 2008–2018), artistic education offered by the Secretary of State for Education "continues to be a curricular area, with it is own content and objectives, that is taught at all levels and modalities of the educational Dominican system to over two million students" (Ministerio de Cultura, 2010, 68).

Recently, what was formerly known as the SEEBAC was divided into two independent secretaries: Secretary of State for Education and the Secretary of State for Culture. Both Secretaries of State are responsible for artistic education. The Secretary of State for Education offers school artistic education to all Dominican students within the academic program in the preschool, elementary, and secondary levels with the objective of developing creativity, expression, appreciation, aptitudes, and attitudes toward the four different artistic expressions. On the other hand, the Secretary of State for Culture offers students (children and adolescents) specialized artistic training outside the school setting in one of the four artistic disciplines.

Artistic education that is offered by the Secretary of State for Culture is available through nineteen fine arts schools and twenty-three municipal music academies, all state-owned. Out of the nineteen fine arts schools, the five national schools are located in the Distrito Nacional (capital area): *Conservatorio Nacional de Música* (National Conservatory of Music), *Escuela Elemental de Música Elila Mena* (Elila Mena Elemental School of Music), *Escuela Nacional de Teatro* (National School of Theatre), *Escuela Nacional de Danza* (National School of Dance), and the *Escuela Nacional de Bellas Artes para Artes Plásticas* (National School of Fine Arts for Plastic Arts). The remaining fourteen fine arts schools are located in important provinces in the north, south, and east regions of the country: Puerto Plata, Santiago, Moca, Cotui, San Francisco de Macorís, La Vega, San Juan de la Maguana, San José de Ocoa, Azua, and San Cristóbal y La Romana. At the present time, these fine arts schools have an enrollment of 2,611 students, of which 43 percent are music students (Ministerio de Cultura, 2010, 76–77).

The twenty-two state-owned municipal music academies have been mostly established in areas near the border with Haiti, in economically deprived communities such as Restauración, Loma de Cabrera, Santiago Rodriguez, Monte Cristi, Villa Vásquez, Neiba, Cabral, Vicente Noble, Pedernales, Villa Jaragua, Los Rios, Duvergé, La Descubierta, El Cercado, Las Matas de Farfán, Vallejuelo, Elias Piña, Hondo Valle, Tamayo, Barahona, Sabana de la Mar, and San Pedro de Macorís y Sánchez. These municipal academies provide instrumental and theoretical teaching for preschool and elementary students. These academies have an approximate enrollment of 1,300 students (Ministerio de Cultura, 2010).

In 1997, after the creation of the artistic education program, the DEMI was no longer allowed to function as an independent branch within education. It became a unit within the department for artistic education. Its name changed to the Unit of Integral Music Education (UDEMI). The unit's approach to music education had to change drastically to fit the new philosophy outlined by the department of artistic education, and many of the advances that had been accomplished in music education by the DEMI were pushed back (Acra-Brache, January 2010).

From 1994 up to the date of this writing, artistic education teachers are classroom teachers who are expected to teach all four arts disciplines. Regardless, it is common for a classroom teacher to focus on teaching the art discipline with which he or she is most comfortable or has the greatest knowledge. It is also common to hear a classroom teacher sing out of tune and with a poor sense of rhythm. The vast majority of classroom teachers do not play an accompanying instrument and cannot read, write, or improvise music.

In an effort to increase the number of artistic teachers available, the Decennial Plan of Education led to the licensure of artistic teachers with only basic forms of training, rather than a university degree (Guzmán, 1999, 30).

The members from UDEMI created a collection of series books (one for every grade level) for the teaching of artistic education. This collection of series books was published by the government and is currently being used nationwide by teachers and students. In these books, the teaching of music is approached theoretically, contradicting a sound-before-symbol approach, and does not reflect contemporary approaches in music education.

FORMAL MUSIC TRAINING IN OFFICIAL INSTITUTIONS

For the past six decades Dominican students have had access to formal music training both at public and private music institutions. Many of these institutions have graduated musicians that in turn have become very actively involved in the musical and cultural development of the Dominican Republic. These institutions are the *Conservatorio Nacional de Música* (National Conservatory of Music), the *Escuela Elemental de Música Elila Mena* (Elila Mena Elemental Music School), and the *Liceos Musicales Oficiales* (Official Musical Schools).

National Conservatory of Music

In 1941, the *Liceo Musical* was closed for remodeling and restructuring, and upon its reopening on February 12, 1942, under Decree No. 599-42 it became the *Conservatorio Nacional de Música* (National Conservatory of Music) with 441 students enrolled (Jorge, 1982, 109).

The first appointed director of the National Conservatory of Music was German orchestra conductor Eduard Fendler (1942–1944). The conservatory directors following Fendler have been all recognized Dominican musicians and are presented in chronological order: Juan Francisco García (1944–1955), Manuel Simó (1955–1959), Manuel Rueda (1959–1978), Floralba Del Monte (1978–1978), Manuel Marino Miniño (1978–1980), Manuel Simó (1980–1981), Manuel Marino Miniño (1981–1982), Licinio Mancebo (1982–1984), Margarita Luna (1984–1984), Frank Hernández (1986–1987), Floralba Del Monte (1987–2000), José Enrique Espín (2000), and María Irene Blanco (2000–) (Acra-Brache, January 2011).

The National Conservatory of Music has a classical department in instrumental performance and a department of folkloric and popular music. The teachers are musicians mostly from the Dominican Republic, Yugoslavia, Cuba, Romania, and Russia. Entrance requirements specify that the student must have completed the eighth grade and have successfully passed the admission test on their instrument. Instruction is offered at the *Nivel Medio* (intermediate level) and *Nivel Superior* (superior level) (SEEBAC, 2000, 45).

The intermediate level is the same for all students regardless of their instrument. This level is composed of two cycles of six semesters each cycle. By the end of the successful completion of the twelve semesters, the student receives the degree of *Instrumentista y Profesor de Música* (Instrumentalist and Professor of Music). At this level, a student may also specialize in choral conducting. This program enables students with the musical skills necessary to perform with the National Symphony Orchestra (entrance by auditions), concert bands, chamber orchestras, and other musical ensembles and venues available in the country (SEEBAC, 2000, 39).

The degree that is given upon graduation of the intermediate level enables graduates to teach instruments or conduct choirs in private or public academies, departments of music of fine arts public schools, and in private or public elementary or secondary schools. Unfortunately, this degree is not recognized as a bachelor's degree, and so students who graduate from high school need to divide their time between their university studies, work responsibilities, and conservatory studies. This situation has led some students to either drop out or take too long to complete the program. By the year 2000, only eighty-six students had graduated from the intermediate level since 1942 (SEEBAC, 2000, 40), and forty-eight more graduated between the year 2000 to 2010 (Acra-Brache, January 2011).

Students who graduate from the intermediate level may enroll in the superior level, which comprises the third cycle. This last cycle may last from one to three years depending on the instrument or specialty chosen: instrumentalist, composition, or orchestral conducting. After completion of this last cycle, students receive the degree of *Profesor de Instrumento y Cursos Superiores de Música* (Professor of Instrument and Higher Studies in Music). These students may teach at the Conservatory and any other music institution and are expected to have the skills necessary to perform as soloists. From 1942 to 2000, thirty-three students have graduated from this level (SEEBAC, 2000, 40) and thirteen more between 2000 to 2010 (Acra-Brache, January 2011).

The program of study for those enrolled in the department of folkloric and popular music has a duration of four years, and upon graduation they receive a degree of *Instrumentista en instrumento aplicado* (Instrumentalist in Applied Instrument). These musicians receive the necessary training to perform in all kinds of popular ensembles and in recording studios, and have the skills to arrange music and compose in the style of jazz, rock, *son*, and *merengue*, among others (SEEBAC, 2000, 41).

There are various performing ensembles within the National Conservatory of Music that allow students to have exposure to repertoire and performing opportunities. There are chamber ensembles, a jazz orchestra, solo performing opportunities, a symphonic orchestra, and a choral ensemble.

The *Orquesta Sinfónica Juan Pablo Duarte* (Juan Pablo Duarte Symphonic Orchestra) is an important ensemble and is composed of the students of the conservatory. This orchestra was created on October 1, 1993, as a result of an initiative that developed toward the end of an orchestral workshop that was offered by eight Venezuelan musicians who traveled to the country to provide orchestral training. Its first director was Cuban conductor Antonio Fals, followed by Fernando Geraldes and Dante Cucurullo (current), who are both Dominican musicians. Since then, the orchestra remains active, performing both in the *Sala Juan Francisco García* auditorium of the conservatory and in the various concert halls around the country. To date, the orchestra has over sixty student musicians from the conservatory between fourteen and twenty-five years of age.

The *Coro del Conservatorio* and *Coro de Cámara del Conservatorio* (Conservatory Choir and the Chamber Choir of the Conservatory) are two choral ensembles made up of voice, piano, guitar, percussion, and choral conducting students. The students that are most eligible for the chamber choir are the voice and choral conducting students. Its conductors have been Licinio Mancebo, Miguel Pichardo, Mayra Peguero, and Iluminada Jimenez (Acra-Brache, November 2011).

Elila Mena Elemental Music School

Juan Francisco García, who was the director of the conservatory during the early 1940s, grew concerned that in time there would not be sufficient students with the required level and skills to enter the conservatory, and so he convinced Dominican authorities to create an official music school offering a beginning music program for young students with the objective of preparing them for the conservatory.

Thus, in 1947, the *Escuela Elemental de Música Elila Mena* (EEMEM) was created to provide formal instrumental music instruction for young children. Since then, recognized Dominican musicians such as María de Fátima Geraldes, Liliam Brugal, Michel Camilo, Dante Cucurullo, Jorge Taveras, José Antonio Molina, Catana Pérez, Ana Silfa, and Ivan Domínguez, among others, have graduated from this school, and most of them currently hold important positions in musical institutions. In the past fifteen years, other students have graduated and have also become actively involved in music-making, and some have even found new venues in which to pursue their art.

The directors of the EEMEM since its beginnings have been Olivia Pichardo, Julio Alberto Hernández, Elila Mena, Licinio Mancebo, Gracita Senior de Pellerano, María Irene Blanco, Margarita Heredia, Bernarda Jorge, Iván Domínguez, Altabeira Polanco, and Jacqueline Huguet (appointed in September 2010).

FORMAL MUSIC TRAINING IN PRIVATE ACADEMIES

The first private music academy after the Trujillo regime was the *Academia Internacional de Música* (International Academy of Music), founded in 1969 by pianists Edith Hernández, Milagros Beras, and Tania Báez. All three had studied piano at the National Conservatory of Music. In 1976 the founders separated, and Tania Báez founded *Academia de Música Tania Báez*. *Academia Dominicana de Música* was founded under the director-ship of Edith Hernández and Milagros Beras. Milagros Beras passed away in 1996, and Edith Hernández has been the sole director since. Edith Hernandez also graduated with a degree in piano performance from the *Real Conservatorio Superior de Música* in Madrid and studied the Orff-Schulwerk methodology at Western Carolina University with Konnie Saliba. The *Academia Dominicana de Música* currently specializes in the training of instrumentalists.

In 1970, Dominican pianist Samia Abkarian, who had studied piano at the National Conservatory of Music, founded the *Instituto de Educación Musical* (Music Education Institute) in her home. Samia Abkarian is currently a piano professor at the National Conservatory of Music but continues to provide piano lessons from her home.

In 1983, Farida Diná (studied piano with Manuel Rueda, Santos Ojeda, and graduated from the *Academia Dominicana de Música*) founded the *Estudio Diná de Educación Musical* (EDEM) (Diná Studio of Music Education). Along with the support from Diná's daughters, the EDEM was able to open two more branches. The second branch was opened in Santiago in 2003 and is directed by Gislem Linares Diná. The third branch was opened in 2010 in the Zona Oriental in Santo Domingo and is directed by Farida Peña Diná. EDEM is the only private music academy in the country to have more than one branch. The academy is known as a center of instrumental training, but it has also contributed greatly to the development of choral singing in the country through its yearly three-day choral festivals that involve the participation of children, youth, and adult nonpro-fessional choirs. In addition to the festivals, the EDEM organizes Instrumental Performance Competitions for piano, strings, woodwind, and voice. In 2010, it hosted the *Concurso Iberoamericano para Jovenes Pianistas* (Latin American Competition for Young Pianists), the first international piano competition ever held in the country.

The *Centro de Educación Musical Moderna* (CEMM) was founded in October 1991 by Dominican pianists Laurina Vásquez (studied piano at the Academia Dominicana de Música), Pascale Denis (studied piano in Haiti), and María del Pilar Domíngo (studied piano at the National Conservatory of Music). All three of these musicians took the music education course that the INTEM offered in Santo Domingo and also traveled for several summers to Western Carolina University to study Orff-Schulwerk methodology with Konnie Saliba. Laurina Vásquez also studied Orff with Jos Wytac at the same university. In 1999 the founders separated, and Laurina Vásquez has remained director ever since. This academy was the first private academy to offer voice classes and choral training to children through their *Escuela de Canto Coral* (School of Choral Singing) program in 1991 and was also the first to offer music education to beginning music students following the methodologies and instruments of the Orff approach.

The *Centro de Pedagogía Musical* (CPMusical) was founded by Susana Acra-Brache in 1999. The center began to offer *Bebé Musical*, the first early childhood music program in the country. The center was also known for introducing piano lessons using Francis Clark's materials and for offering piano lessons to adults in a piano lab setting. Since 2001, Jacqueline Huguet has been the director of CPMusical and has been recently appointed director of the *Escuela Elemental de Música Elila Mena* (Elila Mena Elementary School of Music). Jacqueline Huguet is a pianist who graduated from the National Conservatory of Music and earned a master's degree in piano pedagogy from Columbus State University and a master's degree in piano accompaniment from East Carolina University. CPMusical is mostly recognized for piano teaching following the precepts of Francis Clark and string lessons following the Suzuki method.

In 2001, Susana Acra-Brache founded *Crescendo*, a center that specialized only in early childhood music education. This center also served as a training site for musicians in the country to learn about this field. In the years between 2005 and 2008, *Crescendo* offered the program *Cantabile Prescolar* to preschool teachers, a teacher training program in music, with the objective of improving singing and movement activities at the preschool level. *Crescendo* has been under the directorship of María del Carmen Domínguez since January 2008. María del Carmen Domínguez is a Cuban musician who acquired bachelor's and master's in music degrees from the *Instituto Superior de Arte* (Higher Education of Art) at Habana, Cuba.

Dominican violinist Caonex Peguero (born in Santo Domingo in 1963) is a recognized violin player, conductor, composer, and arranger who initiated his violin studies with Frank Hernandez and later obtained bachelor's and master's in music degrees from the Julliard School of Music. In the year 2001, he founded his private academy called *Tecladíssimo*. His academy was the first to begin offering classes in pop, rock, and jazz. Up to that time, all the academies offered classical music training alone, and his program created a demand for instruction in popular genres. His piano and drum classes in laboratory settings attract many students. Peguero has been National Director of Music and also executive director of the National System of Youth Orchestras. He has founded various orchestral ensembles, among which are the *Orquesta Filarmónica del Cibao*, *Orquesta Nacional Juvenil* (Philharmonic Orchestra of Cibao), and the *Orquesta Juan Pablo Duarte* (Juan Pablo Duarte Orchestra).

Two recent private academies that focus on musical theatre (voice, dance, and acting) are *Escuela de Formación Artística Amaury Sánchez* (Amaury Sánchez Arts School), recently opened in 2010 by Amaury Sánchez, and JAM (Joy and Music) Academy, founded in 2009 by American voice teacher Elizabeth Sanchez.

Other private music academies include *Mubarak* founded by Berenice Mubarak de Ricart (studied piano at the National Conservatory of Music); *Do, Re, Mi Centro de Educacion Artistica de La Tia Nancy* founded by Nancy Peña in 2007; *Centro de Enseñanza Musical* founded in 2010 by trumpet player Andres Vidal and wife, Camelia Perez; *Academia de Música Patricia Logroño* founded in 2009 by Patricia Logroño (studied piano at the Estudio Diná de Educación Musical); *Gocessa* founded in 1992 by Hipólito Mejía (studied violin in Russia); *My Little Music House* founded by Xiomara Mayo in 1998; *Hogar Armonía* founded by Katy Disla; and *Academia de Musica ICA* (the latter two located in the city of Santiago). Many more private academies and music studios are located throughout the country.

HIGHER EDUCATION IN MUSIC EDUCATION

In 1994, the *Universidad Autónoma de Santo Domingo* (UASD) [Autonomous University of Santo Domingo], the oldest university in the New World founded in 1538, and the only public university of the Dominican Republic, approved the first undergraduate degree program in music in the country (Acra-Brache, February 2010). Enrolled students earn a bachelor's degree in music with concentration on music theory and music education. Initially, less than ten students enrolled and began the program of study. To date, fifty-two students have graduated since (Acra-Brache, March 2010).

The Faculty of Arts of the UASD is composed of seven schools with an enrollment of approximately seven thousand students. Data for the year 2010, provided by Ana Branagan, director of OPLASEFA (Office of Sectorial Planification of the Art Faculty), showed that by fall of 2009 there were 5,853 students enrolled in the Faculty of Art. Enrollment by school was as follows: School of Advertising (4,335 students), School of Industrial Design and Fashion (607 students), School of Film, Television, and Photography (317 students), School of Music (264 students), School of Art (84 students), School of Theatre and Dance (55 students), and School of Art History (9 students) (Acra-Brache, April 2010).

The bachelor in music with concentration on music theory and music education is a five-year program that is comprised of courses in music history, music theory, ear training, harmony, choral conducting, complimentary piano, music education (limited to the methods of Orff, Kodály, Dalcroze, and Bon Departe), and instrumental practice, among others. The only two requisites are to have a high school degree and to pass the admission test of the university that measures achievement in non-music-related fields. There is no musical requisite to enter the school of music (Acra-Brache, February 2010).

The majority of the students who enroll have had no previous training in music and thus neither play an instrument nor read or write music. Throughout the course of study they learn to sing, play the recorder, play classroom percussion instruments, and perform a variety of songs on the piano and the guitar. The final requisite for graduation after having completed the course credits by the end of the fifth year is to write and present a thesis on a music-related topic. Student teaching is not part of the program of study (Acra-Brache, June 2010).

Nevertheless, given the economic circumstances of most of the student population, it is common that university students work during hours when they are not in school. Many of these students are already teaching at schools and academies. Therefore, although there is no formal student teaching program, some students do graduate with teaching experience in the field (Acra-Brache, June 2010).

One of the challenges that has existed since the Bachelor in Music was initially offered to the population in 1994 was that the Dominican specialists in music who were going to become the professors of the program did not have a university degree in music. Many of them had studied music at the conservatory and were professors at the conservatory and private academies, and some had also taken courses and seminars in music abroad, but none had had access to formal university training in music (Acra-Brache, February 2010).

The first specialists to teach at the Bachelor in Music program were Bernarda Jorge, Miguel Pichardo Vicioso, Manuel Marino Miniño, and Fausto Vizcaino. The latter two have passed away. Other specialists who in the past taught for a brief period of time are Rafael Scarfullery, Dante Cucurullo, Iluminada Jiménez, and José Méndez.

However, in 2000, the Ministerio de Educación Superior de Ciencia y Tecnología (MESCIT) [Ministry of Higher Education of Science and Technology] mandated that all university professors must have a master's degree in order to have permission to teach at the university level. Professors without university degrees were expected to have completed their bachelor's degree by the year 2003, and by the year 2005, they were supposed to have obtained a master's degree (Acra-Brache, February 2010).

In response to this, the UASD quickly put together a one-time only master's degree in Musical Pedagogy that was offered between 2004 and 2006, consisting of forty-eight course credits and ten thesis credits. According to Victor Encarnación, director of Graduate Studies in Humanities, forty-four students enrolled in that master's program, and none have been able to obtain their master's degree yet. Out of the forty-four students, thirty were able to complete all the courses but were not allowed to complete their theses because the university discovered irregularities with the program, such as the fact that most of the students that had enrolled did not have a bachelor's degree.

The university could not award a master's degree to a student without a bachelor's degree and therefore, the students enrolled did not pursue the realization of their thesis beyond the completion of the courses. To solve this dilemma, the UASD has just offered an extra official, one-time-only, two-year special bachelor's program for these students (Acra-Brache, February 2010). Not a single student has graduated yet, and the master's program has not been offered again since.

At the present time, the music faculty for the bachelor in music degree of the UASD is limited to eight professors who have obtained a bachelor's degree in humanities, a master's degree or "specialty" degree in music, and all of them are currently enrolled in a doctorate degree in education offered by the UASD. The names of the faculty members and the countries where they obtained musical training are: María del Pilar Domingo (Dominican Republic, Chile), Hipólito Javier (Russia), Leovigildo Javier (Dominican Republic, Puerto Rico), Leini Guerrero (Dominican Republic), Gordana Vujcic (Yugoslavia), Larisa Jouk (Russia), Santiago Fals (Cuba, Russia), Mercedes Arostegui (Cuba, Russia) and Gladys Pérez (Dominican Republic, Italy). Paula Jacqueline Báez and Julio Báez, who graduated from the bachelor's degree program, are now teaching assistants. The faculty of music of the UASD has been enriched by the presence of foreign musicians trained in their native countries who now live in the Dominican Republic and who are contributing to the development of music.

The students enrolled in the regular bachelor's program have the opportunity to sing in a choral ensemble, instrumental chamber ensembles, or band. There is no music library, listening library, or computer lab, nor are there practice rooms. The university library has a very limited availability of music books and reference books, and so most of the students work on their research papers and thesis through material accessible through the internet (Acra-Brache, June 2010).

At the present time, the UASD is still the only university in the Dominican Republic to offer a bachelor's program in music education.

OFFICIAL INSTRUMENTAL PERFORMING ENSEMBLES

There are several performing ensembles in the country, both private and public, but it is the same group of musicians that performs in most of them. The official ensembles are the *Orquesta Sinfónica Nacional* (National Symphony Orchestra) and the *Orquesta Sinfónica Juvenil e Infantil* (Children and Youth Symphony Orchestra).

National Symphony Orchestra

On February 13, 1932, the *Orquesta Sinfónica de Santo Domingo* (Symphony Orchestra of Santo Domingo) was formed by Enríque Mejía Arredondo and Julio Alberto Hernández, but in 1940, due to economic reasons, the group ceased to perform. In 1941, the state decided to support this organization and named it *Orquesta Sinfónica Nacional* (OSN) (National Symphony Orchestra) under the directorship of Enrique Casals Chapí, who had arrived in the country as a Spanish refugee (Jorge, 1982, 111).

Between 1941 and 1959, the orchestra had three foreign conductors: Spanish conductor Enrique Casals Chapí (1941–1945), Mexican conductor Abel Eisenberg (1946–1951), and Italian conductor Roberto Caggiano (1951–1959). Following them, the orchestra performed under Dominican conductors: Manuel Simó (1959–1980), Jacinto Gimbernard (1980–1984), Carlos Piantini (1985–1994), Rafael Villanueva (1994–1995), Julio De Windt (1996–2000), Ecuatorian conductor Álvaro Manzano (2001–2004 and 2007–2009), Carlos Piantini (2001–2006 as laureate appointed director), and José Antonio Molina, who has been the current conductor since 2009. Some of the assistant directors have been Fernando Geraldes, Amaury Sánchez, and Dante Cucurullo (Pérez, 1993, 511).

Around the mid-1980s the OSN was reinforced by foreign musicians. Many of the foreign musicians come from Yugoslavia, and the first to arrive were Pavle Vujcic (concertino), Zvezdana Radojkovic and Yolanda Yankar (violinists), and Slobodan Vejkovic (cellist). Other foreign musicians have been John Clifford Huxford (American horn player) and Francois Bahuad (French cellist). New foreigners and fine Dominicans musicians have entered the orchestra since then, and together they deserve credit for the vast majority of symphonic music that is performed in the country. Many of them are also music teachers at the conservatory and private music academies and perform at private events as well.

The OSN has been able to accomplish much throughout the years thanks to the *Fundación Sinfonía*, a private, nonprofit organization founded by a group of music lovers with the purpose of fostering the presentation of classical music and the National Symphony Orchestra of the Dominican Republic. Pedro Rodríguez Villacañas and his wife, Margarita Copello de Rodríguez, founded the *Fundación Sinfonía* (Symphony Foundation) on November 24, 1986, gaining legal status by the Presidential Decree No. 505 on December 23, 1986.

Later, Decree 35-93, issued on January 29, 1993, gave the foundation the management of the National Symphony Orchestra until the creation of the Secretary of State of Culture in 2000. Since then, *Fundación Sinfonía* has been working in close collaboration with the Ministry of Culture to support the development of classical music and the National Symphony Orchestra of the Dominican Republic. The successful management of *Fundación Sinfonía* has enriched the musical life of the nation, inviting soloists, directors, and artists of international fame who alternate with the most distinguished musicians and national classical artists, an effort that reaches its peak every two years with the Santo Domingo Music Festival (SEEBAC, 2000).

Symphonic Youth Orchestra

On March 1997, the *Sistema Nacional de Orquestas Sinfónicas Infantiles y Juveniles* (SNOSIJ) (National System of Early Childhood and Youth Symphony Orchestras) was created under the efforts of Bernarda Jorge (music educator, pianist, recognized musicologist, and active promoter of the arts within official institutions) following UNESCO's program *Towards a Culture of Peace*. Its objective is the education and sociocultural development of human resources in the music field through orchestral performance practice. Dominican composer, educator, and conductor Juan Tony Guzmán was the first conductor of the SNOSIJ.

On April 13, 1997, the youth orchestra had its debut in Santo Domingo with more than a hundred children and adolescent music students from all over the country who participated in a workshop of orchestral practice offered by musicians of the Symphony Youth Orchestra Foundation of Venezuela. The Presidential Council for Culture and the Secretary of State for Education and Culture sponsored this workshop. It was officially established on May 1999 under the Executive Decree 193-99 and has since been active in the training of new generations of musicians.

On December 1998, the *Sistema Nacional de Orquestas Sinfónicas Infantiles y Juveniles*, under the directorship of Susana Acra-Brache, performed for Dr. Federico Mayor, general director of UNESCO. After the performance, Dr. Federico Mayor awarded the orchestra with the title "Young Artists for Peace" and named

Susana Acra-Brache an "Artist for Peace." These were the first two important recognitions that UNESCO had awarded in the field of Dominican art and culture (SEEBAC, 2000, 131).

The SNOSIJ has produced over one hundred workshops and concerts throughout the country. They rehearse on a regular basis and perform in formal settings such as the National Palace, National Theatre, and in other places such as cultural centers, municipal auditoriums, churches, and parks of the capital and other important cities of the country. They continue to be active in the training and practice of orchestral performance in the east, Cibao, and Santo Domingo, having achieved an increase in the number of orchestras and youth bands throughout the country. Dominican composer and conductor Darwin Aquino is responsible for keeping the orchestra active and engaged. Alongside him is Fernando Herrera as associate director.

OFFICIAL CHORAL PERFORMING ENSEMBLES

Choral singing has had the greatest development in the country in terms of the number of choral groups that are currently active. Many banks, universities, and other private institutions have amateur choirs comprised of their own employees. The official choral ensemble is the *Coro Nacional* (National Choir).

National Chorus

The National Choir was founded on March 1, 1995, as the *Coro Nacional del Conservatorio* (National Chorus of the Conservatory) under the Spanish director Juan Urteaga. After 1957, Dominican director Luis Rivera (1957–1962) directed the choir, and its name was changed to *Coro Nacional* (National Chorus). Its main role is to promote choral music representative of all genres. Some seventy Dominican singers comprise the choir. The following are or have been conductors: Luis Frías (1962–1966), José del Monte (1966–1980), Miguel Pichardo (1980–1982), César Hilario (1982–1984), Florencia Pierret (1984), José Manuel Joa (1984–1998), Fernando Geraldes (1998–2000), Mayra Peguero (2000–2002), Jesus Vizcaíno (2002–2004), Mayra Peguero (2004–2005), and José Enrique Espín (2005–) who is the current conductor (Acra-Brache, November 2010).

Lyrical Singers

The *Cantantes Líricos* (Lyrical Singers) are a group of artists incorporated by the state in 1979 with the objective of performing operatic repertoire and vocal songs of both international and Dominican composers under the directorship of Aristides Inchaustegui (tenor). The musicians of the group were Ivonne Haza (soprano), Gladys Pérez (soprano), Marianela Sánchez (soprano), Rafael Sánchez Cestero (tenor), Henry Ely (tenor), Frank Lendor (baritone), Fausto Cepeda (baritone), Vicente Grisolia (pianist), and Ramón Díaz (pianist). The group of singers that currently comprise the *Cantantes Lyricos* include Ondina Matos, Pura Tyson, Marianela Sánchez, Belkis Hernández, Vivian Lovelace, Dorka Quezada, Antonia Chabebe, Paola González, Carolina Camacho, Juan Tomás Reyes, Eduardo Mejía, Otilio Castro, and Juan Cuevas y Modesto Acosta.

EARLY CHILDHOOD MUSIC EDUCATION

The concept of early childhood music education was introduced in the country in 1999 by Dominican music educator and conductor Susana Acra-Brache. She had studied early childhood music education in the United States with Beth Bolton, John Feierabend, and Edwin Gordon. Upon her return to the country, Susana Acra-Brache began to offer the first classes of early childhood music to children ages birth through six during the fall of 1999 through a program called *Bebe Musical* (Musical Baby), described by her as an early childhood stimulation program through music.

Susana Acra-Brache's advocacy for early stimulation and music education through her involvement in workshops, seminars, and interviews on newspaper, television, and radio programs caught the attention of the entire community, especially the attention of educators in general. By the year 2001 many preschools had modified their names to include the words *Centro de Estimulación Temprana* (Center of Early Stimulation).

As a result of her work and training opportunities, other educators have learned about early childhood music education, and some have opened their own programs. Some of the educators who received training or were directly influenced by her work are María del Carmen Domínguez, Eliana González, Stephany Ortega, Nancy Peña, Karla Herrera, Nadia Nicola, Jacqueline Huguet, Farida Peña Diná, and Rita de los Santos. Some of these educators are currently working in the field of early childhood music education, and many Dominican families and educators are benefiting from their work.

On 2002 Farida Diná brought the first *Kindermusik* program into the country. She began to offer classes to children over eighteen months at the *Estudio Dina de Educación Musical*. In September 2005, together with Rita de los Santos, Farida Peña Dina founded the second early childhood center in the country, called *Aula Musical Creativa*, following the Kindermusik curriculum and implementing some of the Music Learning Theory techniques. In 2010, *Aula Musical Creativa* was closed and each of the founders opened their own practices. Rita de los Santos has recently opened *Kindermusik Studio*, and Farida Peña Dina continues to provide her Kindermusik program at the *Estudio Dina de Educación Musical*. Between the years 2000 and 2006, Xiomara Mayo provided outsourcing services in early childhood music to preschools of Santo Domingo and Santiago.

ADDITIONAL TRAINING IN CONTEMPORARY MUSIC EDUCATION

Most of the influential music educators of the nation received training at the INTEM in Chile between the 1960s and the 1980s. Some of them also participated in workshops offered in the country by foreign specialists. In 1999, Susana Acra-Brache offered a more recent intensive training in music education. She conducted a 120-hour course titled *Fundamentos de la Educación Musical* (Foundations of Music Education) to thirty-six musicians from private and public schools, private and public music academies, and state official institutions.

The course content provided an overview of contemporary music education as conceived in the United States.The content included but was not limited to: introduction to music education, early childhood music education, singing and movement, learning theories (Brunner, Gagne, Piaget, Pestalozzi, Gardner, and Gestalt), curriculum planning, lesson planning, measurement and evaluation, the singing voice, movement activities and folk dancing, movable do, music methodologies and techniques (Gordon, Kodály, Orff, Jaques-Dalcroze), peer teaching, teaching observations, choral conducting practicum, and the realization of a final project.

The music teachers who participated were: Leila Pérez y Pérez, Sonia Peralta de Piña, Santiago Fals, Juana Reyes, Adamilka Victoria, Iris Díaz, Ezequiel Sánchez, Marlene Méndez, Altabeira Polanco, Ramón Eladio Restituyo, Farida Peña, María del Carmen Domínguez, Carmen Xenia Rivera, Nancy Peña, Stephany Ortega, Eglass Francisco, Ylsa Peña, Angela Reyes, Amelia Aybar A., Isabel Aybar L., Tania Bonilla, Angel Daniel Calderón, Esmeralda Compres, Joel del Orbe, Rita de los Santos, Joselito del Rosario, Luis Cruz, José Oscar Cuevas, Baron Luis Rodríguez, Aymara García, Marcos González, Evelyn Levasseur, Ramón Osorio, and Juan Esteban Martínez.

Many of these participants were already distinguished members of the Dominican music education community, and others between 1999 and 2010 found ways to contribute to the development of music education in the Dominican Republic and currently hold important positions in the field of music and music education.

MUSIC FESTIVALS

In 1976, the Carol Morgan Music Festival was organized under the initiative of American music educator John Walker (a Luther College graduate), who was the secondary choir and orchestra conductor at the Carol Morgan School of Santo Domingo (the first American school of the country, founded in 1933 by American missionary Carol Morgan). The event involved choirs, ensembles, solos, student conductors, guest clinicians, a combined student orchestra, and a mass chorus of five hundred voices. Each festival had a different thematic focus, which served as a focus for the repertory. As the festival grew over the years, musicians came from all over the country to participate along with musicians from abroad. The festival took place at the Carol Morgan School facilities.

The objective of the Carol Morgan Festival was to create a space for musical encounter that bridged the demographics of age, class, geography, and culture. This event contributed to a wide range of possibilities that encouraged musical development at the grassroots level. While the repertory largely reflected the genre of "musica docta," the level of participatory enthusiasm and democratic nature of the event soon took on the character of "music-making by and for the people." One keen international observer from the United Nations Singers dubbed the Carol Morgan Music Festival as the "Super Bowl of Music." The National Youth Orchestra of the Dominican Republic had its genesis in the mass orchestra of this festival. The festival was held for sixteen consecutive years from 1976 until 1991, and as a result of this festival and others that later were inspired by it, the choral and instrumental movement achieved a deeper level of penetration in the society as a whole.

Since 1979, every year during the entire month of October the Secretary of State for Education celebrates *El Mes de la Canción Escolar* (the Month of School Song). During that month a variety of workshops and regional and district choral encounters are held throughout public schools nationwide. The activities culminate with the *Festival de Coros José de Jesús Ravelo*, usually toward the end of the month. Every year, the festival is dedicated to a Dominican musician, and the 2010 festival was dedicated to Dominican music educator and promoter of choral singing Leila Pérez y Pérez.

The *Festival de Coros Infantiles y Juveniles* (Festival of Children and Youth Choirs) has been organized by the *Estudio Dina de Educación Musical* since 1990 for nonprofessional choral groups. The festival is held over a period of three consecutive days every year and includes adult choirs as well. It is a festival but also a competition, and the three finalists of each category receive an award. The jury is made up of local, and on occasions international, musicians who during the festival conduct workshops. This festival usually takes place at the *Palacio de Bellas Artes* (Fine Arts Palace). This festival was put on hold in 2002 but was reactivated in 2010. The *Festival de Coros Infantiles y Juveniles* for 2010 was dedicated to Jose del Monte (longtime conductor of the *Coro de La Catedral*) (Acra-Brache, July 2010).

Andres Vidal, Cuban trumpet player, started in 2005 a nonprofit organization called Festi-Band with the purpose of creating and supporting youth bands all throughout the nation. To date, five festivals have successfully been held where over 3,500 young musicians have had the opportunity to participate. The last festival held in 2010 included the participation of twenty-nine bands. The *Orquesta Dominicana de Vientos* (Dominican Wind Orchestra) is the official orchestra of Festi-Band and is composed of sixty-four young musicians from all over the country between the ages of ten to twenty-five. Festi-Band receives support from Yamaha Music Latin America, World Association of Bands, and American conductor John Alden Stanley (Acra-Brache, October 2011).

MUSICAL THEATRE

Dominican percussionist, arranger, and composer Amaury Sánchez (born in Santo Domingo in 1963) has been responsible for the recent active development of musical theatre in the Dominican Republic in the past decade. He studied music at the *Academia de Música* de Tania Baez and also with Miriam Ariza and Sonia de Piña. He studied composition and conducting in the United States and Spain. He has staged *The Sound of Music, Jesus Christ Superstar, Evita, Beauty and the Beast, Peter Pan, Annie, Cabaret, Cats, Cinderella* and *Chicago*. In addition, he has been a promoter of pop-symphonic music through his performances with the Santo Domingo Pops. Sanchez has composed a variety of works, among them *Misa Festiva Dominicana* and *Ballet 12 Basados en Los Estados de Animo*, and he has composed music for five films.

For over ten years he has been producing musicals, and as a result of his work many young amateur musicians are formally studying music for theatre, movie, and television. Due to the demand in voice, theatre, and dance training, Amaury Sánchez recently opened in 2010 a private academy for the arts called *Escuela de Formación Artística Amaury Sánchez* (Amaury Sánchez Arts School).

Other theatre artists and musicians who are also active in the musical theatre field have produced other musicals as well. Guillermo Cordero produced *Fiddler on the Roof, Victor Victoria*, and *The Kiss of the Spider Woman*. Danilo Reynoso produced *El Milagro de Fátima*, and Carolina Rivas and Luichy Guzmán produced *Les Miserables*. All the musicals mentioned above were performed in Spanish.

OPERA

The first opera performances were presented during the 1950s through *La Voz Dominicana* television program during Trujillo's regime. Vito Castorina and Roberto Caggiano produced a few complete operas (*Cavalleria Rusticana*, *La Traviata*, and *Rigoletto*) that were staged and transmitted from the television studio. Some of the singers who participated in those opera performances were Violeta Stephen, Elenita Santos, Geronimo Pellerano, Armando Recio, Tony Curiel, Olga Azar, Fausto Cepeda, and Rafael Sanchez Cestero (Acra-Brache, February 2011).

The next important period in the development of opera in the Dominican Republic took place between the 1970s and the late 1980s. Conductor Carlos Piantini (1927–2010), who was artistic director of the National Theatre upon its opening in August 1973, was highly committed to turning the National Theatre into a world-class arts center. Four months after the inauguration of the theatre, he staged and conducted *La Traviata*, premiering Diana Reed, Henry Ely, Adib Fazah, Virginia Kamer, Noel Ramírez, Omar Franco, Ramón Figueroa, Austria Calderón, and Francisco Cassanova. In the ten years that followed, Carlos Piantini conducted an extensive number of operas including *Rigoletto* (1974), the zarzuela *Los Gavilanes* (1974), *The Barber of Seville* (1975), *Tosca* (1975 and 1981), *Il Tabarro* (1975), *Madama Butterfly* (1975), *La Traviata* (again in 1977 and later in 1998), *Carmen* (1977), *L'Elisir d'Amore* (1979), *La Boheme* (1980), *Don Pasquale* (1980), and *Il Trovatore* (1982) (Teatro Nacional, 1998).

During this period many foreign musicians were invited to perform at the various opera performances and participate alongside Dominican lyric singers such as Rafael Sanchez Cestero, Henry Ely, Ivonne Haza, Fausto Cepeda, Aristides Inchaustegui, Frank Lendor, Marianela Sánchez, Teresita Pérez Frangie, Francisco Cassanova, and Gladys Pérez.

A number of other opera performances have been staged since 1985 (including *Aida*) and new singers have emerged, but unfortunately opera in general has had a decline since then. The performances are very costly, and the audience that appreciates the art and can afford to attend is very limited (Acra-Brache, February 2011).

NATIONAL ARCHIVES

The *Archivo Nacional de Música* (National Archive of Music) was created on November 15, 1968, and is the department responsible for investigating, recollecting, classifying, and preserving Dominican musical compositions that existed since the 1800s. It was installed at the *Palacio de Bellas Artes* (Fine Arts Palace) and later moved to a building on the grounds of the National Conservatory of Music. In November of 2006, under the Decree 536-06, the Archive had to merge with the *Centro de Recuperación, Conservación y Difusión de la Música Dominicana*, which had been created in 1999 as a department within the National Theatre. Unfortunately, most of the materials from the National Archive had been lost or were in bad shape and were taken to a repository where they wait to be restored. The *Centro de Recuperación, Conservación y Difusión de la Música Dominicana* (Center for Research, Conservation and Diffusion of Dominican Music) remains active under the care of Leila J. Pérez y Pérez, who has been in charge of the center since the year 2000. The center is no longer the property of the National Theatre but of the Ministry of Culture (Acra-Brache, February 2010).

PERFORMING ARTS CENTERS

The important and well-equipped performing arts centers in the Dominican Republic are located in Santo Domingo and Santiago. These centers have been very active since their inaugurations and have served as a platform for many Dominican and international classical and popular musicians to expose their art to the Dominican community.

The *Teatro Nacional* (National Theatre), located in Santo Domingo, was designed by Dominican arquitect Teófilo Carbonell and was inaugurated on August 16, 1973 (Teatro Nacional, 1998, 19). It has three performance halls: the main hall recently named *Sala Principal Carlos Piantini* (Carlos Piantini Principal Hall, 1,589 seats); the *Sala Ravelo* (Ravelo Hall, 190 seats); and the *Sala de la Cultura* (Hall of Culture, 228 seats). Every year a variety of performances are presented in the theatre, including symphonic concerts, operas, ballets, musicals, theatre plays, and concerts with popular artists.

The *Palacio de Bellas Artes* (Fine Arts Palace) was built in 1955 under the supervision of engineer Virgilio Pérez Bernal during the Trujillo Regime and inaugurated on May 15, 1956. It has a 650 seating hall auditorium that is also used for symphonic and choral concerts as well as all other types of concerts. Many offices of the various department of the Secretary of State for Fine Arts and Culture are located within this building. The offices of the National Symphony Orchestra and the National Choir are located here (SEEBAC, 2000, 22).

In Santiago there are two important art centers. The eldest is the *Centro de la Cultura* (Center of Culture), which was inaugurated on March 30, 1979. Its first director was Margarita Luna, and it is a center where many cultural activities take place. The *Gran Teatro Regional del Cibao* (Great Regional Theatre of Cibao) is almost an exact replica of the National Theatre in Santo Domingo. It was also built by Teófilo Carbonell and inaugurated on August 16, 1995.

MUSIC APPRECIATION COURSES FOR THE COMMUNITY

The first music appreciation courses were offered to the community by Julio Ernesto Ravelo de la Fuente (1910–2000). For over twenty years he offered free *Cursos de Cultura Musical* (Courses in Musical Culture) at the *Sala de la Cultura* Hall of the National Theatre to persons of all social status. He contributed significantly to developing a more informed audience and consumers of classical music. He also wrote all the program notes for the National Symphony Orchestra up to his death. These program notes were published in 2000 in a book titled *Apreciación Musical—Notas al Programa de la Orquesta Sinfónica Nacional* (Program Notes of the National Symphony Orchestra).

Following Ravelo's legacy, Catana Pérez de Cuello, ex-director of the National Theatre and author of *El Universo de la Música*, continued his tradition of providing free courses to the public between 1998 to 2000. Her courses were titled *Programa de Apreciacion Musical Profesor Julio Ravelo* (Program of Music Appreciation Professor Julio Ravelo) and were offered at the *Sala de la Cultura*. Italian composer and musicologist Antonio Braga also provided free appreciation courses in ballet and opera also at the *Sala de la Cultura* from 1996 until 2009, the year of his death. Two other musicians known for offering music appreciation courses are Aida Bonelly de Diaz and Gracita Senior de Pellerano (the latter offered her courses at the National Library during the 1980s).

DOCTORAL DISSERTATIONS ON DOMINICAN MUSIC EDUCATION

Juan-Tony Guzmán's 1999 doctoral dissertation is titled "Music Education in the Dominican Republic Schools: A Survey Appraisal." The data obtained from the surveys led to some of the following conclusions: that there is a great interest in music education regardless of current serious deficiencies; that music instruction should be taught to all students, not just the musically talented or those interested in music; that there is a strong support for large instrumental ensembles in schools, alongside choral ensembles; that all groups are willing to pay for the acquisition of their musical instrument without depending upon complete government support; that according to school stakeholders, music and the arts should be taught separately and not integrated into the artistic education class; that the training of music educators is imperative since Dominicans preferred a music educator as the person responsible for teaching music in the classroom; that, while there are few choirs, most Dominican schools do not have musical activities, music classes, or ensembles; that most students, parents, teachers, and administrators have not had a good music education; and that music teachers, instruments, and facilities are the main needs for the improvement of music education in the schools (Guzmán, 1999).

In Susana Acra-Brache's 2004 doctoral dissertation titled "Toward a Contemporary Vision of Music Education in the Dominican Republic," she asserts that the study provided the following evidence: that music education in the Dominican Republic lacks a contemporary vision and that its practice is not approached systematically; that it is very difficult to be a music educator in the Dominican Republic given inadequate facilities, resources, salaries, and teacher training opportunities; that there is a serious shortage of adequately trained music educators; that the concept of Artistic Education should be revised so that the art disciplines be taught separate from one another by a well-trained specialist in the field; that the National Conservatory of Music should be allowed to award bachelor's and master's in music and music education; and that teacher training in contemporary practices of music education is imperative (Acra-Brache, 2004).

CONCLUSION

Spanish colonization influenced the musical culture of the Dominican Republic since 1492. During the sixteenth and seventeenth centuries music performance and teaching was in the Western European tradition and was available mostly in monasteries and convents, with the objective of training musicians for the Church for sacred purposes.

Music-making in the Dominican Republic has evolved significantly over time, especially since the 1800s, with an increase in the number of performers, composers, conductors, and teachers. This music evolution took place not only in the capital city of Santo Domingo but in other cities and towns as well, and most of the musicians, despite their city of birth, have contributed greatly in one way or another to the development of music in the country. Thus, music education and performance opportunities in cities outside the capital should not be neglected.

Most of the musicians of the nineteenth century performed in municipal or military bands, and this participation clearly inspired a large number of them to become professional musicians. This indicates that the provision of school bands and municipal bands may be one of the ways to increase the number of music students in the country at the present time. This is particularly important given that in actuality there is an extremely limited number of trained musicians and music educators in comparison to the total population of the country. Therefore, these musicians are not able to meet the demands of a country that wants to develop musically.

The creation of official music schools such as the *Escuela Elemental de Música Elila Mena*, the *Conservatorio Nacional de Música*, as well as the other public and private music academies, provided training for most of the accomplished Dominican musicians. The official schools are important, and the state needs to provide a much stronger commitment and budget allocation to them so that they may be properly maintained and sustained over time in terms of physical and human resources, facilities, and adequately trained teachers.

The presence of both foreign-trained musicians and Dominican musicians who received training abroad elevated the musical level of proficiency and knowledge of many Dominican musicians in the fields of performance, conducting, music education, and composition. Many of the pioneers in music education received training at the INTEM from the University of Chile in collaboration with the Organization of American Studies (OEA) between 1967 and 1989. This illustrates that international music exchange provides a successful means to elevate music standards, and such practice should be maintained.

During the Trujillo regime there were many opportunities for music learning and performing because music and cultural development was a priority for the state. Since the 1960s there has been limited funding for music, and little has been done to provide adequate training for professionals in the field of music. Music and education in general need to receive stronger support from government authorities.

Many of the achievements obtained during the 1960s up to 1997 toward the inclusion of music education as a separate and important subject in the school curriculum were dissolved with the implementation of artistic education in schools during the mid-1990s. It should be taken into consideration that any school subject will only contribute to child development if it is taught in such a way that a child may understand its importance and usefulness in their lives.

Dominican authorities recognize that the various art disciplines have the potential to benefit the development of the whole child, but unfortunately that benefit will only be obtained if each of the art disciplines is taught well, and to that end, a separate specialist for each of the arts is necessary. The National Association for Music Education (NAfME) has designed a set of standards for each art and does not recommend teaching all of them at once (visit http://bit.ly/2014Standards).

Perhaps Dominican authorities have not considered separating the arts because the fact is that there are not enough trained specialists to cover all public schools nationwide. A substantial amount of teacher training in music and music education is necessary.

The future development of music in the Dominican Republic will depend on the number of musicians that are adequately trained within the next decades. Significantly larger numbers of trained musicians and music educators are needed. School music education practice needs to move toward a more comprehensive and contemporary approach to music teaching. Many great advances have been achieved, and many more will continue to push Dominican music forward given a strong commitment to improve music education from the government and the entire Dominican population, and hopefully with support from the international community as well.

REFERENCES

Acra-Brache, Susana. (January 2010). Interview with Leila Perez y Perez, Director of *Centro de Recuperacion, Conservacion y Difusion de la Musica Dominicana*. Santo Domingo.

————. (February 2010). Interview with Maria del Pilar Dominguez, Dean of the Art Faculty of the UASD. Santo Domingo.

————. (March, 2010). Interview with Luis Alberto Rodriguez, Director of Thesis Department of the UASD. Santo Domingo.

————. (April, 2010). Data obtained from Ana Branagan, Director of the Office of Sectorial Planification of the Art Faculty. Santo Domingo.

————. (May 2010). Interview with Victor Encarnacion, Director of Graduate Studies of the UASD. Santo Domingo.

————. (June, 2010). Interview with Leini Guerrero, President of the Teachers Association of the Art Faculty of the UASD. Santo Domingo.

————. (October, 2010). Interview with Andres Vidal, Director of Festi-Band. Santo Domingo.

————. (November, 2011). Interview with Mayra Peguero, Past Conductor of the National Choir and Choir of the National Conservatory of Musica. Santo Domingo.

————. (January, 2011). Data obtained from Maria Irene Blanco, Director of the National Conservatory of Music. Santo Domingo.

————. (February, 2011). Interview with Ivonne Haza, Past Director of the National Theater and Lyrical Singer. Santo Domingo.

————. (2004). *Towards a Contemporary Vision of Music Education in the Dominican Republic*. Published Doctoral Dissertation. Temple University.

Alberti, Luis. (1975). *De Música y Orquestas Bailables Dominicanas. 1910-1959*. Santo Domingo.

Coopersmith, J.M. (1949). *Música y Músicos de la República Dominicana*.

Dirección General de Bellas Artes. (2005). *Foro Nacional Sobre la Enseñanza Artística*. Santo Domingo.

————. (2007). *Reglamento de la Formación Artística Especializada*. Santo Domingo.

Fernández de Oviedo, Gonzalo. (1959). *Historia General y Natural de las Indias y Tierra – Firme del Mar Oceano*. Edición Biblioteca de Autores Españoles.

Guzmán, Juan-Tony. (1999). *Music Education in the Dominican Republic Schools: A Survey Appraisal*. Doctoral Dissertation. Florida State University.

Henríquez-Ureña, Pedro. (1960). *Obra Critica*. México, D.F.: Fondo de Cultura Económica.

————. (1977). *Obras Completas Tomo III*. Santo Domingo: Editora de la Universidad Nacional Pedro Henríquez Ureña.

Jorge, Bernarda. (1982). *La Música Dominicana: Siglos XIX-XX*. Colección Arte y Sociedad No. 10. Santo Domingo: Editora de la Universidad Autónoma de Santo Domingo.

Lebrón Saviñon, Mariano. (1981). *Historia de la Cultura Dominicana. Primer Tomo*. Santo Domingo: Editora Universidad Nacional Pedro Henríquez Ureña.

Luna, Margarita. (1973). *Por el Mundo de la Orquesta*. Santo Domingo: Editora Cultural Dominicana.

Ministerio de Cultura . (2010). *Metas Educativas. Consulta Nacional*. Santo Domingo.

Nolasco, Flerida de. (1948). *Vibraciones con el Tiempo*. Ciudad Trujillo.

Pérez, Catana. (1993). *El Universo de la Música*. Tomo II. Santo Domingo: Editora Taller.

Perez, Odalis G. (2010). *Pedro Henríquez Ureña. Historia Cultural, Historiografía y Crítica Literaria*. Santo Domingo: Archivo General de la Nación. Vol. CXIV.

Persinal, Carlos Andújar. (1997). *La Presencia Negra en Santo Domingo*. Santo Domingo: Editora BUHO.

Rodríguez-Demorizi, Emilio. (1971). *Música y Baile en Santo Domingo*. Santo Domingo: Editora Santo Domingo.

Secretaría de Estado de Educación, Bellas Artes y Cultura (SEEBAC). (1976). *Decreto 1141. Octubre, "Mes de la Cancion Escolar"*. Santo Domingo.

————. (1987). Pamphlet *Curso de Formacion y Capacitacion Musical para Docentes Musicales en Ejercicio*. Santo Domingo.

————. (1994). *Fundamento del Curriculo. Tomo I. Serie INNOVA 2000*. Santo Domingo.

————. (1994). *Fundamento del Currículo. Tomo II. Serie INNOVA. 2000*. Santo Domingo.

————. (1994). *¿Por Qué? ¿Para Qué? De la Trasformación Curricular. INNOVA. 2000*. Santo Domingo.

————. (1995). *Propuesta De Orientación Educativa Y Psicológica*. Santo Domingo.

————. (1996). *¿Cómo Promover la Transformación Curricular en los Centros Educativos? . Serie INNOVA. 2000*. Santo Domingo.

————. (1997). *Ley General De Educación No. 66"97*. Santo Domingo.

Teatro Nacional. (1998). *Veinticinco Años de Teatro Nacional*. Santo Domingo.

Chapter Three

Puerto Rico

Raymond Torres-Santos

INTRODUCTION

This chapter presents a historical perspective of music education in Puerto Rico. The research focuses on how music education evolved in Puerto Rican society and made its way into the public schools. To broaden the scope of this study, it became necessary to examine the embryonic forms of musical activities, which emerged in the home, church, and community, as well as other institutional structures and organizations; this expanded the range of possibilities not available within the context of public education. In order to present a historical view it was also necessary to recognize the role and contribution of private teachers, performers, composers, directors, and other community musicians. In addition, the traditions of ethnic groups were included for their profound influence on music education.

EARLY DAYS: TAÍNO HERITAGE

The history of music education in Puerto Rico began with the *Taíno* natives approximately 1,500 years ago, when they called the island *Borikén*. Anthropological and educational studies indicate that through *areytos*—magical, religious, and entertainment rituals—*Taínos* narrated the origins of their deities—*cemís*—and, with music and dance, celebrated the triumph of war and their history (Alegría, 1950; Brau, 1904; Coll y Toste, 1907 and 1910; The International Institute of Teachers College, 1926; Mellado Parson, 1948 and 1976; Osuna, 1949; The Institute of Field Studies of Teachers' College, 1950; Gallardo, 1975).

The instruments used during these celebrations consisted of percussion and wind instruments. Among those instruments were *magüey* (drum made of a hollow tree and played with a wooden stick); *amaraca* (a maraca); *guajey* (a scraper made of a gourd, known today as *güiro*); *guamo* (a sea conch); *sonajero* (a bunch of conches, snails, bones, and dry seed, used to keep the beat); and a consort of flutes and whistles made of human bones among other materials (Muñoz, 1966, 11–12). This tradition was passed on from generation to generation in a society in which making music was part of daily life.

DISCOVERY, SPANISH COLONIALISM, AND MUSIC IN THE ROMAN CATHOLIC CHURCH

A year after the discovery of the New World in 1492, Christopher Columbus, on his second voyage, landed in Puerto Rico (*Borikén*) on November 19, 1493. Immediately Spaniards secured the conversion of natives to Christianity through education provided by mostly Dominican and Franciscan friars and nuns. Grammar and the arts were taught in addition to the fundaments of the Catholic religion. As in many cases in history, music was used as the best "weapon" for the conversion. Natives were taught to read music and sing solo or in chorus, and later to play organ, woodwind (particularly *chirimías*), and string instruments (such as the *vihuela*). The

43

friar-educators learned the native language and allowed in some instances the inclusion of native words and music to the special religious events. Therefore, an exchange between cultures started to take place, eventually resulting in new, mixed, *syncretic* music styles, autochthonous to the island.

The seventeenth century saw the founding of towns. A chapel master and cantor position were soon open in the Cathedral of San Juan to distinguished trained musicians who not only provided music for mass and other liturgical occasions but also music training to the Puerto Rican youth. Eventually, church services provided the opportunity for local composers to perform and disseminate their compositions. During this century an examination was given to those students interested in graduating after their training. However, education was still for a few and nothing had been achieved for the population at large (Fitzmaurice, 1970, 54).

In the eighteenth century there was an active emigration and immigration and, therefore, a great demand for secondary education. It is known that few women taught in the homes of a small number of young women (Fitzmaurice, 1970). Even so, church, through clergy and some laymen, remained as the main provider of education on the island all the way to the 1800s. The first appointed Spanish chapel master at the San Juan Cathedral was Domingo Delgado (1814–1856). Although born in the Canary Islands, Delgado is considered the first Puerto Rican master composer of sacred music, composing many works for vocal soloists, chorus, and orchestra (Rivera, 2006, 7–8).

THE EMERGENCE OF BAND MUSIC

As the military troops settled in strategic geographical locations on the island, they brought with them *bandas de regimiento* (military bands). By the nineteenth century, when many Spanish colonies were getting their independence through revolutionary forces, additional military backup was added to Puerto Rico, and therefore more military bands. These bands became the most important generator of musical activities on the island through *retretas* (open-air concerts). Their music directors provided much of the music training and performance opportunities for local musicians. As a result there was an evident switch of roles from sacred church— that is, vocal music—to instrumental music by means of military bands. The instrumentation and repertoire of the bands had an enormous influence on the development of Puerto Rican dance and popular music.

PUBLIC AND PRIVATE MUSIC INSTRUCTION

The nineteenth century marked the beginning of an education sponsored by the state and an interest in the fine arts. This was particularly evident through the *Decreto Orgánico* [Organic Decree] of 1865. However, education was inefficient as related to clearly dividing the functions between elementary and secondary schools. Furthermore, music was not part of the public education system. This kind of educational system, including the selection and training of teachers, was similar to any Spanish colony. Therefore, it was the private schools and church schools that provided the most meaningful contributions to education during this time (Fitzmaurice, 1970, 118). By 1837, there were many private schools and academies (*liceos*) founded on the island.

Population increased further with the arrival of people from mainland Spain, the Canary Islands, Majorca, Corsica, and other countries in Europe. Among them, there were fine musicians who provided private lessons to both women and men. Thanks to public and private scholarships, some male students coming from bourgeois families pursued music as a profession, studying at the Paris Conservatory of Music. At their return, they also became active music advocates, performers, composers, and educators of other Puerto Rican musicians not able to study abroad. Among those musicians who studied at the Paris Conservatory were Manuel G. Tavárez (1846–1883); Gonzalo Nuñez (1850–1915); and Julio Carlos de Arteaga (1873–1923), who studied with Cesar Franck and Jules Massenet, and both settled in the United States; Arístides Chavier Arévalo (1865–1942); and Francisco Pedro Cortés González (1873–1950). Felipe Guitierrez y Espinosa (1825–1900), who became the first Puerto Rican composer to write an opera (*Guarionex*, 1856, although *Macías*, probably dating from the 1860s, is indeed the earliest extant opera) and authored a text on music theory (*Teoría de la Música*, 1875), studied briefly in Europe as well (Callejo Ferrer, 1977).

Curiously, some of the most remarkable Puerto Rican composers rarely left the island but were the beneficiaries of the knowledge acquired by those who studied abroad. Among those were Juan Morel Campos (1857–1896), who studied with Tavárez in Ponce; Braulio Dueño Colón (1854–1934), who studied with Rosario Aruti, an Italian impresario and music teacher in Bayamón; and José Ignacio Quintón (1881–1925), who studied with Ernesto del Castillo in Coamo (Callejo Ferrer, 1977). Some other music teachers also worth mentioning were the Catalonian José Cabrizas, who taught Manuel G. Tavárez and Gonzalo Nuñez; Dr. Ermelindo Salazar, teacher of Julio C. de Arteaga; José Oriol Pasarell and José Fornós, who taught Francisco Cortés González; and Antonio Egipciaco, one of the professors of Juan Morel Campos. In addition, musicologist Héctor Campos-Parsi acknowledges other teachers scattered around the island. Some of these were Jesús Muñoz in Utuado, Hermógenes in Caguas, Alejandro Romero in Arecibo, José María Scwarkoff in Cayey, and Santiago Espada in San Germán (Campos-Parsi, 1976, 176). In addition, printed music essays, books, and educational materials were translated from French and published on the island. These publications provided the impetus for the development of music educators.

PIANO, INSTRUMENTAL MUSIC, AND OPERA: AN ACTIVE CULTURAL LIFE

By the nineteenth century, the piano became the most popular instrument. Nevertheless, the active performance of string, woodwind, and brass music during the previous century led to the establishment of good orchestras, like the one conducted by Felipe Gutiérrez y Espinosa. These orchestras not only played music of Puerto Rican composers but also important works from the European repertoire. Along with music societies and academies, they served to accelerate music education on the island. In 1823 a philharmonic society was established; in 1865 the *Sociedad Artística* offered a series of concerts and music studies; and in 1871 the *Academia de Música de Puerto Rico*, led by Gutierrez Espinosa, provided music instruction. Accordingly to Héctor Campos-Parsi, the *Sociedad* was "the predecessor of the Federation of Musicians in that it provided medical health to its members," and the *Academia* was "the predecessor of the Puerto Rico Conservatory of Music created nearly a hundred years later" (1976, 178). Other supporting cultural organizations also emerged. In 1832 the *Teatro Municipal* (Tapia Theater) in San Juan was founded, and in 1876 the *Ateneo Puertorriqueño* (Puerto Rican Athenium) became the most distinguished and prestigious center of culture until the end of the century.

Italian operas and Spanish zarzuelas flourished during the nineteenth century. Puerto Rican port cities as well as coffee, sugar, and tobacco *haciendas* built their own theaters, artistic circles, and private musical academies, at which wealthy families sponsored recitals, concerts, and musical *soirées* (*veladas musicales* or *tertulias*). Puerto Rico became a hub for many opera companies and artists. In 1857, for instance, child prodigy Italian singer Adelina Patti visited the island. Her accompanist, prominent pianist, and composer Louis Moreau Gottschalk was singular for encouraging local singers, musicians, and composers. Simultaneously Gottschalk was influenced by Puerto Rico, composing four works using local themes or based on incidents on the island (Fitzmaurice, 1970, 70). Other European visitors included Isaac Albéniz in 1875, Albert Friedenthal in 1885, and violinist Luisa Terzi in 1892 (Thompson, Musical Puerto Rico, 1998, 3).

Many operatic productions were also staged by local singers, musicians, and impresarios, resulting in the proliferation of many opera singers and teachers. Antonio Paoli (1873–1946), who used the stage name Ermogene Imleghi Bascarán, emerged as the first Puerto Rican tenor with an international reputation. In 1912 Ruggiero Leoncavallo himself, composer of the opera *I Pagliacci*, came to Puerto Rico to conduct and record his opera for the first time. His sister, soprano Amalia Paoli (1861–1942), who studied in Spain, also enjoyed an international career and took an active part in Puerto Rico (Thompson, Musical Puerto Rico, 5).

MUSIC IN THE COMMUNITY

Spanish-Derived Folk Music

Meanwhile, peasants who settled on the mountains and are known as *jíbaros* had kept aspects of folk Spanish music and musical practices in the form of *aguinaldos*, *seises*, and *villancicos* (Christmas carols) along with native instruments such as the *típle* (a small variant of the guitar from the Canary Islands), *cuatro* (a medium variant that originally had four strings but later had five double strings), *bordonua* (a large variant), and guitar as well as *maracas* (gourd rattles) and *güiro* (a gourd scraper, descendant of both the *Taíno* and African cultures). The singers were *trovadores* (troubadours) who improvised based on a *pie forzao* (a given obbligato theme). Glasser confirms that "like much of Latin American music, [this music] was permeated by melodic and harmonic elements of southern Spain, which themselves bore a strong Moorish influence." She adds, "Puerto Rican peasants could not read music but preserved their history, transmitted the content of the Bible down through the generations, and commented on life around them" (1995, 20–21). This tradition was kept in the form of *parrandas* (sprees), *fiestas del acabe* (end of harvest parties), *rosaries* (nightly celebration where the rosary was sung), *fiestas de cruz* (sacred rituals), and *fiestas patronales* (patron saint festivals), among others.

African-Derived Folk Music

Puerto Rico also benefited from the arrival of a new ethic group: Africans. Following the colonization of Spain, the imposed agricultural economy of sugar and coffee brought a society with profound class differences, which were in tune with the political structure of European monarchies. The *Taíno* native force had diminished to such a degree that by the middle of the sixteenth century they were practically nonexistent (Fitzmaurice, 1970). In the first decade of slavery (1509–1519), Spaniards brought African slaves already Christianized and assimilated from Seville. In the second decade (1519–1529), slaves came from a spectrum of western, central, and northern African societies to work on the coastal regions, dominated by large sugar plantations. Just as in Cuba and Brazil, many of them were descendent of the Sudan and Bantu cultures from Angola, Congo, and Mozambique (Torres-Santos, 2010). This new influence had a significant impact on music and, therefore, on education. Just like the *Taíno* natives, singing, playing music, and dancing were inseparable and played a major role in their daily lives. When slavery was abolished in 1873 African tradition was well preserved, as it had been passed on from generation to generation and kept alive in carnivals and religious festivities.

Bomba was the synthesis of those African traditions. It was characterized by polyrhythmic drumming and call-and-response vocal style, in which a chorus in unison answered a lead singer. It featured improvisation and a complex interaction between the drummer and dancers. The *Bomba* drums or *barriles* (conga drums) were played in pairs. The large drum is called *tambor macho, seguidor,* or *burlador;* while the small drum is called *tambor hembra, requinto,* or *suvidor.* Other instruments included the *cuá* (a piece of wood struck with two wooden sticks) and rattles. Another instrument related to this tradition was the *marímbula* or *marímba,* a descendant of the African *mbira* or thump piano, just like the xylophone. *Bomba* is played and danced following different rhythmic patterns (or *toques*). At least nine toques have been identified: *güembé, leró, gracimá, holandé, calindá, yubá, belén, cunyá,* and *mariandá.*

Folk Music and Syncretic Music

By the late nineteenth century a cultural exchange between local Africans and Europeans resulted in new, hybrid music genres reflective of the complexity of race, class, and nationality in Puerto Rico. The first of those genres was the *danza,* a popular dance music. Glasser reports, "The form itself was the product of multiple migrations, with roots in the English 'country music,' the *contradanza* of Spain and Cuba, and the *contradanse* brought to Puerto Rico by French planters fleeing the Haitian revolution" (1995). María Luisa Muñoz adds that "in the *contradanse* was contained the rhythmic and melodic germ of the Cuban *habanera* [and the] Dominican Republic's *merengue*" (1966). A multisectioned music, *Danza* began with a *paseo,* or introduction, followed by a melodic section known as a *merengue.* A contrasting melodic section usually followed, and the piece closed with the original *merengue.* The orchestras playing the *danza* usually presented a strong martial influence, consisting of brass instruments, particularly the baritone horn as an *obbligato* instrument, clarinets, violins, piano, and *güiro.* However, piano versions were widely edited, published, and popularized for the immediate facility of performance. The most prolific composer of *danzas* was Juan Morel Campos (1875–1896).

The exchange between freed slaves and peasants of primarily European descent resulted in another genre, the *plena,* developed among an economically deprived *mulatto* population on the southern coast. The *plena* combined the narrative structure found in Spanish music with the call-and-response and the emphatic percussion of African music. *Plenas* were then "musical newspapers" commenting on daily matters in a humorous manner. Its instrumentation presented the hybrid mixture of its influences: *pandero* (a jingle-less tambourine), *güiro*, guitar, and the accordion (an European instrument invented in the first decades of the nineteenth century and immediately introduced into Puerto Rico).

A dance called *Puertorrico* possibly traveled abroad along commercial and military channels and was referred to in seventeenth-century Mexico. There were other *Portorricos* or Puerto Ricos in Spanish America with no documentation for any geographical referent for the dance (Thompson, Musical Puerto Rico, 2).

MUSICAL FAMILIES

Most of the municipal bandleaders were also prolific parents, nurturing their own musical families. Some of those were Manuel Tizol in San Juan; Carmen Sanabria and Jesús Figueroa in Aguadilla; Juan Peña Reyes in Humacao; Francisco, Casimiro, and Angel Duchesne in Cayey and Fajardo; and Simón Madera in Mayaguez and Guayama. Another musical family worth mentioning was that of Juan Inés Ramos in Arecibo and his sons Adolfo Heraclio and Federico Ramos. This tradition was continued by the Hutchinson family (Henry, Luz, and Henry Jr.) and most recently by the Morales Matos family (Mariano, Sonia, Jaime, Rolando, Ricardo, and Jesús), the Cepeda family, and the Ayala family. These families contributed to the legacy of the cultural traditions on the island and abroad.

THE ROLE OF FEMALE MUSIC EDUCATORS

The role of female teachers was significant for the music education of young Puerto Ricans. Amalia Paoli (1861–1942), sister of Antonio Paoli, became a respectable singing teacher for the new generation of singers. Four other female teachers worth mentioning were pianist Elisa Tavárez (1879–1960), Carmen Sanábria (1882–1954), Ana Otero (1861–1905), and Monserrate Ferrer Otero (1885–1966). Elisa Tavárez was the daughter of the eminent composer Manuel G. Tavárez. She created her own academy where many talented young musicians studied. Carmen Sanábria, together with her husband, Jesús Figueroa, opened a music school in Puerta de Tierra, San Juan. They raised sons (José, Kachiro, Guillermo, and Rafael) and daughters (Angelina, Carmelina, and Leonor) who became practitioners of the highest standards of orchestral string instruments (violin, viola, and cello) and piano on the island. They are affectionately known as the Figueroa family. In summary, by the end of the nineteenth century Puerto Rico relied on an infrastructure that provided sufficient formal and informal music training to singers and instrumentalists as well as performance opportunities through ensembles, bands, and orchestras. In the twentieth century, the Negrón sisters: Luz Negrón de Hutchinson (1919) and Cecilia Negrón de Talavera (1917), produced many skillful pianists at the Puerto Rico Conservatory of Music.

THE INFLUENCE OF THE UNITED STATES

In 1898, just a few months after Spain had granted autonomy to the island through the *Carta Autonómica* [Letter of Autonomy] of 1897, Puerto Rico became a territory of the United States as one of the agreements of the Treatise of Paris, which ended the Spanish-American War (quoted in Delgado Cintrón, 1976). The change of sovereign—from Spain to the United States—had a profound impact on Puerto Rican society and culture.

New social and political changes affecting education throughout the twentieth century included: change of official language from Spanish to English—although eventually both were accepted; the acculturation of US values and attitudes; the constitutional state of three sharing powers: executive, legislature, and judicial; the separation of church and state, which resulted in the emergence of Protestant music and the proliferation of choruses; and the transformation from an agricultural economy to industrialization and urbanization (Montilla de Negrón, 1977).

In 1900, the US Congress approved the Foraker Law, which imposed a civil government for Puerto Rico. It also approved the creation of the *Departamento de Instrucción Pública* (Department of Public Instruction) and the position of Commissioner of Education with absolute control over Puerto Rican education at all levels. In 1901, the compiled School Law was approved and adjudicated the power to the commissioner to supervise, appoint, and administer in matters related to courses, tests, textbooks, materials, equipment, and facilities (Montalvo, 1991, 13). The educational system was structured into school districts under the supervision of superintendents, following the American model. The new educational system imposed on the island was targeted to provide a universal education accessible to all children (Mellado, 1976, 17–20).

The first attempt to set an educational philosophy was not drafted until 1942 under the leadership of Dr. José M. Gallardo through the Carta Circular No. 1 of July 1, 1954 (Mellado, 1976, 84). The second attempt was in 1954 under the leadership of Mr. Mariano Villaronga through the Carta Circular No. 17 of September 2, 1954 (Mellado, 1976, 85).

Impact on Music Education

At first, the new government rejected most of the cultural practices and efforts set forth by the Spanish government. Funds for orchestras and ensembles as well as scholarships for talented students were suddenly discontinued. Fernando Callejo designed a curriculum for establishing a conservatory of music (Callejo Ferrer, 1977). The proposal was equally rejected. As a witness of this transition, Callejo recognized that the common practice of the United States had not been that of directly sponsoring the arts (68). Therefore, at the beginning of the century there were no official bands, besides the police, the national guard, and a few others (Vega Martínez, Carlos, and Malagón Meléndez, 2001, 55). However, Puerto Rican citizens responded by taking the necessary steps to keep the cultural spirit alive. The Musical Association was organized to coordinate all musical efforts. Those involved with this organization were Callejo, Arteaga, Chavier, and José Pasarell, among others. Some of the efforts included sponsoring talented students. The most salient students were child prodigies, such as pianist Jesús María Sanromá (1902–1984), who studied with Alfred Cortot and Artur Schnabel and became one of the most important pianists in the United States with the Boston Symphony under the direction of Serge Koussevitzky; and violinist José Pepito Figueroa (1905–1998), from the Figueroa family, who studied with George Enesco and had a brilliant career in Europe.

In the absence of an official music conservatory or music school, military bands from the Spanish colonial regime were taken as models. Municipal and school bands were soon formed practically in every town. Just as in the previous century, public bands were once again the hub of most of the town's musical life and teaching opportunities. Their musical leaders, who were often talented composers and performers, also wrote the music and trained schoolchildren and adults to perform in town plazas and on tours around the island, as well as to participate in festivals and contests. Band musicians read music and were able to even play multiple instruments. Dance bands were drawn from these public bands, and through them Puerto Rican popular music was polished. However, Callejo complained that at times bands tended to be more for entertainment than for instruction (1977).

Americanization: Acculturation

Initially, music education was used as a vehicle for the Americanization of Puerto Ricans. Just as on the US mainland, music in the public school was based, at first, on American and European patriotic and folk songs as well as dancing. Bands' performing calendars were congruent with American holidays, and their repertoire included patriotic songs. However, music in the schools soon became more open to the use of native materials (Thompson, 1998). Local songs included the collection of songs *Canciones infantiles* by Braulio Dueño Colón with words by Manuel Fernández Juncos (in two volumes, 1901 and 1904) and *Juegos y canciones infantiles de Puerto Rico* (Games and Songs of Puerto Rico) by María Cadilla de Martínez (1940).

In 1944, radios were installed to provide some means of musical development in the public school (Inglefield, 1962, 86). Synchronized radio music was broadcasted in the classroom through the service of the School of the Air (Searle Lamb, 1948, 66). The School of the Air programming included Western music as well as

Puerto Rican music performed by local musicians and ensembles. It also included songs for first-through-sixth-grade students and a listening course of works by great composers (Inglefield, 1962, 86). In 1945, the government founded the government-supported WIPR radio station, which still provides high-quality cultural and educational programs.

The Park and Recreation Commission's Cinema and Graphics Workshop was another important educational program, which operated within this administrated structure from 1946 to 1949. Under the direction of Irene and Jack Délano (1914–1997), this program used various artistic media with educational functions on health and other social aspects. In 1949, it became part of the *Departmento de Instruccion Publica* as the Division de Educación de la Comunidad, DIVEDCO (Division of Education for the Community). It provided the first opportunity for local composers to write music for films (Thompson, 2005, 117). Among those were: Héctor Campos-Parsi (1922–1998), Amaury Veray (1923–1995), Jack Delano (1914–1997), Luis Antonio Ramírez (1923–1994), Angel "Lito" Peña (1921–2002), and José Raúl Ramírez (1920).

Protestant Church and the Flourishing of Choral Music

Another measure affecting education and music was the American separation of state and church. The Catholic Church, which had led the religious life of the Puerto Rican society and sponsored composers and ensembles, was suddenly one of many other religious options. Soon Protestant churches began to appear and with them "the practice of singing hymns at services was soon adopted, enabling the fast development of choral singing in newly formed evangelical churches" (Rivera, 2006, 12).

The twentieth century was indeed witness to a staggering proliferation of choral groups, many associated with religion. Therefore, there was an evident shift from band and orchestral music to the return of choral music; this time it was accomplished at a very high performance level. According to Olivieri, the choirs at the Evangelical Seminary of Puerto Rico (1920), the Segunda Iglesia Cristiana de Bayamón (Second Mission Church of Bayamón, 1928), and the Primera Iglesia Bautista de Río Piedras (First Baptist Church of Río Piedras, 1928) served as models for future chorus choirs. Other choral groups soon emerged, such as Caguas Church Choir (1939), Interdenominational Choir of San Juan (1944), Christian Church of Bayamón (1948), and the Bayamón Lutheran Choir (Coro de Bayamón) to name a few (2002).

Directors of these choral groups were key in improving the existing performance practices. Dr. Bartolomé Bover (1903–1984) has been recognized as the "initiator" of the modern era of choral music in Puerto Rico. According to Mattos, his exemplary teaching and commitment to choral music performance inspired many of his students, some of whom eventually became prominent musicians. These included: soprano María Esther Robles, conductor Angel Mattos Nieves, composer Pablo Fernández Badillo, and baritone Pablo Elvira. Bover also encouraged conductor Augusto Rodríguez to organize the University of Puerto Rico Chorus in 1936 (Mattos, 1993, 7–9).

Musicologist, composer, pianist, and choral arranger Augusto Rodríguez (1904–1993) became an exponent of exposing native choral music to the international audiences and established an undisputed tradition of choral excellence at one of the oldest institutions of the island (González Padró, 1999, 8–9). Inspired by Rodríguez, other choirs began to emerge in other colleges and universities. These included: the Inter-American University, the Catholic University of Puerto Rico led by Abel di Marco; the Conservatory of Music led by the Yugoslavian Sergije Rainis; the Metropolitan University led by Luis Olivieri; Turabo University, Polytechnic University; and the Adventist University of the Antilles (Rivera, 2006, 15).

Independent choirs included: Glee Club del Aire (1951) founded by Dr. Bartolomé Bover; Coral Polifónica de Ponce (1964); and Coral de Augusto Rodriguez (1970); Coro Sinfónico de Puerto Rico (1982) led by James Rawie; Coral Filarmónica de San Juan led by Carmen Acevedo; Pablo Casals Festival Chorus (1986); Camerata Coral (1991) led by Amarilis Pagán; Coro Schola Cantorum (1992) led by Luis Olivieri; and Escalonia Filarmónica, Coral Bel Canto, and Orfeón Bautista (1994) led by Guarionex Morales-Matos.

In addition, the end of the twentieth century saw the emergence of fine children choirs. Among those were: El Coro de Niños de San Juan led by Eva Lucío, and the Coro de Niños de Caguas led by Ana Avilés.

Prominent choral arranging included: Bartolomé Bover, Augusto Rodriguez, Pablo Fernández Badillo (1919), Rubén Colón Tarrants (1940), and Esther Alejandro (1947).

Music in Higher Education and Other Institutions

Public higher education institutions also began to appear on the musical scene, such as the Normal School in 1900, which became the only higher education public system in the island, the University of Puerto Rico, Rio Piedras campus, in 1903. Music and art were included in the curriculum as part of teacher training, a common practice in the United States, which was embraced in Puerto Rico. In 1923 Allena Luce directed the music courses at the University of Puerto Rico. She published *A Course of Study in Music for the Public School of Puerto Rico* (1920) and the folksong collection *Canciones populares* (1921). Later, music researcher Monserrate Delíz joined the University of Puerto Rico. Bands and orchestras were either elements of a corps of military cadets or as ad hoc social ensembles (Thompson, 1998, 125). In the 1920s, the University of Puerto Rico established cultural activities and events for students, faculty, and the community in general. Eventually, a music department was established with the first electronic music studio in Puerto Rico in the 1960s.

Similarly, private universities like the Catholic University in Ponce and Inter-American/Poly University in San Germán emerged. The Inter-American University was originally founded in 1912 as a Presbyterian mission school. Later in 1960, under the leadership of President Ronald Bauer, an ambitious music program was implemented under the direction of pianist Johana Harris. Two closely related programs were also conceived: the International Institute of Music and the International String Congress, under the direction of the eminent American composer Roy Harris. In addition, some talented students began to pursue studies in the United States. Such was the case of Elías López Sobá (1927), Irma Isern (1924), and Nydia Font (1927).

THE CREATION OF A SPECIAL MUSIC PROGRAM

Spearheaded by Senator Ernesto Ramos Antonini, Law No. 365 of 1946 created the special *Escuelas libre de música* with the objective of providing Puerto Rican talented children with a structured music education along with a favorable environment appropriate for their development. Not surprising, the main goal was to build a strong band program. For this purpose the curriculum included the performance of instruments as well as voice, ear training, theory, harmony, history, dance, and chorus. These schools became the definite music emporium of popular and classical musicians. The music director of the one in San Juan was given to Carmelina Figueroa, from the prestigious Figueroa family. Despite this major effort, specialized music education was just offered for the most talented students.

GROWTH AND EXPANSION: A CULTURAL RENAISSANCE

In 1917, through the Jones Law, Puerto Ricans had been granted US citizenship, and the relationship between Puerto Rico and the mainland began to improve. As a result, favorable changes occurred: from granting more autonomy at the governmental level to the establishment of education laws protecting all children. In 1948, the Popular Democratic Party (*Partido Popular Democrático*, PPD), under the leadership of Luis Muñoz Marín, came to power as a result of general elections and change began to occur very rapidly. During the 1940s and 1950s, the economy experienced the most dramatic change in its phases of industrialization in the areas of manufacturing, petrochemical, pharmaceutical, and electronics through the *Manos a la obra* (Operation Bootstrap) program. In 1952, the United States granted Puerto Rico Commonwealth status, which reordered the political structure with autonomous features and set up important vehicles of social transformation. Moreover, the Constitution of the Commonwealth transferred educational matters to the local government (Mellado, 1976, 85).

The development of a capitalist economy offered, for the first time, a consumerism, which transformed a great part of all facets of social life in the course of the century. A new urban distribution had repercussions in the traditional culture of families in terms of the role of couples and its effect on the care of children and elderly people (Department of Education, "Marco," 2003a, 20). These events also unleashed a chain of economic activities led by government-sponsored institutions. Particularly, the local government showed an unparalleled interest in education and cultural activities, resulting in a renaissance of the arts.

Music Festivals, Conservatory, and Other Public Institutions

As previously mentioned, independent societies and educational organizations had already appeared at the beginning of the twentieth century. For instance, since 1932, *Pro arte musical de Puerto Rico* sponsored performances by American artists as well as European, South American, and native performers (Thompson, 1998, 132). However, things changed even more rapidly when the PPD came to legislative power. In 1955 the *Instituto de Cultura Puertorriqueña* was created to promote culture and the arts. This enabled the promotion of Puerto Rican music and musicians through editions, publications, recordings, festivals, and concerts. The year 1957 marked the beginning of the *Festival Casals*, in honor of the presence of the renowned cellist Pablo Casals on the island, and in 1958 the creation of the Puerto Rico Symphony. Both efforts promoted and presented the best performers from the classical music world. In 1959 the government opened the WIPR television station, providing a wealth of educational, social, and artistic programming as well as broadcasting the Casals Festival and other similar foreign performances. In addition, during this time the Puerto Rico Philharmonic Orchestra was developed under the direction of Arturo Somohano, offering popular music within a symphonic context. Many other festivals were eventually produced, such as the Inter-American Arts Festival.

In this cultural milieu and awaited for nearly a century, in 1960 the Puerto Rico Conservatory of Music finally opened its doors to provide music education to instrumentalists, vocalists, composers, and educators. A university-level curriculum taught by a mixture of local and foreign professors who were, initially, simultaneously members of the symphony, the Conservatory of Music provided a fertile landscape for the development of music education at an intensive and higher level. Along with the *Escuelas libre de música*, the Conservatory of Music and the symphony formed the vehicles to develop orchestral performers. To secure the development of a strong native string section, a youth string program was added to the conservatory in the 1970s. This last initiative continued the efforts begun by fine musicians such as the Figueroa and Hutchinson families, among others. Professor Nellie Justicia was appointed as director of the Music Education program. Other subsequent directors are Amilcar Rivera, Ricardo López, Ariel Guzmán, and Nellie Lebron-Robles.

Composers

The path begun by Manuel G. Tavárez, Juan Morel Campos, Braulio Dueño Colón, and José Ignacio Quintón, and later by Arístides Chavier (1867–1942), Monserrate (Monsita) Ferrer (1885–1966), and José Enrique Pedreira (1904–1959), was solidified by the emergence of a Puerto Rican national school of composers at the middle of the twentieth century. The dean of this movement was represented by Héctor Campos-Parsi (1922–1998), who studied at the New England Conservatory, and with Nadia Boulanger in France. Other composers in this movement were Amaury Veray (1923–1995), Luis Antonio Ramírez (1923–1994), and the Ukraine-American, who had settled in Puerto Rico, Jack Délano (1914–1997). These composers incorporated and blended native rhythmic and melodic elements into modern classical music. Ortíz asserts, "The leadership and pedagogy of these seminal figures opened a new world of possibilities for future generations of composers to explore, enrich and transform" (Ortiz, 1996, 2).

An avant-garde approach to composition was introduced by American-born Francis Schwartz (1940), Rafael Aponte Ledée (1938), and Luis Manuel Álvarez (1939) in the second half of the twentieth century. On the other hand, Ernesto Cordero (1946) kept a conservative approach through many guitar works, including guitar concerti performed by many prestigious performers from around the world.

Toward the end of the twentieth century there were many successful works by William Ortíz (1947), Esther Alejandro (1947), Carlos Cabrer (1950), Carlos Vázquez (1952), and Roberto Sierra (1953), who became one of the most important names in the classical music scene with commissions, performances, and recordings by prestigious performers and orchestras from around the world. The twentieth century closed with the voices of Alfonso Fuentes (1954), Raymond Torres-Santos (1958), and Mariano Morales-Matos (1960); while at the beginning of the twenty-first century Carlos Carrillo (1968), Loyda Camacho (1960), Sonia Morales-Matos (1961), and Luis Prado (1968) kept the torch lit.

Other foreign composers who contributed to composition in the island were Ignacio Morales Nieva (1928–2006), Father Abel Di Marco (1931), and Roberto Milano (1936–2000). These composers not only supplied original music to instrumentalists and singers but also didactic material for the new generation of musicians.

Opera and Singers

Also in the 1960s, many island-based companies were formed and devoted to the production of operas calling upon both local and imported forces, the later including stellar figures from the international world of opera (Thompson, 2005, 132). Puerto Rico soon produced a healthy number of bel canto singers. Among these were soprano Graciela Rivera Padilla (1921), soprano Rina de Toledo (1925–2011), bass-baritone Justino Díaz (1940), barítono Pablo Elvira (1945–2000), tenor Eduardo Valdés (1956), soprano Margarita Castro-Alberty (1960), tenor Antonio Barasorda Barceló (1965), tenor César Hernández (1970), bass-baritone Carlos Conde (1970), lyric soprano Ana María Martínez Colón (1975), and Hilda Ramos (1960), among many others. Many of these singers have appeared in important opera houses around the world, including the Metropolitan Opera House; thus elevating the image of Puerto Rico as an emporium of talented musicians and singers.

Instrumentalists and Conductors

At the beginning of the twenty-first century, Puerto Rico had surpassed the original goal of the Law No. 35 of June 12, 1959, of forming instrumentalists to supply musicians to the Puerto Rico Symphony as well as composers and teachers needed to support the cultural life of the island. Today the symphony comprises more than 80 percent of native players and music directors.

Distinguished instrumentalists include: pianists Vanessa Vassallo and José Ramos Santana; violinists Narciso Figueroa (nephew), Henry Hutchinson Jr., José Cueto, and Wilfredo Deglans; cellist Rafael Figueroa; violists Francisco Figueroa and Christian Colberg; trumpeters Orlando Cora and Roberto Ramírez; trombonists Aldo Torres and Luis Fred; horn players Luis Arroyo and Javier Gándara; flutists Rubén López and Milton Dávila; oboists Gloria Navarro, Harry Rosario, and Pedro Díaz; clarinetist Ricardo Morales; harpist Elisa Torres; and percussionists José Alicea and Freddie Santiago. Conductors include: Roselín Pabón, Carlos Molina, Luis Caro, Roberto González, Kerlinda Deglans, Genesio Riboldi, Raymond Torres-Santos, Rafael E. Irizarry, and Guillermo Figueroa Jr., among others.

CURRICULUM DEVELOPMENT, TEACHER TRAINING, AND PRIVATE INSTRUCTION

Today, Puerto Rico enjoys healthy music education through programs provided by many public and private educational institutions, which offer both baccalaureate and master's degrees in music; many with performing arts facilities and opportunities to pursue a variety of music careers.

The Puerto Rico Conservatory of Music opened in 2009 state-of-the-art facilities and a new theater in 2012, which is used for recitals by students, faculty, and distinguished guest artists. It currently offers a baccalaureate degree in performance (bel canto voice, flute, oboe, clarinet, bassoon, saxophone, trumpet, French horn, trombone, tuba, piano, organ, harp, percussion, violin, viola, cello, bass), composition, jazz, Caribbean music, and music education. It also offers a master's degree in music education. New York University's David Elliot, renowned music educator scholar, was instrumental in development its curriculum. A diploma degree is also offered in performance. The conservatory also provides a Continuing Education Program to serve alumni, public school music teachers, and professional musicians. The Teachers Certification Program offers an alternative to professional musicians who wish to teach in the public school. In addition to the higher education programs, the conservatory offers a Preparatory Program. The Preparatory Program includes individual and group lessons. Private lessons are offered in flute, oboe, bassoon, saxophone, harp, electric bass, electric guitar, drums, trumpet, trombone, French horn, baritone horn, tuba, popular singing, classical singing, cello, violin, bass, *cuatro*, piano, organ, Latin percussion, and vocal technique. Group lessons include theory, children's choir (ages eight to seventeen), children's orchestra (ages eight to seventeen), bell choir, *criollo* ensemble, wind ensemble, guitar ensemble, piano in group, plus *Kindermusik* for newborn to six years old. It also offers dance courses, such as creative movement, baby ballet, dance for children, and jazz for youngsters and adults (http://

www.cmpr.edu/cmpr/index.htm). The conservatory also houses the *Centro Empresarial para Músicos Cultu-rArte* (CEMCA) [CulturArte Business Center for Musicians] and the *Música 100x35: Sistema de Orquestas y Coros Juveniles e Infantiles* (100x35: System of Youth and Children Orchestras and Choirs). CEMCA focuses on the business of music by means of publishing music through *Editorial Conservatorio* (Conservatory Publishing) and producing recordings through the CEMCA Records. 100x35 was designed to promote social awareness by providing music performance opportunities to financially deprived youth (http://www.cmpr.edu). Modeled after the *El Sistema* from Venezuela, in 2014 it offers classes in San Juan, Bayamón, Cataño, and Guayama of choir, rhythmic band, and orchestra in various levels up to the advanced Puerto Rico Youth Symphony Orchestra (Conservatorio de Música, Brochure 2014). Some concerns have been raised by students and parents worried that the institutions may be loosely focused on its primarily goal, that of training students at a higher education level (Aponte Ledée, 2013, 58).

The University of Puerto Rico, with campuses in Río Piedras, Mayaguez, Aguadilla, Arecibo, Bayamón, Carolina, Cayey, Humacao, Ponce, and Utuado, offers a baccalaureate degree in arts with a major in music. Students in the master's degree in education may choose to do research in music education. Through its extension program, the University offers courses in music business, notation, and arranging using technology (http://www.upr.edu).

The Ana G. Mendez University System, which includes Universidad Metropolitana, Universidad del Este, and Universidad del Turabo, offers a master's degree in education, and students could choose music education as their area of research (http://www.suagm.edu). The Inter-American University with campuses in San Juan (Metro), San Germán, Aguadilla, Barranquitas, Fajardo, Arecibo, Bayamón, Guayama, and Ponce offers a baccalaureate degree in arts in popular music and a master's degree in arts in music education at the Metro campus, and a baccalaureate degree in applied music, general music education/vocal, general music education/instrumental, as well as a baccalaureate degree in arts in music at the San German campus (http://www.inter.edu).

On the other hand, the Pontifical Catholic University in Ponce offers a baccalaureate and a master's degrees in music (http://www.pucpr.edu), and the Adventist University of the Americas offered a baccalaureate degree in arts, majoring in music performance, composition, and music education, plus a master's degree in music education, but according to the University's website its curriculum is currently in flux (http://www.uaa.edu). Furthermore, other universities have emerged such as Phoenix University and Cambridge College, which offer a master's degree in education and allows students to concentrate on topics in music education.

In addition, there are also many private academies and schools. Some offer a variety of pedagogical approaches as proposed by Orff, Kodaly, Dalcroze, Suzuki, and Gordon as well as new musical alternatives like *Kindermusik*. In addition, many *alcaldías* (townships) currently provide music programs to youth and adults.

THE EMERGENCE OF POPULAR MUSIC

The beginning of the twentieth century marks the beginning of the *canción romántica*, a romantic song influenced by the arias of the zarzuela and operas and later by Broadway. The *canción romántica* underwent changes accordingly to the influences coming from the United States: jazz, Cuba; *habanera, guaracha, son*, México; Veracruzan *bolero*; and Colombia *canción criolla*. Soon, the *canción romántica* emerged into the *bolero* and later as *balada*. At first it was sung in duo—a man and a woman—accompanied by a *trío* or *cuarteto*. But later big band and full orchestras performed it (Campos-Parsi, 1976, 121–22).

Famous *duos*, *trios*, and *cuartetos* included: Duo Irizarry de Córdova, Trío San Juan, Trío Vegabajeño, Cuarteto Marcano, Cuarteto Victoria, and Cuarteto Mayarí. Famous big band orchestras were those by Rafael Muñoz, Mingo and his Whoppee Kids, Ramón "Moncho" Usera Orchestra, José "Pepito" Torres and Siboney, César Concepción, and Angel "Lito" Peña and the Pan-American Orchestra.

Some of the most important songwriters were: Rafael Hernández (1892–1965), Pedro Flores (1894–1979), Silvia Rexach (1922–1961), Bobby Capó (1922–1989), Noel Estrada (1919–1979), Plácido Acevedo (1903–1974), Tito Henríquez (1920), Benito de Jesús (1912–2010), and Julio "Chago" Alvarado (1886–1970), Puchi Balseiro (1926–2007), Tite Curet Alonso (1926–2003). Some of the most important interpreters were:

Myrta Silva (1927–1987), Ruth Fernández (1919–2012), Tito Lara (1932–1987), Nydia Caro (1950), Wilkins (1954), Danny Rivera (1945), Lucecita Benítez (1942), Chucho Avellanet (1941), Sophy Hernández (1948), Yolandita Monge (1955), and Ednita Narazio (1955); as well as the vocal quartet Los Hispanos.

To satisfy the demand of the music and to assist the growing number of songwriters, it was necessary to rely on trained musicians who could notate, expand, and orchestrate their music ideas, thus producing the birth of the music arranger. Skillful arrangers included: Ramón "Moncho" Usera (1904–1972), Pedro Rivera Toledo (1942), José Pujals (1951), Enrique "Quique" Talavera (1948), Martín Nieves (1952), Wisón Torres Jr. (1952), Nicky Aponte (1956), Raymond Torres-Santos (1958), Ito Serrano (1961), Milton Sesentón (1962), Angel "Lito" Peña (1921–2002), and Angel "Cucco" Peña (1948). The last two are members of the prominent Peña Reyes family, from the days of the municipal bands in Humacao.

The new century saw a patriotic awakening toward *Jíbaro* music. There is much interest in the research and dissemination of this music, with Dr. Francisco López Cruz (1909–1988) as one of the major researchers and promoters along with Cristobal Santiago and his *La Casa del Cuatro*. Many virtuosic *cuatristas* emerged, among them: Ladislao "Ladí" Martínez (1898–1975?) and Tomás "Maso" Rivera (1927–2001); *guirero*, like Patricio "Toribi" Rijos (1897–1970); and fine vocalists/improvisers (*improvisadores*) such as Florencio "Ramito" Morales (1915–1989) and Jesús "Chuito el de Bayamón" Sánchez (1900–1979). The new generation, influenced by the US folk revival and the Latin American *nueva canción*, embraces it as well. The group *Haciendo Punto en Otro Son*, Antonio "El Topo" Cabán Vale (1942), Roy Brown (1945), and Andrés "Jíbaro" Jiménez (1947) were the most popular. There were also families, such as the Colón Zayas and Sanabria, committed to preserving this music genre. Toward the end of the century young *cuatristas* included Modesto Nieves (1951), Christian Nieves (1982), Prodigio Claudio (1968), Edwin Colón Zayas (1969), Pedro Guzmán (1956), and Quique Domenech (1974).

The development of African- and *mulatto*-related music—*Bomba*, and particularly *plena*—did not remain behind. Manuel "Canario" Jiménez (1895–1975) made of *plena* a popular genre, while Rafael Cortijo and his Combo, together with singer Ismael Rivera (1931–1987), transformed it into an urban sound played by a small ensemble. Monserrate "Mon" Rivera (1899–1978) added roguishness, and César Concepción (1909–1974) brought it to the "big band" dance ballroom. Distinguished families, like the Cepeda and Ayala, dedicated themselves to preserve and disseminate *Bomba*.

The strategic geographical position of the island, coupled with its relation with the United States, made of Puerto Rico a basin for many musical exchanges. In addition, because of the American citizenship awarded by birth to Puerto Ricans, there was an easy mobility between the island and the mainland. Puerto Rican popular music was and is impacted by influences from the United States, the Caribbean, and Latin America as well as the world today. African-related music was influenced by Cuban *son* and United States jazz and rhythm and blues among others, producing a new sound known as *salsa*. It became the most salient expression of the spirit of the youth (Campos-Parsi, 1976, 152). Important exponents of this genre working in Puerto Rico or in the United States mainland were: Tito Puente (1923–2000), Tito Rodríguez (1923–1973), Eddie Palmieri (1936), Ritchie Ray (1945), Bobby Cruz (1937), Santos Colón (1922–1998), Willie Colón (1950), Héctor Lavoe (1946–1993), Ismael Miranda (1950), El Gran Combo, Sonora Ponceña, Cheo Feliciano (1935), Willie Rosario (1930), Tommy Olivencia (1938–2006), Roberto Roena (1940) y Apollo Sound, and Gilberto Santa Rosa (1962). Fine arrangers of this genre included: Tito Puente (1923–2000), Louis Ramírez (1938–1993), Máximo Torres (1938), Ray Santos (1928), Mario Ortíz (1935–1999), José Febles (1949–2011), José Madera (1951), Bobby Valentín (1941), Jorge Millet (1939–1981), Enrique "Papo" Lucca (1946), Elias Lopes (1945), Luis "Perico" Ortíz (1949), Oscar Hernández (1954), Sergio George (1961), Julio "Gunda" Merced (1953), Louis García (1951), Cuto Soto (1955), Humberto Ramírez (1963), Ramón Sánchez (1961), Tommy Villarini (1957), Ernesto Sánchez (1961), and José Lugo (1960).

The globalization and the influences of other contemporary musical forms had led Puerto Rico to be known for pop artists, such as Menudo, Ricky Martin (1972), Jennifer López (1969), and Marc Anthony (1968). The influence of reggae, rap, and hip hop has resulted in a new genre: reggaetón, with Daddy Yankee (1976), Tego Calderón (1972), and Don Omar (1978) as its major performers.

MUSIC AND THE MEDIA

Technological advancement, such as the gramophone, cinema, and radio and television had a tremendous impact on popular music. The first transmission of the radio station WKAQ began transmission in 1922. Television arrived on the island in 1954 with WKAQ Telemundo and later WAPA Television. At the beginning films were accompanied by pianists and a small ensemble. Later, local composers and musicians provided original soundtracks.

Equally, the record industry flourished and launched the careers of many singers and orchestras. Recognizing the wealth of talent on the island, national recording companies opened local offices. Some were: RCA, Sony, EMI, and Universal. Radio—through radio theatres—and television—through live shows—served as the best advertising vehicles of dissemination of their products.

In the 1960s, Puerto Rico counted on the Puerto Rican Society of Music Authors, Composers and Publishers to monitor and distribute the performance royalties of composer members. Local and international music publishers also emerged. Peer Music and Southern Music were some of the most famous publishers. Similarly, the business of music was so active that the US performing rights organization, ASCAP (American Society of Composers, Authors and Publishers), also opened a local office.

In addition, already during the 1960s the island enjoyed a healthy tourist activity. Most hotels housed a big band to accompany local and international entertainers. It provided job opportunities to musicians and a platform to develop their music skills and to be exposed to many music genres.

MUSIC IN THE PUBLIC SCHOOLS

Coinciding with the curriculum survey by the Institute of Field Studies of Teachers' College at Columbia University, in 1950 the Department of Public Instruction created the Music Program to provide a music curriculum to the public school (The Institute of Field Studies Teachers' College, 1950). The *Escuelas libre de música* (Free School of Music) in San Juan, Ponce, and Mayaguez were incorporated to the Department of Public Instruction (Department of Education "Marco," 2003, 21). María Luisa Muñoz, educated at Columbia University, served as the first music superintendent. The program was devised for elementary, junior, and high school students. Music activities included singing, listening, rhythmic activities (mostly maracas, guiro, and claves), band instrument lessons, and folk dances and songs for elementary school; general music classes, band, and chorus for junior high schools; and band, chorus music appreciation, and history for high schools (Inglefield, 1962, 86). Under Muñoz's direction, the first manuals, guides, and official songbooks were developed (Oliver, 1999, 5). Together with Angeles Pastor she wrote *Canta conmigo*, which was also used in Latin America. Other books used at school included *Puerto Rican Singer*, containing Latin American and Puerto Rican songs in both English and Spanish (Searle Lamb, 1948, 65–66); *Renadío del cantar folklórico Puertorriqueño* (1952); *Cantos infantiles* (1924) by Monserrate Delíz; *Canciones de Navidad, Vols. I and II*, edited by Sister Mariana, OP (1953 and 1967); and *Canciones Hispanoamericanas*, consisting of a collection of songs from Spain and Latin America, arranged by Francisco López Cruz, Haydée Morales, María Mercedes Moreno, and Edward Heth (Inglefield, 1962, 86). According to Muñoz, the majority of the classroom teachers had inadequate training. Most of them had just studied music courses as part of their studies of a normal diploma (1953, 560)

In 1955, the *Manual and Guide for the Music Education Program* was designed to be used by first-grade teachers (Department of Public Instruction of Puerto Rico, 1955). Evangeline Oliver acknowledges, "It emphasized singing and interpretation of folkloric repertoire. Songs were the fundamental basis of the music education program. Listening activities, rhythmic band, singing and dancing traditional rounds complemented the program" (Oliver, 1999).

Toward the end of the 1950s, the Music Program underwent a series of reorganization changes (Oliver, 1999, 5). In 1960, the duties of teachers were redefined by means of *Carta Circular No. 15* (Department of Public Instruction of Puerto Rico, 1960). However, a series of activities had a great impact during this decade. Among those were the Chorus and Band Festivals under the leadership of Augusto Rodríguez and Ramón Collado, respectively (Department of Education of Puerto Rico, "Marco," 2003a, 219). Robert M. Fitzmaurice argues that, in general, choral groups "seldom rose above the level of the tuna" [or *rondalla*, a Spanish ensemble associated to academia, formed by mostly male students playing stringed instruments such as *bandurria*, *laúd*, *octavina*, and guitar] (Fitzmaurice, 1970, 10).

In 1961, Haydée Morales, educated at Miami University, acted as Music Supervisor of the Music Program, and published the first comprehensive manual on music education in Puerto Rico, *Music Education Manual for Elementary Schools in Puerto Rico* (Department of Public Instruction of Puerto Rico, 1961) in collaboration with Ana Dolores Maldonado. It presented materials in sequence by grades, interests, and teaching areas. Several books were published in the 1960s. Among them were: *Canciones favoritas*, *Nuevas aventuras en canción*, *Canciones para tí*, *Cantemos*, and *Todos los pueblos cantan* (Montalvo, 1991, 27).

In 1970, *The Manual and Guide for Elementary School Music Teachers* (Department of Public Instruction of Puerto Rico, 1970) updated and reorganized the 1955 *Manual and Guide for the Music Education Program* (Oliver, 1999, 6). The Music, Theatrical Arts, and Visual Arts Programs were also consolidated into one program, the Fine Arts Program (Department of Education of Puerto Rico, "Marco," 2003). In 1972, *Carta Circular No. 75-71-72* took without effect previous *Cartas Circulares* and provided new standards of duties for the Fine Arts Program (Department of Public Instruction of Puerto Rico, "Carta Circular," 1972). It emphasized singing activities and spontaneous physical expression of the body for the elementary school; musical literacy for intermediate school; and performing in bands and choirs for the high school level (Oliver, 1999, 6–7).

In 1974, the different areas were separate and independent. From 1978 to 1979 a process of consolidation of the three areas started, leading into a single unit, the Fine Arts Division with an executive director. From 1985 to 1994 the Fine Arts Program was again separated and led by individual executive directors (Department of Education of Puerto Rico, "Marco," 2003a, 220).

In 1986, *Carta Circular No. 4-85-86* brought extra guidance in pedagogical methods and administration structure (Department of Public Instruction of Puerto Rico, "Carta Circular," 1986). In 1987 the Arts Education Project (K–3) was created. It placed 260 fine arts teachers in 65 districts. This innovated project introduced, for the first time, students in elementary school to a formal learning of all the arts (Department of Education of Puerto Rico, "Marco," 2003a, 220). During the 1980s, many educational materials appeared. Among them were the guide, *Nuestra tradición musical*; the songbooks, *Canciones de ayer y hoy para los niños de Puerto Rico*; and the manuals, *Manual de movimiento*, *Curso de música general*, and *Manual de banda rítmica*.

Oliver notes, "In 1987, a revision of the manual, *Music at the Elementary Level* (Department of Public Instruction of Puerto Rico, "Music," 1970), stated a list of fundamental musical, kinesthetic, and singing skills to be acquired in three levels of development: K–III, IV, V–VI. Basic competencies were established in "singing, moving, instrumental experiences, and reading music." She adds, "In 1989, the Department of Education published the document *Principles for Integration of the Curriculum* (Department of Education of Puerto Rico, "Principles," 1989), as part of the Educational Reform. It was guided by three principles: (1) the continuity and reconstruction of daily life; (2) the development of thinking skills; and (3) the development of values (Oliver, 1999, 7–8). "The Curricular Music Guide at K–III level offered strategies to follow the exploration, conceptualization, and application model, known as ECA" (Rodríguez Arocho, 1989).

During the decade of the 1980s, the Arts Programs began to develop, together with the University of Puerto Rico's Continuing Education Program, a study proposal to certify new teachers and those who had not finished their academic degrees (Department of Education, "Marco," 2003a, 220). During this time the manuals *El mundo de la música* and *Manual de banda rítmica* and a guide for the teaching of melodic bells were prepared. Other efforts included professional development for band directors on orchestration and instrument maintenance as well as for choral directors on preparation of choral arrangements. In addition, an Electro-Acoustic project was implanted (Sistema Educativo de Puerto Rico, 1992, 132). Yet by the end of the 1980s teachers showed dissatisfaction with the status of music education in the public schools. Among the greatest needs identified were adequate materials and appropriate equipment (Montalvo, 1991, 123–27).

Through Law 68 of August 28, 1990, and Law 18 of June 16, 1993, the Department of Public Instruction, now under the new name, Department of Education, created the School of the Community and established education as one to discover and lead the attitudes and talents of youth with activities that would enrich their lives and promote the quality of life and harmony of the community. In 1995, the separate arts programs are once again consolidated into the Fine Arts Program under an executive director and three coordinators per each area (Department of Education of Puerto Rico, "Marco," 2003a, 220).

In 1999, the Department of Education underwent a curricular reform by means of the Law 149 of July 15, 1999. The curricular reform promoted an integral development of the educational process with a holistic vision of the human being (Department of Education of Puerto Rico, "Marco," 2003a, 10). The new institutional mission established that education was to be geared toward the development and integral formation of the physical, mental, social, emotional, and ethical and moral levels of students. The new legislation allowed setting standards of excellence for all curricular areas. This disposition was in tune with the third goal of Puerto Rico Goal 2000 as a result of the United States Federal Goal 2000, Educate America Act of March 31, 1994. The major purpose was to direct the curricula offering in the direction of the cognitive-humanistic learning theory and the constructivist approach. Another federal legislative instrument affecting the curricular offering was Law 103-182, Improving American School Act 1994, which required more accountability to schools regarding student academic performance (Department of Education of Puerto Rico "Carta Circular," 2003b).

Carta Circular No. 1-1999-2000 set the direction of the teaching and administration of the Fine Arts Program at the elementary and secondary public schools, which included visual arts, dance and movement, music, and theater (Department of Education of Puerto Rico, "Carta Circular," 2000). It presented the principles, objectives, organization, and skills to be assessed. The programmatic area of music mentioned the existence of a Center for Training and Fine Arts at Ramey Base on the eastern region of Aguadilla and a Youth Choral Project. The curricular music content was divided into two levels: (1) elementary, consisting of general music, vocal, and instrumental experiences as well as rhythmic, ear training, and creative; and (2) practical experiences. The organization of the curriculum was also organized in two cycles. The first cycle included fundaments of music, harmony, and an introduction to art, pop, and folk music. The second cycle included history of music from Middle Age to present. Band music, still the central performing ensemble, was organized in four levels: elemental, intermediate, advanced, and superior. Technology was encouraged but no resources assigned (Department of Education, "Carta Circular," 2000).

In 2000, *Carta Circular No. 3-2000-2001* revealed academic and technological standards of excellence (Department of Education of Puerto Rico, "Carta Circular," 2000). The new curricular design consisted of eight basic aspects: (1) knowledge; (2) values, attitudes, and human virtue; (3) skills and competencies; (4) cultural diversity; (5) environment; (6) work study; (7) technology; and (8) economics. The document presented seven institutional goals. The standards were classified in terms of content, performance, and assessment. The content standards for the fine arts related to: (1) educational aesthetics; (2) historical, cultural, and social research; (3) creative expression and performance; and 4) aesthetic judgment.

The four performance standards for music were: (1) the student listens and analyzes music using the effective language and vocabulary; (2) the student develops skills of research and understands the relationship between music, history, and culture; (3) the student reads and notates music, sings or plays musical instruments in a varied repertoire, improvises melodies, variations, and accompaniments, composes and arranges music, develops knowledge and the necessary skills to understand and perform music from other cultures; and (4) the student applies knowledge, skills, and understanding at the moment of making judgments and determining the quality of the musical experience and performance.

The three assessment standards were: (1) diagnostic evaluation of the previous repertoire of knowledge; (2) formative evaluation through four techniques ranging from cooperative, concrete poem, public exhibition/presentations, public speaking, list, daily journal, anecdote record, rubrics, modeling, interview, auto-evaluation, and research; (3) summative evaluation using three criteria: end of semester grades, the Puerto Rican Academic Competencies Test, and/or the submission of a portfolio.

Band music was still the vehicle to provide group and individual performance skills to middle and high school students. In the 2000, there were sixty-five bands in the public school system (Department of Education of Puerto Rico "Brochure," 2006). However, some songbooks also appeared, among them: *Canciones y cantos infantiles* (Bou de Blanco, 2006), *Despertar musical* (García Casillas, Hernández Candelas, and Andújar, 2004), and *Juegos infantiles de Puerto Rico* (Vélez-Adorno, 2005).

Finally, the latest document setting philosophical principles, fundamentals, approaches, and basic curriculum from K–12, for the standards of excellence already established, was published in 2003, in the *Marco*

Curricular del Programa de Bellas Artes (Department of Education of Puerto Rico, "Marco," 2003a). It presents an integral scope of the curriculum in terms of vision and goals, area of studies in levels, the organization, depth, and content sequence, general recommendations on teaching strategies and methodology as well as evaluation criteria. It also establishes the public policy regarding goals and required curriculum in pursuit of a Puerto Rican education. This document teaches principles, which serve as a foundation for the fine arts program. These include: psychology, psycho-psychology, neurology, and multiple intelligences, and the Mozart effect. It also offers methods and strategies, such as Dalcroze, Orff, Martenot, and Suzuki. In addition, the document presents strategies on how to incorporate technology to the classroom. The strategies include: MIDI (Musical Instrument Digital Interface), Band-in-a-Box, Cakewalk, and ProTools. However, schools are still awaiting financial resources to successfully accomplish the mandates.

A 2014 research addressing some of the aspects that may describe the reality of music education in public schools at the primary or elementary level in Puerto Rico described a gap between "schools' reality and the academic expectation gathered in the proposals of music education in manuals, guides, circular letters, and other material published by the Department of Education in Puerto Rico" (Lopez-León et al., 2013, 13). Findings in this study revealed that "80 percent of students between kindergarten and third grade and 77 percent of children from fourth to sixth grade did not have any formal music education throughout the school year." This is a strikingly low rate if compared with other geographically near islands with cultural similarities, such as Cuba. The study expands that some of the reasons for the lack of academic exposure to music experienced by Puerto Rican children may be the lack of: (1) supervision and remedial administration of artistic education; (2) educational philosophy; and (3) teachers using musical teaching methodologies, despite institutions offering degrees in music education, expose future teachers to different methodologies as part of their studies (López-León et al., 2015, 14).

CONCLUSION

By the end of the twentieth century, some of the shortcomings reflected in previous studies on some aspects of music education in Puerto Rico were addressed by the Department of Education (Bragg, 1971; Bonano, 1982; Rodríguez Arocho, 1989; Alicea y de Jesús, 1991; Villarini, 1991; and Montalvo, 1991). However, there are still issues to be examined. First, there has been too much disruption in the administration of the Music Program at the Department of Education during its sixty years of existence. There is an apparent indecision on whether music should be a stand-alone program or one of the areas within the fine arts. These constant administrative changes have created confusion among music educators as related to curricular implementation, expectations, and outcomes. Therefore, the Department of Education needs to work on building up its credibility among music educators. Second, music education in Puerto Rico has been primarily focused on performance. Educational institutions must foster an interest in music pedagogy as they provide an adequate education for those wanting to teach. Teaching music should not be an appendix to singers and instrumentalists. It should be a vocation nurtured through years of study, observation, and practice. Third, communication pipelines must be opened up to music educators so that they could establish a sincere dialogue and share sources, resources, books, and materials among themselves. With the aid of technology, music educators must be encouraged to be in touch with their internal and external worlds and experiences. Fourth, there is an absence of early childhood music policy for the education of children ages birth to eight, which could guarantee the development of the emotional, expressive, cultural, social, intellectual, and creative needs of all children (Hernández-Candelas, 2008, 27–32). However, some private schools offer commercial early childhood education programs, such as *Kindermusic*.

On the other hand, today Puerto Rico enjoys the educational music transformation from the past four hundred years. It has positioned itself in the world by the efforts of many Puerto Ricans who have excelled as singers, instrumentalists, composers, conductors, arrangers, copyists, and producers in the classical and popular worlds. In addition, as a territory of the United States, the island has benefited financially and culturally. Many Puerto Ricans are educated, bilingual, and bicultural. By the 1980s nearly 90 percent of the population was literate, compared with some 67 percent in 1940, and public schools annually enrolled 486,200 elementary pupils and about 165,000 secondary students (Puerto Rico; Colleges in Puerto Rico; Education in Puerto Rico). This by itself places them in a valuable position to compete in the global markets. Since all US federal laws apply to the island, there is financial aid for students to access postsecondary education at a reasonable cost and in accredited institutions.

External influences force educational institutions to develop and implement curricular innovations as they prepare future teachers. In recent years, the preparation of teachers, including music teachers, underwent deep transformation as a result of the US federal law known as the No Child Left Behind Act (NCLB). Local public education schools are required to hire high-quality teachers. Therefore, it has a direct impact on the education and certification of teachers as well as on public education agencies as they must show accountability in the progress of projects and the use of federal funding. It affected music teachers as well as those in the other areas: language, math, science, social studies, and special education. Today, Puerto Rico follows national standards for all areas of music education.

In Puerto Rico there are thirty-one higher education institutions offering studies in education. Out of these there are five institutions offering music education. In 2006, at least 71 percent of public school teachers were well qualified (Shokooh Valle, 2006, 8). However, there is still a need to keep up with the changes in curriculum and assessment of student learning in order to continue nurturing good and effective teachers. On the other hand, the proliferation of private music academies and schools, which are not regulated by accrediting agencies or required to hire certified teachers, should be reviewed. Furthermore, it is necessary to examine how the political, economic, and technological changes are affecting education now. In the twenty-first century, a real challenge to the teaching of music is the changing roles in the music professions and the few demands for musicians due to technology, which are producing less interest for a career in music and, therefore, a decline in enrollment in music educational institutions. Under these circumstances, it will be necessary to design a music education that makes sense and is meaningful to students' lives and experiences as well as to the community at large. As audiences are changing, so is the musical landscape.

REFERENCES

Adventist University of the Americas. http://www.uaa.edu. December 25, 2012.
Alegría, Ricardo E. (1950). *Historia de nuestros indios*. San Juan, Puerto Rico: Departmento de Instrucción Pública.
Alicea y De Jesús, Mercedes. (1991). *An Overview and Analysis of the Choral Program of the Department of Education. A Music Teachers' Resource Manual, Grades 1–6*. New York: Teachers College, Columbia University (Doctoral dissertation).
Ana G. Mendez University System. http://www.suagm.edu. December 25, 2012.
Aponte-Ledée, Rafael. (2013, Mayo). "100x35 es igual a . . . " *El nuevo día* 30, no. 58.
Bonano, Rubén. (1982). *El rol de la música en la escuela elemental pública de Puerto Rico*. Rio Piedras: University of Puerto Rico (Master thesis).
Bou de Blanco, G. (2006). *Canciones y cantos-juegos infantiles*. San Juan, Puerto Rico: Avemar.
Bragg, David A. (1971). *The Teaching of Music Concepts in the Elementary Schools of Puerto Rico*. Tallahassee: The Florida State University (Doctoral dissertation).
Brau, Salvador. (1904). *Historia de Puerto Rico*. New York: D. Appleton, Co.
Cadilla de Martínez, María. (1940). *Juegos y canciones infantiles de Puerto Rico*. San Juan, Puerto Rico: Talleres Gráficos Casa Baldrich.
Callejo Ferrer, Fernando. (1977). *Música y músicos puertorriqueños*. San Juan, Puerto Rico: Ediciones Borinquen/Editorial Coquí.
Campos-Parsi, Héctor. (1976). "Música," vol. 7. *La Gran Enciclopedia de Puerto Rico*. Madrid: Ediciones R. 14 vols.
Coll y Toste, Cayetano. (1907). *Prehistoria de Puerto Rico*. San Juan, Puerto Rico: Tip. Mercantil.
———. (1910). *Historia de la instrucción en Puerto Rico hasta el año 1898*. San Juan, Puerto Rico: Talleres Tip. Boletín Mercantil.
Conservatorio de Música de Puerto Rico. http://www.cmpr.edu/. December 25, 2012.
———. Brochure, March 2014.
Delgado Cintrón, Carmelo. (1976). "Política," vol. 2. *La Gran Enciclopedia de Puerto Rico*. Madrid, Spain: Ediciones R. 14 vols.
Delíz, Monserrate. (1924). *Cantos infantiles*. New York: Heath and Co.
———. (1952). *Renadio del cantar folklórico Puertorriqueño*. San Juan, Puerto Rico: S.A. Ediciones Espectaculares de América.
———. (1963). *Guía para el maestro: ABC cantos infantiles*. San Juan: Departamento de Instrucción Pública.
Department of Education of Puerto Rico (DEPR). (1989). *Principles for the Integration of the Curriculum*. San Juan, Puerto Rico: DEPR.
———. (2000). *Carta Circular No. 1-1999-2000*. San Juan, Puerto Rico: DEPR.
———. (2003a). *Marco Curricular del Programa de Bellas Artes*. San Juan, Puerto Rico: DEPR.
———. (2003b). *Carta Circular No. 3-2000-2001*. San Juan, Puerto Rico: DEPR.
———. (2006). *Brochure–Fine Arts Program*. San Juan, Puerto Rico: DEPR.
Department of Public Instruction of Puerto Rico (DPIPR). (1954a). *Carta Circular Num. 1*. San Juan, Puerto Rico: DRIPR.
———. (1954b). *Carta Circular No. 17*. San Juan, Puerto Rico: DRIPR.
———. (1955) *Manual and Guide for the Music Education Program*. San Juan, Puerto Rico: DRIPR.

————. (January 4, 1960). *Carta Circular No. 15*. San Juan, Puerto Rico: DPIPR.

————. (1961). *Music Education Manual for Elementary Schools in Puerto Rico*. San Juan, Puerto Rico: DPIPR.

————. (1970) *The Manual and Guide for Elementary School Music Teachers*. San Juan, Puerto Rico: DPIPR.

————. (1972). *Carta Circular No. 75-71-72*. San Juan, Puerto Rico: DPIPR.

————. (1986). *Carta Circular No. 4-85-86*. San Juan, Puerto Rico: DPIPR.

Dueño Colón, Braulio. (1901). *Canciones Infantiles*. New York: Silver Burdett and Co. and ed. San Juan: Departmento de Instrucción Pública.

————. (1904). *Canciones Infantiles*. San Juan: Departmento de Instrucción Pública.

Fitzmaurice, Robert M. (1970). *Music Education in Puerto Rico: A Historical Survey with Guidelines for and Exemplary Curriculum*. Tallahassee, Florida: Florida State University (Doctoral dissertation).

Gallardo, José M. (Ed.) (1975). "Proceedings of the Conference on Education of Puerto Rican Children on the Mainland." *The Puerto Rican Experience*. New York: Arno Press.

García Casillas, G., M. Hernández Candellas, and S. L. Andújar. (2004). *Despertar musical*. San Juan, Puerto Rico: Conservatorio de Música de Puerto Rico.

Glasser, Ruth. (1995). *My Music Is My Flag*. Berkeley: University of California Press.

González Padró, Pedro. (1999). "A la memoria de Augusto Rodríguez." *Coral* 11, no. 2: 8–9.

Hernández-Candelas, Marta. (2008). "Policies for Early Childhood Music Education in Puerto Rico." *Arts Education Policy Review* 109, no. 2 (November/December): 27–32.

Inglefield, Bonita. (1962). "Music in the Public Schools of Puerto Rico." *Music Educators Journal* 48 (November): 86.

The Institute of Field Studies of Teachers' College. (1950). *Public Education and the Future of Puerto Rico: A Curriculum Survey 1948–1949*. New York: Bureau of Publications, Teachers' College, Columbia University.

Inter-American University. http://www.inter.edu. December 25, 2012.

The International Institute of Teachers College. (1926). *A Survey of the Public Educational System of Puerto Rico*. New York: Bureau of Publications, Teachers' College, Columbia University.

López Cruz, Francisco, et al. (1962). *Canciones Hispanoamericanas*. San Juan, Puerto Rico: Departamento de Instrucción Pública.

Lopez-León, Ricardo, Oswaldo Lorenzo-Quiles, and Anna Rita Addessi. (2015). "Music Education in Puerto Rico Elementary Schools: A Study from the Perspective of Music Teachers." *International Journal of Music Education* 33, no. 2: 146–62.

Luce, Allena. (1920). *A Course of Study in Music for the Public School of Puerto Rico*. San Juan, Puerto Rico.

————. (1921). *Canciones populares*. San Juan, Puerto Rico: Government of Puerto Rico, Department of Education.

Mattos, Angel. (1993). "Semblanza de Bartolomé Bover: Iniciador de una era coral." *Coral* 1, no. 1: 7–9.

Mellado Parson, Ramón A. (1948). *Culture and Education in Puerto Rico* (Educational Monograph No. 1). San Juan, Puerto Rico: Bureau of Publications Puerto Rico Teachers Associations, Educational Monographs No. 1.

————. (1976). "La Educacion en Puerto Rico," vol. 10: Education/Ateneo/Bandera/Economía/Fauna/Flora. *La Gran Enciclopedia de Puerto Rico*. Madrid: Ediciones R. 14 vols.

Montalvo, Rachel. (1991). "An Assessment of the Status and Needs of K-12 Public School Music Education in Puerto Rico." Miami, Florida: University of Miami (Doctoral dissertation).

Montilla de Negrón, Aida. (1977). *La Americanización de Puerto Rico y el sistema de instrucción pública 1900–1930*. Rio Piedras: Editorial Universitario.

Muñoz, María Luisa. (1953, April/May). "Music Education in Puerto Rico." *Music Educators Journal* 39: 56–57.

————. (1966). *La Música en Puerto Rico; panorama historico-cultural*. Sharon, Connecticut: Troutman Press.

Oliver, Evangeline. (1999). *Curricular Resource Guide for Upper Elementary and Intermediate School Music Teachers in Puerto Rico*. New York: Columbia University's Teachers College (Doctoral dissertation).

Olivieri, Luis. (2002). "A Short History of Choral Music in Puerto Rico." *International Choral Bulletin* 20, no. 2.

Ortíz, William. (1996, September). "A Panoramic View of Puerto Rican New Music." *World New Music Magazine* 6.

Osuna, Juan José. (1949). *A History of Education in Puerto Rico*. 2nd edition. Rio Piedras, Puerto Rico: Editorial de la Universidad de Puerto Rico.

Pontifical Catholic University. http://www.pucpr.edu. December 25, 2012.

Rivera, Jose. (2006). *Roberto Sierra's Missa Latina: Musical Analysis and Historical Perspectives*. Tallahassee, Florida: Florida State University (Doctoral dissertation).

Rodríguez Arocho, W. C. (1989). *La zona del desarrollo potencial y su importancia en la evaluación de destrezas del pensamiento*. In A. Villarini and A. Rios (Eds.), *Ponencias primer encuentro nacional sobre la investigación y la enseñanza orientada al desarrollo del pensamiento*. San Juan, Puerto Rico: Centro para el Desarrollo de la Docencia.

Searle Lamb, Elizabeth. (1948). "Music Education in Puerto Rico." *Music Educators Journal* 34, no. 4 (February–March): 65–66.

Shokooh Valle, Firuzeh. (2006, August). "Ajustes a nivel universitario." *Primera Hora* 14: 8.

Sistema Educativo de Puerto Rico. (1992). Trayectoria de Realidades y Necesidades. San Juan, Puerto Rico: Consejo de Educación Superior de Puerto Rico.

Sister Mariana. (1953). *Canciones de Navidad, Vol. I*. San Juan: Departamento de Instrucción Pública.

————. (1967). *Canciones de Navidad. Vol. II: Navidad en Europa*. Hato Rey; Departamento de Instrucción Pública.

Thompson, Donald. (1998). The Arts in the American Presence in Puerto Rico. In Lynn-Darrell Bender (Ed.), *Puerto Rico, USA Centennial Commission*, 108–34. San Juan, Puerto Rico: Institute of Puerto Rican Culture/Publicaciones Puertorriqueñas.

————. (1998). Musical Puerto Rico: Microcosm in the Mainstream. Unpublished Manuscript.

————. (2005). "Film Music and Community Development in Rural Puerto Rico: The DIVEDCO Program (1948–1991)." *Latin American Music Review* 26, no. 1 (Spring/Summer): 102–14.

Torres-Santos, Raymond. (2010). The Influence of African Music in the Americas. In *African Presence and Influence on the Cultures of the Americas*. Cambridge, England: Cambridge Scholars Publishing.

University of Puerto Rico. http://www.upr.edu. December 25, 2012.

Vega Martínez, Juan Carlos, and Ramíro Malagón Meléndez. (2001). *Breve Historia de la Música en Puerto Rico*. San Juan, Puerto Rico: Colegio San Ignacio de Loyola.

Vélez Adorno, C. (2005). Juegos infantiles de Puerto Rico. Rio Piedras, Puerto Rico: Editorial de la Universidad.

Villarini, A. R. (1991). *Manual para la enseñanza de pensamiento.* San Juan, Puerto Rico: Proyecto de Educación Liberal Liberadora.

Chapter Four

Jamaica

Marilyn J. Anderson

INTRODUCTION

The arrival of Admiral Christopher Columbus in the New World with his fleet of three small ships—the *Niña*, the *Pinta*, and the *Santa Maria*—and the landing on the small Bahamian island he called San Salvador on Friday, October 12, 1492 (Halsall, 1966), set in motion a series of events that are tragically familiar in so many instances of human intercultural contact. They are typified by unequal and strongly hegemonic relations—themes of exploitation and domination, outright slavery, resistance, and rebellion—which were to have the most profound impact imaginable on members of three of the old, established cultures on the planet: the African, indigenous Amerindian, and the European.

The fact that all three of these cultures have survived in the New World, when looked at as a whole, and have even prospered despite the initial years of abrasive, violence-filled contact down the intervening centuries, without descending into outright barbarism and permanent coarsening of human behavior is, of course, testimony to the resilience of the human spirit and the inherent human tendency to moral recovery and improvement, but the true cost in terms of human lives and misery can hardly be properly calculated.

Columbus had always felt that it was a better plan to reach Asia by sailing west across the Atlantic, instead of going around the Horn of Africa and into the Indian Ocean, and so after being unable to find suitable sponsors elsewhere in Europe he took his ideas to the Spanish Royal Court and convinced King Ferdinand and Queen Isabella of Spain of the feasibility of his plans. They made an agreement to sponsor his first trip with the understanding that he was to be given the titles of admiral and governor of any lands discovered, and also that he would receive a 10 percent tax-free portion of any riches discovered (*Voyages of Christopher Columbus*, 2011).

The exploits of the early Spanish explorers in the New World revealed to the rest of Europe the extent to which there were vast expanses of undeveloped, mineral-rich, and fertile lands that were then occupied by Amerindian tribes lightly armed with only primitive weapons. This scenario served to usher in a rush and scramble by other European nations to annex and defend territory, as best they could, in the name of their royal sponsors. The early centuries of post-Columbus colonial settlement were therefore marked by both fierce, small-scale conflicts and wars of conquest between European powers. The dominant powers of the day—the Spanish, British, French, Dutch, and Portuguese—each sought to establish zones of dominance in the region with the aim of enriching themselves as explorers and bringing wealth and glory to their sponsoring regimes.

Even piracy was used as a tool to challenge Spain's ownership of the New World, and the exploits of famous English-sponsored buccaneers, such as Blackbeard, Captain Morgan, and Calico Jack, have been portrayed as heroic romantic adventures that have captured public attention for centuries. The often celebrated Francis Drake (later knighted by Queen Elizabeth I) carried a lifelong grudge against the Spanish after he and his mentor in the contraband slave trade, John Hawkins, barely escaped with their lives following their defeat at the battle of San Juan de Ulna (Groepl, 2010).

In pursuit of their aims of territorial exploitation, the labor needed by the Spanish for heavy work in the mines, and/or on the plantations, was at first obtained by enslaving the indigenous Amerindian peoples (Tainos, Kalingos, Mayans, etc.), some communities of whom were thereby driven to the edge of extinction in some of the islands, including Jamaica, by the sudden loss of freedom to pursue their centuries-old way of life, therefore resulting in the destruction of important elements of their culture and the intolerable harshness of the forced work regimes. The labor shortage that became evident as a result of the demise of the Taino civilization in Jamaica led to the idea of importing slaves from Africa as a sustainable labor resource. The usual mode of acquisition was that these were either kidnapped by European slavers or were bought from African rulers eager to get rid of troublesome prisoners-of-war, criminals, and enemies of different tribal ethnicity.

It may seem odd, prima facie, that a discourse on slavery, wars, violence, bloody suppressions, and reprisals should be so prominently interwoven with a narrative on an aesthetic subject area such as the development and practice of music in Jamaica. An examination of the present case reveals, however, that due to the special circumstances of territorial settlement and slavery-supported development in Jamaica, first as a colony of Spain then of Britain, both cultural aesthetics and violence are inescapably interlinked.

The tenacious practice of their music, and other culture by the African slaves, was not done merely for vocal aesthetic appreciation, nor to display virtuosity in polyrhythmic drumming, but was in fact a deadly serious enterprise that supported their very concept of positive self-identity and their mental stability in an ambience of severe dehumanizing challenges. Were it not for the spiritually uplifting influence of their music, dance, and vocal expressions, the slaves could have descended into becoming mere units of labor, with a robotic mind-set, and no overarching mental vision of ultimate liberation and societal viability and might therefore have gone the way of the Jamaican Tainos.

Some of the music of the slaves in preemancipation Jamaica represented a neo-African fusion of different ethnic styles not heard in Africa. Indeed, as the planters forced people from different and historically hostile tribes to live together as a means of control, mutual survival interests, more often than not, led to cultural and musical accommodations. According to Stowell (2000):

> Slavery, while raping cultural practices, suppressing artistic expression and causing ethnic groups to combine for survival, could not entirely control the succession of music which is woven inseparably with the thought and action of Jamaica's African population. A history of rebellion contributed immeasurably to this musical retention. (4)

In the case of the indigenous Amerindian Tainos in Jamaica, their swift decline in numbers, while even more Africans continued to be imported to support the plantation system, meant that their culture, including their music, would have no large-scale impact on music in post-Hispanic Jamaica, down the generations. The burgeoning knowledge of Taino musical practice today is therefore largely due to modern reconstructions based on artifacts reclaimed from the fossil record (Institute of Jamaica, 2010).

In the case of the musical legacy of Europe, it must be noted that European music, especially of the "art genre," was not an oral phenomenon amenable to instant variation according to ambient circumstances. It was typically invented and set down in writing, in Europe, by highly trained musicians using a spatiotemporal notational system that recognized no intervals smaller than a semitone, thereby making it useless for recording the microtones prevalent in some African music. Moreover, it is intuitively clear that in order to preserve social distance and hegemony, such high musical culture would be regarded by settlers as the domain of the ruling Europeans, and so there would be no serious attempt to teach such music to African slaves. The reality is that though the dissenting voices of nationalism became increasingly strident as agitation for political independence gathered broad support, this aspect of European sociocultural hegemony would last well into the initial decades of the postcolonial/independence era.

While European musical forms, not surprisingly, given the circumstances, always had pride of place where social acceptance was concerned, other ethnic minorities, inclusive of the Spanish or Portuguese Jews who fled to Jamaica to escape the Inquisition, the Chinese and East Indians who were hired as indentured servants to provide labor on the deserted plantations after Emancipation, and the Syrian and Lebanese immigrants from the Middle East, have had relatively little national impact on music in Jamaica. This may be due to the lack of common musical bases for engendering meaningful amalgamation or syncretism.

The major focus of this narration of centuries-long musical development in Jamaica will therefore be on the African-derived forms, their "culture clash" with the socially dominant European music, especially the "art" genre, their functional use as aids to social cohesion, mental image of self-worth, and finally their full social acceptance and coexistence with European music in school curricula.

In sum, the history of music in Jamaica is inextricably bound up with the multifaceted historical realities of the country itself, and the reality of the vast sonic wealth of Africa, which was imported mentally into Jamaica on the slave ships. A study of the historical linkages between rebellion and resistance, and the supporting cultural retention of musical roots that reaffirmed positive perceptions of selfhood, should therefore be part of a broad cultural inquiry.

THE FIRST JAMAICANS WERE AMERINDIANS

Since we gather from recent anthropological studies that the arrival of the first Amerindians in Jamaica was as early as 5,000 BC (Woodley, 2001), it is plausible to posit that a musical Amerindian culture existed in Jamaica and the Americas, predating many of the defining musical events of the ancient world, such as the musical teachings of the celebrated Egyptian Mystery System in which Moses was trained (James, 1954).

These studies have also shown that Amerindian culture was brought to the New World by migrating tribes from Asia, seeking game and other supplies of food during the early phases of the last postglacial global warming period. The first Americans were therefore Asians who walked to America—that is, to Alaska, from Siberia, across a now submerged land bridge across the Bering Straits thousands of years ago, at the end of the last Ice Age (Elias, 1997).

The first Jamaicans to have left traces on the fossil record were descendants of these early intrepid migrants. These were the Ciboney (Guanahuatebey) people who came to Jamaica across a now submerged chain of islands stretching from Eastern Yucatan to Cuba and Jamaica between 5000 and 4000 BC. The Arawakan Tainos came to Jamaica, from South America, at about the third century AD, and then came the Caribs, who were the third wave of Amerindian settlers, in about the seventh to the ninth centuries. The Caribs were a fierce warrior people who launched many raids against the Arawak/Tainos, capturing the Taino men for use as slaves and women for sexual dalliance and childbearing (Woodley, 2001).

SPAIN OPENS UP THE NEW WORLD

Modern historians now believe that Leif Ericson, son of Eric the Red, preceded Columbus into the New World by some five hundred years. Indeed, in 1964, the US Congress led by President Lyndon B. Johnson unananimously honored Ericson as the first European to set foot in the New World by naming October 9 Leif Ericson Day (Ryne, 2000). Nevertheless, it was Spain, ousting the Moors at the battle of Granada in 1492, that led the robust expansion of a revitalized, postmedieval Europe into the vast territories of the underdeveloped New World.

The Moors were direct descendants of the ancient Carthaginians who fought under Hannibal. They were aided by battle-proven Senegalese troops from the South. These combined forces invaded Europe by way of the Iberian Peninsula in 711AD, under the leadership of Tarik-bin-Zaid. The Muslims scored notable victories when they defeated the Germanic Visigoths and also sacked the Vatican. However, the Battle of Tours, also known as the Battle of Poitiers in 732 AD, was won by the Franks led by Charles Martel. This Arab-African alliance remained in Europe for over 700 years, and traded an estimated two million slaves during this period, until they were decisively defeated and driven out of Europe by the Spanish forces at the battle of Granada in 1492 (Hyman, 1994).

Detailed accounts from the personal journals of Christopher Columbus narrate the providences through which he arrived in the "New World," a providence that appears to have been the result of a Royal suggestion:

> Whereas Most Christian, High, Excellent, and Powerful Princes, King and Queen of Spain . . . this present year 1492, after your Highnesses had terminated the war with the Moors reigning in Europe, the same having been brought to an

end in the great city of Granada . . . determined to send me, Christopher Columbus, to the . . . countries of India . . . and furthermore directed that I should not proceed by land to the East, as is customary, but by a Westerly route, in which direction we have hitherto no certain evidence that any one has gone. (Halsall, 1966, 1)

The Spanish sailors, in attempting to reach the East Indies "by a Westerly route" through uncharted sea lanes, found themselves enmeshed in the legendary navigational mishap that led Columbus's arrival in the Caribbean in 1492; an area he named the Indies, believing he had reached Asia. He made landfall on a small island in what is now known as the Bahamas, claimed it for Spain, and named it San Salvador. The Tainos living on San Salvador told him about a large island to the south, now known as Cuba.

Columbus sailed to Jamaica during his second voyage in May 1494, having been directed to the island by Tainos living in Cuba, who also told him that gold in abundance was to be had in *Yamaye*, a Taino term meaning "land of springs," which was transliterated into *Xaymaca* by the Spanish. When no large deposits of gold were found, the Spanish lost interest in the long-term development of Jamaica, which they called Santiago. The island was thereafter regarded as a minor, backwater property in the Spanish Empire. It was widely used, however, as a convenient supply staging post for launching expeditions and for transporting African slaves to the more lucrative gold and silver mines of the Spanish Main.

A LOOK AT TWO EARLY JAMAICAN SONIC CULTURES

The Tainos

We now know that the Taino tribes people, a subgroup of the Arawkian Indians, were not extinct at the time of the English invasion, that some had already joined the Maroons in their strongholds, and that some degree of cultural fusion and knowledge interchange (in language, food staples, bush medicine pharmacology, and especially in music) had indeed been taking place at this critical point (Satchell, 1999).

Taino musical forms were, as is common in Amerindian music, monophonic (with a single melodic line) and strophic (where the lyrics for each verse of song changed but the melody remained the same). In some Taino songs, a feature found across the Americas is that a lead singer would be accompanied by other singers in a "call-and-response" style, which was also a noted and celebrated song style among the Africans who were brought to Jamaica as slaves from the early sixteenth century onward. Taino singers would be accompanied by *mayohuacanes* (wood drums), *guiras* (scrapers), seashells, and different kinds of flutes and whistles (Guitar, 2006–2007).

Flutes were made from various hollow plants, wild cane, and the trumpet tree, and during sacred *areytos* (ceremonial dances) only the *Cacique* (chief of a village) would play the *maguey* (tambourine). Taino oral traditions—their histories, creation myths, and stories about the origins of their gods—were preserved in the songs, movements of dances, and the rituals of the *areytos*. The maracas, which is today much loved by Jamaican schoolchildren, was an important instrument during sacred *cohoba* rituals. Preceding these religious rituals were extensive cleansing regimes—fasting for eight days, ritual bathing, and inner cleansing with the use of "vomiting sticks." In the focal event of these rituals, the *Cacique* inhaled *cohoba*—a sacred hallucinatory powder—which would put him in a trance state, during which he was believed to be receiving special visions on behalf of the tribe (Martyr de Angliera, 1989).

Taino music then, served them in the business of their daily round of existence, religious and secular, providing cohesion in social relations and facilitating the people's relationship to their celestial gods of both sexes, or cemis. The writer therefore posits that the disruption of their free practice of their music, religion, and other and cultural rituals was a key factor in the almost complete Taino social collapse, and that the lack of these deprived them of the mental fortitude and determination needed to persevere in their desire for self-autonomy and survival.

The Maroons

After seizing Jamaica from the Spanish in 1655 (though Spanish resistance continued for the next five years), the English forces were unable to establish control over large tracts of the entire island due to the defense of these areas by Maroons. Maroons (from French and Spanish terms supposedly meaning "wild" or "hunters of wild animals") were runaway slaves turned freedom fighters, who had escaped from the Spanish plantations all over the Caribbean and had made homes in the defendable mountainous interiors of Hispaniola, Jamaica, Cuba, and even as far south as Suriname and Brazil. In their fortifications, Maroons in Jamaica, as elsewhere, practiced their African-based sonic cultures, religious and secular, featuring religious dances and pounding their huge war drums (Groepl, 2010).

In Jamaica, the maroons took advantage of the five years of hostilities between the British and remnants of the Spanish settlers to set up strongholds in Portland, the Cockpit Mountains in the northwest, the Blue Mountains, and the John Crow Mountains in the northeast. They also launched frequent harassing raids on plantations to secure food and weapons and to free slaves, especially women, who were in short supply in their strongholds. Finally, acknowledging the unlikelihood of military victory over the Maroons, the British formalized the realities on the battlefields by a Peace Treaty negotiated in 1739 to 1740 (Patterson, 1970).

However, it seems that the Maroons were not as skilled at negotiation as they were as warriors and they were out maneuvered by the British. They probably conceded more than they could have gotten away with. In exchange for self-management, consent was given to allow British supervisors to live in their towns, the Maroons were to support British military action against European pirate raids on the island, and most importantly they were to act as slave catchers and return runaway slaves for a price per head to be paid by the British. Despite these onerous terms agreed by the Maroons in exchange for peace and autonomy, it is nevertheless true that a section of the black population had thereby achieved a great measure of independence, and the right to govern themselves, as early as the mid-eighteenth century (Patterson, 1970).

In the Cockpit Mountains, a Maroon stronghold that British forces found very difficult to penetrate because of difficulty of access and therefore the uncertainty of victory coupled with the danger of unacceptable losses, music served the full diverse range of practices typical of a thriving community. There were grave songs, work songs, antiphonal call-and-response songs, chants derived from the ancient traditions of the Coromante tribe, and songs and dances related to Myal religious rites. Myal dances were religious in focus and venerated minor deities subordinate to the principal deity of the Maroons who were known as Nyankopon (also Nyame or Accompong). Prominent instruments were the *Gumbe* and *Ebo* drums, bamboo flutes, Coromante nose flutes, the Abeng (made from a cow's horn), shakers, scrapers, and graters. The grater was a rhythm instrument made by scraping a piece of metal or other hard substance in which holes had been bored.

The "sugar islands" (Caribbean islands, such as Jamaica and Barbados where sugar manufacturing made massive fortunes for planters using slave labor) were at one time among the most treasured possessions in the British Empire, and the wealth generated from them may well have laid the foundation for the industrial success of the Western world. According to Satchell (1999):

> The profit generated by the "triangular trade" (involving sugar and tropical produce from the British Caribbean colonies, the trade in manufactured goods for slaves in Africa, and the trade of slaves in the British Caribbean) financed the Industrial Revolution in Britain. (para. 11)

This is an amazing datum, for it means that black slave labor in the Caribbean, and by extension the folk music that aided their survival in the most desperate of circumstances imaginable, indirectly at least, provided the springboard for the success of the early factory system and the subsequent prosperity of modern Britain and her former colonies, including the American states that originally depended on Britain for both capital goods and manufactured products.

RELIGIO-CULTURAL TRADITIONS

Folk music had its genesis in a diversity of circumstances. The model here was the ubiquitous use of music in African traditions relating to birth and death, harvest, worship, work, and entertainment (Anderson, 2008). However, some of the music and dance expressions formerly regarded as mere cultist activities are now seen by some researchers as having deeper spiritual meanings. For example, Kumina dances (a Bantu-related practice) are now typically treated as cultural events that are choreographed for performance dances in the theatre, but some scholars insist that the deeper meaning of Kumina rituals is indicative of a religion. Kumina is so regarded because of its coherent system of beliefs, religious ritual, and spiritual practices that are based on metaphysical principles and cultural norms of adherents (Stewart, 2005).

In this scenario we may note that some scholars now assert that there are deposits of African religious culture in many of Jamaica's music forms apparently treated as vehicles for entertainment or cultural purposes only. These include Jonkunnu, Burru, Gumbay, Tambu, Dinki Mini, Gerreh, Nine Nite, Ettu, and even Ananse (Stewart, 2005). Some of these music forms, for example, Jonkunnu, make sense to the modern onlooker, even without consideration of the spiritual meanings.

Jonkunnu is one of the oldest styles of African-Jamaican folk music, and it emerged during slavery. Various forms and related traditions existed of this formerly popular form among Caribbean peoples of African descent. Jonkunno was a moving dance and music tradition, exhibiting features of British mime, and which featured various characters doing their specific dances that had symbolic meanings; for example, "Pitchy-patchy," who did quick steps and cartwheels, and was all things to all men as it were; "Cowhead," who did "bucking" motions, was symbolic of the African tradition of attributing power to horned animals, and these were also linked by tradition to rites of circumcision; "Devil," performing quick steps, and quick turns and jabs with his pitchfork, reminded of the need to be vigilant against attacks by evil, malevolent spirits; "Belly woman," who moved her belly in time with the music (which may have been a tribute to the life-renewing reproductive urge); and the "Set girls" with red and blue costumes and parasols (usually played by mulatto women) who symbolized European finery and the aspiration of many such mixed-race women to become mistresses of planters or plantation officials.

MUSIC AND REBELLION

The planters came to realize that the frequent slave riots, sabotages to the plantation system, and the spirit of rebellion all presented serious threats to the viability of the plantation economy. These were in large part fueled by the African musical and other cultural traditions that helped to maintain and uplift the morale and the spirit of freedom evident in the resistance struggles of the slaves and that became manifest in violent antislavery actions such as riots, rebellions, poisonings, assassinations, escapes, and even the refusal of some women to have children (Stowell, 2000).

A series of laws were therefore passed by the English colonists who sought to increasingly reinforce and intensify the restrictions imposed on the slaves. Many detailed clauses intended to suppress the music of the slaves, as well as preempt antislavery resistance by prescribing harsh punishments for even attempted acts of rebellion. An Act of 1717 provided that no "proprietor, attorney, or overseer suffer any beating on drums, barrels, gourds, or other such like instruments of noise on the plantations and settlements aforesaid" (*Acts of Assembly*, 1743, 108). However, though closely supervised, the Africans found ways to pass on their musical traditions to the young.

By happenstance, moderns can get a reasonably good idea of an authentic performance of African music in the seventeenth century in Jamaica. During one such performance in the year 1688, Dr. Hans Sloane, an English physician, musician, and naturalist, who was then living at King's Hall on the governor's estate in Spanish Town, went to visit the owner of a sugar plantation some distance away, intending to make use of the visit to garner notes for his book of field studies (Sloane, 1707). The plantation owner invited Sloane and his guest at the Great House (a name given to the residence of a plantation owner), a French musician named Baptiste, to witness a festival of music the slaves were due to perform that very afternoon. The planter was somewhat apprehensive at attending the festival because there had been recent riots at nearby plantations; nevertheless, the Europeans were so intrigued at the prospect of seeing the performance that, despite the potential for danger, the small party set out for the clearing where the event was to take place (Rath, 1993).

Sloane's journals of the event described two African musicians sitting on a log around a small fire while about a dozen men and women having rattles on their legs, wrists, and hands danced in a circle of people. The others clapped, scraped sticks, or shook bean pods, or beat on an iron shoe blade as the dancers and percussionists made "noise keeping time with one who made a sound answering on the mouth of an empty gourd or jar with his hand" (Rath, 1993, 700).

The French musician Baptiste wrote the music as he heard it, using the European spatiotemporal system of lines and spaces; and through Baptiste's undertaking, the Jamaican plantation music of the late seventeenth century was preserved down through the centuries, thus giving some idea of the music of those times. Baptiste's three transcriptions were titled *Koromanti, Angola,* and *Papa,* supposedly to identify the place of origin of each piece (Rath, 1993).

The Koromanti style typically employed the heptatonic scale, however, as regard to Angola music, Baptiste could only record intervals of a semitone, or more, not those of smaller intervals since his transcription was hampered by the fact that the European notation system could not record the microtones (i.e., tones less than a semitone) often found in music from the region referred to as Angola (Rath, 1993). Baptiste's work has not been fully endorsed by modern researchers. Rath writes:

> I claim no special objectivity on Baptiste's part, nor do I contend that his transcriptions are more accurate (or even nearly as accurate) as those of modern ethnomusicologists. Western musical notation is unable to capture many features of non-European musics, and I have no evidence that Baptiste's recording transcended any of these limits. However, the interpretation accounts for the many non-European features that are present in his transcriptions, features also found in modern ethno musicological studies of West Africa, Central Africa, and Jamaica. (707)

It seems that the predilection of modern popular Jamaican musicians, such as "dancehall" artists, for the use of "slackness" (bawdy lyrics often accompanied by overtly suggestive dance choreography) was also a well-established feature of ancient African lineage, so to speak. In Sloane's notes (as cited in Rath, 1993) we find the following:

> The Negros are much given to Venery, and also hard-wrought, will at nights, or on Feast days Dance and Sing; their Songs are all bawdy. . . . They have several sorts of instruments in imitation of lutes, made of small Gourds fitted with Necks, strung with horse hairs or the peeled stalks of climbing Plants or Withs. Their instruments are sometimes made of hollowed Timber covered with Parchment or other Skin wetted, having a Bow for its Neck. (712)

CHRISTIANITY: CULTURE CLASHES, CONVERTING/EDUCATING THE SLAVES

The Roman Catholics had come with the Spanish settlers in 1509, fifteen years after conquest, and had set up the first Christian Church on the island at Seville Nueva (later St. Ann's Bay) by 1526. An Abbey was established at the request of the Spanish king for the purpose of converting the Taino Arawaks to Christianity, but this royal attempt to convert and educate the natives was unsuccessful because the indigenous people were naturally skeptical of the wisdom of abandoning their own religion for that of the Spanish, who were relentlessly driving them to almost complete extinction by means of the harsh labor regime, gratuitous cruelty by the Spanish, and also the ravages of European diseases to which they were unaccustomed. Furthermore, the Tainos believed that a better life awaited them, beyond the physical, in the hereafter, and therefore parents and their children often committed suicide when driven to desperation (Thomas, Vaitilingam & Brown, 2003).

When the English monarchy was restored, after the Cromwellian hiatus, Charles II ordered that the Anglican Church, which had previously been banned in England by Oliver Cromwell, be established in Jamaica as an antidote to the licentious behavior, drunkenness, and other vices that was reported to have been rampant among the English settlers, thereby constituting an obstacle to the proper development of the colony. However, from 1655 to 1816 the English Church in Jamaica refused to either Christianize or educate the slaves. They did so for the same reasons that the Anglican hierarchy in England opposed the education of the lower classes in England at the time. They feared that Christian teaching of the fundamental equality of all mankind in the sight of God would make the lower classes in England, or slaves in Jamaica, think that they were as good as their social superiors. As late as 1807, therefore, the year of cessation of the Atlantic Slave Trade, only one in seventeen people in England could write at all (Icke, 1994).

The nonconformist Moravians (in 1754) were the first to seriously teach Christianity to the slaves in Jamaica, and they were followed by the Methodists in 1759. The Scottish Presbyterians (1823) and the Congregationalists were also active in teaching the slaves.

However, the white missionaries often faced a credibility challenge, in that they were seen as ambivalent toward the liberation aspirations of the slaves. For example, the slaves noted that while many failed to condemn the extreme evils of the slavery system publicly, they were not reticent about preaching against perceived moral lapses of the slaves. In addition, the worship music of the missionaries was European in orientation and did not make allowance for the practice of the sacred music of the slaves (Stewart, 2005).

In 1782, two African American slaves, Moses Baker and John Lisle, came to Jamaica and started the "Native Baptist Movement." In the Baptist organizational structure leaders were called "Daddies" and "Mammies." The Native Baptist faith easily resonated with the sacred Myal music of the slaves, to the extent that the white missionaries worried that by their rituals and teachings Native Baptist churches were becoming more African than Christian. However, English Baptists such as Wilberforce, Knibb, and Burchell were fervent abolitionists and were leaders of the Abolitionist movement in England. The Baptists were involved in both Myal music and the liberation aspirations of the slaves. The practice of Myal was a morale-building factor in Jamaican freedom struggles from the Tacky rebellion in 1760 to the Morant Bay rebellion in 1865. It also played a part in the antislavery resistance when Daddy Sharpe, a Baptist deacon, organized and led the Baptist rebellion in 1831 (also known as the Christmas rebellion), just a few years before emancipation in 1834.

MUSIC: THE POSTEMANCIPATION ERA

With regard to the musical training of the majority of Jamaicans up to the early nineteenth century, we cannot plausibly apply the term *music education* in the usual sense of an integrated educational benefit in organized courses of study in an educational system. There was still tension between the African-based orally transmitted forms that were percussive and rhythmical and post-Renaissance European music that emphasized melodic supremacy and strict written formal structure and was the socially dominant genre of music in Jamaica—the music of the gentry and upper-class elite.

There were a few private schools operated exclusively for the education of whites, and it was the practice that those white Jamaicans who could afford to do so would then send their children to schools in Britain for professional training. The study of European music, leading to some proficiency in playing an instrument, was regarded as conferring a distinct social advantage and was desirable in terms of a rounded education, but music was not seen as viable in terms of an occupation for life.

THE TWENTIETH CENTURY: MUSIC, NATIONALISM, AND POSTCOLONIAL CONSCIOUSNESS

In the twentieth century there was much accelerated musical activity in both popular and art music in Jamaica. A growing ethos of nationalistic fervor eventually led to ever more strident calls for political independence from Britain, and this was, of course, the logical ultimate step in liberation consequent on emancipation in the nineteenth century. In parallel to these political ambitions there emerged demands from those with a burning desire for cultural independence as well, for formal recognition and inclusion of historically important African-derived forms in school curricula.

However, such cultural nationalism and enthusiasm for local music was not everywhere evident among all classes in the society. For example, locally based public radio broadcasting, which began at about the start of World War II, was a new technology owned and operated, for the most part, by Englishmen, or local anglophiles, and as a result little notice was taken of local music. A shortwave radio station, ZQI, was set up in

November 1939 and began broadcasting one hour per week in 1940. It played classical music, and then added relays from the BBC so that by 1947 it was broadcasting four hours daily during daylight hours only.

The impact of ZQI on local music was minimal. In July 1950, the first commercial radio station in Jamaica, Radio Jamaica and Rediffusion (RJR), was established. RJR also started out largely ignoring local Afro-Jamaican music. An example of its musical programming follows: Calypso Corner, Treasure Isle Time, Reynolds Hour, Les Paul and Mary Ford, Bing Sings, Sweet and Swing, Nat King Cole's Court, Hit of the Day, and Music by Manitoban. There is a story popular among old-timers that the relevant Minister for Culture threatened to revoke the station's licence if it continued to refuse to play local music. By 1956, however, RJR had an estimated six hundred thousand listeners, or almost half of the population over nine years of age (Chang & Chen, 1998).

IMPACT OF MUSIC FESTIVALS ON CULTURE CONSCIOUSNESS

From the opening decades of the twentieth century the music taught in Jamaican schools was a subject called "Singing." Singing as taught in Jamaican schools adhered closely to British music pedagogy in vogue at the time, and its model, as in England, was nineteenth-century British choral tradition. It was not until the 1960s when the burgeoning flame of passionate nationalism led to political independence in many territories of the Anglophone Caribbean, including Jamaica (1962), that there was a move to introduce folk music in the schools (Tucker & Bowen, 2001).

Music in the "singing" class became an important part of the primary (elementary) school common core of skills to be acquired, and had been recognized as such at that level for some time. The variety of local music used in the curriculum at the primary school level resonated with young students and engendered enthusiastic participation from them in music classes. Not surprisingly the more anglicized music offerings of curricula in the high schools did not generate the enthusiasm for the subject that was evident at the primary level. National policy in promoting mass cultural events, however, generated much enthusiasm in both the high schools and the wider society.

THE JAMAICA FESTIVAL OF THE ARTS

Following the grand Festival of Arts that was staged in celebration of independence in August 1962, Edward Seaga, a cultural visionary, then Minister of Development and Welfare in the government (the Jamaica Labour Party), decided that it would be a good idea to have such a festival on an annual basis. In 1968, Seaga took a bill to the House of Representatives proposing the setting up of a Jamaica Festival Commission. The Act was passed without opposition. In 1980 another bill was passed changing the Festival Commission into the Jamaica Cultural Development Commission (JCDC), an entity with much broader responsibilities, which unearthed a wealth of talented performers, many of whom are now icons of cultural expression in Jamaica. This Festival also provides opportunities for all schools, with or without a music program, to present their ensembles (vocal and instrumental) as well as individual presentations by their students for adjudication, with the aim of developing musical skill that will lead to high performance standards.

In 1990, there was major reform in school curricula due to the implementation of a Curriculum Guide for use throughout the Jamaican public school system. This related to both the aesthetic subjects as music, drama, and dance as well as the so-called grammar school subjects (the three R's), and was supported by major stakeholders such as principals, university lecturers, school teachers, education officers, and of course, parents, who were eager to see upgrades in the school system to meet the challenges of the fast-developing Jamaican society.

Among the developments in music education and practice in Jamaica during the twentieth century were the following:

1. **From *Solfège* to the Use of Written Scores:** It used to be the practice before the wide availability of sheet music that school choirs, from the primary level through high school and teacher training colleges,

taught musical literacy using the solfa system. This made it possible for teachers to collect material for use in the classroom through *solfège*, and thereafter transfer it to a written document. This practice, though now made largely obsolete by the availability of written scores, laid the foundation for excellent high school choirs such as those of Kingston College, Jamaica College, and Glenmuir High School, which have toured Europe and the Americas.

2. **Communications Media, a Medium for Music Education:** Many Jamaican music educators have made it their mission, both in face-to-face interactions in the classroom and via communications media, to ensure that a diversified offering of both Jamaican folk music and popular forms coexist and are passed on to coming generations. The recently deceased Lloyd Hall for many years operated as a national music teacher by doing a series of government-sponsored radio broadcasts to schools, in which he dealt with various aspects of folk music for both junior and senior schools.

3. **A Songbook Used to Teach Music and Storytelling:** *Jamaica Song and Story*, a much respected compilation by Walter Jekyll, organist at the Hanover Parish Church, was published in 1907 and immediately was used as a key resource for teaching songs and the storyteller tradition in the schools. It was still relevant when it was republished in the 1960s (by Sangster's Publishers), this time including prefatory essays by respected historian Phillip Sherlock and internationally known social commentator and dance choreographer, the late Rex Nettleford.

4. **A Published Work Focuses on the Sociohistorical Development:** Marjorie Whylie published the important work *Mento: The Who, the What, and Why* (Whylie Communications), which analyzed the sociohistorical development and the form, transcriptions and arrangements of Mento. Mento is a form going back into the early days of slavery.

5. **A Television Program, *All Together Sing*:** A television program, *All Together Sing*, has for the past three years (2008–2010) showcased musical talent in the high schools islandwide with musical performances in classical, folk, and popular genres.

6. **An Orchestra and a Choral Group Developed:** The Jamaica Philharmonic Orchestra and the Y Choral Group, which were conducted by the late Sibthorpe Beckett, gave young Jamaican instrumentalists, in the schools and the wider society, an opportunity to hear and participate in playing a wide range of orchestral music that spanned the art music genre from the Baroque and Classical Romantic eras to the early twentieth century.

7. **The National Chorale and Orchestra Leads the Way:** The National Chorale and Orchestra has been led by many notable conductors, including the late Vibart Seaforth, a member of the Jamaica Regiment and the Jamaica Folk Singers, and eventual head of the Jamaica School of Music, who taught voice, woodwind, and the use of the recorder as a functional instrument for classroom teachers.

At the tertiary level there are now serious ongoing attempts to organize studies of local music forms. The University of the West Indies (UWI) now offers a Level 1 course in the Faculty of Humanities and Education—An Introduction to Music—which teaches the elements of African music. The Level 2 program, "Music of the English-Speaking Caribbean," includes the teaching of art music and examines traditional folk forms—ritual, work, social, and socioreligious—as well as gospel music, jazz, and popular music.

Another course offered at the UWI is Music and Dance in the Primary School, which explores the use of music and dance as catalysts in the learning experience. At the Mico University College, undergraduates who so elect are prepared for teaching music in the school system by a degree program in heritage studies that examines artifacts, architecture, and music and dance forms with their sociocultural underpinnings.

The Little Theatre Movement has been creating scripts, scores, productions, and recordings of the National Pantomime's annual end-of-year presentations since the 1940s. These very popular pantomimes, originally based on the British pantomime tradition but now with wholly local content, have been using topical local themes and draw on the melodic contours and rhythmic complexity of the traditional and popular music of Jamaica. They provide vehicles for showcasing local music/dance culture and are models for smaller productions of similar aesthetics in the school system.

After independence, Jamaica continued the system of parliamentary democracy inherited from the British, and with the elected representatives of the people now solely in charge of policy directives in all spheres of national life, elected governments moved to give increasing formal recognition in the school system to the folk music of the overwhelming majority of voters; namely, people of African descent. So while there is indeed a long tradition of support for classical music in Jamaica, the island is now most known internationally for its popular forms such as reggae and dancehall.

AFRO-JAMAICAN FOLK MUSIC MATURES AS ART

As may be expected, there came a time when many of these previously functional neo-African folk forms were bereft of their functional, practical associations, as with gradual emergence of industrialization, at least in urban areas, their utility was not directly relevant to the new challenges. They later found a secure place in the culture that was far removed from their original use; that is, they became useful for their historical value in preserving links with ancestral culture and for entertainment purposes. Some of the same work songs originally used by urban slaves while loading produce on ships bound for Europe were later reworked into a more sophisticated Euro-African muted call-and-response format by performers such as Jamaican-born Harry Belafonte. This format achieved tremendous success in live concerts, recordings, and cinematic presentations in the United States and Europe.

Groups such as the Frats Quintet were requested to sing at the United Nations General Assembly. The Jamaica Folk Singers led by Olive Lewin, the theatrical dance theatre pioneered by the visionary Ivy Baxter, the National Dance Theatre Company founded by Rex Nettleford and Eddie Thomas in 1960, and the pianist/musicologist noted for her jazz and folk stylings, Marjorie Whylie (2005), all forged highly respected international reputations based on their creativity and ability to express the materials and inspiration of indigenous culture into art forms in music and dance.

Jamaican folk music has always been widely accepted and practiced from the earliest days by Afro-Jamaicans. In modern times, musical ring games such as "Ring Ding," delivered in riveting interactive format on live television with studio audiences of Jamaican school-age youngsters by Miss Lou (Louise Bennett, a folk culture icon) and Marjorie Whylie, were immensely popular, and served to inspire the coming generation to maintain links with their root culture.

Forms associated with the religious rites of Revivalist Afro-Christian cults such as *Pukkumina* and Zion had less popular acceptance. One major hindrance preventing popular acceptance was that these African-based cults were polytheistic in outlook, while the overwhelming majority of Jamaicans were, and are, Christians with a religious culture of monotheism. However, on the other hand, this spiritual plurality meant that the Afro-Christian cults were able, from their perspective, to incorporate central icons of Christian beliefs including a hierarchy of angels and a plural Trinitarian godhead. Nevertheless, the cultists were dissatisfied with the staid hymnic culture of the Christians. Consequently, they adapted the melodies, harmonies, and rhythms of European religious music to suit the dynamism of their own ethos and practice, resulting in an unmistakably African presentation (Seaga, 1969).

In this postindependence era there was a flowering of popular acceptance by people of all classes for the popular music and dance forms associated with, or invented by, the African majority. The Mento rhythm produced the rhythmic inspiration for the modern popular form of *ska*—a primarily Mento-influenced combination with elements of American jazz and rhythm and blues. The advent of rock and roll in the United States led to a decline in the popularity of jazz, and this spurred jazz-loving Jamaican musicians and record producers to come up with their own creative alternatives. Foremost among these were Sir Clement "Coxone" Dodd, Duke Reid, and Prince Buster. It is said anecdotally that the use of syncopated rhythms—that is, stress on the "offbeat" as used in reggae—was first initiated by Prince Buster in a studio rehearsal.

Rocksteady was a form of limited longevity, featuring the so-called dred the "rude boy" slower tempo. The "rude boy" was typically an unemployed urban youth who haunted venues where "sound systems" played for dances and sometimes "toasted" (rapped) over a basic driving "riddim." The dancehall genre is very popular among all social classes in Jamaica and now typically uses drum machines rather than acoustic sets.

Reggae is a music form known for its rhythmic emphasis on the offbeat, and this syncopation effect grabbed the attention of the popular music world and gave the Caribbean its first superstar, in the person of the

Rastafarian Bob Marley. Marley's *Exodus* was voted best popular music album of the twentieth century, and his song "One Love" was voted the song of the century. Rastafarians also hold Haille Selassie I as the son of God of the Second Advent. They believe that the birthplace of *Homo sapiens* was in Africa, and that this human survived and spread through the world by adapting physically to ambient local environmental conditions; this is also the view of a majority of modern anthropologists. Of course, many Marley music fans in Europe and America, who were participants in the drug culture, were also intrigued by the novelty of a religious practice that proclaims ganja (marijuana) as a legitimate religious sacrament.

THE FORMAL CURRICULUM

Up to the mid-twentieth century there was still inadequate interest in designing curricula that incorporated Afro-Jamaican music materials into the formal high school curriculum structure. This was still the habitat of the music of post-Renaissance European culture, and in this lofty perch of establishment monoculturalism a powerful vanguard of the middle class and wealthy elite in Jamaican society saw no real benefit in ascribing cultural parity to African-derived forms in the formal curriculum in the schools. Some expressed fears that this could lead to the "vulgarization" of music and diminished appreciation of the necessity to study the technical foundations of the art.

However, the winds of change would not be denied. The heady days of political independence were indeed at hand, and it was recognized by influential persons comprising what may be dubbed the "liberal/progressive" intellectual elite that a national music idiom needed to be articulated and implemented at the formal curriculum level. They provided the leadership for the broadening of the formal curricular offerings at the tertiary level of studies, which were designed to train performers and also teachers who would then be instrumental, so to speak, in disseminating their knowledge throughout the Jamaican school system.

Many visionary Jamaican music educators and ethnomusicologists, and friends of goodwill from overseas tertiary institutions and conservatories, have participated in the transformational process and have designed a multicultural approach to studies and performance offerings that reflects the richness of our historical legacy. A roster of notables and their contributions cannot be dealt with comprehensively in the space available, but, prominent among those pioneers who have disseminated their ideas in writing for curriculum reform, and have taught (academic, vocal, or instrumental subject areas in the broadened curriculum) at the first conservatory-level institution of music in the English-speaking Caribbean (the Jamaica School of Music) are Joan Tucker, Audrey Cooper, Ivy Baxter, Vibart Seaforth, Rex Nettleford, Marjorie Whylie, and afterward, maintaining the tradition, Winston Ewart, former head, and Roger Williams, current head, of the Edna Manley School of Music (formerly the Jamaica School of Music).

However, the most outstanding contributor to, and visionary of, the process was certainly the late Pamela O'Gorman, born in Brisbane, Australia, in 1935, who became a naturalized Jamaican citizen in 1972. Pamela O'Gorman's passion for Jamaican culture and the indigenous music of the people was readily apparent to all who met her. She started her music career in 1958 in Jamaica immediately after completing studies in England at the Trinity College where she became an associate, licentate, and fellow of that institution. O'Gorman was never happy with being just another teacher in the European music tradition, and made innovative curricular impact during her years as director of the Music Unit of the University of the West Indies (1970–1976) and as head of the Jamaica School of Music (1976–1989). She is recognized as a driving force behind the transformation of the curriculum of the Jamaica School of Music (Hickling-Hudson, 2000).

The Jamaica School of Music (the musical arm of what was to become a Culture Complex comprising tertiary-level schools of Art, Drama, and Dance) was founded by Vera Moodie in 1961 to 1962, the year before independence, and even then, though ostensibly mandated to devise an inclusive multicultural curriculum, British musical influence was overwhelming, and the curriculum was modeled on that of the Royal Schools of Music. The School of Art was founded in the 1950s by Edna Manley, and in the 1970s there followed the establishment of the Jamaica National School of Drama founded by the Little Theater Movement, and the Jamaica School of Dance, which was established by the National Dance Theater Company (Hickling-Hudson, 2000).

It was not until 1972 when a thorough reorganization of the curriculum led by O'Gorman and supported by other enthusiasts such as Marjorie Whylie, who taught conga drumming (a core requirement), was undertaken, that the curriculum took on aspects befitting the multicultural historical roots of a Caribbean conservatory of music. Some of the highlights of the updated offerings that then represented Jamaica's multicultural diversity were: Afro-American music, Jamaican folk traditions, conga drumming (which brought protests from the Jamaican middle class), jazz, popular Jamaican forms, and Western classical music. Students taking the classical stream had to take minors in jazz and pop, and vice versa.

These transformational approaches to the music curriculum attracted the attention of music educators in England. Professors John Blacking and John Paynter from the University of Cambridge, after attending a seminar series in Jamaica, were impressed with the philosophy, curriculum designs, and methodology of delivery in the ferment of postcolonial innovations to the extent that they wrote about them in the *British Journal of Music Education*, commending such methods to British educators.

At present, the faculty of humanities and education at the University of the West Indies is offering courses in music that are well-designed to equip teachers with firm foundational bases in the European art musics as well as the emergent forms arising from the historical legacy. These courses provide extensive exposure to topics such as Art Music from ancient times, through the medieval, Renaissance, baroque/rococo, classical, Romantic/Post-Romantic, and twentieth-century eras. In studies dealing with regional musics there are Caribbean traditional forms such as social and socioreligious music, gospel, theatre and art music, jazz and popular forms. "Music and Dance in the Primary School" is intended to study these forms as a catalyst in the learning process.

ROSE/CXC: THE BROADENED CURRICULUM IN THE SCHOOLS

As noted, although the process was initially tentative and overly dependent on British models and notions of education, genuine steps forward have been made in the general as well as music education of the Jamaican and Caribbean people. Successive Jamaican governments—the Jamaica Labour Party (JLP) and the People's National Party (PNP)—have made critical innovations and interventions to enhance the delivery of a quality product, and to include the musical culture of the formerly excluded Afro-Jamaican element within the formal structure.

The Reform of Secondary Education (ROSE) Project I (1993–1998) and ROSE II (continuing and updating the reforms of ROSE I) have introduced musical syllabi that, in content, seem light years in advance of the state of affairs at independence in 1962, where local forms were largely unwritten and marginalized. In addition, songs and music of other music cultures globally are also to be found in the ROSE-promoted CXC syllabi (*Reform*, 2000).

The Caribbean Examinations Council (CXC) music syllabus is organized under three major areas: Listening and Appraising (LIAP); Performing (PERF); and Composing (COMP).

Candidates are required to complete papers in LIAP, PERF, COMP, and a school-based assessment (SBA) comprising LIAF and PERF profile dimensions. The CXC (Music) is intended to provide students with opportunities to develop practical knowledge of music and skills of analysis that can form the basis for further studies in teaching, performing, conducting, composing, and/or arranging; the music business and related fields; and is rooted in Caribbean musical expressions and those of other cultures (MOEYC, 2004).

CXC now views music as an essential subject and proposes to make it a compulsory subject. To mark the two-hundredth anniversary of the abolition of the transatlantic slave trade in 2007, the CXC produced a seminal multidisciplinary work, *Let These Things Be Written Down*. The work was first performed on October 6, 2007, at the University Chapel, by a sixty-voice choir, and it combines traditional Jamaican melodies, lyrics, and rhythms and uses texts by outstanding Jamaican and Caribbean writers and cultural icons including Louise Bennett-Coverly (Miss Lou), Dennis Scott, Derek Walcott, and Una Marsden. The work is the most important and brilliantly conceived musical element in the CXC music syllabus. Items from the work will be selected and used all over the Caribbean in the CXC music syllabus.

In commenting on this work, funded by the British High Commission and as a result of which music teachers in eleven Caribbean countries were trained, Jeremy Cresswell, British High Commissioner said:

Music can uplift the soul in a way, dare I say, and that literature barely can. Music is something that is probably more easily accessible irrespective of language and irrespective of language ability. So the notion that music should not just be an option is something that I can certainly share very strongly. (JIS News, 2009, para. 8)

We have come full circle from the dire situation of official suppression outlined at the beginning of this chapter. The late Professor Barry Chevannes, chairman of the Institute of Jamaica, summarizes the positive opinion all around to *Let These Things Be Known*. He said that the Institute was very proud to be associated with the project and that it could be held accountable for ensuring that the work would be widely distributed (JIS News, 2009).

Jamaican music is a work-in-progress. The typical music for which Jamaica is known is of the popular genre, and little attempt at creating "art music" for aesthetic pleasure is now evident. However, there are signs of intent to do so, and the work, *Let These Things Be Known*, is a brilliant attempt in this regard. It is truly a work of art on a large scale, and uses themes arising from the melodic ideas and delivery styles of the people themselves, worked into an aesthetic whole, and as such it gives much hope for the musical future of Jamaica.

CONCLUSION

Caribbean peoples have shown themselves to be marvelously inventive in the sonic culture of music. Most of the Caribbean territories that, like Jamaica, were appropriated and directly administered by various European powers—the Spanish, English, French, Dutch, and Portuguese—which came to the region in the post-Columbus era, are now independent political entities. Large numbers of Africans brought in originally as slaves carried with them, on the slave ships, the only possessions they could—the mentally held indelible memories of their particular tribal musical culture. These musics have developed down the generations, over centuries, proving their worth during the severe challenges of chattel servitude, destruction of family ties, violence, and colonialism, and now after emerging, tested and purified in the freedom of independence, have flowered and contributed significantly to world music.

This "flowering" of musical culture, despite antecedent prejudice, is evident in Jamaica, as after a tentative start in multicultural designs to school curricula a flood of strategies have been devised to ensure full dissemination of historically relevant music of the people. One such strategy is the establishment of the Jamaica Field Service Project (JAFSP). With the help of students and professors from participating American universities and institutions such as the Peace Corps Volunteers, many rural and urban primary schools are receiving organized tutoring in the use of recorders, guitars, drums, and vocal ensemble singing in their own native musical forms. This cross-cultural rapport has deepened the musical insights and appreciation of both the overseas participants and Jamaican school children (JAFSP, 2009).

Jamaica has produced many world-renowned musicians in many genres, including classical performers/ interpreters now performing internationally, as well as performers in the tradition of native inventions in the popular forms such as reggae, which has a large international fan base and a Grammy category of its own. There is therefore ample evidence for optimism regarding future significant contributions to world music by Jamaican musicians.

REFERENCES

Acts of Assembly, passed in the Island of Jamaica, from 1681 to 1737, inclusive. (1743). London. 1.c., 108.

Anderson, M. (2008). *Readings in music education: Philosophical and educational perspectives*. Mandeville, Jamaica: Northern Caribbean Press.

Chang, K., & Chen, W. (1998). *Reggae routes: The story of Jamaican music*. Pennsylvania: Temple University Press.

Elias, S. (1997, April). Bridge to the past. *Earth*. 51–55.

Groepl, J. (2010). *Caribbean slave trade: John Hawkins's first Caribbean voyages*. Retrieved from http://www.suite101.com/content/cimaroons-or-maroons-from-slavery-to-freedom-in-the-caribbean-a309815

Guitar, L. (2006–2007). New notes about Taino music and its influence on contemporary Dominican life. *Issues in Caribbean Amerindian Studies (ICAS)*, 7(1). Retrieved January 2, 2011, from http://www.centrelink.org/GuitarTainoMusicEN.html

Halsall, P. (1966). *Medieval source book*. Bronx, NY: Fordham University, Centre for Medieval Studies.

Hickling-Hudson, A. (2000). Post colonialism, hybridity, and transferability: The contribution of Pamela O'Gorman to music education in the Caribbean. *Caribbean Journal of Education, 1&2*, 36–55.

Hylton-Tomlinson, O. (1975). *Mango walk: Jamaican folk songs and games*. Kingston, Jamaica: Jamaica Publishing House Ltd.

Hyman, M. (1994). *Blacks before America*. Trenton, NJ: Africa World Press, Inc.

Icke, D. (1994). *The robot's rebellion: The story of the spiritual Renaissance*. Bath, UK: Gateway Books.

Institute of Jamaica. (2010, September). *The Jamaica music museum presents "The music of Jamaica: People, Voice, Song."* Retrieved January 2, 2011, from http://instituteofjamaica.org.jm/ioj_wp/?p=1

JIS News. (2009, November 4). *Bicentenary anniversary musical piece to be added to CXC syllabus.*

Jamaica Field Service Project (JAFSP). (2009, July 26). *Service learning in Jamaica.* Retrieved February 20, 2011, from http://www.youtube.com/user/JAFSProject

James, G. (1954). *Stolen legacy.* New York: Philosophical Library.

Martyr de Angliera, P. (1989). Primorcronista de Indias: Decades del nuevomundo. *Sociedad Dominicana de Bibliofilos, 1*: 351. Santo Domingo.

Ministry of Education, Youth and Culture [MOEYC]. (2004, August 15). *National report of Jamaica.* Kingston, Jamaica: Author.

Patterson, O. (1970). *Slavery and slave revolts: A socio-historical analysis of the first Maroon war.* New York: Anchor Books.

Rath, R. C. (1993, October). African music in seventeenth-century Jamaica: Cultural transit and transition. *The William and Mary Quarterly (3rd Seer), 50*(4), 700–26.

Reform of Secondary Education [ROSE] Paper. (2000, October). Kingston, Jamaica: Government of Jamaica/World Bank.

Ryne, L. (2000). *Leif Ericson: Columbus' predecessor by nearly 500 years.* Retrieved January 2, 2011, from http://www.mnc.net/norway/ericson.htm

Satchell, V. (1999). *Jamaica.* Retrieved November 20, 2011, from http://africana.com/tt/1122.htm

Seaga, E. (1969). *Revival cults in Jamaica.* Kingston, Jamaica: The Institute of Jamaica Publications.

Sloane, H. (1707). *A voyage to the islands Madera, Barbados, Nieves, St. Christopher and Jamaica with the natural history of the herbs and trees of the last of those islands*, xlvii–lvii. London: B. M. Printers.

Stewart, D. (2005). *Three eyes for the journey.* Oxford University Press Inc.

Stowell, C. R. (2000, August). *Retention and preservation of African roots in Jamaican folk music.* University of Vermont. Retrieved January 2, 2011, from http://debate.uvm.edu/dreadlibrary/stowell.html

Thomas, P., Vaitilingam, A., & Brown, P. R. (2003). *The rough guide to Jamaica.* London: Rough Guides.

Tucker, J., & Bowen, C. (2001, September). *Music education in Jamaica and the Commonwealth Caribbean.* UNESCO.

Voyages of Christopher Columbus. (2011). Retrieved January 2, 2011, from http://www.enotes.com/topics/christopher-columbus

Whylie, M. (2005). *Our musical heritage: The power of the beat.* Jamaica: Grace Kennedy Foundation.

Woodley, G. (2001). *The Taino of Jamaica.* Retrieved November 20, 2011, from http://www.jamaicans.com/articles/primearticles/taino.shtml

Chapter Five

Trinidad and Tobago

Hollis Liverpool

INTRODUCTION

Like the other countries of the British Caribbean, Trinidad and Tobago was made known to the outer world in the late fifteenth century when the Italian navigator, Christopher Columbus, laid anchor on its shores and sought to enslave the indigenous, Amerindian population. By his actions, Columbus opened up the islands of the Caribbean to European explorers who, anxious to make money from trade and exploitation of the natives, came to the islands bringing their European customs and traditions. As such, throughout the sixteenth and seventeenth centuries, mainly Spaniards, Frenchmen, and Englishmen poured into the island as planters, merchants, missionaries, and administrators and, in the course of time, inevitably stamped on the islands their musical structures. To find laborers for their plantations, the Europeans looked to other less privileged and lowly placed Europeans, Africans, and, later, Asians. In the course of time, it was only natural that as Europeans influenced this oppressed, laboring population with their music, they too would become influenced by the music of the oppressed classes.

THE EARLY DAYS

Amerindian Influence

The first sound of music heard in the islands was that of the first peoples, the Amerindians. History records that in the Caribbean they sang and danced particularly after registering a victory over their enemies whose bodies some Caribs ate as a sign of victory and resilience. Famed ethnomusicologist Peter Manuel (1995) noted:

> Indigenous Caribbean music centered around a socioreligious ceremony called arieto, in which as many as a thousand participants would dance in concentric circles around a group of musicians. The musicians sang mythological chants in call-and-response style, playing rattles (later called maracas), gourd scrapers (guiros), and slit drums called mayohuacan. These last were hollowed logs with H-shaped tongues cut into them. Although most scholars think the Indians of the Caribbean originally came from what is now Venezuela, the use of slit drums suggests some affinity with Aztecs and other Mexican groups, who played similar instruments called teponaztli. (3)

In Trinidad, young historian Linda Newson (1976) recorded the presence of mainly friendly Arawaks, although there were pockets of more fierce Caribs (19). The Amerindians were so badly treated by the Spaniards that although by 1553 there were 6,000 of them, by 1797 only 1,082 were left. By 1826, only 655 of them could be found (Liverpool, 2001, 28). Nevertheless, according to planter Pierre Borde (1876), they held parties at which they sang and danced all night. Borde noted that the Spaniards called these parties "bebidas or drinking bouts" and that they lasted for "several days and nights," during which time "no pains were spared to

79

amuse their guests." Their intoxicating drinks were made from cassava and corn, and their songs "were love and war ballads" (51).

A Spaniard who accompanied Columbus to Trinidad noted that the Amerindians held "public and private dances" and "kept time with wonderful precision." He went on to say that Amerindians in Trinidad "accompanied their dances with historical songs . . . their musical instruments consisted of a rude drum and different conch shells." The historical evidence shows that at victory celebrations especially, Amerindians smoked tobacco, drank intoxicating alcoholic drinks, kept up a musical rhythm by beating a large drum made from the trunk of a tree with a huge stick, played flutes made from bones and the stems of trees, and blew conch shells and danced with shells attached to their feet, the shells keeping up a rhythm relevant to that of the drum being struck (Liverpool, 2001, 142, 143). Notable historian Gertrude Carmichael (1961) also noted that the Amerindians made music from drums and conch shells, but such music slowly disappeared in the face of Spanish aggression (16).

Although early twentieth-century writer Andrew Pearse (1956) records that the Amerindians took no part in the later carnivals of the nineteenth century, he noted that an earlier writer and researcher, Mitto Sampson, recorded that in the mid-nineteenth century an Amerindian calypsonian, named Surisima, organized a procession of Caribs into Port of Spain and sang calypsoes throughout, in memory of one of their heroes, Caziria, who was killed by the Spaniards. According to Sampson, as mentioned by Pearse, the Amerindians sang joyous "Carietos" that were used not only to heal the sick but also to embolden the warriors and seduce the women (154–55). The Spaniards feared these Amerindian singers, who saw them as spirit-possessed souls capable of harming them. The Spaniards, therefore, killed many.

It would appear that the British also feared the Amerindian music makers for, by the 1850s, with England in firm control of the island, the procession in honor of Caziria was stopped by the police, the caciques were killed, and the singing Amerindians were brought to court (153). Thus, although the Amerindians did not live long enough to impact on the modern-day music of Trinidad and Tobago, Surisima sang calypsoes as late as 1859. In addition, their lives and times now provide data for many modern-day songs and fodder for the masquerades of today's carnivalists.

EUROPEAN INFLUENCES

Spanish

Of all the European inputs, Trinidad and Tobago first felt the impact of the Spaniards on its culture, music, and customs, they having colonized the island in the sixteenth century and reigned supreme until 1797 when the British took over the reins of government. In addition to those who came from Spain, hundreds of Creole Spaniards from Cumana and Carrapano provinces in Northern Venezuela as well as town dwellers from Caracas and Angostura migrated to Trinidad. Revolutionary upheavals along the Spanish Main as well as wars in New Granada caused many Spaniards, both Whites and Creoles, to come to nearby Trinidad. Of the 2,261 Whites in Trinidad in 1805, 505 were Spaniards. Between 1814 and 1817, 3,823 more free people, mostly Creole Spaniards, were allowed to stay in Trinidad. They, staunchly Catholic, moved into the foothills of the Northern Range to cultivate crops, chiefly cocoa, and to serenade their loved ones after work and at Catholic festivals, in their churches and homes (Wood, 1968, 33).

Like the other Europeans, the Spaniards were fond of partying around Christmastime, and both peninsular as well as local Spaniards or Peons, as they were called, went house to house visiting. There, they serenaded their friends and families with guitar, cuatro,[1] and shac-shac,[2] and sang special carols based on the birth of the Christchild called *Aguinaldos*. Many Spanish dances were also introduced. These included the "Manzanare," the "Joropo," and the "Galleron" (Carr, August 1965).

House-to-house visits by the Spaniards at Christmastime developed into what is known today as the *Parang* from the Spanish word *parrandear*, meaning to go out partying. The musicians are aptly referred to as *paranderos*. Further trade linkages between the Spaniards of Trinidad and those in Venezuela entrenched the parang tradition to the extent that today, parang is a national festival to which all citizens of Trinidad and Tobago anxiously look forward at Christmastime (the last week of November to January 6).

In Spanish times in Trinidad, the Spaniards utilized, besides the guitar, the lute and the African box bass (when African were brought in). They also sang ballads and carols, mainly in three-four, waltz-like tempo at their Catholic masses and celebrations. The use of the African box bass is significant for it shows the African impact on the music, Africans having formed the major laboring class on the islands of Trinidad and Tobago then. Moreover, parang music today, though structured around the traditional, triple-rhythm pattern of the Spaniards, is heavily laced with the African duple rhythms that are especially intoned by the cuatro, guitar, and chac-chac. In fact, while most of the parang songs are written and sung in three-four and six-eight rhythms, many are played in the traditional African-based tempos of two-two and four-four meters.[3] Other instruments used by paranderos include the mandolin, the bandolin, the violin, the bandola, and sometimes the cello (Taylor, 1977, 15).

Peninsular Spaniards had a further impact on Trinidad's music; laws passed by the Spaniards relegated the Carnival to three days preceding Ash Wednesday, as was the custom in Spain then (*Port of Spain Gazette* (Trinidad), 1833, 2). Spanish landowners who came directly from Spain would have known of the carnivals in many Spanish towns and provinces such as Madrid, Barcelona, Aragon, Galicia, Toledo, Andalusia, and Valencia, where the challenge of the African Moors and the subsequent Christian conquests were celebrated through simulated battles that later became part of the carnival festivities. The Spaniards, therefore, looked forward to the festival that was celebrated in the islands by the Africans and other Europeans. Thus, during the preemancipation period in Trinidad and Tobago, the Carnival lasted for three days. It was changed later to two days of festivity since it was felt that the Africans were desecrating the Sunday or first day of Carnival.

French

The Spaniards in Trinidad and Tobago knew of the benefits of plantation agriculture, particularly that of sugar, but did not have the manpower necessary to cultivate crops successfully. As such, they resolved to attract foreigners to the islands by way of a scheme known in history as the Cedula of Population. By this scheme, Frenchmen from the neighboring islands of Martinique and Guadeloupe were encouraged to come to Trinidad with their enslaved laborers and till the fertile but neglected soils in return for grants of land. As early as 1777, groups of Frenchmen led by Roume de St. Laurent migrated to Trinidad with their African enslaved men and women. By 1779, there were 523 of them with 973 Africans (Williams, 1962, 12). From then on, the islands became thriving colonies of sugar, coffee, and cocoa to the extent that by 1796, the coffee lands yielded 330,000 pounds (Williams, 17). To improve their living conditions as well as the relationships between master and enslaved, the French Code Noir[4] of 1789 that governed the relationships was replaced by a new one on behalf of the Spaniards. This code allowed the Frenchmen to practice their musical habits in full view of the enslaved who at times were anxious to mimic them.

Even before the Cedula of Population, however, Frenchmen from French towns such as Lyons and Paris brought to Trinidad elements of the carnival practiced in France. There, on the days preceding Ash Wednesday, Frenchmen observed the carnival as "a farewell to the flesh" ritual, in preparation for the strict observances that underscored the Lenten period. The origins of this carnival lay in Egypt, Africa, from whence it went to Greece, then to Rome, and to all parts of Europe (Tallant, 1948, 83–85). In France especially, the carnival was celebrated as a form of protest against the ruling classes. To portray them, the masqueraders paraded in mud, ashes, and flour and transformed themselves into various effigies such as goats, dummies, and asses, in keeping with their satiric, political portrayals.

In addition, Frenchmen held in France grand balls marked by dancing in elaborate, expensive costumes and masks on their faces. These "Mardi Gras"[5] balls were lavishly staged in Trinidad especially because, following the French Revolution, the carnival in France was banned by Napoleon when he came on the political scene. It meant that Frenchmen who came to the islands looked forward anxiously to the practice of balls, feasting, concerts, picnics, dancing, and house-to-house visits between Christmas and Ash Wednesday (Liverpool, 2001, 85–87). All such amusements were held "in an atmosphere of general gaiety . . . laughter . . . happy sallies and comic stories" (Borde, 1876, 306–7).

Besides sex games at their dinners and balls, the Frenchmen, both Creole and native, contributed much to the carnivals of Trinidad and Tobago by way of musical concerts, dancing, costuming, and masking. The *Port of Spain Gazette* (1881) noted that "the favourite costume of the ladies was the graceful and courtly *mula-tresse*,"[6] while the men opted for "the *negre jardin* or garden negro . . . (while) dancing the *belair*[7] to the African drum" (March 19, 3). Moreover, at their dances and balls, the African drum and shac-shac, the Spanish cuatro, the guitar, the violin, the bandol, and mandolin were the instruments used (Liverpool 2001, 127). This evidences the acculturation process taking place in Trinidad and Tobago then between the customs of Whites and Africans, especially in the early carnivals of the islands. Moreover, history records that the French, in portraying the Africans on Carnival day, did so as a way of displaying their awesome political, social, and economic power over the Africans. They were laughing at the tattered dress of the field slave, and they degraded the courtly dress of the mulatresse. By allowing their enslaved men and women to participate in the carnivals was also indicative of their assumption that the Africans were subordinates to them. It was, therefore, an awesome display of power (Liverpool, 2001, 131–32).

British

The English and Scots, as missionaries, introduced many English hymns, carols, and what was known as "sankies" to the people of the islands. Such sankies, carols, and hymns were sung at their English-Catholic rituals, particularly on festive days such as Easter and Christmas. They also celebrated the New Year and Carnival with rowdy balls and fetes and introduced martial law during the Christmas period to allow them to do so (*Port of Spain Gazette*, January 10, 1821). Besides the military maneuvers that coincided with the passing of martial law, the English balls were described as "elegant," with an assemblage of ladies "that formed a scene highly interesting." The governor himself held a ball attended by a "select party" with music played by the resident army band.[8] There were "fireworks on the lawn . . . tents to accommodate the many guests" (Pearse, 1955, 14), and the band that comprised string, brass, and wind instruments played music such as the "minuet, gavotte, quadrille, polka and the waltz" (Liverpool, 2001, 133). At their elaborate balls too, the English continued the Whites's custom of disguising and wearing masks as well as house-to-house visiting and street promenades. Like the French, the English also allowed their enslaved Africans to participate in Carnival and, by way of costumes, laughed at the misfortunes of Africans. There were a few Africans in the Regiment band, and the mere fact that the band played a variety of French and African music showed again the acculturation process at work in early Trinidad and Tobago.

Free Coloreds or mixed persons of color also held dance balls of their own and tried desperately by their lavish spending and numbers to outdo the Whites, especially because they suffered from the discriminatory acts done to them by the upper-class elite. Free Coloreds, for example, had to obtain a license to hold a dance (Liverpool, 2001, 140–41). By 1822, the census accounted for 13,392 of them as against 3,341 Whites, and by 1834, their numbers rose to 18,724 as against 3,632 Whites (Liverpool, 2001, 138). Because of the number of Free Coloreds participating in the carnivals, Whites, who sought to put an end to the early postemancipation festivities, could not do so for fear that there might have been uprisings by the populous Free Coloreds. As a result, the festive spaces of the Africans grew tremendously. In any case, the "carnival remained for them (Free Coloreds) an important season of festivity and sociality, consisting of house to house visiting with small combinations of musical instruments, playing in the tradition of the Spanish Main, and also a variety of 19th century dances from Europe" (Pearse, 1955, 23). Both Frenchmen and Free Coloreds of French origin loved the sight of African women dancing and defended the Carnival from being legally obliterated by the Whites simply because they loved to see the African women dance (Personal Communication, Carr, 1965).

African Influence

Caribbean history has shown that Africans did not come to the Caribbean to engage in musical practices; rather, they were brought by force by Europeans to supply labor for Whites on estates of sugar and cocoa mainly, and as servants for white households. In coming to the islands of the Caribbean in general and to Trinidad and Tobago in particular, the Africans inevitably brought with them, as adults, their African cultural traits that included dancing, masking, and music. To Trinidad and Tobago came hordes of persons from the Mandinka, Fulbe, Kwakwa, Yoruba, Hausa, Igbo, Allada, and Kongo peoples. All such persons had centuries-old carnival and masking traditions and common forms of music. History shows that the Africans brought to Trinidad and Tobago many drums, thumb pianos, flutes, bamboo fifes, xylophones, quills, bagpipes, and tambourines, as well as the art of making them. In addition, they composed many songs and musical pieces in keeping with their accustomed time signatures (usually two-four and four-four meters and sung in polyrhythmic style) (Abrahams and Szwed, 1983, 256).

Proprietor Mrs. A. C. Carmichael, who owned land and enslaved persons in Trinidad, also noticed that "their songs and dances were of their own composition" (Liverpool, 2010, 70). Melville Herskovits (1990), who carried out research in Trinidad in 1939, recorded and analyzed 325 melodies. These he found to be African in character in terms of modulation and the manner in which they were sung (267). Richard Waterman (1990), who carried out research into Trinidad's music in the 1940s and found that most of the songs used by Trinidadians were African in character, also mentioned the art of syncopation or "off beat phrasing of melodic accents" common to the music of the people. This syncopation, common to African music, is especially present in calypso music, as is the call-and-response pattern found all over West Africa and in Trinidad and Tobago as well (88).

The links between Africa and Trinidad and Tobago have resulted in much collective and indeed affective forms of singing such as hocketing,[9] clapping, ring shouts, and dancing as well as forms of Kongo and Rada,[10] polyrhythmic music. Kongo music traditions underscore three-part harmony singing at wakes, weddings, and baptisms while the Rada (Allada) tradition is marked by drumming, singing, and spirit possession. Rattles and iron-beating are sometimes added. Similarly, links with the Yorubas have produced the religious music of the Shango or Orisa tradition where the ritual is also marked by drumming, singing, and spirit possession.

Tobago, the other island in the twin state of the Republic, was merged with Trinidad in 1888 for administrative purposes. Independence was gained in 1962. In 1974, the state opted for a Republican status within the Commonwealth.[11] Tobago's history is in some ways different from Trinidad in terms of colonial ownership, despite its closeness. In terms of its Africanisms, however, because of the overwhelming presence of Africans on both islands, the two islands share most things in common, including music, masking, masquerading, dancing, and singing. Tobago today boasts of its speech band music whereby speechmakers give humorous four-line speech ditties to the listeners before calling upon the musicians to "drag yuh bow." Dragging the bow is an ebonic term that means "play your fiddle." The polyrhythmic music that follows is usually played by fiddles, shac-shacs, and tambrins (tambourines), with the speechmakers dancing in unison.

One of the singing traditions common to both islands is that of the work song, which accompanied the pulling of seines on the seashore, the building of homes, and the digging of lands in preparation for planting. These songs, common to Sierra Leone, the Kongo, and Nigeria, are yet sung in Trinidad and Tobago in the time signature of most African music, and seem to ease the woes of the workers. In the eighteenth and nineteenth centuries especially, Africans all over Trinidad and Tobago used them lavishly. In some instances the songs were of a satirical nature, as is the character of most African songs, and were used particularly in the eighteenth and nineteenth centuries to lampoon cruel, tyrannical, or otherwise political leaders and the elite (Liverpool 2001, 80–81).

The Calypso and Its Development

Another common form of music that has descended from the African tradition of Carnival is that of the Kalenda or music associated with stickfighting. On Carnival day particularly in the pre- and postemancipation eras, stickfighters accompanied the band of revelers who paraded throughout the streets and plantations and fought one another in organized stickfights for turf, to display their prowess and fighting skills, and for esteem. As they fought, bands of singing men and women urged them on with song and ritualistic dancing steps accompanied by drums.

Stickfight or Kalenda songs had a rebellious appeal; the accompanying singers chanted them in a warlike manner and boasted of the feats of the fighter whom they supported. It was from such music carried out in the call-and-response pattern of African singing that, according to J. D. Elder (1966), the calypso emerged (7; 91–92). Hence, it can be said that some aspects of calypso, particularly the "war" calypsoes whereby two singers engage each other in verbal onslaught, is derived directly from the Kalenda. Whites participated in the stickfight and allowed the Africans to do so until the 1880s when it was eventually banned. Despite the ban, however, the stickfight and the Kalenda songs continue to be a part of Trinidad and Tobago's musical legacy, based mainly on the polyrhythms of African music.

Besides the native Africans, there were, after the North American War of 1812, several African American soldiers who had fought on the side of Britain refusing to go back to the slave system of the United States. They preferred to live in Trinidad and thus began a small but significant migration of approximately eight hundred souls who were placed in villages in South Trinidad. There, as small independent farmers, they mixed their Baptist melodies gained from the United States with those of Trinidad and Africa to impact on the religious African music of the colony. Their songs have thus "enhanced the song repertoire of the Trinidad Spiritual Baptists" (McDaniel, 1991, 2).[12] Calypsonian Super Blue understood this and must have certainly felt the beat when, in the mid-1970s, he sang a calypso that he aptly termed "Soca Baptist." In it, he mentioned that the Baptists of South Trinidad were singing European hymns and sankeys with a *soca*[13] beat.

This beat is derived from by far the most prominent form of music that has developed in Trinidad and Tobago, that of the calypso. Moreover, today, the calypso is associated with the Carnival that has developed, over time, to the extent that it is considered the principal music of the festivity. The calypso stemmed from enslaved singers who onboard ships on the journeys from Africa to the Caribbean sang songs of satire, mystery, history, praise, and derision in keeping with the griot tradition in West Africa whereby court singers lambasted or praised their chiefs and reminded them of society's ideals at official ceremonies and state functions (Liverpool, 1993, 256–57; Hill, 1972, 73). They thus continued to compose and sing these songs on the estates where they labored, first in the call-and-response pattern and then placed the tunes into sixteen- and eight-bar frames accompanied by African, polyrhythmic music sung in major and minor key melodies. By singing these songs at their early Kalenda and Cannes Brulees[14] processions, the songs and music became associated with Trinidad and Tobago's Carnival and the Carnival tradition.

The truth is, Africans sang wherever they went. They sang at the markets where they sold their produce. They sang to celebrate the sugarcane harvest. They sang in mockery of their masters. They sang at the Great House where they worked as they launched blistering attacks on the plantation system (Elder, 1966, 89–111). In the nineteenth century, the calypso became part of the response of Africans to the pressures exerted upon them by the privileged classes who were themselves pressured by the British in their zeal to anglicize the islands (Elder, 1966, 87–90, 113).

Creolization and Acculturation

After emancipation, when the black population flocked to the cities to gain jobs and to earn a living from their skills, the calypsonian, following in the tracks of the *chantuelle*,[15] assumed greater significance as the voice of the urbanized oppressed. He had to deal too with the relationships and conflicts that developed between the landed gentry and the landless, the European and the African, the haves and the have-nots (Liverpool 1994, 180–82). It would be true to say that the calypso must be seen as the large pot that caught all the rhythms that developed in Trinidad and Tobago following the creolization and acculturation processes that developed and created social change throughout the eighteenth, nineteenth, and twentieth centuries. Picong[16] and wit were the calypsonian's chief weapons as he strode from urban yard to urban tent singing and introducing various forms of calypso such as the oratorical or ballad type, the narrative, the political and social commentary, the extemporaneous, and the smutty compositions. The single and double tone songs[17] were then added to the Kalenda-type call-and-response features.

As the twentieth century unfolded and so many changes, political and otherwise, became part of the maturing society, the calypsonian moved from the barrack yards of the cities to specially constructed calypso tents where he sang eight-line and sixteen-line songs and became in the process a professional entertainer. String and brass instruments replaced the drum and flute ensemble and, by the 1950s, sheet music was introduced in the calypso tent. The period 1914 to 1918 gave calypsonians new themes to sing about, and businessmen and politicians "began to exploit calypso as a means of advertisement or propaganda" (Elder, 1969, 15). As early as 1914 too, American companies made recordings of the art so that by the 1930s the calypso spread to numerous cities and countries in Europe and North America and was consequently seen and accepted in many circles as world music.

For the budding calypsonian then, and even today, the question arose: How were they to learn the skill of calypso singing or the music deposited by the French, Spaniards, and English? Some privileged children of the elite were able to attend schools in France and England during the nineteenth and twentieth centuries and there become exposed to European forms of music and notation. For the lesser privileged with no money to travel overseas, there was no such opportunity. In terms of local schooling, it is true that the colonial government assisted by the local religious denominations had started a system of primary education after emancipation in 1838. By 1846, there were fifty-four primary schools in Trinidad and fewer in Tobago. By 1851, a series of Ward schools run by a public board came into being. These numbered thirty by 1870. For all the good intent of the government then, the education offered the citizens little chance for social mobility, and many children, particularly those of East Indians who came in 1845, never attended primary schools (Brereton, 1981, 125–26).

MUSIC EDUCATION IN THE NINETEENTH CENTURY

Informal Training

In terms of music education, there was absolutely no formal structure put in place to teach either the old or the young. The period 1838 to the 1960s was thus a blank one for music education in the nation's schools. With no formal secondary education available to the majority of African youths especially, and with no training in music offered at public schools, it was only inevitable that the urban landless and uneducated would turn to any form of music that, where and when available, would satisfy their basic instincts. The Carnival with its emphasis on music and masquerading filled that need.

Formal Training

Perhaps the first institution to teach music formally was that of the Trinidad and Tobago Police Military Band, which was founded in 1866 to provide military music for the police force units. It must be understood that in colonial times, in the absence of a resident army, the police carried out all the duties of a military establishment and thus there was a need for music at parades. In time, however, the Police Band became a separate section of the Trinidad and Tobago police force, and all types of music, especially European, was played. It was fashionable for people, up to the 1970s, to gather on a Sunday evening to listen to the regular weekly concerts of the band at a bandstand outside of the governor's residence. There, military marches, waltzes, and even the polka formed part of the musical agenda. In time too, the Police Band began to teach music to its young trainees and to members of the community, particularly the orphanages[18] then situated at Belmont and Tacarigua in Trinidad.

Besides the Police Band, a few music-minded, primary-school headteachers would engage their charges in singing mainly Irish songs, English sankeys, and Christmas carols, especially on a Friday evening when the heat of the day or the heavy rains made it almost impossible to get pupils to fully concentrate on the main subjects of reading, writing, arithmetic, and religion. Many persons received their first lessons in music in Trinidad and Tobago thusly. With one exception, it was not until the late twentieth and early twenty-first centuries that formal music was introduced into primary schools and training colleges for teachers.

Secondary education between the years 1838 to 1973 suffered the same fate; there were no formal structures to teach any form of music on the curricula of the schools. From the onset of secondary schools in Trinidad in 1857 when Queen's Royal College was established for the sons of white planters to 1863 when College of the Immaculate Conception came into being to satisfy the Catholics, down to the twentieth century when African and East Indian children won scholarships to secondary public and private schools, education was based mainly on secular subjects and not any of the arts. During the era, however, a few wealthy, private, and privileged schools engaged some of their pupils in music education, particularly the reading and writing of European music as well as the playing of the piano. A few persons, too, who were able to write music, gave private lessons in notation after school hours and on weekends, turning out in the process many of today's music educators.

The exception in terms of music teaching was that of the two orphanages where members of the Police Band taught music to the orphans. There was the Tacarigua Orphanage in East Trinidad set up in 1857 for the children of East Indians and the Belmont Orphanage in Belmont, *Port of Spain* set up for homeless orphans in general by Roman Catholic Fr. Forrestier in 1871. Belmont Orphanage in particular was run by the Dominican Sisters and started very early teaching music to the orphans with the help of members of the Police Band. Music was seen by the orphanage leaders as a medium to pacify the more violent or depressed ones and a way to stop those with a penchant for running away (Personal Communication, Cape, 1984).[19]

MUSIC EDUCATION IN THE TWENTIETH CENTURY

It is a truism that from the turn of the twentieth century to the present, the majority of top musicians and bandleaders in Trinidad and Tobago have all come from the Belmont Orphanage. They include well-known names such as Carl Bariteau, who became famous in Britain; world-class trumpeter Errol Ince; world-traveled saxophonist Roy Cape; steelband arranger Artie Shaw; Police Band leader Anthony Prospect; band leader Frankie Francis; and calypsonians DeFosto and deceased Lord Melody, to name a few.

In the 1960s, it took a visionary abbot, Dom Basil Matthews, as principal of St. Benedict's Boys in San Fernando, South Trinidad, to start a band where under Major Rupert Dennison of the Police Band boys were taught the rudiments of European music and learned to play European musical instruments. The band of Dom Basil Matthews was "a complete brass ensemble with tubas, clarinets, trombones, euphoniums, drums, and trumpets. After Major Dennison, famed musicians Ernie Castello and Milton Thorpe took over the reins of teaching while many of the young musicians played after leaving school in the famous Dennis Carr Orchestra" (Personal Communication, Figaro, 2010). There were also bands of bugles and drums associated with Presentation College in South Trinidad in the 1960s and the Cadets of North Trinidad in the 1950s.

It was not until the year 1972, with the advent of the Junior Secondary and a few Senior Secondary schools in Trinidad and Tobago, that music was officially placed on the curricula of secondary schools. Moreover, when these schools started, there was, inevitably, a huge shortage of music teachers so that many schools did not have any music teachers. An acclaimed musician, Mr. Melvin Robbin, trained the teachers in music education over a three-month period, in preparation for teaching in the nation's schools (Personal Communication, Albino-DeCoteau, 2010).[20]

Pulling from the French, English, and Spaniards, the Africans through the process of creolization constructed their Carnival characters and portrayals in the urban cities and displayed them with music and dance on the two days before Ash Wednesday. In doing so, all their African attributes of drumming, masking, spirit intonation, stickfighting, dance, calypso composition, and music making come into play. Music is the driving force behind the masquerade procession so that during the preemancipation and early postemancipation eras mainly drums supplied the music. After emancipation, various assortments of percussive instruments and strings (boxbass, lute, violin, guitar, fife) were added until the year 1881 when, through fear, the Whites banned the use of drums. It is a known fact that the resonation of drums incites many people to the extent that they become possessed by spirits and other ancestors, and they display dances and other acts that can only be described as supernatural.

The Emergence of the Steel Drum

The banning of drums gave rise to the *tamboo-bamboo*[21] band where percussion was achieved by striking lengths of bamboo on the ground and hitting shorter lengths against the sides of other pieces. The bamboo cut into different lengths produced mainly three tones, aptly named the bass, the foule (foulay), and the cutter. The bamboo thus took the place of drums while the African rhythms it produced continued. "To increase the overall orchestral pitch and to provide a melody instrument, the musicians included the jin bottle" which they beat "with a large tablespoon" (Elder, 1969, 14).

Around the mid-1930s, to create louder and more percussive sounds for a growing number of revelers on the road, dustbins, biscuit and kerosene tins, and motorcar hubs were all beaten. At first called iron bands, the beaters noticed that different tones were obtained when the tins were pounded in. The beaters had noted too that "melodic sounds were produced" in the bottle and spoon bands "by striking partly filled bottles of water with spoons" (Elder, 1969, 19). All such beating and experimenting eventually gave rise to the beaters grooving two and then three and, afterward, four notes on the paint pans, kerosene tins, and biscuit drums. Later, oil drums were tuned and notes put in to the extent that by 1945, following the war,[22] simple, melodic tunes were played.[23]

By 1946, road marches were played on sixteen-note ping pongs,[24] and a forty-five-gallon oil pan was tuned by Ellie Mannette of the Invaders Steel Band. Between 1945 and 1951, development of the steel orchestra was rapid to the extent that by then, a national band of mainly pan tuners from Trinidad, TASPO,[25] went to England and played at the Festival of Britain. During this period too, the steelbandsmen, through experimentation, developed three new pans to substitute for the tamboo-bamboo bass, foule, and the cutter. They were the cuff bass made from an eighteen-inch biscuit drum; the *tenor kittle*, made from a paint pan and that developed later into the ping pong and today's lead soprano; and a *bass kittle* or *dud-oup* made from a caustic soda pan.

In the 1950s and 1960s, several new pans developed to facilitate the playing of tunes that called for more chords and more notes. These tunes were those heard especially from films and from radio (Personal Communication, Borde, 2010). By the mid-1940s, with more and more college boys and sons of elite Whites joining the steelband movement, the steelband, which before was looked upon by the elite and a few religious groups in the society as something degenerate, grew slowly into acceptance by the middle and upper classes. By the 1960s, with fewer and fewer fights among steelbandsmen, with more and more sponsorships from the businessmen, and with steelbandsmen displaying their ability to master many of the European classics, the steelband was identified with the development of the state to become in the 1980s the national instrument. Thus can be traced a continuous development of music making by Africans from the Congo drums to the steelband "within the context of change, variation and evolution of carnival and calypso production and presentation" (Elder, 1969, 14).

National Identity

National development was associated too with the Prime Minister's Better Village Government awards, as the then prime minister searched the various villages of the islands for cultural skills in order to preserve the country's legacy. Beginning in 1963 under Prime Minister Eric Williams's leadership, items of dance, folk literature, drama, and music were staged annually. In doing so, music of all kinds came to the forefront as prizes were awarded for the many genres that the twin-island state possessed. As classified by Andrew Pearse, the musics of Trinidad, as revealed in the historical names, include the categories congo, rada, shango, yarraba, bele, bongo, pass-play, work song, chanty, reel dance, quesh, sankey, trumpet, veiquoix, fandang, calypso, parang, and steelband (Pearse, 1955).

To a large extent, then, all these above-mentioned forms of music showed up in the Better Village Programme as practitioners, unable to learn them formally in public schools and in any curricula approved by the government's Education Ministry, wallowed in their historical and meaningful tones and sounds. To these African, French, and Spanish forms were added many East Indian forms by the 1970s, for by then it was made known to the program's practitioners that many traditional songs and tales from Northern India celebrating marriage, childbirth (*sohar*), agriculture (*khajri*), and seasons (*chowtal* or spring) as well as older Indian classics and game songs all survived in Trinidad.

East Indian Influence

East Indians, as indentured laborers, came to Trinidad from 1845 and deposited on the island's shores their Indian traits of music especially. Researcher and famed sitarist Mungal Patasar has always spoken of the fact that indentured Indians brought "many of the elements of classical Indian music" to Trinidad such as *murkhi*, *gamak*, *zamzama*, and *ragas*. In addition, they composed over time many folk songs based on their relations with their environment (Patasar, 1997, 69). Many of the Indians in Trinidad sang and spoke *Bhojpuri*; many sang the Hindu *bhajan* hymns that today are taught in Hindi schools while many creolized the forms introducing Trinidadian Creole into the lyrics. All such Indian songs were sung to the accompaniment of instruments such as the harmonium, the *dholak* or double-headed drum, the *kartal* or clappers with jingles, the *manjira* or small cymbals, and the larger *tassa* or goatskin drum.

The advent of Indian films such as *Bala Joban* in 1935 changed the low esteem that local Indians held for their own culture, and it motivated them too into composing their own (Gooptar, 2010).[26] The establishment of the first radio station in Trinidad in 1947 (Radio Trinidad) with radio broadcasters and DJs such as Kamaluddin Mohammed and his brother Sham, the establishment of the first Indian orchestra in 1944 (Naya Zamana),[27] as well as the holding of competitions featuring the songs of famous Indian singers all led to an upsurge of Indian music in Trinidad. In addition, the introduction of the television show *Mastana Bahar* that featured local Indian singing and Indian culture produced a number of local stars and increased the desire for and the spread of Indian music. At weddings especially, the music of the Indians were heard as the singers, accompanied by the dholak, the dantal, and the harmonium, would sing a mixture of old folk songs from North India mixed with elements of Indian classical music and local idioms and features. This was described as *Tan* singing (Manuel, 1995, 215).

The development of Indian music in Trinidad and Tobago, according to Patasar, spans four outstanding periods. During the first period 1917 to 1940, many songs associated with the birth dates of children took precedence. Events such as *chuthee* and *barahee*[28] gave women the opportunity to compose, sing, and celebrate. During the period 1940 to 1960, songs from films dominated; nevertheless, a few were changed with the introduction of a few English words. During the period 1960 to 1980, Shri H. S. Adesh came to Trinidad, taught Hindi, and established the "Bharatiya Vidya Sansthaan, an institution to teach the elements of Indian music." In the period 1980 to 1988, the basis of what today is called *chutney* music developed from the chuthee and barahee songs. A product of Indian Classical music in the bhojpuri style, chutney actually means "hot and spicy," and so these songs were dominated by up-tempo music (Patasar, 1997, 70).

Chutney music became prominent in the year 1970 especially, when a singer named Sundar Popo brought out a recording titled "Nana and Nani" that underscored some of the folk traditions and behavioral patterns of Indians. The song was hailed by most persons, and it became an instant hit even among the African population, since the term *nani* is a colloquial one for the vagina on the one hand and also since the calypso-like, percussive, chutney beat appealed to most people. In fact, most chutney songs were sung originally by women at weddings to advise the young bride of marriage's expectations. Some of the suggestive lyrics became enmeshed in the song traditions of the society and thus caused chutney singing to rise to new and higher heights to the extent that today there is chutney-soca[29] and chutney-soca contests.

While Patasar (1997) notes four outstanding periods of Indian music in Trinidad, researcher Primnath Gooptar[30] focuses mainly on three, beginning with the advent of the first Indian film to be shown in Trinidad in the year 1935. For him, during the first period, 1935 to 1948, films from India impacted heavily on the local Indian population, to the extent that the first, local, Indian orchestra was formed in 1939. Gooptar calls the second period, 1949 to 1969, the Golden Era. It was a time when Indian films gave rise to local Indians in Trinidad imitating the musicians, singers, and dancers seen in films. The third period, 1970 to 2010, Gooptar describes as the period of decline since most of the cinemas where Indian films were shown went out of business owing to the advent of television, the computer, as well as the rise in music-technology globally. According to Gooptar, by the 1980s, Indian melodies from films were reproduced in Trinidad with a local rhythmic beat. Later, English lyrics replaced the Hindi. As such, to a large extent, the Indian tunes accompanied by the local rhythms and lyrics underscore what is known as chutney music today (Gooptar, December 2010).

Another form of Indian music that developed in the mid-1990s and is unique to Trinidad and Tobago is the *pitchakaree*. Though it came into prominence in the 1990s through the Phagwa celebrations and compositions of community worker Ravindranath Maraj (Ravi-Ji) and singer Gita Ramsingh, its roots go back thousands of years to India, the word *pitchakaree* being used in an early Phagwa song sung "2,000 years ago." According to Ravi-Ji, a pitchakaree is the instrument used to squirt the "abir" on adherents and the songs "came to us from India." As used by Ravi-Ji and the participants, the pitchakaree captures many of the Phagwa song-types such as the *Bidahar*, a contestual type of song that had its origins in romantic songs sung by cowherds in the fields and their wives at home; chowtal[31] songs, performed at the vernal Phagwa (Holi) festival; and the *jumar* and the *jaiti*, which were performed by guests on their way home from the village weddings using a mixture of "English words which were bhojpurized and Bhojpuri words that were anglicized." According to Ravi-Ji, most of the chutney songs were all meant to entertain. The chutney did not capture the serious "ideological base of the Indian community" in Trinidad and Tobago; rather they were of "a primary and simple nature." As a result, Ravi-Ji got his students to compose and set to poetry all the ideas and issues that impacted on their behavior and identity and put them into song, the result of which, sung at Phagwa festivals, they called pitchakaree (Ravi-Ji, 1997, 73–76).

Pluralism and Eclecticism

Similar to the Hindu links with bhajans, the Muslims carry bamboo-framed and ornamentally decorated tadjahs through the streets accompanied by the beating of tassa[32] drums and cymbals at their annual Hosay (Hosein) festival, where they celebrate the martyrdom of the grandsons of the Prophet Mohammed. Traditionally, women followed the procession singing (*marseehas*) laments. The laments, tassa drumming, and gatka (stick-fighting) is a reminder of the fierce jihad battle of Karbala. Many Africans have partaken in the beating of the tassa drumming ensemble so that the festival today is one of a multicultural nature (McDaniel, 1991, 73–74).

Similar to the Muslims and Hindus, the Baptists and Orishas in Trinidad and Tobago have produced and continue to produce African music. Known for their style of dress that include head ties, gowns with belts, sashes, and aprons, the Baptists sing and chant throughout their religious services followed by hand-clapping, drumming, spiritual shouts, hocketing,[33] and doption. Among the several song types, "lining" the hymn whereby the words are first intoned by a leader as a prompt for the congregation is fairly common. So too is "doption," whereby the European sankey is adopted and "Africanized" into a fast African tempo replacing the words with eighth-note syllables (bi-mi-bam-bam-bi mi-bam-bi-mi-bam). "Often, two songs flowing simultaneously may be joined by a third, to form a distinctive polyphonic texture" (McDaniel, 1991, 74–75).

The Orisas or Shango faith worship powerful Orisas (powers) including Ogun, Obatala, Yemanja, Osun, Elephon, Sakpana, and Shango (Sango), whom most Trinidadian followers of the faith claim as their own—their patron saint. Many of the followers have, through acculturation, joined their religion with that of the Catholics, to the extent that they have given Catholic saints African names and syncretized them with their own Orisas. The Orisa faith is mostly practiced in Trinidad by Yorubas from whom, in Africa, it was derived. They thus worship their ancestors and Powers by formal ceremonies that last at times for four days and involve drumming, singing, hocketing, praying, and spirit possession. "Music is continuous and essential during the all-night feast." Various-sized drums are played, some with Yoruba-type curved sticks to accompany the call-and-response chants of the prayerful participants (McDaniel, 1991, 70–71). Spirit possession is usually accompanied by singing and dancing whereby dancers shake and bend their supple torsos while making steps in unison with the rhythmic beat, at times holding and juggling cutlasses or jugs of water. Colonial Laws in 1917 outlawed the Shouter Baptists and Orisas, and it was not until 1951 that they were allowed to practice their faiths openly. Such a ban, however, did not dull the passion of the Baptist adherents for making music.

Religious Music

The history and development of music in Trinidad and Tobago thus shows that, from the Amerindians to the indentured Indians, migrants have, by their enthusiasm and passion for music, overfilled the music armory of the twin state of Trinidad and Tobago with religious and secular music. The presence of both religious and secular music operating side by side makes Trinidad and Tobago a bimusical state. The emphasis on percussion and percussive instruments of all kinds provides the glue that binds this bimusicality. The question therefore remains: How is all this music being passed on to the youth? How are our peoples being trained to become musically literate? The answer lies in our public and private institutions as well as in our social and religious festivities.

Religious music is today carried out by the many religious groups all over Trinidad and Tobago. In keeping with the many feasts and holidays of obligation, the many Christian groups learn and sing hymns for all occasions. The choirs are mostly accompanied by organs, synthesizers, guitars, and drums and in the ecumenical spirit of today's rituals, members shake, clap, and even dance at the many holy events. The Baptist and Orisa groups, however, are the more jubilant; they not only clap and dance but also use their throats as trumpets and for hocketing and doption purposes. They are adept too, in spiritual shouts or songs derived from spirituals "brought to Trinidad by ex-slave American soldiers liberated after the war of 1812" (McDaniel, 1991, 75). The Catholics and other Christian groups pass on their European-style hymns and music to their followers in preparation for the celebration of their feasts. In the case of Catholics, the Holy Mass is the main form of worship that involves the singing of hymns while other Christian groups introduce their hymns at their many rituals.

Secular Music

In terms of secular music, there is first of all the Prime Minister's Better Village Programme that is held annually in districts throughout Trinidad and Tobago. During the year, Better Village officers, operating out of the Ministry of Culture (now called Arts and Multiculturalism), organize the villagers through workshops to learn and practice the music for the competition. By providing the teachers for these workshops, villagers study aspects of Amerindian, Spanish, French, African, and Indian music and dances with a view to gaining financial awards and other prizes at the national contest. Outstanding performers are sometimes given scholarships to study overseas while the winning villages gain much from the esteem and fame that follow. Overall too, a village is named the winner, and the gaining of this title is usually preceded by endless sleeping nights whereby musical performances turn many an ordinary citizen into a musician of note.

Music Festivals

Side by side with the Better Village competition is the Tobago Festival where in open contests villagers reproduce in dance, music, and social customs the cultural landmarks for which the island has become famous. Thus is seen the bele, the reel, and other creolized dances, and there can be heard the calypso, the tambrin (tambourine) drum beats, the Tobago speech band, and the African Baptist shouts amid the European waltzes and polkas. Bele dances stem from the creolized movements of the French and the African and are preserved by stage productions such as those held by the Tobago Heritage and Better Village festivals. The Bele dance features "elegant solo and ensemble performances rather than those of grass-root ritual participation" (McDaniel, 1991, 75–76). The reel dance is performed as a "vehicle for ancestor worship and veneration at a pre-wedding or a healing ritual. Ancestors are thereby invoked to validate a union or to heal the sick and the violin, tambourine, triangle and shac-shac support the dancers" (McDaniel, 1991, 75).

Music Associations

Side by side with the Better Village Programmes are the various associations that promote their indigenous music throughout the year. These are the Parang Association of Trinidad and Tobago in the area of Parang music; Indian groups such as the NCIC and the Tassa Association promoting Indian music; the Trinidad and Tobago Unified Calypsonians' Association (TUCO) in the field of calypso; the National Drama Association in the field of drama and its relevant music; Pan Trinbago in the realm of steelband music; the Trinidad and Tobago Arts festival groups and the Music Teachers' Association promoting European music and song festivals; the National Carnival Bandleaders Association promoting carnival music; the Gospel Music Association for gospel music; and the Jazz Alliance promoting jazz. All these groups further the interests of their members by promoting the different genres of music in the state through competitions, festivals, and concerts. In preparing for same, they hold seminars, workshops, and classes whereby their members are schooled and thus become more adept in their particular genre of music.

Steeldrums and Education

In terms of music associated with the steelband, besides steelband concerts, many have learned the art of pan playing, as members of steelbands practicing for the annual Panorama competition held annually around Carnival time. In doing so, several of them, especially overseas members, learn to play the selected Panorama tunes by reading the scores; others too, learn to read musical scores in tandem with their musical playing. Apart from the music learned in steelband yards, the Ministry of Education has for the past thirty years or so initiated a "Pan in the Classroom Project" that allows students to use the pan to learn music in schools. This project also facilitates youngsters who take music as a subject at the Caribbean Examination Council examination.

Within a steelband, one finds pans of different sizes, tuned to emit different ranges and functions. There is the "tenor pan" or melody pan that approximates the soprano voice and plays the melody. Derived from the early ping pong, it is today a pan with about twenty-eight to thirty pitches and sunk to about six inches in depth. Next is the "double tenor," a set of two pans playing harmony and counterpoint. The pan known as the "second pan" is in the alto voice range and is about eight inches in depth. "Double seconds" play harmony; they are a set of two drums providing the upper register of chords. In the background, there is first the "guitar pan" about fourteen inches deep playing rhythmic chords in the lower register; the "cello pan" in the tenor voice range, three drums tuned to cover about twenty-one pitches; and the "tenor bass" that, as a set of four drums, plays the rhythm. Finally, there is the "bass pan" that is made with the full size of the oil drum. Rhythm and bass notes are obtained from bass sets that are usually six and up to nine drums in number (Aho, 1987, 28).

Brass Bands

Just as steelband yards assist in music education, so too are the various brass bands that prepare for Carnival. These bands practice for many hours nightly with a view to accompanying the bands of revelers and masqueraders on the two days of Carnival. In the early carnivals of the nineteenth century, music was played by membrane-drum ensembles and string bands with the masqueraders singing mostly Kalenda songs and Road March[34] calypsos. History shows that many costumed fancy bands, especially those catering for the elites, followed their chosen chantuelle who led the kings, queens, and members of the court in singing specially composed call-and-response songs, distinct from those of the lower classes who thrived on the more bawdy and obscene tunes. History also shows that these bands practiced the tunes at pre-Carnival events, and on Carnival day, some of the elite were even seen "on horseback playing Scottish tunes on bagpipes" (McDaniel, 1991, 84).

At Carnival time, a few of the bands also accompany calypsonians at the various calypso tents all over the state and so must practice for a considerable length of time in order to master the musical scores of the hundreds of calypsonians who strive annually to win the various calypso contests, some national and others private. To achieve this level of musicianship calls for musicians of a high caliber in reading musical scores, for very often, calypsonians, without having the necessary rehearsals, change their tunes in response to the appeal of audiences.

Carnival and Education

Carnival in Trinidad and Tobago is therefore a music-filled occasion with musical ensembles, including string bands, pan orchestras, brass bands, as well as nonmusical bands of costumed participants re-creating themes historical, mythological, and imaginative. By playing music at calypso tents, steelband yards, and mass camps before the Carnival, the citizens arrive on the streets on Carnival day "musically alert and prepared for a season of national artistic involvement" (McDaniel, 1991, 87). Many children in Trinidad and Tobago, then, get their first taste of music from the prevailing carnival to which they are exposed either at home or at school.

Music Schools

It is a well-known fact too that children who are exposed to music, particularly at an early age, usually perform better holistically. Thus, besides Carnival, there are many music teachers in Trinidad and Tobago who, with pans, flutes, and pianos, provide music lessons for children on afternoons and on weekends, in the serenity of their homes. The Pan Pipers Music School at St. Augustine, Trinidad, founded by Ms. Louise McIntosh, and the Albino School of Music at Laventille, Trinidad, run by Ms. Merle Albino-DeCoteau, are two formidable examples of structured music teaching that is applied to students from age five to the adult stage. Many have left these hallowed halls and have made a name for themselves in Europe and elsewhere as world-class musicians, arrangers, and music conductors. One such person who came through these ranks is Dr. Kwame Ryan. Ryan has conducted orchestras in Germany, Scotland, and England and is now a director of the Orchestre Francais des Jeunes in France.

Higher Education

In terms of professional music training at university level, the University of the West Indies at St. Augustine, Trinidad, has, beginning in the mid-1980s, provided musical training for educators, administrators, and policy-makers associated with the teaching of music. There, students can gain a BA degree with a major in the musical arts or a Certificate in Music with a concentration on the steelband. The programs for the degree and certificate include courses in arranging, studies on the calypso, pan, and parang music, as well as lessons in ethnomusicology. Recently too, another university, the College of Science, Technology and Applied Arts of Trinidad and Tobago (COSTAATT), have included courses leading to students gaining degrees and certificates in music and music education. Not to be outdone is the University of Trinidad and Tobago (UTT) that has recently laid down plans for a four-year program leading to the Bachelor of Fine Arts Award in music, particularly Caribbean Music. The program calls for all students to read in their first year a core course in music education. The university has also begun, in September 2010, to bring music to children aged seven to twelve through its National Youth Music Education Service (NYMES), a special institute designed to enrich the minds of the youth by exposing them to music and thereby helping them to achieve their full potential.

CONCLUSION

Trinidad and Tobago then, through its many historical struggles and conflicts, through its many ethnic voices, and through its many and varied customs associated with race, ethnicity, and class interactions has emerged with music of all types: European, Indian, African, creolized, and original. Such music is today available to all through the many musical institutions, public and private, that promote music education at all levels, primary, secondary, and tertiary. It is available too, through the many religious and secular groups that practice music for entertainment, religion, and for mere aesthetic enjoyment.

NOTES

1. A four-stringed instrument originating from Venezuela. It is tuned A, D, F#, and B.
2. Sometimes called "maracas."
3. This knowledge I gained from personal observation and from discussions with paranderos.
4. The "Black Code." Laws passed by France to govern their relationships with the enslaved Africans.
5. French for "Fat Tuesday." Balls were held to celebrate the end of Carnival.
6. Biological mixtures of French Whites and Africans.
7. A creolized dance found in Trinidad and many parts of the French and British Caribbean. Sometimes spelled *Bele*.
8. The band of the Third West Indian Regiment of the British army.
9. Guttural rhythmic sounds made with the throat.
10. A popular term in Trinidad for music from the Allada peoples.
11. The family of nations that were formerly owned/colonized by Britain.
12. Lorna McDaniel is an American ethnomusicologist who studied the music of Trinidad and Tobago.
13. One of the several varieties of calypso music. It was called thus by Lord Shorty (Ras Shorty I) to underscore the mixture of the soul music he felt within him and with which he infused the calypso. In doing so, Indian rhythms also contributed to the soul music for which he searched.
14. French for "Canes burning." The canes were burned in preparation for the cutting and harvesting of the stems that contained the juice from which sugar was made. The event became for Africans a processional carnival.
15. The leader of the singers in the Kalenda band.
16. From the French *piquant* meaning spicy and hot, it is today a colloquialism for a humorous banter.
17. Eight- and sixteen-bar songs were termed as such.

18. Homes set up for orphans or otherwise homeless children.

19. Musician Roy Cape attended the Belmont Orphanage and learned his music there.

20. Merle Albino-DeCoteau was one of the students in Mr. Robbin's class.

21. From the French word for a drum: *tambour*.

22. World War II (1939–1945).

23. Eyewitnesses say that around 1941, Winston "Spree" Simon of John John Iron Band, Port of Spain, played the tune "Mary Had a Little Lamb" on a four-note ping pong pan tuned C, D, E, and G.

24. The lead pan that carried the melody; the forerunner of today's tenor pan.

25. Trinidad All-Steel Percussion Orchestra.

26. Gooptar is currently a PhD candidate at the Academy of Arts, Letters, Culture and Public Affairs of the University of Trinidad and Tobago (UTT) researching the impact of Indian films on Trinidadians.

27. For researcher Gooptar, the first Indian orchestra started as far back as 1939.

28. These are celebrations held on the sixth and twelfth day after a child is born.

29. Chutney songs reproduced with or accompanied by the soca rhythm.

30. Now reading for a PhD in Cultural Studies at UTT.

31. A seven-beat song sung at Phagwa celebrations. Usually it contains three beats plus an additive of four.

32. Large goatskin kettledrums.

33. A guttural sound from the throat that keeps the rhythm.

34. Road Marches are those calypsos played on the road for Carnival. However, the calypso played the most on the two Carnival days wins the Road March prize.

REFERENCES

Abrahams, Roger, and John Szwed. *After Africa*. New Haven: Yale University Press. 1983.

Aho, William. "Steelband Music in Trinidad and Tobago: The Creation of a People's Music." *Revista de Musica Latino Americana/Latin American Music Review* 8, no. 1 (1987): 26–58.

Albino-DeCoteau, Merle. Telephone Conversation. Trinidad, November 30, 2010.

Borde, Hugh. Telephone Conversation. Michigan, USA. November 28, 2010.

Borde, P. G. L. *Histoire de L'Isle de La Trinidad sous Le Government Espagnol*. Paris: Maisonneuve et Cie, Libraires, 1876. Reprint, Port of Spain: Paria Publishing Co., 1982.

Brereton, Bridget. *A History of Modern Trinidad, 1783–1962*. Port of Spain: Heinemann, 1981.

Cape, Roy. Conversations with Roy Cape. Sweden, September 1984.

Carmichael, Gertrude. *The History of the West Indian Islands of Trinidad and Tobago*. London: Redman. 1961.

Carr, Andrew. Personal Communication. Port of Spain: Trinidad, August 1965.

Elder, J. D. "Evolution of the Traditional Calypso of Trinidad and Tobago: A Socio-Historical Analysis of Song Change." PhD Diss. University of Pennsylvania, 1966.

Elder, J. D. *From Congo Drum to Steelband*. Trinidad: UWI, St. Augustine, 1969.

Figaro, Gil. Telephone Conversation. New Jersey, USA, November 29, 2010.

Gooptar, Primnath. Lecture at UTT. Barataria, August 2010.

Gooptar, Primnath. "75 Years of Indian Films in Trinidad." Public Lecture Series, Academy of Letters and Public Affairs, UTT. NAPA, December 1, 2010.

Herskovits, Melville. *The Myth of the Negro Past*. Boston: Beacon Press, 1990.

Hill, Errol. *The Trinidad Carnival: Mandate for a National Theatre*. Austin: University of Texas Press, 1972.

Liverpool, Hollis. "Rituals of Power and Rebellion." PhD Diss. University of Michigan, 1993.

Liverpool, Hollis. "Researching Steelband and Calypso Music." *BMR Journal* 14, no. 2 (1994): 179–201.

Liverpool, Hollis. *Rituals of Power and Rebellion: The Carnival Tradition in Trinidad and Tobago, 1763–1962*. Chicago: Frontline, 2001.

Manuel, Peter. *Caribbean Currents: Caribbean Music from Rumba to Reggae*. Philadelphia: Temple University Press, 1995.

McDaniel, Lorna. "Trinidad and Tobago." *Music of the Caribbean*. MHM Course (Fall 1991): University of Michigan, 65–87.

Newson, Linda. *Spanish and Aboriginal Colonial Trinidad: A Study in Culture Contact*. London: Academic Press, 1976.

Patasar, Mungal. "The Development of Indian Music in Trinidad and Tobago." *Caribbean Dialogue* 3, no. 4 (Oct/Dec. 1997): 67–71.

Pearse, Andrew. "Aspects of Change in Caribbean Folk Music." *Journal of the International Folk Music Council* 7, 1955.

Pearse, Andrew. "Carnival in 19th Century Trinidad." *Caribbean Quarterly* 4, nos. 3 & 4 (May/June 1956). Reprint, *Trinidad Carnival*. Trinidad: Paria Publishing Co., 1988.

Pearse, Andrew. "Mitto Sampson on Calypso Legends." *Trinidad Carnival*. Trinidad: Paria Publishing Co., 1988.

Port of Spain Gazette (Trinidad), January 22, 1833.

Ravi-Ji. "The Development of Pitchakaree in Trinidad and Tobago." *Caribbean Dialogue* 3, no. 4 (October/December 1997): 73–76.

Tallant, Robert. *Mardi Gras*. New York: Doubleday & Co., Inc., 1948.

Taylor, Daphne Pawan. *Parang of Trinidad*. Port of Spain: National Cultural Council of Tinidad and Tobago, 1977.

Waterman, Richard. "African Influence on the Music of the Americas." *Mother Wit from the Laughing Barrel*, ed. Alan Dundes. Jackson: University Press of Mississippi, 1990.

Williams, Eric. *History of the People of Trinidad and Tobago*. Port of Spain: PNM Publishing Co., 1962.

Wood, Donald. *Trinidad in Transition*. London: Oxford University Press, 1968.

Part II

Central America

Chapter Six

Costa Rica

Guillermo Rosabal-Coto

INTRODUCTION

The present chapter intends to analyze the historical origin and development of formal music education practices in Costa Rica, with particular attention to the economic, social, and political context of instructional goals and policy and their sociocultural implications. A description of the context and social functions of pre-Hispanic and Colonial music practices is presented at the beginning. At the end, the author makes recommendations to interrogate and strengthen recent educational practices in relation to sociocultural challenges within Costa Rican society. Since literature on Costa Rican music education is almost nonexistent, the author interprets literature on music practices in Costa Rica drawn from historical musicology and ethnomusicology, against the backdrop of scholarship on social history.

PRE-HISPANIC CONTEXT (EARLY SIXTEENTH CENTURY)

When the Spanish first arrived at this territory, in 1502, they encountered native groups of Mesoamerican and Southern origin, of hundreds of thousands, such as the *chorotegas*, *bruncas*, and *huetares*, among others, scattered mostly on the North Pacific region and Central Valley of the territory. Their life was arrayed in exuberant nature and was subject to a sociopolitical organization centered on the chieftainship, which contrasted with the sophisticated urban and technological developments of the neighboring Maya civilization in the north of the Central American isthmus.[1]

While linguistic study reveals that some surviving indigenous[2] languages included words that depicted specific ways of music making, such as *to sing* and *to dance*,[3] archeology provides evidence of several pre-Hispanic instruments, ranging from ocarinas, whistles, shakers, jingles, snail shells, and a variety of drums.[4] Although sonorous records or evidence of music notation are lacking, the study of the pitch range of existing ocarinas suggests that melodies may have been mostly pentatonic.[5] According to Cervantes-Gamboa (1995), pre-Hispanic indigenous music may have been mostly vocal and monodic, with some instance of instrumental accompaniment and very few examples of solely instrumental performance.

Music practices of pre-Hispanic ethnic groups were associated with economic, political, and socialization rituals and activities,[6] such as harvesting, religious ritual (for example, funerals and spiritual purification), as well as festivities and recreation. The social function of religious and profane genres seem to have entailed specialization and gender division:[7] from ritual practices presided by shamans, priests—which may have required some specialized musical instruction—to dance, work, and other daily-life-related songs specific to males or females.[8]

The intrusion of the colonizers into the territory at the beginning of the sixteenth century[9] initiated an era of resistance of the natives against foreign and violent physical and material domination that threatened their physical integrity, their economics, social rites, political structures, and culture[10] (Molina-Jiménez and Palmer,

2007, 19–28). It is not difficult to imagine how the autochthonous music practices that were at the core of relevant personal and communal experiences would be marginalized or strategically blended into the outsiders' practices, as will be explained in the next section.[11]

MUSIC PRACTICES BEFORE INDEPENDENCE (CA. MID-SIXTEENTH CENTURY TO NINETEENTH CENTURY)

The economy during this period relied on the exploitation of the indigenous through the *encomienda* regime: a servile relationship through which the natives were forced to provide products and work to the conquerors. The native population was highly resistant to this imposition and was reduced considerably due to severe diseases brought by the Spanish.[12] The workforce shortage in the *encomienda* was then compensated with the import of slaves of African descent, from Caribbean markets (Molina-Jiménez and Palmer, 2007, 35–38).[13]

Despite the forced subordination of both natives and African-descent slaves, foreign and native music practices did not seem to be sharply antagonistic since early colonization. While the colonizers witnessed native musical and dance practices such as those that "ended in ceremonial sacrifice" (Flores-Zeller, 1978, 31), a music component was essential within the newly imposed Catholic cult.[14] Music practices within the Church would remain fairly rudimentary throughout this period due to fact that Costa Rica was a peripheral colony without a bishop and lacked cathedrals. The few parish churches probably had very small ensembles of heterogeneous make-up.[15]

Mainly due to some degree of economic development with the insertion of the province into the broader colonial economy, it was possible to establish other foreign music practices, associated with political control or recreation, in the sixteenth and seventeenth centuries: military music was required for civic celebrations of the Spanish Crown[16] and dance music was featured at profane gatherings in major villages.[17]

The above practices were carried out in precarious material conditions, as the territory remained a geographically isolated,[18] nonwealthy,[19] and politically unimportant colony.[20] An example of this situation is the fact that the same musicians had to perform in all the above contexts and received insufficient financial retribution.[21] In fact, it is highly unlikely that professional musicians from Spain or the main musical centers of the Spanish colonies—Mexico and Perú—would settle in this land, although a few amateurs may have,[22] without a major impact. In accordance with this context and the lack of historical and documentary evidence, no significant impact seems to have been made in terms of music instruction of the population under Spanish control.

Music is not the subject matter of the existing accounts on religious or political spaces of sociability, and the terms of description of music practices is quite vague.[23] This suggests the possibility that given the insufficient material limitations, music may have somehow had an accessory connotation in the official culture of the new colonial society, despite music's undeniably functional character in the cult and government rituals. Therefore, ecclesiastical or government efforts for music's further development or specialization, such as the systematic organization of music at a larger scale than parishes or villages, or the establishment of teaching centers, must have been unthinkable.[24]

The above argument only finds support in contemporary perceptions of music by government officers, recorded not only in documents on Church or state activities but also in legal documentation regarding felonies. In the latter, musicians were often considered truants and "good-for-nothings" because they were responsible for providing music at noisy, pernicious social gatherings,[25] and were treated and punished as such. This kind of judgment seems to confirm the contradiction between the role and status of music in this society.

Despite the natural cultural clashes brought by processes of colonization, the scarce evidence that has become available helps to suggest that a fairly conservative and "respectful" degree of musical *mestizaje*[26] seems to have taken place, first, because music may have been an effective means to indoctrinate natives and Afro-Caribbean slaves in the foreign religion. For example, some of the few surviving indigenous melodies show some influence of the foreign music, such as tonality or plainchant style.[27] Moreover, by the end of the seventeenth century the marimba of African origin had been incorporated in at least one mixed instrumental-vocal ensemble in a Catholic cult, perhaps fulfilling the harmonic support to chant in the absence of an organ.[28]

Cultural coexistence may have also been exercised as a mechanism to control resistant subordinates: a few existing indigenous practices in their own right may have become elements of civic celebrations and profane practices.[29] It is also feasible that both indigenous and Afro-Caribbean instruments and practices were particularly appealing to the colonizers for social activities and that some natives decided to "play the new rules of the game" for the sake of survival. For instance, an indigenous chirimía seemed to mingle with Spanish instruments in profane practices.[30] Also, *mestizos* and *mulatos*,[31] who were among the lowest social strata, may have learned to play Iberian instruments for profane entertainment, joining some nonwealthy settlers.[32] No further evidence suggests that a more vital and intricate musical coexistence took place.

To date, no material vestige of instruments, music scores, or traces of composers, original compositions,[33] or written accounts attest to sophisticated music making or systematic music instruction associated with the three metropolitan-based practices—religious cult, military institutions, or profane music ensembles—in this territory during the colonial period.[34] Even though some evidence suggests some kind of musical *mestizaje* in this period, the native music practices and the new-coming Afro-Caribbean culture would undergo severe marginalization within the economic and political order to come.

TOWARD GOAL-ORIENTED MUSIC EDUCATION[35] (1821 TO CA. 1940)

Bourgeois Taste and the Rise of Private Music Instruction

The early decades of transition from a Spanish colony to an independent nation after 1821[36] did not bring significant changes in terms of the role and status of music in social, religious, and political rituals of the new society. Practices in the Catholic rite and traditions and the civic protocol were associated with the old colonial material conditions,[37] mainly because Costa Rica relied on an incipient agrarian economy and continued to be fairly geographically and culturally isolated. Some music teaching featured on the short-term contracts of some Church musicians.[38] Due to the terms and scope of such contracts, it is not yet possible to speak of systematic music education.[39]

In the second half of the nineteenth century, the young nation positioned itself within the world economy as an important producer and exporter of coffee beans. A wealthy elite rose,[40] which adopted and was able to afford the European bourgeois tastes,[41] such as imported fancy clothing, trendy books, musical instruments—mainly pianos—and musical scores.[42] By the end of the century, the use of music for entertainment purposes featured at drama and poetry performances at theatres, hotels, clubs, and elite homes, for activities such as movie exhibitions, balls, sports, and picnics.[43] Music was often provided by small salon ensembles, whose repertoire included opera, operetta, and zarzuela arrangements as well as marches, waltzes, mazurkas, and other European dance music.

Music instruction for elite offspring also became an object of private consumption. Instructional needs were mostly fulfilled by Central American musicians[44] contracted by municipalities and religious groups to take over the music component in diverse community activities, as well as several Costa Ricans, who returned from music studies in Europe, and staff members of foreign touring opera companies who decided to remain in Costa Rica.[45] On the other hand, local choristers and instrumentalists were often employed by the latter companies and had the opportunity to broaden their repertoire with the current European trends and improve their performance abilities through contact with professional musicians.

Instrumental instruction in European art music was officially institutionalized when the Costa Rican state decided to subsidize the creation of the National School of Music in 1890,[46] with the specific goal of training instrumentalists to establish the first symphony orchestra in the country.[47] Despite the apparent enthusiasm of the Costa Rican society, which called for more study openings and teacher positions, some teachers and civilians argued that the school had become an academy for wealthy, amateur young ladies, and thus its original goal was not being accomplished. The antagonism among teachers in regard to educational goals and the lack of consistency of government funding caused the school to close down for four years later.

The *Escuela de Música de Santa Cecilia*,[48] a private music school, was immediately founded in 1894. Its work during more than sixty years proved very productive in comparison with previous private schools of very ephemeral existence: it held regular concerts featuring students and teachers, started the first and only working-class people choral society, and expanded its instructional offer out of the capital city, despite never-ending financial limitations. On the other hand, numerous philharmonic societies of brief existence[49] too contributed to the rise of the first local professional instrumentalists. The first symphony concerts by a Costa Rican ensemble finally took place in 1926, thanks to the "Musical Society of Costa Rica."

As evidenced in this section, music instruction first rose privately and was soon instituted by the government in order to educate performers of European art music. Whether private or public, ephemeral or lasting, the projects directed to this aim were elitist and discriminatory: they reached only a small portion of the population, reproduced foreign sociocultural trends associated with a modern economy and state organization, and furthered the colonial exclusion of the indigenous and Afro-Caribbean cultural legacy. While influences of European derivation would serve a "national identity" discourse, marginalization of local musics would soon be endorsed through state policy.

THE INVENTION OF A NATION PROJECT

Military Bands, School Music,[50] and "The" National Music

The ruling political elite believed that the European concept of "the nation"[51] was the model to best gather and define a political community, and that nationalism was useful in mobilizing popular classes.[52] Through liberal policies, they disseminated a cultural discourse in order to promote the solidarity and consensus to support the collective identity that would guarantee the desired political order. This discourse was based on mystified memories,[53] traits and values,[54] and was systematically disseminated by several subsequent governments through journalism, philosophical and political writings, historiography, visual arts, music, and education (168).[55] Exaltation of nationalistic symbols and icons, such as the national flag, shield, local heroic figures, and national songs and anthems became crucial to the invention of "the nation."[56]

Since then, official historical discourse propagated a narrative of racial homogeneity,[57] which perpetuated the inherited indigenous marginality[58] and legitimized it through official history.[59] The Afro-Caribbean cultural legacy, which includes African-derived folklore, Protestant religious practices, a language based on Jamaican English, and of course, music practices, underwent the same marginalization.[60] It is important to mention that a considerable number of Afro-Caribbean people had arrived to the port of the Caribbean province of Limón[61] in the early 1870s[62] as the workforce for the construction of a national railroad, and definitely were established in the province when banana and cacao plantations later increased in the region and a workforce for these activities were needed.[63]

The role of the former colonial military wind ensembles, which summoned the population to civic meetings,[64] was also recast within the national identity project. The military ensemble, "comprised by well-dressed musicians, with sonorous and brilliant instruments, was a visual and aural spectacle of great impact that reinforced the image of grandeur and power that the State needed to consolidate" (Vargas-Cullell, 2004, 208). Its new duties comprised performing military music, the national anthem, and national songs at civic and state ceremonies[65] and providing live music at weekly community social gatherings,[66] as well as in some religious feasts and celebrations[67] in major cities.[68]

A crucial action aimed at increasing the number of skilled musicians and the quality of performance of bands was the establishment of the Military Music School, in San José[69] in 1909.[70] Music instruction would encounter significant problems associated with the unpractical work division inherent to the military body: apprentices held the lowest rank in the military headquarters and were thus in charge of inferior duties, such as ornate,[71] which they had to perform aside from music learning. Other significant problems derived from insufficient policy: bad quality instruments, excessive workloads and schedules, very low salaries, and abusive physical punishments as part of the military training protocol.[72] The State's inability to suffice the salary and material needs of military bands due to World War I further magnified these problems.[73]

Despite the important role music played in the "identity project," music may have ironically been taken for granted when it came to fund allotment. Perhaps if the goal of music instruction had not been so detached from the broader education of the population this "national" music project would have flourished more steadily in accordance with a more significant social role. Another national project, to be discussed next, would serve to demonstrate this.

Among the gamut of means to generate and reproduce the consensus and cultural integration sought by the Liberal political elite, education was deemed the most effective. According to Álvarez (2006, 148–53), education in many developing countries has served as an institutional agency for creating national uniformities among the heterogeneous class and status grouping of a society by transmitting a national culture through the construction and glorification of national history, teaching of national symbols, and of a national language.

Rather than using expensive military means to guarantee the survival of "the nation" political project, the institutionalization of a lay, universal, and practical school education seemed a less costly means to persuade for the acceptance of a system of norms of the Liberal state. To this aim, educational reform was enforced between 1885 and 1889,[74] through which a new elementary school curriculum was drawn and several secondary schools were founded. Such a measure would also allow the government to promote productivity through "the moral and intellectual progress of the citizenry" (Álvarez, 2006, 177).

School music seemed appropriate to the above purpose, given its notable influence on individuals and their character and its potential to instill civic and moral messages clothed in attractive melodies. While the teaching of music was first enforced only in the education of girls, it later became mandatory in both elementary and secondary school education, in the form of the subject "Singing."[75] Teaching songs would be a way to "elevate the child's soul, instil love for study, abnegation for the motherland, and enthusiasm for virtue and the noble actions" (Vargas-Cullell 2004, 213). The State funded the publication of textbooks focused on rudiments of music theory, reading, and notation, and songs that dealt with hygiene norms or contained civic and moral messages.[76]

Provisions were also made by the government for stable appointments of music teachers and music school inspectors at the major provinces, who would supervise both teaching of music at schools as well as repertoire choice. According to accounts by inspectors, teachers often preferred to teach very complex songs, such as choruses from Spanish zarzuela or other "mundane" genres, unsuitable to the tessitura and performing capacities of young children, as opposed to "the more appropriate and simple melodies of easier retention, of noble maxims and thinking" [sic] (*Archivo Nacional de Costa Rica*, 1898) that were in accordance with the high Western aesthetic culture.[77]

As can be perceived in the preceding analysis, the degree of governmental resource allotment and organization toward the launching of school music within an educational project aimed at consolidating "the" national identity was impressive. Such action contrasts strikingly with past, erratic efforts to organize musical practices within a military context that was somehow incompatible with broader educational goals. This strongly suggests that awareness on the sociocultural and educational "power" of music would be necessary to trigger any worthwhile effort of systematizing music instruction in the country. Let us now discuss another facet of this political project, one where music would continue to be essential.

Until 1927, Costa Rican salon and concert music reproduced the elements and traits of European music. Partly motivated by nationalistic movements in Latin America, numerous authoritative musicians and composers considered that Costa Rica needed to have its own "national" rhythms and musical genres. The local "invasion" of contemporary foreign musics, such as foxtrot and jazz, only added to this concern. These arguments called for the "invention" of a national music. Invention—rather than collection—was once again deemed necessary within the State's project. In accordance with the now official marginality of old autochthonous musics, quite a few intellectuals and composers considered that the indigenous music did not seem to reflect "the feelings and melancholies" of the Costa Rican people.[78]

The task of such invention was commissioned by the government to a group of composers—many of them graduates of European conservatoires—in 1927.[79] The *tambito* rhythm[80] from the North Pacific province of Guanacaste was ascribed the status of "national music." Deliberately disregarding the traditions and legacy of other old and even newer music practices outside one single province[81] only served to support the myth of the nation's racial and cultural homogeneity, and finally condemned the musics of the indigenous and Afro-Caribbean populations to absolute invisibility and oblivion.[82]

The government sought to strengthen the above action by holding competitions for the composition of national music from 1927 until the late 1930s. The outcome was the creation and dissemination of numerous chamber and concert works that allegedly reflected what was "national." "National music" was also brought into school music through the publication of songbooks by the National Secretariat of Education.[83] The most important song was the National Anthem, which formed a "symbolic trilogy" along with the national shield and flag (Vargas-Cullell, 2004, 220) and became a mandatory content within the subject "Singing."[84] The anthem was a crucial component of civic gatherings. It was customary that groups of as many as three thousand school children would sing it at civic ceremonies, so they would interiorize the concept "Homeland."[85]

The "national" discourse analyzed so far, disseminated and imposed upon the population through art music and music education, served to instill values and ideologies presumably needed to consolidate an apparently "consensual" nation project. The exclusion of local musics incompatible with the liberal political project was somehow assumed as a value crucial to the "nation." In the particular case of music education policy—the first consistent, systematic, and stable policy in this regard ever—it appears that the intensity of the political agenda considerably overshadowed any other possible educational goals.

STATE-FUNDED MUSIC SCHOOLS[86] (1940 TO THE PRESENT)

The "Association of Musical Culture," made up mostly of graduates from European conservatories, founded in 1942 the National Conservatoire, which was incorporated into the Faculty of Fine Arts of the University of Costa Rica two years later, and in 1974 took the name "School of Musical Arts." Despite the new academic setting, the school's curriculum remained basically a conservatory program until 1968, when the curriculum was organized as a university program leading to a bachelor's degree in music performance.[87]

A music department was founded in 1974 at the National Autonomous University of Heredia,[88] another state-funded institution that attends mostly to students from the province of Heredia and in recent years founded a precollege program. A new conservatoire-modeled music school was opened in 1972 by the newly created Ministry of Culture, Youth, and Sports of Costa Rica. Its goal was to educate orchestral instrumentalists for a national youth symphony orchestra. The school's teaching staff was composed of a large number of foreign professional musicians, mostly from the United States, also contracted by the government to play in a renewed symphony orchestra. An isolated milestone during this period was the foundation of the only public arts elementary and secondary school to this date, in 1953: the *Castella* Conservatory.

Due to a severe financial crisis in the late 1970s, caused by the second world petroleum crisis and the fall in the price of coffee beans,[89] most of these foreign musicians decided to return to their native countries. As a result, Costa Ricans trained in the Symphony Youth Program soon took over the vacant positions.[90] At present, the National Symphony Orchestra and its Youth Symphony School staff are constituted largely of professional Costa Rican musicians. Both orchestra and school are now programs of the National Center of Music, which also houses the National Opera Company and the National Symphony Choir. Since the 1990s, graduates from the school obtain a bachelor and licentiate degrees in music granted by the *Universidad Estatal a Distancia* (State Distance University).

Until the late 1990s, publicly funded music schools were only available in the major cities of Costa Rica's central provinces: San José, Heredia, Alajuela, and Cartago. For people interested in studying music who were not living within the central area of the country, the location of the schools was an obstacle. In view of this, and after conducting a one-year pilot plan in 1995 in the province of Cartago,[91] municipal music schools were created a year later in outlying areas of the country (Chinchilla-Solano, 2009). This project involves material, staff, and resource provisions by both ministries of Culture and Education and the specific communities.

The municipal school curriculum, strongly modeled after the precollege program of the University of Costa Rica, has a twofold major.[92] The "main" major leads to a certification that allows graduates to play in bands and orchestras and teach elementary and secondary schools, municipal music schools, or other music institutions. A "special" major is directed to people of any age who wish to pursue studies in music as a secondary or nonprofessional activity. To date, more than fifteen municipal schools have been established in fifteen munici-palities.

In 2007, as one strategic measure within the National Development Plan 2006 to 2010[93] proposed by the Costa Rican Ministry of Planning and Financial Policy, the Ministry of Culture of Costa Rica founded the

National Music Education System or *Sistema Nacional de Educación Musical* (SINEM), which consists in a network of municipal music schools that offer instrument and theory instruction to children and youth. It follows the curricular model of the already existing Youth Symphony Program School and is inspired on the ideals and practices of the Youth and Children Orchestras System of Venezuela (FESNOJIV), particularly in the development of social and life skills through instrumental education and ensemble performance.

SINEM's goal is not to train music professionals; it is concerned with educating future citizens in social values and toward artistic skills through music engagements (Vargas-González, 2007, 4). The System gathers twelve already existing municipal schools and has opened over ten more in cities or towns with considerable population of youth at social risk after its foundation. SINEM has established a network between the Ministry of Culture, municipalities, and private agencies in order to warrant enough funding, teachers, and fluent operations. It has expanded state-funded music education out of the capital city and targets mainly socially vulnerable populations. SINEM seems to fully embrace the idea of a far-reaching and more participatory music education model at a national level.

State-funded music instruction after 1940 has remained goal oriented. Although it continued to be directed to the training of instrumentalists, it has spanned beyond the ideal of conservatory education of instrumentalists to professional education at university and municipal music schools to attend to socially vulnerable children and young people. Unlike past educational projects, the social scope of more recent programs has been much broader, and the educational goals are more closely related with art education values. This seems to be a more consistent national project at the service of education of the population.

CRISIS OF SCHOOL MUSIC (1980–2000)

After the second decade of the twentieth century, school music instruction (elementary and secondary),[94] in the form of the subject "music," emphasizes the learning of national songs and anthems and the elements of music, especially in regard to Western canon (Rosabal-Coto, 2001, 3). Moreover, to this day, the national music education program for elementary school emanated from the Costa Rican Ministry of Education envisioned the music classroom as the setting where children and young people develop aural, vocal, psychomotor, intellectual and affective skills, learn disciplinary habits, assimilate civic, moral, ethic and spiritual values, and interiorize attitudes of respect, tolerance, and cooperation, considered indispensable for family and social growth (Rosabal-Coto, 2001).[95]

During the last two decades of the last century, school music suffered because of government policy (De Couve, Dal Pino, Fernández, Frega, and Souza, 1999). As several governments considered arts education as accessory and thus secondary to general education, more attention and resources was given to increasing the teaching time to English, computer literacy, and other subjects that were supposed to develop in students the necessary skills for a more successful insertion of the country into globalization processes. An alternative to reduction of teaching positions and instructional time has been the opening of positions of extracurricular music activities—locally known as "clubs"—such as marching bands, conventional and nonconventional instrumental ensembles, choirs, and student dance groups.

The once politically legitimate role of school music within the broader education of the national population no longer would seem relevant to late twentieth-century governments, whose interests shifted considerably from the liberal project of "identity formation" to cultural insertion into the dynamics of a new economic order. Once more, music education would suffer because of a political agenda, partly rooted in extraneous forces and values. This time music education, once a priority means for political action, would not be excluding; it would somehow be *excluded* from the stately projects.

RECASTING "IDENTITY" AND MARGINAL MUSICS IN SECONDARY SCHOOL MUSIC (2009 TO THE PRESENT)

A curricular reform implemented in 2009, called "Education in Arts, Ethical, and Citizen Values"[96] in secondary school education, attempts to contribute to social awareness in light of a rise in school dropout and rise in crime and citizen insecurity experienced by the Costa Rican society in the last decade. [97] The reform seeks to engage the students in learning and socialization practices, such as dialogue, cooperation, and negotiation, in which knowledge is constructed by the students themselves through research, active engagement, reflection and criticism, and close interaction with their community. It aims at educating citizens who are not only socially aware but are able to make responsible individual and collective choices and engage in healthy social relationships.

The music curriculum within the reform [98] aims at instilling and developing self-knowledge, self-realization, criticism, as well as dialogue and negotiation skills through musically embodied agency. [99] The musical engagement is regarded as a valuable setting for transforming the individual self, and through the self, the social order. [100] The educational and assessment practices encourage students to examine who they are, how, and why within a lived-by musical space and extend empowering experience acting upon individual and collective realities. Students can engage in exploring, understanding, performing, creating *their* music, the musics in the community, as well as past and present musics of society at large *and* their self in music engagements—that is, their subjectivity and identity. [101]

Besides social awareness among future citizens, another expected outcome of the new secondary music curriculum is the critical exploration and interrogation of the nature, role, influences, and acculturation processes of the host of musics that make up the Costa Rican culture. First and foremost, their mostly popular and urban music they engage with are: rock, rap, jazz, and Caribbean genres such as salsa, *merengue, cumbia, vallenato,* reggae, calypso, soca, and *punta,* among many. Of course, of undeniable importance is traditional Costa Rican music. According to Cervantes-Gamboa and Flores-Zeller (2007), this music is mainly derived of Hispanic traditions and also Afro-Caribbean and indigenous traditions. [102] The above musical and educational endeavors acknowledge that Costa Rica is a multiethnic and multicultural country. [103]

It is expected that the implementation of this curriculum will promote awareness on a multiplicity of musics and identities, and that such awareness will be developed by the students themselves as protagonists of the educational processes, rather than by vertical imposition. Prominent among such multiple musics and identities are, of course, the indigenous and Afro-Caribbean legacies.

CONCLUSION

This chapter has critically addressed the historical itinerary of music education in Costa Rica, with particular interest in the context and social and political implications of instructional goals and policy. After the precolonial years that witnessed modestly organized and apparently socially relevant local musical activities within the religious, political, and civil life, the itinerary of goals and policy begins a cyclic journey up to the late twentieth century, in which the following patterns of colonialism and exclusion in the social and cultural milieus are recurrent and outstanding:

1. Metropolitan cultural trends and music instruction models were adopted with intensity and officially legitimated.
2. Goals of music culture and music instruction were impacted and shaped by extraneous influences, the interests of socially or politically hegemonic groups, and the vicissitudes of both private and public resource organization and provision. Perhaps due to these, instruction has not necessarily been connected to aims as artistically or social development directed education.
3. The indigenous and Afro-Caribbean culture and legacy was gradually excluded from the official culture and state educational projects.
4. Most educational projects involving music were rampant in terms of resources and organization, and of ephemeral duration, despite their alleged significance to diverse social and political purposes.
5. Educational enterprises involving music were not carried out consensually.

When looked at more closely, the above music- and education-related trends, in subsequent cycles, acquire certain intensity, and yield very specific sociocultural consequences. For instance, the music practices in the colonial period were associated mostly with the foreign religion and political control and allowed to some extent a coexistence of local and newcomers' practices. However, their precarious degree of material and artistic development did not warrant systematic music instruction. After the independence, an elitist European-based culture was imposed, first through private music performance and music instructions and later through state policy. The latter fulfilled social status differentiation needs and state control mechanisms. Next, the same foreign culture and political model of a state would serve as a basis for the creation of a "national identity" within a liberal project of "the nation." This project claimed to reach consensus by imposing a cultural discourse from within, particularly through artistic and intellectual endeavors, education, and school music.

In the latter part of the twentieth century, the itinerary opens up into broader outreach. Since educational goals and their supporting organizational structures seem to somehow detach from inherited patterns of colonialism and exclusion, a broader population has access to music instruction: from municipal music schools for socially vulnerable youth and children to professional music education at the university level.

Since then, educational endeavors also seem to be better prepared to face social contradictions and overcome past erratic practices. For instance, even though school music loses significance within a national project and was on the verge of reduction, a social-awareness-oriented music curriculum for secondary school attempts to recast the concept "identity" among young people and revalue the local musics that were marginalized since colonial times and later banned from history through a narrative of "ethnic purity." Such enterprises are fairly recent, and thus several recommendations can be formulated in order to enhance their social potential and warrant their sustainability.

RECOMMENDATIONS FOR FURTHER DIRECTIONS

Given the nature of the issues discussed in this chapter, Costa Rican formal music education would benefit greatly from critical examination of educational goals and policy from the perspective of social justice and equity issues in education. Focusing on the sociocultural implications of past and present educational processes may allow better understanding of the relevance of goals and policy, as well as their possibility for social and cultural change through music education practices.[104]

Such scrutiny might be enriched through international dialogue and comparative music education research (Cajas, 2007)[105] involving Latin American countries, as well as other national contexts.[106] Comparative research should go beyond formal music schooling and instrumental education and draw from recent international trends that focus on the participation and creative agency of learners, such as informal and community music education. In fact, developments in learning in informal or community environments in Costa Rica are topics not at all explored. Also, the time is ripe for educational practices, curricula, teaching materials, and teacher preparation to be researched systematically.

Along the lines of comparative studies, some strategic actions of a practical nature—not historically yet undertaken—such as cooperative alliances with private or nongovernmental education and development agencies to assess the current music practices, might be one potentially successful way to prevent embracing officially legitimated paradigms related to social and political hegemony and exclusion.

Goal establishment and policy making would also benefit from assuming creativity and participation as foundational values, promoting dialogue and among diverse social sectors in regard to their sociocultural needs, thus detaching from insufficient historical actions. For instance, the recent milestones in music schools and secondary music would benefit from ongoing critical reflection on the multiplicity of identities encompassed in the Costa Rican population so as to ensure effective connections with the challenges of a society that is not and has never been socially or culturally homogeneous.

NOTES

1. For a thorough discussion on the organization and development of pre-Hispanic societies in Costa Rica, see Molina-Jiménez and Palmer (2007), 1–28.

2. Within this context, the term *indigenous* must be understood as autochthonous Amerindian.

3. See Arroyo, V. M. (1972), *Lenguas indigenas de Costa Rica* [Indigenous Languages of Costa Rice]. San José, Costa Rica: Editorial Cultural Centroamericana.

4. Flores-Zeller (1978, 23–29) provides iconographic materials on pre-Hispanic and colonial indigenous instruments. Cervantes-Gamboa (1995) discusses an organological classification, and provides information on their design, manufactured materials, and pitch range, among other relevant characteristics. See also Acevedo-Vargas (1986) and Salazar-Salvatierra (1992).

5. Flores-Zeller (1978, 29) transcribes and comments on some presumably post-Hispanic indigenous melodies, collected between the nineteenth and twentieth centuries.

6. See Acevedo-Vargas (1986) for a collection of accounts from chroniclers.

7. Flores-Zeller (1978) provides several examples in the first chapter of his book.

8. Anthropologist and ethnomusicologist Cervantes-Gamboa (1995) provides a discussion on indigenous musical genres, their structure, as well as some performance practices of music of particular ethnic groups. Other relevant works on these topics, by this and other authors, are listed in this source.

9. The first Spanish arrived at this territory in 1502.

10. In fact, the colonization process has often been equated by some early historians to "the conquest," and is associated with attempts of domination known as "pacification," hence the process' violent connotation. The dissemination and indoctrination of natives in the foreign religion (Catholicism) during this period has been called "evangelization."

11. Unfortunately, thorough studies on this phenomenon are lacking.

12. In fact, the pace of the colonization process and its consequent ethnic and cultural blend were considerably slow owing to this situation, in comparison with other colonial provinces.

13. See the work by Duncan and Meléndez (1972) for a thorough discussion on the subject. Due to emancipation mechanisms, much of this population would be incorporated ethnically and socially between 1750 and 1850. Unfortunately, no studies are available to date to attest for specific musical practices of the African slaves of African descent and their potential impact on the existing culture.

14. Music featured in the liturgical services, such as the Ordinary of the Mass, Mass for the Dead, Te Deums, Vespers, patron saint feasts, and other festivities (e.g., Holy Week services and processions, and Christmas), and popular devotions such as the Rosary. M. Peralta provides perhaps the first evidence of a sung Mass in the territory, in 1526. Some of this music may have been required and funded by *cofradías*, religious fraternities gathered around the cult to a saint, or for charity purposes. See Flores-Zeller (1978), 33–35.

15. It is worth adding that music was one of many liturgical elements that required material investment, next to consecration wine, wax for candles, flour for making hosts, ornaments and statues, and liturgical garments, all of which many times may have come before music performance and instruments on a priority list. Recorded accounts of the liturgy during the period fail to provide further details on how music practices were carried out. See work by Carvajal-Mena and Arroyo-Muñoz (1985).

16. Upon royal instruction, parish churches celebrated the birth, death, or spouse of the Spanish royal family members, as well as their victories at armed conflicts. A typical ensemble for this purpose comprised rudimentary snare drums, shawms, fifers, bugles, and clarinets. See Blanco-Segura, R. (1983) and González-Flores, L. F. (1945) for accounts on music, musicians, and instruments in specific celebrations, such as the welcoming of Spanish bishops or religious representatives.

17. For example, sarabandes, fandangos, or *saraos*. Secular celebrations would include parades, bullfighting, and drama, also supported by music. Interestingly enough, evidences of musical activities in profane contexts are provided in documents related to the regulation of public order, since often such gatherings their music was considered "pernicious" or a "source of sin" due to the morale of society. For several accounts, see Blanco-Segura, R. (1983).

18. The characteristics of the territory were quite adverse to the Spanish settlers. Both the terrain and climate were arid.

19. The absence of precious metals or material wealth made the territory of little economic significance to Spain.

20. Recent scholarship (Flores-Zeller and Acevedo-Vargas, 2000; Vargas-Cullell, 2004; Vargas-Cullell and Madrigal-Muñoz, 2008) emphasizes the negative impact of insufficient material conditions and overall development upon music practices.

21. It is very probable that the strong link between religion and state would also be another logical reason why the same musicians had to take over music in both religious and profane contexts. Vargas-Cullell (2004, 27–32) provides numerous accounts.

22. For example, Spaniards such as Diego de Nicuesa, an aggressive Spanish conqueror, who happened to be a "great vihuela performer" (Flores-Zeller, 1978, 31).

23. Some official sources, such as the chronicles by Spaniards and church inventories, specify the name of instruments, and sometimes the number of musicians at specific activities or circumstances, at the most.

24. This is a striking possibility considering that in most colonial Latin America countries the Catholic Church was the one institution that organized music. See Béhague (1983), 7.

25. See accounts in the article by Vargas-Cullell and Madrigal-Muñoz (2008).

26. Process of ethnic or cultural blending.

27. See Flores-Zeller (1978), 34.

28. A 1785 inventory in Orosi, the main religious center of the time, reports one viol, a marimba, three violins, two guitars, a bugle, and two *chirimías* in the church ensemble (Flores-Zeller, 1978, 33).

29. See account by Acevedo-Vargas (1986), 55–56.

30. See Flores-Zeller (1978), 34.

31. Terms for Spanish-indigenous and Spanish-Afro-Caribbean ethnic mixes.

32. See article by Vargas-Cullell and Madrigal-Muñoz (2008).

33. Vargas-Cullell and Madrigal-Muñoz (2008) speculate that the absence of printed music for religious ritual may be due to the fact that Costa Rica was subordinated to Guatemala in both religious and political matters. It is feasible that music for ritual came from this territory.

34. In fact, according to Vargas-Cullell and Madrigal-Muñoz (2008), the existing accounts of music in social rituals are quite vague perhaps because music seemed to have been overshadowed by the rituals themselves and taken for granted by chroniclers or writers. This may be another strong argument to think of a very modest musical component in social and religious rituals during this period.

35. In this chapter, the expression *goal oriented* refers to music education directed specifically to the production of instrumentalists.

36. Costa Rica was one of several Central American provinces that jointly declared their independence from Spain.

37. See chapter 1 of the work by Vargas-Cullell (2004).

38. Unlike developed music chapels in colonial Latin America, the term *church musician* in this context should not be equated to *chapel master* but rather understood as a multifaceted empirical instrumentalist.

39. See accounts by Vargas-Cullell and Madrigal-Muñoz (2008).

40. Needell (1987) provides insight to understand elite habits in newly independent Latin American countries.

41. See the works by Fumero-Vargas (1994), and Molina-Jiménez and Palmer (2004) for exhaustive analyses on these trends.

42. According to Moritz and Scherzer (1853), the first piano was brought to Costa Rica in 1835 (Flores-Zeller, 1978, 43).

43. See discussion in Vargas-Cullell (2004), 95–110.

44. They came mainly from the neighboring country of Nicaragua. The need to hire foreign musicians strongly suggests that conditions and quality of music making were still modest and that systematic instruction was nonexistent.

45. See discussions on this subject by Flores-Zeller (1978) and Vargas-Cullell (2004).

46. Two types of students were accepted: "effective" ones [*sic*], who wished to become professionals in music, and the "assistants," who desired to enrich their education with music instruction (Decree X, March 12, 1890).

47. An indirect motivation for consolidating a symphony orchestra was the fact that the construction of the National Theater, a performance house modeled after European standards, was already in progress. It only seemed reasonable that a refined and cult nation would be able to display its own orchestra at its national theatre.

48. "Saint Cecilia Music School."

49. Sociedad Santa Cecilia (1902), Sociedad Musical de Costa Rica (1911), Sociedad Filarmónica Josefina (1914), Asociación Musical (1915), Conservatorio de Música y Declamación (1915–1917), Asociación Musical de Costa Rica (1926–1927), Conservatorio Euterpe (1934), and Asociación de Cultura Musical (1934–1946). These institutions usually followed the French conservatoire curriculum model.

50. The curricular goals and contents of school music and institutions involved in this period has been addressed in the study by Chacón-Solís (2009).

51. This "nation" discourse was inherent to the eighteenth- and nineteenth-century political movements in Europe, and the ideals of Liberalism and the Illustration.

52. See discussion in Álvarez (2006), 163.

53. The departing concept for the invention of "the nation" in Costa Rica was the small homeland, whose roots were to be found in the administrative divisions inherited from the colonial past (See Torres-Rivas and Pino, 1983, 171–75, and Álvarez, 2006, 149).

54. The adoption of the idea of "rural democracy," based on the perception that Costa Ricans were peaceful and diligent people, served to promote the image that the political system was consensual and that conflicts among societal groups were nonexistent. Coincidentally, a considerable part of the population shared these traits. The rural democracy was incarnated by small and medium agricultural producers, mainly coffee growers, who were owners and who were considered to be the fundamental group in the nation's history. See Álvarez (2006).

55. Molina-Jiménez and Palmer (2004), 257–13, discuss thoroughly state policies in art and education.

56. See Anderson (1991) for further explanation on the role of nationalism in the formation of "the nation."

57. The population was "bleached" and depicted as a homogeneous race: the indigenous were transformed into "ladinos" to make the bridge. "Mestizos"—the mix between European white and indigenous—were called "white." See discussion in Álvarez (2006), 156–59.

58. See *Situación de la música en las reservas indígenas* (Status of Music in Indigenous Reservations), in Flores-Zeller and Acevedo (2000), for a discussion on acculturation and developments in indigenous music in the contemporary era.

59. See Álvarez (2006), 157–58.

60. It is worth noting that this population is the largest Costa Rican ethnic minority group (Cervantes-Gamboa and Flores-Zeller, 2007).

61. The country's main commercial port at that time.

62. They came from Jamaica, Saint Kitts, and Barbados (Monestel-Ramírez, 2005).

63. According to Monestel-Ramírez (2005), the newcomers faced hardships of work with songs, whistling, cajón rhythms, *marimbulas*, and perhaps guitars, and developed their own local music practices. Their musical legacy to this date comprises work songs, *mento* rhythm, square dance, and Christian and *pocomía* (a Jamaican religion) songs. Of later influence, the calypso was adopted from Trinidad, and blended with *mento*. At present, this population comprises the largest ethnic minority in the country, and about 2 percent of the overall population.

64. Several policy and material efforts by the Costa Rican state to rule and improve its military wind ensembles began in 1845. In this year, the Costa Rican government made the first significant purchase ever of a big lot of woodwind, brass, and percussion instruments, and contracted a foreign specialist to take over organization and musical instruction of military bands. It also provided the bands with uniforms suitable for playing at official ceremonies. By the 1860s each of the main four provinces of Costa Rica had one military band.

65. For example: Independence Day celebrations, political speeches, and presentation of decorative arches and flower offerings at public places and monuments (*La Gaceta Oficial de Costa Rica*, August 26, 1871, 4).

66. Mainly *recreos* ("recesses") and *retretas* ("retreats").

67. For example, Sunday morning Mass, and processions in Holy Week.

68. Similar to colonial times, and up the present, the State has had a significant relationship with the Catholic Church, thus it is not strange that the duties of state-funded military bands include performing in both religious and civil contexts.

69. Capital city of Costa Rica.

70. The School's four-year study plan focused in reading and writing skills and performance of scales, intervals, and repertoire on several band instruments.

71. This work division in the military band entailed five ranks, from apprentice—the lowest—to "first class." Mobility was subject to progress in performance. See Flores-Zeller (1978), 42.

72. See Vargas-Cullell (2004), 133–48, for detailed accounts.

73. When in 1948 the Costa Rican government declared the abolition of the army, the military bands became part of the Education and Culture Secretariat. At present, each of the seven provinces of the country has one national band. They usually perform weekly *retretas* (evening concerts) and *recreos* (Sunday morning concerts). Their repertory includes traditional music similar to that of the *cimarronas*

(small, festive civil brass ensembles) with more military and symphonic music, national hymns, and even music from zarzuelas (Cervantes-Gamboa and Flores-Zeller, 2007), and lately, more popular and commercial music.

74. See Fischel-Volio's 1990 work that deals in depth with the education reform, its context, and development.

75. This seems to reflect some contradiction: despite its alleged political and cultural importance, music somehow still holds an accessory status through policy, as it was not first considered relevant to the entire educational population.

76. See work by Chacón-Solís (2009) for a detailed description on these actions.

77. With the purpose of alleviating this situation, in 1906 the National Music School Inspector was sent out by the government on a journey to important cities in North America and Europe to observe school music education and interact with school authorities in those cities. It was expected that he would promote the incorporation of novel pedagogical methodologies and materials into the local school music instruction. A few decades later the inspector position changed into a "National Coordinator." Currently, the Ministry of Public Education appoints national coordinators of school music for both elementary and secondary school, as well as regional coordinators in most school districts.

78. As stated by composer J. Fonseca, in *La Nueva Prensa* daily, October 1927, 6.

79. Vargas-Cullell (2004) discusses exhaustively this situation (231–37).

80. A fast, joyful hemiola rhythm that shows the 6/8 ambivalence on much Latin American music, characteristic of *parranderas* (parties) (Cervantes-Gamboa and Flores-Zeller, 2007).

81. The composers commissioned to this task made several field research trips to the North Pacific province of Guanacaste and neglected the musics in the rest of the territory in their quest.

82. This action is highly contrasting with nationalistic music movements in Latin America, which turned their attention primarily to the indigenous, Amerindian legacy.

83. Vargas Cullell (2004) describes these actions exhaustively (237–48).

84. In fact, the National Inspector of Music had the responsibility of overseeing the learning of the Anthem at schools.

85. See specific accounts by Vargas-Cullell (2004), 225–30.

86. Private music schools have flourished in Costa Rica since the last decades of the twentieth century. They are not addressed in this chapter, as they do not respond to state policy.

87. The Music Education program opened in 1971, and later came Composition and Conducting. A Licentiate program in every major and a precollege program were soon opened. Currently, the university offers undergraduate and graduate degrees in music.

88. The department became a School of Music in 1977. It offers degrees in performance, music education, and choral conducting.

89. See Molina-Jiménez and Palmer (2005), 39.

90. Murillo-Torres's work (1986) deals with the creation and trajectory of the symphony orchestra and its youth music school.

91. Eastern province, neighboring the province of San José, site of the capital city.

92. These schools usually implement a program of studies that was created in 1996 by a group of teachers who participated in the pilot project.

93. See Ministerio de Planificación y Política Económica (2007). The Plan is geared toward an efficient use of state funds in addressing a gamut of government priorities: (a) strengthening public institutions and eradicating corruption in the public sector, (b) reduction of poverty and inequality, (c) increasing economy growth and employment, (d) increasing the quality and coverage of education, (e) fighting the rise in crime, drug traffic, drug addiction, and citizen insecurity, among others.

94. Music education is not offered in the preschool level in the public school system in Costa Rica.

95. The official school music curricula have also enforced reading, writing, and performing music, as well as music appreciation, mostly of Western art music, as part of their prescribed contents.

96. The curricular reform comprises the so-called soft subjects in the public secondary school system (grades seven to eleven): physical education, civic education, industrial arts, visual arts, home education, and music education. Such subjects, traditionally known as "recreational" or "nonacademic" are allotted one to two forty-minute lessons per week. Despite being mandatory subjects, their status has been inferior to the "hard" core subjects: Spanish, mathematics, social studies, sciences (physics, biology, and chemistry), computer science, and English-as-a-second-language.

97. Rosabal-Coto (2010) describes in detail the sociopolitical context and rationale of the project.

98. The entire curriculum document is available from the Ministry of Public Education of Costa Rica and the author of this chapter.

99. Rodriguez-Ramirez's study (2007) on the psychosocial role of music in the development of Coata Rican adolescents provides this curriculum with considerable background on music-embodied agency.

100. In consonance with this foundational premise, the curriculum has adopted an expanded praxial philosophy of music education and drawn from implications of postmodernism and premises from critical pedagogy, liberation theology, and cultural studies in education.

101. See Rosabal-Coto (2010) for a critical description and explanation on the educational practices of the curriculum, from a philosophical and sociological point of view.

102. African influence can be traced in both the rhythmic structures of many genres and in the rise of particular instruments. Iberian polyphony in parallel thirds, Hispanic melodies, and Western harmony predominate most Costa Rican traditional music. The influence of indigenous music has rarely extended to other national groups or to art music composers (Cervantes-Gamboa and Flores-Zeller, 2007). The most recent study in popular music in Costa Rica is by Marín-Hernández (2009). See also Flores-Zeller and Acevedo (2000).

103. Molina-Jiménez and Palmer (2007, 175) discuss the outcome of awareness on this diversity among contemporary Costa Rican society.

104. Pérez-Mora (2007) has addressed some of these issues from the perspective of critical theory.

105. See Kertz-Welzel (2008) for a discussion on the potential advantage of international dialogue and research in international, comparative music education.

106. Rosabal-Coto (2009) has already taken a step forward by comparing instrumental music education in Costa Rica with its Finnish counterpart.

REFERENCES

Acevedo-Vargas, J. L. (1986). *La música en las reservas indígenas de Costa Rica* [Music in the Indigenous Reservations of Costa Rica]. San José, Costa Rica: Editorial de la Universidad de Costa Rica.

Álvarez, R. (2006). *The Relationship between Processes of National State Consolidation and the Development and Expansion of Systems of Public Education during the Nineteenth Century in Central America: Nicaragua and Costa Rica in Comparison.* Doctoral dissertation, University of Columbia, New York.

Anderson, B. (1991). *Imagined Communities: Reflections on the Origin and Spread of Nationalism.* London: Verso.

Archivo Nacional de Costa Rica [National Archives of Costa Rica]. (1898). Serie Educación [Education Series], No. 5317, San José, Costa Rica.

Arroyo, V. M. (1972). *Lenguas indígenas de Costa Rica* [Indigenous Languages of Costa Rica]. San José, Costa Rica: Editorial Cultural Centroamericana.

Béhague, G. (1983). *La Música en América Latina* [Music in Latin America]. Venezuela: Monte Ávila Editores.

Blanco-Segura, R. (1983). (2nd ed.) *Historia eclesiástica de Costa Rica* [Ecclesiastical History of Costa Rica]. San José, Costa Rica: Editorial Costa Rica.

Cajas, E. J. (2007). *Music Education in Central America: A Comparative Study of Educational Policies and Practices in Guatemala, Honduras, and Costa Rica.* Doctoral dissertation, University of Oklahoma.

Carvajal-Mena, L., and Arroyo-Muñoz, G. (1985). *La cofradía en el Valle Central: Principal obra pía de la colonia* [The *Cofradía* of the Central Valley: Main Pious Work of the Colonial Era]. Licentiate thesis, University of Costa Rica, San José, Costa Rica.

Cervantes-Gamboa, L., and Flores-Zeller, B. (2007). Costa Rica. In Oxford Music Online.

Cervantes-Gamboa, L. (1995). Información básica acerca de la música indígena de Costa Rica [Basic Information about Indigenous Music of Costa Rica]. In *Káñina* 19, no. 1, 155–73.

Chacón-Solís, L. (2009). Inclusión-afianzamiento de la asignatura "Música" en el currículo de la educación pública primaria y secundaria. Actores determinantes y visiones sobre su importancia. Costa Rica, 1849–1925 [Incorporation and Consolidation of the Subject "Music" in the Primary and Secondary Education Curriculum. Determinant Actors and Visions on Its Importance. Costa Rica, 1849–1925]. In *Káñina*, XXIV (in press).

Chinchilla-Solano, C. (2009). An Examination of the Program of Studies Developed for the Municipal Music Schools in Costa Rica. Unpublished manuscript.

De Couve, A. C., Dal Pino, C., Fernández, D., Frega, A. L., and Souza, J. (1999). Arts Education Policy in Latin America. In *Arts Education Policy Review* 99, no. 4, 18–28.

Duncan, Q., and Meléndez, C. (1972). *El negro en Costa Rica* [The Black in Costa Rica]. San José, Costa Rica: Editorial Costa Rica.

Fischel-Volio, A. (1990). *Consenso y represión: Una interpretación sociopolítica de la educación costarricense* [Consensus and Repression: A Socio-Political Interpretation of Costa Rican Education]. San José, Costa Rica: Editorial Costa Rica.

Flores-Zeller, B. (1978). *La Música en Costa Rica* [Music in Costa Rica]. San José, Costa Rica: Editorial Costa Rica.

Flores-Zeller, B., and Acevedo-Vargas, J. L. (2000). Costa Rica. In *Diccionario de la Música Española e Hispanoamericana* 6, 122–35. Madrid, Spain: Sociedad General de Autores y Editores.

Fumero-Vargas, P. (1994). *Teatro, público, y estado en San José, 1880–1914* [Theater, Audience, and State in San José, 1880–1914]. San José, Costa Rica: Editorial de la Universidad de Costa Rica.

González-Flores, L. F. (1945). *Historia del desarrollo de la instrucción pública en Costa Rica. Tomo I. La colonia* [History of the Development of Public Instruction in Costa Rica. Vol. I. Colonial Period]. San José, Costa Rica: Imprenta Nacional.

Kertz-Welzel, A. (2008). Music Education in the Twenty-First Century: A Cross-Cultural Comparison of German and American Music Education towards a New Concept of International Dialogue. In *Music Education Research* 10, no. 4, 439–49.

La Gaceta Oficial de Costa Rica [The Official Gazette of Costa Rica]. (August 26, 1871), San José, Costa Rica, 4.

La Nueva Prensa [The New Press Daily]. (1927, October 28), San José, Costa Rica, 6.

Marín-Hernández, J. J. (2009). *Melodías de perversión y subversión. La música popular en Costa Rica, 1932–1960* [Melodies of Perversion and Subversion. Popular Music in Costa Rica, 1932–1960]. San José, Costa Rica: Editorial Alma Mater.

Ministerio de Planificación y Política Económica. [Ministry of Planning and Financial Policy]. (2007). *Plan nacional de desarrollo 2006–2010 "Jorge Manuel Dengo Obregón"* ["Jorge Manuel Dengo Obregón," National Development Plan 2006–2010]. Available: http://www.mideplan.go.cr/content/view/69/371/

Molina-Jiménez, I., and Palmer, S. (eds.). (2004). *Héroes al gusto y libros de moda: Sociedad y cambio social en Costa Rica, 1750–1900* [Pleasing Heroes and Books in Fashion: Society and Cultural Change in Costa Rica, 1750–1900]. San José, Costa Rica: Editorial de la Universidad Estatal a Distancia.

———. (2005). *Costa Rica del siglo XX al XXI: Historia de una sociedad* [Costa Rica from the Twentieth to the Twenty-First Century: History of a Society]. San José, Costa Rica: Editorial de la Universidad Estatal a Distancia.

———. (2007). *Historia de Costa Rica* [History of Costa Rica]. San José, Costa Rica: Editorial de la Universidad de Costa Rica.

Monestel-Ramírez, M. (2005). *Ritmo, canción, identidad. Una historia sociocultural del calypso limonense* [Rhythm, Song, Identity. A Socio-Cultural History of Limón's Calypso]. San José, Costa Rica: Editorial Universidad Estatal a Distancia.

Moritz, W., and Scherzer, C. (1974). *La República de Costa Rica en la América Central.* San José, Costa Rica: Ministerio de Cultura, Juventud y Deportes.

Murillo-Torres, L. F. (1986). *La Orquesta Sinfónica Nacional de Costa Rica* [The National Symphony Orchestra of Costa Rica]. San José, Costa Rica. Licentiate thesis, University of Costa Rica, San José, Costa Rica.

Needell, J. D. (1987). *A Tropical Belle Époque: Elite Culture and Society in Turn-of-the-Century Rio de Janeiro.* New York: Cambridge University Press.

Pérez-Mora, Y. (2007). Análisis crítico del quehacer docente de los músicos [Critical Analysis of the Educational Task of Musicians]. In *Actualidades Investigativas en Educación* 7, no. 1, 1–20. Available: http://revista.inie.ucr.ac.cr/articulos/1-2007/archivos/musicos.pdf

Rodríguez-Ramírez, M. (2007). *El papel psicosocial de la música en el desarrollo adolescente: Un estudio exploratorio en un colegio privado del cantón de La Unión de la provincia de Cartago* [The Psychosocial Role of Music in Adolescent Development: An

Exploratory Study in a Private School of La Unión Canton of the Province of Cartago]. Licentiate thesis, University of Costa Rica, San José, Costa Rica.

Rosabal-Coto, G. (2001). *A Liturgical Music Education Component for the Central Seminary of Costa Rica.* Master's thesis, Brandon University, Manitoba, Canada.

———. (2009). Instrumental Music Education in Costa Rica and Finland: A Discussion and Comparison of Contexts and Goals. In *Musiikkikasvatus* (Finnish Journal of Music Education) 9, no. 2, 84–94.

———. (2010). Music Education for Social Change in the Secondary Public Schools of Costa Rica. In *Action, Criticism, and Theory for Music Education* 9, no. 3. Available: http://act.maydaygroup.org/articles/Rosabal-Coto9_3.pdf

Salazar-Salvatierra, R. (1992). *Instrumentos musicales del folclor costarricense* [Musical Instruments of Costa Rican Folklore]. Costa Rica: Editorial Tecnológica.

Torres-Rivas, E., and Pino, J. C. (1983). *Problemas en la formación del estado nacional en Centroamérica* [Problems in the Formation of the National State in Central America]. San José, Costa Rica: Instituto Centroamericano de Administración Pública.

Vargas-Cullell, M.C. (2004). *De las fanfarrias a las salas de concierto: Música en Costa Rica (1840–1940)* [From Fanfares to Concert Halls: Music in Costa Rica (1840–1940)]. San José, Costa Rica: Editorial de la Universidad de Costa Rica.

Vargas Cullell, M. C., and Madrigal-Muñoz, E. (2008). De rituales y festividades: Música colonial en la provincia de Costarrica [From Rituals to Festivities: Colonial Music in the Province of Costarrica]. In *Revista de Historia*, 57–58, 109–34.

Vargas-González, R. (2007). *Proyecto Sistema Nacional de Educación Musical* [Project: National Music Education System]. Unpublished manuscript.

Chapter Seven

El Salvador

Cristian Daniel Guandique Araniva

INTRODUCTION

In this chapter, the history of Salvadorian music education is presented, especially from the author's view as a witness of the events of the late decade of the twentieth century.

In El Salvador a real history is hard to be read in official documents without any issue with the organization of the historical memory, not to mention with the different political factors that, in order not to show their failures during their actions, prefer to keep confidential any event that evinces their faults in the unrest of the artistic manifestations in the country.

Naturally, it is also impossible to make any statement without documents proving it. This is why, while a certain criticism of those events is made, and impartiality being impossible to achieve, I have tried, to the best of my possibilities, to include data that is both relevant and verifiable. In the same way, skimming through the history of El Salvador will be enough to see that violence has marked Salvador's society, which, in spite of the ceasefire and the signing of the Chapultepec Peace Accords between the Armed Forces and the Farabundo Martí National Liberation Front (FMLN),[1] peace, not even an imaginary one, has never been obtained. Lack of education, employment, and overall social insurance have led to the country being stricken with drug trafficking and the "Maras."[2] However, artists have striven to fight on with a message of artistic commitment to both the Salvadorian people and Salvadorian society. They have also tried to conserve traditions of the utmost importance to national identity, as well as the sense conveyed by music such as discipline, union, and brotherhood. Artists in El Salvador have plenty to say and to communicate, but little opportunities to do so, and, even worse, little resources and national support too.

One of the main problems for Salvadorian artists is that society lives striving to meet the most basic needs such as security, food, health, regular education, and household (an alienating life, Marxistly speaking), making it more difficult to think of more spiritual, aesthetic, and meaningful artistic needs. For this reason, artistic practices are deemed as practices of "little production," not only by the Salvadorian State but also by most of the population. Additionally, the higher class and bourgeoisie deem art as a simply status-defining expression, or as a way to picture themselves belonging to a European higher class or bourgeoisie stereotype. Therefore, Salvadorian higher class seems to have little interest in preserving any value of what is Salvadorian, and of what is national.

Arts in El Salvador, particularly music, have not been able to integrate to the day-to-day life in its "natural" way. While very appreciated by many, generally students and pundits, they have not been able to give music the place it deserves in Salvadorian society by themselves. Music continues, for many, as something for minorities.

Although many dates and years are found in this chapter, there are many sources with misleading or inaccurate information. However, there have been efforts to give the most accurate information hereinafter.

As for the part of the overall history of Central America, so many were the events that made the environment during independence time so confusing, and one could just not tackle them in this chapter. However, efforts to mention relevant information for the thread of the chapter have been made, especially for the aspects that have to deal with the most important part within the formation of the Salvadorian identity.

The last part has an almost testimonial sense of the events, practically since the new foundation of the Salvador Youth Symphony Orchestra. Special emphasis will be laid on this topic with no further financial or political details, because, although for many countries arts are a reflection of society and are worth capturing and recording, in El Salvador recordings talking about society were practically of no importance to the government.

Salvadorian musicians have shown dissatisfaction with the few opportunities that the government provides children and youngsters with the development of their artistic skills, not to mention the lack of job opportunities for those who, with great effort, have specialized abroad.

Therefore, El Salvador, a country of only 21,200 square kilometers and a current population of over six million people, has had, like the other countries in Central America, a social and political history of strong and violent social clashes and class struggles. Although the first music school was founded in 1700, people interested in music studies needed to learn to live in a double reality: that of creating and cultivating music and artistic activities in general while striving for their lives in a political system that has shown little interest in providing people in El Salvador with a developed musical culture that can go beyond the practices of the eighteenth- and nineteenth-century European bourgeois societies.

PRE-HISPANIC PERIOD

Little information is available on the music practices in El Salvador, if any, before the arrival of Spaniards (in Andres Niño's 1522 expedition). Records of the languages spoken therein exist, but there is little information regarding the aboriginals' day-by-day activities and the meaning they would give to music.

Mayas' influence arrived to the western area of the country. The Nahya and Pipil people were the rulers of the Valle de Chalchiapa, Cerrón Grande, and the downstream Rio Lempa. By the 1500s, Spaniards divided these territories in provinces: Eastern and Western Lempa, Cuscatlán and Izalco, and San Miguel.[3] Vital statistics show that by 1519,[4] population in the Rio Lempa sector was 450,000 in the west and 300,000 in the eastern side.

Aboriginal peoples in El Salvador dedicated to the trading of products such as animals, clothing, salt, fish, and others for their survival. Unlike Spaniards, aboriginals deemed golden and finished objects as ornamental pieces, with no monetary value at all.

They were very well organized religiously and politically. Chroniclers named in various ways the *caciques* (Indian chief) of the regions, with names such as "tecti" for the Pipiles, "teyte" for the Nicaraos. In El Salvador, they called them "papa," which means, basically, "the lord of all the land." This was the highest political position, followed by their subordinates, who ruled the smaller parts of the land.[5]

Samuel Martí, in his book *Instrumentos Musicales Precortesianos*, comments on instruments classified by Vicente T. Mendoza (a Mexican researcher). Among them are percussion, wind, and bowed string instruments as well as resources such as water and resounding objects:

> The Pre-Hispanic aboriginal musical organography in chroniclers' descriptions, codexes and recent archaeological findings are remarkable for the use of resources and technical development unknown in other peoples of a parallel evolution such as the use of resounding and vibrators or the use of water, either in percussion and wind instruments; teponaztlis with two, three and four reeds, some times with a water gourd.[6]

While Mendoza was referring in the first place to instruments in the Aztecan and Mayan regions, and not about any other instrument group, up to the point of discreetly excluding—as he says—parallel cultures, one can think, through the Mesoamerica's settlement theories, that other cultures in the region had such instruments.

COLONIAL PERIOD

Turning our sights to the past, to the colony times specifically, music practice in Latin America was used as an evangelizing tool on aboriginal peoples. Probably, Spaniards' intention was never that of spreading musical practices for the people's cultural development, much less for the creation of inclusive programs for the different groups aboriginal society was divided in: Ladinos,[7] Mestizos,[8] Spaniards, and others. No information is found about a musical tendency trying to include the Latin American aboriginal ways and styles to European music. Conversely, it is well known that the colonization was so voracious that it tried to destroy any indigenous trait among Latin American inhabitants. Naturally and fortunately for all of us, in spite of that, they had no success.

It is known that the region of the Captaincy General of Guatemala was one with the strongest anticolonial movements, whereby aboriginals showed their disagreement with the domination practices imposed thereon. To such an extent was its support that it was one of the regions that supported the independence movement between 1821 and 1823. Evidently, these movements would conclude generally in a strong crackdown by Spaniards. However, the germ of Enlightenment was already sown in the European thought, creating, after chaos due to the revolutionary ideas, the necessary crisis for the anticolonialist groups.[9]

INDEPENDENCE AND NATIONAL IDENTITY

After the events in the Spanish territory for the 1808 French invasion, many pundits adopted the Enlightenment ideas and encouraged many aboriginal uprisings, such as the 1811 uprising. But Spanish domain would not end there, and tough clashes between Spanish monarchs and French liberals were pivotal for the events in America.[10]

Throughout the whole independence process in Central America, which was very confusing and turbulent in nature, art practice, and, in a certain way, music practice were not an emancipating activity themselves, but quite the contrary—it was a way of supporting the European ideals in Latin America. In other Latin American countries such as Mexico, Venezuela, and Cuba, however, music was studied at a professional level, and it is even known that scholarships to different European countries[11] were granted to interested parties to deepen their knowledge.

No wonder why, then, the first music school founded in El Salvador was in the city of Sonsonate, with a large amount of aboriginal inhabitants and relatively far from San Salvador, the capital.

In more urbanized areas new groups started to appear, such as military groups, and their main function was playing in official events, and probably playing in nationalist parades. Among them was the *Banda de los Supremos Poderes* (Band of the Supreme Powers), founded in 1841.

José Escolástico Andrino[12] (1817–1862) founded the first music school in San Salvador in 1846. El Salvador had just become an independent republic in 1841. This first school was a private one, and so its maintenance was not the State's responsibility. Andrino, who besides being a musician was also an expert in other arts, showed great interest in music cultivation in El Salvador. It was him who founded in 1860 the first orchestra in El Salvador. From a musical family, Andrino's education was enough to teach students competently in his school.

Andrino had a very important role in music development in El Salvador, as he was the driving force behind a musical culture yet unknown in the country. Invited by San Salvador's bishop, he was appointed as both chapel master and organist to the San Salvador Cathedral.[13]

Little is known about the musical activities in El Salvador before the arrival of Jose Escolástico Andrino. Andrino himself made important publications, where there was evidence of the lack of historical and musical projects in the region. Existence of musical activity cannot be dismissed, however, as insufficient documents do not show its nonexistence. And as in all musical history, a great part of the musical activities was in charge of the people; that is, the people's activities with music.

In any case, Andrino was the starting point for the academic music education in El Salvador. This tradition was increasingly centralized and moved to San Salvador, where other projects were given the approval, and the development of the music school in El Salvador was planned.

Sonsonate is known for a great number of traditions ranging from craft to dances and music of *Izalco* aboriginal origins. Although surrounded by commercial areas such as the Acajtla, San Salvador, and Santa Ana ports, there are many towns that preserve many traditions such as the Nahuizalco, Juayua, San Pedro Masahuat, Santa Catarina Masahuat, and other hinterland towns of this department. Although pillaged by uprisings and colonialist practices, the region was able to keep its own culture and ethnic identity.

Traditions such as towns' typical dishes, patronage festivals,[14] always come with dances and folkloric attires, where mainly the "piteros"[15] and drum players execute traditional melodies or stylizations of Catholic melodies.

As described by David Díaz Arias in his article, "Entre la guerra de castas y la ladinización. La imagen del Indígena en la Centroamérica liberal, 1870–1944,"[16] during the early twentieth century, efforts to incorporate aboriginal features through artistic means were carried out in El Salvador. It was so because of the existing racism between social classes, and even between ethnic groups. This campaign was of conciliatory purposes, using art as a conciliatory means.

Writer Miguel Ángel Espino published in 1919, with a conciliatory purpose, his work *Mitologia de Cuscatlan*, with a series of national stories about the aboriginal mythology. In the area of music, folklorist María de Baratta, who had studied in both the United States and Europe, made efforts to highlight aboriginal figures in her creations.

However, urbanism and the great economic needs led to a dramatic proletarianization of aboriginals, who needed to move to cities to look for jobs.

EL SALVADOR AND MUSICAL ACTIVITY FROM THE TWENTIETH CENTURY TO PRESENT

From the Military Dictatorships to the 1980–1992 Civil War

Twentieth-century musical tradition in El Salvador is not but the reflection of this country's struggle for survival. It must be highlighted that music education had many artistic bonanza periods in spite of the long range of military regimes. The most representative one, because of bloodthirstiness, was General Maximiliano Hernández Martínez's, who started precisely in 1931.

In 1930 the National School of Music was created. As years passed, it would remain active, only changing names as administrations passed. In 1950 the Dirección General de Bellas Artes (General Fine Arts Department) was created. It already had a variety of artistic disciplines.[17] In 1952 the Conservatorio Nacional de Música (National Music Conservatory) was created. In 1967 both of them were shut down. However, the projects were not given up for dead, and they kept working although their institutional room in the State was not yet defined. With the 1968 educational reform, the high school program in arts was quickly included as part of the diversified cycle. In the program, students were given a diploma that enabled them to teach music (and others in performing and plastic arts) in regular education institutions. The National Center of Arts not only took care of music education but also of the education of students of other artistic areas such as visual arts, dance, and theater. The program included since early education a series of areas that would help students to get into art studies. The institution also offered a high school program with technical schools where students were given both music education courses and regular education courses. Regular and music lessons, as well as visual arts, dance, and dramatic arts, were taught in different buildings, far away from the other, and in poor conditions.[18]

The Centro Nacional de Artes (CENAR), the National Center for the Arts, was formally founded in 1970. In this phase, the CENAR took some responsibilities and made clear its mission of promoting artistic activities as a cultural experience[19] originally from the Fine Arts General Department.

Soon, the CENAR became the cradle for many projects of a deep artistic interest. It was then that the children's program was introduced to the school's program (1971), first as plastic arts, and then with added performing arts and music. The "Educación Básica en Música" programs, and the similar programs in plastic arts, a High School of Arts, specifically in the area of music that lasted from 1973 to 1978, are all part of this phase.

The CENAR had a gestation period, which was not so long as much as difficult and in which the government took no direct participation as the project manager of arts. Instead, as the 1980s drew closer, rulers realized that arts make people free, is a identity creator, and is an intellectual and critical-mentality creator, but it is a capital generator to become of the "state's interest." Many times and with different purposes this institution was almost shut down, first on grounds of being of no national interest (1981), and then on the basis of the program reformation (1985).

During this time, the school was moved to many places, generally unsuitable for a proper teaching process. The different CENAR headquarters were intended to remain closer for better management of the different artistic areas. Although in different places, it was kept in the capital, just in San Salvador's downtown.

By 1985, the goal was to detach high school from the art's program, and therefore the institution's ideology was changed and transformed exclusively into an art school. CENAR became thus the Instituto de Formación Artística (IFA). However, the education structure endured no major changes, and even some financial support was given under the name of IFA.

The first national band, the Banda de los Supremos Poderes, was founded in 1841. The band had the most important duties in the country. It was the symbol of the music tradition in El Salvador. In 1952, the Banda de la Fuerza Armada (Armed Force Band) was created, which would become the National Symphonic Orchestra in 1960.

Although of poor technical musical development, it can be said it was in the period before the civil war that national and especially international artists became popular in El Salvador. Even many musicians would travel abroad to perfect their music knowledge.

Postwar Music Situation

Although the war was over after the January 1992 Peace Accords, the postwar years were very tough for people, and therefore for musical activity. With unsuitable facilities and lack of instruments and teachers, the music school began a process of musical growth and renaissance. The country was still mourning the victims of the conflict. Many former combatants needed to get back to a civilian life, most of them with many psychological traumas due to the war's cruelty.

Many boys attended the Suzuki Method programs, which, although not applied in full extension with this methodology's philosophy, it was sowing enjoyment through music practice into society again. A new generation was emerging after the years of war, in which, luckily for these children, musical-related activities had not been totally razed.

Many regional or cantonal music schools opened. Although far from professionalizing students, these schools would encourage people in the consumption of art. Many times, the music taught in those schools was band songs or Salvadorian traditional music. Naturally, bands continued with their purposes generally of a military nature, and towns with a majority aboriginal population preserved music, dances, and instruments among their traditions. Bands played in Christian religious traditions such as Easter processions and the celebration of patron saints in these towns.

In 1994 the building that would be home of the CENAR was finished, with facilities that were more suitable to artistic activities. There was plenty of room in that building—for the student population at that time, at least—to accommodate plastic arts and music students.

One of the pivotal events during this phase was the refoundation of the El Salvador's Youth Symphonic Orchestra that was cured by a commission of Venezuelan maestros, and held in 1995 with the support of the Pro Arte de El Salvador Foundation.[20]

The Youth Symphonic Orchestra rose again in just one week, when many national musicians, of all instruments, gathered like never seen before at the CENAR. Recorders, piano, choirs, and other orchestral instruments—they gathered to welcome to the new orchestra.

At the end of the Venezuelans' commission mission, the orchestra went under the command of violinist Elmer Amaya. Mr. Amaya is popular in El Salvador because of his initiatives at the Suzuki Academy. During this phase, many tours were held in the country for the orchestra to become popular, and for children's and youngster's involvement. The Pro Arte Association helped enormously in the accommodation of students from

El Salvador's hinterland. As expected, the Youth Orchestra downsized little by little because of the difficulty in students' transportation to their rehearsal. Additionally, social problems were making free transit more difficult, and one of the major problems scourging El Salvador now was starting to emerge: organized crime and Maras.

Despite the social and financial unrest in the country, the Youth Orchestra was able to continue, and they even received a new conductor, Cuban master Julián Blanco, who started the orchestra direction in 1996. With him, many Cuban outstanding maestros in the music area arrived. Their training and aptitude provided some help to many students. Among them were the Cuban maestros Jose Iglesias and the deceased Cuban musicologist Pedro Martínez.

This new acquisition by the orchestra allowed the project's consolidation. These well-trained people helped the orchestra when they were not touring in the hinterland to get familiar with a more difficult repertoire as well as to show this repertoire to people.

One characteristic of the Salvadorian society is the great stratification in social groups, and obviously, the Youth Orchestra was the scenario for social clashes. Little importance was perceived toward students coming from schools from other Salvadorian departments,[21] and priority was given to students coming from private schools in the capital. Music education was under the service of a minority coming from the most well-off social circle. As throughout El Salvador's history, well-off people were the ones that could afford education abroad for their musician sons. Many students sought ways to perfect themselves in countries such as Costa Rica, Mexico, Guatemala, or the United States, and doing music is just a good excuse for the union between those social classes. One criticism of that time toward students was their evident elitism among the most well-off members of the group.

But not only mismanagement by governments has affected arts negatively; geographical vulnerability, intrinsic to this region, has caused natural disasters that have hit economies in the region tremendously, and have left their own mark in the different areas of life in Central America. By 1999, El Salvador's financial situation was a very critical one. With the pass of the Mitch hurricane, both agricultural production and tourism decreased, affecting El Salvador directly or indirectly. By 2001, earthquakes in January and February left the country in a tight situation. Many national projects were not possible to carry out, and with them, music progress.

By 2000, a music academy was created, and it was a part of the Youth Symphonic Orchestra. This effort helped students refresh their knowledge.

By 2002, the Youth Symphonic Orchestra's direction changed to Maestro Germán Cáceres. Maestro Cáceres had been the principal director of El Salvador's National Symphonic Orchestra for many years (1985–1999, 2002 to present). By 2003, Uruguayan maestro Martín Rodrígo Jorge was hired. He is the current principal conductor of the El Salvador Youth Symphonic Orchestra.

On the other hand, music education in public schools is primarily focused on teaching and learning some nationalist or people's songs. There is no interest by the state to create a program of real education in popular, folk, or classical music.

There is no higher education in music in El Salvador. There is not a university program in music, and there is no national conservatory that can give people the opportunity to get an advanced education at a professional music level.

Currently, music environment in El Salvador has changed in many aspects. Art as an elite's symbol has increasingly become a common practice, with no social difference at all. It probably has become a more supportive environment. Concerts by the National Symphonic are free now, and music is merely a vehicle to escape from violence.

There are efforts to establish a social inclusion program in El Salvador, which basically consists in the creation of musical groups that can carry children and youngsters away from violence. These should be of small wonder, as many other Latin American countries such as Mexico and Costa Rica have carried out similar plans, presumably inspired by Venezuela's *El Sistema*.

Many musicians have struggled for the continuation of this musical activity in El Salvador, but more time is yet to pass before we can see an important change in El Salvador's musical area.

CONCLUSION

For many decades, music education in El Salvador has suffered remarkable deficiencies in several aspects—little advertisement, no level staff, little financial support by the State, exclusion of regular education programs, and others. Even so, many musicians—who, in the best of the cases, have had the chance to study abroad—remain with the idea that there should always be an artistic outlet for society, as music and other arts. However, social problems overwhelming the population directly affect musicians. Personal insecurity affects both children and youngsters to such an extent that it makes it impossible to think of playing an instrument when you know basic food for survival is not guaranteed. Music appreciation, much less playing an instrument or becoming professional musicians, are not among most Salvadorians' priorities. Simply put, there is no a way leading to musical professionalism without traveling abroad. The music market is, therefore, very small. There is only one professional orchestra, which now the State makes efforts to support.

El Salvador could aspire to have music as a way to reach those outsiders in society. It is not an easy task, but by observing the orchestral movements that have emerged in Latin America one can argue that music has a certain effect and helps in people's awareness-raising process. No limits have been proven yet about music's benefits. The best example is, evidently, Venezuela's *El Sistema*.

El Salvador has a long and important history to tell about both its experience and traditions. However, a way for the protection, diffusion, and for growth encouragement of El Salvador's traditions should be sought. Time will pass before music in El Salvador can reach a good and competitive level.

NOTES

1. The FMLN is a Leftist political party formed after the 1980s conflict, a conflict that concluded in 1992. It was called Farabundo after Farabundo Marti, who led the 1932 peasant uprising. He was executed by orders of President Maximiliano Hernandez Martinez that same year, alongside other peasant leaders such as Mario Zapata and Alfonso Luna Calderon, accused of communism.

2. Gangs wresting for territorial dominance of drug-dealing control and the subjugation of their rivals. They are very violent. Their presence became more relevant after the 1980s civil war. They first originated in Los Angeles, and arrived in El Salvador through criminals deported from the United States.

3. G. Hasemann and Gl. Lara Pinto, "Historia General de Centroamérica," tom. I (Siruela, Madrid, 1993).

4. L. Rosero-Bixby, A. Pebley, and A. Bermudez Mendez, "De los Mayas a la planificación familiar" (San Jose, Costa Rica: University of Costa Rica, 1997).

5. Hasemann and Pinto, "Historia General de Centroamérica," 195.

6. S. Marti, *Instrumentos Musicales Precortesianos* (Mexico: Instituto Nacional de Antropologia, 1955), 19.

7. Initially, a Ladino was someone who spoke more than one tongue. Later, in the seventeenth and eighteenth century, it would be used for individuals of mixed race. The term *Ladino* can also be applied to aboriginals who would dress up like Spaniards. Aboriginals would use it to define individuals that did not belong to their community.

8. *Mestizo* was the son/daughter of an aboriginal and a Spaniard.

9. Julio Cesar Pinto Soría, "La Independencia y la federación (1810–1840)," in *Historia General de Centroamérica*, vol. 3, ed. Hector Pérez Brignoli (Ediciones Siruela S. A., Madrid 1993), 85.

10. E. Fonseca, *Centroamerica: Su historia* (San Jose, Costa Rica: FLACSO, 1996), 127.

11. Alicia C. de Couve and Claudia Dal Pino, "Panorama histórico de la educación musical en Latinoamérica: Las instituciones de formación musical," *International Journal of Music Education* 34 (1999): 30–46.

12. T. M. Scruggs, "El Salvador," In Grove Music Online. Oxford Music Online, http://www.oxfordmusiconline.com/subscriber/article/grove/music/08745

13. I. de Gandarias, "Homenaje. Jose Escolástico Andrino. Datos biograficos," http://redmusical.org/homenaje/escolastico/index.php

14. Catholic Church saint's versions.

15. A player of a wooden fipple flute very similar to recorders.

16. David Díaz Arias, "Entre la guerra de castas y la ladinización. La imagen del Indígena en la Centroamérica liberal, 1870–1944," *Revista de Estudios Sociales* (Abril núm. 026, Universidad de Los Andes, Bogota, Colombia).

17. "Aspectos generales sobre el Centro Nacional de Artes," http://ri.ufg.edu.sv/jspui/bitstream/11592/7091/2/790.2-F475d-Capitulo%20I.pdf (accessed January 2, 2012).

18. Interview with former students of the Centro Nacional de Artes, March 2011.

19. "Aspectos generales sobre el Centro Nacional de Artes."

20. Author's personal experience.

21. *Department* is the name of the political divisions of El Salvador's provinces.

REFERENCES

Arias Gomez, J. (2005). *Farabundo Martí*. San Salvador, El Salvador: Editorial Abril Uno.

"Aspectos generales sobre el Centro Nacional de Artes." (2011). Accessed May 10. http://ri.ufg.edu.sv/jspui/bitstream/11592/7091/2/790.2-F475d-Capitulo%20I.pdf

de Couve, A. C., & Claudia Dal Pino. (1999). "Panorama histórico de la educación musical en Latinoamérica: Las instituciones de formación musical." *International Journal of Music Education 34*:30–46.

de Gandarias, I. (2011). "Homenaje. Jose Escolástico Andrino. Datos biográficos." redmusical.org. Accessed May 10. http://redmusical.org/homenaje/escolastico/index.php

Diaz Arias, D. *Entre la guerra de castas y la ladinización. La imagen del Indígena en la Centroamérica liberal. 1870–1944*. Revista de Estudios Sociales, IV, 26. Bogota, Colombia: Universidad de Los Andes.

Fonseca, E. (1996). *Centroamerica: Su historia*. San Jose, Costa Rica: FLACSO.

Hasemann, G. & Gl. Lara Pinto. (1993). *Historia General de Centroamérica*. Vol. 6. Madrid: Sirulea.

Marti, S. (1955). *Instrumentos musicales precortesianos*. Mexico City, Mexico: Instituto Nacional de Antropología.

Pinto Soría, J. C. "La Independencia y la federación (1810–1840)," in *Historia General de Centroamérica*, vol. 3, ed. Hector Pérez Brignoli (Ediciones Siruela S. A., Madrid, 1993), 85.

Rosero-Bixby, L., A. Pebley, & A. Bermúdez Méndez. (1997). *De los Mayas a la planificación familiar*. San José, Costa Rica: UCR.

Sheridan Prieto, C. (2002). "Diversidad nativa, territorios y fronteras en el Noroeste novohispánico." *Desacatos* 10 (Fall–Winter). Mexico City, Mexico: Centro de Investigaciones y Estudios Superiores en Antropología Social.

Velázques, C. (2005). *Diccionario de términos coloniales*. San Jose, Costa Rica: UCR.

Chapter Eight

Guatemala

Edgar Cajas

INTRODUCTION

Guatemala has a long tradition of music. This can be seen in pre-Columbian times when the Mayan civilization flourished in music and the arts, in the production of European-inspired sacred compositions by natives during colonial times, in the musicians who wrote symphonies during the classical and romantic eras, and in the twentieth-century composers whose musical works have been played around the world. The marimba, considered a national instrument by Guatemalans, has reached high levels of performance and musicality, and rich music folklore is present in the daily lives of the Guatemalan people.

These aspects of musical life in Guatemala have been documented in several books, articles, and other publications. However, the process of teaching/learning music has not been adequately studied. In this chapter a panoramic view of the historical development of music education from pre-Hispanic to current times will be presented. A special emphasis will be given in this chapter to the role of music in the school curriculum rather than in artistic or professional formation.

Guatemala, situated south of Mexico and neighboring El Salvador and Honduras, is the largest country in Central America (42,042 square miles, about the size of Tennessee). It has a population of 14,361,666 (Instituto Nacional de Estadística, 2010), 40 percent of which are of Mayan descent and the other 60 percent *mestizo* (mixed European and indigenous ancestry). Guatemala and its neighboring countries in Central America were a colony of Spain for almost three hundred years, from its conquest in the sixteenth century until its independence in 1821. Its importance is demonstrated by the fact that it was the seat of the colonial Kingdom of Guatemala, exerting political and religious control over the rest of provinces at that time (Salvador, Honduras, Nicaragua, and Costa Rica).

THE BEGINNINGS OF MUSIC EDUCATION

Although many studies document the musical life of the ancient Mayans, who settled and flourished in the Middle America region, there is no historical information about formal music education among the indigenous peoples (Cabello & Martínez, 1988; O'Brien-Rothe, 2000; Olsen & Sheehy, 2000). This is true in part because their musical activities had a utilitarian purpose rather than a purely aesthetic one and because their songs were transmitted in an oral tradition.

According to Estrada (cited in Cabello & Martínez, 1988), the music from Central America, including Mexico, was deeply embedded in religion. Well-trained priest-musicians, both men and women, who were usually older, practiced music. Musicians were held in high esteem by society, evidenced by the fact that they were tax exempt. A perfect musical performance was expected from them and mistakes, which were sometimes punished by death, were considered an offense to the gods and an alteration to the harmony of the universe.

Diverse instruments such as drums, flutes, sea shells used as trumpets, and rattles were used for ceremonies, as the archeological findings show.

The study of chronicles transcribed as early as AD 1500 by Catholic priests who accompanied the conquistadors reveals that music and dance were used in specific rituals: magical, therapeutic, agricultural, and those related to war. One of these chronicles is the Mayan sacred book titled *Popol Vuh* (The Book of Counsel or Book of the Community), a sixteenth-century account of the creation and history of the world. In this book there is mention of singers, chanters, and flute players, but there is no description of how music was taught (O'Brien-Rothe, 2000). It is inferred that music was transmitted orally from generation to generation.

Music was present in the process of the discovery and conquest of the New World. Yurchenko (1996) describes the policy Spaniards used to conquer and colonize this part of the world: to destroy the Indian cultures, both rural and urban, and at the same time to enlist the surviving artists in building a new civilization to replace the old. In Central America, as well as in other regions of Latin America, Spanish Roman Catholic missionaries who accompanied the conquistadores introduced Spanish religious music traditions to the natives with little respect for local culture (Stevenson, cited in O'Brien-Rothe, 2000). These Catholic missionaries used music to spread their religion to aboriginals in two different ways: adults who participated by praying and singing in Christian ceremonies but did not receive formal musical instruction, and children who were taught to sing, write, and compose music and to play instruments (De Couve, Dal Pino & Frega, 1997). In some instances, local folk elements such as rhythms and melodies were incorporated in these music compositions. Lenhoff (2000) has done extensive research on the religious and secular compositions in which these local musical elements were introduced.

During the colonial period, Guatemala was part of a political unit known as *Audiencia* (Superior Court) or the Kingdom of Guatemala, a territory including Chiapas, currently a part of Mexico, through Costa Rica. Guatemala, the capital city of the Kingdom of Guatemala (now known as Antigua Guatemala), was also the center of musical life for the whole area. Its cathedral had an organist and a chanter since the time of its construction in 1534 (Behague, 2005). Colonial archives document the rich sacred repertoire performed there and in other churches from both European and local composers (Lenhoff, 2000). As in other countries, the process of colonization and the establishment of a European culture in Guatemala included a reproduction of the European system of music practice and training (Yurchenco, 1996).

Instruction in singing and in playing wind instruments for the performance of the sacred polyphony of Western Europe began early in the *Audiencia* of Guatemala (Stevenson, cited in O'Brien-Rothe, 2000). The teaching of plainchant is documented in the *Tratado de Santa Eulalia*, a manuscript from the sixteenth century that was discovered in 1963 in Huehuetenango (a town located in the northwestern part of the country). An interesting fact is that this music theory treatise was written in Nahuatl, a pre-Columbian language.

The learning of music by Guatemalan natives was facilitated by their natural inclination toward music, which was part of their cultural heritage, and by external conditions such as the exemption from severe tax laws for those who served in churches. This situation, according to Lenhoff (2000), led King Philip II to order a limit on the number of young natives admitted to musical education in churches and monasteries in the city of Santiago, formerly the capital of Guatemala. One of the most outstanding native musicians from the last part of the sixteenth century was Tomás Pascual (c. 1595–1635), born in San Juan Ixcoy, an Indian town in the west highlands of Guatemala. He became chapel master of one of the churches there. Some of his original compositions are well represented in the Huehuetenango manuscript mentioned above, both in Castilian and Indian languages (Behague, 2005; Flores, 2004a).

During the colonial period in Guatemala (sixteenth to the early part of the eighteenth century), musical instruction took place in an artisanship guild system. The young aspiring musician entered as an apprentice to serve his teacher-master in the choir. The teacher was in charge of providing him with general education and musical training, in addition to room and board. Sometimes the church helped with these expenses. After the student became proficient in music reading, writing, and instrument playing, he was promoted to an official position where he would spend the rest of his life. However, very few of these musicians became teachers. In addition to this system, there were other avenues of how music was taught: one through priesthood preparation and the other through family heritage. One example of the latter is the eighteenth-century Guatemalan composer Manuel Joseph Quiroz, whose nephew Rafael Antonio Castellanos y Quiroz became a famous singer, violinist, and composer. Maestro Castellanos trained many pupils under the apprentice system (Lenhoff, 2000). Almost all the academic music written up to this time was related to the Church: sacred music sung in Latin and other types of music such as semisecular cantatas and "villancicos."

In the early nineteenth century, which includes the period of independence from Spain and the establishment of the Republic of Guatemala in 1821, the training of professional musicians was done inside musical families. One of the most important families in local music in Guatemala at that time was the Sáenz family. Benedicto Sáenz, who died prematurely in 1831, and Benedicto Sáenz Jr. (1815–1857), a cathedral organist and *maestro de capilla* (chapel master) respectively, were both influential music teachers. The latter also contributed to the diffusion of Italian opera in Guatemala (Behague, 2005).

Starting around 1830, the musical instruction that previously was taught mainly by the mentorship modality was now taught in private music schools or academies started by prominent musicians. One of the schools most notable for the number and quality of students was that of Maximo Andrino. José Eulalio Samayoa, Rafael España, and Mateo Sáenz started other well-known schools of that time (Todo sobre musica marcial, 2009).

The liberal revolution of 1871 led by Justo Rufino Barrios brought many changes, including educational ones. A significant change was that public education became nonreligious, mandatory, and free. In 1880, music became part of the national curriculum and began to be taught in public schools. In the same year, the Public Instruction Office elaborated a music curriculum for all of the country. It was implemented in 1881 and included songs about nature, animals, and important persons. In spite of this law, few schools in the rural areas implemented this subject in their curricula (Educación Musical en el Área Rural, 2000).

One of the first school music teachers on record was a cornet player from one of the military bands. His salary was two reales per school (8 reales = 1 US silver dollar) (Ruiz, 2001).

Also at this time, the training of musicians for the military bands began. When an Italian opera company came to one of theaters in the city during the 1870 to 1871 season, the Italian Pedro Visoni came as director. The government of that time asked Maestro Visoni to direct one of the military bands. He realized that a school to train new musicians for these bands was necessary, and a "school of substitutes" was formed in 1872. In 1875, the German musician Emilio Dressner became the director of the principal military band in the city and also of the "substitute" school. He was so successful in instrumental music education that he was able to organize a concert in which at least 273 musicians participated. In this school, notable composers such as German Alcantara and Rafael Alvarez (composer of the national anthem) did their musical studies. Dressner later became the director of the National Conservatory of Music (Lenhoff, 2005).

In the same year, Juan Aberle, an Italian musician who immigrated to El Salvador, began a private school of music in Guatemala, which in turn became the National Conservatory of Music (Lenhoff, 2000). Some Guatemalan musicians, especially pianist-composers, went to Europe for musical training, such as Luis Felipe Arias (1876–1908) and Herculano Alvarado (1879–1921). Later they became teachers at the conservatory.

In the early twentieth century, National Conservatory of Music graduates carried out school music teaching. The conservatory provided exams and supervised the *maestros de canto* (song teachers), who taught music in the public schools. The emphasis on singing was probably due to the influence of bel canto and opera that flourished in the capital, especially in the upper and middle classes. The rest of the country, which was largely rural, did not get any of these music opportunities. Other teachers were members of the military bands or self-taught musicians. The first songbooks for children were published in the 1930s (Alvarado, 2004). Composers of educational songs during this period are Jesús María Alvarado (1896–1977), José Castaneda (1898–1983), and Miguel Sandoval (1903–1953) (Hoover, 2010).

The beginning of a more systematized training of music teachers can be traced to 1945, when Maestro Oscar Vargas, who received a music teacher degree in Spain, was asked to create a Fine Arts Office by the government. The same year a specific office for Aesthetic Education was created, and all the "music preceptors" (music teachers who were teaching music without a certificate) were called to receive music and pedagogy courses and thus become licensed music teachers.

In 1953, a Central America Music Teacher conference was held in La Ceiba, Honduras. After the conference, Guatemalan music education professors Héctor Waldemar Lainfiesta, Luis Alfonso Alvarado, and Rafael Sánchez asked the assistance of OEA (Latin American State Organization) to create a school for music teachers. They received scholarships from this organization to do specialized courses in music education in Mexico and Chile (50 Años de Rítmo y Alegría, 2009).

In 1959, the National Normal School for Music Teachers was founded under the Aesthetic Education Office with Jesús María Alvarado as its director; eight students were enrolled and only two graduated from this first class. Manuel Alvarado, upon his return from a study trip to England in 1960, became the director of this school and, along with his brother Alfonso Alvarado, reformed its course study plan. The curriculum, which they designed, included two main areas: an artistic area, which included music, literature, and instrumental courses, and a psycho-pedagogical area with pedagogy, methodology, and psychology courses. Students would take music theory, harmony, recorder, guitar, dance, drama, choir, marimba, and piano, plus courses on children's literature, music education methods, and practice teaching. The current curricula for music teacher training still include these areas. In 1966, this school became part of the Normal School system in Guatemala.[1] Currently, music teachers who teach at the elementary level need to be graduates of this kind of school.

In the twentieth century, several music textbooks for use in elementary and middle schools have been written and published in Guatemala. The following are some of the authors of these textbooks: Jesús María Alvarado, Roberto Valle, Antonio Vidal, Aníbal Delgado Requena, Dolores Batres de Zea, and Eduardo Tánchez. Manuel Gómez designed an early method of music training based on eurhythmics for children at the National Conservatory of Music during the 1970s. Manuel Alvarado has published books on music pedagogy (Flores, 2004b). More recently, the series of music textbooks most commonly used by elementary and middle school music teachers is Ethel Batres's *Viva la Música* (Cajas, 2010).

MUSIC TEACHER TRAINING INSTITUTIONS

Guatemala is one of the few countries in Latin America where music teacher training still takes place at the high school level. These schools are called Normal Schools, and all elementary teacher training is done following this modality.

As was stated earlier, the first national school for music teachers was founded in 1959 in Guatemala City. Currently there are two sections of this school: one functions in the mornings and the other in the evenings. In 1995, the first private school for music teachers in the city was opened under the direction of Dr. Edgar Cajas. There are four other schools of this nature in the rest of the country.

Another option to get a degree in music education is the *profesorado*, a three-year program after high school designed for those who will teach music in secondary schools. Two universities in Guatemala offer this degree: San Carlos State University and Universidad Del Valle. Due to the scarcity of music teachers, graduates from these programs teach on the elementary level as well, but without the necessary training to effectively teach this age group.

Currently the institution that prepares professional musicians is the National Conservatory of Music in Guatemala City, which offers a diploma at a high school level in each of the orchestral instruments.

In 2006, a music school sponsored by the municipality of Guatemala City was founded with the purpose of reaching at-risk children and youth and providing them with musical opportunities such as a youth orchestra and choir. Besides this school, there are six other municipal schools of music throughout the city. These schools follow the model of the Venezuela Youth Orchestra movement. There are other community music projects such as the Youth Orchestra of Santa Cruz Balanya, an Indian town in the west highlands of Guatemala. A farmer started this project, which was motivated by his love for music and education. The Philharmonic Chorus of Guatemala, a children's choir for high-risk children and youth in the outskirts of Guatemala City led by two young music teachers, performs classical choral music of the most sophisticated level. These two community projects were started and originally sponsored by evangelical churches.

The "Escuela Superior de Arte," a department of the San Carlos University Humanities School (the only state university in Guatemala), offers a five-year program (*licenciatura*) in diverse musical instruments. One of the private universities in the city, the Universidad del Valle de Guatemala, also offers a *licenciatura* in music to students who have completed the *profesorado* described above.

MUSIC EDUCATION IN THE SCHOOL CURRICULA

The first music curriculum published by the Ministry of Education dates from 1970. An interesting fact that shows the lack of clear objectives for music as a school subject is how the name has changed over time. At first it was called "Aesthetic Education," then it was part of "Practical Areas," and subsequently "Beauty, Work and Recreation," which included art, crafts, and music (Cajas, 2010).

As a result of the latest educational reform (2002–2005), music as a separate subject has been integrated into a broader area called Artistic Expression. According to the Ministry of Education, this reform was the result of the "peace agreements" signed in 1997 between the leftist guerillas and the government. This reform was also based on the cultural identity and rights of the indigenous groups in the country. Guatemala has twenty-two ethnic groups, each with its own language. One of the topics of the educational reform is the intercultural component, or the decision to apply the effects of interculturalism in the classroom. (R. D. Flores interview June 2, 2005, in Cajas, 2010).

Music education is now one of the five subareas of this subject. The other four are dance and movement, theater, visual art, and Guatemalan cultures. These five subareas are presented as a group of actions, which a teacher can use to develop artistic expression in the students. According to Ministry of Education officials, the students do not necessarily have to receive all these subareas. A grade teacher could choose two to three out of the five different areas that are suggested and work on them for 2.5 to 3 hours a week (R. D. Flores interview, June 23, 2006, in Cajas, 2010). On January 2005, this new curriculum came into effect for the first three grades of the elementary level.

Although a curriculum guide for the area of Artistic Expression has already been published to complement core subjects such as mathematics and social studies, there is no specific curriculum for music. Similar reforms and the inclusion of music in broader areas have also taken place in other countries such as El Salvador and Honduras. However, in Guatemala the subject of Artistic Expression has well-defined subareas and not much integration with other subjects (E. Batres interview, June 2006, in Cajas, 2010).

The Ministry's intention is that the classroom teacher should teach the area of Artistic Expression, or the music teacher, if one is available. Adequate training in the new curricula has been one of the problems. Currently the only specialized teacher training that exists is in musical education; there are no credentials to teach the other subareas (R. D. Flores interview, January 18, 2005, in Cajas, 2010). According to the director for curricular development of the Ministry of Education, the intention of the new national curricula was to dedicate two hours a week to the Artistic Expression area, as was done for the other subjects in the curriculum.

A more recent study (Cujcuy, 2010) on the classroom teacher's perspective of the implementation of this new area shows that most teachers have not been prepared to teach this area. They are mainly focusing on visual art since it is what they feel more comfortable doing. However, they are not following a sequence in the art concepts, nor are they developing creativity in their work with the children.

CURRENT SITUATION OF SCHOOL MUSIC EDUCATION

The whole country of Guatemala has a disproportionately low number of music teachers who work at the elementary level. According to the Ministry of Education's music coordinator for the area of Artistic Expression, in 2005 there were nineteen thousand public primary schools with ninety thousand primary teachers. Of these nineteen thousand schools, only 763 have music teachers, meaning that more than eighteen thousand schools have none. For these 763 schools there are only 204 music teachers, and therefore most of these music teachers work in more than one school (R. D. Flores interview, January 18, 2005, on Cajas, 2010).

The extremely low number of music teachers in the country has been recognized as the main problem affecting music education in Guatemala. This scarcity of music teachers is due in part to the crisis that affects education in Guatemala in general. The following interview excerpt demonstrates the dilemma of hiring music teachers versus general classroom teachers:

> The problem in Guatemala is that there is still a crisis in covering all levels of education. In the face of this crisis, what should the Ministry of Education do? Should it appoint a music teacher or a classroom teacher who will cover all the

areas of the curriculum? As you know, in Guatemala we still have schools with only one room and schools with multi-grade classrooms. (H. Reyes interview, January 17, 2005, on Cajas, 2010)

Additional factors that contribute to the minimal coverage of music education in the country are that most music teachers stay in the city and only a limited number of class periods are available for music in each public school.

Especially in its capital city, Guatemala has a large percentage of private schools, both at the elementary and secondary levels. However, the number of music teachers working in the private sector is unknown even to the Ministry of Education officials. Flores (2004b) estimates that approximately 1,200 music teachers are working at private schools. Among the 105 music teachers who participated in a survey in Guatemala during 2005 to 2006 (Cajas, 2010), thirty-four (32.4 percent) taught in public schools and seventy-one (67.6 percent) in private schools. These figures demonstrate the greater availability of teachers to work in private institutions compared with teachers in the public sector. Private schools generally offer a better quality of education, including artistic subjects like music, due to a greater availability of resources (more equipment, better salaries for teachers, etc.).

In the same survey for music teachers (Cajas, 2010), results showed that a large majority of the teachers participating in the study were male (66.8 percent). A possible explanation for this finding is that in Central America, males generally have more access to education. This is especially true in Guatemala where, according to *Eduquemos a la niña*, published by the Ministry of Education, the average indigenous female received an average of 0.9 years of education, and nearly 70 percent of indigenous women never completed primary school. In Guatemala, more than one-third of the population is indigenous, most of them being of Mayan origin.

Concerning the teachers' ages, most surveyed teachers (35.1 percent) fell in the bracket of twenty-one to thirty years old, and another 30.9 percent were between thirty-one and forty years old. Guatemala, in comparison to countries such as Honduras and Costa Rica, had the largest percentage of teachers between the ages of twenty-one and thirty (45.7 percent) (Cajas, 2010).

Regarding instrumental school groups, the most common ensembles are percussion bands. Traditionally in Guatemala, and especially at secondary schools, percussion marching ensembles or "bands" participate in the *15 de Septiembre* (September 15) holiday parade. This parade has existed for many years to commemorate the independence of Central American countries from Spain in 1821. The main instruments used in these ensembles are drums, cornets, and portable glockenspiels called "lyras." These groups are typically called *bandas de guerra* ("war bands").

> Before they used those little trumpets called cornets, but now they buy trumpets and they add a tuba, and some buy a drum set. I would dare to guess that 90% of all public secondary schools in the country have a band, although the figure would be lower in private schools. (E. Batres, interview, July 2, 2006, in Cajas, 2010)

Marimba, considered the national instrument of Guatemala, is another musical ensemble used in schools, mainly at the secondary level.[2] Some schools will have choirs, and a few private schools will have wind or string ensembles.

Recently, the Ministry of Education, through the Artistic and Corporal Education Program (*Programa de educación artística y corporal [APRENDO]*), has published manuals for these musical ensembles. The project, called the National Program for Choirs, Bands, Orchestras and School Ensembles (*Programa nacional de coros, bandas, orquestas y conjuntos escolares*), is funded by several international organizations.

The Ministry of Education's budget for music is designated only to pay teachers' salaries. There is no provision to buy equipment or other materials or to improve the teachers' professional level. It is up to the schools to look for funds to buy their instruments and other materials to teach music. The main instruments used in schools are the recorder (generally the plastic model), electronic keyboards, and basic percussion instruments.

Due to the high educational deficit in the areas of reading and writing in Guatemala and the low budget for education, there are no plans for the future to include budgetary provisions to buy equipment or to print textbooks for music. However, it is interesting that there are textbooks for other areas considered "fundamental," such as mathematics, natural science, language, and social studies.

You know that among Central American countries, we are next to last in how much money we spend on education. We were spending 2.98% of the national income when the peace agreements were signed. By the year 2000 we should have been spending 6% . . . compared with 1999, but we are still a long way off. (H. Reyes, interview, January 17, 2005, in Cajas, 2010)

Part of the problem faced by music education in Guatemala (i.e., low number of music teachers, lack of financial support to buy equipment and materials) is that although the Ministry of Education would be interested in promoting and supporting all areas of the curriculum, including the new area of Artistic Expression, the current priority is to ensure that students finish their elementary education.

Currently, there is no evaluation or supervision system for music teachers. In the past, the Aesthetic Education Office of the Ministry of Education was in charge of supervising the work of the music teachers, as well as theater, art, and dance teachers. Another obstacle in the advancement of music education programs and projects, according to the opinion of one of the music educators interviewed, is the lack of continuity in the programs due to political interests.

The Ministry of Education, financed by international institutions such as the World Bank, has begun a professional development program for music teachers, especially those serving in the areas of Escuintla, Sacatepéquez, and Chimaltenango (three *departamentos* in Guatemala). Music teachers from these areas will come to Guatemala City to receive the courses to update their training and will receive a certificate after having completed one hundred hours of study. The requirements to participate are to have graduated as music teachers from a Normal School and to be teaching in any school, whether public or private.

The Ministry of Education has designed another proposal to help classroom teachers integrate music in the teaching of other subjects in the curriculum. These guides do not lay out a curriculum with a specific content; they are more like anthologies of simple activities. As E. Batres explained:

You cannot have complicated activities with people who know nothing about music. These guides contain rhythmic games, a lot of oral tradition, and very pleasant songs with ideas on how to use them. It also includes goals, the activity itself, and how to relate the activity to mathematics, for example. It is definitely a useful resource because they assume that the classroom teacher will not be teaching music. They assume it will be a musical activity that will motivate the class or activate the other hemisphere of the brain. (E. Batres interview, July 2, 2006, in Cajas, 2010)

Since 2006, there has been a general coordinator for the Artistic Expression area and a second coordinator to work with the preschool level. These offices were created as an outcome of the latest educational reform.

Another new program sponsored by the new Artistic Expression Unit is the "Musical Classroom" project, an extension of the "Schools of Excellence" program started by the former government. Approximately fifty public schools are involved in this program, the emphases of which include mathematics, Spanish, and technology.

The Latin American Forum for Music Education (FLADEM), created in Costa Rica in 1995, is a network of music educators in Latin America, which organizes yearly congresses in different countries and promotes conferences and workshops in each country. The Guatemalan chapter has organized several conferences and workshops not only in the city but also in other parts of the country. Local initiatives and contextualized pedagogical approaches are presented in these meetings as well as new materials such as recordings and publications for children's music. This nongovernment organization has provided the music educator community with professional development, fellowship, and networking opportunities. Almost every music teacher in the country is now a member of this organization.

Private schools such as the Christian School for Music Teachers "Alfredo Colom" have organized workshops with international music education specialists.

Although music has been incorporated as a component in the new national curriculum, the low number of music specialists, the limited training in music offered to classroom teachers, and the lack of logistic support from the government authorities means that music education remains unavailable to the majority of the student population, especially at the elementary level. At the secondary level, music is still an independent subject and is compulsory.

One possible means of alleviating this situation could be to implement a national advocacy campaign for music education, emphasizing the worth of music in the whole education of a child—for example, the importance of music in cultural identity, boosting achievement in other academic areas, and combating attrition without losing the intrinsic values of music education.

CONCLUSION

In summary, we have seen that Guatemala has had a long tradition of music: the ancient Mayans' used music, both vocal and instrumental, in everyday activities; natives during colonial times wrote highly complex church music after the European model of the time; national composers created classical symphonies; works by more recent composers such as Jorge Sarmientos and Joaquín Orellana have been played in international venues; and pop singers such as Ricardo Arjona are well known throughout Latin America. All these facts show that musical potential in Guatemala clearly exists. This long musical tradition needs to be preserved and new musical outputs encouraged through a broader and more inclusive music education.

There is a pressing need to offer to the majority of children and young people an opportunity to profit from the numerous values of music. Music education should be a right of every person in our country; therefore, the government should more decisively support the music component in the new "artistic expression" area of the school curriculum, hire more music teachers, and encourage the production and dissemination of new approaches to teach music in the context of our culture. Community music projects need to be supported and funded by local businesses and the international community, and music training institutions need to be renovated to improve the existing study programs.

In spite of present limitations, including a lack of resources to provide the basics for more efficient music teaching, the limited number of music teachers employed by the government, the training of music teachers that is done at the tertiary level, and scarce or no support by the government for the arts in general, music education enthusiastically takes place in the country by resilient music educators who share a vision and a deep conviction that music can help form better and more well-rounded persons. This in turn will make Guatemala a better place to live, knowing that we are heirs of a rich and long musical tradition and that, since music still plays a crucial role in our daily lives, music is paramount in the education of the generations to come.

NOTES

1. In Guatemala, in order to become a kindergarten, elementary, PE, music, or any other type of teacher at the elementary level, the student must finish three years of middle school and enter a three-year program. Music Education is a four-year program.

2. In Guatemala, a marimba band includes a smaller marimba for three players and a larger marimba for four players. Sometimes a drum set and a string bass are added.

REFERENCES

50 Años de Ritmo y Alegría en la Educacion en Guatemala. (2009). Retrieved December 2, 2010, from http://enmemjesusmariaalvaradoji50.blogspot.com

Alvarado, M. (1992). *Hechos . . . Verdades* [Facts . . . Truths]. Guatemala: Técnicos en Comunicaciones Graficas.

Alvarado, M. (2004). *Los años de mi vida: Memorias de Manuel Alvarado* [The Years of My Life: Memories of Manuel Alvarado]. Guatemala City: Magna Terra Editores.

Behague, G. (2005). Guatemala, I Art Music. In L. Macy (Ed.), *Grove Music Online*. Retrieved September 5, 2005, from http://www.grovemusic.com

Cabello, P., & Martínez, C. (1988). *Música y Arqueología en América Pre-Colombina* [Music and Archeology in Pre-Colombian America]. Oxford, England: Bar International Series.

Cajas, E. (2010). *Music Education in Central America.* Saarbrucken, Germany: LAP Lambert Academic Publishing.

Cujcuy, M. A. (2010). Expresión Artística y Práctica Educativa de Educación Primaria en Escuelas Oficiales de Guatemala. Unpublished master's thesis, Universidad de San Carlos de Guatemala.

De Couve, A. C., Dal Pino, C., & Frega, A. L. (1997). An Approach to the History of Music Education in Latin America. *The Bulletin of Historical Research in Music Education, 19*(1), 10–30.

Educación Musical en el Área Rural: Docencia Experimental en Escuelas de Nivel Primario [Music Education in Rural Areas: Experimental Teaching in Elementary Schools]. (2000). Escuela Nacional para Maestros de Educación Musical [ENMEM] Jesús María Alvarado Seminario, XV Promoción Jornada Matutina. Unpublished manuscript, Guatemala.

Eduquemos a la Niña. (2007). Centroamerica: Guatemala. Asocaicion Eduqemos a la Niña. Retrieved June 3, 2007 from http://eduqemosalanina.centroamerica.com

Flores, R. (2004a). *Análisis Practico-Didáctico de la Metodología utilizada por Maestros de Educación Musical en las Escuelas Primarias de la Ciudad de Guatemala* [Analysis Practical-Pedagogical in Elementary Schools in Guatemala City]. Unpublished master's thesis, Universidad Rafael Landívar, Guatemala, Guatemala.

Flores, R. (2004b). *La Docencia Musical en Guatemala, Problemas y Perspectivas.* Unpublished manuscript.

Hoover, M. (2010). *A Guide to the Latin American Art Song Repertoire: An Annotated Catalogue of 29th Century Art Songs for Voice and Piano.* Bloomington, IN: Indiana University Press.

Instituto Nacional de Estadística. (2010). *Población.* Retrieved from https://www.ine.gob.gt/sistema/uploads/2014/02/26/L5pNHMXzxy5FFWmk9NHCrK9x7E5Qqvvy.pdf

Lenhoff, D. (2000). Guatemala. In *Diccionario de la Música Española e Hispanoamericana* (Vol. 6, 1–11). Madrid, Spain: Sociedad General de Autores y Editores.

Lenhoff, D. (2005). *Creación musical en Guatemala.* Guatemala: Universidad Rafael Landívar y Fundación G&T Continental, Editorial Galería Guatemala.

O'Brien-Rothe, L. (2000). Guatemala. In D. A. Olsen & D. E. Sheehy (Eds.), *The Garland Handbook of Latin American Music* (175–90). New York: Garland Publishing, Inc.

Olsen, D. A., & Sheehy, D. E. (Eds.). (2000). Guatemala. In *The Garland Handbook of Latin American Music.* New York: Garland Publishing, Inc.

Ruiz, B. C. (2001). *Spanish Colonial Currency.* Retrieved November 2, 2010, from http://bellsouthpwp.net/r/u/ruiz_b/colonial_currency/colonial_currency_index.htm

Todo sobre música marcial: Escuela Militar de Musica Rafael Alvarez Ovalle. (2009). Retrieved November 30, 2010, from http://todomusicamarcial.blogspot.com/2009/01/escuela-militar-de-msica-rafael-alvarez.html

Yurchenco, H. (1996). An Introduction to Indian Mexico and Guatemala from Pre-Hispanic Times to the Present. *The Sonneck Society for American Music, 12*(3), 1–10.

Chapter Nine

Mexico

Antonio Fermín

INTRODUCTION

This chapter examines the various musical and sociocultural developments that have influenced music education in Mexico—from its early stages in the pre-Conquest era to modern times. It recognizes the value of social movements in defining the nation's musical urgency by providing an understanding of music teaching and learning in broad historical and cultural contexts. With the largest media industry in Latin America, modern Mexican society displays a wide and diverse musical spectrum; it spans from the traditional *mariachi, banda, norteño, ranchera,* and *corridos* to Mexican rock.

The study of musical education in Mexico signifies a collective awareness of its immense impact on the lives of children and young adults today. An ethically diverse culture, Mexico embraces more than sixty indigenous languages that are still spoken in the country. This diversity has notably influenced the scope of attitudes in providing educational opportunities to urban and rural communities alike. But the core element of Mexican national identity is formed on the basis of a synthesis of European culture with indigenous culture in a process known as *mestizaje*.

This process was further stressed through the efforts of postrevolutionary reformers toward building a true Mexican national identity. Each Mexican region exhibits distinct musical characteristics. In the Huatesca region, for example, the Spanish influence, particularly that of Andalucia, is apparent with its lively rhythms and melodic cadences. In the mountain regions, the music is more sad and monotonous, in contrast with that of coastal areas where it is happy due to the strong African and Spanish influences.

In Chiapas and Oaxaca the *marimba*, a percussion instrument of African origins, plays a significant role. In the Indigenous region Mixe of Oaxaca, state band music is passed on from generation to generation, and children learn how to read a musical score in parallel with learning the Spanish language. Thus, music education functions at its best in this social setting—family traditions such as weddings, christenings, or funerals are essential events in this process. The only commercial music is that heard on radios and televisions, which people try to imitate by ear (Villanueva Pezet and Bañuelos Calvo, 2007).

Mexican society is firmly based upon the home and the family, and the musical skills of Mexican children are directly related to the abilities of the adults that immediately surround them. As a result, the transmission of traditional music has been historically embedded in the oral tradition. Through this informal process, music is learned primarily through observation, followed by imitation. Children's songs and games play critical roles for learning opportunities and musical growth. Enculturation plays a crucial role in this transmission, with music and dancing permeating every social activity from youth to old age.

Baily and Doubleday (1987) maintain that "the study of musical enculturation is one of the keys to understanding musical systems as cognitive phenomena, for it shows how cognitive schemata are built up and reveals the kinds of information necessary for their development." Beginning with the process of conversion led by the Franciscan friars in 1523, the Indians assimilated and altered the European art forms, making them a part of their "ancestral traditions" (Truit, 2010, 311–30). Since then, Mexican culture has experienced important sociocultural reforms that link this new national identity with educational practices. More evident, however, are the correlations encountered in subsequent periods—all of which have emerged and manifested distinct signs of musical developments. In addition, an acculturation process extended during the three hundred years of the colonial era and the years following independence in 1810. This process involved the rhythms and melodies of Indians, Spaniards, and Blacks to produce a music that eventually evolved into distinctly Mexican (or *mestizo*) forms (George, 1987, 195).

Several studies have contributed greatly to the understanding of the educational processes occurring in the field of Mexican music. Pointing to the earliest periods, Gabriel Saldívar (1934) broke new ground in colonial and early independence era history with his publication, *Historia de la Música de México*. In his essential monograph, *Music in Mexico* (1952) and *Music in Aztec and Inca Territory* (1976), Robert Stevenson focuses on indigenous music in the pre-Hispanic and colonial periods. *La Conquista Musical de México* (1993) by Lourdes Turrent examines music in its symbolic and social roles, the changes it underwent during the early colonial period, and its use as a tool of conquest and evangelization. In contrast, Jonathan Truitt (2010) addresses the issue of music being used not just as a tool for evangelization but also how it was adopted into the everyday lives of normal people.

MUSICAL CONDITIONS IN THE PRE-CONQUEST PERIOD (1492–1519)

Music was an integral activity at all levels of society prior to the arrival of the Spaniards. Evidence found in paintings, artifacts, and Spanish chronicles indicates that music was a central activity in Mayan culture (Bourg, 2005). Ceremonial music was often related with sun worship, battles, and crop harvest, in addition to labor of various kinds and with public expressions of joy or mourning (Hague, 1934, 66).

Moreover, Nettl (2004) explains that, often, listening was not the objective of music during the pre-Columbian period. Instead, it was a cultural activity performed by both child and adult, commoner and elite. One function of music was therefore to indicate prestige through the use of music and musical instruments. Cultural characteristics are evidenced particularly through the various musical instruments preserved today (Stevenson, 1952, 17–19). For instance, Bishop Landa of Yucatan, (1524–1579), an early writer, commented on the instruments he found among the Mayas as "small kettledrums, played with the hand, and another made of hollow wood, played with a wooden sticks, with a small ball on the end made from the milk of a certain tree" (Hague, 1934, 17).

Instrumental resources found in ancient Mexico are grouped into three categories: (1) *Winds*: flutes, *Chili-lihtli* (large flutes); and *ocarinas* and pan flute, *Tlapitzalli* (small flutes); sea shells, *Atecocoli*; (2) *Percussion*: vertical drum, *Huehuetl*; horizontal drum, *Teponaxtle*; pumpkin rattles, *Tzicahuaztli*; *güiros* made with human bones, *Omichitzicahuaztli*; gourds filled with grains, *Ayacaztli*; and (3) *Strings*: a resonant box with five strings, *Tinya*. In this regard, Stevenson (1952) maintains that "music was used solely in a functional capacity, dealing with religious and cult rituals . . . music was a communal, not an individual expression and some instruments such as the *huehuetl* (vertical drum) and *iteponatzli* (slit drum) were considered sacred."

Instruments of percussion dictated in many ways the spirit and function of many levels of society with rhythm performed in a succession of steady, quick beats. The large bands of drums (*chunk'u*) are depicted in murals, codices, and burials as being instruments of ceremonial significance. Percussion instruments were now replaced with the new instruments with melodic possibilities. The latter categorization has references of early aerophones that include ceramic whistles, *ocarinas*, and flutes. The pentatonic scale seems to have been predominant, with some flutes producing diatonic and chromatic intervals. Similarly, Aztec singing was characterized by monophonic, pentatonic vocalizations that were rhythmic and accompanied by wind instruments and drums.

Daniel Castañeda and Vicente T. Mendoza (1933) published the first volume of *Instrumental Precortesiano*, an extended work with numerous illustrations, diagrams, and measurements of pre-Cortesian instruments. Several nationalistic composers incorporated the coloristic sounds of these ancient instruments into their compositions. Among them, Carlos Chávez (1899–1978) used the *huehuetl* (tubular drum) and the *tyeponaxtle* (drum carved from hollow trunk) in *Cuatro Soles* (1925) and the *jícara de agua* (gourd drum) in the *Sinfonía India* (1935–1936). Some insights as to how Aztec music might have sounded can be heard in the music of present-day Indian tribes who have remained outside of mainstream of contemporary life, such as the *Cora* and *Huichol* Indians. Songs and dances served as a diversion and as a way of communication; young people would gather at the *cuicacalli*, educational centers where they could learn about history and heroic deeds through music and dance.

SPANISH CONQUEST AND COLONIZATION (1519–1810)

The influence of the Catholic Church in Mexico during this extended period tended strongly toward intense conservatism. The opportunities for cultural contacts with the rest of the world were limited. Spain restricted the commercial and cultural contacts of the colonies by forbidding all trade and limiting the number of fleets during the year. The result of such prohibitions, from the musical standpoint, was that the colonies clung to archaic types of instruments or songs long after Spain itself had evolved new kinds (Hague, 1934, 62).

Music was a necessary part of the Church ritual, and many of the Christian missionaries sent to Mexico placed emphasis on the musical training of the Indians since music was an integral part of Church ceremony. They brought with them their own music, including Masses, *Magnificats*, and other Church-related forms that were faithfully copied, thus establishing congregational singing, Western harmonies, and choirs. The first printing press in Mexico had already been introduced in 1536 with many of the early books devoted to church music. In fact, Mexico was the first country in the Western Hemisphere to publish a book with musical notation; it was an Ordinary of the Mass printed in Mexico City in 1556. The printing of another volume with Gregorian chants for the Holy Week followed in 1604 (Slonimsky, 1947, 255).

Pedro de Gante (1480–1572) established a school for church music in Texcoco—the first of its kind in the Western hemisphere. His aim was the teaching of hymns, liturgical chants, and Gregorian musical notation to the Indians. In 1527, he moved the school to Mexico City to educate the natives and sons of Spanish officials. A gradual synthesis of native and Spanish elements emerged in the music of the time. Nettl (1985) examines these pedagogical developments and asserts that "as musical styles converged, traditional practices by which music was taught and learned began a transformation."

Whether indigenous music changed as a result of modifications in educational practices or whether changes in music and music training occurred simultaneously is not all together clear" (Campbell, 1991, 192). Similarly, Turrent (1993, 128) eloquently points out, "There is no doubt that, music was the ideal tool to attract the indigenous people to the newly imposed religion; the adjoining schools to the monasteries were useful in this initial conversion. There, friars learned the native languages and gave rise to the development of the music that served them well during the first years of evangelization."

Singing and vocal music played important roles, particularly at this time when Europeans had already enlarged the scale from the prevailing pentatonic and introduced harmony. Indigenous *cantores* were prominent during the sixteenth and seventeenth centuries and possessed a guaranteed income for their weekly responsibilities (Truitt, 2010, 311–30). Women, excluded during the sixteenth century were now included as participants in this tradition by the end of the seventeenth century.

In the *Alabanzas* (Christian praise songs), native instruments were used evidencing stylistic influences from the liturgical music of the Church. Other forms, including the *motet, madrigal, cantiga,* and *villancico*, were introduced to the Indians. During the first century of the conquest, the militant Church opposed dances and ritualistic songs. Saldívar (1934, 253) mentions a case in 1623 in the province of Zapotitlán, where a notary of the Inquisition informed his superiors about the "inappropriate" dances among the Indians, recommending penalties and deportation. Thus, European salon dances continued to cause concern about public morals owing to the nature of both sexes partnering, until 1779 when such dances were prohibited (Slonimsky, 1947, 256). By the last decade of the eighteenth century, pianos were being imported into Mexico, and in 1796 a piano factory was established in Mexico City. Learning and playing the piano became a fashionable pasttime among well-to-do families. Its impact on the musical life of the country would be evidenced in the piano literature of Mexican nationals during the subsequent century, echoing Schumann and Chopin. Other instruments of the period included the flute, trumpet, *vihuela*, guitar, clavichord, and organ.

MEXICAN INDEPENDENCE AND THE NINETEENTH CENTURY (1810–1910)

From 1820 to 1910 Mexico was being formed, appearing as if "a seething mass of indigenous culture was brewing under a thin crust of European veneer" (Mayer Serra, 1942). During this period, while in the countryside popular music bands performed all kinds of marches and popular tunes, the elites of the urban societies assumed the "nacional airs" as their cultural status (Márquez Carrillo, 2006, 2). The new Constitution of 1857 proclaimed traditional liberal political ideals and severely restricted the Catholic Church. This period of liberal legislation in Mexico is known as *La Reforma* (the Reform). Three years of civil war followed until Benito Juárez (1806–1872) emerged as liberal leader and president (Eakin, 2007, 223).

Throughout the nineteenth century, early advocates of school music instruction promoted the Pestallozian philosophy of "learning by doing" and of proceeding from practice to theory. Having teachers that would actively engage students in learning by sensory experiences guaranteed an education of well-rounded individuals, intellectually, morally, and physically. Many musicians from Italy and Germany established themselves as teachers in Mexico (Slonimsky, 1947, 257). Significant social events and musical developments occurred during the thirty-four-year dictatorial period of Porfirio Díaz (1830–1915). From 1876 until the Revolution of 1910, Mexico lived in bondage to this feudalistic reign: the government, foreign businessmen, and large landowners were at the top, the Mexican peasant at the bottom. Díaz encouraged foreign exploitation of Mexico's natural wealth while modernizing the economy and establishing public education. This granted students opportunity and access to basic education. Thus, in 1891 with the passing of the Education Bill, instruction became free and mandatory. During this period composers pleased to the elite classes, particularly with music for dances featuring waltzes and polkas.

The father of musical education in Mexico was José Mariano Elízaga (1786–1842). His efforts in the field of music education predate that of Lowell Mason (1792–1872) in the United States. A true innovator and active in church music, Elízaga wrote and published the first treatise on musical theory, *Elementos de Música* (1823). He created the Sociedad Filarmónica in 1824 and a year later established the Academia Filarmónica de México, the first music conservatory in the nation.

In 1826, he organized the first secular printing press in Mexico where his works and those of other Mexican composers were published. In 1835, he published his treatise *Principios de la armonía y de la melodía* (Principles of Harmony and Melody), establishing an important musical base. In 1877, the Conservatorio Nacional de Música was founded in Mexico City, with Melesio Morales (1838–1908) leading the school during its beginning stages. Morales's exclusive promulgation of an Italian style of composition led to a rebellious movement headed by one of his disciples, Gustavo Campa (1863–1934), leaning toward the French style of composition in opposition. During this period, Julian Carrillo (1875–1965) also developed a progressive and revolutionary theory of composition, *Sonido 13* (1895), that was characterized by the search of musical possibilities outside of conventional harmony and the structure of conventional scales (Slonimsky, 1947, 49–50, 258). He was the first Mexican composer to undertake formal research on tonal organization and the division of the scale into smaller units. This work consequently led to numerous treatises.

These progressive new thoughts signaled new grounds for creativity. As Eakin (2007, 223) states, "No other country in Latin America in the late 19th and early 20th centuries surpasses Mexico in its combination of liberal and positivism ideals, economic growth, brutal authoritarian rule, and imposition of Europeanization and modernity on the non-European peoples of the countryside. By 1910, Mexico was on the verge of one of the most profound political and social revolutions of modern times." Toward the end of the nineteenth century, musical themes of nationalistic tendencies reached their peak, with close ties to more popular and cultivated genres.

CONTEMPORARY MEXICO (1910–PRESENT)

In the beginning of the twentieth century and before 1910, Mexico was highly influenced by European music. Composers trained in the Romantic fashion produced works that were mere imitations of the Europeans. However, their music lacked a distinctive or unique musical identity. Waltzes, salon pieces, *gavottes*, marches, and *romanzas* were written mostly for the piano. The popular manifestations generated by the Revolution and the struggle for power caused a parenthesis to the musical activities in the country. According to Slonimsky (1947, 257), with the Revolution, new musical forces unraveled among the Mexican people. Popular *corridos* as *La Adelita*, a form of musical folk ballad ingrained in Mexican life, became associated with the Revolution through its lyric, epic, and narrative qualities.

One of the most notable songs of that period was the anonymous "La Cucaracha," a tune that would become associated with the revolutionary days of General Pancho Villa (1878–1923). Mayer-Serra (1941) assigns the year 1912 as the beginning of Mexico's Nationalistic musical era. This coincides with a concert given by Manuel Ponce (1882–1948), where he offered for the first time selections of his own works. Ponce's compositions are the most representative repertoire of the period, particularly those written for the piano and for the guitar.

According to Chávez, "Ponce not only initiated 'musical nationalism' . . . [but] it was he who created a real consciousness of the richness of Mexican folk music, and gave orientation to the process of integrating that music into the higher forms of composition" (Mayer-Serra, 1941, 125). Until then, Mexican folklore had been considered exotic material to be treated in the European manner. However, Ponce's handling and treatment revealed a different approach—an intimate interpretation of musical art. Both Ponce and Chávez (1899–1978) continued to explore with national themes utilizing modern musical techniques. Other composers that followed that movement include some of Chavez's disciples, including Daniel Ayala (1906–1975), Salvador Contreras (1910–1982), Pablo Moncayo (1912–1958), and Blas Galindo (1910–1993). These four composers formed the *Grupo de los Cuatro* (The Group of Four), whereby native folklore was enhanced by contemporary techniques. The year 1920 marks the culmination of the Revolution and the beginning of relative political stability. The government of President Alvaro Obregon (1880–1928) initiated important reforms, including free and secular education.

Cultural nationalism was built on the recognition of the indigenous roots of the nation, with José Vasconcelos (1882–1959) as the architect of this movement. A Minister of Education in the early 1920s, Vasconcelos initiated a government-sponsored cultural project that would last for decades, one that used art and aesthetics to promote a new sense of Mexican identity. It was an agency devoted to the full-time study of musical folklore, and the Department of Music and Folklore was his creation under the Secretaría de Educación Pública in 1923. Its objective was the study and preservation of music, song texts, dance movements, musical artifacts, instruments, and cultural information relevant to the indigenous music and peoples of Mexico. Other research centers followed this interest and were established at the Universidad Nacional Autónoma de México (UNAM) and the Conservatorio Nacional de Música. In 1923, Ponce and other composers became associated with the Department of Music and Folklore founded by Vasconcelos.

Their work was the study of the cultural manifestations of the two most representative national groups—Indians and *Mestizos*—with an emphasis on providing educational opportunities to these groups. Based on Ponce's beliefs, Mexican music had to dignify the sounds of the people using its folklore as the basis of its own art. Chávez's aims, on the contrary, were to capture their spirit, and with this foundation expand on the artistic expression to reflect their indigenous essence (Márquez Carrillo, 2006, 2). Although Ponce began creating music during the revolutionary years, the mainstream of musical nationalism began after the nationalistic school of painting had been established following the Revolution.

The murals of artists such as Diego Rivera (1886–1957), José Clemente Orozco (1883–1949), and David Alfaro Siqueiros (1896–1974) are particularly important because they express the government's and the artists' nationalistic sentiments and, due to strength and revolutionary validity of the symbolism used, helped initiate a powerful nationalistic movement in the arts (Frary, 2001, 3). Chávez, a friend and ideological ally of Rivera, remarked, "Our attempt at a similar program in music took place some years later after the Mexican painters had started their movement" (Chávez, 1961, 97). Because of Chávez's position as a government official, educator, composer, and conductor, he became the most influential member of Mexico's musical community from the 1920s to the 1950s. His compositional style—an austere blending of Indianism, Neoclassism, Primitivism, and modernistic elements, as well as the singular work of Silvestre Revueltas (1899–1940)—set an important precedent for up-and-coming composers. His postrevolutionary compositions of those and his disciples—Revueltas, Moncayo, Galindo, Ayala, and Contreras—were products of government ideology. Ponce's music, instead, was a personal evocation of the music of the *mestizo* in a neoromantic setting usually devoid of strong political messages (Frary, 2001, 3).

Vicente T. Mendoza (1953, 57) remembers that "around that time the young musicians of Mexico were going through a crisis of unfulfilled dreams . . . musical nationalism excited our curiosity at the same time that more modern trends with its avant-garde tendencies claimed our attention on the opposite direction." In reality, what was formally paved during the presidency of Porfirio Díaz was pure musical nationalism, but now the argument centered on how to express it.

As Frary (2001) explains, "Unlike European Nationalism, where national consciousness grew from common bonds of language and culture, Mexican Nationalism resulted from the necessity of unifying diverse cultural groups in the struggle of foreign domination. Because of a long history of foreign oppression, a predominant feature of this nationalism is its distinctly anti-foreign attitude." Tovey (1999, 1–11) describes the efforts of this social movement:

> In 1923 the government established a program of traveling *misiones culturales* in an attempt to prepare citizens in remote rural areas for the introduction of modern public schools. Music education held a central position in the activities of the missions. Music specialists organized vocal and instrumental ensembles; they arranged music for such groups; taught singing, *solfège*, harmony and instrumental techniques. They also taught patriotic songs to support the left-leaning state. Music specialists also helped locals to prepare music for church use, thus easing anti-mission hostilities fueled by Catholic clergy and other conservatives who resented the socialistic vision espoused at that time by the Mexican state.

This consciousness permeated the various pedagogical reforms in both rural and urban regions. Under Chávez's leadership, the most progressive school at the time was the Conservatorio Nacional de Música. Between 1928 and 1934, Chávez introduced an innovative method of instruction that encouraged students to compose in all the styles while paying close attention to the national Mexican rhythms and melodies. In 1936, he described this experience:

> We do not use any texts. All the students worked tirelessly writing melodies in all the diatonic modes, melodic scale of twelve tones and all the pentatonic scales. We had instruments in the classroom and the melodies were performed by the students themselves, finding limitations or advantages according to the potential of the instruments. The end result is that now the young composers are able to write melodies with an incredible dexterity and instrumental sensibility. (Meierovich, 1995)

Under his leadership, teaching became more practice and less theory. New developments included the creation of a chorus and the incorporation of musical research into Mexican music—an integral aspect of the musical studies. Other accomplishments during his tenure as director included the academic revamping in orchestral studies and conducting and pedagogical studies. Chávez established the Orquesta Sinfónica de México in 1928 with himself as director and Silvestre Revueltas as codirector.

The orchestra adopted the politic of performing compositions by Mexican composers. Thus, from that year until 1943, the orchestra presented more than seventy works from thirty-one Mexican composers. In addition, another organization, the *Orquesta Mejicana*, was founded in 1933 with the sole objective of reviving the performance of ancient Mexican instruments. Many national composers, including Chávez, Ayala, Luis Sandi (1905–1996), and Galindo, wrote special commissions for this particular ensemble (Slonimsky, 1947, 37, 252). After Chávez's departure from the conservatory in 1934, his pedagogical ideas were sustained and further developed. Later on, during the presidency of Lázaro Cárdenas (1934–1940), the conservatory's function was aimed toward the masses, reflecting the populist project of a nation, as accomplished by decree in 1937. The academic activities of the time encouraged the preservation and study of Indigenous music—a trait of the social urgency of the time. In 1945, musicologist Henrietta Yurchenco (2003) reported:

> Unlike many Indian regions of Mexico, the Tzotzil and Tzeltal regions still adhere to a musical culture, which has vitality. It is a folk music, which not only serves a definite social function within the community but is also a personal expression. Everyone in these Indian towns knows and participates in the singing—men, women, and children. Music has to a large extent broken away from the rigidly ritual concept of music typical of homogeneous primitive societies. Although it was impossible to ascertain exactly how old the songs were or who created them, there can be no doubt that some free invention is practised [*sic*] by musicians. This gives birth to new songs from time to time.

This interest in the musical roots of the country will be later formalized at the Conservatorio Nacional de Música (CNM) in the 1942 to 1945 plan when Mexican Folklore would develop into a formal subject of academic interest for the first time in the curriculum. In this regard, the conservatory has played an important role in the curricular designs toward music teaching education in the country. Since its beginnings in 1866, the school has had twenty-four curricular revisions.

By 1946, the conservatory had already firmly established Musical Research as a pertinent career at the technical level, coinciding with the establishment of the General Professional Section, where the first licenses were given to graduates from music professions. In the plan implemented in 1951, objectives included the professional training of specialized music teachers and the creation of several new departments: Introduction to Music for ages eight to fourteen; Secondary Studies, aimed toward vocational training in musical education; Technical Studies, intended for singers and performers; Advanced Technical Studies, for concert performers and researchers; and Pedagogical Studies, for the training of specialized music instructors. In 1979, the process of advancing music education at the conservatory experienced a crucial moment evidenced in a revised plan that encompassed four principal areas: Interpretation, Pedagogy, Research, and Creativity. This served as an important step in the advancement of the profession by offering for the first time at the conservatory an undergraduate degree corresponding to the bachelor of music in the United States.

Presently, according to the General Education Law of Mexico (Article 3), the government has the responsibility to offer a basic, free, and secular education to all students equally. Beginning at ages three to five, children are enrolled at preschool—the foundation of formal education for three years. Then, during ages six to eleven, primary education is offered for six years. The last segment of compulsory and free education is the secondary school for students ages twelve to fourteen. It is interesting to note that, already on July 16, 1937, by official decree in the *Diario Oficial de la Federación*, President Lázaro Cárdenas (1895–1970) had established that music learning be given in a compulsory and free manner in all the schools of the Mexican Republic. Unfortunately, this measure has not been implemented in many public schools because, as the Secretary of Public Education argues, the budget and a lack of music teachers remain issues. However, the real problem is that an updated and official music education program is missing (Villanueva Pezet, 2004). González Alcántara (2004) emphasized the importance of a reliable music curriculum, stating, "We must insist in providing a systematic music education program aimed primarily to children and young adults. They constitute the majority of those ignoring the music of the masters, both nationals and foreign." He believed strongly in "safeguarding the authentic and valuable Mexican music from those outside influences that distort its essence."

By now there are several convincing proposals concerning the collective needs to gather and utilize native musical materials in the curriculum. An example of this pedagogical thought is the method *Micropauta* developed by César Tort (1928). He incorporates the principles of Carl Orff (1895–1982) by using the Mexican folklore and native instruments as the basis for his didactic principles. Other methods currently in use in Mexico emphasize the importance of a grounded elementary music education—the work of Gunild Keetman (1904–1990), Soltan Kodaly (1882–1967), Edgar Willems (1890–1978), and Shinichi Suzuki (1898–1998) all underline the importance of early exposure and training. The adoption and adaptation of traditional Spanish songs in the classroom is common practice in the country and throughout Latin America. Mexican composer Francisco Gabilondo Soler (1907–1990) wrote over 150 songs sang by over three generations of children that significantly enhanced the repertoire. In addition, the proximity to the United States has allowed for the implementation of many translated American traditional songs that are now valid material in schools. An attempt to implement more age-appropriate materials took place in the 1960s, for instance, with *Cantos y*

Juegos (Songs and Games), a program intended for all preschoolers but which only lasted until the early 1990s when educational authorities eliminated it from the curriculum. At the elementary level music instruction is dependent upon the individual resources of private or public schools. The latter, unfortunately, has lacked the resources to offer adequate programs for this population.

At this time, the Ministry of Public Education determines the curriculum for elementary, secondary, and teacher education for the entire Republic. According to the Education Development Program (SEP, 1994), music was not included within the national curriculum as a subject (Devroop and Aguilar, 2006). Recent studies of Mexican schools provide further insights on music education as being absent of the indicators of curricular programs (Robles Vásquez et al., 2007), or being at the edge of the curriculum with both students and teachers, holding lower expectations for success in learning and teaching this subject (González Moreno, 2009).

However, in 2000, the Ministry of Public Education in Mexico promoted a reform to improve secondary music education by encouraging student participation and improving the conditions for the professional development of teachers. This initiative has lead to recent studies that compare previous educational programs with the new proposed changes. For example, new attitudes were observed in teachers' performance and self-evaluations, including "assessing students' opportunities to express their viewpoints, to improvise and create music, and to participate in decisions and self-assessment activities that appeared to have a positive effect in the classroom" (Vargas Mendoza, 2010).

For the past few decades, however, music has been recognized at the secondary level (high school) as part of the general curriculum, despite struggles to afford teachers and make musical instruments available for students. This reality is not unique to Mexican schools. Music as a formal subject remains on the periphery of curricular planning with many educational reforms underlining the importance of standardized tests on the competitive subjects such mathematics, science, and language, thus leaving behind the formidable legacy of music education previously established in earlier periods. The challenge is to provide a more sustainable framework toward the development of systematized music teacher-training programs to serve the needs of a hugely diverse population based on their cultural identity.

There is an enormous demand for music teachers throughout Mexico's educational system at various levels throughout the various regions. However, the number of graduating students from existing music education programs does not meet the needs found in both urban and rural sectors. The Escuela Nacional de Música (ENM), created in 1929, is affiliated to the Universidad Autónoma de México (UNAM) and presently plays a crucial role in the formation of music teachers that serve the many schools throughout the country.

Although music education has played formal and informal roles in Mexico's educational system, it has only been since 1996 that it has been welcomed as an independent area of research. At the undergraduate level, the music education program at UNAM began in 1996 providing students with a wide exposure to pedagogical skills, including all theoretical subjects, Mexican music history, choral training, educational research, and philosophy to strengthen methodological awareness. The program stresses the musical as well as the ethical and creative processes that make learning effective within the national reality to achieve a coherent musical education curriculum.

The graduate program began in 2004 and stressed the coupling of interdisciplinary research, artistic work, and pedagogy. In 2008, the restructuring of curricular programs was finalized serving an extended population of 1,739 students, distributed among its main programs: Cycle of Musical Initiation, Pre-College, and Undergraduate Studies. In the same year and for the first time in the history of the UNAM an innovative academic structure was implemented with the creation of the masters and doctoral programs, bringing together into one single program three main divisions: Arts (Escuela Nacional de Música), Science (Centro de Ciencias Aplicadas y Desarrollo Tecnológico), and Social Sciences (Instituto de Investigaciones Antropológicas). Taking into account the social needs of music education in Mexico, this program provides evidence to its perception—from strengthening the artistic and academic levels to the preservation and promotion of its national musical heritage (UNAM, 2008, 4).

CONCLUSION

An ethnically diverse culture, the identity of the Mexican people is the synthesis of European influence and indigenous culture. Acculturation played a vital role in defining their national character and the musical characteristics encountered in the various regions. The conversion process that began with the Franciscans friars in 1523 led to the gradual assimilation of rhythms and melodies from Indians, Spaniards, and Blacks. Music was used in a functional capacity during the Pre-Conquest period with singing typified by monophonic and rhythmic pentatonic vocalizations. Together with dancing, singing served as both diversion and communication.

The conquest and colonization exhibited intense conservatism through the dominating presence of the Catholic Church. Thus, the training of Indians on liturgical chants proved useful in the evangelization process. Cultural isolation typified this period, causing musical stagnation in instrumental and vocal practices. The expansion from the pentatonic scale to more diatonic modes and harmonic progressions became more pronounced. Indigenous singers held prominent positions, and women were included in the music liturgy for the first time as equal participants. As early as 1536 the printing press had already been introduced in Mexico, with many of the early books devoted to Church music. Certain dances and ritualistic songs caused public concern due to moral issues of both sexes partnering.

The process of independence gave birth to musical nationalism. The liberal and positivist ideals established in the Constitution of 1857 damped the conventional pronouncements of the Catholic Church in juxtaposition to an authoritarian rule and the imposing of European values. The Pestallozian approach of learning by doing was favored among early advocates of music instruction. The Sociedad Filarmónica established in 1825 and the Conservatorio Nacional de Música created in 1877 positioned music education at its beginning stages. Free and compulsory public education, established after the passing of the Education Bill in 1891, became a national priority under the administration of Porfirio Díaz. In 1895, *Sonido 13*, the revolutionary theory of the composition of Julian Carrillo, was developed in search of musical possibilities outside prevalent conventions.

In the twentieth century, with the Revolution new musical forces unraveled the potential of nationalistic music. Manuel Ponce, the most representative composer of his generation, integrated folk material into higher forms of composition. Other relevant figures, such as Carlos Chávez, utilized native Mexican folklore within a more contemporary compositional context. Cultural Nationalism, a government-sponsored cultural project, saw an uprising in the 1920s toward the defense of indigenous music. This movement awoke an unarguable sense of national identity among other cultural institutions, including the Universidad Nacional Autónoma de México and the Conservatorio Nacional de Música. Between 1928 and 1934, Chávez introduced innovative methodologies at the conservatory and created the Orquesta Sinfónica de México—a tool to promote works by Mexican composers. In 1937, President Lázaro Cárdenas reestablished learning music in a compulsory and free manner in all schools of the Mexican Republic. New disciplines such as Mexican Folklore and Musical Research developed into more formal subjects of study in the conservatory's curricular modifications of 1942 to 1945. Today, the Escuela Nacional de Música, through its affiliation with the Universidad Nacional Autónoma de México, plays a central role in the training of music teachers offering music education programs at the undergraduate and graduate levels, underscoring its rightful mission in the lives of children and young adults.

REFERENCES

Baily, John, and Doubleday, Veronica. 1987. "Patterns of Musical Enculturation in Afghanistan in Music and Child Development," ed. Frank R. Wilson and Franz L. Roehmann. The Biology of Music Making. Proceedings of the Denver Conference.

Béhague, Gerard H. 1973. "Latin American Folk Music," in *Folk and Traditional Music of the Western Continents*, 2nd ed., ed. Bruno Nettl. Englewood Cliffs, NJ: Prentice-Hall.

Bourg, Cameron Hideo. 2005. "Ancient Maya Music Now with Sound." Master's theses, Louisiana State University.

Campbell, Patricia Shehan. 1991. *Lessons from the World: A Cross-Cultural Guide to Music Teaching and Learning*. New York: Schirmer Books.

Castañeda, Daniel, and Vicente T. Mendoza. 1933. *Instrumental Precortesiano*. México: Imprenta del Museo Nacional de Arqueología, Historia y Etnografía.

Chávez, Carlos. 1949. "Discurso de Carlos Chávez en la inaguración de la sede del Conservatorio Nacional." Retrieved from http://conservatorianos.com.mx/3documento.htm

————. 1961. *Musical Thought*. Cambridge, MA: Harvard University Press.

Devroop, Karendra, and Aguilar, Beatriz. "The Occupational Aspirations and Expectations of Music Education Majors in Mexico." *Research and Issues in Music Education*, vol. 4, no. 1 (September 2006): 2.

Eakin, Marshall C. 2007. *The History of Latin America: Collision of Cultures*. New York: Palgrave Macmillan.

Frary, Peter Kun. 2001. "Music & The Socio-Cultural Environment of Post-Revolutionary Mexico." Retrieved from http://emedia.leeward.hawaii.edu/frary/social_envir_mex.htm

George, Luvenia A. 1987. *Teaching the Music of Six Different Cultures*. Danbury, CT: World Music Press.

González Alcántara y Carranca, Juan Luís. 2004. "La tradición musical en México." *Conservatorianos* 2, no. 7: 65.

González Moreno, Patricia A. 2009. "Motivational Beliefs about Music and Six Other School Subjects: The Mexican Content." PhD dissertation, University of Illinois at Urbana–Champaign.

Hague, Eleanor. 1934. *Latin American Music*. Santa Ana, California: The Fine Arts Press.

Kivy, Peter. 1991. "Music and the Liberal Education." *Journal of Aesthetic Education* 25, no. 3 (Fall): 79–93.

Márquez Carrillo, Jesús. 2006. "Creación artística o enseñanza profesional: Los orígenes de la Escuela Nacional de Música, 1929–1934." *Graffylia: Revista de la Facultad de Filosofía y Letras* no. 6: 156–63.

Mayer Serra, Otto. 1941. Panorama de la música mexicana. México, D.F.: Fondo de Cultura Económica.

————. 1941. "Silvestre Revueltas and Musical Nationalism in Mexico." *Musical Quarterly* 27 (April): 125.

————. 1942. "Music Made in Mexico." *The Rotarian* (January): 29–30.

————. 1960. *The Present State of Music in Mexico*. Washington, DC: Pan American Union.

Meierovich, Clara. 1995. *Vicente T. Mendoza, artista y primer folclórogo musical*. México, D.F.: Coordinación de Humanidades de la UNAM, 1995.

Mendoza, Vicente T. 1953. "La Investigación folklórica-musical." *Aportaciones a la investigación folklórica de México*. Mexico, D.F.: UNAM, 57–69.

Nettl, Bruno. 1985. *The Western Impact on World Music*. New York: Schirmer Books.

————. 2004. "American Indian Music." *The Harvard Dictionary of Music*. Cambridge: Belknap.

Robles Vásquez, Héctor. 2007. *Panorama Educativo del México 2007: Indicadores del Sistema Educativo Nacional*. México, D.F.: Instituto Nacional para la Evaluación de la Educación.

Saldívar, Gabriel. 1934. *Historia de la Música de México*. México: Secretaría de Educación Pública.

Schwaller, John F. 2010. "Evangelization as Performance: Making Music, Telling Stories." *The Americas* 66, no. 3 (January): 305–10.

Slonimsky, Nicolas. 1947. *La Música de América Latina*, trans. M. Eloísa González Kraak. Buenos Aires: Librería y Editorial El Ateneo.

Stevenson, Robert. 1952. *Music in Mexico: A Historical Survey*. New York: Thomas Y. Crowell Company.

————. 1976. *Music in Aztec and Inca Territory*. Berkeley: University of California Press.

Tovey, David G. 1999. "The Role of the Music Educator in Mexico's Cultural Missions." *Bulletin of the Council for Research in Music Education* 139 (Winter): 1–11.

————. 1997. "José Mariano Elízaga and Music Education in Early Nineteenth-Century Mexico." *The Bulletin of Historical Research in Music Education* 18, no. 2 (January): 126–36.

Truitt, Jonathan. 2010. "Adopted Pedagogies: Incorporation of European Music and Theater in Colonial Mexico City." *The Americas* 6, no. 3 (January): 311–30.

Turrent, Lourdes. 1993. *La conquista musical de México*. México, D.F.: Fondo de Cultura Económica.

Universidad Nacional Autónoma de México. 2008. *Memorias*: 4.

Vargas Mendoza, Mariana de Jesús. 2010. "Evaluation of the Impact of the New Music Program of the Ministry of Public Education in Mexico." Paper presented at the 29th International Society of Music Education World Conference, Beijing, China.

Villanueva Pezet, René. 2004. "Profesionalización del maestro de educación artística escolar." *Conservatorianos* 2, no. 7 (January–February):70–73.

Villanueva Pezet, René, and José Bañuelos Calvo. 2007. "La Educación Musical en el Medio Rural de México." *Conservatorianos*: 80–84.

Yurchenco, Henrietta. 2003. *La Vuelta al Mundo en 80 Años*. México: Comisión Nacional para el Desarrollo de los Pueblos Indígenas.

Chapter Ten

Nicaragua

Lylliam Meza de Rocha

INTRODUCTION

Nicaragua is a country with a great musical potential; however, its history curiously has been challenging. Nicaragua's territory occupies a land extension of 130,000 square kilometers with a population that exceeds six million. The country is known as the "Land of Lakes and Volcanoes," but it could be also known as the "Land of Musicians and Poets." Nicarguan poet Ruben Dario shines in the world of writers as a star of great magnitude, and the universal literature and music of Nicaragua is well known in the Central American region.

It seems as if the nineteenth century was the gold century of Nicaragua. Many musicians distinguished themselves, composing masses, symphonies, operas, and ballroom music. Nicaragua was deeply influenced by Spain and Italy, mostly because of the arrival of the Spanish "conquistadores" and some Italian writers. Evidence of this influence is the discovery of the dance comedy *El Güegüence* from colonial times. Probably written in the seventeenth century, it incorporates all artistic manifestations. It is the only composition found in the eighteenth century and one that was proclaimed by the United Nations Educational, Scientific and Cultural Organization (UNESCO) as an Intangible Patrimony of Humanity. The work presents many characteristics of Italian music (Arellano, 1982). Similarly, many romance compositions and childhood and religious songs were found during the nineteenth and twentieth centuries (Mejia Sanchez, 1946). This chapter lets us visualize the musical education of Nicaragua with its artistic and historical backgrounds.

EARLY DAYS

Gonzalo Fernandez de Oviedo, the foremost Spanish chronicle writer, witnessed a celebration with songs and dances accompanied by drums and *atabales* (kettledrums), which took place in what today is known as Chinandega, previously known as Tezoatega, a village of the Nahuatl people. Even though information regarding the music from Nicaragua is scarce, all those informed coincide in that the feeling and musical style of Nicaraguan music is nostalgic and sad (Barrera, 2009).

In a visit to the Tenderi Museum of Archaeology located in the city of Nindiri, a few kilometers from Managua, anthropomorphic and zoomorphic ocarinas can be found, which have been found to be from the years 500 to 700 of our era and are unique to the museums of Nicaragua. They are made of a black ceramic, unknown to the area, since that type of ceramic is only found in the northern part of Nicaragua. It is believed that invading tribes left these instruments buried. This museum just celebrated its one hundred years of existence and its founder, José María Gutierrez Arancibia, who was the person to discover these artifacts.

It is a pity that musical instruments used in the pre-Colombian period have not been preserved. However, it is known that the following instruments were used in Nicaragua: the *chirimía*, a kind of oboe made of clay; the *quijongo*, a percussion instrument; and an instrument similar to the guitar (Peña Hernández, 1968). Today, some examples of these instruments could be seen at the Nindiri Museum. The emergence of the marimba, quite known in Nicaragua, came much later after the Spanish arrival.

COLONIZATION

Bernal Diaz del Castillo in his *Verdadera Historia de la Conquista de la Nueva España* (Mejia Sanchez, 1946) states that the *romances* and *corridos* came from Spain by way of the *conquistadores*, and they stayed in both its original form and those created by the indigenous people. Romances described the life and passion of the people, and they are sung even today. They propelled the corridos, songs in two beats, which described the cultural identity of the people from Mexico to Costa Rica. In the colonial dance comedy *Gueguence*, there are already references to the corridos.

The colonial religious music arrived with the missionaries, and they brought with them *alabados* (praises), *villancicos* (Christmas carols), and *cantos* (chants). It is known by word of mouth that a Francescan friar from Toledo, Spain, brought with him a psalm, which was sung and played in a solemn and dignified rhythm, profoundly mystical, which in 1910 gave way to the Nicaraguan national anthem.

INDEPENDENCE

The independence of Central American countries was very uncertain since these countries would frequently switch from declaring independence to later rejoining their "motherland," Spain. The real independence occurred in 1821. At that time, "La Granadera," a very solemn song and music with definite European influence, was sung during military masses and during the doing and undoing of the flag. But "La Antífona de los colores" was the real hymn of the Central American Federation, and it is still heard in Guatamela to honor the president of the country. The "Banda de los Supremos Poderes," which was very relevant in Nicaragua until 1979, was performed as a hymn for a long time. It is considered a historical relic. Of course, the influence of the Church was very obvious in all facets of the people's lives: art, music, literature, poetry, and their beliefs and customs.

TODAY'S WORLD

The educational system in Nicaragua started with the arrival of the De la Salle Christian brothers at the end of the nineteenth century. They founded the first Normal School, which developed teachers with a more scientific than humanistic vision. They came from the Illustration period, and their philosophy was based on science rather than on humanities as the important factor in the development of teachers.

The first study plan was developed in 1938 and was still in use until the middle of the 1960s, when UNESCO sent a group of education experts to the country, mostly composed of Chileans, Brazilians, and Ecuadoreans, and the first educational reform was introduced. In this study plan there was a class of music and song. The Ministry would contract self-taught musicians to teach in the schools. Of course, these "music teachers," which were men only, did not necessarily teach songs appropriate to the age and interests of students. They just taught hymns used in celebrations, songs they composed, or known melodies they adapted, such as "The Blue Danube," "Stories of the Vienna Forests," "Ojos negros," and others.

In 1967, this study plan was reformed. Even though the music class continued under the same guidelines, the UNESCO experts gave education a new focus. Musical education as a concept still did not exist, but the classes of music and song would be considered among the study courses available. In other words, there was an interdisciplinary concept (D'Hainaut, 1998). The students, however, began to familiarize themselves with significant songs more in tune with their interests, even though the music class was more recreational than formative. It really did not meet the desired objectives. The basic principles of education—freedom, activity, and creativity—were very much present in the other classes of their curriculum, but not in the music class.

In 1970, the Organization of American States (OEA in Spanish) started a musical education movement in Nicaragua with the visit of Dr. Maria Luisa Muñoz, the first Puerto Rican musicologist who was working as a consultant to Maestro Guillermo Espinosa, director of the music unit of the OEA at the time. She was a member of the International Society of Music Education (ISME) and came with new ideas. During her visit to Nicaragua and the Central American region, she detected a big need for music education in all countries. Some more than others, Nicaragua was the one with the most need since there were no programs at all.

At the Third International Conference of the International Private Center for Education and Culture (CIEP-CIE), and within the sponsorship of the Conferencia International de Edución Musical (CIDEM), Music Education Center, a project was approved to assist in overcoming the deficiencies found in the study plans and programs in Central America.

In 1971, under the sponsorship of the OEA, the first pilot course of Central American music education was organized. It was based in Nicaragua, and the participants were all teachers of music or another study area, from all five Central American countries and Panama. It lasted five weeks from January to mid-February 1971. It was forged by the faculty of Sciences and Musical Arts at the University of Chile where the Inter-American Institute of Music Education (INTEM) was in operation. Dr. Muñoz, along with other teachers, directed it: Maria Eliana Breitler and Jarah Schmidt from Chile; Patricia Stokóe from Argentina; and Cecilia Cabezas from Costa Rica (the first postgrant recipient from INTEM). The curriculum consisted of: basic music and music appreciation; guitar (collective and folkloric); special education; the Dalcroze method; recorder; choir direction; and school repetoire. There definitely was a change in music education in Nicaragua and the other Central American countries.

In 1972, while working for the Ministry of Education, Lylliam Meza de Rocha was selected to partake in the Musical Education specialty in Chile. Of course, she was motivated, and there were high expectations about her contribution to the country upon her return. Unfortunately, the December 22, 1972, earthquake interrupted my stay. When she returned, the city of Managua was almost destroyed. Despite the almost total destruction of the city's infrastructure, international assistance was bountiful, including the reconstruction of schools.

In the months following the earthquake, a group of experts in the field of education and psychologists and sociologists arrived to help children and young adults return to a "normal" life. This group of specialists from Switzerland, England, and Germany, called the Andromeda Group, recommended that the government initiate recreational and occupational programs for children to facilitate their recovery from trauma; especially psychological treatment for those children who had lost their family, their home, and all their belongings. Of course, the educational system was halted.

In August 1973, the school year started with school buildings almost finished. The support received was unconditional. Music education seminars were organized for teachers. In the following years new programs, supporting materials, songbooks, and musical instruments made with recycled materials were produced, in addition to resources from neighboring countries. Achievements and successes were disseminated in a tri-monthly bulletin, culminating in 1974 with the first Choir Festival with the participation of choirs from the schools in Managua.

In 1975, the OEA in conjunction with the INTEM organized a course on the Approach to Musical Education. Students from Mexico, Central America, and some Latin American countries attended, fostering diverse points of view regarding musical education. Nicaragua continued working on this issue with impetus and received the support from colleagues from Honduras and Colombia.

Fortunately, the political changes of ministers of the following years did not affect the restoration of the country. Thanks to the enthusiasm of its citizens, music education was institutionalized in high schools and somewhat in elementary and middle school. However, childhood education, which is the most important for the full development of children, was almost nonexistent except in the private sector.

In 1978, the first signs of the revolution began, and the Minister of Education transferred Professor Meza de Rocha to the National Music Conservatory as director, where she remained as such until 1979. The conservatory, founded in the 1950s, was reorganized, study plans were written, objectives were defined, and monthly didactic concerts were instituted. In 1979, after the Sandinista Front assumed the government, the education system was changed. The directors that followed concentrated their efforts in developing massive activities to support the arts for people. It was in that way that groups such as Los Palacguina and others became known for their political music.

With the change in government in 1990, the new education policies and curriculum took two years to develop. UNESCO returned again to Nicaragua with the support of The Netherlands and initiated the *Proyecto*

Sistema de Mejoramiento de la Educación Nicaragüense (SIMEN), the Nicaragua Education Improvement Project, which together with the BASE Project, from AID, and the "APRENDE" Project from the World Bank, started the curriculum transformation for preschool, elementary, and teacher formation education (Meza de Rocha, 1997). The project lasted nine years and produced study plans based on humanistic approach curriculum, and trained teachers from preschool, elementary, and Normal Schools with the technical assistance of international consultants. Music education was at its best moment; it was revitalized.

In this educational and curriculum transformation, the open education concept was instituted and the teaching methods were transformed into open, active, and participatory ones. Now study plans included the class Practical Activities, with music education, dance, and visual arts. The opening of eight Normal Schools in the country helped teachers evolve into professionals. The curriculum in the Normal Schools included how to teach music education. Professor Meza de Rocha served as consultant to the SIMEN Project and assisted in the elaboration and implementation of these programs, not only because these programs were her responsibility but also because the Ministry of Education lacked the human resources to fulfill this need.

At the same time, in the 1990s the Catholic Redemptoris Mater University initiated the conversion to professionals of its teachers on duty. Professor Meza de Rocha was appointed as teacher and years later was appointed as a thesis advisor. This motivated her to write a thesis regarding the state of musical education in Nicaragua, and in this manner to try to create a general awareness of the importance of musical education in education in general. The professional formation of teachers was part of the curriculum transformation taking place in the 1990s.

In 2000, the idea of grouping the three artistic courses into one simple name, Arts Education, was pondered (Meza de Rocha, 1989). Students had the option of selecting between music, dance, and visual arts. This is mostly a Latin American point of view because there are other countries that have not permitted the elimination of musical education in their programs. It is a pity, but it is also a reality that information management and languages are substituting music education.

THE INSTITUTE OF CULTURE AND SPORTS

In the 1990s and 2000, the Culture and Sports Ministry, established by the previous government, was converted into the Nicaragua Institute of Culture, part of the Ministry of Education, Culture and Sports (MECD in Spanish). The field of music was composed of:

The National School of Music (known before as the National Conservatory of Music)
The National Orchestra of Music
The National Choir of Nicaragua
The Youth Symphony Orchestra

The Youth Symphony Orchestra was based at the Batahola Cultural Center in Managua, which was founded by Father Agnel Torreillas, a Spanish Dominican priest who came to Managua to support the revolution and stayed. This center, which is still open and supported by Germany, trained and still trains many good musicians. From this center many projects have emerged, such as: the Music in the Suburbs; The House of the Three Worlds located in Granada; and the school housing the Education, Faith and Happiness Project, which trains teachers. There is also the Youth Symphony Orchestra with branches in Jinotega, Granada, Masaya, and Chinandega, and with more independence from the Nicaragua Institute of Culture because of external support from Germany, Spain, and other countries.

In 1993, the Japanese donated musical instruments and materials with a value of $35,000 to the music department of the Nicaragua Institute of Culture. These donations have continued to come from different European countries. The National School of Music offers courses in clarinet, violin, bassoon, trombone, trumpet, cello, flute, piano, oboe, saxophone, English horn, and bass. The Nicaragua Institute of Culture operates the Ruben Dario National Theater, the National Museum, the National Archives, and the Music Museum. All these institutions stimulate culture at all levels.

PRESCHOOL EDUCATION AND MUSIC

In the 1990s, preschool education received a great incentive from the Ministry of Education, including those preschool centers not owned by the government. Once a month, two to three teachers from each center were offered training, which included musical education. The objective was for them to convey the knowledge acquired to other teachers and centers. As a result, the preschool education situation changed dramatically. However, the problem today is that no follow-up was given to this educational strategy. But what is really worse is that the Ministry of Education is eliminating preschool education, and only those centers that are privately owned exist, and they still have musical education in their programs.

ELEMENTARY SCHOOL AND MUSIC

Primary education has suffered the same fate as preschool education. Students elect folk dance since there are no music teachers. The teachers that were trained between 1973 and 1979 have immigrated to other countries or have abandoned the field of teaching because of low wages and other reasons. There are still some elders that remember how the music class was integrated with the other classes and how every now and then, there were schools with choirs and musical groups.

It is a pity that the musical education at this level is nonexistent because as Violeta Hemsy de Gainza affirmed in a conference given in October 2010, "Together with the advancement of electro-acoustic technology, the capacity of our youth to distinguish quality and profoundness and to be able to discern has diminished." As a musical educator, I completely agree with this statement, since it is in primary school where values are built—but more than built, the range of values is extended so when students complete primary school they take with them these values to their next educational level. Values such as respect for others, the conservation of the environment, and their good taste in music are very important today and forever (Meza de Rocha, 1994).

In some schools the teaching of the recorder is predominant because students take private music lessons or attend the National School of Music, but they are few. As is the case of preschool education, private primary schools, those not owned by the government, include music education in their programs, and a musician or a music educator who trained under the previous government when the National School of Music trained music educators teaches the class. However, the majority of Nicaraguan children and teenagers do not know the minimum content of a music education program (Meza de Rocha, 1998).

HIGH SCHOOL EDUCATION AND MUSIC

With the predominance of Information Management, there was no place for human studies—music among them—in intermediate or high school programs. The priority is given to the study of computers and English, which are two of the skills young people, many of whom do not pursue higher education, need to get jobs. In the 1970s there was an attempt to offer special performance activities in institutes. However, only dance was the artistic manifestation that prevailed. Musical bands were present in each secondary school, where they practiced all year round in preparation for the National Festivals. Since these bands lacked musical education, their rhythm was of a very bad quality and they were monotonous (Meza de Rocha, 1998).

Young people at this level should at least know how to read music in order to play their musical instruments with precision. They are young girls and boys, which requires in-depth knowledge of human studies since they have been culturally deprived since childhood. They need music to occupy their free time in order to stimulate their creativity and other aspects that are so valuable at the ages of fourteen through eighteen.

THE DEVELOPMENT OF TEACHERS AND MUSIC

In the past, there were two Normal Schools: one for boys and the other for young women. Both had music and song classes; teachers would teach how to read music and how to sing. In the 1970s when music education started, programs included choir activities, which already existed but was more relevant while the existence of the Music Aesthetics Department of the Ministry of Education. With the curriculum and education reforms of the 1990s, all eight Normal Schools were converted into music education centers so that students starting their professional career could, one year before graduation, take the message of musical education to the schools they were assigned to teach. This practice continues to this day. Nowadays, there is the support from the *Corporación Española*, the Spanish Corporation, to provide technical assistance in the area of the arts, but they do not provide music education due to the lack of trained personnel needed.

CULTURAL INSTITUTIONS AND MUSICAL GROUPS

Nicaragua presents many popular festivals. This custom is considered to be a Spanish heritage. Some have religious connotations, and others are folk in nature. Each city celebrates their festivals with the music of *chicheros*, amateur musicians with no formal training and who play by ear. They normally consist of six musicians, and the instruments played are the fluegelhorn, trombone, clarinet, trumpet, and percussion. They are considered to be the most popular group of Nicaragua because they exist everywhere in the country. They play Easter songs and bullfight songs and popular music in general. The Ruben Dario National Theater has an interesting and varied musical offering. It presents two seasons a year: the classical music season and the choir season. International groups are invited, but also national groups are featured.

Other centers such as the French Alliance and the Nicaragua Institute of Hispanic Culture are centers that offer time and space so national musical groups can present their concerts at a reasonable price. The French Alliance celebrates the Week of Music every year. The explosive festivities of these musical groups momentarily change the pace of the capital city. This activity travels slowly from city to city spreading happiness to young and old through music.

There are other musical groups such as the chamber ensemble, Kinteto, whose mission is to interpret only Nicaraguan art music, especially that of the nineteenth and twentieth centuries, in chamber music format. This group is part of the consortium APC, FONMUNIC, and Kinteto. APC is the Association of Culture Promoters, and FONMUNIC is the Nicaragua Music Trust Fund. The Norweigan Embassy finances these groups. In past years this society has put their focus on music research and the conservation and dissemination of Nicaraguan music. Maestro Alfredo Barrera is the founder of FONMUNIC. The Guardabarranco Duet is a duo of songwriters of ecological music of very good quality. The BACH Camerata is a very successful musical group, which through the years has staged operas, played North American music from the 1940s, music from the Beatles, and others. They play with an excellent high quality and focus to conserve Nicaraguan folk and popular peasant melodies.

MUSIC IN THE UNIVERSITY

Until the mid-2000s, the Universidad Nacional de Nicaragua (UNAN), Nicaragua National University, initiated the subject of music education as a minor degree in the College of Educational Sciences. The profession did not have a great demand because the emphasis was on education and not on the music, but at least it filled a void.

The Universidad Politécnica de Nicaragua (UPOLI), Nicaragua Polytechnic University, has a music conservatory where specialists in orchestra instruments and in voice are trained. The offering is good, and it is accredited to offer a degree in music. For many teachers and others interested in the subject, this degree is much more attractive than the UNAN since the music conservatory has resources and materials necessary to offer a sound music education.

MUSIC EDUCATION TODAY

In 1995, a meeting of musical experts, sponsored by UNESCO and supported by Consejo Nacional de Cultura de Venezuela (CONAC), was held in Caracas, Venezuela. In that one-week meeting, which had forty experts from all over Latin American in attendance, very interesting themes around the subject of musical education were discussed and the idea of a Latin American organization was formed. At the end of this meeting, Violeta

Hemsy de Gainza (Argentina) traveled to Costa Rica and met with Carmen Méndez, Gloria Valencia (Colombia), and Margarita Fernández (Chile). At the end of this meeting, these four women founded the Foro Latinoamericano de Educación Musical (FLADEM), Latin American Forum of Musical Education.

The next year, FLADEM began to grow and evolve, and began to invite other Latin American countries to join the forum. FLADEM is an accessible platform at which music educators have the opportunity to collaborate and share ideas with other colleagues from other countries. The meetings are indeed very interesting, and even though FLADEM began small, today many practitioners from many Latin American countries have joined.

In 1999, the FLADEM-Nicaragua was founded, and in 2000 it was tasked with organizing the International Congress on Musical Education in Managua. Some 360 teachers from Nicaragua, Costa Rica, Guatemala, and Honduras were in attendance, and it had the support of Ricardo López (Puerto Rico), Ethel Batres (Guatemala), Violeta Hemsy de Gainza (Argentina), Victoria Santa Cruz (Peru), Carmen Méndez, Nuria Zúñiga, and Mario Alfaguell (Costa Rica), and Eduardo Robles (Mexico). It was quite an international affair.

A major achievement was to stimulate the degree in Musical Education with the Universidad Juan Pablo II, John Paul II University, and the FLADEMNIC. In this case, the University awards a postgraduate degree with a major in Musical Education. It was a titanic effort but one that advanced music education as part of the country's educational system.

CONCLUSION

We can conclude that Nicaragua was and still is a country with great musical richness. It has evolved but does not have a history that can compare with other Latin American countries. The lack of an institutionalized music education program has been the reason for Nicaragua's struggle in Latin America. The reforms that have taken place have treated music with indifference, but there are strides being made so that new generations learn about their cultural past.

The people from Nicaragua are proud of their *Gueguence* since it is a unique piece of its kind in America. The Minister of Education in Nicaragua is gaining knowledge of the significance of music education as a formative subject in schools. The organizations that helped Nicaragua are no longer there. They showed the people of Nicaragua the way, and it is up to them to ensure that they have musical education as a part of schools' curricula.

REFERENCES

Arellano, Jorge Eduardo. (1982). *La Música en la Historia de Nicaragua*. Boletín Nicaragüense de Bibliografía y Documentación. Managua: BCN.

Barrera, Alfredo. (2009). *Breviario de Investigaciones Bibliográficas Musicales Nicaragüenses*. Managua: Asociación Promotores de la Cultura.

D'Hainaut, Louis. (1998). *La Interdisciplinariedad en la Enseñanza General*. París: UNESCO.

Ibarra Mayorga, Salomón. (1955). *Monografía del Himno Nacional de Nicaragua*. Managua.

Lacayo, Francisco. (1977). *Reflexiones sobre la Cultura Nicaragüense*. La Prensa Literaria, 16 de marzo. Managua: Diario La Prensa.

Mejia Sanchez, Ernesto. (1946). *Romances y Corridos Nicaragüenses*. México.

Meza Ruiz de Rocha, Lylliam. (1989). *Guía Metodológica de 1° a 6° grado*. Área Humanística. Managua: MED.

———. (1993). *Seminario Taller de Educación Musical*. Dirección de Educación Preescolar. Managua: MED.

———. (1994). *La Educación Estética: Una Propuesta para su Desarrollo*. Tesis de Maestría (No publicada). Salamanca: Universidad de Salamanca.

———. (1997). *Informe de Progreso del Proyecto SIMEN*. Managua: SIMEN-MED.

———. (1998). *Informe sobre la Educación en Nicaragua*. Managua: MED.

———. (2000). *Memoria del Congreso Internacional de Educación Musical*. FLADEM-NICARAGUA. Managua: MED.

Peña Hernández, Enrique. (1968). *El Folklore en Nicaragua*. Managua.

Scrubs, T. M. (1999). *Disfrutemos como Nicas*. Managua: Diario La Prensa, 18 de mayo, 3.

Willems, Edgard. (1981). *El Valor Humano de la Dirección*. Buenos Aires: Paidós.

Chapter Eleven

Panama

Jaime Ingram Jaén and Néstor Castillo

Note: Most of the information has been taken from the book written by yours truly, Jaime Ingram Jaén, *La Música de Panamá* (República de Panamá: Editorial Universitaria Carlos Manuel Gasteazoro, 2008).

INTRODUCTION

In the middle of the month of national celebration, it is also customary to commemorate the day of the musician every November 22 in Panama. Around the same time, Music Week also unfolds, with musical performances; delivering baskets for newborns; Mass at St. Cecilia, the Patroness of Musicians; and a pilgrimage to the mausoleum promoted by the labor union. The "Day of Rest for All Musicians in the Country" is also observed. This celebration was approved by Law No. 24 of February 11, 1955, in recognition of the contribution given by musicians to strengthening the cultural identity of Panamanian men and women. It urges us to remember the reasons why people are led to be musicians—to make music, to facilitate its learning, and to promote the happiness of so many others. The causes of such an important decision are still there, reminding us how we have built structures and continued to open channels of communication so that this beautiful art may express ineffable feelings and touch the sensibility of each human being on this isthmus so small and beyond.

EARLY DAYS AND DISCOVERY

According to the general history of Panama, Rodrigo de Bastidas, after visiting the Kuna (Guna) Yala Coast, an indigenous province inhabited by the Kuna people in northern Panama, arrived on October 5, 1501, at the Punta de Escribano, known during that time as *Retete*. Alonso de Ojeda's trip followed his. Later, on October 5, 1502, the conqueror Christopher Columbus, in his last voyage, arrived at the Bocas del Toro Coast. After fifty-two days of exploring new lands he also arrived at Punta de Escribano, near the Yeba River in the northern coast of Veragua, and founded Saint María de Belén, which was considered the first Spanish mainland (not island) discovered in the American continent (Ingram, 19).

Given the extensive pre-Columbian musical instruments discovered in Central America, we might conclude that there was a rich artistic and musical expression by the original inhabitants of the Meso-American region, a cultural legacy that has been lost, probably forever, due to the lack of documentation from the conquerors and evidence of written music prior to the arrival of the Europeans. With the exception of the ocarina and some variety of other wind instruments, some drums of different sizes and shapes, rattles, and some percussion instruments, we do not have too much knowledge of the musical creation of the pre-Columbian artistic development (Ingram, 20).

It is precisely with Columbus's last trip that the first precise and detailed account about the Old and New World encountered began. European conquistadores (explorers) started to come to the area via the Caribbean

Sea, which is the name given to the Atlantic Ocean in the north of the Panamanian isthmus (a narrow piece of land connecting two larger areas across an expanse of water that otherwise separates them) (Ingram, 19).

SPANISH COLONIALISM

Along with the explorers and conquerors, representatives of the clergy arrived at the isthmus with the purpose of evangelizing to the indigenous people. The most important step toward this direction was the introduction of liturgical chants. Vocal music is considered to be the first European musical expression in the Americas. Only a few explorers and religious practitioners could play some of the instruments. The exception was Ortíz the Musician as described by Bernal Díaz del Castillo in his celebrated writing *La Conquista de Nueva España* (The Conquer of New Spain) (Ingram, 20).

However, it is known that with the arrival of liturgical and sacred books there were a proliferation of Spanish instrumental music scores, such as the *Orphénica Lyra* by Miguel de Fuenllana and *Seis Libros del Delfín de la Música de Cifras para Tañer Vihuela* (the six books of tablatures to play the vihuela) by Luis de Narváez, two of the most prominent instrumental composers of the time in Europe. Besides sacred and religious music there are very rare references made by the chroniclers about popular songs and the performance of other instruments such as the *chirimías* (shawm), *dulzainas* (recorder), and *sacabuches* (sackbut). Of course, these were aside from the trumpet and drums, which were used for military purposes (Ingram, 21).

MUSIC IN CHURCH

With the signing of the *Pastorali Bula Oficii* (Official Papal Bull), a letter patent or charter by Pope Leon X on August 28, 1513 (a month before the discovery of the South Ocean by Vasco Núñez de Balboa on September 25, 1513, in the Darién Coast), as requested by King Ferdinand the Catholic, the Santa María La Antigua del Darién Archidiocesis was created, the first of its kind in the Americas, known by the name of *Primada de Tierra Firme* (Primitial Mainland). It gave the impetus to create the Bishop of Santa María de la Antigua del Darién and appointed the first bishop of the New World, Fray Juan de Quevedo, named by Pope Leon X (Ingram, 22).

After his installation as bishop, Fray Juan de Quevedo ordered *"seis libros del Canto Toledano, seis antifonarios y seis salterios toledanos"* (six Toledan chants, six antiphonals, and six Toledan salterios) for the church choir of Santa María la Antigua del Darién as well as *"un pesado clavecímbalo con fuelles"* (a heavy clavichord with bellows) that probably constitutes the first piano instrument that arrived in the New World (Ingram, 23).

FOUNDATION OF THE CITY OF PANAMA

In 1519, Governor Pedrarias Dávila, following the orders from the Spanish king of creating new cities in the New World and aware of the discoveries of the South Ocean already discovered by Vasco Núñez de Balboa in 1513, decided to found a new city in the south coast near an indigenous fishing town and called it Nuestra Señora de la Asunción. This was the first European city in the Pacific Ocean coast of the continent, today known as *La Vieja* (The Old). This city replaced Santa María la Antigua de Darién as the largest and most important city in the new mainland world.

It is interesting to underscore that at the beginning of 1535 indigenous people from the nearby town of Santa Marta, Colombia, were surprised in the morning by a concert as a result of a mandate of Pedro Fernández de Lugo, which ordered the troops to execute a work with a military character using *"con trompetas, chirimías y sacabuches"* (trumpets, shawms, and sackbuts). Some of the scholars believe that given the evidence examined, conquerors brought the instrumentation used by the military exercises: *pífanos, clarines, tambores, trompetas,* and *chirimías y sacabuches* (fifes, clarinets, drums, and trumpets), in addition to the instruments brought by the clergy, such as: *violas de arco, arpas, rabeles, bajones,* and *así como órganos pequeños o portátiles* (violas, harps, ravels, basses, and organs). We must be reminded that in 1496 the Catholic King and Queen traveled to

La Española (present-day Haiti and Dominican Republic), and according to the chronics of Las Casas some musical instruments were available for people to be happy and to share the instruments with others. Even though we may not know for certain, it was probable that the population already preferred such instruments as *vihuelas de arco y de mano, guitarras de cuatro y cinco cuerdas, laudes, flautas, arpas, dulcemelos*, and others (*vihuelas*, four- and five-string guitars, lutes, flutes, harps, and dulcimer) (Ingram, 24).

Some of the conquerors received musical instruction prior to arrival in the new world. This was the case of Diego de Nicuesa, founder of the *Nombre de Dios* (name of God) and governor of Veragua in 1508, who had an education as a "cortesan and *vihuela* musician." Notwithstanding in the second half of the century, some of the dignitaries of the New World hired the services of instrumentalists of the flute, guitar, or vihuela for their personal entertainment (Ingram, 25).

SEVENTEENTH-CENTURY MUSIC: A MUSIC INSTRUMENT INVENTORY

There are personal inventories of the seventeenth century that mentioned harps and vihelas in addition to violins and guitars, and other popular instruments, such as drums, flutes, and shawns, as referenced in festive activities. On the other hand, we know by the chronists that instruments accompanied liturgical processions, and the most common one was the vihuela, with its rich repertoire widely developed in the Spanish Peninsula with first-rate composers. Soon, the guitar and violin became very popular, while shawns and drums continued to be popular (Ingram, 27).

THE GREAT CHAPEL MASTER JUAN DE ARAUJO

Juan de Araujo (1646–1712), one of the prominent composers of American Baroque music, arrived as the Chapel's Maestro for the Cathedral in 1676, with over two hundred musical scores (Ingram, 29).

CITY POPULATION

The musical activity that took place in the majority of the villages and urban cities of the colonies was primarily that made in churches and convents with liturgical and sacred character, aside from dance music. This precarious situation in the musical arts, in addition to the constant destruction of records and archives in offices and personal residences, created a vacuum of information. However, it is known that the most popular domestic instruments were the guitar, the harp, and the vihuela or Flandes guitar as well as some keyboard instruments, such as clavichord and harpsichord, which were known as virginals because they were exported from England (Ingram, 31).

EIGHTEENTH-CENTURY MUSIC: MUSIC ACTIVITIES

Although it has been impossible to present precise references about Panama, it is known that the principal musical activity that took place at different villages of the colonies was, as already established, that practiced at Church. In addition to the contribution of diverse denominations, congregations, and *cofradias* (brotherhoods) by which all social classes were exposed to in Panama, we cannot forget the contributions of *mestizos*, blacks, and indigenous workers in general (Ingram, 36).

NINETEENTH-CENTURY MUSIC: THE FIRST PANAMANIAN CANTOR

At the end of the Illustration Age and the beginning of the nineteenth century, Dr. Rafael Lasso de la Vega (1758–1831), originally from the city of Santiago de Veraguas after being the doctoral clergyman of the Metropolitan Church in Bogotá, was named chantre of the Cathedral in Panama, a position he occupied for a limited amount of time since he was named Bishop of Mérida in October 1814. He is the only Panamanian that we are aware of that became chantre, an honor bestowed to him to direct the chorus and the music at Church. There was another musician by the name of Joseph Fernández de Miñano, but we cannot ascertain if he is originally from the Americas (Ingram, 39).

EMANCIPATION FROM SPAIN

Panama declared its independence from Spain on November 28, 1821, and became part of the "Bolivian" community of the Great Colombia, which was comprised of modern Panama, Colombia, Venezuela, Ecuador, northern Peru, and northern Brazil. Therefore, when describing the nineteenth-century music of Panama, it has to be within the context of the music activities in the towns of Bogota, Cartagena, and Boyaca in Colombia. In 1560 rises what could be considered the first music book in the Americas, *Tratado de Canto llano y polifonía* (Monophonic and Polyphonic Music Treatise) by Juan Pérez Materano, the publication of which was authorized by Joan of Austria, sister of Philip II on December 19, 1559, in Valladolid (Ingram, 40).

The poor concept about music that prevailed in most Latin American countries after a few centuries of history may be attributed to the kingdom of Ferdinand VII. It is enough to remember that by introducing the tauromachy, the traditional spectacle of one or more bulls fighting in a bull ring, the king best known as the "the Desired" declared that he did it to "counteract the negative reaction which may produce among his citizens the creation of a conservatory of music by his fourth wife Mary Christina of Borbon" (Ingram, 41).

FIRST PANAMANIAN COMPOSER

There is not much evidence about music activities right after independence. Many musicians were from abroad. We know that around 1830 there appeared the first composer from Panama, the guitar player Porras (full name unknown). Known as *El Maestro* (The Master), he taught guitar to ladies from high society in a time when piano was still unknown in the region and guitar was the preferred instrument (Ingram, 41).

FIRST MUSIC INSTITUTION

Coming from one of the many groups traveling for recreational functions, such as the operetta and zarzuela companies, a well-known French musician, Jean Marie Victor Dubarry, settled in the isthmus and is credited with founding the first Academy of Music. The Academy of Music was created to prepare young people who would form the Band of the Sovereign State Guard of the Isthmus of Panama in 1867, later known as the Public Force Band from 1882 to 1886 and from 1886 to May 1903 as the Presidential Band. Decree No. 110 of August 10, 1904, named it Republican Band (Ingram, 43). Since its founding, the band has played an important role in the artistic and cultural development of the new nation, running repertoire for protocol and ceremonial acts of the State, parades, retreats, and educational concerts and galas. Besides the names mentioned herein as directors of this band, so were the horn player, Luis Antonio García; the clarinet players, Rafael García and Silvestre Lugo; the renowned trumpet player José Luis Cajar Antillón, who had held the post from 1979 to 1990; and his deputy Ventura Delgado and the current director Virgilio Escala.

CREATION OF THE PHILHARMONIC SOCIETY

In March 1875, the Sociedad Filarmónica de Panamá (Philharmonic Society of Panama) was created. The first concert was presented on April 19, 1875, with the appearance of pianist Rosendo Arosemena (Ingram, 46). The society not only sponsored many subsequent concerts by Bach, Handel, Beethoven, and Verdi, but also gave piano lessons.

POPULAR MUSIC COMPOSERS

In the last two decades of the nineteenth century, Lino Boza migrated from the island of Cuba with his son Pablo Boza and his nephew Máximo Herculano Arrate Boza (born November 7, 1859, and died on August 9, 1936), who were musical cornerstones of the new nation in the making: Panama. Don Máximo Herculano, nicknamed Maestro "Chichito" in 1910, opened an academy to train musicians that would later integrate the Band of the Fire Department of Panama.

The Colombian José Manuel Rodríguez was another composer of the time who cultivated small musical forms such as *corridos, mazurkas, polkas, waltzes, gallops, habaneras, rumbas, dances, pasodobles,* and *school hymns*. He was a teacher of Régulo Ríos, who years later edited a book on music education.

FIRE DEPARTMENT BAND OF PANAMA

In the celebration on November 28, 1891, of the anniversary of the founding of the Fire Department of Panama, Commander Juan Antonio Guizado took the initiative to make the institution march to the beat of a brass band. The activity was entrusted to the director of the Colombia Battalion Military Band, Lucio Bonnel. The commander of the Fire Department, Don Florencio Arosemena, enthusiastic about the idea, organized on August 4, 1892, the first band of the Fire Department of Panama, although the band was officially founded on November 1, 1909, under the baton of Maestro Máximo H. Arrate B.

FIRST MUSIC TEACHERS

The Spanish Francisco Cebamanos came to the isthmus accompanied by the Soler brothers. When the group disintegrated, he settled in Chitre where he formed an artistic and comedy group that offered free functions for charities. He also taught music and musical instruments free of charge. That is how he formed the Band of the Fire and Police of Chitre, Herrera, and Los Santos. Daniel Cárdenas was one of his students, who later became a great accordionist and songwriter of typical Panamanian music for over fifty years.

The last decade of the nineteenth century welcomes two musicians of Spanish origin, first Don Santos Jorge Amatrian (1870–1941), to whom the School of Music of Madrid channeled its inspiration. Around the same time, Angel Julio R., to whom is owed a widespread treatise on music theory, and the versatile Esteban Peralta, featured as a pianist, organist, and composer, also became known (Ingram, 45).

DISTINGUISHED MUSICIAN

Careen Key or Carenero Island, an island in the province of Bocas del Toro, brought to the music world the pianist Luis Carl Russell, on August 5, 1902. Like many in his day, he began studies with his father, Alexander Russell, a church organist. Upon moving to Colón in 1918 and immigrating to the United States the following year, thanks to his own efforts and determination, he developed the jazz orchestral style known as New Orleans style. He played with the best bands of the fabulous 1920s as the Dixie Syncopators of the trumpeter "King" Oliver in 1926, and he even led his own band, touring from 1935 to 1943, joined by the great trumpeter Louis "Satchmo" Armstrong.

TWENTIETH-CENTURY MUSIC: EMANCIPATION FROM THE GREAT COLOMBIA AND THE FIRST OFFICIAL MUSIC SCHOOL

By the month of March, just four months after November 3, 1903, the date of the separation of Panama from Colombia after becoming independent from Spain on November 28, 1821, the National Constituent Act dictated the first public education Act 11 of March 23, 1904, Article 56, authorizing the Executive power to establish an Institute of Fine Arts in the capital of the Republic, comprised of a School of Fine Arts and a School of Music and Rhetoric (Ingram, 61).

NATIONAL THEATER

In 1906 the National Constituent Convention featured the construction of the National Theater of Panama culminating in 1908, with an official opening on October 1 of that year on the occasion of the inauguration of the second constitutional president of the new Republic, Don Domingo of Obaldía. Twenty days later, the art opening was made with the opera *Aida* by Giuseppe Verdi by Italy's Mario Lambardi, which remained until 1910. Besides this, several Italian opera companies acted on the isthmus, namely: Sigaldi (1910), Morton Opera Co mpany (1913), the Grand Italian Opera Company of Manzini (1915), and in the same year Cleo Vicini and the Grand Opera Company of Bracale Adolfo (1917–1920, 1922, 1928, and 1930) (Ingram, 63).

FIRST MUSIC PERSONALITY IN PANAMA

The violinist, organist, and music critic Narciso Garay Díaz was appointed as the first director (1876–1953) of the School of Fine Arts. Since 1891 he received lessons in harmony, philosophy, and law in Bogotá, Colombia. In 1897 he left for Paris, France, to continue studying music. He later advanced his education in Brussels, Belgium, and returned to Paris under the tutelage of Vincent d'Indy. He returned briefly to the country and went back to Paris to attend the composition course of the eminent Gabriel Fauré, with classmates such as Maurice Ravel, George Enesco, and Florent Schmitt (Ingram, 43, 59).

OTHER MUSIC INSTITUTIONS

At that time there were two musical educational institutions: a music academy directed by Jean Marie Victor Dubarry and the National School of Music lead by Don Narciso Garay Díaz. The latter had flutist Arturo Dubarry (1858–1911), the most talented son of Jean Marie Victor Dubarry and the first Panamanian composer of music for bands born in the nineteenth century, and who influenced the beginning of the twentieth century with dancing forms of the time and teaching woodwinds.

Don Julio J. Fábrega, Secretary of Education, issued the Organic Decree No. 23 on May 13, 1904, organizing and regulating the National School of Music and Rhetoric. During the following year the first evening of music took place, where the country's first polyphonic choir performed and Don Narciso Garay Díaz sang the Solemn Mass of Gioacchino Rossini.

In 1906 a group of students founded the Philharmonic Circle, and in 1908 the Alumni Society. These groups acquired improvements in all areas until orchestra classes opened, culminating in a gala concert on August 7, 1909, at the newly opened National Theatre. The program included European classics such as Wagner, Schumann, Gounod, Boito, Mendelssohn, Bizet, Beethoven, Thomas, Viotti, Massenet, Verdi, Chopin, Weber, a movement of Mozart's Symphony No. 21, and the premiere of the "Patriotic March" of Narciso Garay, under his direction. The full orchestra intervened while the Choir of the National School of Music and Rhetoric was heard in a Bach chorale. On January 21, 1910, the first orchestral symphony of the School of Music took place at the National Theatre, marking the anniversary of the founding of the new City of Panama. The orchestral symphony included sixty-one musicians, distributed as follows: five flutes, three oboes, three clarinets, three bassoons, five horns, two trumpets, three trombones, one timpani, two percussionists, one harp, twenty violinists between first and second, three violas, five cellos, and five basses.

NATIONAL CONSERVATORY OF MUSIC AND RHETORIC

The Concert Society was created toward the end of the first decade (1910) of the nascent twentieth century that united a large number of amateur musicians, professionals, and students. This group made its premiere on

February 22, 1910, at the National Theatre, offering numerous programs of symphonic quality. That same year, the National Assembly issued Law 46 of 1910 that created the National Conservatory of Music and Rhetoric. As a result, in 1911 the National School of Music became the National Conservatory of Music and Rhetoric. The following year the highest-known seat of learning music was regulated and organized: the Panama National Conservatory. In September 1912, a presentation of the first act of the opera *Faust* by Charles Gounod took place, with the participation of students, soloists, corps de ballet, and a full orchestra.

END OF THE FIRST CONSERVATORY OF MUSIC

In 1918, the conservatory was forced to close due to a budget cut of the national government, but their work was carried out privately until 1921, under the direction of María Nicolasa de Las Mercedes and Nicole Garay, daughter of the painter Don Epifanio and sister of Don Narciso Garay Díaz (Ingram, 71). Narciso Garay Díaz— who led the symphony that originated the first conservatory—consistently continued giving a variety of monthly concerts. The withdrawal of government support for music education hindered orchestral activities; therefore, intellectuals and artists joined forces to prevent the country from remaining inactive musically. Dr. José Dolores Moscote, rector of the National Institute (prestigious grammar school that in 1935 hosted the birth of the University of Panama), gave warmth to Literary-Musical Saturdays of the National Institute in the years 1926 and 1927. In 1927 the National Institute received the services of Madrilenian Ricardo Sosaya (1887–1946), pianist, teacher, and choir director, who, among his many artistic activities, brought together a symphony orchestra that took part in paying tribute on November 28, 1929, to the National poet María Olimpia de Obaldía, playing the overture *Rienzi* by Richard Wagner and Johannes Brahms's *Hungarian Dance No. 6*. During this hiatus, Paul and Máximo Arrate Boza, Walter Myers, and Antonio Henríquez developed activities with the National Orchestra; there were zarzuela presentations by the Academy or Conservatory of Music, Song and Rhetoric (1928); institution of musical education Arturo Merel Murt (1898–1963), pianist of Catalan origin; and operas by the National School of Opera (1926–1938), founded by Italian-born tenor Alfredo Graziani (1878–1957). It also privately operated the Alcove Conservatory (Colón, pianist María Alcové).

SECOND CONSERVATORY OF MUSIC

Dr. Arnulfo Arias Madrid, president, created by Executive Decree No. 100 of 1941 the Conservatory of Music and Rhetoric and appointed as director the already famous violinist Alfredo de Saint Malo Orillac. His fellow violinist, Teodoro Haengel, dedicated his "Serenade for Violin and Piano," made on July 28, 1941, to the institution and was secretary to the cellist Walter Myers. Don Alfredo assigned the Italian-born and nationalized US citizen cellist Mosa Chavivi the leadership of this second conservatory. Years later, the violinist Alexander Feinland replaced him and was able to bring the orchestral ensemble to an amazing artistic level, as witnesses say (Ingram, 85).

NATIONAL INSTITUTE OF MUSIC

Also during the 1940s there were some organizations related to art, highlighting the Concert Society Daniels promoted by Don Herbert de Castro; Musical Art Society; and the Pro Musical Art Society (1942) founded by Federico Jimeno and directed by Alfredo de Saint Malo Orillac. It originated in 1945 with the quartet of Don Alfredo Saint Malo and Alexander Feinland as violinists, Ernst Baker on the viola, and cello by Walter Myers, as well as newspaper articles and musical guidance written by Edwin de la Guardia, professor of the Second Conservatory. Because of this promotion, the conservatory achieved an approximate enrollment of 1,200 students served by thirty-seven teachers. However, a 1953 law decree left all teachers ineffectual, but they reappeared twenty-four hours later with the title of National Institute of Music, with professor Roque Cordero as CEO, together with Jorge Luis McKay (1891–1965) as managing director, who contributed to the musical literature with his ballet *Anayansi* and for years maintained a warehouse under his name that supplied musical instruments to its customers who held him in high esteem as a gentleman of fine treatment (Ingram, 91). As advisory director, Gonzalo Augustín "Chalo" Brenes Candanedo (David 1907, Chiriquí 2003), on his return from the Conservatory of Leipzig, Germany, with a grant from the national government presided by Don Rodolfo Chiari, bequeathed his interest in the study of folklore, a field in which the couple Manuel Fernando Zárate (University Professor of Chemistry, Guararé 1899, 1968 in Panama) and Dora "Eda Nela" Pérez de Zárate (Spanish teacher, Panama 1912, 2001) ventured in meritorious research, in his prolific output spearheading the musical farce *The Cockroach Mandinga* joined by the poet Rogelio Sinán (pseudonym Don Bernardo Domínguez Alba, born in Taboga, the magical island, on April 25, 1902, and died in Panama on October 7, 1994), and his "Songs" collected in a volume called *Tonadas del Trópico Niño*.

Later on, the sixth decade of the twentieth century shows an exodus of teachers and a decrease in enrollment to three hundred students. The Education Minister, Alfredo Ramírez, replaced in 1961 the name of INM with School of Musical Education, and a new manager came in from 1965 to 1972, organist Damián Carles P., who graduated with a master's degree from the University of Chicago. In the 1980s, with Professor Marcos Aguilera as director, a movement of teachers concerned about the fate of the National School of Music and with the consent of the then director of the National Institute of Culture, Dr. Diógenes Cedeño Cenci, rescued the name of National Institute of Music, which remains to this day and is run by the pianist María Elena Carles, who holds a Master of Music obtained from Illinois State University followed by the director, Ricardo Risco R. and subdirector Maestra Ariadna Nuñez.

NATIONAL SYMPHONY ORCHESTRA

Investigating the beginning of the symphony orchestra involves trying to tie up loose ends. Just as it is to remember the Philharmonic Society of Panama, whose founding members in 1911 were Narciso Garay and Máximo Herculano Arrate Boza, the operetta and zarzuela companies that performed between 1910 and 1927 and the late 1930s when, after seven years of study ing music in Paris with teachers such as Albert Roussell and Arthur Honegger, came to the isthmus Herbert de Castro (1905–1969). He organized chamber concerts, which included the Panameño Quartet, composed of violinists Antonio Alberto Andrete and Antonio Henríquez, violist Gilberto Pérez, and cellist Walter Myers, which constituted the basis of the future orchestra. In its literary musical evenings in 1932, participated figures were novelist Rogelio Sinán, Octavio Méndez Pereira (in 1935 he became the first rector of the University of Panama), Professor Otilia Arosemena, Abbie de Linares as pianist, flutist Jacques de Castro, pianist and organist Avelino Muñoz Barrios (born in La Mesa de Veraguas on December 20, 1912, and died in Puerto Rico on January 24, 1962, as his widow, Mrs. Xenia, kindly informed us during a telephone interview through "Especiales de Crisol" Monday morning January 25, 2010), Pablo Garrido, and baritone Federico Jimeno, a Colombian, who died in Panama on January 13, 1979.

The enthusiasm of Don Herbert managed to attract more units to form a small orchestra to make public presentations. Two prominent musicians focused their musical concern from the point of view of the trade union. Pedro Rebolledo and Luis (" Lucho") Azcárraga (pianist born December 31, 1899) grouped several musical units, and on September 7, 1934, they met in the house of H Street No. 51 to form a musical partnership to which they gave the name of Musical Union of Panama. The president of the Union organized the orchestra and choir that premiered at the Cathedral Church on November 22, 1936, during the solemn mass in honor of the patron saint of musicians, Santa Cecilia.

The Musical Union decided to seek the free collaboration of Herbert de Castro. By accepting the request, Herbert de Castro became the organizer and first director of the orchestra of the Musical Union of Panama. The rehearsals did not wait. They acquired new premises on top of Bar Puerta de Oro (Golden Gate), corner of J Street and Central Avenue. Thus, on November 22, 1938, the Orchestra of the Musical Union was ready, composed of enthusiastic local musicians. Both orchestra and choir directed by De Castro sang Glory Mass in the Cathedral Church in honor of St. Cecilia. The work of De Castro leading the Orchestra of the Musical Union uninterruptedly continued, offering quality concerts. When the Musical Union was no longer able to keep its own premises, the orchestra continued to rehearse at the private house of Mr. De Castro, at the National Institute, in the rehearsal room of the band of the Fire Department, and at the National Theatre—in short, wherever the time and the willingness of people interested in this cultural work allowed it. As director of the

Orchestra Union Musical, Herbert de Castro worked without interruption from 1938 until 1941, when decree No. 65, signed by President Arnulfo Arias, officially established the Symphony (National) Orchestra of Panama and empowered once again Herbert de Castro to organize and conduct the first official symphonic grouping of the Republic of Panama. On August 18, 1941, at the National Theater, the Symphony (National) Orchestra of Panama offered its first concert to the local audience. In 1944 Walter Myers (1891–1973) took over the management of the orchestra to just over 1952. These were beneficial years for orchestral activities due to military and civilian personnel stationed in the former Canal Zone that constantly moved to the capital to interact musically.

A strategy similar to that used with the second conservatory is used with the orchestra. It was renamed National Orchestra in 1953, and was redirected by Don Herbert—who had returned to his homeland years before—until 1964, when he resigned to qualify for retirement and died some years later. Roque Cordero took over the direction from 1964 to 1966, when he left for the United States, and Maestro Eduardo Charpentier became chief conductor of the National Symphony Orchestra (NSO) until June 1988, assisted by Néstor Castillo and Jorge Ledezma Bradley, who currently directs the orchestra.

THE BAND OF THE NATIONAL POLICE

At the initiative of the president of the Republic, Don Juan Demóstenes Arosemena, and the then head of the National Police, Colonel Manuel Pino, on September 20, 1938, the Band of the National Police was founded in order to promote two principles: the cultural and the military. As the parent corporation continued evolving, functional and artistic subgroups developed. These groups included the concert band, popular music groups Pearl and Latino Heritage, the Band of Bugles and Drums, the Band Voices and Strings, and the folk group.

CLASSICAL MUSICIANS

Born August 16, 1917, and raised in Panama and the United States (died in the United States on December 27, 2008), Roque Cordero won international awards. His bountiful productions include *Capricho Interiorano* (1939), *Eight Miniatures* for a small orchestra (1948), *Duet 1954* for two pianos (dedicated to Kelly and Jaime Ingram, 1954), *String Quartet No. 1* (commissioned by the Coolidge Foundation, 1960), *Concerto for Violin and Orchestra* (commissioned by the Koussevitzky Foundation, 1962), *Cantata for Peace* (commissioned by the National Arts Endowment, 1979), *Fourth Symphony* (Panama) for orchestra (1986), and *Jubilant Fanfare for Brass, Wood and Percussion* (commissioned by the Cincinnati Symphony Orchestra, 1994) (Ingram, 92–95). He was director of the Latin American Music Center (LAMúsiCa) and professor of composition at Indiana University, and from 1972, he was distinguished professor emeritus at Illinois State University. His pedagogical contributions include the music books *Curso de Teoría* (Theory Course) and *Tratado de Armonía* (Harmony Treatise). Written in Spanish, they served as textbooks to thousands of musicians in Latin America.

With transcendent work as a bassist in the NSO and teacher at the National Institute of Music, arranger and director Clarence Martin (1922–1980) is greatly remembered for "The Fugitive's Hideaway." Martin came from a musical family atmosphere, and so did Victor Everton "Boa" McRae (died on June 12, 2004), better known as Victor Boa, pianist, in the orchestra for "The Perfect" of Armando Boza, Avelino Muñoz, and international stars such as Woody Herman, Gerry Mulligan, and Charlie "Bird" Parker, and arranger of classic jazz and fusions with other musical genres. He is the composer of more than three hundred experimental subjects genres creating "tambo jazz" and "pana jazz," and is the director of the group Down Beat Five.

On March 12, 1927, Eduardo Charpentier, son of Eduardo Charpentier de Castro, was born in Panama. He studied at the National Conservatory of Music and Rhetoric in Panama, Roosevelt College in Chicago, Marlboro College in Vermont, Eastman School of Music, University of Rochester, Conservatoire National de Musique, Paris, and Columbia Pacific University in California, where he received his Doctor of Philosophy with a major in Music and Education. The State Department of the United States awarded him the US Government Research Professor Grant. He was a member of the National Association of Composers and Conductors of New York, the American Federation of Musicians of the United States, among many other achievements and awards national and abroad. From September 1966 to June 1988 he served as director of the NSO of Panama. From 1972 to 1990 he was founding director of the Department of Music (1972) and Chamber Orchestra (1992) of the University of Panama.

Jaime Ricardo Ingram Jaén was born in Panama City, Panama, in 1928. He began piano studies with his mother, and he continued at the National Conservatory of Music and Rhetoric of Panama with Orillac Adriana Orillac J., Ethel Carbone, and Alberto Sciarretti. In 1947 he traveled to New York on a state scholarship, and with the aid of the Pro Art Society, he furthered his studies at the renowned Juilliard Institute, where he obtained by competition the Olga Samaroff scholarship, with whom he studied until her death. He then continued his studies with Professor Joseph Bloch, until he received the Diploma of Piano. When traveling to Paris, he won another scholarship to study with pianist Yves Nat, in the Conservatory of Music, and later spent two years with Professor Bruno Seidlhofer in Vienna, Austria. His piano career took him through the major cities of America, Europe, and the Middle East, giving recitals and concerts with orchestra, and he was the founder and first director of Kinder Music and Conservatory of Music James Ingram S.A. (1961), the National Association of Music (1962), and the National Institute of Culture (1973). He has participated in international festivals and organizations. He is the author of numerous articles on music, and was Ambassador Extraordinary and Plenipotentiary of Panama in the Kingdom of Spain, in Argentina, in the Kingdom of Morocco, the Vatican, and the Sovereign Order of Malta, in addition to being awarded several awards and honors, and he has appeared in prestigious publications. His teaching experience developed in reputable centers as associate professor in the Department of Music of the Faculty of Fine Arts of the University of Panama.

POPULAR MUSICIANS

The experienced Panamanian trumpeter Victor "Vitín" Paz scored a career as one of the most sought after trumpeters in the world of commercial recording in New York.

Danilo Pérez Enrico, after completing his primary and secondary music education, obtained a scholarship to study classical piano, which led him to the University of Indiana. He concentrated on jazz at Berklee College of Music in Boston, sponsored by the Quincy Jones and Oscar Peterson grants. His musicality allowed him to alternate with a long list of stars led by Paquito D'Rivera, "Dizzy" Gillespie, Roy Haynes, Charlie Haden, Lionel Hampton, Freddie Hubbard, Dave Valentin, and Flora Purim. He has continued the triumphant journey traced by Panamanians predecessors such as Luis Carl Russel and Victor Boa. The Jazz Festival organized by pianist Pérez and his delegation is in its seventeenth edition in Panama in 2016, and was preluded by the radio programs of "Roberto Mariette, Ernesto Crouch, Ray Fernández, César Villalobos, yours truly (Edward Irwin, MA), and more recently Noris Miranda, Derek Irving and Octavio Arosemena (and probably many more, perhaps since the beginning of radio transmission in Panama) are faithful testimony to this reality" (Ingram 140). Associations such as Jazz Unlimited, the Embassy of the United States, and the Boquete Jazz Festival have promoted presentations of true giants elsewhere.

UNIVERSITY OF PANAMA

The Music Department of the University of Panama first opened its doors in July 1972, with its founding director Maestro Eduardo Charpentier. Since then and to strengthen the foundation of this novel department, originally attached to the Faculty of Arts, Humanities and Education (later Faculty of Humanities), there was a great collaborative effort that, over the years, allowed it to evolve—with its Music School and School of Musical Instruments and Singing—into the backbone of the novel Faculty of Fine Arts. The school offered a Bachelor in Music Education, Bachelor in Teaching Musical Instruments or Singing, and Bachelor of Teaching Musical Instruments or Singing along with the Master of Music.

The musical extension function of the department was developed by the Guitar Chamber ensemble, and until 2002 the Philharmonic Choir (1991–2002), the Rondalla (1993–2002), and the Quintet "Mendez Pereira" (2001–2003), the Panama Saxophone Quartet (2001), and the most recent group, the Slide Trombone Quartet (2001).

With the main objective of promoting national artists, in 1984 a group of enthusiastic music lovers such as the late architect René Brenes, with piano training at the Conservatory of Santiago de Chile; the pianist Carmen Linares; and soprano Alicia Sáenz, among other Panamanian professionals, founded the Pro Music Society.

The Philharmonic Orchestra of the University of Panama was a high-standards music teaching project that started on August 8, 1988, by Maestro Néstor J. Castillo Restrepo, intended so that the House Méndez Pereira could develop within the short, medium, and long term, and framed on its needs, greatness, and limitations. It is one of the most specialized tools to increase cultural efforts, as is expected of a university orchestra.

This University Philharmonic began with the accumulated experience in the Philharmonic Chamber Orchestra Association (Philharmonic Chamber Orchestra) of a small group of teachers, students, and administrators, called Musical Circle of Latin American Studies, which is dedicated to research, composition, and performance of regional and universal music. Backed by the current central government, it has incorporated orchestral sections such as Bronzes of the Hill, the 2 in Sax, digital interface instruments, percussion, violin, and singing, along with technical support—while the Council Academic No. 44-99 of October 6, 1999, adopted Resolution No. 40-99 GSP, by which it is constituted and regulated—and continues to gradually improve through its multiple presentations at the national and international level, thus fulfilling its ideals of closer artistic and cultural ties among sister nations and friends of the institution through the art of music and harmony of women and men of good will.

In November 2003, with the support of the International Soka Gakkai of Panama, the first compact disc of the orchestra was produced, titled "Centennial Philharmonic" as a joint tribute to the University of Panama and the SGIP at the Centennial of the Republic.

The Symphonic Band was created on October 16, 1992, with twenty-four musicians and a director, thus being officially formed. The Capital District mayor instructed to place the Band in the Municipal House, where they worked out and did relevant studies and functions; namely, conducting retreat programs, concerts, and varied musical activities in municipal institutions, parks, streets, and other government entities. At the same time a specific budget was established for the purchase of instruments and a bus that served to fulfill its many activities. Thus was born the musical group of the Municipality of Panama that proudly stood among the best, with professionals in this discipline as their music directors, beginning with its founder Maestro Efraín S. Cruz de Gracia, Moisés Salas (died January 2004), and Dino Nugent, who graduated in 1998 in Composition from the Federal University of Minas Gerais, Brazil, and who directed numerous concerts with its symphony orchestra.

The Faculty of Fine Arts of the University of Panama was created on October 28, 1992, by resolution of the Academic Council at its Session No. 35-92. It is the Panama University's academic response to the unblemished need of the artistic community. It is dedicated to improving the status and accreditation of the national artist, to a vision of excellence aimed at raising the cultural level of the Panamanians, and to educate society to the usufruct of the aesthetic expressions. Hence it has a flexible administrative and academic structure to allow for practical and conceptual innovations and developments in the different fields of the arts. It continues highlighting its mission that the "Faculty of Fine Arts exists to provide spaces and meeting places for cultural diversity, national production and to generate a sustainable movement with local and international projection."

In its framework of principles are found the values that could serve as guidelines for faculty: artistic excellence, dedication, harmony, flexibility, creativity, cultural influence, and recognition. The University's "window of the soul," as some have called it, is composed of the Department of Music (1972), Department of Visual Arts (1988), the Department of Theater Arts (1992), and the Department of Dance (1992), in chronological order of creation and magnitude. The school offers a Bachelor of Fine Arts majoring in Theater Arts, Bachelor of Fine Arts majoring in Visual Arts with an emphasis in drawing and painting or print or sculpture, or Visual Art Design, Bachelor of Fine Arts majoring in dance with an emphasis on classical ballet, modern dance or jazz, and character dance or folklore or ethnic dance. It also offers a Bachelor (Teaching) of Music, Bachelor (Teaching) Musical Instruments or (of) Singing, and the Master of Music. It offers services at a national level, especially in the Regional University Center of Columbus, Regional University Center of Los Santos, and the Regional University Center of Veraguas.

The award "Women in the Arts" was approved by the Board of the Faculty of Fine Arts (University of Panama) No. 2 on June 1, 2001, to honor Panamanian ladies or resident s of the isthmus for their training and experience in any of the artistic expressions. The first three ladies honored were Ginela Vásquez in dance, Ileana Solís in theater, and Xenia Muñoz in visual arts. On 2003 this award honored a lady in music. Also generated and approved are the Departmental Board of Music, No. 1-02 on May 21, 2002; Board of School of Fine Arts No. 1-02 on April 2, 2002; Academic Affairs Committee on May 9, 2002; and Academic Council of the University of Panama No. 20-02 on May 15, 2002. The Centennial Memorial Lecture of the Republic, which honors Panamanian citizens—preferably while they are alive—that thanks to their talents, dedication, and personal sacrifices have excelled musically in the country and abroad, launched on June 1, 2002, with a tribute to Maestro Victor "Vitín" Paz, followed by the homage on October 26, 2002, to the Panamanian divas Marta Estela Paredes and Leona Herrera, and in 2003 a tribute (posthumous) to Mauricio Smith and others. Similarly, the Board of the School of Fine Arts No. 1-03 on May 9, 2003, unanimously approved the request to the Honorable Academic Council to grant the title of Honorary Professor of the University of Panama in the Faculty of Fine Arts to the following personalities: Victor Nicolás "Vitín" Paz and Solanilla (Music).

At 7 p.m., the Gregorian calendar marked the day December 17, 1992, and twenty-four hours before the Extraordinary Administrative Council of 12/18/92, No. 10-92 by Resolution No. 67-92, approved the creation of the Chamber Orchestra of the University of Panama. This novel musical group gave its inaugural concert in the staff room of the Faculty of Humanities, under the direction of Maestro Eduardo Charpentier and as assistant oboist Luis Efrain Castro de León, who was born in Juan Díaz, Panama, August 19, 1935, and currently directs with great dedication. Castro began his studies at the National Conservatory of Music, and continued with American musicians until graduating in the Music Department of the University of Panama. He has given recitals and performed as a soloist with orchestras in cities across the continent, besides being first oboist of the NSO, and he is the creator—along with Marco A. Aguilera—of the Youth Plan of the NSO for the study of string instruments and teacher at INM and the Faculty of Fine Arts where he became vice dean (1994–1997) and dean (1997–2000 and 2003–2006).

The Symphonic Band of the office of Student Affairs at the University of Panama was founded in March 1996 and was directed from its inception by Maestro Efraín Cruz de Gracia. The band was mostly comprised of students from various university academic units, as well as faculty and staff, playing woodwinds, brass, and percussion. With its varied repertoire, ranging from classical to modern and from national to international, the band gave concerts across the country, in addition to special events for Educational Radio and Television Channel 11 and National Television (TVN) Channel 2.

It is necessary to emphasize the contribution of the music bands of centers, cycles, colleges, schools, and public institutions and individuals incorporated as the center band of Vista Alegre under the baton of Leoni Delgado; the music band "The Lion of Judah" of the Bilingual Center of Vista Alegre directed by Carlos Rodríguez; the music band of the School Cristóbal Adán Urriola under the direction of Nicolás A. Montero; the music band "Victor Raúl González O." of Moisés Castillo Ocaña College directed by Dimas Rodríguez; the music band "Herbert Smith" of José Daniel Crespo College with Julio Zamora's baton; the band of the college of La Salle led by Leopoldo Elías Moreno; the band of St. Christopher Episcopal College under the direction of Earl Graves; the music band "Virgilio Escala" of Pedro Sánchez College led by Virgilio Escala; the band of the College Saint George led by Luis Lugo; the band of Jose María Tejada Roca led by Juan E. Salazar; the music band "Ascanio Arosemena" of the Professional School "Isabel Herrera Obaldía" directed by Ameth Shreeves; the music band of the American Institute led by Maestro Manuel Palma; the band and of the Institute Justo Arosemena originally directed by Ricauter "Palito" Hayes, later by Fernando "Tito" Rodríguez Cabrera, Manuel Moreno, Alfonso Lewis, and currently Roberto Zuñiga; the music band of Benigno Jiménez Garay Institute led by Elliot Simpson; the music band of José Dolores Moscote Institute under the baton of Rafael Tejada; the music band of the National Institute (BAMIN) directed by Antonio "Periquillo" Paredes and in 2009 by José Antonio Reyna; the music band "Armando Villa" of the Fermín Naudeau Institute who was led Ronaldo Ivan Ceville, later José Manuel Caballero Pérez and currently Isaac Reyes; the music band of the Pan American Institute under the direction of Rafael Tejada; the band of the *Instituto Panameño de Turismo* (IPT, Panamanian Tourist Institute) of the Chorrerra under the baton of Faustino Sánchez; the music band "Glory" of the *Soka Gakkai Internacional de Panamá* (SGIP, Soka Gakkai International of Panama) directed by Dámaso Vergara; the band of the Urraca Institute led by Omar Morales, and many more where youth musical talent parades.

Another festival is noteworthy: the Panama III International Guitar Encounter (1999). Its founder and current artistic director, the Panamanian guitarist and composer Emiliano Pardo Tristán, was born in Santiago de Veraguas and trained at the Panama National Institute of Music, the Royal Conservatory of Music in Madrid, Spain, and Temple University, Philadelphia. This enriching experience that has Panama as its headquarters periodically finds Panamanian artists and artists from other latitudes, who make the guitar a means of expression and transmission of musical art. The administrative director is Don Enrique Téllez.

SCANNING THE HORIZON

New musical groups were formed comprised of young musicians. The year 2001 saw the birth of the Bel Canto Foundation, led by communicator and cultural and sports promoter Juan Carlos Tapia Rodríguez to promote opera singing in Panama.

In parallel emerged the Foundation Friends of the Arts, an organization with legal personality granted by the Ministry of Government and Justice. It is a private entity, independent and nonprofit, that promotes and develops artistic and cultural activities to raise the level of cultural life of the Panamanian population. And finally, the Foundation of Fine Arts organized the First World Song Festival, whose president and CEO was the promoter Alfonso "Papito" Almanza Serrato.

Maestro Jaime Ingram created and chaired the Panama First International Piano Competition, staged at the National Theatre from November 15 to 21, 2004, thanks to the generosity of Yamaha, Maxell, the National Brewery, SA, Multi Credit Bank, General Bank, Manzanillo International Terminal, National Institute of Culture, Municipality of Panama, Emily Motta Foundation, Inocencio Galindo V., and María Quelquejeu de Galindo, Juan Carlos Tapia, Allegro, and Farallón Aquaculture. The second competition was scheduled for November 2006.

The singing enthusiasts are proud of the birth in 2008 of a Panamanian Opera Foundation and the reappearance of the Hei Group, SA that promote artistic services such as the First National Competition of Music Bands.

CONCLUSION

We ask Saint Cecilia to reconcile us with the past and to forgive the involuntary omissions or sacrificed gestures and details for lack of space, and to strengthen present ties and to grant a better future for all for whom music is a universal but abstract language. Similarly music is one, as is the electrical current that we can see, feel, and handle; human beings have given names to these expressions, but underneath is unique. Hence, from Luis Carl Russell and Victor Boa to pianists Jaime Ingram, Carlos Dutary, and Ricardo Noriega Cuevas; from harpsichordist Julieta Alvarado de Rieppel to Danilo Pérez and Juan Carlos de León; or from Narciso Garay Díaz, Eduardo Charpentier, and Efraín Cruz to Ildemaro Correa, Carlos Tovar Pérez, Samuel Iván Robles, and José Manuel Caballero; all have made and continue to produce quality music. That was their intention—giving rise to new generations. We owe it to this country so dear that deserves and needs it.

REFERENCES

Ingram Jaén, Jaime. (2008). *La Música de Panamá*, Panamá, República de Panamá: Editorial Universitaria Carlos Manuel Gasteazoro.
Castillo, Nestor. (2010). Telephone interview with Mrs. Xenia Muñoz through "Especiales de Crisol."

Part III

South America

Chapter Twelve

Argentina

Alicia de Couve and Claudia Dal Pino

INTRODUCTION

The purpose of this chapter is to provide a general perspective of the development of music teaching in the Argentine Republic from the pre-Hispanic period up to the present.

The following periodization has the aim of facilitating the temporal localization of facts. The dates are a mere setting for the referred events.

PRE-HISPANIC PERIOD (FROM ABOUT 11,000 BC UP TO THE SIXTEENTH CENTURY AD)

The data presented in this section allows us to make some speculations that are nowadays built upon the remaining documents and materials from the pre-Hispanic cultures because, as stated by Gudemos (1998), "It is difficult to understand and approach the complex of social, natural and supernatural realities that demand man an active participation according to the cultural norms established or concerted in each social core."

Several cultures settled in various times and locations in the vast territory of the present Argentine Republic (almost 2,800,000 square kilometers without taking into account the 970,000 kilometers corresponding to the Antarctic Sector and the 3,900 of the continental islands). The first signs of people were found in the south of the country, in the Patagonia, and date from 11,000 BC.

On the arrival of the Spaniards to these lands, the *Guarani* lived at the Northeast, while other American Indians as the *Diaguitas*, the *Quilmes*, the *Cafayates*, the *Yocaviles*, the *Andalgalaes*, the *Amaichas*, and the *Guachitas* lived in the *Puna* and the *Quebradas* (downs) of the Northwest. They used aerophones (several flutes, horns, *sikus*—a kind of panpipes), idiophones (bells, rattles), membranophones, and chordophones (stretched strings) made of bones, ceramics, and metal, as it appears from many archaeological sites. It is assumed that they played them in vocal and instrumental expressions with sacred, festive, or war intentions. According to the testimony of some European evangelists, as the letters by Father Martin Schmid (1694–1773) referred to the Guarani, these music performances were accompanied by dance (Guillermo Furlong, Josefina Pla, Szarán and Ruiz Nestosa, and others).

Over the centuries, different peoples settled in the Patagonia, as for example the *Tehuelches*, the *Onas*, and the *Mapuches*, who were nomad pickers and hunters. With regard to the Mapuches, it is known that there is not a word for music in their language, possibly because it was linked to religious beliefs, though they also developed vocal and instrumental music with loving or festive character. Mapuche musical instruments comprise aerophones (*tutruca, loquin, cullcull, pifilca, pinquilhue*), membranophones (*caquel cultrum* and *kultrum*), idiophones (the *huala*—a kind of maraca—and the *cada cada*—sea shells), and chordophones (the *quinquercahue* or araucanian—violin). These instruments might be played alone or in groups in ceremonies such as the *Nguillatún*, which is still performed in villages belonging to the Mapuche community, such as Chiuquilihuín (Avaca, 2009, 18).

In short, we can infer that aboriginal people addressed music as one of the expressive languages that was passed from generation to generation through informal teaching (by diffuse influence of the environment or without an expressed educative intention) or through nonformal teaching (set of educational activities with more or less degrees of systematization).

PERIOD OF THE CONQUEST AND EVANGELIZATION (1536–1776)

The Spanish Crown, for which the territorial conquest and religion went hand in hand, dominated part of the territories of present-day Argentina from the sixteenth century through three colonizing streams—on the north from the Viceroyalty of Peru, on the west from the General Captaincy of Chile, and on the east from the Atlantic—which derived from the foundation of villages and cities in different chronological moments. The Spanish settlers brought their songs, dances, and instruments. Roman Catholic priests who were in charge of celebrating religious services for the Spaniards and to convert indigenous populations to the Christian faith accompanied them.

Music was present from the very beginning of the conquest, even when Pedro de Mendoza (1499?–1537) founded for the first time Buenos Aires near the River Plate in 1536. In this village they erected a temple and founded a school where, according to a record of 1536, Father Gabriel Lezcano, who was born in Valladolid, "devoted himself to teach those people and took the chiefs and their sons to the big house where they learned to read and write, and to recite the Lord's Prayer, the Hail Mary, the Hail and the Creed, the Commandments and finally all the Doctrine. He composed chants for them against their vices, that is in order not to eat human flesh, not to paint their bodies and not to kill" (Furlong, 1957, 28). The indigenous tribes of the area (Querandis and Guarani) soon destroyed this first settlement, but not before some of the conquerors had gone north with the expeditionary Juan de Salazar de Espinosa (1508–1560), who was accompanied by Father Gabriel Lezcano who continued his missionary work in a new settlement called Asunción founded in 1537. There he was appointed chapel master in 1540 and founded a house and school for native children.

In addition to the religious songs, the conquerors set up farces, which were a kind of play based on actual events where the situations were exaggerated, usually with a comic tinge. According to Josefina Pla (1990, 15), Juan Gabriel de Lezcano set up an Auto Sacramental (allegorical or religious play) on the feast of Corpus Christi in which a satire was performed criticizing the government of the *Adelantado* (Governor) Alvar Nuñez Cabeza de Vaca (1507–1559). These performances were intended to accompany certain salient facts of the life of the community (such as relevant weddings, outstanding visits, changes of government, etc.).

After the second foundation of Buenos Aires by Juan de Garay (1528–1583) in 1580, churches, convents, and schools were built in the main settlements. In parallel, they carried on the evangelization of the Indian people, appealing to all means including the arts. There was the aim to provide the artistic expressions necessary for worship, applying them in the communication and teaching of the new faith in order to facilitate the adaptation of the indigenous societies to the social and cultural standards/patterns of the conquerors. Thus Father Martin Schmid wrote: "We teach people all these worldly things to get rid of their rude behaviour and look like civilized people, predisposed to Christianity" (Szarán and Ruiz Nestosa, 1996, 31).

Religious orders such as the Franciscans established indigenous population centers in the Litoral, Buenos Aires, Tucumán, Cuyo, and Alto Peru. It is noteworthy the music educational work carried out by San Francisco Solano (1549–1610), who through the violin and probably the *quena* (indigenous wind instrument) succeeded in evangelizing to the native people of the actual territories of the provinces of La Rioja, Tucumán, Santiago del Estero, and Catamarca, making them get in contact not only with Catholicism but also with the art of music.

As for the Jesuits, from 1609 they installed sixty-one Indian towns called Reductions or Missions. There music education was part of everyday life through the teaching of instrumental performance, vocal performance, instrument construction, dance, and theatre. The educators were priests from Europe who had a broad education that included one or more of the aforementioned arts, such as Antón Sepp (1655–1733), Florian Paucke (1703–1769), and Domenico Zipoli (1688–1726), among others. In addition to choral chants and instrumental music, they set up plays and operalike performances as part of the religious ceremonies held at

Christmas, Easter week, Corpus, and many other holidays where other profane expressions, like comedies, *entremeses* (interludes), and operas were included.

The Jesuits considered these people naturally suited for music, as Father Sepp pointed out: "I have observed that these Indians keep the beat and rhythm even more accurately than the Europeans, and that they also pronounce the text in Latin with precision though they are illiterate" (Szarán and Ruiz Nestosa, 1996, 26). Their teaching obtained excellent results both in the vocal and the instrumental fields. That is what Father Sepp said in his text *De cómo están constituidos los pueblos de los indios conversos de Paracuaria*: "In each town there is a choir of thirty or forty musicians, counting the singers and the chord and wind instruments. In every case, the instruments are four or up to six violins, six or eight high and bass horns in total, three or four harps, one or two organs, two or three bugles" (Szarán and Ruiz Nestosa, 1996, 27). The repertoire comprised works by European composers such as Corelli, Locatelli, or Brentner, and other vocal and instrumental pieces composed by priests such as Schmid, Sepp, and Zipoli.

Lutherie (the art of constructing musical instruments) was another field of training developed in the Missions. Apparently, the learning method used for the construction of instruments was the imitation of those brought from Europe. They manufactured flutes, violins, harps, and organs. In that respect Father Schmid pointed out: "My organs resound in every village. I made a lot of musical instruments of all kinds and I have taught the Indians to play them (. . .) and I sing and play the organ, the zither, the flute, the trumpet, the psaltery and the lyre both in major and minor mode. All musical arts that I did not previously totally know, now I practice them and teach them to the native sons" (Schmid in Szarán and Nestosa, 1996, 25–26). These instruments supplied much of the instrumental needs of the region.

The labor of the Jesuits was the result of a synthesis and adaptation to the Indian idiosyncrasies of those elements of the European culture that were useful to carry out their educational and evangelistic aims.

COLONIAL PERIOD AND THE VICEROYALTY (SEVENTEENTH AND EIGHTEENTH CENTURIES)

Much of the current Argentine territory was part of the Viceroyalty of Peru. Since 1776 the king of Spain, Charles III, established the jurisdiction of the Viceroyalty of River Plate with Buenos Aires as the capital city. The growth of this city was favored by viceroys such as Juan José de Vertiz y Salcedo (1719–1799), who ruled between 1770 and 1783. During his tenure, art and culture were promoted; for example, through the founding of the first theatre, *Teatro de la Ranchería* (1771) and the creation of the *Real Colegio de San Carlos* [Royal School of Saint Charles]. At the same time, European musicians arrived and offered their services, including educational ones, to the aristocratic sectors of society (Roldan, Vicente Gesualdo, among others).

In cities such as Buenos Aires, Córdoba, Corrientes, Santiago del Estero, La Rioja, Salta, Santa Fe, Tucumán, Catamarca, Mendoza, San Juan, and San Luis the religious orders such as the Franciscans, the Mercedarians, the Dominicans, and the Jesuits established educational institutions in which music education was present. The Jesuits founded in Buenos Aires in 1617 the *Primer Colegio de Segunda Enseñanza* (First School of Secondary Education) and the *Colegio del Salvador* (School of Salvador), in which they taught reading, writing, singing, and Christian doctrine. In these religious educational centers plainchant was prioritized as its daily practice was closely associated with religious instruction. Music education was in the hands of clerics, often with limited knowledge on the subject, so it is inferred that they resorted to intuition as a teaching method (Roldán, 1988). Such was the situation at Buenos Aires but not at Cordoba, where highly trained musicians such as Domenico Zipoli settled.

In the cathedrals and major churches, the work of chapel masters and organists was crucial. In the creation record of Buenos Aires Cathedral, the organist's functions are detailed: "He will play the organ all holidays and their eves and whenever necessary or ordered by the Cabildo and he will play all the times the bishop enters the church as prescribed by the ceremonial" (Fontana, 1985, 49). Gesualdo states that the chapel master should be "skillfull at plainchant and at organ chant and four singers to whom he will conduct keeping the time singing and playing the organ during the services hold in relevant days and their eves, and he should also give lessons of plainchant to the Seminar students" (Gesualdo, 1961, 677). He should also sing the canonic hours, conducting singing of diverse Masses.

Roldán, in his research on music in the colonial period, noted that in some cases slaves were taught to play instruments in religious institutions: "In the expenses account of the Betlemitas' Convent and Hospital of Santa Catalina in Buenos Aires there is a record of the payment to the teacher of José, the black, who is learning to play the organ" (*Temporalidades* in Roldán, 1988, 13). There are no further details about the training they received.

At the major cities of the viceroyalty, the Cabildos (Spanish colonial institution in charge of government, administration, and justice in the district, town, or city) favored the realization of ceremonial and festive events to mark the change of monarch, viceroy, governor, and others. These celebrations included symbolic acts, pantomimes, allegorical or commemorative street parades, and more in which the arts (music, dance, visual arts, theatre) were present in full. During the heyday of the Jesuit missions at the Mesopotamia region, such as San Ignacio Mission, their Indian vocal and instrumental ensembles were called for these events. For example, the Jesuit Father Florián Paucke referred to the performance of his musicians in Buenos Aires: "The music my boys placed was the admiration and delight of the guests who never thought that among these barbarians could be found such a difficult and harmonious art, had they not seen and heard them. They were treated so cordially as if they belonged to distinguished families" (Roldán, 1988, 46).

Another function of the Cabildos was to allow individuals to carry out teaching and to install schools under their own dependency. There is no evidence of music teaching in these private educational institutions.

The expulsion of the Jesuits in 1768 by order of the Bourbon crown involved in most of the reductions they had founded the culmination of their project, as the priests who replaced them eliminated or could not sustain the work of the Jesuits, which caused the dispersal of the natives. Some of them migrated to the cities and exercised the artistic professions they learned with the clergymen; that is, instrument construction and vocal and instrumental performances, which enabled them to earn their living and integrate themselves into urban society.

In some cases, as in Mojos, the civilian authorities tried to give some continuity to the musical practices introduced by the Jesuits. Several evidences have been preserved; for example, fragments of the repertoire, records of the musical chapel configuration, instruments, and more (for more details see Antón Priasco, 2002; de Couve and Dal Pino, 1999; de Couve, Dal Pino, and Frega, 1997).

PERIOD FROM THE PRO-INDEPENDENCE PROCESS UP TO 1853

In the early part of the nineteenth century began the process of Argentine independence. Its chief events were on May 25, 1810, when the first patriotic government formed a governing board, and on July 9, 1816, when, after six years of consolidation of the self-governing ideal, independence was declared as a result of the Creoles' pressure. This process was accompanied from the musical point of view by the composition of patriotic songs such as "La Azulada Bandera del Plata" (The Blue Flag of Plata), attributed to the Spanish musician Blas Parera (1777–1820), and "La Canción Patriótica de 1810" (Patriot Song of 1810) attributed to Esteban de Luca (1786–1924), which was intoned as a patriotic song until the Constituent General Assembly of 1813 approved the National Anthem. These were some of the music expressions of the time that manifested a sense of belonging in construction.

In the aristocratic salons, such as Mariquita Sánchez de Thompson's (1786–1868), the literary and musical works by local and foreign artists were unveiled (Frega, 1994). Many musicians and music teachers arrived from Europe to Buenos Aires port, especially from Spain as Manuel Espinosa, and in a lesser extent from France and Italy as Cayetano Lino Loforte. Most of them settled in Buenos Aires, as it was the case of the Spanish flutist and clarinettist Víctor de la Prada. But music teachers were not only European immigrants but also Creoles and Indians *Nos parece correcto el remplazo, negros, mulattos, sambos* (sons of a native and a negro), who worked as servants in family houses, convents, churches, and in the army. It must be noticed that the referred black population came from the slave trade and that in 1813 the Constituent General Assembly declared the abolition of slavery.

In this period the first specialized music teaching institutions emerged. The above-mentioned Víctor de la Prada, after playing at Cordoba Cathedral, founded an *Academia de Música* in Buenos Aires in 1806. It functioned in the room belonging to the Protomedicato (court where future physicians were examined). There studied, among others, the black musicians from Mendoza who formed the Band of the Eighteenth Battalion of the Andes Army in 1816. Years later the Spanish presbyter José Antonio Picasarri (1769–1834), who had just returned from Europe thanks to the amnesty law enacted by the government of Martín Rodríguez and his ministry, Bernardino Rivadavia, together with his nephew Juan Pedro Esnaola (1808–1878), created in 1822 the *Escuela de Música y Canto* (Music and Singing School) where young men and women attended their classes separately and the best pupils gave concerts for the authorities and the public (see Gesualdo, 1961).

Music performance and teaching continued to be cultivated in the religious sphere in major cities. The Ecclesiastical Cabildo (collegiate religious institution that functions in the more important urban centers and was in charge of the government of the cathedral and of liturgical tasks ordered by the canon law and the bishop) comprised, among other officials, the chantre (chapel master), who controlled the level and quality of the musical practice and the teaching carried on in the cathedral and other important churches. Among those who played prominent roles in the House of Lords in this period is highlighted Spanish José Antonio Picassarri (1769–1849), who was teacher, singer, instrumentalist, and composer. He arrived to Buenos Aires in 1783 after being called by his uncle, the dean of the Cathedral and principal of the *Real Seminario de San Carlos*. There he studied music with Father Juan Pedro Goiburu (1759–1813); in 1795 he was appointed singer at the Cathedral and in 1807 became the chapel master. In 1823 he resumed his duties at the Cathedral and opened and conducted the salon of the Philharmonic Society. He was later chapel master of Santo Domingo Chapel (1823), of San Nicolás de Bari Church (1828), and of San Ignacio (1834). Among the laymen stood Catalán Blas Parera (1765–1840?), who settled in Buenos Aires in 1797 and was organist at the Cathedral and the churches of La Merced and San Ignacio. He also taught music to many families of the society and in 1804 was hired as a performer, composer, and conductor by the theatre, *Coliseo Provisional* of Buenos Aires (see Gesualdo, 1961).

Researchers such as Furlong and Roldán considered that Buenos Aires Cathedral was a training and presentation center for Argentine organists and singers, such as Juan Vizcaino de Agüero, who was born in Tucumán in 1606 and was organist in Buenos Aires Cathedral since 1629 and chorister from 1637. Other examples were the colored brothers Bernardo and Roque Jacinto Pintos. Bernardo was organist in the Church of Monserrat and since the beginning of the eighteenth century acted in the services at the Cathedral, while his brother Roque played the violin in the Cathedral since 1790 and in the orchestra of the *Coliseo* since 1804.

With regard to schools not under the Catholic Church, there is no precise information about music teaching, save for the founds by Gesualdo (1978), who wrote in his *Historia de la música en la Argentina* that "'La Canción Patriótica' by López and Parera (the National Anthem) was intoned for the first time in public, the 25th of May 1813 at the Victory Square, near the Pyramid of May, by the pupils of Don Rufino Sánchez's school" (133). This data could not be confirmed in any other documentary source.

PERIOD OF THE NATIONAL ORGANIZATION (1853–1900)

During the second half of the nineteenth century the nation was organized after the enactment of the National Constitution in 1853. Prominent men of politics and national culture, such as Juan Bautista Alberdi (1810–1884, lawyer, politician, author of the *Bases para la organización política de la Confederación Argentina* [Basis for the Political Organization of the Argentine Conferedate], the text that became the theoretic column of the National Constitution), and Domingo Faustino Sarmiento (1811–1888, pedagogue, writer, journalist, politician, and president of the nation between 1868–1874), considered that the country was in the process of being civilized; that is, to become a land inhabited by men with a cultural level similar to the European societies of the time. In order to obtain a data base, Sarmiento ordered the first national census in 1869 from which there is the following information: there was a population of 1,836,490 people, 31 percent of them were settled in the province of Buenos Aires, 71 percent were illiterate; 5 percent were Indians and 8 percent Europeans; 75 percent of the families lived in poverty, in ranchos (huts made of mud and straw); and professionals accounted for only 1 percent of the population. The information collected in this census showed that the population was sparse, poorly geographically distributed, and poorly educated. Given these data Sarmiento wanted to promote the arrival of English immigrants, which might boost the industrial and cultural development, but most of the immigrants were Italian, Spanish, Russian, and French farmers who settled in the major cities or in the countryside. Men such as Sarmiento and Alberdi encouraged the development of a prosperous and cultured citizenship. So they supported education in general and music teaching particularly as it was a valuable cultural component (see Suárez Urtubey, 1989).

Juan Bautista Alberdi published two works on music teaching: *Ensayo de un método nuevo para aprender a tocar el piano con la mayor facilidad* (Essay on a New Method of Learning to Play the Piano Easily) and the *Espíritu de la música a la capacidad de todo el mundo* (The Spirit of Music within the Reach of Everybody), both in 1832. *Ensayo* is an introduction to his piano method that takes an important premise: practice must precede theory. "My disciple will know how to play the piano before knowing a single note, in the same way he has learnt to talk without knowing a letter, that is, giving him the example before giving him the rules" (Alberdi in Suárez Urtubey, 1989, 165). After this active approach to music the pupil began to learn musical theory. With regard to *El espíritu*, it is an attempt to bring the reader to topics such as genres, styles, and aesthetic aspects of music, tinged with the author's judgments. This publication would probably have the aim of helping the common man to appreciate the art of music as it was an important aspect of human education. Such was the point of view of many Argentine people as expressed in a letter published in *El Lucero* on September 4, 1832, in which a reader of this book said that it "can strongly influence in the prompt and easy propagation of the art that contributes more than any other to polish and soften the manners of a country" (Suárez Urtubey, 1989, 179).

Domingo Faustino Sarmiento gave importance to music education in basic training. In 1839 he was principal of the girls' school *Colegio de Pensionistas de Santa Rosa de Lima* in San Juan, in which music was a mandatory subject,

> because the idea that had preceded the foundation of this *pensionado* (boarding school) was to give the pupils a complete education, without letting in [the] hands of the parents' ignorance or to concern the selection of the subjects. Music must be learned in the more complete and scientific way. A collection of blackboards contained the scale and the first *solfège* scales, which all students practice daily; the piano takes other part of the lesson [and] pupils taking turn to do their exercises. A little music treatise printed in Buenos Aires first and then the catechism of music by Ackerman were the text for the technical section. There were also some ruled blackboards to show the values of the notes, the metres, etc. and the teacher wrote the lesson on it and the pupils copy it in their ruled copybooks, [a] task in which they have acquire[d] such a skill to dictate that to copy the lesson was not more difficult than any other dictation. A stopwatch taught to measure time and nothing seemed to be missing so that this education was even more complete than the ordinary one in which ladies aspire more to a careful performance than to know the science of music. In their first exam they have to perform the Third Act of the *Gazza ladra* and the teachers can say how much study it is necessary to get the girls and beginners to play their roles with precision in such a variety of compositions. (Sarmiento, 1849, 155)

In his text *Enseñanza de la Música a los jóvenes* (Teaching Music to Youth) he argued over the necessity of music education as, "in one word, we have no judgement in musical matters, we are not cultivated men if we ignore such an essential aspect of civilization. Is it not a great void in our education?" (1896) He considered that music was a moral hobby, as "he who does not know how to fight for days up to obtain nice sounds from a musical instrument that reflect the idea of the author of a famous piece, will end in the coffee shops, in dissipation and in reprehensible distractions, as a way to escape from the hours of boredom left by the society and the occupations as a resource to flee from themselves and engulf in the maelstrom that excite passions and encourage leisure" (1896).

In the 1880s the country was in a consolidation process, with economic prosperity and receiving European immigrants looking for better opportunities. This scenario led politicians and thinkers, who belonged to the so-called generation of the eighty, to establish an educative system with the goal of homogenizing the population by providing highly significant knowledge, because "the school is the organism from which the State can and should develop more intense and effective action to print in the future a national character considered in all its social, political, cultural and economic aspects" (Consejo Nacional de Educación [CNE], 1938, 54).

In 1884 *Ley No. 1420 de Educación Común* [Law N° 1420 of Common Education] was enacted. It provided compulsory, free, and grade primary education for all children between the ages of six and fourteen. It stated that it must be granted in accordance with the precepts of hygiene and with an aim "to favour and direct simultaneously the moral, intellectual and physical development of children" (Article 1). "It established the following as mandatory subjects: Reading and Writing; Arithmetic; Argentine and basic World Geography; Argentine and basic World History; Spanish Language; morals and good manners; basic notions of Mathematics, Physics and Natural Sciences; basic notions of Drawing and Vocal Music [literal translation, in current wording: Singing]; physical training and knowledge of the National Constitution" (Article 6). The Law also stated "that daily lessons at public schools will alternate with breaks, physical training and singing" (Article 14).

The inclusion of music within the subjects of compulsory education was due to several reasons, mainly because it was considered as a means of promoting national identity as "school singing helped to revive patriotic feeling . . . some patriotic songs that had been sung by the people and the Argentine armies in the struggles for freedom arose from their memories" (CNE, 1913, 10). Furthermore, musical activity favored the practice of breathing and pronunciation, facilitating good communication as "it would modify with time the unpleasantness of the provincial accent" (Torres, 1887, 61).

Law No. 1420 focused music education on singing, but unfortunately there are no records available on the contents taught in each grade of compulsory education during the first years this law was in force. Some contemporary texts reported that the pupil sing in unison or at voices according to their age. There was a debate upon learning theoretic contents at school as "to teach pupils to sing by ear is to incur into empiricism and routine, to guide them with a method that is completely sterile and baleful for their faculties (. . .) Singing demands the knowledge of music notation and this one the knowledge of the grammar and prosody of the language of sounds" (CNE, 1888, 242). It also suggested the use of the piano or the violin in order to improve choral practice and to apply *solfège*.

The National Council of Education, at that moment the higher institution in charge of education, had jurisdiction over the schools at the capital city, the colonies, and national territories. In 1905, by Law No. 4874, known as Lainez, it extended its competency to the provinces as new national primary schools were created all over the country. Thus it became a national organization with significant resources, a large staff, and a vertical organizational structure that came to the uttermost parts of the country. It has also the function of approving the repertoire applied at schools. For this there was a Committee of Text and a Committee of Didactics that raised their reports to the council giving the list of approved texts (CNE, 1889, 713–14). The repertoire consisted of patriotic songs as the Argentine National Anthem, the "Saludo a la Bandera" [Greeting to the Flag], "Viva la Patria" [Long Live Our Country], and "La Canción Patriótica de 1810" [The Patriotic Song of 1810]. There was also a repertoire of songs to sing in unison, two or three voices with instrumental accompaniment (piano or violin) with lyrics in the national language and strong moralizing texts because they were used to transmit those values considered relevant for social life.

The decision of the national government to provide mandatory basic or primary education required teachers' training at special kinds of secondary schools created in 1869 and called *Escuelas Normales*. The first Escuela Normal opened in Paraná City, in Entre Ríos, in 1870 under the direction of the American educator George A. Stearns. The second one was founded in Buenos Aires in 1874. Initially these schools comprised a six grades application department (primary school) and a teachers' training level that lasted four years. Teachers' training included music, as was stated in the syllabi of 1903. The first year of study was devoted to the revision of the musical knowledge acquired at primary school and to the deepening of theoretical contents (such as rhythmic values, triplets, dots, two times meters, rhythmic and melodic music notation) as well as practical ones (such as the performance of major and minor scales and a vocal repertoire). For the following years the curriculum included singing pieces at several voices with or without instrumental accompaniment.

These syllabi included comments like: "For the girls, singing with text in unison and at two voices, with an extension between the C under the staff up to the F in the fifth line of the staff, in treble clef. For the boys, an extension between F under the staff and G or A in the second space of the staff in treble clef" (Ministerio de Justicia e Instrucción Pública de la Nación, 1903). During the first decades from the enactment of Law No. 1420, music lessons were in charge of primary teachers, as there were no graduated music educators.

With regard to music training, many European musicians who settled in Argentina devoted to teach music, as for example, the pianist Clementino del Ponte (1858–1914), the Napolitalian violinist Gaetano Gaito (1852–1915) who arrived in 1874, and the violinist and conductor Pietro Melani (1854–1900), who trained very important Argentine musicians such as Constantino Gaito (1878–1945).

With regard to specialized music training institutions, in 1869 Juan Horacio Reinen founded and directed the *Conservatorio de Música* and in 1880 the *Conservatorio de Música de Buenos Aires* opened, while the *Instituto de Estudios Musicales* functioned in the province of Córdoba since 1883. In Buenos Aires, the composer Alberto Williams (1862–1952), who had won the Prize Europa to the Arts granted by the national government, founded in 1893 the *Conservatorio de Música de Buenos Aires*, whose staff was integrated by distinguished musicians of the time. Some of their pupils became notable musicians, for example, Celestino Piaggio (1886–1931), Celia Torrá (1899–1962), Pascual de Rogatis (1880–1980), and Ernesto Drangosch (1882–1925). By the end of the nineteenth century there were other private conservatories in Buenos Aires, like the *Escuela de Música* founded by Ricardo Pérez Camino in 1886 and the *Conservatorio Santa Cecilia* created in 1894 by Luis Forino (1868–1936). These institutions' graduates and professors not only played instruments, conducted, or composed but also devoted themselves to music teaching.

PERIOD OF CONSOLIDATION OF MUSIC EDUCATION (1900–1990)

During the twentieth century, despite the variable political and social situation of the country, including the ruling of several de facto governments, music education consolidated as a subject in the different educational levels both in private and public schools. The educational system comprised the following levels: primary school (seven grades), secondary school (five or six grades, with different options or modalities: baccalaureate, *magisterio*, or Normal School (teachers' training school), commerce and technical), tertiary level (superior studies not belonging to the university), and university.

Music education went on being a mandatory subject in primary school, giving priority to choral activity (in unison or several voices) and to musical literacy that was taught in the higher grades, including the following contents: "Staff, treble chef, four times metre, notes, rests, bar lines, dots, ties, additional lines, accidentals, two and three times metres and dynamics" (CNE, 1910, 34). These contents were essentially applied in *solfège* exercises.

Since the beginning of the twentieth century national and local authorities intended to exercise a greater control over the activities carried on in the arts subjects at schools. New decisions were added to the official approval of bibliography and scores to be used at schools, which were published at *El Monitor de la Educación Común* (The Common Education Monitor) and were in force for three years. One of them was the creation of the *Oficina de Ilustraciones y Decorado Escolar* (School Pictures and Scenery Office) that supervised the supply of decorative material to the schools for the diverse celebrations and events; other examples were the music teachers' duty to play the National Anthem and the patriotic songs approved by the Council, the resolution dated on March 1909 that fixed that "in order to pass Grade 3 of primary school the pupils should know the National Anthem by heart" (CNE, 1913, 74), and the approval of an official version of the Argentine National Anthem in 1944. The increasing number of official syllabi, detailing contents and repertoire for each school grade, was another evidence of the authorities' control on music education.

At the already mentioned repertoire of patriotic songs, anthems, and moralizing songs, it must be added many foreigner children songs; for example, anonymous French and Spanish lullabies or games with music. At the first half of the twentieth century there was more interest in bringing to the classrooms works by academic Argentine composers inspired by folk music (as in the case of Alberto Williams, Carlos López Buchardo, Julián Aguirre, Athos Palma, Felipe Boero, etc.). In parallel many composers made vocal music for the schools. Such was the case of Leopoldo Corretjer (1862–1941), composer, orchestra conductor, and chorus conductor, who had studied at the *Real Conservatorio Isabel II* in Condal, Spain, and settled in Buenos Aires in 1887. He taught music at *Sarmiento* School and became Music Inspector of the National Council of Education. He composed school songs, some of them inspired by folk melodies, such as "El gaucho" and "El ombú," and several outstanding titles of the patriotic repertoire such as "Himno a Sarmiento," "Saludo a la Bandera," and "¡Viva la

Patria!" "At the celebration of the centenary of the May Revolution he conducted a chorus of thirty thousands voices who sang the National Anthem at the Two Congress square in Buenos Aires city" (Arizaga, 1972, 100).

The inclusion of authentic folk songs was also encouraged. For that reason the National Council of Education issued a resolution on March 10, 1921, ordering a recollection of popular literature with the help of the teachers of the schools located in Buenos Aires and the national territories, and of those individuals who could bring folk elements. The collected material was donated to the Faculty of Philosophy and Languages of Buenos Aires University. The Committee of Didactics of the National Council of Education published a series of little books with compositions addressed to the children and another one for adults, under the title of *Antología Folklórica Argentina* (Argentine Folk Anthology) for schools for adults in 1940.

Throughout the twentieth century the formal approval of repertoire continued, especially during the times of de facto governments when some authors were banned. These official limits were not always fulfilled.

In terms of objectives, in addition to the consolidation of educated citizens with a clear national spirit, from the 1960s the curricula expanded the aims mentioning the integral formation of human beings, the development of aesthetic taste, and the use of musical language as a means of communication and expression. "To consider music as a language or medium of human communication and therefore to aspire to a comprehensive understanding in detail of musical messages and to express themselves musically through his voice, his body and the different instruments, according to a growing progression in the complexity of musical structures" (CNE, 1972, 357). From the 1960s this broadening of objectives led to including activities centered on musical instrument performance (mainly recorders), appreciation, mixed productions, and some improvisations. As an example, here are the objectives of the Curricular Document for primary schools elaborated in 1972, where it is expected that the child would "develop his imagination and inventiveness when he expresses himself through music in a spontaneous and correct way in individual or collective improvisations and musical creations and in developing his own musical material and examples" (CNE, 1972, 358). It should be noted that although the prescribed curriculum promoted a change, it took its time to become evident in the real curriculum for several reasons, including teachers' lack of preparation to carry on activities focused on creation.

With regard to the editorial field, some European books on music education were translated into Spanish and published in Argentina; for example, *El niño y la música* (The Child and Music) (1947), *Síntesis del saber musical* (Synthesis of the Musical Knowledge) (1948) both by Kurt Pahlen (1907–2003), and *La Educación Musical* (Music Education) (1950) by Albert Lavignac (1846–1916). In the following decades some European methods, such as those by Carl Orff (1895–1982), Maurice Martenot (1898–1980), Zoltan Kodaly (1882–1967), and Emile Jacques-Dalcroze (1865–1950) gained diffusion, followed later by the pedagogical approaches of Murray Schafer (1933), Brian Dennis (1941–1998), John Paynter (1944), and François Delalande (1941), among others. Prominent national educators such as Ana Lucia Frega (1935), Silvia Malbrán (1943), Violeta Hemsy de Gainza (1930), María del Carmen Aguilar (1945), Emma Garmendia, and Marta Varela made their own contributions teaching, giving lectures, and publishing articles and books in which they presented their didactic ideas and made a synthesis of the above mentioned foreign proposals leading the way in a national music education pedagogy focused on promoting pupils' participation and emphasizing direct experience before getting to theory (from many sources).

During the twentieth century, kindergarten education gradually became an independent level from primary school and extended its educational offerings, including three-year-old children and younger groups, from the 1980s. Music teaching was always present, focused on singing and playful activities involving body movements.

In secondary school, which generally comprised five years of study, music teaching was included in all the modalities except technical schools. It has more presence in the schedule of the baccalaureate (secondary school with an humanistic orientation) and the *magisterio* (secondary school with pedagogical subjects that granted up to 1969 the grade of teacher for primary school) than in the commercial modality (secondary school that granted the title of *Perito Mercantil*, commercial expert). In the 1950s the curricula included contents that referred to the history of Argentine and occidental music, national folklore, singing at one or more voices, musical theory, and *solfège* (similar to those applied at the conservatories). In the 1970s instrumental performances and dance were included in the syllabi. When the curriculum was changed in 1988 pupils began to choose among the workshops of two artistic languages, being the music contents focalized on musical performances. This pedagogical approach is still in force. In parallel, the editorial curriculum developed different textbooks devoted to music learning at secondary school (for more details see de Couve and Dal Pino, 2001, 2005, 2006, and 2007).

As for the music teacher training, many private and public conservatories were created during the first decades of the twentieth century. In 1919 the *Escuelas Municipales de Música* were opened. In 1924 the National Ministry of Public Instruction Dr. Antonio Sagarna created the *Conservatorio Nacional de Música Danza y Arte Escénico*, based on the former *Escuela de Arte Lírico y Escénico del Teatro Colón*. Its first principal was Carlos López Buchardo, who was in charge of the institution until his death in 1948. In the same year, the Departments and Superior Schools of Music of the National Universities of La Plata, Córdoba, Tucumán, Mendoza, San Juan, and Santa Fe were established, and the *Conservatorio Provincial de Música Julián Aguirre* was founded in the city of Rio Cuarto, Province of Cordoba. In 1927 the Town Hall of Buenos Aires created the *Conservatorio Municipal de Música Manuel de Falla*. These institutions granted official titles of professor in several instruments, singing or composition, which enabled them to teach music in all educational levels. So, gradually, specialized music teachers replaced nongraduate and amateur musicians, although there was always an insufficient number of music teachers and nongraduates were allowed to give music lessons at schools if they passed an examination.

In the private sphere the *Collegium Musicum de Buenos Aires* was created in 1946 and developed an educational offer for children and adults.

PERIOD OF REFORMS IN MUSIC EDUCATION (1990 UP TO PRESENT)

During the last decade of the twentieth century a series of reforms were carried out in order to renovate and modernize the educational system. The Laws of Transference of Educative Services from the nation sphere to the provinces and jurisdictions (1978 and 1992), the *Ley Federal de Educación* [Federal Law of Education] (1993), and the *Ley de Educación Superior* [Law of Superior Education] (1996) were enacted, as well as some official documents such as the National Basic Common Contents (1995) and new provincial curricula were approved.

The Federal Law of Education substituted Law No. 1420. It established a new structure for the educative system, with the following levels: Initial Level (including nursery school and kindergarten), General Basic Education (nine grades), Polymodal Level (three grades), and Superior Level (including university and nonuniversity studies). Compulsory education comprised kindergarten to five-years-old children and the Basic General Education, reaching a total of ten years of studies (Federal Law of Education).

In the Initial Level music education continued to have as its goal the comprehensive training of children as well as the teaching of an expressive language through vocal and instrumental performance, appreciation, and creation, focusing on sound exploration and playful aspects.

In the General Basic Education Level the traditional subjects (Music and Drawing) were sustained, but the time devoted to artistic expressions in the schedule was not increased (forty minutes per week in half-day schools and twice a week in whole-day ones). Corporal Expression and Theatre were added as possible artistic subjects as the schools may modify every three years their offer of two artistic languages. As a consequence, in some cases music was not included in the nine grades of E.G.B. or it has a disrupted offer as it was held only in some of the grades.

The Federal Council of Culture and Education approved the Basic Common Contents in which those relevant contents, that must be included in every provincial or jurisdictional curricula, were listed. The four artistic languages mentioned above were present in these official documents. The goals stated in the new provincial curricula incorporate the knowledge, performance, and respect for the music expressions of regional, national, Latin American, and universal cultures. There was also an emphasis on the comprehensive training considering music as a vehicle of expression and communication. In addition to vocal and instrumental performances and creation, contextualization of musical expressions through analyses and reflection was proposed.

The educative reform stated at the Federal Law of Education was resisted by some jurisdictions as the Autonomous City of Buenos Aires, where it was not fully applied. Professional musical training also showed changes. The Law of Superior Education affected music studies at the conservatories as it stated that nobody could study a teaching career unless he has completed his secondary school (polymodal in this period), and this criteria led to a rise in the age of the students as they could study the music teacher career in parallel with secondary schools as they used to. Another change was the increment of the schedule of the teaching careers, with a minimum of 2,800 hours, which implied an increase in the number of subjects' resting time from the study of musical instruments. In parallel, teachers' pedagogical training was revalued, including new subjects such as Educational Policy, General Didactics, and more. In parallel, additional training opportunities were raised as nonuniversity tertiary technical programs with no pedagogical subjects. That was the case of *Conservatorio Superior de Música de la Ciudad de Buenos Aires Astor Piazzolla*, which offers not only a teacher's training career but also a *tecnicatura* (superior nonpedagogical music career) centered on instrumental performance.

The educative reform focused on lifelong learning and on the need to have postgraduate offers. For that reason specializations were opened in nonuniversity institutions, as well as specializations, masters, and PhD at the universities. The university titles, as that of Licentiate, were revalued, and the traditional *Conservatorio Nacional de Música* of Buenos Aires became a Department of the new *Instituto Universitario Nacional del Arte* (IUNA). The Federal Law of Education contemplated nonformal education as a valuable social option. Music education assumed the role in this field, promoting free projects such as the Infant and Youth Orchestras, the Music Schools for children, music teaching at cultural centers, and others.

In 2006 a new law, called *Ley de Educación Nacional No. 26.206* [Law of National Education], was enacted. Its objectives comprise the preservation of the natural and cultural patrimony (Article 11, Subsection c), the strengthening of the national identity based on the respect for cultural diversity (Article 11, Subsection d), and to provide training that stimulates the creativity, the taste, and the understanding of the different manifestations of the art and the culture (Article 11, Subsection t).

With regard to the educative system (Article 17), the Initial Level continue, the General Basic Education disappeared because the former Primary and Secondary levels returned, both as compulsory education. Therefore there are thirteen years of compulsory education (Article 16) in which there are at least two artistic subjects per year as a minimum, to chose between music, dance, visual arts, theatre, and any other that may be incorporated (Article 41). The proposals formulated in this law and the consequent changes in the provincial curricula are still in process.

With regard to superior education, the *Instituto Nacional de Formación Docente* (INFOD) was created by the Ministry of Education to be in charge of planning and executing the public policies dealing with teachers' training (Article 71). This institution determined that music teachers' training careers as well as any other teachers' training plans would have at least 2,600 hours distributed over four years of study with a strong presence in pedagogic matters and teaching practices.

CONCLUSION

As noted in this study, music education was a continuum in the history of education in the Argentine Republic. Its inclusion in basic education not only has the aim of consolidating the national spirit but also managing an expressive language within comprehensive training. As time went by and different educative reforms were applied, the artistic educational offer was diversified, but music remains always present.

Therefore, we can ensure that music education is in good health in the Argentine educational system and continues in force in a transformation process that seeks to reconcile the local tradition with the training demands of the globalized world of the twenty-first century.

REFERENCES

Antón Priasco, S. (2002). "La herencia jesuítica en las Misiones de Mojos El archivo musical de San Ignacio en la actualidad." Paper presented at *El libro en el protopaís (1536–1810): Tradición clásica, cosmovisión eclesiástica e ilustración*. Primer simposio nacional de bibliografía y cultura coloniales, November 4–6, 2002. In http://www.bn.gov.ar/descargas/publicaciones/mat/MyP03.htm

Arizaga, R. (1972). *Enciclopedia de la música argentina*. Buenos Aires: Fondo Nacional de las Artes.

Avaca, M. (2009). "Los instrumentos musicales mapuche en el Nguillatún de Chiuquilihuín." Paper presented at *Todas las músicas*. VII Encuentro Regional Latinoamericano ISME 2009. Buenos Aires, Argentina, August 12–15, 2009.

Consejo Nacional de Educación. (1888). *El Monitor de la Educación Común, 8, No. 126.*

Consejo Nacional de Educación. (1889). *El Monitor de la Educación Común, 9, No. 154.*

Consejo Nacional de Educación. (1910). *Programa de Estudios.* Buenos Aires: Consejo Nacional de Educación.

Consejo Nacional de Educación. (1913). *La Educación común en la República argentina. Años 1909–1910, presidencia del doctor don José María Ramos.* Buenos Aires: Penitenciaría Nacional.

Consejo Nacional de Educación. (1938). *Cincuentenario de la Ley 1420. Tomo II. Memoria sobre el desarrollo de las escuelas primarias desde 1884 a 1934.* Buenos Aires: Consejo Nacional de Educación.

Consejo Nacional de Educación. (1972). *Lineamientos Curriculares 1° a 7° Grado.* Buenos Aires: Consejo Nacional de Educación.

de Couve, A., and Dal Pino, C. (1999). "Historical Panorama of Music Education in Latin America: Music Training Institutions." *International Journal of Music Education* 34: 30–46.

de Couve, A., and Dal Pino, C. (2001). "La música en el octavo año de la EGB (ex primer año del nivel medio): Estudio comparativo de las propuestas curriculares nacionales (1952–1995)." *Boletín de Investigación Educativo-Musical* 8, no. 24: 16–22.

de Couve, A., and Dal Pino, C. (2005). "La música en el ex primer año del nivel medio: Estudio comparativo de la propuesta curricular nacional y la propuesta editorial expresada en los libros de texto (1952–1977)." *Boletín de Investigación Educativo-Musical* 12, no. 35: 32–41.

de Couve, A., and Dal Pino, C. (2006). "La música argentina en el ex primer año del nivel medio: Estudio comparativo de la propuesta curricular nacional y la propuesta editorial expresada en los libros de texto (1952–1977)." In *Primer Congreso Nacional de Artes Musicales. El arte musical argentino: retrospectiva y proyecciones al siglo XXI*, comp. Z. Noli and M. C. Albini (181–89). Buenos Aires: Instituto Universitario Nacional del Arte.

de Couve, A., and Dal Pino, C. (2007). "La música en el ex primer año del nivel medio: Estudio comparativo de la propuesta curricular nacional y la propuesta editorial expresada en los libros de texto (1978–1988)." *Boletín de Investigación Educativo-Musical* 14, no. 40 (Buenos Aires), 33–42.

de Couve, A., Dal Pino, C., and Frega, A. L. (1997). "An Approach to the History of Music Education in Latin America." *Bulletin of Historical Research in Music Education* 19, no. 1: 10–39.

de Couve, A., Dal Pino, C., and Frega, A. L. (2010). "Argentina: From 'Vocal Music' to 'Educación Artística: Música.'" In *The Origins and Foundations of Music Education*, ed. G. Cox and R. Stevens (139–51). London: Continuum International Publishing Group.

Fontana, A. (1985). "El órgano en la Argentina–Época colonial y siglo XIX." *Revista del Instituto de Investigación Musicológica Carlos Vega* 5, no. 5: 49–50.

Frega, A. L. (1994). *Mujeres de la Música.* Buenos Aires: Planeta.

Furlong, G. (1957). *La tradición religiosa en la escuela argentina.* Buenos Aires: Theoría.

Gesualdo, V. (1961). *Historia de la música en la Argentina 1852–1900. Tomo 2.* Buenos Aires: Editorial Beta.

Gesualdo, V. (1978). *Historia de la música en la Argentina, II La independencia y la época de Rivadavia, 1810–1829.* Buenos Aires: Libros de Hispanoamérica.

Gudemos, M. (1998). *Antiguos Sonidos: El material arqueológico musical del Museo Dr. Eduardo Casanova.* Tilcara, Jujuy, Argentina: Instituto Universitario Tilcaraqa, Universidad de Buenos Aires.

Ley N° 1420 de Educación Común (Law of Common Education N° 1420). (1884).www.bnm.me.gov.ar/giga1/normas/5421.pdf.

Ley de Educación Nacional No. 26.206 [Law of National Education No. 26.206]. (2006). Buenos Aires: Ministerio de Cultura y Educación.

Ley Federal de Educación No. 24.195 [Federal Law of Education No. 24.195]. (1993). Buenos Aires: Ministerio de Cultura y Educación.

Ley de Educación Superior No. 24.521 [Law of Higher Education No. 24.521]. (1996). Buenos Aires: Ministerio de Cultura y Educación.

Ministerio de Justicia e Instrucción Pública de la Nación. (1903). *Plan de Estudios y Programas para las Escuelas Normales de la República Argentina.* Buenos Aires: Ministerio de Justicia e Instrucción Pública de la Nación.

Pla, J. (1990). *Cuatro siglos de teatro en el Paraguay. Tomo 1.* Asunción: Universidad Católica Nuestra Señora de la Asunción.

Roldán, W. A. (1988). *Música colonial en la Argentina: La enseñanza musical.* Buenos Aires: El Ateneo.

Sarmiento, D. F. (1849). *De la educación popular.* Santiago: Julio Belín i Compañía.

Sarmiento, D. F. (1896). *Obras Completas.* Buenos Aires: Imprenta Mariano Moreno.

Suárez Urtubey, P. (1989). "Juan Bautista Alberdi, Teoría y Praxis de la Música." *Revista del Instituto de Investigación Musicológica Carlos Vega*, no. 10: 157–200.

Szarán, L., and Ruiz Nestosa, J. (1996). Música en las Reducciones Jesuíticas. Colección de instrumentos de Chiquitos, Bolivia. Asunción: Fundación Paracuaria Missions Prokur S. J. Nurenberg.

Torres, J. M. (1887). *Primeros Elementos de Educación.* Buenos Aires: Imprenta de M. Biedma.

Chapter Thirteen

Brazil

Sergio Figueiredo

INTRODUCTION

This text intends to offer a general overview on Brazilian music education, without the pretension of being an exhaustive report. Divided into seven parts, the text explores:

1. Historical perspectives, presenting aspects of the history of music education in Brazil, tracing a time line from the discovery—1500—until today
2. Aspects of the educational legislation regarding music education in Brazil, showing the main topics of each change
3. Music in Basic Education, presenting aspects of the school organization
4. Music schools, discussing the role of conservatories, music schools, and private teaching in Brazil
5. Music in the community, bringing some research reports that discuss the role of music in social projects in diverse contexts
6. Music teacher preparation, with the main factors that are considered in the preparation of music teachers and also generalist teachers
7. Music curriculum, where some of the current orientation is discussed in terms of music education in schools

Final considerations summarize the discussion presented in each part, indicating the new phase of Brazilian music education, after the approval of legislation that established it as a compulsory content in the curriculum.

HISTORICAL PERSPECTIVES

The presence or absence of music education in Brazilian schools can be found in the literature, although the research on the history of music education in Brazil could be extended. Different authors analyze major aspects that indicate the strength and the weakness of music as part of the education in Brazil in different periods.

Pedro Álvares Cabral, a Portuguese navigator, discovered Brazil in 1500. Indigenous people from diverse ethnic groups were in the country, and musical activities from those groups were not very well known until today. Jesuits came to the country from 1549 and, according to Oliveira (2007, 3), they "were the educational leaders in Brazil until their expulsion, in 1759." During this long period, music was part of education delivered by Jesuits with the aim of establishing the Catholic religion among the indigenous. Music in the Jesuit period followed principles brought from Europe, emphasizing, obviously, religious practices. The local values and culture, including the indigenous values and culture, were not considered in that methodology, and the European tradition in terms of education and music was imposed on the people.

In 1808, the Portuguese Royal Family came to Brazil, bringing other musical practices to the society. Gradually popular manifestations were becoming stronger in Brazilian society, in addition to the musical European tradition established during the settlement period (Fonterrada, 2005). Coming mainly from Congo and Angola, Africans were brought to Brazil as slaves—in the eighteenth and nineteenth centuries—and their musical manifestations were incorporated especially in popular music practices in Brazil. Musical instruments such as *berimbau, agogô,* and *atabaque* were part of those musical traditions brought by Africans, gradually becoming a part of the Brazilian musical practice from that time until today. *Lundu, maxixe,* and *jongo,* for example, are types of music and dance derived from African tradition incorporated to the Brazilian culture in the nineteenth century.

The first conservatory in Brazil (*Conservatório de Música do Rio de Janeiro*) was established in 1841. The European model of music teaching was adopted, keeping the tradition of emphasizing the instrumental preparation for classical music. It is important to mention that the conservatory served a small number of participants compared to the Brazilian population at large.

One of the first educational legislations—*Decreto n. 1331-A de 17 de fevereiro de 1854*—that included officially the teaching of music in schools was published in the nineteenth century, establishing that notions of music and singing exercises should be part of primary education (Brasil, 1854). In 1890 another official document indicated the necessity of specific preparation for teachers responsible for music in schools (Brasil, 1890).

At the end of the nineteenth century, the period of the Republic proclamation in Brazil, musical practices continued to be related to European tradition, and Brazilian composers were strongly influenced by that tradition. In parallel, popular music continued to be developed with a variety of forms and styles.

Wisnick (1977) analyzes music concepts in the beginning of the twentieth century, considering *description, nationalism,* and *civism* as the most relevant characteristics of the period. The *Semana de Arte Moderna* (Modern Art Week), in 1922, represents a benchmark for the arts in Brazil because prominent artists contested the strong conservative approach for diverse types of art manifestations. Music was included in this event, and the ideas discussed in 1922 influenced generations of artists.

The Modernist movement in Brazil, in the first decades of the twentieth century, brought new ideas for music education, valuing the social function of music and the importance and value of both folk and popular music. At the same time, new proposals in terms of education, under the influence of John Dewey (1859–1952), were developed in many contexts, including Brazil; music should be accessible to everyone and not a privilege of the talented, "contributing to the integral preparation of the human being" (Fonterrada, 2005, 194).

Heitor Villa-Lobos (1887–1959), one of the most well-known Brazilian composers in the beginning of the twentieth century, participated in the modernist movement and was one of the most important musicians in that period, developing his music with an emphasis on popular and folk tradition and producing a large number of pieces for diverse instrumental and vocal groups. His background included experiences with popular music, and his production assumed classical and popular elements; his music also reinforces the ideas of nationalism, showing diverse perspectives of sounds and rhythms found in diverse Brazilian contexts. Aside from his intense activity as a composer, he was responsible for the creation and implementation of a musical practice in Brazilian schools called *Canto Orfeônico* (Choral Singing). Singing was an activity already present in music programs since 1854, when music was established as a compulsory subject in schools (Fuks, 2007).

The *Canto Orfeônico* was implemented in 1931, supported by the political administration of the country. Souza (2007) affirms that in that period—named as *Estado Novo* (New State)—education was used as "a political instrument for the State control" (14); the music was also used to eliminate social differences. Hentshcke and Oliveira (2000) consider that "the political-ideological objective of the musical practice of the *Canto Orfeônico* was the congregation of masses, exalting the sense of collectivity, patriotism and discipline" (47). The national folk anthems and patriotic songs were the basic repertoire of the *Canto Orfeônico.*

Methodologically, the *Canto Orfeônico* was a "traditional model, based on imitative processes, directed to determined objectives and goals, and that explored the functional aspect of music in terms of the accommodation of the individuals to the current governmental system" (Hentschke and Oliveira, 2000, 47–48). The proposed methodology could be identified with some of Kodály's principles, especially those related to nationalism through folk music and singing.

Educação Musical (Music Education) was the name of the subject that substituted the *Canto Orfeônico* in the schools, over approximately ten years. This short period was marked by different approaches to music education, including the new methodologies developed by Dalcroze (1865–1950), Willems (1890–1978), Kodály (1882–1967), and Orff (1895–1982). Once again these methodologies were not spread to all public education in Brazil, and was restricted to a small segment of the population.

New legislations were produced in the 1970s and will be briefly discussed in the next topic of this text.

ASPECTS OF THE EDUCATIONAL LEGISLATION REGARDING MUSIC EDUCATION IN BRAZIL

The aim of this part is to show how some aspects of the Brazilian legislation have influenced music education in schools. Diverse documents published from the decade of the 1970s were not necessarily favoring music education in diverse contexts because they did not present enough orientation in terms of music; some of those documents are too strict, limiting the action of teachers and curricula; others are too flexible, allowing multiple interpretations about what would be music education in schools. Some of those documents will be briefly discussed below.

Although changes in legislation occurred for some period of time, some aspects of the former legislation are still present in the educational context. Some practices remain strongly attached to the arts teaching, and new documents are not necessarily followed in schools. The reasons could be related to: (a) the low status of the arts in terms of the school curricula; (b) the unsuitable preparation of the arts/music teachers; (c) the inadequate physical space to develop the arts in schools; and (d) the lack of equipment and musical instruments in schools to develop musical activities.

In 1971, the federal law number 5692 established the *Educação Artística* (Artistic Education), a curricular activity that should include music, drama, visual arts, and geometric drawing. Penna (2002) gives a panoramic view of the context of the time that this law was conceived:

> The Law 5692 was the first to establish the duty of the State with the public and free education for eight years . . . that law represented a significant progress in the fight for the right to the education, bringing, as a consequence, an effective expansion of the education. . . . Like this, popular classes sat down in the school banks, putting in check pedagogic practices previously appropriate to an elitist school—as the schools of Getúlio Vargas's time, in which the *Canto Orfeônico* had place, or in the specialized music schools. A fundamental education with larger popular reach demands, therefore, a "new" pedagogic posture for the music teaching, different from the traditional patterns, still effective. (Penna, 2002, 18)

Specific university courses were created to prepare teachers to deliver the *Educação Artística* in schools. Those courses offered two types of certificates: a short course—two years—prepared teachers in all the arts areas, with an integrative approach to teach in the first years of regular school (ages seven to ten); and a long course—more than two years—specialized teachers in one of the arts, allowing them to teach upper levels, including the secondary years (ages eleven to seventeen). The results of this preparation, according to Fonterrada (2005, 202), were that teachers were not prepared to meet the educational expectations and went to schools "with big gaps in their formation." Under the idea of "arts integration" (Oliveira, 2007), the *Educação Artística* had "devastating effects, that our area is resented until today" (Duprat, 2007, 30). One of the most important problems was the idea of *polivalência*; that is, one teacher should be *polyvalent*, teaching all the arts subjects. Barbosa (2001) considers that the *polivalência* is "a reduced and incorrect version of the interdisciplinary principle" (48) that was developed in North American schools but introduced in Brazil with a distorted view.

According to Fonterrada (2005, 202), "the discourse of *Educação Artística* was based on the modernist concept (the enlargement of the sound universe, musical expression committed to the practice and free experimentation)." Beyond this, "the experience incentivized the emotional liberation, the valorization of folk and popular music" (Fonterrada, 2005, 202). The practice emphasized the spontaneity, understanding it as a lack of planning and perspectives, without rigor; free expression was the objective, functioning as "an open space for the freedom of expression, that, however, it didn't really happen, but as imitation" (203).

Educação Artística and *polivalência* have been discussed and criticized by many authors in the Brazilian context (Figueiredo, 2004a, 2004b, 2007; Fonterrada, 2005; Hentschke and Oliveira, 1999; Penna, 2002, Tourinho, 1993). This period brought to the Brazilian education a strong presence of the visual arts tradition in schools. Music educators preferred to direct their activities to specialized schools, such as conservatories and music schools, or to private music teaching. The lack of suitable conditions to the development of music classes—such as adequate equipment, appropriate rooms, and musical instruments—established gradually an absence of music in regular schools in many parts of Brazil. Besides the lack of conditions, Penna (2002) emphasizes the lack of commitment of the music education area with basic education and regular schools.

Unfortunately, the *Educação Artística* period brought a very simplistic notion for the arts in education as these areas have occupied an insignificant space inside the school curricula in many educational systems. Despite of the criticism and the unsuitable outcomes, some teachers are satisfied with the practice that involves several arts delivered by one teacher, sustaining the *polivalência* until today, even after new changes in legislation. Thus, the Brazilian educational context is still strongly attached to the idea of the arts as superficial activities, without relevance in the preparation of students, functioning more like entertainment in special moments and parties in schools. Evidently some exceptions can be found and good arts programs are developed in different parts of the country, but they do not represent the majority.

MUSIC IN BASIC EDUCATION

The current legislation in Brazil was approved in 1996, and, since then, the arts are included at different levels of Brazilian education: "The arts teaching will consist as a compulsory curricular subject in the diverse levels of basic education to promote the cultural development of students" (Brasil, 1996, art. 26). This legislation is valid until today, and some changes have been approved to be included in the law as a constant effort for the improvement of the Brazilian education. Such legislation orients all aspects of education, including the teachers to be allowed to teach in different levels and the preparation of teachers.

Basic education in Brazil is divided into three main periods: (1) Early Childhood Education—ages zero to five; (2) Fundamental Teaching—ages six to fourteen; (3) Middle Teaching—ages fifteen to seventeen. Commonly, generalist teachers are in Early Childhood Education (ages zero to five) and the initial four years of Fundamental Teaching (ages six to nine); some schools could have specialists in those phases of schooling (Early Childhood and the first four years of Fundamental Teaching) for the arts, physical education, and foreign languages, when applicable, but this depends on the context. Specialist teachers are in the final five years of Fundamental Teaching (ages ten to fourteen) and during the Middle Teaching (ages fifteen to seventeen).

Generalist teachers are usually prepared in universities, and their courses include some arts preparation but not necessarily music preparation. The Brazilian literature has discussed the music preparation for generalists in diverse contexts, showing the necessity of improving such courses, considering initial and continuing education. The literature points to the lack of confidence and competence of generalist teachers with music, generated by the lack of preparation in this area during their preparation in universities; and also continuing music education is rarely offered to the teachers in schools. At the same time, the literature discusses the current situation of generalist teachers' music preparation, including reports with good results of music courses for generalist teachers—preservice and in-service experiences—showing that the music preparation of those teachers could be a very important aspect to be considered in the Brazilian context (Bellochio et al., 2003; Figueiredo, 2002, 2003, 2004a, 2004b; Figueiredo, Bellochio, and Souza, 2008; Godoy and Figueiredo, 2005; Souza, 2002).

Specialist teachers are prepared in universities by different areas. In the case of the arts, universities offer specific preparation in music, visual arts, drama, or dance. Nowadays the idea of *polivalência* is extinct from the university courses, and all students must choose one art form of study in their undergraduate studies. Although the model of *polivalência* is not offered anymore, many educational systems still recruit teachers with that preparation, ignoring the current orientation of separate art preparation in universities. This is possible in the Brazilian context because the educational systems in different states and cities have autonomy to decide about their curriculum, following general orientation from the national legislation. The current legislation establishes that the arts must be taught, but educational systems have the freedom to decide which art forms must be taught at each level. The choice could be related to the number of hours in the curriculum and the availability of teachers. Economic factors usually restrict the number of arts teachers in schools, and until today the visual arts are much more established in many educational systems as the main focus of arts teaching.

Recently a complementary new legislation was approved regarding music education. It adds—to the article that establishes the arts teaching as a compulsory curricular component—music as a compulsory content, but not exclusive (Brasil, 2008). This means that music must be compulsory at all Brazilian educational systems, but not substituting other forms of arts teaching. The approval of this law brings a new perspective for the arts teaching established in 1996. Some schools already offer music as a curricular component. Some others have music as an optional, extracurricular activity that is not for all students. Others do not offer any music activity at all. The new legislation to be implemented depends on several factors, including financial resources for the recruitment of music teachers. In addition to economic aspects, it will be necessary to reorganize the school's offerings, adding music in the school activities at diverse levels. This will demand new orientations organized by the Ministry of Education, followed by states' and cities' regulations.

Although music education in Brazilian schools has been inconsistent and frequently out of the regular curriculum, there is plenty of music in the school environment, as research has shown (Figueiredo, 2008). Santos (2005) affirms that "musical activities are frequent and occupy a prominent place in parties and in the quotidian of the schools, carrying out different functions" (31).

MUSIC SCHOOLS

Music schools can be found in Brazil, offering opportunities for students from different ages and levels. There are conservatories, music schools, and also a number of private teachers developing a very important task in terms of music education, as music has not been regularly offered in basic education for all students.

The majority of music teaching out of the regular school is private. A small number of Brazilian cities run public music schools, attending a selective number of students. Because of the lack of music education in the regular schools and the small number of public music schools in Brazil, this type of teaching does not reach a considerable amount of students. The private music teaching, delivered out of the regular schools, could be assumed as an elitist activity. Therefore, the private music schools are frequented by a minimal part of the population that has financial conditions to afford such type of study.

With diverse characteristics, music schools and conservatories tend to emphasize instrumental teaching. Children, young adults, and adults could find music courses that are adapted to their interest and the availability of teachers. In general, popular and classical music can be studied in many music schools, even though some of them are specialized.

Methodologies are also varied in terms of music teaching, in the context of music schools and conservatories and according to the teachers and the proposal. Some schools have a curriculum that includes practice (instrumental classes, group activities such as choirs, bands, orchestras) and theory (reading and writing music, harmony, music history, among others). In many schools, curricular proposals are connected to the methodologies of prominent educators like Dalcroze (1865–1950), Willems (1890–1978), Kodály (1882–1967), Orff (1895–1982), Suzuki (1989–1998), and Schafer (1933–), among others. Brazilian proposals with specific approaches are also present in the context of music schools and conservatories, but it is not possible to affirm that there are currently Brazilian methodologies in the same sense that elements of the quoted educators can be found, identified, and developed by music teachers in Brazil. It is evident that Brazilian materials have been increased in diverse directions, and publications, CDs, DVDs, and other resources are available for the delivery of teaching different topics in music—repertoire, exercises, theory, and so on.

Music schools have full autonomy to develop their curriculum, methodologies, and to set the criteria to hire teachers in terms of their education, musical background, and music studies. However, there is one exception to this point: that is, the possibility of having music schools that offer courses related to professional education in music. For instance, the music program offered in a conservatory is connected to a regular school (Middle Teaching—ages fifteen to seventeen), and students must attend classes in both institutions. There are some cases in which both preparations are offered in the same school. The intended result is that at the end of Middle Teaching, the student has been prepared to begin in the music profession. The courses in this specific situation are regulated by national legislation, and the schools must follow a number of hours and subjects in terms of music preparation (Brasil, 2005). Although this possibility can be found in different parts of Brazil, it is unlikely that students enroll in such a program. Many prefer to continue studies in their instruments, parallel to the regular school (Middle Teaching), not linked to the profession. It is not necessary to have this type of music certification to enter the university or to play in an orchestra or a band. Therefore, the demand for this type of program is not so popular among young students.

MUSIC IN THE COMMUNITY

Research has shown the importance of music in different school contexts. Social projects, established and developed by NGOs (nongovernmental organizations), are important examples of the role of music education in the people's lives in the Brazilian context. These organizations are part of the Third Sector, which means that they are not part of the First Sector—the State and public—and neither the Second Sector—the market and private. In other words, these organizations belong to the civil society, with public and nonprofit ends; NGOs work with a diversity of goals, offering activities that in many cases include music and education.

Grossi and Barbosa (2004) affirm that due to

> the little efficiency, in Brazil and in other countries, of the First and Second sectors to supply the needs of the marginalized groups, part of the civil society transferred its expectations in the solution of certain problems to assistance organizations without lucrative ends among which are inserted NGOs.

Music has diverse objectives in social projects offered to the community, but in many of them "it has been presented as a form of moving away [from] social delinquency, as a professionalization alternative, as an instrument of valorization of the popular culture, of improving the quality of life of the assisted population" (Santos, 2005, 32).

The literature in this area discusses a contradictory situation that can be found in the Brazilian context. At the same time music is absent of the school curriculum but is present as special projects in many schools. Santos (2005) considers that the government does not assume the responsibility in terms of music education for all, determining little resources to finance musical activities developed by NGOS. "To the others," criticizes Santos, "the wide majority of students in the public nets of teaching, remains a poor school for poor people" (32). Müller (2005) also emphasizes such contradiction, showing that the resources that allow NGOs to survive are predominantly coming from the government.

Several authors have studied music in social projects, bringing important contributions to music education in the Brazilian context, understanding and publicizing different perspectives of music teaching and learning. The publications of ABEM—The Brazilian Association of Music Education—present a number of texts with discussion of social projects and music education. Some examples of those texts are: Almeida (2005); Araldi and Maltauro (2006); Azuelos, Avelino, and Menezes (2006); Braga (1997); Fialho (2004); Garcia (2004); Grossi and Barbosa (2004); Joly et al. (2002); Kleber (2005, 2006); Lima (2002, 2003); Müller (2000); Silva (2002); Souza (2002, 2005); and Stein (2001). The synthesis of these studies can be found in Figueiredo (2008), offering a general overview on the topic.

MUSIC TEACHER PREPARATION

Music teachers who teach at Basic Education in Brazil are prepared in a university program called *licenciatura* (teacher training course). There is a continuous debate whether or not learners should be prepared to be both a musician and a teacher. Recent reforms on the preparation of music teachers have been presented, and all universities are adapting their curricula continuously to abide by the new legislation and also to improve the quality of the curriculum.

The main document regarding music preparation in universities is called *Diretrizes Curriculares Nacionais do Curso de Graduação em Música*—National Curriculum Guidelines of the Undergraduate Music Course (Brasil, 2004). All universities that offer undergraduate courses in music must follow the orientations established in the guidelines. Among the several aspects presented in the document, the general organization of the course must consider the inclusion of the following three points:

1. Basic contents: studies connected with the Culture and the Arts, also involving Human and Social Sciences, with emphasis in Anthropology and Psycho-pedagogy
2. Specific contents: studies that particularize and give consistence to the area of Music, including Instrumental, Compositional, Aesthetic, and Conducting Knowledge
3. Theoretical-practical contents: studies that allow theory and practice integration related to the exercise of the musical art and of professional acting, also including Supervised Teaching Preparation, Teaching Practice, Scientific Initiation, and use of new Technologies (Brasil, 2004, art. 5)

The guidelines also establish that the undergraduate music course must guarantee a professional preparation that reveals competences and abilities:

1. to intervene in the society in agreement with their cultural manifestations, demonstrating sensibility and artistic creation and practical excellence
2. to make possible scientific and technological research in music, seeking to the creation, understanding, and diffusion of the culture and its development
3. to act, in a significant way, in the instituted or merging musical manifestations
4. to act in differentiated cultural spaces and, especially, in articulation with institutions of specific teaching of music
5. to stimulate musical creations and their popularization as manifestation of the artistic potential (Brasil, 2004, art. 4)

In practice, universities are always revising their curricula, reorganizing the compulsory and optional subjects to be offered for students. Beyond this document from 2004—the guidelines for music quoted before—other guidelines orient universities about courses that prepare teachers for all areas of the school's curriculum. These other documents—guidelines for the preparation of teachers in Brazil (Brasil, 2002)—reaffirm the importance of the preparation for teaching, not only for the content of a specific area. The balance between musical and pedagogical preparation offered in the Brazilian universities is a permanent challenge, and the teaching practice has been considered as a central issue to be addressed during all years of the program.

MUSIC CURRICULUM

The Brazilian educational legislation has not formulated core contents for any area of school knowledge. The notion of a National Curriculum is not present in the Brazilian context. The Law 9394/1996 establishes that the curricula must have a "common national base, to be complemented, in each education system and school, with a diversified part, demanded by the regional characteristic and places of the society, of the culture, of the economy and of the clientele" (Brasil, 1996, art. 26). The curricula must include "the study of the Portuguese language and Mathematics, the knowledge of the physical and natural world and the social and political reality, especially of Brazil . . . the arts teaching will constitute compulsory curricular component" (Brasil, 1996, art. 26).

The Ministry of Education produced other documents regarding specifically curricular orientation. These documents, called *Parâmetros Curriculares Nacionais* (PCN—National Curriculum Parameters) (Brasil, 1997, 1998), present orientation for all areas to be included in the school curricula. One of the volumes of this publication is dedicated to the arts, bringing separately issues of music, dance, visual arts, and theatre. The orientations are open and flexible, allowing educational systems to adapt the objectives and contents according to their interest and availability of teachers. These documents—PCN—are only suggestive, not compulsory, and therefore they do not constitute a national curriculum. In different Brazilian contexts, when music is part of the curriculum, the objectives and contents could be quite diverse.

The orientation for music in the document named PCN is divided into three main topics:

- Communication and expression in music: interpretation, improvisation, and composition
- Significant appreciation in music: listening, involvement, and comprehension of the musical language
- Music as a cultural and historic product: music and sounds of the world (Brasil, 1997)

In each of these topics, general orientation is suggested considering a variety of elements that could be part of the curriculum; for instance, interpretation of music from diverse sources, arrangements, improvisation and composition, music notations, music perception, identification of musical instruments, styles and elements of the musical language, music history, music and society, music events, music practice, and research, among others. All these indicators can be organized by educational systems with flexibility and freedom.

Even though some orientation is offered, and the legislation allows freedom and flexibility of the educational systems, music education remains in a low position in terms of curriculum. It is necessary to foster the review of concepts on music and the arts in the school, and this is a huge task because people are habituated to understand the arts in general only for fun and not as a serious component in the school curriculum. To change this view is necessary to rebuild the perspectives of the arts teaching in many Brazilian schools. In diverse contexts, this different perspective, where the arts occupy a more significant place in the curriculum, is already established. The big challenge is to reach all schools in terms of the arts and music education.

FINAL CONSIDERATIONS

Diversity and discontinuity are two concepts that could represent a summary of the situation of music education in Brazil. In different periods music was part of the school curriculum, emphasizing several aspects that were considered suitable for music teaching. In all periods briefly described in this text, music education assumed different roles and functions: religious practice, nationalism and civicism, creativity and spontaneity, cultural development, and so on.

To sum up:

- Diversity can be seen in the functions, and consequently in the approaches, defined to the development of music in the curriculum. At the same time, music out of the curriculum was and continues being a permanent presence in schools. It can also be found in terms of the contents to be addressed, considering that Brazil is a huge country with specific characteristics in each region. When the idea of folk and popular music is presented as music content, the result is a wide range of possibilities.
- Diversity could be related to the comprehension of music as an autonomous subject or a part of the arts teaching, delivered by one or various specialist teachers. Generalist teachers are also responsible for the integration of the subjects in the curriculum, which means that they should deal with music in some sense. It is also present when the flexibility and freedom given by the legislation allow a multiplicity of approaches, objectives, and methodologies, producing a myriad of practices in the educational environment. As a consequence of the diversity, discontinuity is a common issue in the history of music education in Brazil. The understanding of the importance and relevance of music in school is far from an agreement among teachers, administrators, and society.
- Discontinuity has been a problematic aspect of music education in Brazil. As a result, generations of students were in schools without any musical education, promoting an idea that this subject area is not relevant in the preparation of students.
- Because of discontinuity, it is very common to find people that consider learning music as an issue of talent, and this is enough to accept that music is not in the school curriculum.

Apart from the problems announced and discussed in this text, Brazilian music is a very strong social activity, and the wide majority of people in Brazil deal with music somehow. This point could be seen as a kind of impediment for music in education because many people argue that music is already sufficient in the life of people, and it is not necessary to include it as a curricular component. Others argue that exactly because music is so present in people's lives it should be more relevant in terms of education, to enlarge this experience of students in schools.

The debate is on. There is an expectation on the new legislation approved in August 2008 establishing music as a compulsory component of the curriculum. The Ministry of Education and Secretaries of Education in states and cities in Brazil will regulate this new topic. Different interpretations and applications certainly will be part of this debate, and the expectation is that, even though the agreement in some topics is necessary, the diversity must be pursued and assumed, respecting specific contexts, regionalities, and singularities in the process of music education.

The regulation is now being organized and future studies will show its effects on school life. The hope is that music education could be offered to all Brazilian citizens, contributing to the development of a fair society, with equal opportunities for all where education—and music education—have a fundamental role in the construction of a better Brazilian and world society.

REFERENCES

Almeida, C. (2005). Educação musical não-formal e atuação profissional. *Revista da ABEM* 13, 49–56.

Araldi, J., and Maltauro, J. P. (2006). Traz um rap aí professora, que aí sim eu canto! *Anais do XV Encontro Anual da ABEM*, CD ROM. João Pessoa: ABEM.

Azuelos, E. S., Avelino, N. C., and Menezes, B. S. (2006). Projeto de musicalização: Melodia da vida, harmonia da alma. *Anais do XV Encontro Anual da ABEM*, CD ROM. João Pessoa: ABEM.

Barbosa, A. M. (2001). *John Dewey e o ensino de arte no Brasil*. São Paulo, Brazil: Cortez Editora.

Bellochio, C. R. et al. (2003). Pensar e realizar em Educação Musical: Desafios do professor dos anos iniciais do Ensino Fundamental. *Revista da FUNDARTE* 5, 42–46.

Braga, J. M. (1997). Projeto Tocando a Vida. *Anais do VI Encontro Anual da ABEM e I Encontro Latino-Americano de Educação Musical*, 134. Salvador: ABEM.

Brasil. (1854). Decreto No 1.331-A de 17 de fevereiro de 1854 que "Approva o Regulamento para a reforma do ensino primario e secundario do Municipio da Côrte." Available from http://www.histedbr.fae.unicamp.br/navegando/fontes_escritas/3_Imperio/artigo_004.html

Brasil. (1890). Decreto No 981 que "Aprova o Regulamento da Instrucção Primaria e Secundaria do Districto Federal." Available from http://www.camara.gov.br/internet/infdoc/novoconteudo/legislacao/republica/decretos1890_1a30nov/pdf31.pdf

Brasil. (1996). *Lei 9394/96—Lei de Diretrizes e Bases da Educação Nacional*. Brasília: Ministério da Educação. Available from http://www.mec.gov.br)

Brasil. (1997). *Parâmetros Curriculares Nacionais*. Brasília: MEC: Secretaria de Educação Fundamental.

Brasil. (1998). *Parâmetros Curriculares Nacionais*. Brasília: MEC: Secretaria de Educação Fundamental.

Brasil. (2002). *Diretrizes Curriculares Nacionais para a formação de Professores da Educação Básica*. Brasília: MEC—Ministry of Education.

Brasil. (2004). *Diretrizes Curriculares Nacionais para os Cursos de Graduação em Música*. Brasília: MEC.

Brasil. (2005) *Resolução n. 1, de 3 de fevereiro de 2005. Atualiza as Diretrizes Curriculares Nacionais definidas pelo Conselho Nacional de Educação para o Ensino Médio e para a Educação Profissional Técnica de nível médio às disposições do Decreto no. 5.154/2004*. Brasília: Ministério da Educação. Available from http://www.mec.gov.br

Brasil. (2008). Lei 11.769/08. *Altera a Lei no. 9.394, de 20 de dezembro de 1996, Lei de Diretrizes e Bases da Educação, para dispor sobre a obrigatoriedade do ensino da música na educação básica*. Brasília: Ministério da Educação. Available from http://www.mec.gov.br

Duprat, R. (2007). A pós-graduação em música no Brasil. In A. Oliveira and R. Cajazeira (orgs.), *Educação Musical no Brasil* (29–36). Salvador: P&A.

Fialho, V. M. (2004). O *rap* na vida dos *rappers*: "Eu carrego o *rap* como a minha vida, sem ele eu acho que não vivo." *Anais do XIII Encontro Anual da ABEM*, CD ROM. Rio de Janeiro: ABEM.

Figueiredo, S. L. F. (2002). Generalist Teacher Music Preparation: A Brazilian Investigation. In G. F. Welch and G. Folkestad (eds.), *A World of Music Education Research: The 19th ISME Research Seminar* (77–82). Goteborg, Sweden: Goteborg University.

Figueiredo, S. L. F. (2003). *The Music Preparation of Generalist Teachers in Brazil*. Unpublished PhD Thesis. RMIT University—Faculty of Education, Melbourne, Australia.

Figueiredo, S. L. F. (2004a). Teaching Music in the Preparation of Generalist Teachers: A Brazilian Experience. *Bulletin of the Council for Research in Music Education* 161/162, 73–81.

Figueiredo, S. L. F. (2004b). A preparação musical de professores generalistas no Brasil. *Revista da ABEM*. Porto Alegre, 11, 55–62.

Figueiredo, S. L. F. (2007). A legislação brasileira para a educação musical nos anos iniciais da escola. *Anais do XVI Congresso da ANPPOM*, CD ROM. São Paulo: UNESP/ANPPOM.

Figueiredo, S. L. F. (2008). Educación musical y proyectos sociales em Brasil. *Eufonia* 42, 32–47. Barcelona, Espanha.

Figueiredo, S. L. F., Bellochio, C. R., and Souza, C. V. C. (2008). Music Education and Teacher Preparation for Childhood: Research and Practice in Brazil. *28th ISME Conference Proceedings*, CD ROM. Bologna, Italy: ISME.

Fonterrada, M. (2005). *De tramas e fios*: Um ensaio sobre música e educação. São Paulo: Editora da UNESP, 2005.

Fuks, R. (2007). A educação musical da Era Vargas: Seus precursores. In A. Oliveira and R. Cajazeira (orgs.), *Educação Musical no Brasil* (18–23). Salvador: P&A.

Garcia, E. C. P. (2004). Música & ações sociais: Experiências em Cuiabá–MT. *Anais do XIII Encontro Anual da ABEM*, CD ROM. Rio de Janeiro: ABEM.

Godoy, V. L. F. M., and Figueiredo, S. L. F. (2005). Música nas séries iniciais: Quem vai ensinar? *Anais do XIV Encontro Anual da ABEM*, CD ROM. Belo Horizonte: ABEM.

Grossi, C. S., and Barbosa, P. I. R. (2004). Educação musical nas ONGs do Distrito Federal: Campo de trabalho e perfil profissional. *Anais do XIII Encontro Anual da ABEM*, CD ROM. Rio de Janeiro: ABEM.

Hentschke, L., and Oliveira, A. (1999). Music curriculum development and evaluation based on Swanwick's theory. *International Journal of Music Education* 34, 14–29.

Hentschke, L., and Oliveira, A. (2000). A educação musical no Brasil. In L. Hentschke (ed.), *Educação musical em países de línguas neolatinas* (47–64). Porto Alegre: Editora da Universidade/UFRGS.

Joly, I. Z. L., Santiago, G. L. A., Penteado, E. D. L., and Joly, M. C. L. (2002). Formação de orquestras com crianças de classes populares: Uma proposta para constituição da cidadania. *Anais do XI Encontro Anual da ABEM*, CD ROM. Natal: ABEM.

Kleber, M. O. (2005). Práticas musicais em ONGs: Reflexões sobre percurso metodológico na coleta de dados. *Anais do VIII Encontro Regional da ABEM Sul*, CD ROM. Pelotas: ABEM.

Kleber, M. O. (2006). A prática de educação musical em ONGs: Dois estudos de caso no contexto urbano brasileiro. *Anais do XV Encontro Anual da ABEM*, CD ROM. João Pessoa: ABEM.

Lima, M. H. (2002). Projeto Música & Cidadania: Uma proposta de movimento. *Anais do XI Encontro Anual da ABEM*, CD ROM. Natal: ABEM.

Lima, M. H. (2003). Educação musical/educação popular: Projeto música & cidadania, uma proposta de movimento. *Anais do XI Encontro Anual da ABEM*, CD ROM. Florianópolis: ABEM.

Müller, V. B. (2000). "A vida é, bem dizê, a vida da gente": Um estudo sobre a relação de crianças e adolescentes em situação de rua com a música. *Anais do 7. Simpósio Paranaense de Educação Musical* (123–33). Londrina: UEL.

Müller, V. B. (2005). Por uma educação musical implicada com os modos de vida de seus cenários de atuação. *Revista da ABEM* 12, 43–47.

Oliveira, A. (2007). Aspectos históricos da educação musical no Brasil e na América do Sul. In A. Oliveira and R. Cajazeira (orgs.), *Educação Musical no Brasil* (3–12). Salvador: P&A.

Penna, M. (2002). Professores de música nas escolas públicas de ensino fundamental e médio: Uma ausência significativa. *Revista da ABEM* 7, 7–19.

Santos, M. A. C. (2005). Educação musical na escola e nos projetos comunitários e sociais. *Revista da ABEM* 12, 31–34.

Silva, D. G. (2002). Pau e lata: projeto artístico–pedagógico. *Anais do XI Encontro Anual da ABEM*, CD ROM. Natal: ABEM.

Souza, C. V. C. (2002). A música na formação dos professores dos anos iniciais do ensino fundamental: Uma visita à literatura de educação musical. *Linhas Críticas. Revista Semestral da Faculdade de Educação da UNB* 8(14).

Souza, J. (2007). A educação musical no Brasil dos anos 1930–45. In A. Oliveira and R. Cajazeira (orgs.), *Educação Musical no Brasil* (13–17). Salvador: P&A.

Souza, R. D. (2005). Federação de Bandas do Rio Grande do Sul: "Não curto drogas–curto Bandas." *Anais do VIII Encontro Regional da ABEM Sul*, CD ROM. Pelotas: ABEM.

Stein, M. (2001). OUVIRAVIDA: Um projeto da Fundação Orquestra Sinfônica de Porto Alegre de educação musical em bairros populares. *Anais do IV Encontro Regional da ABEM Sul e I Encontro do Laboratório de Ensino de Música/LEM-CE-UFSM* (108–16). Santa Maria: UFSM.

Tourinho, I. (1993). Usos e funções da música na escola pública de 1o grau. *Fundamentos da Educação Musical, ABEM* 1, 91–113.

Wisnick, J. M. (1977). *O coro dos Contrários: A música em torno da Semana de 22*. São Paulo: Duas Cidades.

Chapter Fourteen

Chile

Ana Teresa Sepúlveda Cofré

INTRODUCTION

Music education in Chile could be viewed through the strength it has acquired throughout its history and the opportunities brought by the demands established by pop culture and its technological advances. In the same fashion it has confronted difficulties simultaneously with the education system and its development as a vehicle for the personal and collective growth of the nation. Therefore, in order to observe various aspects of its presence, it is necessary to take a look at its history since pre-Hispanic Chile, continuing with colonial Chile and focusing on today's independent state, which in conjunction with other Latin American nations celebrated its bicentennial in 2011.

PRE-HISPANIC CULTURE

Tales of travelers, studies made by diverse histories, and recent investigative reports have discovered an earlier life filled with wonders through the American territory back to the BC years (Villalobos, 1995: 15). Historian Francisco Antonio Encina (1983: 37) suggests that the clergy member Juan Ignacio Molina (1788) "suspected about the existence of a civilization in the Chilean territory established way before the Inca conquest." He goes on to say that it is not possible to pinpoint with any certainty what ethnic groups arrived at the Chilean territory. According to their geographic location, it seems that the immigration took place from north to south and by sea. But some took place from the south. The *Tehuelches* were a mere "consequence" of invading groups from south to the north (Encina, 1983: 40). The only certainty was that the ethnic groups were being continuously transformed given the "tradition of exogamy or marriage outside the tribe and by women being the prizes of war." Given that this practice was seemingly common in Chile, the racial group that was found in our territory by the Spaniards was not, in an anthropological or cultural sense, aboriginal (Encina, 1983: 41) but only in part pre-Incan. Encina argues that what is important is their differences. For example, the *Picunches* and *Huilliches* southern cultures are very different from the *Mapuche* cultures that inhabit a region to the north of the aforementioned two ethnic cultures (1983).

For this reason, when the Incas arrived to this territory in the mid-sixteenth century, and later by 1536 the Spaniards, they found diverse groups (Villalobos, 1995) who were different in physical and moral characteristics that were evident to the researcher or conqueror (Encina, 1983). A land like *una loca geografía*, as it is defined by the historian Benjamin Subercaseaux (1956), with varied climates and ecological areas, harbored various ethnic groups, be it nomadic or sedentary and people dedicated to agriculture, hunting, and fishing. From north to south, *Changos, Atacameños, Diaguitas, Picunches, Mapuche, Hulliches, Pehuenches, Puelches, Thuelches o Patagones, Selk'nam* (Onas), *Chonos, Alcalufes, Yaganes,* or *Yamanas* created a multicultural coexistence. These cultures, a few of them now defunct, have left testimonials of their existence by way of objects of architectural, ethnic, and musical interest (Marquez, 2000: 13–29).

These objects or "archaeological remnants" (Cabello and Martínez, 1988: 1), like domestic utensils for hunting, fishing, safety, for rituals and celebrations, allow us to get closer to the music of aboriginal peoples now vanished. This study allows us to get closer "in a more intimate way to how those people are, feel and sound" (Perez de Arce, 1995:11). Archaeologists and physical anthropologists have conducted research, findings, and analyses of such objects. Ethnomusicology provides an inside look at the role music plays by way of the study of musical instruments and artistic iconography. People were transformed, as mentioned in the Aldunate del Solar (1982), into "inconsistent phenomena belonging to groups who have disappeared and have not left any written evidence of their history. . . . The only evidence that the pre-Columbian musicians have left us is their instruments. Their plethora of imaginative forms, frequently associated with animals, plants and other elements of nature, such as the common portrayal of musicians and dancers in pre-Columbian paintings and sculptures, gives a glimpse of how important the music was amongst those ethnic groups and the role it played in the festivities, religious or pagan ceremonies and small or large scale activities."

MUSIC IN COLONIAL CHILE

Religious Music

According to researchers in colonial times (from 1601 to 1810), the religious orders that arrived in Chile were pivotal in evangelization as well as education. It was during those two centuries and part of the nineteenth century when the culture gave life to the emerging Chilean society (Villalobos, 1995: 83). The Jesuits stand out for their preparedness and tastefulness. The musical activity that they developed during the colonization was accomplished by three of their religious endeavors: catechism, festivities, and religious services (Rondón, 1997a). The missionary works of the Mercedes were notable as well as the Franciscans, Dominicans, and Augustans. Their labor as well as of the Jesuits continues to have a strong presence in the churches and schools in Chile today. Their contribution to education was disseminated throughout the entire country (Eyzaguirre, 1997: 38), and music had a great presence in the pastoral work of such religious groups.

Catechism played a pivotal role in evangelization, and therefore in music, particularly in singing. We know by Pereira Salas that both Father Luis de Valdivia and Father Hernando de Aguilera sang their doctrines on the streets and town squares of Santiago as soon as they arrived to the city in 1593. The Jesuit O. Vecci, who was a missionary and martyr of Italian origin, referred to the results of his work done during his two months in Arauco in 1610 while narrating his apostolic activity. He states that during the teaching of catechism, he educated more than two hundred people. He also expresses that it was of major relief to see "those infidel children learning the four prayers and the catechism, and sing songs from the doctrine in their own mother tongue" (cited by Rondón, 1997b). It is my belief that one of the great values instilled by the Jesuit missionary work in the *Mapuche* was learning their language and translating texts with songs, catechisms, and devotional works to the *Mapudungun* language. Those documents indeed contain valuable information for researchers today. Flutist and musicologist Victor Rondón studied the music in the Jesuit missions in the southern part of Chile as well as the musical legacy left by those religious musicians more than three centuries ago.

COLONIAL SOCIAL LIFE

Colonial social life was developed based upon religious, official, civilian, and military ceremonies. The religious ceremonies were based upon the rhythm of life and death, celebrating baptisms, marriages, and wakes. Such ceremonies were numerous and marked important social events (Villalobos, 2000). The traditional seasons such as Christmas, Lent, and Holy Week had a special significance. Claro Valdés states, "During the colonial Christmas time all America enjoyed to the beat of villancicos and chants interpreted by the best artists of the day who sang various choirs accompanied by instruments and compositions created for such occasion" (Claro Valdés, 1976).[1] "The festivities were outfitted with the best religious ornaments, the objects were generally made out of silver. The church interiors were luxuriously outfitted with rugs provided by neighbors, flowers meticulously arranged by nuns and ladies of the church . . . Silver candelabras and candleholders showcased high priced candles . . . Every time an event was to be upgraded to a higher level, a higher expense in music, wax and fragrances went along with it" (Claro Valdés, 1976: 308). Villalobos noted the popularity of religious festivities and the enthusiasm with which they were embraced by all classes within society. Yet by the same token, there was a strict distance kept among classes due to the prevalent stratification. He also points out that processions were where the differences were most evidently exhibited.

Many rivaling congregations competed among themselves by the way they dressed. The poorest congregations were the native Indians, blacks, and mulattos who organized the venues that were characterized by the "noise" they made with their "singing and screaming" (Claro Valdés, 1976: 310). He also emphasizes the social inequality made evident in these festivities (Claro Valdés, 1976: 311). Victor Rondón (1997c) points out the following quote by the Jesuit Father Ovalle, who speaks about the care with which the native Indians and blacks would put together the congregations; this explanation would differ from the opinion held by Villalobos. He states:

> The very superiors, even the highest religious superior, are the first to speak during the services and sermons during the days of the festivities and congregations, and about giving them a confession and to join in the processions with crucifixes on hand [. . .] The processions are very exuberant and there is a lot to see in them. In comparison, the native Indians put together their congregation the morning of Easter Sunday, two hours before sunrise they gather up with their white candle sticks, though all very well dressed and outfitted. The procession is comprised by a lot of floats and flags adorned by a lot of artificial silk flowers, silver and gold. And the one with the baby Jesus sporting the wears of the native Indians; the Virgin Mary is dressed gloriously with rich adornments and surrounded by other devotional iconography. All this with plenty of music, dance, and various instruments made out of boxes, flutes and clarinets [clarines] as the procession goes by a monastery, it is acknowledged by nuns and religious members by bell tolls, organs and good music.

It is necessary to add a very interesting fact in regard to the Jesuit musicians from the missions. These religious men played a significant role not only by providing their talent and musical knowledge but also convincing people about the influence of music to their wellness. They also provided the interpretation and teaching of the musical instruments they brought as well as the ones they built with local raw materials. In addition to boxes, flutes, and clarinets [clarines], they brought flutes, *chirimias* (double-reed instruments), and trumpets; laud, sitars, violin, and more frequently the violoncello, which could be the *viola da gamba* as a bass and/or ravel (a string instrument). The brother Jorge Krazer, organist and organ maker, constructed a baroque organ. The original construction techniques are still preserved by the Cathedral Church of Santiago. In Chile there were also churches devoid of bells and organs, facts compiled by Victor Rondón (1997b).

Very established customs during colonial times were the *tertulias* and *chinganas*. The *tertulias*, which took place in homes, were a gathering of family and friends for having conversations and listening to musical works interpreted by a family member. The *chinganas* in turn were popular public places where music was livelier, more spontaneous, and flamboyant; the type of venues that young ladies of high society did not take part of (Sepúlveda, 2004). Villalobos states, "During colonial times, art was constrained to social guidelines and requirements more than any other time. The artist was not free to exhibit their inspiration, instead he had to express himself within the confines of what was defined by the collective thought and feelings of the Church and State and no one dared steer away from such confines and limitations" (Villalobos, 2006:196).

MILITARY BANDS

Military bands performed hymns and marches with their drums and trumpets. In doing so they provided another avenue for music during colonial life. The sound filled the city streets, and the children would follow the beats by imitating the steps of the military. Many of the religious, civilian, and military customs of the time were practiced well into the nineteenth century. In fact Jose Zapiola (1997), through his biographer Guillermo Blanco, tells the story of how his musical experience started in such *correrias* next to a band that came across town every day. His mother, seeing his enthusiasm, sold a silver mate gourd to buy him and old fife [pífano], and a soldier gave him basic music knowledge.

Villalobos (2006: 314) states that "music of fifes [pífanos] and trumpets" entertained along with the fire of rifles the atmosphere during a very important official ceremony in which the governor took oath as well as entertained the people in attendance. Music played a very ornamental role in private schools where children of high-society families attended, and it was thought and learned voluntarily. The results of such teaching were showcased in school festivities. There were no official curriculum or programs for the teaching of music. According to Victor Rondón, the doctrine teachings to students in public schools may not have been too dissimilar to the teaching given to the natives and colored slaves, since the students participated in popular religious festivities and therefore they practiced processional singing and dancing (Rondón, 1997b).

MUSIC EDUCATION IN THE SCHOOLS OF REPUBLICAN CHILE

To write about music education in Chilean schools prompts many questions about the three areas that it covers, in formal education and in the context of its two hundred years. The first area is the regulations that dictate its presence in the Chilean school system. The second lies in the private school classrooms where music takes a fuller life. The third is the public perception of the state of music presence and its inclusion within the school system. Those questions also arise within the historical context.

INCORPORATION OF MUSIC IN THE CHILEAN EDUCATION SYSTEM

Music was not part of the curriculum in the school system during a long period after the Republic's inception. Upon the 1810 independence, Chilean intellectuals and governing figures took it upon themselves to quickly address this issue. They had the conviction that education was the way to form the new citizens of a country being born. A republican society required cultured citizens, and the culture needed to be incremented and disseminated throughout all social classes (Villalobos, 1995: 224). In 1847, a crucial event takes place in Chilean education when music makes its official appearance in the burgeoning education system. Two artists were responsible for such an event because they were convinced of the need and importance that music had in schools.

On one hand, the tenacious musician Jose Zapiola was the passionate composer of the revolution for independence. He spoke on behalf of many contemporary intellectuals by emphasizing how music could be a positive influence in the education of a nation's citizens. On the other hand, Salvador Sanfuente, a man who was part musician and part poet, while he was Minister of Public Education declared the inclusion of music as part of the program for primary schools (A. T. Sepúlveda, 2004). The expectation for such teaching was really high. One can say that it prompted the birth of music education in Chile as the official discipline named *Canto Llano* (Plainchant). Even its name was a simple way to refer to it. It is now criticized as being part of today's problems since music was thought of as being more suitable for civic and religious festivities rather than for education. Zapiola was frustrated by the gap between reality and fantasy and complained about its achievements. He states that,

> Since singing classes of the Escuela Nacional de Preceptores [The National School of Private Teachers] started in 1848 and having reduced the teachings in school, there was plenty of time in twenty four continuous years for those who did not have a singing ability to learn an instrument. After the thousands of singers that by Mr. Sanfuente's calculation would perform in civic and religious festivities, readers do you want to know how many state or local schools teach music? None. (Zapiola, 1997)

Without a doubt, to celebrate and honor the festivities represents an undeniable societal value that sparks profound motivation and sense of identity.

In 1874 an article was published in the newspaper named *El Santa Lucia*. The article was dedicated to teaching, and it revealed the reality, failures, and needs of the moment. That was a duofold reality. On one hand there was an absence of music in school programs, and on the other hand there was a lack of interest by the government to establish music in school. That need has a very particular foreshadowing that pointed directly to the objective and fundamental presence of music in the Chilean educational system during those years. The opinions and solutions presented in the newspaper were very interesting:

> Without a doubt the study of fine arts could transform society's landscape of society once it becomes part of the regular teaching.
>
> It is time that the study of music in public education gets the support from the government.
>
> It is necessary to correct instead of repressing, reward instead of penalize, and encourage people with the noble sources of art, and to not abstain them from that which could elevate them, console them and propelled them toward their well being.
>
> Another vehicle for that is to establish a vocal and instrumental musical class in the two main schools in Santiago, whose students become teachers at the state schools once they finish their studies. It is evident that while music study has not only been barely noticeable in education, yet it has not been taught and organized in a serious manner in order to popularize it and to make it an element of general prosperity. But now that this art form is part of public teaching in the most civilized nations and that its influence in society is one of the most beautiful conquests of the present century, we do not see any reason why Chile should not give it the attention that it deserves. [2]

Finally in 1887 the decision was made to include music in primary school. In 1889, fifteen years after the article in *El Santa Lucia*, a very important teaching congress took place. On that occasion, some of the preoccupations of the newspaper were addressed and music was part of the discourse. It was present in the subject: "Musical teaching in primary schools." Congress goers studied the way music was implemented in different grades of primary school and in Normal Schools. It was concluded that there were four declarations regarding primary students, and two declarations referring to the professorship.

> I. The teaching of music in schools will be focused in singing, that given its great educational value it is part of a proper and mandatory study subject.
>
> II. The singing of simple hymns, songs related to life, and kids games could now be sung in elementary schools.
>
> III. In primary school singing is to be done in a single voice. Only in advanced courses the singing could be done in two voices.
>
> IV. In the lower levels kids will sing by ear. Learning notes may take place in mid- to high-level courses.
>
> V. So there is adequate direction, the teachers must know how to play the violin.
>
> VI. In schools having both genders, the teachings should be given covering as much material as possible including singing, violin, and music theory. [3]

It is evident that when it comes to the future professor, they should be familiarized with the teaching of singing so that way the existing void is filled. Before the 1889 congress, singing classes did not have a specific method for teachers in school, nor was there a musical instrument to accompany and give harmonic support. Four out of the six points from such declarations were oriented toward methodology.

The reports say that the subject of including music in the school system prompted heated arguments and debate among congress goers. While one group advocated that music in primary school should have had a wide presence, another group thought the contrary. At the end, what remained viable was the teaching of singing as a modality of choice. The reason why such an option still held so much weight is revealed in the first conclusion as "its great educational value." There was a trend that suggested that there was a need by primary teachers to use an instrument to accompany the teaching in class. At that time the violin was the only instrument considered to be the most suited for the "best direction for singing class." The most interesting trend or modality was that it was necessary to acquire a "singing method for teaching." This helped the repertoire in a very significant way. The employment of routine methods was one of the deficiencies of primary teaching (Ahumada, 1886).

It is often the opinion that congresses do not have a lot of influence in educational issues. However, in 1893, just five years later, an educational reform took place and music became part of the official Study Plans for Secondary School Teaching. As a result, musical programs were created. This clearly shows that those reforms followed the conclusions and recommendations made at that congress in 1888.

> More important than the method is the requirement that the professor must know how to sing and produce sounds in tune with the violin because that is what matters in art. Practice is of essence, which suggests a great working model and imitation exercise. The phonetic guidelines take second place. . . . The text on the songs has to be learned by

memory after the teacher has made the necessary explanations. . . . Each class has to make systematic exercises before engaging in singing. The songs learned will be repeated frequently. (1893 Program)

The incorporation of music in the school programs was a great achievement since popular classes also had a more complete education. The prevalent social differences during those times were deeply felt in the process of relaying the culture and the music. Even though schools did not have an obligation to teach music, children coming from well-off families would get private classes by teachers in their homes or schools. Some of the programs of the end of the school year at the Silesian school, *Patrocinio de San José*, and from the private school *Sagrado Corazón*, were conserved and archived at the Fondo de Música (Music Archive) that is kept by the Biblioteca del Congreso (Congress Library), which in turn was transferred to the National Library. The private nonreligious schools available to the regular folk also were preoccupied with the musical aspect of teaching, but always as an optional feature for education (Sepúlveda, 2004: 73). Such schools offered their very exclusive alumni regular classes for instrument and children choirs. Magazines of the time give an account of the role teaching in those schools was used as a form of marketing the schools: "We offer a suggestion [tp] the parents . . . visit the school of Miss Quintana R. de Zubicuate . . . where you will hear little kids singing and play the piano with an admirable mastery" (*El Santa Lucia*, 1874).

Before the reform in 1893, middle-class students did not have the same possibilities. They did not have any alternatives for musical development. That was in part due to the exclusivity of the high class, and the fact that public schools did not have music as a subject. But that gap was closed when the reform took place. The contribution that primary schools had in a repertory appeared in two books that contained traditional German songs. These books were adapted and translated into Spanish as a series of Chilean patriotic hymns for the use of the *Clase de Canto* (Singing Class). *Cien Canciones Escolares* was titled by its author Bernardo Göhle and published in 1888. The book was intended for schools, and it contained the harmony for national themes (Sepúlveda, 2004: 73).

The conclusions from the 1888 congress had an influence into several decades in the beginning of the twentieth century. The reform programs of 1935 were titled "Music and Singing." That is indicative of the place singing occupied and it would continue to occupy in music at the school system. Still the programs were in need of being renovated. The high school programs present a window into the reality and where their vision for the future of singing lies in teaching: "If we study the great gaps in the musical culture in secondary school, we would discover the precarious teaching method that is used frequently in music and singing classes. This program was based on an active method and it assumes that songs have been learned by memory and the musical elements would be learned after. Singing and following the beat as the rhythm is written in the songs would then be analyzed and constructed. The intervals would be discovered and that would continue to go deeper into learning the hues and the power of expression of music" (Ministerio de Educación, 1955: 1).

These programs have a curious element as they are open to new technology suggesting the use of a *vitrola* (victrola) and radio so the students would listen to a piece of music as reference for study. "It is more than the professor simply speaking about music," the Ministerio (Ministry) commented as a solid argument (1955: 4).

The artistic context of the times was a fundamental cornerstone for the development courses in the educational system. The Bach Society was created in 1927, propelled by musician Domingo Santa Cruz and with a group of amateur musicians. They forged the work that benefited music and education by promoting chamber music and regular concerts for the national and universal musical movement. Its society members recorded in history their work and education (Allende, 1932: [2]7). The presence of music in the schools was put under a lot of scrutiny, and the society worked hard to reach a course that was more efficient, musically based, more national, and more Americanized. Their efforts are reflected in the study programs of 1935. The new principles guiding these programs were based on the belief that music has a direct effect on the senses, emotions, and intelligence.

The *Asociación the Educadores Musicales* (AEM, Association for Music Educators) was born in 1946 thanks to the works and mutual interest from distinguished musicians such as Domingo Santa Cruz and music professors in the school system. It continued to function until the end of the 1970s, and it became the supporter for pushing the idea that music is valuable. This postulate affirms that the sonic-rhythmic expression that music encompasses provides the capacity to relay perceptions of beauty of joy and harmony, and that the spiritual power of feelings contained in music compositions affects the emotional capacity directly.

A search for the aesthetic reasons that motivate the creation of music along with the study of elements that form its expressive language and the materials that make up the beauty produced by the creative endeavor—all of these were considered as an intellectual endeavor (Rodriguez, 1947: 4). The categories that exist in music are worthy of study in a humanities class. According to the source, the program is comprised of music for vocals, instruments, mechanical, mixed, artistic, popular, vulgar, according to quality, national, universal, according to regions, sacred, profane (danceable or not), and according to objective.

In 1952, the AEM held an important gathering in Santiago with professional musicians and music professors. This *Primer Congreso de Educación Musical* (First Congress of Music Education) looked into the problem that affected the music education in schools at that time. The programs for the course as well as a lack of good teaching methods, the lack of professional orientation, the apathy of the authorities, and the lack of incentives to the professors of music education were cemented in four issues in which the study subject depended on. Those four issues were: techno-pedagogic preparedness, the revision of teaching programs, the organization of the Music Education (Educación Musical) in the country, and the formation of a leadership structure for professors (Cárcamo, 1946). A great contribution to the school music education at the time was the display of the Chilean music magazine *Revista Musical Chilena*, created in 1942 at the Universidad de Chile and given to the AEM in its musicological pages, which reveals the common interest that both music teachers and university academicians had for music and education (Sepúlveda, 2004).

Some of the issues the studies agreed upon at the AEM congress were later considered in the education reform of 1955. Those music programs represented a major change and were reflected by the title *Educación Musical* (Musical Education). That name was given in the 1949 programs, and with this new plan the name was solidified. Its meaning is expressed in the description of the study program, and it started with: "The music education as a course is destined to contribute to the integral development of the learner. As such, its realization in high school intends to cultivate the vocal capacities and interests and to gain an artistic appreciation in the field. It also hopes to provide a historic accounting that would revolve around the notion that this is an art for human cultural expression" (Ministerio de Educación, 1955: 1). This introduction points out four aspects of the development of learners: the psychophysical aspects, language, aesthetic appreciation, and artistic expression and critical spirit. It clarifies that the activities were oriented toward stimulating the artistic interests and the development of habits that the programs deem valuable. Such activities were recreation, social cooperation, responsibility, and focus. It also mentions that the course as a cultural vehicle intended to provide a wide view of the cultural contribution that music offers in the physical, psychological, and the social. In terms of the contents, they were varied, but it suggests that the professor could select and customize to make them fit into the reality of "human material, and the circumstances with which they count on." The musical repertory did not delve into that selection and customization for each of those courses in high school teaching (Ministerio de Educación, 1955: 1).

According to the new pedagogic theories, an integrated education was important. They made teaching so that teaching would revolve around the one who was teaching rather than emphasizing the discipline characteristics or its expectations. They also proposed a correlation between the study material and active teaching. Still, by reducing the amount of hours, it reduced the amount of time dedicated to music. In comparison with the programs established before that were comprised of two hours of teaching weekly (ninety minutes) as they were for all classes, the programs in 1995 established one hour for the end of the high school years (grades four, five, and six). This reduction came coupled with new study subjects followed up with a new way of teaching high school. A reduction does not agree with the pedagogic ideas of that time. All and all, for some contemporaries, the new programs meant an advance in the course (Margaño Mena, 1946).

An interesting aspect of these programs was the addition of folklore as a study subject and as a repertory of songs and dances, either national, American and European, or pre-Columbian and colonial; and as a trend, the American "folklorism" of Latin American composers Castro, Chávez, Villalobos, Allende, Sepúlveda, Isamitt, and Santa Cruz (Ministerio de Educación, 1955). This in some way opened up the education that was given to a different sound than what was given by European music, even though it was still a cornerstone of music's history. Another support given to the music professors by the AEM was a bulletin newspaper, which along with the teaching and musical materials, it was comprised of a music score with harmonized songs. That bulletin was distributed throughout Chile.

A NEW ORDER IN THE EDUCATIONAL SYSTEM

There was an in-depth educational reform of 1965 that brought significant changes in various aspects of the school system. One of those was the systems' structure. Elementary education was expanded from six to eight years to reinforce the obligatory teachings; hence secondary school was reduced from six to four years as inspired by the idea of having a new middle school (Livacic, 1966). There was a very important change in the university selection process favoring the acceptance of those who had attended such a middle school after taking an academic aptitude test, the *Prueba de Aptitudes Académicas* (PAA, Academic Aptitude Test), as opposed to the selection test for a bachelor's degree in the previous system. In 1969, the new system encouraged students to study different careers in pedagogy. Musical education was also encouraged without having the previous strict knowledge-based requirements. Instead, admission was allowed by means of a musical aptitudes exam and the minimum score required by the PAA (Sepúlveda, 2004).

The reform had a very important economic support, and schools were built, personnel was sent abroad to acquire expertise, and didactic materials were purchased to implement different study programs, among other reforms. This was the moment where new methods (some called them systems) started to be used, namely Dalcroze, Martenot, Orff, and Kodaly. Professors within the system in summer schools taught the learning of those methodologies, especially Orff and Kodaly, while it remained a novelty and/or the budget was available. From Orff, the Chilean schools followed the use of reciting chants and rhythms for several years; from Kodaly, the use of solmization, phonomimic, metalophones, and the recorder. Teachers working in kindergartens or elementary schools are still using the last two musical instruments. The Education Musical professors who were interested in folk music have been replacing the recorder for the *quena* and *zampoñas* (pipe flutes). They taught students not only to play but also to construct these Andean air instruments with PVC and incorporated them into musical groups in school. During this time, Chilean composer and pianist Estela Cabezas created a system to teach music to young children based on the order and colors of the rainbow. She created clever didactic and short materials, but beautiful songs. Those materials are still in use today in private schools around the country (http://www.musicaencolores.com).

FORTHCOMING CHANGES

In the year 1970 the government of Frey Montalva, who was a promoter of the education reform of 1965, ended. He was followed by Salvador Allende during a socialist government that planned a new educational reform with the purpose of making more radical changes than its predecessor with the project *Escuela Nacional Unificada* (ENU, Unified National School). Allende was heavily criticized by the opposition and swiftly extricated by the dictatorship of Augusto Pinochet in 1973. The school system remained party-sided during those years and kept an eight-year structure for the elementary studies and four years for middle schooling. Both levels were divided into two cycles. The standards established for university admission by the PAA in the 1965 reform still remained.

In the meantime, Chilean society witnessed, from many political angles and approaches—amid the pain of some and passing of others—changes and replacements on the voices and styles of singers and musicians, be they professional, popular, or folkloric. The microphones and TV sets entertained some but disregarded some others according to political trends. But like a subterranean river, music, with its socializing effect in everyday life, in the school, church, and the military, followed its course because the "singer may die but his singing never will."

So the education, plans, and school programs for the Frey reform continued until 1981, which had modifications during the dictatorship that also affected musical education. The rules of the new plan of study for the first cycle (first and second of middle school: ages fifteen to sixteen) reduced six hours of artistic education (music, crafts, and plastic arts) to a total of three hours. At the same time, as an effect of this modified plan, students could only elect one of the three artistic subjects. Therefore, children lost four hours of artistic education.

The second cycle of middle school (third and fourth year of middle school: ages seventeen to eighteen) offers two possibilities by way of a unified plan with mandatory study subjects without any artistic studies and another one with electives for workshops of various subjects. For Music Education, there were four possibilities that every private school could implement based on the know-how of the professors and the infrastructure available. The four are: Folk Music (folkloric dance fell under Physical Education), Music Appreciation, Musical Instruments, and Choir Workshop (Ministerio de Educación, 1981).

It is interesting that in a totalitarian system the educational system is focused toward students. The text states that students could take "whatever they responded with most interest" (Ministerio de Educación, 1981: Art. 3), the workshop should consider the "preferred interest of the students," and the infrastructure and resources available should be considered "without any prejudice for the needs of the country or the zone that it belongs to" (Ministerio de Educación, 1981: Art. 4). Among the stipulations are also the acknowledgment that the curriculum be based on the individual and in the integration of intra- and extracurricular learning. It is then obvious that teachers were the ultimate designers of the curriculum (Sepúlveda, 2004: 314).

A NEW CHANCE FOR EDUCATION

These programs were in place until the end of the dictatorship, which gives way to democracy with yet another new reform and with plans and programs that are in use today. In addition to going back to the optional aspect, as it was in 1981, it takes away the mandatory requirements in all study levels. It loses its traditional name of *Educación Musical* (Musical Education) and becomes *Artes Musicales* (Musical Arts). It also loses its category as a study subject and becomes an Area of Study (*Sectores de Aprendizaje*).

Instead, it is paired with Visual Arts, thus jeopardizing both disciplines, considering the freedom given by the Minister of Education to private schools to create their own courses. But today we have something worse with the establishment of rules imposed by the current government. The new law has not been passed and already private schools have been obligated to reduce the Artistic Education Sector (*Sector de Educación Artística*) to three hours as is planned for the law. With the marriage of the arts, some questions emerge about the three hours designated for such sectors: An hour and half for each artistic discipline? Are there possibilities for cross-pollination between the two disciplines? Who would designate the hours? and How would the hours be assigned? It is easy to imagine the sense of uncertainty among the professors for these disciplines.

CURRENT STATE

Music has experienced several changes and modifications during the 162 years of the official presence of the Chilean education system. One of those changes has been the new name given to the school program, as was mentioned before. Such names have been without a doubt a reflection of the times. In the beginning it was named *Canto Llano* (Plainchant); later *Música y Canto*, later *Música y Gimnasia*. From 1937 to 1996 it was called *Educación Musical*, at the end of which it was changed due to the educational reform now in place. Now it is called *Artes Musicales* (Musical Arts), and it coexists with the *Artes Visuales* (Visual Arts), dance, and *Artes Escénicas* (Scenic Arts), all in the area of *Educación Artística* (Artistic Education). These permutations are used in the school system from elementary to high school levels.

Today, suffice to say, there is no obligation to engage in such school programs. In regard to the private schools, according to their educational projects or *Proyectos Educativos Institucionales* (PEI, Institutional Education Projects) and with the system's consent, they could bypass what is mandatory through the Matriz Curricular (Curricular Matrix), "an instrument designed to regulate the liberties allowed by law for every establishment to decide their study plans and programs."[4] With that end, private schools have other options for the arts, be it visual arts, theater or dance, or other nonartistic curriculum such as multimedia and/or English or Mandarin Chinese. Some private schools believe that they are fulfilling the students' need for artistic musical education by way of extracurricular activities offered in various systematic workshops. Among those are some optional musical workshops.

Within the *Marco Curricular* (Curricular Frame) that is stipulated by the *Objetivos Fundamentales* (OF, Fundamental Objectives) and the *Contenidos Mínimos Obligatorios* (CMO, Minimum Contents Required) for each educational level of the Chilean school system, music is along with other teachings established in the *Matriz Curricular Básica* (MCB, Basic Curricular Matrix). The MCB is bound by the *Principios Básicos* under the guise of anthropology and educational value, hence based in the principles of liberty, dignity, and equality of human rights (Ministerio de Educación, 2002b: 2).

The selection, organization, and operation of the OF and CMO function according to four guidelines: the knowledge structure, the types of learning that students should reach progressively, the interests of the State, and the interests of each of the educational centers (Ministerio de Educación, 2002b: 2). It is worthy of noting that this curricular framework does not mention the student's personal development.

The hourly workload given in the plan of studies is deemed obligatory only in certain subsectors in each learning level. The remaining time is based upon a flexible schedule. According to the Basic Curricular Matrix, "Each school determines within the total time that is given, to their convenience, the amount of hours distributed amongst all the learning sectors outside what is already established" (Ministerio de Educación, 2002b: 17). Note the disclaimer "to their convenience." The arts belong to "those" available hours. That explains the chaotic state of music in some Chilean schools and lyceums. This does not conform with the requirements established for music by the reform in each educational level throughout the *Ministerio de Educación* (MINE-DUC, Ministry of Education), presented by the Chilean government in the year 2002.

CHILDHOOD MUSIC EDUCATION

The curricular basis for small children's music education appears in the regulations called *Núcleo de aprendizaje* (Learning Cell), a niche within Basic Artistic Languages. The general objective of this department formulates the hope that children achieve the capacity to create and express reality by acquiring aesthetic sensibilities, artistic appreciation, and creative capacity through various artistic languages, and that they could imagine ideas and experience and transform these ideas based on their feelings (Ministerio de Educación, 2002c: 65).

The learning children should achieve is interpreted in three integrated areas in which music is the "vehicle of communication" in the first cycle from ages zero to three, as well as in the second cycle from three to six years of age or until their elementary education is attained. This integration hopes to be in concert with the way children of these ages perceive the world, even though children since the age of four should be close to having specific experiences in those "learning sectors" (Ministerio de Educación, 2002c: 29–30). It is here where there is space to start with musical experiences given that this is where certain aspects of the language and music matters are addressed. Also it is where fifteen *expected skills* appear as a requirement for the first and the second cycle of this pre-elementary level. These curricular bases proposed that children progressively experience certain musical elements such as speed, intensities, and sonic timbre through simple songs, dance, and corporal expression. It is interesting that the kind of pedagogic orientations have in relation to the natural integration of children's schoolwork. In order to give way to the development of artistic sensibility and to promote the development of creativity, the children should be provided access to different musical expressions: "music from different types and periods, painting reproduction of famous artists, harmonic environments, and attractive objects with interesting details among others" (Ministerio de Educación, 2002c: 66–67).

The orientations for the second cycle clarifies that if the focus is to integrate the artistic languages, the possibility of detailed work should be considered so that it could benefit a very specific artistic language (Ministerio de Educación, 2002c: 69). This opens the possibility to a more specific end result in music.

MUSIC EDUCATION IN ELEMENTARY SCHOOL

According to the Basic Curricular Matrix, music at this educational level is a *learning sector* referred to as *Musical Arts*, that in turn belongs to the "Arts" Sector. Each level has a number of hours deemed as "hours of free disposition." The arts are part of this disposition during eight years of the elementary school system (Ministerio de Educación, 2002b: 19–21). The Arts Sector does not offer separate guidelines for the separate subsectors, but under the same umbrella lie the following general objectives: (1) Comprehension for human being's aesthetic expression. (2) Stimulate the sensibility and enjoyment of aesthetics, especially in the visual arts, music, dance, and representational arts. (3) Develop the capacities in the field of arts and appreciate the values contained in the production of each of them. (4) Develop the creative imagination, perception of the surroundings, and the communication capacity through expression and artistic appreciation. The intention is to give emphasis to the knowledge and appreciation of a proper culture and a sense of national identity in a world where culture tends to be globalized (Ministerio de Educación, 2002b: 155). The first four years of elementary education have the following goals: capacity of artistic expression, initiation of the aesthetic appreciation of the surroundings, and the appreciation of works through an intuitive experience. According to the document, the artistic perception should be tied to exploration, spontaneous invention, and play.

It is important that the alum develop a capacity for expression and artistic appreciation in relation to the different subjects and art languages. The document clarifies that the concept of *artistic expression* is used with the intention to include in this form of expression certain proper characteristics: freedom, creativity, play, and especially the manifestation of feeling and emotions," also the notions of order, discipline, and rigor that are proper of the creative work (Ministerio de Educación, 2002b: 55–156). In terms of the themes indicated as fundamental objectives or as minimum contents, the following are mentioned as specific aspects regarding music:

NB1 (first and second): Folklore as a resource of expression.

NB2 (third and fourth): Folklore and expression through dance and the organization of sound.

NB3 (fifth): Regional Folklore; basic structure of music.

NB4 (sixth): Know-how and acknowledgment of Chilean and Latin American traditional musical expressions.

NB5 (seventh): Aural discrimination of large selections of music.

NB6 (eighth): Knowledge and appreciation of musical works from the popular and concert repertories through the interpretation and hearing establishing relationships with other artistic languages.

It is necessary to point out that the Musical Arts subsector is not established in the first six years, but it is part of the Artistic Education subsector that shares the same objectives as the Visual Arts subsector. It is in seventh and eighth grades that a title is established for each course so that it differentiates them from the other arts.

MUSIC IN MIDDLE SCHOOL

At this level the Visual Arts and Musical Arts have their own study programs even though they are under the same umbrella as Artistic Education. It is true that the objectives and contents go deeper than on the previous teaching level, but in reality there is no deepening of the learning. In some cases the classes comprise an instrumental group, school band, or choir practice according to the knowledge or the professor. This is a reality often seen in professional practice when students do investigative projects similar to the practicing student-teacher (De la Barra, 2008). Still there are classes where there is very authentic music teaching and where it is practiced in a very integrated way. Such classes offer a space for listening, singing, instrumental performance, percussion, dance, and reflection from and with music.

According to the Curricular Frame for middle school, the scientific knowledge, art, and technique are expressed in the sector and are understood as a human expression. Seeking a concrete and contemporary vision of the learning and creative process, the new curricular framework provides different interpretations of historical events and exercises designs and the realization of various research and projects (Ministerio de Educación, 2002a: 16).

The Curricular Frame also proposes to focus the pedagogic endeavors to the learning more than teaching. It points out that this requires the use of varied pedagogic strategies that are adapted to the students' pace and styles of learning. It continues to state that there is a need to reinforce and prompt students to search and create

(Ministerio de Educación, 2002a: 17). For this new curricular framework, the freedom that private schools have to elect and design their study plans has to be coordinated with the State. In this manner, there is room for the educational policies concerned about solving the problems of the quality of learning and equal opportunity with the participation of their own educational agents (Ministerio de Educación, 2002a: 18).

The document also mentions the importance of learning as a way to integrate *knowledge, abilities*, and *attitudes*. This suggestion for integration is present in the *Objetivos Fundamentales* (Fundamental Objectives) and *Contenidos Mínimos Obligatorios* (Fundamental Objective and Minimum Contents Required) (Marco Curricular, Enseñanza Media). It indicates that the Artistic Education sector, comprised of the Visual Arts and Musical Arts, has as a mission to collaborate in the development of the youth's aesthetic sensibility and expressive and creative capacity. It also intends to achieve a balance between the development of a capacity for expression and art appreciation through a workshop-like systematic work in which awareness is given to the artistic/cultural tradition at different levels, be it regional, national, Latin American, and global.

The Curricula Framework of the Artistic Education Sector for this middle level declares that, in a world dominated by the audiovisual, the arts, aside from building a unique way of knowledge and a unique way of portraying reality, offers a privileged space for the development of creative and expressive capacity. The arts with its diverse language and aesthetic symbols reveal ideas, feelings, and emotions that bring to light fundamental aspects of the human experience that could otherwise not be understood with other forms of knowledge. For this reason, the arts benefit the development of thought as well as the mental and spiritual growth (Ministerio de Educación, 2002a: 185).

In this new curriculum, students are the principal characters in the creative experience of constant discovery of music and its perceptive and expressive capacities. Music should be viewed under two complementary dimensions, music as an artistic discipline and music as a culture. The importance is given to the sonic consciousness in the music learning as a formative element that promotes the capacity to learn, express, and communicate.

Music learning should be engaged through various perspectives: (a) ample musical knowledge as an artistic product and a sociocultural phenomena; (b) music perception and appreciation through comprehensive listening that would provide an enjoyable aesthetic; (c) experiencing diverse ways of emotional expression, symbolic processing, creative works, and communication through sonic resources used in the interpretation and composition; (d) awareness of the meaning of music in people's lives and the community; of its diverse manifestation to open us up to multiculturalism; and of its links with other areas of knowledge, for example, art and philosophy, science and technology, and its multiple uses (i.e., in communication and the reinforcement of identity).

Three related areas give structure to the Music Arts curriculum: (1) appreciation (perception and the appreciation of music); (2) interpretation; and (3) composition. There are some criteria to follow as well, including an open mind to all music and all types of music repertoires; for example, music from all levels: concert, popular/urban, and oral tradition, also, music from Chile, Latin America, and other places and cultures, from the past to present. Given those criteria, there is an attempt to give the students the following development objectives:

1. to reinforce and widen the personal attachment to music by actively practicing it, enjoying and knowing it, developing listening skills, interpretation, and music compositions
2. to develop a perception and the skills to analyze and listen with a wide array of musical expressions, identifying the language elements, and basic levels of music organization
3. to develop a consciousness and respect for the sonic environment, the acknowledgment of silence and the awareness of problems related to acoustic pollution
4. to comprehend and value the role music has in the livelihood of towns, and the diverse contexts and musical manifestations in different places and times
5. to understand the history of the artistic/music knowledge and value the contribution of dialog in various musical cultures in human history
6. to know and use the musical information as a means and source of cultural information, and as a resource for the interpretation and musical composition (Ministerio de Educación, 2002a: 198).

Music education is organized in each year of middle school teaching in four fundamental areas that are very representative in the history of artistic creation: nature and creation; person and society; surroundings and everyday life; culture and technology. These four thematic groups spell out the minimum contents for the teaching of Visual Arts and the Musical Arts within midlevel education (Ministerio de Educación, 2002a: 197–98).

First: Music — Nature and Creation

1. Vocal and instrumental interpretation with a varied repertoire that considers music revolving around society and culture so that the students could contribute to it.
2. Project design: steps and activities. Development of musical ideas, exploring and organizing sounds and simple structures with different styles and techniques, thus stimulating different creative avenues. Create projects for the enhancement of the sound quality and the environment.
3. Basic notions of psychoacoustic and its repercussion in human beings (tolerable levels of audio, acoustic shock, partial or total deafness, ultrasound, etc.). Inquiry, experimentation, and comprehension of the basic properties of sound (pitch, duration, timbre, intensity, and transient). Conduct research on improving the quality of sound in the environment.
4. Principles for construction and luthiery notions applied to the fabrication of simple sonic objects or the repair of instruments.
5. Listening skills and exercising basic procedures of music construction (imitation, repetitions, variation, improvization, etc.) and its aesthetic appreciation in works at all levels: concerts, urban popular, oral tradition, ethnic (Ministerio de Educación, 2002a: 199–200).

Second: Music — Person and Society

1. Music and its relation to the development of an identity (individual group, regional, national, etc.). Music as a cultural heritage, referring specially to the traditions of music and dance from Chile, Latin America, and other countries.
2. Singing tradition and singing throughout time (video, lied, aria, music by troubadours, countryside songs, dancing, etc.). Constructive and interpretive characteristics. Listening to different styles and singing traditions (concert, popular, and folk).
3. Development for the capacity of musical expression (in individuals and in groups) of the interpretation and composition, applying diverse structures and stylistic elements with emphasis in the song genre.
4. Music and timbre: luthiery notions and basic applications. Systems for the classification of musical instruments. Selection of musical groups (vocals, instruments, or mixed) used in various traditions and music repertoires. Inquiry on the form of sonic reproduction in the American music traditions.
5. Singing and vocal/instrument improvisation. Formation of musical groups around songs, applying the basic properties of sound (pitch, duration, timbre, intensity, and transient) and basic procedures of music construction (imitation, repetition, variation, improvisation, etc.), keeping in mind its aesthetic dimension.
6. Development of projects for interpretation and composition, applied according to preference as established (Ministerio de Educación, 2002a: 201).

Third: Music — Surroundings and Everyday Life

1. Music, everyday life, and modern society. Cultural industry and mass media: its influence in contemporary music culture.
2. Main genres and movements of the twentieth century. Listening to discriminate key languages and styles. Relevant Latin American examples.
3. Understanding the history of artistic/musical knowledge. Musical functions in other historical eras (Middle Ages, Renaissance, Baroque, Classicism, Romanticism). Relevant example for listening recognition

of improvisations and entertainment music (arrangements and versions). Inquiries about diverse trends on improvisation and entertainment styles used in today's music. Development of application for music projects for video, theater, dance, and more.

4. Notation forms and musical register: information about the uses for register, control, and coordination of interpretation and composition (Ministerio de Educación, 2002a: 202–3).

Fourth: Music—Culture and Technology

1. Music and technology. Primary applications for the electronic and digital technology. Evaluate the impact in composition, interpretation, and reception in the way of life and the individual behavior.
2. Music and communication. The music in the phenomena of global communication. The growth and mass appeal of multimedia and the digital technology and its relation with the current habits in the communication of music.
3. Music and multiculturalism. Listening identification of current expressions (in concert, popular, ethnic, etc.) of music in Chile and other countries, with emphasis in Latin American music. Acknowledgment of the cultural diversity in music expression.
4. The musical medium. Selection, record keeping, and analysis of musical events including those youth identify with. Critical reflection about the characteristic of the current musical medium.
5. Cultivate the interpretation and musical composition. Formulation and creation of projects to integrate other expressions that promote the exploration and systematic application of computers and technological resources (Ministerio de Educación, 2002a: 203–4).

Today, a new reform being implemented with the new right-wing government is being questioned, just as the current system in place for seventeen years was questioned. Its development must be observed.

FORMATION OF MUSIC PROFESSORS

Music professors come from fourteen universities throughout the country. Three of those are state institutions: in the north, La Serena University in Valparaiso the Playa Ancha University (UPLACED); in Santiago the *Universidad Metropolitana de Ciencias de la Educación* (UMCE, Metropolitan Education Sciences University); and in the south, the Talca University. Some universities offer the career of Music Pedagogy for Elementary Education; others a general degree such as Music Education for Elementary and Middle School. But the majority offers the Music Education for Middle School degree.

The formation process for Music Education professorship in the diverse careers takes approximately fours years, and the practical training varies depending on the institution. In the *Universidad Metropolitana de Ciencias de la Educación*, the students must do a "tesina" (a type of investigation project) in the third year in order to finish their degree. In the fifth year students must do a Final Professional Practice (that is the last practice of all realized throughout their studies). In it students will be in charge of two courses of different levels, offer workshops for choir or instruments, and serve as a lead professor to one of the courses that they are attending and conduct tutoring. At the end of the practice the students turn in a portfolio with the material used for the process to be evaluated. To obtain the professional degree, they have to make a presentation to a committee and take a test. In 2003, university institutions began undergoing a process of auto evaluation as well as an external evaluation in order to get an accreditation for the careers offered. The intention is to ensure a high-quality turnout of professionals. This process seeks to perfect the curriculum design, including the careers for music pedagogy.

Since the 1990s the creation of a professorship for music education has been an issue and reason for reflection in the national and international congresses for Music Education and Artistic Education as well as in gatherings with directors and people in charge of creating methods for music education. Currently, these gatherings and meetings have been formalized by the body named *Asociación de Directores de Carreras de*

Pedagogia en Música (Association for Directors of Pedagogy Music Careers). They hold meetings for all private and public universities in Chile.

CONCLUSION

By studying the evolution of the pedagogic history of music in the Chilean schools we can observe the transformation that music education has undertaken over different educational reforms. In my view, even the names represent a sign of significant change and clear evidence of the perception legislators have had about music in the classroom. From the beginning of the nineteenth century it was called *Canto Llano* (plainchant), *Clase de Canto* (voice class), *Canto y Gimnasia* (Singing and Gymnastics), *Educación Musical* (Music Education), and *Artes Musicales* (Musical Arts).

From its inception 160 years ago, music education in Chile has had many strengths and at the same time has provided opportunities in the area. Some of those opportunities are: the 1965 reform, which was a breath of fresh air for music education and the push given by the Bach Society during that time. Also the incorporation of folklore into the school programs during the 1945 and 1955 reforms; the professors that came from the Association for Musical Educators between 1946 and 1968; the anthropological aspect of the programs of Musical Arts; the formation of professors with university degrees; and of course, the existence of music in schools, even when there is resistance from the administration to increase the contact hours in order for these disciplines to flourish and provide what is necessary to adequately form citizens.

However, there is still a difficult and paradoxical situation that could transform the current reality into a threat and a weakness. One of those is the proliferation of private schools offering music teaching as a career. Certainly, this expansion is not negative. The danger lies in the saturation that is taking place in the workforce, and it is already happening in an alarming way since new professors are having a hard time finding jobs within the school system. The reason?: The managers and directors of those institutions have been benefiting other areas. That is not the only problem. Today, any professional that knows music could teach a class. So there are more music professors than there are jobs since there is no interest in making music a priority. Another threat is the unawareness that ministry directors have about the way in which the music experience benefits individuals. That could be seen as a dead end; still those challenges could be transformed into possibilities. Once those challenges are studied they could be a vehicle to better understand the relation between music education and the Chilean educational system, its positive aspects and struggles.

POSITIVE ASPECTS IN THE EDUCATIONAL SYSTEM IN CHILE

A positive aspect is the history that has been developing by the presence of music in the school system since the country became an independent republic. Once the country became independent, the nation began to organize a school system. In the mid-nineteenth century, music was included in the schools. In 1858, music and plans officially arrived in the six years of high school. Since then its presence became mandatory until it was changed with the *free hours of disposition* by the new educational reform.

Its presence has had a history of ups and downs, and it has been at the mercy of different trends in the various education projects. Sometimes it has been at the mercy of the music teachers themselves. Even though some teachers do not get the appropriate education or the minimum music education, the educational system provides opportunities for historical and pedagogical research that could reveal future decisions and approaches of pedagogical and musical value.

Moreover, there is a wide array of successful examples of schooling that could be replicated, especially the ones that have been developed by teachers with extensive teaching experience or by very well-prepared young professors who have the talent for teaching.

Successful didactic experiences within the private schools and the history for the area of study to be mandatory in the previous years is a guarantee that school directors will continue to add music in their plans. There has been very interesting examples of teachers that with their teaching and artistic accomplishments have sparked the interest of authorities to make the decision to implement special opportunities for music classes and workshops.

CHALLENGES IN THE SCHOOL SYSTEM

Here are the current challenges or debts in the Chilean school system:

1. Reestablish the mandatory requirement of music in the school system, not just plans and agendas, but also in all educational projects in colleges around the country in which music is seen as a subject matter essential to students' education. As a result, it should provide space and time required for its implementation. Today many educational projects truncate students' education in favor of subject matters required for standardized academic rankings in all levels. Rankings are the main concern of many education centers and institution directors, thus neglecting the integral education that every school should provide to students.
2. Bring back integrated music education into the schools. That is, develop a subject matter where all children and youth can have the opportunity to sing, listen, play, dance, follow the beat, create, read, search, think music, think with music, and enjoy music. It is very common to reduce musical learning to just one aspect of the musical experience: into a choral or instrumental activity, or art music takes a priority over the folk music or vice versa, forgetting the value of an integrated and global approach of experiences and learning. Therefore, it is imperative that specialized teachers achieve a didactic/musical balance for all students for the sake of music and learners.
3. In relation to the formation of specialized teachers, tenacious curricula have to be created, with the capacity to break away from old-fashioned norms. There is a need to loosen up the fear to change that exists in institutions of higher education. It is necessary to dream and be willing to take new sound didactic paths as well as new curricular and administrative paths. To accomplish it, it is necessary to collaborate as a group in common projects to unite isolated efforts. A great challenge is to reach equilibrium between the pedagogic and musical formation of future teachers, considering that this is an autonomous discipline with a long trajectory at the international level.
4. To work considering the pedagogic knowledge of music teachers, graduated from the universities and working in the school system. This will open up an environment for new encounters, conversations, and exchanges for and by teachers. Such space should take into consideration the ethnographic tools teachers acquire during the teaching practice, a teacher forged in school with the passion for teaching learners to listen and ask intelligent questions as a very capable active observer. Thus, it is necessary to open up ways for collaborative investigative projects between university academicians and schoolteachers in order to establish connections with the reality of schools. That in turn would illuminate and guide teaching and research work in the universities.
5. To open up the discipline of Music Education with its double function of teaching and music to reach beyond instrumental music; to reach the study or areas, situations, and problems in society in a visionary way. Observing from and with music situations and problems that society would face in the future.
6. To offer opportunities to perfect the discipline at a postgraduate level. Concentrating in projects that have been put aside in designs or previous design phases without reaching fruition.

NOTES

1. *El Mercurio*, domingo, 26-XII-1976, Suplemento Cultural, VII.
2. Periódico "El Santa Lucía," no. 9, Santiago de Chile, junio de 1874.
3. Revista de Instrucción Primaria, Tomo IV, 1889: 139.
4. Ministerio de Educación (2002): *Marco Curricular para la Enseñanza Media*, Gobierno de Chile 13.

REFERENCES

Ahumada, M. R., (1886), "Métodos de Instrucción," *Revista de Instrucción Primaria*, II (11), 159-161, Santiago de Chile.

Aldunate del Solar, Carlos, (1982), *La Música en el arte precolombino*, Museo de Arte Contemporáneo Precolombino, Santiago de Chile.

Allende, Pedro Humberto, (1932), Sociedades Musicales, *Revista Aulos*, (2)7, Santiago de Chile.

———, (1973), *Historia de la música en Chile*, Ed. Orbe, Santiago de Chile; Ed. Yunque, Buenos Aires.

Cabello, Paz, and Martínez, Cruz, (1998), *Música y arqueología precolombina: un estudio de una colección de instrumentos y escenas musicales*, BAR International Series, Eds. A. R. Hands and D. R. Walker, printed in Great Britain.

Cárcamo, F., (1946), "Enseñanza de la música en las escuelas," *Revista Musical Chilena*, No. 2 (10), 26-29, Recuperado: http://www.revistamusicalchilena.uchile.cl/index.php/RMCH/article/view/11126/11454

Claro Valdés, Samuel, (1976), "Festividades coloniales," Diario *El Mercurio*, Domingo 26-XII, Suplemento Cultural, Santiago de Chile.

———, (1997), *Oyendo a Chile*, Ed. Andrés Bello, Santiago de Chile.

Claro Valdés, Samuel, and Urrutia Blondel, Jorge, (1973), *Historia de la Música en Chile*, Ed. Orbe, Santiago de Chile, Ed. Yunque, Buenos Aires.

De la Barra, René, and Borlone, Ma. Paz, (2008), *La integración curricular en y desde la clase de educación musical y su aplicación en dos colegios donde se realizó la Práctica IV, en la especialidad de Artes Musicales*. Tesina para optar al grado de Licenciados en Educación, UMCE.

Encina, Francisco Antonio, (1983), *Gran Historia de Chile Ilustrada*, Periódico *Las Ultimas Noticias*, Santiago de Chile.

Eyzaguirre, Jaime, (1979), *Fisonomía histórica de Chile*, Ed. Universitaria, Santiago de Chile.

———, (1982), *Historia de Chile*, Ed. Zig-Zag, Santiago de Chile.

———, (1986), *Ideario y ruta de la emancipación chilena*, Ed. Universitaria, Santiago de Chile.

———, (1997), *Breve historia de las fronteras de Chile*, Ed. Universitaria, Santiago de Chile.

Göhler, Bernardo, (1888), *Cien canciones escolares*, edición especial, imprenta Cervantes, Santiago de Chile.

Grebe, María Esther, (1974), "Instrumentos precolombinos musicales de Chile." *Revista Musical Chilena*, No. 128, año XXVIII, Universidad de Chile, 5–55, Santiago de Chile.

Guevara, Tomás, (1929), *Chile Prehispánico*, T. I, Universidad de Chile.

Krazer, Jorge, (1767), construye el segundo órgano de la Catedral de Santiago; *Historia de la música en Chile*, de Samuel Claro Valdés y Jorge Urrutia Blondel, 1973, p. 66.

Livacic, (1966), *Narrativa Hispanoamericana, 1816-1981: La generación de 1910-1939*, editado por Ángel Flores.

Margaño Mena, Luis, (1946), "Carta abierta a un profesor de música." *Boletín de Educación Musical, Asociación de Educadores Musicales* (AEM) (2) 10, Santiago de Chile.

Marquez, Antonio, (2000), *Historia de Chile ilustrada*, Ed. Ercilla, Santiago de Chile.

———, (2009), *¡Fuego!*, Novela histórica, Fondo de Cultura Económica Chile S.A., Santiago de Chile.

Ministerio de Educación, (1935), *Programas de Música y Canto*, Gobierno de Chile.

———, (1955), *Programas de Educación Musical para la Enseñanza Secundaria*, Santiago de Chile.

———, (1981), *Decreto No. 300*, Gobierno de Chile.

———, (2002a), *Marco Curricular para la Enseñanza Media*, Gobierno de Chile.

———, (2002b), *Marco Curricular para la Educación Básica*, Gobierno de Chile.

———, (2002c), *Marco Curricular para la Educación Preescolar*, Gobierno de Chile.

Molina, Juan Ignacio, (2000), *Compendio de la Historia Geográfica, Natural y Civil de Chile*, primera parte, Ed. Pehuén, Santiago de Chile. (1st edición en castellano, 1878).

Pereira Salas, Eugenio, (1941), *Los orígenes del arte musical en Chile*, Santiago, Imprenta Universitaria.

Perez de Arce, José, (1982), *La Música en el arte precolombino*. Catálogo de instrumentos musicales. Museo de Arte Precolombino. Ilustre Municipalidad de Santiago. Fundación Familia Larraín Echeñique, Chile.

———, (1995), *Música en la piedra. Música Prehispánica y sus ecos en Chile actual*. Museo Chileno de Arte Precolombino, Ilustre, Municipalidad de Santiago, fundación Familia Larraín Echeñique, Chile.

El Santa Lucía, Periódico, No. 9, Junio de 1874, Santiago de Chile.

Revista de Instrucción Primaria, (1889), Tomo IV, No. 139.

Rodriguez, E., (1947), Audición musical, *Boletín de Educación Musical*, Asociación de Ecuadores Musicales (AEM), Santiago de Chile.

Rondón, Víctor, (1997a), "Diecinueve Canciones Misionales en Mapudungun contenidas en el Chilidugu (1777), del misionero jesuita en la Araucanía, Bernardo Havestadt (1714–1781)", FONDART, *Revista Musical Chilena*, Santiago de Chile.

———, (1997b), *Música jesuita en Chile en los siglos XVII y XVIII: Primera aproximación*, Revista Musical Chilena, p.51, No. 188, Santiago de Chile.

———, (1997c), *Música Misional en Chile 1583–1767*. Tesis de Magister en Artes con mención en Musicología, Universidad de Chile, Santiago de Chile.

———, (2001), *Música y Evangelización en el Cancionero Chilidugu* (1777) del Padre Havestadt, Misionero Jesuita en la Araucanía, durante el sg. XVIII." In *Los Jesuitas expulsos. Su imagen y su contribución al saber sobre el mundo hispánico en la Europa del sg. VIII*, Manfred Tietz y Dietrich Brisemeister, eds., Madrid, Frankfurt Iberoamericana, Vervuet, 557–79, Santiago de Chile.

Santa Cruz W. Domingo, (1941), Prólogo a *Los orígenes del arte musical en Chile*, de Eugenio Pereira Salas, Ed. Universitaria, Santiago de Chile.

———, (2007), *Mi vida en la Música: contribución al estudio de la vida musical chilena durante el siglo XX*, edición y revisión musicológica, Raquel Bustos Valderrama, Consejo Nacional de la Cultura, Gobierno de Chile.

———, (1983), *La Sociedad Bach y su significado histórico*, Ed. Universitaria, Santiago de Chile.

Sepúlveda Cofré, Ana Teresa, (2004), *La presencia de la música en el sistema educativo secundario chileno, a través de cinco reformas educativas*. Tesis doctoral, Universidad Pontificia de Salamanca, España.

Subercaseaux, Benjamín, (1956), *Chile o una loca geografía*, Ed. Ercilla 11th ed., Santiago de Chile.

———, (2004), Historia de las Ideas y de la Cultura en Chile. Editorial Universitaria, Santiago de Chile.

Victoriano, Monserrat, (2009), *El sentido y función de la música Rapanui,* Memoria para obtener el título de profesora de Educación Musical, Universidad Metropolitana de Ciencias de la Educación, Dpto. de Música, Santiago de Chile.

Villalobos R., Sergio, (1995), *Chile y su historia.* Editorial Universitaria, Santiago de Chile.

———, (2000), *Historia del Pueblo Chileno.* T. IV, Editorial Universitaria, Santiago de Chile.

———, (2006), *Historia de los chilenos.* T. I, Taurus, Santiago de Chile.

Zapiola, José, (1997), *Recuerdos de treinta años, 1810-1840,* Ed. Guillermo Miranda, 5th edición, Santiago de Chile.

Chapter Fifteen

Colombia

Constanza Rincón

INTRODUCTION

The history of music education in Colombia is a topic relatively unexplored. There is very little literature on the history of Colombian music, which focuses on the evolution and characteristics of music education in the country. Very few studies that focus on musicological aspects include, at the same time, themes related to the teaching and learning of musical skills. In the same way, very few of these works have given importance to the study of the different methods of music teaching and learning that have influenced the evolution of music in Colombia.

To understand the development of the musical culture and the diverse processes of musical education in Colombia, it is essential to consider two variables: first, the conditions that influenced the configuration of the country under the influence of three cultures: the Amerindians, the Spanish, and the African; second, the specific geographical characteristics of the country.

The geographical configuration of Colombia has influenced a territorial cultural fragmentation. Therefore, what one day was only a strain in communication between regions turned into a cultural dislocation with social, political, and cultural differences. The country is divided into five geographic regions—Atlantic, Andes, Pacific, Orinoco, and the Amazon—that delimit, in a way, communities with cultural differences.

The musical manifestations of each one of these regions are the result of the mixture of native and foreign cultures—significant historical events such as Spanish colonization and the commerce of slaves brought from Africa. This mixture gave birth to new cultures that created their own musical and cultural traditions.

INDIGENOUS PRE-COLUMBIAN CULTURE

Musical activity in the region that now belongs to modern Colombia before the Spanish conquest is barely known through anthropological and ethno-musicological research studies. From their findings—pictographic evidences, and sculptures reflecting any musical and dancing practices in pre-Columbian indigenous communities, and the recovering of sound-producing objects—it is possible to infer some characteristics of the musical practices that existed in Colombia before the colonial period (Escobar, 1925/1993; Martínez, 2004).

Despite the large amount of indigenous groups still in existence and living in the contemporary region of Colombia—around eighty well-preserved indigenous communities spread within thirty-two of the country's departments (Chávez, Morales & Calle, 1995, 229)—it is not possible to completely connect their musical genres and practices with those belonging to the pre-Columbian period and their inhabitants. This is due to the large influence that European and African cultures have had on the evolution of Colombian music and culture for the past five hundred years.

The only direct sources of descriptions of indigenous pre-Columbian musical practices are found in the writings of chroniclers such as Juan de Castellanos (De Castellanos, circa 1565–1944), Fray Pedro de Aguado

(De Aguado, circa 1570–1930), and Fernández de Piedrahita (Fernández de Piedrahita, 1688). According to Perdomo (Perdomo, 1976), it is possible to draw parallelisms and establish common points in their writings, which offer a stark knowledge of the indigenous music.

From the study of these narratives, in which it is described some of the occasions during which the natives used music, it can be concluded that the use of manifestations and musical expressions had a significant meaning beyond their mere execution. According to Bermúdez (1993), music accompanied with flutes and drums during ceremonial acts in religious, war, funeral, and festive occasions was very common. And there is no concrete data that describes the methods used by the indigenous to transmit their musical knowledge to their descendants, other than the presence of onomatopoeia (the use of the mouth and vocal chords as the primary musical instrument) and the use of gestures in their performances.

Since the arrival of the Spaniards and the development of their culture in American territory, the native pre-Columbian culture was modified, giving way to a new one in which the instrumental and vocal performances as well as the function and use of music were influenced by the European ideology of the time. The concept of teaching formal music was established following the canons of the old world; the European scholastic system was introduced through the creation of new educational institutions.

SPANISH COLONIALISM

During the colonial period, the Catholic Church was one of the most powerful institutions, only after the Spanish royalty. Its presence in American territory exercised a decisive leadership role in the ruling and acculturation of the natives. The initial relationships between the Catholic Church and the different religious manifestations of the natives were established through symbolic manifestations. Among them, music presence in religious ceremonies was one of the most important and conclusive tools for religious conversion of the natives. In other words, music was a tool of evangelization. In the words of Perdomo (1976),

> The missionaries mixed Christian doctrine with rudiments of art and linguistics. The natives were taught some ecclesiastic hymns to solemnize religious acts. Wherever they went to preach, they indoctrinated the natives with the notion that the best way to praise God was through sung prayers and the Gregorian chants.[1] (21)

The Spanish religious congregation of the Order of Jesuits—Society of Jesus—established the "missions" with the purpose of introducing social order throughout the conquered regions under the European ideal of establishing a homogeneous culture and society ruled by a unique religion. The teaching and practice of different musical genres, imposed in the new land known as *Nuevo Reino*,[2] were derived from the Church and, in turn, they were influenced by the Counter-Reformation processes that occurred in Spain during the sixteenth century.

The consolidation of the musical instruction in the newly founded city of Santafé de Bogotá (1538) occurred with the foundation—around 1581—of the Seminary of San Luis. This theological school was the result of the efforts made by the first archbishop of the city, Fray Luis Zapata de Cardenas, who arrived to the city in the decade of the 1570s. According to Bermúdez (2000), the Seminary of San Luis became the first teaching institution to implement a formal methodology of music education:

> According to the norms established by the Council of Trent: grammar, rhetoric, singing and other things must be taught in such establishments. The school was founded, exclusively, for the sons of Spaniards due to the segregation policies. The natives' musical instruction was done through religious teachings. (39)

Years later, the Society of Jesus with Fr. José Dadey continued with the work of teaching music with the foundation of another seminary school—Colegio Seminario de San Bartolomé—in October 1605.

Plainchant, canticles, and organ playing were part of the school's curriculum, with such importance that it became part of the school's foundation charter (Hernández de Alba, 1969). The students of this seminary school continued spreading the corresponding musical instruction in other places such as Tunja and Fontibón.[3] Additionally, Fr. Dadey supervised the construction of the first pipe organ in Fontibón and established this place as the center of ecclesiastic activities and a music school; other clerics studied there before going to the "missions" in other areas waiting to be conquered. Natives, who attended this music school, were also taught diverse musical practices. In addition to canticles and organ music, they also received violin and flute instruction.

According to some authors, there were other schools of indoctrination, where music was one of the main tools for conversion. Perdomo (1976), identifies the natives from other places such as Cajicá and Gachetá[4] as the first ones to learn rudimentary musical language. In the same way, De la Espriella (1997) mentions other academies and music schools:

> The first school for canticles, founded in Santafé de Bogotá by a mestizo canon in 1575, belonged to Alfonso Garcia Zorro (1548–1617), the son of a famous Spanish conqueror with the same name. His father came to *Subachoque*[5] in 1537 with the expedition of Gonzalo Jiménez de Quesada. From there, he supervised the conquest of the different villages in the Chibcha plains and the ones belonging to the niece of the *Zipa*[6] Tisquesusa, who lived in *Funza.*[7] (870)

THE BIRTH OF TOWNS AND MUSICAL EDUCATION PROCEDURES

During the sixteenth and seventeenth centuries, the increasing urban settlements were strongly influenced by the establishment of the European system of education. The concept of education and knowledge acquisition to belong to a specific place in society was mainly established by the presence of the "missionaries" in the region (1550–1718) and their methods of education. The idea of culture was then conceived as a distinctive status in society that distinguished the well educated from those of poor educative conditions. Culture was then seen as the accumulation of knowledge and the development of skills such as the performance of musical instruments.

Santafé de Bogotá became, during the colonial period, the capital city of the region belonging to the newly named *Nuevo Reino de Granada*; that started to expand until it formed a territory compound by the contemporary regions belonging to the actual countries of Colombia, Venezuela, and some regions of Ecuador (Fernández de Piedrahita, 1688; Millán, 2001). From the moment that it was appointed the capital of Nuevo Reino de Granada in the middle of the sixteenth century, Santafé de Bogotá became the place of residency of Europeans belonging to the Spanish royal family or those with a royal title, high-ranking military, and ecclesiastics. This created the need for creating educative institutions that followed the European system of education in order to keep the standards of the Europeans' schools and to provide the best education possible to the descendants of the Spaniards. New schools, led by religious orders, were established, and the curricula of these schools included the teaching and use of music for religious purposes.

The use of music for religious purposes continued until the end of the first half of the eighteenth century, when the musical practice began to be extended to other sectors of society. That implied other purposes to it, such as that of social entertainment. European music and its practice spread as a symbol of power and distinction among families belonging to the ruling class. In the words of Bermúdez (2000),

> It seems that the teaching of music and musical instruments for the privileged social classes was in the hands of competent enthusiasts who were valued by their musical skills. It was common for musicians, who worked as music teachers and performers, to be linked to religious musical activities in cathedrals and convents. They also participated in the musical instruction of the natives and blacks, who, in turn, later diffused the use of musical compositions, instruments and outlines of traditional European versification schemes in their communities. (50)

During the eighteenth century, musical activities and the increment of musical instruction in the city of Santafé de Bogotá affected the musical development of the country significantly. It is important to mention that up to this point, formal education was conceived and designed aiming to educate religious scholars, the sons of Spaniards, and "missionaries" coming from Spain. Education was, then, for a chosen masculine few.

Aside from some convents that had music instruction, girls' and womens' education mainly focused on the learning of household labor and manual skills. Nevertheless, at the end of the eighteenth century, Maria Gertrudis Clemencia de Caycedo y Vélez founded—in 1783—a school for girls—*Monasterio Colegio de la Enseñanza* (Colegio de la Enseñanza, 2009)—attending the needs of the daughters of those belonging to the ruling society. According to Duque (2000), this school was the first institution dedicated to the education of women, with music as one of the main subjects in its curriculum.

During the nineteenth century, Colombia lived through periods of political and social instability that resulted from the independence wars and the establishment of the different countries in the region. However, toward the middle of this century, the country passed through a period of stability and social calm that allowed people to give special importance to activities of leisure and culture. During this time, foreigners with diverse professions and European customs, traditions, and art practices, like the opera and *soirées*,[8] arrived in the cities, mainly Santafé de Bogotá. Others left the country to go to study in capital cities of Europe and later diffused new European musical genres—symphonies, opera, and chamber music—and musical instruments around the country.

During the first half of the nineteenth century, the musician Juan Antonio de Velasco established a music academy that later became the *Sociedad Lírica*.[9] The main objective of this institution was to keep religious music alive since it had lost its importance compared to older times. However, nonreligious symphonic and musical styles were also taught in this institution (Perdomo, 1976).

Soirées were in style with performances of musical pieces for piano, voice, and even small orchestras. The *soirées* contributed to the development of a European musical taste that enhanced the *classical* repertoire and became at the same time a symbol of distinction for the upper classes of the capital city. Women were given the privilege to learn how to play the piano as a symbol of distinction for the upper classes. It is important to mention that lessons were held at the women's homes since they were not allowed to attend a music academy.

In 1846, the British, Henry Price, and other acknowledged musicians in the country founded the *Sociedad Filarmónica de Santafé*[10] (Pardo Tovar, 1966). The Philharmonic Society was later established as the institution in which all of the other musical institutions around the country based their foundational structures. The main objective of this musical society was to promote and expand the culture of *classical* European music (Duarte & Rodríguez, 1991). It had an orchestra, and it is presumed that around 1847 this society had a music academy as well. According to Duque (2000, 125), the establishment of the Academia—as part of the Philharmonic Society of Santafé—marked a change in the concept of the profession of the musician, since it followed the goal of preparing musicians to have a comfortable living based on their musical practice.

As mentioned before, other music societies were established in other cities such as Medellín, Santa Marta, and Cartagena following the structure of the Philharmonic Society. In the same way, other music societies and/or academies were born in the capital city, such as the *Unión Musical*[11] that was established in 1858—the year after the Philharmonic Society disappeared—and the *Sociedad Filarmónica de Santa Cecilia*[12] created in 1868 ("Colombia," 1999). This last society aimed at working on the teaching and interpretation of religious music, and it was the first one to propose and work on the creation of a children choir.

ACADEMIA NACIONAL DE MÚSICA (NATIONAL MUSIC ACADEMY)

During the government of the president of the United States of Colombia,[13] Rafael Núñez (1880–1882/ 1884–1886), Jorge Price (1853–1953), the son of Henry Price, was in charge of the creation of a new institution for the formal teaching of music. Consequently, the *Academia Nacional de Música*[14] was born in the year 1882 (De la Espriella, 1997). The establishment of this academy marked a new definition for music as a professional occupation and for the field of music education in the country.

The Academia developed a curriculum based on European concepts and methodologies. It included music theory and vocal and instrumental training. During the first years of the Academia, this very formal professional music education was only offered to men, leaving women with the only option of private classes at home and out of what it could constitute a professional occupation. But at the end of the 1880s, an opportunity was given to women by offering music theory, vocal, piano, and violin classes in courses specially designed for them. This aspect was decisive in the incorporation of women into professional musical activities and their strong contribution to the implementation of the profession of the music teacher in the country (Barriga).

The *Academia Nacional de Música* closed its doors at the end of the nineteenth century during the war known as *Guerra de los mil días*[15] (1899–1902) and reopened them in 1905 under the direction of Honorio Alarcón (1859–1920), who, after studying in France, imposed French methodologies. In 1910, the name of the academy changed to *Conservatorio Nacional de Música*[16] (National Music Conservatory), under the direction of the composer Guillermo Uribe Holguín (1880–1971).

The National Music Conservatory later became a section of the Faculty of Fine Arts from the National University of Colombia (founded in 1867), and the symphonic orchestra that belonged to the conservatory was transformed into the National Symphony Orchestra, which, from that moment, belonged to the National Ministry of Education.

Other formal institutions of music education that followed the structure of the National Music Conservatory were established in other cities. Some of them were: the music conservatory *Antonio María Valencia* in Cali, the Music Academy in Cartagena de Indias, the Fine Arts Academy in Medellín, and the music conservatory of *Antioquia*.

MUSIC IN SCHOOLS

It could well be considered that music education has always been present in schools. But music as part of the curriculum cannot be found until the second half of the nineteenth century.

Midway through this century, the *Secretaría de Instrucción Pública*,[17] which later became the Ministry of Education, decided to create a national system of education with the purpose of unifying the methodology and curriculum of public education. Specifically in music, work was done for the development of an educational program focusing on singing.

An educative reform was designed, taking into consideration the creation of the Central School in the capital city of the country and a Normal School in each one of the states of the country. This reform was part of the November 1, 1870, Organic Decree for Public Education (Ministerio de Educación Nacional–Archive(a)). Under this decree, all aspects of the public education system were organized under three branches of intervention, based on the third article: teaching, assessment, and administration. In the article 116, which relates to the subjects that will be included in the curriculum, a singing class was imposed in each school.

One of the most important aspects of this decree was the creation of the Normal School, which had the main objective of training teachers and promoting a diversity of teaching methodologies. In order to support this project, the Colombian government had assistance from German scholars who trained the first teachers and implemented their methodologies in the different cities of the country. This project received the name of the *Primera Misión Pedagógica Alemana*,[18] and it was established throughout the country at the beginning of the 1870s (Rojas, 1982). Through the work of the German teachers, Pestalozzi's teaching methodology was introduced in the country and a system of education similar to that in Germany was imposed. The themes of education were separated in subjects, giving a special and important place to music and singing.

Toward the end of the nineteenth century and until around the 1930s, Catholic pedagogy was imposed in Colombia thanks to a treaty signed in 1887 between the Colombian government and the Holy Catholic Church. Norms and regulations dictated by the Church were outlined in this document with the purpose of establishing a social order ruled by Catholic ideology. According to the October 26, 1903, Law 39 Decree (Ministerio de Educación Nacional–Archive(b)), public education went into the Church's hands, and the preparation of teachers in all areas, including music, was modified according to the needs assessed by the clerics.

The main objective of this new phase in the specific subject of music was to provide singing instruction in the primary stages of education. Its inclusion in the curriculum as an individual subject was limited for the upper classes of society. It had a patriotic component since the national anthem and other patriotic songs were compulsory in the curriculum. Music education belonged to the area of "Music and Singing Training," and it was only taught in urban areas until 1950 (Ministerio de Educación Nacional–Archive(c)), when music and drawing were implemented as individual subjects in rural schools. The music class in elementary schools was scheduled for an hour a week and in the secondary schools for four hours a week (Rojas & López, 2003).

At the beginning of 1920s, a new policy of education was implemented with the goal of strengthening teachers' training. In the same way as before, the government got assistance from German educators. That period is known as *Segunda Misión Pedagógica Alemana*.[19] According to Flórez (2008), in the year 1932, the musician Antonio María Valencia (1902–1952) presented a proposal—based on this policy—for structuring the occupation of music education. This proposal could be considered as one of the first steps toward the beginning of the undergraduate degree of Music Education in the country.

There was a *Tercera Misión Pedagógica Alemana*[20] that was initiated in 1968 under the principles of active pedagogy. A few years before that date, the professional degree of Music Education started to be offered at the National University in Bogotá. It continued to be offered until the end of the twentieth century.

Back to music as a subject in schools, between 1962 and 1994, music as a subject was part of the area of Aesthetics Education, which included choir, music appreciation, calligraphy, vocational crafts, dance, and art history (Ministerio de Educación Nacional–Archive(d)). The decades of the 1970s and 1980s were known for the creation of undergraduate programs in teacher training in general subjects. The curricula for Psycho Pedagogy, Pre-Elementary Education, and Special Education were strengthened, and university programs for the professional development of musicians in areas such as music interpretation, composition, and music education were offered in several universities around the country.

Music in the classrooms benefited from the newly trained music teachers and the implementation of methodologies that originated in Europe, such as Kodaly, Orff, Dalcroze, and Willems, among others. In addition to music in the schools, more symphonic orchestras and ensembles were established in the cities, and the organization of festivals and music competitions, acknowledging traditional popular music, was strengthened. From the beginning of the 1970s, the National Pedagogic University started to offer an undergraduate degree on Music Education.

In 1994, music in the school curriculum became part of the area of Artistic Education. The presence of music in schools suffered a significant change; it was no longer a compulsory subject but a part of a general artistic area. By law, every child must have some training in the area of the arts, through participation in activities including dance, theater, music, sculpture, and literature (Ministerio de Educación Nacional–Archive(e)), with the dilemma that all these subjects share the same time schedule of one or a maximum of two hours per week.

THE TRAINING OF THE PROFESSIONAL MUSICIAN IN THE NINETEENTH AND TWENTIETH CENTURIES

The idea of supporting the musical evolution and the professional training of musicians in the country developed around the European method of written music. This aspect was related to the performance of music in the European styles and was established in the urban areas in the nineteenth and part of the twentieth centuries. The idea of linking professional musical training to the writing process evolved, creating a division between the professional musicians trained in academia and those involved in traditional popular music.

The division between the popular experience and the academic one—supported by the *Academia Nacional de Música*—was manifested during intense polemics at the beginning of the twentieth century. A methodological division in the academic world was marked by those following the ideas of the *Schola Parisiense*, and the partisans of the ideas of looking for a national musical identity. That division resulted in very poor training of musicians and great difficulty in the establishment of national teaching, writing, and performance styles of music in the academia, congruent with the popular music of the country.

However, music with European influences permeated that of African and Indigenous background through informal practice. Outside of the academia teaching and learning methodologies as well as traveling musical performances were supported by the intellectual bohemia at the end of the nineteenth century and the beginning of the twentieth. The need to encourage national and regional music genres and styles and the promotion of the expression of popular roots was established thanks to the influence of *La Gruta Simbólica*, a cultural movement that reunited poets, writers, and musicians (Suárez, 2002, 35).

In the beginning of the twentieth century, there was a generation of musicians who seriously opposed the educational policies of the National Music Conservatory. Their ideas could be found not only in their writings and compositions but also in their musical activities and performances. These musicians infused their symphonic nationalist musical works with traces of Colombian popular music. They contributed significantly to the consolidation of the identity of the country's music composition school.

together once a week for an ensemble rehearsal. Students work toward common goals, and individual technical difficulties are addressed in a collective way during instrument lessons and ensemble rehearsals. Students belong to their orchestral site's symphonic orchestra, and the ones with higher academic achievement apply every six months for a place in the city's youth symphonic orchestra that also belongs to the program.

CONCLUSION

Music education in Colombia has received important social and cultural influences that, over time, have contributed to the evolution of musical practice in the country. The lack of specific data about the use of music and the methods for music learning during the pre-Columbian period marks a difficulty for research studies that inquire about music education in Colombia before the Spanish colonization.

From the time of the Spanish colonization, the inhabitants of the region, their culture, and traditions mixed with that brought to the new continent by European conquerors and African slaves who settled in the new land. The Spanish imposed their culture and beliefs, creating a new style of life based on their European traditions, mainly in urban areas. The Catholic Church was an important institution that contributed to the use of European musical traditions and methods of education. Music was used as a tool of Christian conversion and acculturation.

During the nineteenth century, music represented not only religious aspects but also social status. Performance was taken out of the Church, and it was also used for entertainment purposes. Being educated in European music was recognized as a symbol of distinction of high-class status in the urban social scheme. This phenomenon contributed to the creation of music academies and schools dedicated to the teaching and learning of singing and *classical* instruments such as piano and violin, with an influence, once again, that is highly European.

During the twentieth century, the concept of music practice and education as a professional occupation was established, with the consequent creation of professional music conservatories and undergraduate programs in universities. Furthermore, music was included in the school curriculum, introducing different methods developed in Europe by pedagogues like Orff-Schulwerk and Willems, among others. During this century the division between popular and academic musical practices evolved into a merging of both styles that has acted as a strong contribution to the evolution of Colombian music.

Toward the end of the twentieth century, programs aimed to encourage healthy social development have used active participation in music as a tool for achieving their goals. As a result of a state policy, the creation of four programs based on music education and their implementation around the country have contributed to the number of people with the option of learning music and participating in the cultural life of their respective communities.

NOTES

1. Due to the fact that the majority of the bibliographical sources are in Spanish, the translations of the quotes are mine.
2. New kingdom.
3. Tunja and Fontibón were indigenous settlements during the colonial time. Nowadays, Tunja is a city situated in the middle east of Colombia and Fontibón is a locality that belongs to the city of Bogotá.
4. Towns founded by Spaniards in the places of indigenous settlements. The names belong to the Muisca or Chibcha tribes.
5. Idem iii.
6. Zipa: Royal title given to the governor of the *Muisca* tribe.
7. Idem iii.
8. French tradition. A social meeting in a private house with the objective of listening to life. music performances.
9. Lyric society.
10. Philharmonic Society of Santafé.
11. Musical Union.
12. Philharmonic Society of Saint Cecilia.
13. The name of United States of Colombia was established from 1863 to 1886 to denote the federal republic formed by the contemporary countries of Colombia and Panama.
14. National Music Academy.
15. War of a thousand days. A civil war that ended with the separation of Panama from Colombia.

16. National Music Conservatory.
17. Secretary of Public Instruction.
18. First German pedagogic mission.
19. Second German pedagogic mission.
20. Third German pedagogic mission.
21. Pilot Plan of the Superior Arts Academy of Bogotá.
22. National Music Plan for the Coexistence.
23. National System for Children and Youth Symphonic Orchestras.

REFERENCES

Barriga, M. L. La educación musical de la mujer en Bogotá de 1880 a 1920. Retrieved from http://udistrital.academia.edu/MarthaBarriga/Papers/248840/La_Educacion_Musical_de_la_Mujer_en_Bogota_de_1880_a_1920

Bermúdez, E. (1993). Música: la tradición indígena y el aporte colonial. In C. D. Lectores (Ed.), *Gran Enciclopedia de Colombia-Temática* (Vol. 6, 205–16). Bogotá: Círculo de Lectores.

Bermúdez, E. (2000). *Historia de la música en Santafé y Bogotá 1538–1938*. Bogotá: MVSICA AMERICANA.

Chávez, A., Morales, J., & Calle, H. (1995). *Los indios de Colombia*. Quito: Abya-Yala.

Colegio de la Enseñanza. (2009). *Colegio de la Enseñanza*. Retrieved from http://www.colegiodelaensenanza.edu.co/historia.php

"Colombia." (1999). In E. Casares (Ed.), *Diccionario de la Música Española e Hispanoaméricana*. Madrid: Sociedad General de Autores y Aditores D.L.

Conpes. (2002). *Fortalecimiento del Programa Nacional de Bandas de Vientos. Documento Conpes 3191, Consejo Nacional de Política Económica y Social*. Bogotá: Ministerio de Cultura.

Conpes. (2006). *Lineamentos para el fortalecimiento del Plan Nacional de Música para la Convivencia. Documento Conpes 3409, Consejo Nacional de Política Económica y Social*. Bogotá: Ministerio de Cultura.

De Aguado, P. (circa 1570/1930). *Primera parte de la recopilación resolutoria de Santa Marta y Nuevo Reino de Granada de las Indias del Mar Oceano*. Madrid: Espasa Calpe.

De Castellanos, J. (circa 1565/1944). *Elegías de varones ilustres de Indias*. Madrid: Atlas.

De la Espriella, A. (1997). *Historia de la música en Colombia*. Bogotá: Norma.

Duarte, J., & Rodríguez, M. (1991). *La Sociedad Filarmónica y la cultura musical en Santafé a mediados del siglo XIX. Boletín cultural y bibliográfico, XXVIII*(31).

Duque, E. A. (2000). El estudio de la música *Historia de la música en Santafé y Bogotá 1538–1938* (125–58). Bogotá: MVSICA AMERICANA.

Escobar, L. A. (1925/1993). *La música precolombina*. Bogotá: Fundación Universidad Central, Intergráficas.

Fernández de Piedrahita, L. (1688). *Historia general de las conquistas del Nuevo Reino de Granada*. Amberes: Verdussen.

Flórez, M. A. (2008). *Aproximación a la pedagogía musical en Colombia. Finales del siglo XIX y siglo XX*. Universidad Pedagógica Nacional, Bogotá.

Hernández de Alba, G. (1969). *Documentos para la historia de la educación en Colombia* (Vol. I). Bogotá: Patronato Colombiano de Artes y Ciencias.

Laboratorio Cultural. (2010). *Plan Nacional de Música para la Convivencia*. Retrieved September 15, 2010, from http://www.laboratoriocultural.org/revista/festivales/red/pnmc/index.html

Martínez, E. (2004). *La música precolombina: Un debate cultural después de 1492*. Barcelona: Paidós.

Millán, C. (2001). *Epítome de la Conquista del Nuevo Reino de Granada: La cosmografía española del siglo XVI*. Bogotá: Universidad Javeriana.

Ministerio de Educación Nacional–Archive(a). *Decreto Orgánico de Instrucción Pública 1 de Noviembre de 1870*.

Ministerio de Educación Nacional–Archive(b). *Ley 39 de Octubre 26 de 1903*.

Ministerio de Educación Nacional–Archive(c). *Decreto Orgánico 3468 de 1950 (repealed by law, Decreto 1710 de Julio 25 de 1963)*.

Ministerio de Educación Nacional–Archive(d). *Decreto Orgánico 045 de Enero de 1962*.

Ministerio de Educación Nacional–Archive(e). *Ley 115 de Febrero 8 de 1994*.

Pardo Tovar, A. (1966). *La cultura musical en Colombia*. Bogotá: Ediciones Lerner.

Perdomo, J. I. (1976). *Historia de la música en Colombia*. Bogotá: Ministerio de Educación.

Rojas, M. C. (1982). Análisis de una experiencia: La Misión Pedagógica Alemana. *Revista Colombiana de Educación, 10*(2).

Rojas, D. C., & López, A (2003). *Historia de la Educación Musical: Panorama de las relaciones entre educación, música y educación musical en Colombia durante el siglo XX en la formación básica (1903–1984)*. Universidad Pedagógica Nacional de Colombia, Bogotá.

Suárez, C. A. (2002). *Colombia Andina*. Bogotá: Norma.

Chapter Sixteen

Ecuador

Ketty Wong-Cruz

INTRODUCTION

This chapter presents a brief overview of the development of professional music education in Ecuador in the colonial and republican periods.[1] I will focus on the music training of instrumentalists who play in the symphony orchestras and music bands, drawing special attention to the history of the conservatories and the role of other institutions, such as monasteries, military bands, and music societies, in the instruction of professional musicians.[2]

To these ends, I will concentrate on four major cities that have developed an active musical life with their symphony orchestras and conservatories: Quito, the capital and political center of the country; Guayaquil, the major port city and economic center; and Cuenca and Loja, two southern highland cities with long-standing musical traditions. It is worth noting that while the demand for "classical music"[3] in the major cities of Ecuador has increased significantly in the past two decades, before the 1980s these concerts did not attract large audiences.

This chapter will show how the development of music education in and outside of the conservatories in the 1970s and 1980s, as well as the creation of youth symphony orchestras and bands, has greatly influenced the growth of a general public for classical music concerts. This research is based on archival research, bibliographical sources, and interviews of musicians who play and teach in the conservatories, symphony orchestras, and bands.

THE COLONIAL PERIOD

The Spanish clergy used music to indoctrinate Amerindians into the Catholic faith by teaching them how to sing and play chants for the Mass and offices. In 1555, Fray Jodoco Ricke and Pierre Gosseal of Louvain founded in Quito the *Colegio de San Andrés* (San Andres School) in the Convent of San Francisco, where indigenous people learned basic skills such as carpentry, printing, metal smithing, and how to sing and play the organ, trumpet, and sackbut. For evangelization purposes, Spanish monks used indigenous melodies and translated hymn texts to Quichua, the main indigenous language in Ecuador. Although the Colegio de San Andrés was not a school of music as we understand it today, chronicles from this period highlight the talent of indigenous people in singing and playing various instruments.

The earliest account we have for a music school from this period was founded in 1810 by Tomás Mideros y Miño in the Convent of St. Augustine. Known as "Aula de Música" (Music Classroom), this school required students to enter into monastic life in order to take music lessons. They learned music theory, *solfège*, and how to sing and play the violin, harp, sackbut, and organ (Guerrero, 1876). Although the teaching methods were elemental, they were effective and produced good singers (Moreno, 1996). Mideros formed various choirs and small orchestras with his students. Some became Kapellmeisters of the Cathedral of Quito, while others, such as Antonio Altuna, Crisanto Castro, and José Miño, founded their own music schools.

It is worth noting that in the first half of the nineteenth century, there was an incipient infrastructure for music education outside of the monastery. Little is known about the instruction of secular music in this period, except that foreign musicians were hired to teach private music lessons.

In 1816, Spanish musician José Celles taught harmony and composition, subjects that had never been studied before in Ecuador (Moreno, 1996). Alejandro Sejers, an English violinist who came to Ecuador as a tourist in 1838, was hired by President Juan José Flores to organize a music society, which was headquartered in the convent of Santo Domingo. In 1841, after three years, Sejers left the country and Agustín Baldeón, one of his students, succeeded him as director, retaining the post until his death six years later. In 1847, the society changed its name to *Sociedad Filarmónica de Santa Cecilia* (Saint Cecilia Philharmonic Society) and survived one more decade under the direction of Miguel Pérez, another student of Sejers.

THE REPUBLICAN PERIOD

According to musicologist and composer Segundo Luis Moreno, the music of military bands was unknown in Ecuador before the wars of independence in the early 1820s. It was in 1818 that the Batallón Numancia from Colombia arrived in Ecuador with its military band and impressed Ecuadorian people with their sonorous musical instruments not previously seen in the country. Military and civic bands mushroomed and provided a new venue for the popularization of secular musics, such as marches, waltzes, polkas, and *pasillos*.[4]

In the nineteenth and early twentieth centuries, military bands provided a basic music education to people who were interested in music and enrolled in the army. Recruits learned to play musical instruments and the basic rudiments of music theory from the band conductors, most of whom had studied at the *Conservatorio Nacional de Música* of Quito (National Music Conservatory of Quito (CNM)). Segundo Luis Moreno (1882–1972), for example, was the music instructor and conductor of several military bands in the highland region from 1915 to 1937. He learned how to play the clarinet in a music band in Cotacachi, a small town north of Quito, before he entered the conservatory in the early 1900s to study composition. Also a student of the CNM in this period, composer Francisco Salgado Ayala (1880–1970) conducted the band of the Bolívar Artillery Regiment from 1920 to 1925 and the band of the Yaguachi Cavalry Regiment until 1929. It is safe to say that military bands provided music education to people who, given their social condition, could not afford private music lessons.

Musicians who retire from the army often go on to form their own *bandas de pueblo* (community bands). These are small brass bands made up of amateur musicians that provide music for religious processions and civic festivities in small towns. Musicians usually begin on the drum at an early age, later learning to play other wind instruments. Although informal, this type of music training has had an important role in the preservation and continuity of religious and secular traditions.

Military and civic bands played in the parks every Thursday evening and Sunday morning, entertaining the public that gathered around them in the quiet atmosphere of the little towns. In addition, Italian opera companies traveled to Ecuador to give concert tours, performing a repertoire of *zarzuelas* and operas to the delight of people in Quito and Guayaquil. It was not uncommon to listen to young ladies from aristocratic families perform salon music in social gatherings. They took private piano lessons from local or foreign music instructors. These classes were informal in character and intended only to enhance the ladies' personal attributes.

MUSIC EDUCATION IN THE CONSERVATORIES

While the Spanish clergy provided music training in the convents, Italian musicians had an enormous influence on the establishment of the conservatories in the late nineteenth and first half of the twentieth centuries. The national conservatories in Quito, Guayaquil, Loja, and Cuenca were founded in different decades, but all have encountered similar challenges in establishing themselves as centers of professional music education—from finding a functional building to setting the curriculum for each area of specialization to buying musical instruments and hiring qualified music teachers on a low budget. The following sections will describe the formation of the national conservatories and alternative music schools in these cities.

MUSIC EDUCATION IN QUITO

The first conservatory in Ecuador, the CNM, was founded in 1870 during the regime of President Gabriel García Moreno. The director was Antonio Neumane (1818–1871), a French composer of Italian descent and the composer of Ecuador's national anthem, who died in 1871. Juan Agustín Guerrero, a painter, composer, and subdirector of the conservatory at the time, succeeded him until the arrival of Francisco Rosa, the new director, in 1872. Other Italian musicians, such as Pedro Traversari and Antonio Casarotto, arrived in Quito with Rosa to teach music following the curriculum of the European conservatories. The conservatory was closed in 1877 for economic reasons (Guerrero Gutiérrez, 2001–2005).

The CNM was reopened in 1900 during the government of President Eloy Alfaro and under the direction of violinist Enrique Marconi. He was succeeded by composer Domingo Brescia, who led the institution from 1903 to 1911 and was instrumental in the emergence of the first generation of Ecuadorian nationalist composers. Brescia encouraged his students to compose art music using elements of Ecuadorian folk and vernacular music. Segundo Luis Moreno (1882–1972) and Francisco Salgado (1880–1970), Brescia's two outstanding students in composition, established this nationalist trend and composed piano and orchestral pieces using the rhythms of the *sanjuanito*, the *yaraví*, and other Ecuadorian indigenous and *mestizo*[5] musical genres.

Other important academic composers, performers, and music critics led the conservatory and set the basis for a musical infrastructure in Quito in the first half of the twentieth century. Pedro Pablo Traversari (1874–1956), a flutist and the son of Pedro Traversari, the Italian musician who taught in the first conservatory in the 1870s, directed the CNM on three different occasions. He wrote several essays on indigenous music and the folklore of the Americas, and compiled a large collection of musical instruments of the world, which bears his name.[6]

Sixto María Durán (1875–1947), a nationalist composer, pianist, and lawyer who was designated president of the Supreme Court of Justice in 1909, emphasized the study of *solfège*, music theory, and harmony (Guerrero Gutiérrez, 2001–2005). Juan Pablo Muñoz Sanz (1898–1964), a composer, pianist, and violinist who graduated and taught at the CNM, was also the conductor of the symphony orchestra of this institution. This orchestra became the basis for the formation of the National Symphony Orchestra in 1956. Muñoz Sanz was also a writer, music critic, and cultural promoter who worked intensively toward the creation of the symphony orchestra and music organizations that support activities related to the dissemination of classical music, such as the Philharmonic Society of Quito (Guerrero Gutiérrez, 2007). Other intellectual musicians shared Muñoz Sanz's interests, such as Francisco Alexander (1910–1988), a violinist who gave impulse to these endeavors through his writings and music critiques in the newspapers of Quito.

The composers and performers mentioned above were also influential figures in the direction of other conservatories in the country. The *Conservatorio Antonio Neumane* in Guayaquil was founded in 1928 under the leadership of Pedro Pablo Traversari. In 1938, Segundo Luis Moreno became the first director of the *Conservatorio José María Rodríguez* in Cuenca. Founded in 1944, the *Conservatorio Salvador Bustamante Celi* of Loja was directed by Francisco Salgado (1949–1954) and by Juan Pablo Muñoz Sanz (1954–1956).

From 1900 to 1944 the conservatories belonged to the Ministry of Education and Culture. They were incorporated into the university system[7] from 1944 to 1969, and returned to the Ministry of Education in 1970, where they still remain. These changes of status have had enormous implications for the development of the conservatories, both in terms of autonomy, financial resources, and degrees conferred by the institution. These issues will be discussed later in the chapter (Guerrero Gutiérrez, 2001–2005).

Other institutions besides the CNM have been central to the development of professional music education in Quito. In 1967, Padre Jaime Mola (1918–1991), a Spanish organist and composer of the Franciscan order, founded the *Instituto Interamericano de Música Sacra* (Inter-American Institute of Sacred Music) with the sponsorship of the *Consorcio Internacional de Música Sacra* (International Consortium of Sacred Music) (Reed, 2002). This Instituto was intended to train musicians to serve the church and also to promote a musical culture in Ecuador. For these purposes, the Instituto provided basic classes in music education for children as well as advanced courses in harmony, counterpoint, and composition for adults. In its heyday in the 1970s, renowned Ecuadorian musicians who also worked at the CNM taught at the Instituto, such as Luis Humberto Salgado (1903–1977) and Memé Dávila de Burbano (1917–1980). The quality of music education decreased when Padre Mola left Ecuador in 1979 and the renowned teachers passed away. In 2000, the Instituto changed its name to *Conservatorio Jaime Mola* (Jaime Mola Conservatory).

Many instrumentalists in Quito have been trained outside of the conservatory, particularly in music schools created by the symphony orchestras and bands since the 1970s. Their goal was to recruit and train talented musicians from childhood for the purpose of long-term recruitment. Several young instrumentalists of the National Symphony Orchestra began to study music at the *Centro de Difusión Musical* (Center of Musical Diffusion) with the principal musicians of the orchestra in that period. The Centro de Difusión Musical had a short life span of ten years (1976–1986) (Guerrero Gutiérrez, 2001–2005).

In 1980 in Quito, the Consejo Provincial del Pichincha founded the *Banda Juvenil de Pichincha* (Youth Band of Pichincha), an artistic project directed by Edgar Palacios, a trumpet player and composer who studied in Romania and transformed the music education of the conservatory in Loja, his home city (Palacios, 2001). The Banda Juvenil was created as an alternative model of artistic development outside of the conservatory in order to stimulate the musical interest in Quito and the province of Pichincha. The goal was to engage children and adolescents in actual musical practice by first learning to play an instrument (woodwind, brass, or percussion), and then teaching them music theory. The band started with 120 children age six to eighteen years old. Three institutions made this project possible: the Consejo Provincial offered the use of its buildings, while the national government purchased the musical instruments and the Banco Central del Ecuador paid the conductor's and instructors' fees. The Banda Juvenil rehearsed every day in the afternoon and gave an average of two hundred performances per year in Quito and other provinces of Ecuador.

Essentially, the Banda Juvenil de Pichincha had similar goals to those of the System of Youth Orchestras created by José Antonio Abreu in Venezuela. In addition to a classical music repertoire, the Banda Juvenil played Ecuadorian popular music, thus providing a space for disseminating Ecuadorian popular culture. Many children who played in the Banda Juvenil in the 1980s pursued a musical career and currently play in the National Symphony Orchestra, the Philharmonic Orchestra of Ecuador, and the *Banda Sinfónica Metropolitana de Quito* (Metropolitan Symphonic Band of Quito). In 1989, the Banda Juvenil changed its name to *Orquesta de Vientos y Percusión de Pichincha* (Wind and Percussion Orchestra of Pichincha). The Banda Juvenil project was ambitious and also included a children's choir, the Pichincha Choir, and small musical ensembles (Palacios, 2001). Other *bandas infanto-juveniles* (early child and youth bands) sponsored by the Ministry of Defense and the Ministry of Social Welfare were created in small towns, such as Macará, Huaquillas, Manta, Santo Domingo, and Sangolquí.

A structure similar to the System of Youth Orchestras of Venezuela was implemented in 1995 in Ecuador, called the *Fundación de Orquestás Sinfónicas Juveniles del Ecuador* (Foundation of Youth Symphony Orchestras of Ecuador (FOSJE)), directed by Patricio Aizaga. With the auspices of the government, the FOSJE orchestras were created first in Quito, and then in Guayaquil and Loja. Like its counterpart in Venezuela, FOSJE has created a social program called "Sinfonía por la vida" (Symphony for Life), which seeks to develop the levels of education, self-esteem, discipline, responsibility, and teamwork among children from the marginalized sectors of society. According to FOSJE's website, more than six hundred children and young people have studied in FOSJE's music schools since its foundation. In the late 2000s, the Youth Orchestra changed its name to *Orquesta Filarmónica del Ecuador* (Philharmonic Orchestra of Ecuador).

The Philharmonic Society of Quito (1952) has had an active role in the dissemination of classical music in Quito by sponsoring concerts given by national and foreign musicians and orchestras. In 1993, this society opened a private music school where students took classes in piano, violin, violoncello, flute, and other instruments. National and foreign instructors were hired to teach at this school, which applied the Suzuki method to the violin and flute classes for children (Reed, 2002). This music school also had a short life span.

Besides the conservatories and music schools ascribed to the symphony orchestras and bands, music *institutos* and *colegios* (high schools) of music provide music instruction in small cities. Theoretically, *institutos* are supposed to train K–12 music teachers and *colegios* are basically high schools where students receive a concentration of music classes in addition to the general high school curriculum. However, in actual practice there is no clear distinction between them. According to the Ministry of Education, *institutos* have been founded in the provinces of Chimborazo, Imbabura, Cotopaxi, and Bolívar. *Colegios* are found in Chimborazo, El Oro, Cotopaxi, Pichincha, and Loja (Ministerio de Educación, n/d).

MUSIC EDUCATION IN GUAYAQUIL

Foreign musicians have exerted great influence on the professionalization of musicians, the structuring of the conservatories' music curricula, and the activation of a musical life in Guayaquil. In 1891, the *Sociedad Filantrópica del Guayas* (Philanthropic Society of Guayas) opened the first music school (*clase de música*) for people of low incomes (Guerrero Gutiérrez, 2001–2005). Several musicians who played in the *Círculo Musical Guayaquil* (Guayaquil Music Circle), the first orchestra in the port city, were trained at this school. Claudino Roza, a Portuguese saxophonist and band conductor, successfully directed the school from 1893 until his death in 1931. Although the music school continued under the direction of former students of the Sociedad Filantrópica, by 1940 the student enrollment had substantially decreased. This was partly due to the opening of the *Conservatorio Nacional Antonio Neumane* (Antonio Neumane National Conservatory) in 1928, which started functioning in the Municipal Palace with only a few musical instruments and no furniture at all. According to conservatory reports, it was not unusual for students to bring their own chairs to class! More than eight hundred students were enrolled the first year, when the conservatory had a capacity for less than two hundred students (Monroy, 1952).

Italian composer and conductor Angelo Negri (1878–1947) has been a key figure in the musical development of Guayaquil. In 1932, he arrived while on a concert tour with Lea Candini's opera company and stayed in Guayaquil due to a health condition (Monroy, 1952). An experienced musician and an excellent cultural promoter, he organized a symphony orchestra and an *orfeón* (choral society). He also founded the *Asociación de Música Angelo Negri*, which from 1938 to 1947 produced several Italian operas, including *La Traviata*, *Madame Butterfly*, and *Cavalleria Rusticana*. He taught composition at the Conservatorio Neumane and served as its director from 1937 to 1942. He was dismissed based on false accusations regarding a supposed involvement with Italian fascism. During his directorship, Negri established the curriculum for a three-year music theory program, as well as those for piano and other instruments. He also obtained from the government the economic resources to purchase musical instruments and to establish ten scholarships for instrumentalists in the orchestra. In addition, he hired foreign musicians to teach students how to play the instruments that the orchestra required but did not have at the time to provide instruction for. After leaving the conservatory in 1942, Negri assumed the direction of the music school of the *Sociedad Filantrópica del Guayas* and formed a 250-voice choir. Soon afterward, he founded his own music school, the *Academia de Música Santa Cecilia*, where he taught piano, *solfège*, and music theory. His students remember him as a strict and demanding teacher, but also one who encouraged them to work at their best and study music at a professional level.

Another important musician who made substantial contributions to the way music theory was taught in Guayaquil was Hungarian conductor Györgi Rayki (b. 1921). He came to Ecuador in 1950 as the Technical and Artistic Director of the Conservatorio Neumane and was also the conductor of the Symphony Orchestra of Guayaquil when it was still part of the *Casa de la Cultura Ecuatoriana* (Ecuadorian House of Culture) (Monroy, 1952). Realizing that there was a need for adequate textbooks to teach music theory, he published his own book titled *101 estudios rítmicos de solfeo sobre los intervalos (enseñanza post-elemental)* [101 Rhythmic Studies of *Solfège* on the Intervals (Postelementary education)]. Many generations of students at the Conservatorio Neumane, including myself, have since then used this textbook in the *solfège* class. In addition, Rayki founded the *Coro Mixto* (Mixed Choir) and the *Coro Madrigalista* (Madrigal Choir) at the conservatory, following the choral tradition established by Negri. It is important to note that the conservatory had two directors during this period, one in charge of the technical aspects of music education, and another responsible for administration.

Fleeing fascism in his native Spain, José Barniol (1913–1982), a laureate of the international Sarasate Competition for young violinists, arrived in Ecuador in 1938. He was hired by Negri to teach violin at the conservatory and with other foreign and national musicians formed the Barniol String Quartet, which regularly gave live concerts on the radio (Monroy, 1952). In the 1950s, he was first violin in the Symphony Orchestra and years later became its conductor, a position he held until his death. He was also the director of the Conservatorio Neumane from 1956 to 1961 (Álvarez García, 1986). Most of his students went on to play in the Symphony Orchestra of Guayaquil and teach violin at the conservatory.

Carlos Arijita (1915–1992), a Spanish conductor, composer, and pianist who studied in the Conservatory of Paris, further developed the choral tradition in Guayaquil. He arrived in Guayaquil in 1959 and became the director of the Conservatorio Neumane in 1961 (Álvarez García, 1986). He founded the *Conjunto Lírico de la Casa de la Cultura Ecuatoriana* (Lirical Ensemble of the Ecuadorian House of Culture) and the *Orfeón Universitario* (University Choral Society), which performed in the *zarzuelas* he produced in Guayaquil. While he did not make major changes to the music curricula of the conservatory, the *zarzuela* performances helped to expand the port city's musical activities.

Guayaquil has a long-standing tradition of choral music, as the work of Negri, Rayky, and Arijita demonstrates. This tradition has continued with Enrique Gil Calderón (1935–2008), the director of the choir at the Universidad Estatal de Guayaquil Choir and director of a music school attached to the university. He founded the *Festival Internacional de Coros* (International Choral Festival) in 1979, which brings together choral groups from different Latin American countries and is organized annually in Guayaquil.

In the 1970s, the Conservatorio Neumane experienced serious economic problems and had to operate in a small house that could barely accommodate the large number of students enrolled in this institution. The conservatory was closed in 1978 and reopened in a restored three-story building provided by the government (Álvarez García, 1986). New musical instruments were donated to the conservatory, and foreign musicians were hired to teach piano, violin, classical guitar, voice, and choral conducting. Among the faculty were Avtandil and Irina Tabatadze (piano), Lemo Erendy and Andrei Podgorny (violin), Guillermo Cárdenas and Martha Gordon (choir), Mario Baeza (music history and harmony), and Ryuhei Kobayashi (classical guitar). The discipline, work ethics, and knowledge of these musicians inspired Guayaquilean students to pursue a professional music career. Many obtained scholarships from the former Soviet Union and studied there in undergraduate (*uchilishie*) and graduate (conservatory) institutions in Moscow, St. Petersburg, and Kiev. Others opted for study in the United States and Germany, especially classical guitar and composition. Beatriz Parra, a soprano from Guayaquil who graduated at the Moscow Conservatory, was the director of the institution at the time.

Students from other cities of Ecuador, particularly from Loja and Quito, also pursued music studies in Russia. Most returned to Ecuador and currently work as music teachers and/or instrumentalists in the symphony orchestras. Some have Russian or Ukrainian spouses, who are also professional musicians and teach in conservatories and private music schools. Others opened their own conservatories in the mid-1990s, such as the *Conservatorio Rimsky-Korsakov* (Rimsky-Korsakov Conservatory)[8] in Guayaquil and *Mozarte*[9] in Quito. These private conservatories provide curricula similar to those found in the *uchilishies* from Russia but adapted to the musical realities of Ecuador. It is worth noting that private music schools in Ecuador generally bear the name of "conservatory" but do not necessarily offer the full curriculum of a conservatory.

MUSIC EDUCATION IN LOJA

In 1944, when the conservatories were part of the university system, the *Universidad Nacional de Loja* (National University of Loja)[10] opened a school of music. Due to a lack of economic resources, it was closed in 1956, but then reopened in 1959 under the direction of José María Bustamante. Five years later, the music school joined the *Facultad de Ciencias de Educación* (Educational Sciences Department). Although students received basic instruction of *solfège* and music theory, the curriculum was not sufficient to train professional musicians (Palacios, 2001). In addition, the school had only a few musical instruments and a nascent music library. Edgar Palacios, who studied trumpet and composition at the Conservatory Ciprian Porumbescu in Bucharest-Romania from 1962 to 1967, became the new director of the music school in 1968. The school was closed shortly after due to government reforms, and reopened in 1970 under the name *Conservatorio Nacional de Música* (National Conservatory of Music) and ascribed to the Ministry of Education. In 1971, the conservatory adopted the name Salvador Bustamante Celi, honoring a renowned composer from Loja.

Like Angelo Negri in Guayaquil, Edgar Palacios has been an effective cultural promoter and a major figure in advancing a professional music education in Loja. He found the financial resources to purchase musical instruments and to construct a new functional building with seventy classrooms and a music library (Palacios, 2001). He brought in foreign musicians, especially from Russia and Romania, as teachers and performers of the symphony orchestra, thus imposing a high music standard among the young students. Loja's symphony orchestra, string orchestra, and wind band were created under Palacios's leadership. His project, called "Complejo Musical Loja" (Loja Musical Complex), was ambitious and intended to create the required infrastructure to make Loja an important musical center in Ecuador. In 1979, Palacios quit his position and moved to Quito to establish the *Banda Juvenil del Consejo Provincial de Pichincha* (Youth Band of the Pichincha Provincial Council), mentioned earlier.

Although Palacios was not able to complete his project, the result of his work is seen in the many instrumentalists who studied in the Conservatory of Loja during this period and who currently play in the symphony orchestras of Quito, Cuenca, and Guayaquil. Taking advantage of his close connection with the government of Romania, several students from Loja got scholarships to study in that country. When they returned to Ecuador in the early 1980s, they began to train local students in their areas of specialization, particularly composition and percussion.

MUSIC EDUCATION IN CUENCA

The *Conservatorio José María Rodríguez* (José María Rodríguez Conservatory), which owes its name to an important piano teacher and composer from Cuenca, was founded in 1937 under the direction of Segundo Luis Moreno (Guerrero Gutiérrez, 2003–2005). Unlike in Quito, Guayaquil, and Loja, music education in Cuenca has developed at a slow pace and instrumentalists have had less opportunity to study abroad. Many students from Cuenca received music instruction in the conservatories of Quito and Loja. The Symphony Orchestra of Cuenca was founded in 1972, almost two decades after those of Quito and Guayaquil.

In 2000, the University of Cuenca opened a school of music within the Faculty of Arts, and in 2009 began offering a master's degree in music approved by *Consejo Nacional de Educación Superior Ecuador* (Ecuador National Higher Education Council) (CONESUP). Other public and private universities in Ecuador offer music programs that are somewhat similar to those of the conservatories; however, only a few confer a bachelor's degree in music. The *Universidad San Francisco de Quito* (San Francisco University of Quito) offers a bachelor's degree in jazz music, which they call "contemporary music."

THE CONSERVATORIES TODAY

According to the Agreement 3400 of the Ministry of Education,[11] the mission of the conservatory is "to promote education, outreach, research and musical creation in the country, ensuring the training of professional musicians, teachers and instrumentalists, whose education is recognized nationally and internationally." The conservatories have faced serious challenges in recent decades to fulfill these goals due to several factors, including limited funding, the need to restructure the curriculum of the conservatory, and little understanding of the need of an appropriate musical pedagogy. As already mentioned, many musicians who currently play in the symphony orchestras and bands have been trained either outside of the conservatory or have studied there for only a few years.

The length and structure of the curriculum of the conservatory has changed throughout the twentieth century. Before the 1970s, the minimum age to enter the conservatory was twelve years old; however, since the early 1980s children are accepted at a much earlier age and learn music through a variety of approaches to children's music education, such as the Orff, Kodály, and Dalcroze methods. The creation of a children's conservatory level has required a restructuring of the institution and its curriculum, which now needs to accommodate a new population. It must be noted that the curriculum of the state and private conservatories in Ecuador is under revision by the Ministry of Education (2009).

Currently, the curriculum of the conservatory is divided into three skill levels: *Básico Inicial, Básico,* and *Bachillerato*[12] (equivalent to Basic Preschool, Elementary, and High School), though this structure is not standard for all conservatories . The third level includes two paths: (1) specialization in an instrument or voice, or a general knowledge option (*bachillerato generalista*). Graduates receive a degree as instrumentalists/voice majors or as "generalists" (which certifies them as music teachera).[13] Before the 1980s the conservatories conferred a degree in performance, whereas now it offers a degree called *tecnologado* (musical technician), equivalent to that of a high school degree. This structuring did away with the "superior" (undergraduate) level that the conservatories had before when they were part of the university system.[14]

The national conservatories confront many other problems, such as overcrowded student populations and a high percentage of desertion in the early years of instruction. According to a Ministry of Education report (n/d), the ratio of teachers per students enrolled in the Conservatorio Neumane is 78 per 1,110; it is 50 per 1,011 in the Conservatorio José María Rodríguez. These student/teacher ratios are very low compared with those in a well-resourced music institution in Europe or the United States. As a result, classroom sizes for theoretical subjects, such as music theory and *solfège,* are overcrowded, while individual classes tend to be curtailed in order to accommodate the large number of students. Likewise, the level of student desertion in the early years of study is high compared with the ratio of students who graduate.

There is little understanding of the need to apply a specialized musical pedagogy. For example, students learn to play their musical instruments but receive little training on how to teach them to other students. Other aspects that need to be addressed are the lack of student recitals and class studio hours as important elements of students' musical development. It is also necessary to update textbooks and other teaching materials used in the classroom, which would make student learning more effective and easier.

Despite the structural problems of the conservatories, Ecuador has had talented musicians who have succeeded in their music careers. They have studied either abroad or with foreign musicians who lived in Ecuador. In general, good teachers stimulate good students to become better performers and can create "schools" in their instrument of specialization, as the following examples will show. These examples are not comprehensive and are only meant to illustrate the general music trends in the country.

Ecuador has had excellent pianists, such as Isabel Rosales (1895–1961) and Gustavo Bueno (1904–1984), who studied with Alfred Cortot in Paris in the 1910s and 1920s, respectively. Belisario Peña (1902–1959) studied piano in the Giuseppe Verdi Conservatory in Milan and trained several generations of Ecuadorian pianists in the mid-twentieth century. Luis Humberto Salgado (1903–1977) and Memé Dávila de Burbano (1917–1980) studied in Ecuador and stood out as notable performers and teachers. The first was self-taught in the field of composition, while the latter studied in Quito with a renowned Czech pianist. Some of Dávila de Burbano's students pursued an international piano career, such as Leslie Wright and Carlos Juris, who teach piano in France and Finland. Many young pianists who studied abroad in the 1990s have found teaching positions in the United States and Germany.

In Guayaquil, foreign teachers greatly influenced young Ecuadorian students in their decision to pursue professional musical careers. Many students of Avtandil Tabatadze, a pianist from the country of Georgia (former Soviet Union) who worked at the Conservatorio Neumane from 1978 to 1982, became piano teachers, choral conductors, or musicologists, or have engaged in other music-related activities.

Although choral music has a long tradition in Ecuador, there are no choral conducting programs in the conservatories. Some choral conductors have studied abroad, while others are instrumentalists and singers who apply their music skills to conducting high school, university, and other institutional choirs. Ecuadorian orchestra conductors have been trained abroad, particularly in Russia and the United States. Some conductors are Russians or Americans who have settled in Ecuador.

It is safe to talk about an Ecuadorian flute school founded by Luciano Carrera (b. 1948), director of the CNM in the 1990s and early 2000s. He has organized the International Festival of Flutists in the Middle of the World (Quito) annually since 1990. Many of his students play in Ecuador's symphony orchestras and bands of Ecuador. Likewise, percussion studies have been well developed in Quito by Pablo Valarezo, a percussionist from Loja who studied in Romania. Guayaquil has developed a classical guitar school under the Japanese

Ryuhei Kobayashi (b. 1953), who arrived in Guayaquil in 1978. Some of his first students pursued professional music careers in Germany as guitarists, musicologists, and composers. In Quito, composer Carlos Bonilla is considered the founder of Quito's classical guitar school (Guerrero Gutiérrez, 2001–2005). He also played the double bass and trained the musicians who currently play this instrument in the National Symphony Orchestra.

The study of music composition is centered in Quito. Most Ecuadorian academic composers are either from Quito or have studied there. They have followed distinct musical orientations, particularly in nationalist, postmodernist, and electroacoustic trends. Ecuadorian composers of the first half of the twentieth century were trained in France, Germany, Russia, Romania, and the United States, following different compositional styles and techniques. The *Departamento de Investigación, Creación y Difusión* (Department of Research, Creation and Diffusion) (DIC) of the CNM was founded in 1985 with the mission of training academic composers and music researchers (Guerrero Gutiérrez, 2003–2005). This department has an electro-acoustic studio, which was financed by IBM Ecuador. Many young composers in Ecuador are either self-trained or have studied composition with the above-mentioned composers.

CONCLUSION

Ecuador currently enjoys a vibrant musical life with its various orchestras, choirs, and instrumental ensembles that perform a vast repertoire of classical music on a regular basis. There is also a public eager to attend their concerts, which take place in theaters, concert halls, churches, and open-air venues. This was certainly not the case before the 1990s, when attendance at classical music concerts was low and there were a few orchestras playing a limited repertoire. The creation of youth symphony orchestras and bands as well as music schools providing music education outside of the conservatories have given young people opportunities to get involved in music in ways that were not available before. This, in turn, augmented public interest in listening to these young musicians play a larger repertoire. Students who studied in Russia and Romania in the 1970s and 1980s have returned to Ecuador and teach and play in the symphony orchestras and bands.

As seen in this brief overview of professional music education in Ecuador, the conservatories have had periods of blossom and decay. It must be noted that the leadership and talent of charismatic Ecuadorian musicians and foreign teachers have brought about periods of great development in music education in Ecuador. However, attempts to restructure and standardize the music curriculum are still a work in progress.

NOTES

1. Archeological musical instruments (flutes, panpipes, ocarinas, and drums) demonstrate that ancient indigenous cultures that inhabited current Ecuadorian territories had rich musical traditions long before the Spanish and Inca conquests. Unlike the well-documented studies on Inca music in Peru, research on pre-Hispanic musical practices and education in Ecuador still awaits scholarly study and is beyond the scope of this chapter.

2. In Ecuador, there is no specific regulation on the skills music teachers require in order to teach in K–12 schools. Therefore, this chapter focuses on the music training of professional instrumentalists.

3. The term *classical music* is used here as a generic term for European art music. It does not refer to the music of the "Classical" period.

4. The *pasillo* is urban popular music from Ecuador, which is derived from the European waltz.

5. The term *mestizo* refers to the racial and cultural mixture of indigenous and white people.

6. This collection belongs to the Casa de la Cultura Ecuatoriana in Quito. It includes archaeological instruments of the Andean area and ancient instruments from Europe, Asia, and Africa.

7. The website of the Universidad Central del Ecuador (UCE), Ecuador's oldest university, does not provide a precise year of foundation, though the year 1651 appears in the University's coat of arms. In 1836, during the presidency of Vicente Rocafuerte, this institution changed its name to Universidad Central del Ecuador.

8. Reinaldo Cañizares, a pianist who studied at the St. Petersburg and Moscow Conservatories, is the founder and director of the Conservatorio Rimsky-Korsakov. http://rimsky-korsakov.org/carreras.php

9. Aníbal Landázuri and Natalia Kovalenko are the founders of Mozarte.

10. The National University of Loja was founded in 1859. http://mozarte.edu.ec/

11. Published in the Official Gazette 735 of July 11, 1995.

12. The term *bachillerato* refers to the terminal degree that a student receives when graduating from high school. It should not be confused with the "bachelor's" degree that college students receive in the American college system. In Ecuador, this degree is called *licenciatura*.

13. It is worth noting that in Ecuador music teachers do not require a certification or license to teach in elementary and high schools.

14. The CNM in Quito keeps the term *Superior* as part of its name, but it does not confer an undergraduate degree.

REFERENCES

Álvarez García, Lila. 1986. Historia del Conservatorio Antonio Neumane. Manuscrito.

Conservatorio Nacional de Loja. http://www.vivaloja.com/content/view/395/557/

FOSJE Website. http://www.fosje.org.ec/

Guerrero, Juan Agustín. 1876. *La música ecuatoriana desde su origen hasta 1875.* Quito: Imprenta Nacional.

Guerrero Gutiérrez, Pablo. *Enciclopedia de la música ecuatoriana,* Vol. 1 (2001–2002), Vol. 2 (2004–2005). Quito: Corporación Musicológica Ecuatoriana CONMUSICA.

Guerrero Gutiérrez, Pablo. 2007. *Voces en la Sombra. Juan Pablo Muñoz Sanz.* Quito: Consejo Nacional de Cultura.

Ministerio de Educación. Bachillerato de Arte, n/d.

Ministerio de Educación. 2009. Propuesta de Reestructuración del Conservatorio Nacional de Música. Quito: Comisión de Reestructuración del Ministerio de Educación.

Monroy, César. 1952. "El Conservatorio de Música Antonio Neumane. Sinopsis histórica de sus veinticuatro años de vida." *Revista de la Universidad Estatal de Guayaquil.* Guayaquil: Universidad Estatal de Guayaquil.

Moreno, Segundo Luis. 1996. *Historia de la Música en Ecuador.* Quito: Municipio de Quito.

Palacios, Edgar. 2001. *Edgar Palacios. Toda la vida . . . Toda la música.* Quito: Casa de la Cultura Ecuatoriana.

Reed, Alicia. 2002. *50 Años de la Sociedad Filarmónica de Quito.* Quito: Imprenta Mariscal.

Chapter Seventeen

Peru

Victoria Waxman

INTRODUCTION

Peru is located on South America's western coast on the Pacific Ocean, in between the countries of Chile and Ecuador. Peru's population is 29,907,003, made up of people primarily of Amerindian, mestizo, white, black, Japanese, and Chinese ethnic backgrounds. Peru has two official languages, Spanish and Quechua. Peru's history is ancient; its origins can be traced back to the Incan Empire and earlier. In 1533, Peruvian history changed drastically with the arrival of a Spanish expeditionary force, which led to the downfall of the Incan Empire. The Spanish ruled in Peru until 1821, when Peru declared itself an independent country. Today, Peru is a constitutional republic with its capital in Lima. Peru has a diverse history, and its music and music education history is correspondingly diverse. This chapter will trace this long history and how music tradition and education changed and varied over time.[1]

MUSIC EDUCATION AND THE INCA

Context for Music in Peru and Music Schools in Cuzco and the Use of Song to Aid Memory

For the ancient *Inca*, the word *taki* stood for both song and dance rather than having two separate words.[2] This lack of delineation is significant when considering the context and role of music and performance in Incan culture. Music had many functions; it was a means to learn and memorize history, praise the gods at festivals, and for general entertainment. Musical life was rich and diverse, taking inspiration from the surroundings of the Andes and Peru. The Incas took animals that were important to them, such as llamas, as inspiration. They sang songs of the llamas, *Pucca llama*, in imitation of the sounds llamas make—"y" and "yn" sounds were used to sound like whining llamas.[3] Music and passing the music tradition on to the next generation was a part of Peruvian life from the region's early history, and its role remains central to Peruvian life today.

The Inca were the earliest among the American peoples to create formal music education, beginning from circa 1350. The Inca Roca, who taught noble and royal children, included music as part of their teaching curriculum. Music was taught by rote and had a significant role in educational and court life.[4] Early Incan religion involved ancestor worship, and knowing how to sing played a large role in this worship. Songs were used as a way to retell the stories of these ancestors and functioned as a kind of oral history.[5] These songs included battles and deeds by the ancestors that, again, had to be learned by rote.[6] The Inca Roca realized early on that music was an effective educational tool. Memorization proved easier when in conjunction with melody and intonation.

The integral role of song in nobles' education and the passing down of history is perhaps best demonstrated in a story about Inca (emperor) Huayna Capac. As part of initiating his rule, the emperor wanted to inspect all aspects of his empire in order to learn how best to rule. This included learning about his empire's agriculture, tribute, nobility, and worship institutions and how they functioned. Aside from the officers he sent to all corners of his empire to learn this, he himself went and inspected the institutions of the capital city of Cuzco. At each noble household, the emperor asked the nobles' servants to sing the history of their lords' past deeds so as to educate the emperor. Listening to the servants' songs helped Huayna decide how to reward each lord. The emperor privileged song in teaching him about his empire and his nobility. In this way, the emperor educated himself about his lords and the institutions of his empire through song. [7]

Song functioned in Incan festivals as well. One such festival was for a good harvest, which was dedicated to the celebration of the sun. This festival corresponded with the sun cycle, beginning with sunrise. As the sun rose, the male nobles who had gathered for the festival sang and tapped their feet. They maintained their song until sunset, but the intensity of the song varied depending upon the intensity of the sun. As the sun rose, the nobles' voices continuously increased until noon, when their singing would begin to decrease as the sun began its descent. While singing was certainly a large part of the festival, additionally there were sacrificial offerings such as burning meat offered to the sun to ensure a good harvest. [8]

Incan songs were written anonymously but also by Incan emperors. Indeed, the Inca founder Manco Capac wrote hymns, three of which survive. In particular, sacred poetry was used as the lyrics for songs. For instance, Pachacuti Inca Yupanqui wrote eleven hymns some time between 1440 to 1450, which were used for religious ceremonies. [9] Hymns like these were called *haillikuna* and frequently used instrumental accompaniment. While Incas (emperors) did compose such songs, the majority of the hymns was composed anonymously by priests and used as part of everyday life of the priests in praying to the Creator at each beginning and end of the day. Such hymns asked the gods for prosperity for the people and the empire. *Haillikuna* served religious functions, but there were also secular forms, such as the historical heroic tales discussed above and agricultural *haillikuna*. Farmers and workers sung agricultural *haillikuna* during the workday, which helped them to keep up a steady pace and sometimes work in unison. [10]

It should be noted that the Incan Empire was just that—an empire in which other cultures and peoples lived and had to pay tribute to the central Incan government. The empire itself was a loose formation and covered land from present-day Chile to Colombia. [11] So thus while there was certainly variation in songs and music genres across regions, they were unified by an Incan cultural framework in which they had to function, including the use of the *Quechua* language. [12] Incan nobility did not speak Quechua originally—they had their own "secret" language that they did not wish their subjects to learn. Accordingly, Quechua was used in all government matters rather than the nobility's secret language and became widespread in use under the Inca regime. The language itself is agglutinative, meaning that a root word is taken and syllables are added to the end of the root in order to give it different meanings. [13] In addition to this spoken language of Quechua, the Inca used a recording system called the *quipu*. Quipu was not a written language but rather a kind of mnemonic device that used knots to record historical events, accounts, and other things to preserve such as the tales of an emperor's feats. [14] While quipu could be used to keep track of the basics of historical events, it is really through song that these events were fleshed out and remembered holistically and with detail.

Music Education for Women in Incan Peru

Formal music education for women occurred mainly in the context of the houses of the Virgins of the Sun. This order, whose virgin priestesses were called *mamaconas*, was in many ways similar to that of the Romans' Vestal Virgins. Special houses within the order were devoted to music. Those girls who exhibited musical talent were accordingly educated in these houses and used their skills for religious praise but also to entertain the nobility and the royal family at banquets. [15] The music education girls received consisted primarily of singing and flute performance. [16] While other girls outside of the houses of the Virgins of the Sun could learn music, it is only here that there was more formal, specifically musical education during the Inca regime.

Music Beyond Urban Centers and Instrumentation

Aside from functioning as part of the education for nobles and priestesses and music being used for religious festivals and for entertainment at court, outside the urban centers song was used to tell tales. [17] These kinds of songs usually used responsorial performance techniques, thus encouraging community participation, and had no accompaniment. The notable exception was love songs that usually did have accompaniment.[18] This idea of music and its importance to celebrating and maintaining a sense of community is one that continues throughout the history of Peru, right up until present day, as will be discussed further below.

It is important to know what kinds of instrument the Inca used to make music. Incan musical instruments consisted primarily of recorders, shawms, panpipes, trumpets, percussion, and flutes.[19] Incans invented the most complex musical instrument in the Americas at the time, the *antara*.[20] The antara is made up of cane pipes, and its more modern form is called panpipes; it is perhaps the most well known of Peruvian instruments. Musical instrumentation would change drastically with the Spanish invasion and introduction of entirely new instruments such as guitars and other instruments with more than a single string. Before the Spanish arrived, instruments with multiple strings were unknown in Peru. A complete music group in Incan Peru consisted of "drums, ocarinas, tambourines, bells, trumpets and bean shell anklets."[21]

MUSIC IN A COLONIAL STATE

In 1532, Francisco Pizarro arrived in Peru with a Spanish military force and invaded the Incan Empire. As part of Pizarro's campaign, he kidnapped and killed Inca Atahualpa. A forced Spanish administration was created once conquistadors put down any resistance.[22] In addition to the many new changes this Spanish colonial administration entailed, there were changes in the social makeup of Peru. In addition to native Peruvians and the new Spanish population, there were now also *mestizos*, interracial offspring between Europeans and Native Americans, and *criollos*, persons born in the Americas but of European descent. These different groups and people's identification with their respective groups continued even after the end of Spanish colonial rule. Similarly, musical instruments became diversified with the new influence of the Spanish. String instruments were a completely new phenomenon introduced by the Spanish. Such newly introduced instruments often changed as the Peruvians made the instruments their own. In the 1700s, the *charango*, a version of a guitar, developed. It is smaller and higher pitched due to its shorter string length and is featured in music from the colonial period and beyond.[23]

Goals of Music Education in Colonial Peru

Education was a major aspect of the colonial regime. Music was a way to communicate across class and ethnic lines since not everyone spoke or read the same language.[24] The Spanish, as Catholic Christians, wished to convert all the native Peruvians to Christianity, and music was used as an educational tool to this end.[25] Conversion was important as it was used by the Spanish to justify their invasion and rule of Peru and other regions in the Americas.[26] Schools were established by various religious orders, such as the Franciscan Colegio de San Andres at Quito, and European music was taught at such schools.[27]

As part of this educational endeavor, bridges between Peruvian music and Spanish European music had to be created. In 1598, the *Symbolo Cathólico Indiano* was published in Lima. This book contained the lyrics of European Christian religious songs but had corresponding melodies that were both Spanish-European and Peruvian.[28] Music with Christian texts but in Quechua rather than Spanish or Latin was also used in order to get through to the native population. However, after 1600, this use of bilingualism and cross-cultural music techniques lessened as the native American culture became further dominated by the Spanish and tolerance of the native American cultural expression decreased.[29]

Cathedral Music

Cathedrals were the musical centers of cities under the Spanish regime. The cathedrals furthermore functioned as schools for the native elite. The colonial government targeted the sons of the native elite to be educated. By educating the elite, the government hoped they would cooperate and serve as examples for others in native Peruvian society.[30] For instance, at the Jesuit Colegio de San Jorja, sons of the Peruvian elite were educated about European music.[31] Music was taught and performed by students at the seminaries in cathedrals. The students were themselves centers for music dissemination to other members of their community, such as when they performed in public ceremonies such as the ceremony for the death of the Spanish ruler Philip V. [32] Those students who trained in music at seminaries or other religious centers and who did not become priests could become professional musicians. They could move to parishes, especially outside the cities, that did not have a priest with musical training and accordingly needed someone who did. At these parishes, they aided the performance of music for religious purposes, but could also become the musical educators of the local students, once more spreading music education and Spanish-European music to others. [33]

Parishes, Convents, and Monasteries

Convents were the center of music education for girls. The earliest Peruvian convent founded was that of Santa Clara in 1558. Similar to cathedrals and seminaries, the goal of the convents was to Hispanicize and Christianize its students, and music was once more used to this end. [34] Music performance (and thus education) was a large part of convent life, including singing, organ, and harp playing. Such music was part of ceremonies but also nonceremonial events. [35]

For music education, convents hired outside teachers as well, both native and Spanish. [36] Convents were not just for current and future nuns but also impoverished and orphaned children who would be taught music as well. Learning music was a useful tool, and these girls could earn money with their musical skills. Musical talent could also mean reducing or waiving the dowry fee to become a nun. [37] In this way, although the Spanish-European religious orders saw music education primarily as a way to convert the native population, music education also functioned as a way to move up the social ladder and to find greater success in life.

Rural Music

Spanish-European music education and dissemination continued outside the cities. For instance, in addition to convents, there were *beaterios*, less formal educational organizations for women where they learned, as in convents, about Christianity and European social norms. [38] *Beaterios* were another way in which to gain music education without the same strictures of the convents. Similarly to those who learned how to play and perform music in the convents, musical knowledge was a social steppingstone to better things for these girls and women. Being a member of a *beaterio* choir enhanced one's reputation and involved monetary compensation. [39] Music education was valued outside the context of convents and being a nun; it had a place in the secular world of Peru as well.

In addition to schools for native elites, in the eighteenth century some steps were made toward widening the targeted group for education. The majority of the Spanish population saw the Peruvians as inferior in mind and culture. Accordingly, this majority felt educating more than the children of native elites did not make sense. [40] However, there were those with somewhat different opinions and who were not completely satisfied with the elite educational system as it stood. Bishop Baltazar Jaime Martínez Compañón felt there was an opportunity to use education in order to make native Peruvians into cooperative citizens of the colonial regime. [41] For the bishop, this meant the development of a regional educational project that went beyond education for the elite. [42] Before these regional schools that the bishop formed, primary education was mainly private and for males from the upper class whose families wanted them to either become clergymen or civil servants. This education consisted largely of reading, writing, and basic math while and of this initial group, fewer boys went on to higher education and other subjects. [43] The government was interested only in educating sons of native elites to the point where they could aid the state, which meant learning Spanish and etiquette. [44] Further education was deemed not really necessary; as long as the elites cooperated and showed others how to cooperate, the government did not feel pressed to emphasize higher education or education for others besides the elite.

For girls, there was even less opportunity for education. This education was again usually from private tutors or at convents where girls learned about reading, writing, sewing, singing, and other domestic activities. Only later, and only in large urban centers like the capital, Lima, and cities like Arequipa and Cuzco, did more opportunities for education become available to women. [45]

The important goal for the native population as a whole, according to the colonial government, was to teach native Peruvians about Christianity. Thus, Bishop Martínez Compañón's act of creating primary schools for boys and girls of all backgrounds in the native population was unusual. Again though, this was not so much for these children's benefit as to ensure their conversion to Christianity and learn to be good citizens who would be loyal to the colonial government.[46] Compañón set forth strict requirements for the new students; any boys (aged between five and ten years old) and girls (aged between four and eight years old) had to attend the school if they lived within a radius of half a league from the school. The catechism would be used to teach against vices like vanity, and Spanish would be taught for reading, writing, and counting.[47] Daily mass was also a requirement, and children learned hymns for both the mass and to be sung while in transit to the church.[48] While music education was not a primary goal of these schools, it was once more used as a tool to teach larger goals.

Peruvian Composers

There were opportunities for Peruvians and mestizos to compose music that would be used, but this music had to fit within the ruling Spanish-European framework. Accordingly, the music that survives from these composers is primarily religious in nature and European in genre. For instance, Juan de Fuentes, a choirmaster in Cuzco, composed a religious song for Corpus Christi using a traditional Inca song for sowing. He took the melody of the Inca song and created corresponding polyphonic parts. Even in the song's performance, precolonial elements existed. The eight boys who sang the piece for the feast wore traditional native American garb with a plough as the singers of the original version of the song would have, and the choir added their voices to the refrain as would have been done in the original, native American version.[49] However, while there were certainly compositional opportunities for non-Europeans, it should be noted that discrimination still abounded. In terms of cathedral musicians, native American performers were treated more like servants and did not have the same status as their European counterparts.[50] This discrimination was not as prominent outside the cathedral context, but nevertheless could not be escaped entirely. It is furthermore important to note that this first generation of non-European composers and musicians went on to teach those who came after them.[51]

The Spanish invasion and rule forever changed music and education in Peru. The European influence would, at various times, dominate and be adapted to local genres and techniques. One area in which this is clearly illustrated is the genre of dance drama and its development during and after the colonial period. Dance drama was well established in Incan culture, but its subject and form changed with the Spanish invasion. The Spanish encouraged the creation of a "Dance of the Conquest," which told the story of Pizarro's invasion and the death of the emperor Atahualpa in 1533. The story's ending was intended to be a happy one and help pave the way toward cooperation with the Spanish regime. However, as time passed, the "Conquest Dance" came to be used in a different way. Now the emperor became a tragic, even a Messianic, character and went against the idea of Spanish rule. The dance became a symbol of resistance to Spanish rule and hope of a return not just of an Inca emperor but of a Spanish-free society.[52] These cultural changes reflected larger political ones; in the eighteenth century native Americans claiming descent from the Inca royal family led fellow Peruvians against the colonial regime. Though such uprisings were put down (the last one in the 1780s), the uprisings foreshadowed a later rebellion of the *criollos* in the 1820s against the Spanish regime.[53]

MUSIC AND POLITICS: AN EMERGING NATIONAL IDENTITY

In 1821, Peru declared its independence from Spain and established a new regime, and this new regime was created and dominated by the *criollos*.[54] Education was important to the newly independent Peru; the divisions between the different groups that made up Peruvian society still existed and education was a means of creating united Peruvian citizens. And at first, the regime wanted everyone, as part of this new conception of the Peruvian citizen, to be participants through voting. However, in reality, soon only the wealthy and literate were permitted to vote. Though *criollos* continued to rule and as part of this regime, not all native Peruvians could vote, this began to change particularly with Augusto Leguía's dictatorship from 1919 to 1930. Leguía became more interested in the native Peruvian population and in educating and preserving their rights. However, it was not until the Constitution of 1979 that all Peruvians, including those who were not literate, could vote.[55]

With this new *criollo* regime in 1821, new musical genres continued to develop and old genres continued to be changed and reconstructed. For instance, *criollo* music continued to have a European foundation—such as the use of waltz and polka, but with distinct differences. Aside from the *criollo* music, there are other kinds of music inspired by the social makeup of Peru, such as Afroperuvian and native Peruvian and Andean music. [56] Andean music dominated the music scene, especially outside the cities, in many ways because of the large Andean population, and today it is still used in rituals and ceremonies in more rural contexts. [57] As part of the Andean musical tradition, pre-Spanish musical forms, such as the *harawi*, were preserved. The genre of *harawi* is used in ceremonies such as those dealing with marriage and agriculture. It uses only one musical line (monophonic) and repeats a musical phrase incorporating melismas and glissandos as enhancements to the main musical line. Traditionally older women sing it and in a high, nasal style. [58]

In the Southern part of the Andes Mountains, *wayno* is the best-known musical genre and is perhaps the best-known Andean genre outside of its native land. *Wayno* is versatile; unlike other genres, *wayno* is not particular to a certain context and can exclude or include instrumental accompaniment. *Wayno* usually uses duple meter and a pentatonic scale (A-C-D-E-G). It incorporates a lot of syncopation as part of its rhythmic framework; for instance, it often uses rhythmic phrases such as one eighth note paired with two sixteenth notes or an eighth note sandwiched between a sixteenth note on either side. Like other musical genres of Peru, *wayno* differs from area to area and can have many names. [59] *Herranza* is another preserved pre-Spanish genre, but it incorporates Spanish influence in the form of instrumentation. *Herranza* is used during branding of animals. A woman sings accompanied by a spiral-shaped horn trumpet *wakrapuku* and *tinya*, a European violin. The whole ritual has several steps: marking animals, offerings, rites, music, and dance. [60]

Legacy of the Colonial Regime

While certain pre-Spanish traditions and genres are maintained, the influence of the colonial period is inescapable. As mentioned above, it is made visible in the use of non-Peruvian instruments. In particular, the influence of multistringed instruments is strong, such as the twelve-stringed *charango*, a twelve-stringed, smaller version of a guitar, developed. The *wakrapuku*, a spiral-shaped trumpet, noted above is also from Spain originally. [61] Musical genres that either changed or developed as a result of the Spanish conquest continued under the initial *criollo* regime and beyond. Perhaps one of the best examples of this influence is the *carnaval*, which involves both song and dance. *Carnaval* is a festival during the season of Lent that takes place in February. Though the *carnaval* was introduced by Europeans in the 1920s, it changed and became adapted to its new environs. The *carnaval* involved burlesques focusing on two main characters. In the town of Tarma in Peru, for instance, the character of Don Calixto, a lecherous old man, pursues the young and lovely Ña Pimienta only to discover that she is in fact a cross-dressing man. As part of the story being performed, Don Calixto proclaims three days of celebration with parades, theater, and music. [62] In the 1930s, adaptation and change in the repertoire can be found. Different members of the artisan guilds of Tarma wrote new music, and local instruments such as flutes and tambourines were used instead of Spanish-European-derived instruments. [63]

Outside Musical Influences

Influences on Peruvian music are not entirely from Spain or Europe. Africans' history in Peru began in conjunction with the Spanish conquest. The initial Spanish expeditions included not only soldiers but also slaves. With the new colonial regime, the slave trade added Peru as a destination or at least a stopping point for enslaved Africans. This influx of Africans increased in part as a response to a decrease in the indigenous Peruvian population from European-introduced disease. With Peru's independence in 1812, opportunities for slaves to earn their freedom increased, but it was not until 1854 and 1855 that slavery was officially abolished in Peru. [64] There is controversy over what happened to the Afroperuvian population in Peru in the twentieth century, as the population appeared to significantly decline. Some scholars claim that the decline was due to the poor conditions under slavery and beyond as well as death in action during military service and that the decline was so great it can be labeled as a kind of "disappearance" of the Afroperuvian population. Other scholars, while acknowledging a decline in population, also point out that many Afroperuvians identified more with the *criollo* population, and this explains a fall in population numbers but also a decline in the presence of African or Afroperuvian culture.[65] In terms of music, Afroperuvian music exists in Peru today it was severely affected by the cultural disappearance of Afroperuvians.[66] Afroperuvian music as it existed in the colonial period was largely lost until the 1950s. The Afroperuvian population decreased since the colonial period and the culture and music were less present.[67] Thus much of contemporary Afroperuvian music is reconstructed.[68] In this reconstruction, the history of colonial Peru is played out on stage, though sometimes romanticized.[69] Several artists and scholars helped in this endeavor, using archives, oral histories, song remains, accounts of performances, anthropology, ethnology, and musicology.[70] One scholar, José Durán, put together what pieces he could find from Afroperuvian music and added to them for a work "La Quadrilla Morena de Pancho Fierro." This in turn spurred greater interest in the musical genre and further reconstruction, adding *criollo* and Cuban aspects to the genre.[71]

Furthermore, with the reconstruction of this genre, new organizations and uses for education came to be, as well as the professionalization of Afroperuvian dance and music. For instance, Victoria Santa Cruz created some of the early reconstructed choreographies of Afroperuvian dance using what still existed but also adding techniques she learned at school in Paris.[72] The National School of Folklore in Peru is one newer organization in which genres like Afroperuvian music are taught and preserved. However, at the National School, teaching focuses on following the reconstructed Afroperuvian songs and performances of the twentieth century closely, rather than continuing to develop the art form. The Afroperuvian genre is now deemed by many as "authentic" in its current form and thus leaves little room for further reconstruction or change. In the teaching and passing down of the genre, there is furthermore an emphasis on family. The techniques and forms are taught from generation to generation, and this creates some difficulty in outsiders learning it.[73] However, it should be noted that in its reconstruction, Afroperuvian music supported the idea of collective music making to unite the community, especially in the wake of globalization and modernization.[74] One of its goals was to look to the past to solidify a Peruvian identity in the present.

Musical changes like the reconstruction of Afroperuvian music are helped along by the way the Peruvian musical experience changed over time. In the twentieth century in particular, methods and opportunities to communicate within the country and with areas outside the country increased, often in conjunction with new technology and infrastructure developments. Even more traditional *criollo* music changed over time, especially with increased methods of communication and exposure to other musical genres. For instance, one of the famous *criollo* musicians and composers is Felip Pinglo (1899–1936). Despite his earlier context, he changed the *criollo* tradition, incorporating aspects of tango, jazz, and other genres. With increased communication, Peruvians' exposure to other musical genres increased, and their own music traditions came to reflect these new influences.[75]

Modern Continuity and Change

Looking at Peruvian music today and back on its long history, it is interesting to trace what musical traditions remain over time and how they are adapted in different time periods. For instance, during the precolonial Inca period, a kind of parade would take place in which figures representing the Inca would be carried through the streets. With the colonial period and Christian conversion, religious festivals to celebrate a saint's feast day were celebrated in a similar manner, with a statue of the saint being carried throughout the town.[76] The Dance of the Inca, originally the Death of Atahualpa dance discussed above, as performed on December 24 of each year, came to be used as a way to defy the Spanish colonial regime.[77] As mentioned above, the dance began to use Atahualpa as a tragic figure rather than, as the Spanish wished to portray, as a justifiably killed emperor whose death led to the institution of a great colonial regime. This dance developed still further. In the dance, both the Inca and Spanish are represented by two lines of dancers—the Incas wore headdresses and gold and silver while the Spanish had pantaloons and tricornered hats. The Inca emperor and Pizarro were both at the head of each line. Rather than ending, as in previous versions of the dance, with the death of the emperor, Pizarro instead had to kneel down before the Inca emperor and acknowledge his authority.[78]

Further developments in Andean music occurred as a result of urbanization. For instance, one dance, the *cumbia andiana* (or chica), is a dance developed by Andean migrants to the cities. It is an urban-style dance and music tracing its origins from the 1960s and it synthesizes urban dance with Andean *wayno* and electrical instruments, such as guitars, bass, organ, and percussion.[79] The new art form soon became popular, and by "By 1985 . . . had become the most ubiquitous urban-popular musical form in Peru."[80] The dance is used in many contexts, such as weddings and first haircutting ceremonies.[81] One of the songs developed from the migratory influence is "We Are Students" or "Somos Estudiantes," which discusses the importance of education for promotion and success in life, especially with greater availability of education now.[82]

This dance, as well as some of the other Andean-influenced genres already discussed, are reflective of an interest in Andean culture in Peru, sometimes at the beckoning of the government. During the regime of General Juan Velasco from 1968 to 1975, the government became involved in the dissemination of Andean culture. Quechua became an official national language, and in terms of music, the government had radio stations play more Peruvian music and encouraged its performance throughout the country.[83]

A NOTE ON MODERN MUSIC DISSEMINATION AND TRADITION IN PERU

Panpipes are a major part of modern Peruvian music and identity. Panpipes are the Peruvian instrument and music form that people outside of Peru are exposed to. Panpipes found its way to becoming a representative national instrument and music in part because of its uniqueness and its smooth sound. The panpipes thus became a part of national folklore rather than remaining regional.[84] There are many different kinds of panpipes, and thus here only a selection will be briefly described. The *quena* or *kena* consists of a single piped flute. It has six holes on the top side and a thumb hole on the bottom side. The pipe itself is half-stopped and can come in a variety of sizes. In performance, it is frequently accompanied by a drum. There are also various panpipes that consist of multiple pipes bound together in a row, like *maizus*. These pipes are usually played in pairs. The leading pipe of the duo has a row of three stopped pipes, and the follower pipe has a row of two stopped pipes. Finally, perhaps the best-known panpipe is the *siku* or *zampona*, which consists of a double row of pipes. The top row is stopped and the bottom row (which has the same number of pipes) is unstopped.[85]

Inside Peru, panpipes have come to the fore as a part of the urban migration discussed above. As Peruvians migrated into the cities, in order to establish themselves and create their identity, migrants created regional associations. While these kinds of associations first made an appearance in cities like Lima in the 1920s and 1930s, their presence really became prominent in the 1970s and later. This increased growth can be demonstrated with regional associations in Lima—in 1957 there were about 200 regional associations in the city, which increased to 1,050 by 1970, and then up to 4,000 in 1980.[86] Size was not the only aspect of the regional associations that changed over time. When these associations first developed, they focused on sports, especially soccer, as their mode of expression and way to bring the community together. However, again after 1970, the focus increasingly became music performance instead.[87] While the exact type of song or techniques used by each regional association varies depending on the region it is associated with, primarily they perform *estudiantina music* (string ensemble consisting of guitars and mandolins), costumes of light dances (using a brass band), and traditional Andean wind instrument (panpipes) music.[88] Networks headed by umbrella organizations in turn link these regional associations, connecting the musical life throughout urban centers.[89]

There are public, sometimes government sponsored, musical performances these groups participate in and performances in more private or local events, such as parties, weddings, and first haircutting ceremonies.[90] The roof-raising festival is another such event—it focuses on the community and helping one another within it. Panpipes are used to accompany the event and the *achuqallu* dance.[91] In both the public and more private events, regional associations serve to bring together and celebrate the community.

In terms of public events, perhaps the most important is *Todos los Santos* (All Saints' Day). This is celebrated in different ways by different associations and different locations, but it emphasizes ancestors and other members of the community who have died but are now remembered. The celebration is a way to remember these people but also to comfort those still living who miss them.[92] The regional associations' most frequent performance opportunity is the *festival folklórico*, or folkloric parade, which take place throughout the year on Sundays. This is a public event, sometimes sponsored by the government, and is an opportunity for associations to compete with other associations and to support themselves financially through raising money.

Different regional associations gather on the Sunday afternoon, and an emcee organizes the event.[93] While there is music throughout, the main event is the competition between the different groups. The judges listen to each group for ten minutes and whichever group or organization hosts the event provides prizes to the winners.[94] This contest element was not always a part of the festival; it dates from the 1920s. It can perhaps first be traced to Lima in 1927, when President Augusto B. Leguía supported the *Fiesta de Amancaes*. President Leguía was a major proponent of the native Peruvian traditions, and as part of supporting the *Fiesta de Amancaes*, he helped to organize the first contest.[95] The fact that these festivals furthermore function as a social event should not be overlooked; nor that they are another way in which community is brought together and cemented.[96]

Though panpipes function both as a large part of Peruvian identity and music tradition, and as representation for Peru outside the country, the other musical forms discussed above should not be neglected simply because they are not always as present nor because some forms are only traceable in historical record. Peruvian musical life and tradition is diverse and its history is long and fruitful; it should continue to be taught with this in mind.

CONCLUSION

Peruvian music and music education has a long, rich history. Beginning from the Inca Roca, who taught royal children music as part of their education, music had an important role in Peruvian society. It functioned both as entertainment and as a way to preserve culture and history to be passed on to future generations. With the arrival of the Spanish invaders and the colonial regime they imposed, European styles of music, particularly its Christian elements, both influenced Peruvian music and were adapted to preexisting Peruvian music forms. Music education moved primarily into cathedrals, convents, and other religious centers, but this did not mean that the indigenous music tradition disappeared; there were still opportunities for continuing these traditions. Rather, European music styles, while they certainly could present a strong influence, were also adapted to local genres and techniques. Non-European influences, such as African music traditions, came to be incorporated into Peruvian music traditions as well, creating a diverse music culture. Overall, Peruvian music education's history is a complex one of a process of exposure to new music traditions and the way they come to be incorporated into Peru's own music culture.

NOTES

1. "Peru," *The CIA World Factbook*, last modified January 20, 2011, https://www.cia.gov/library/publications/the-world-factbook/geos/pe.html

2. Gary Tomlinson, *Singing of the New World* (New York: Cambridge University Press, 2007), 135.

3. Tomlinson, *Singing*, 162.

4. Robert M. Stevenson, "Music Instruction in Inca Land," *Journal of Research in Music Education* 8, no. 2 (Autumn, 1960): 110.

5. Tomlinson, *Singing*, 127–28.

6. Tomlinson, *Singing*, 129.

7. Tomlinson, *Singing*, 129.

8. Tomlinson, *Singing*, 134.

9. John Curl, "The Sacred Hymns of Pachacuti: Ancient Inca Poetry," *Bilingual Review* 26, no. 2/3 (May–December 2001–2002): 111.

10. Curl, "The Sacred Hymns," 112.

11. Fiona Wilson, "Indians and Mestizos: Identity and Urban Popular Culture in Andean Peru," *Journal of Southern African Studies* 26, no. 2 (June 2000): 240.

12. Curl, "The Sacred Hymns," 111.

13. Curl, "The Sacred Hymns," 114.

14. Curl, "The Sacred Hymns," 114.

15. Stevenson, "Music Instruction in Inca Land," 110–111.

16. Stevenson, "Music Instruction in Inca Land," 111.

17. Stevenson, "Music Instruction in Inca Land," 111.

18. Stevenson, "Music Instruction in Inca Land," 111.

19. Stevenson, "Music Instruction in Inca Land," 113.

20. Stevenson, "Music Instruction in Inca Land," 110.

21. Curl, "The Sacred Hymns," 112.

22. Raúl R. Romero, "Andean Peru," *Music in Latin American Culture: Regional Tradition*, ed. John M. Schecter (Schirmer Books, 1999), 383.

23. Tomlinson, *Singing*, 38.

24. Geoffrey Baker, *Imposing Harmony: Music and Society in Colonial Cuzco* (Durham, NC: Duke University Press, 2008), 71.

25. Stevenson, "Music Instruction in Inca Land," 112.

26. Bernardo Illari, "Cusco: Colonial Music in Wonderland," *Review: Literature and Arts of the Americas*, vol. 42, no. 2 (2009): 247.

27. Stevenson, "Music Instruction in Inca Land," 15.

28. Stevenson, "Music Instruction in Inca Land," 113.

29. Illari, "Cusco: Colonial Music in Wonderland," 247.

30. Baker, *Imposing Harmony*, 143.

31. Baker, *Imposing Harmony*, 55.

32. Baker, *Imposing Harmony*, 70–71.

33. Baker, *Imposing Harmony*, 177.

34. Baker, *Imposing Harmony*, 112–33.

35. Baker, *Imposing Harmony*, 116.

36. Baker, *Imposing Harmony*, 121.

37. Baker, *Imposing Harmony*, 121–22.

38. Baker, *Imposing Harmony*, 124.

39. Baker, *Imposing Harmony*, 126.

40. Susan E. Ramirez, "To Serve God and King: The Origins of Public Schools for Native Children in Eighteenth-Century Northern Peru," *Colonial Latin American Review* 17, no. 1 (June 2008): 73.

41. Ramirez, "To Serve God and King," 73.

42. Ramirez, "To Serve God and King," 73.

43. Ramirez, "To Serve God and King," 73.

44. Ramirez, "To Serve God and King," 74.

45. Ramirez, "To Serve God and King," 74.

46. Ramirez, "To Serve God and King," 74.

47. Ramirez, "To Serve God and King," 80.

48. Ramirez, "To Serve God and King," 81.

49. Illari, "Cusco: Colonial Music in Wonderland," 247.

50. Illari, "Cusco: Colonial Music in Wonderland," 248.

51. Illari, "Cusco: Colonial Music in Wonderland," 249.

52. Fiona Wilson, "Indians and Mestizos: Identity and Urban Popular Culture in Andean Peru," *Journal of Southern African Studies* 26, no. 2 (June 2000): 242.

53. Wilson, "Indians and Mestizos," 242–43.

54. Romero, "Andean Peru," 383.

55. Wilson, "Indians and Mestizos," 244.

56. Romero, "Andean Peru," 386.

57. Romero, "Andean Peru," 386.

58. Romero, "Andean Peru," 387.

59. Romero, "Andean Peru," 388–89.

60. Romero, "Andean Peru," 392.

61. Romero, "Andean Peru," 401.

62. Wilson, "Indians and Mestizos," 251.

63. Wilson, "Indians and Mestizos," 251.

64. Heidi Feldman, *Black Rhythms of Peru: Reviving African Musical Heritage in the Black Pacific* (Middletown, CT: Wesleyan University Press, 2006), 2.

65. Feldman, *Black Rhythms of Peru*, 2–3.

66. Heidi Feldman, "The International Soul of Black Peru," *Musical Cultures of Latin America: Global Effects, Past and Present: Proceedings of an International Conference University of California, Los Angeles, May 28–30, 1999*, ed. Steven Loza (The Regents of the University of California, 2003), 156.

67. Javier F. León, "The 'Danza de las Cañas': Music, Theatre and Afroperuvian Modernity," *Ethnomusicology Forum* 16, no. 1 (June 2007): 128.

68. León, "The 'Danza de las Cañas.'"

69. León, "The 'Danza de las Cañas,'" 129.

70. León, "The 'Danza de las Cañas,'" 130.

71. Feldman, "The International Soul of Black Peru," 156.

72. León, "The 'Danza de las Cañas,'" 131.

73. Javier F. León, "Roots, Tradition, and the Mass Media: The Future of *Criollo* Popular Music," *Musical Cultures of Latin America: Global Effects, Past and Present: Proceedings of an International Conference University of California, Los Angeles, May 28–30, 1999*, ed. Steven Loza (The Regents of the University of California, 2003), 135.

74. León, "Roots, Tradition, and the Mass Media," 164.

75. León, "Roots, Tradition, and the Mass Media," 166.

76. Wilson, "Indians and Mestizos," 247.

77. Wilson, "Indians and Mestizos," 248.

78. Wilson, "Indians and Mestizos," 248–49.

79. Thomas Turino, "Somos el Peru: 'Cumbia Andina' and the Children of Andean Migrants in Lima," *Studies in Latin American Popular Culture* 9 (1990): 15.

80. Turino, "Somos el Peru."

81. Turino, "Somos el Peru."

82. Turino, "Somos el Peru," 23.
83. Turino, "Somos el Peru," 16.
84. Thomas Turino, *Moving Away from Silence: Music of the Peruvian Altiplano and the Experience of Urban Migration* (Chicago, IL: University of Chicago Press, 1993), 218–19.
85. Max Peter Baumann, "Music and World View of Indian Societies in the Bolivian Andes," *Music in Latin America and the Caribbean: An Encyclopedic History*, ed. Malena Kuss (Austin: University of Texas Press, 2004), 118–19.
86. Baumann, "Music and World View of Indian Societies in the Bolivian Andes," 181.
87. Baumann, "Music and World View of Indian Societies in the Bolivian Andes," 184.
88. Turino, *Moving Away*, 184–85.
89. Turino, *Moving Away*, 187.
90. Turino, *Moving Away*, 232.
91. Turino, *Moving Away*, 193.
92. Turino, *Moving Away*, 233.
93. Turino, *Moving Away*, 220–21.
94. Turino, *Moving Away*, 222.
95. Turino, *Moving Away*, 224.
96. Turino, *Moving Away*, 223.

REFERENCES

Baker, Geoffrey. *Imposing Harmony: Music and Society in Colonial Cuzco*. Durham, NC: Duke University Press, 2008.
Baumann, Max Peter. "Music and World View of Indian Societies in the Bolivian Andes." *Music in Latin America and the Caribbean: An Encyclopedic History*. Edited by Malena Kuss. Austin: University of Texas Press, 2004, 101–22.
Curl, John. "The Sacred Hymns of Pachacuti: Ancient Inca Poetry." *Bilingual Review* 26, no. 2/3 (May–December 2001/2002): 109–47.
Feldman, Heidi. *Black Rhythms of Peru: Reviving African Musical Heritage in the Black Pacific*. Middletown, CT: Wesleyan University Press, 2006.
Feldman, Heidi Feldman. "The International Soul of Black Peru." *Musical Cultures of Latin America: Global Effects, Past and Present: Proceedings of an International Conference University of California, Los Angeles, May 28–30, 1999*. Edited by Steven Loza. California: The Regents of the University of California, 2003.
Illari, Bernardo. "Cusco: Colonial Music in Wonderland." *Review: Literature and Arts of the Americas*. vol. 42, no. 2 (2009): 246–50.
León, Javier F. "The 'Danza de las Cañas': Music, Theatre and Afroperuvian Modernity." *Ethnomusicology Forum* 16, no. 1 (June 2007): 127–55.
León, Javier F. "Roots, Tradition, and the Mass Media: The Future of *Criollo* Popular Music." *Musical Cultures of Latin America: Global Effects, Past and Present: Proceedings of an International Conference University of California, Los Angeles, May 28–30, 1999*. Edited by Steven Loza. California: The Regents of the University of California, 2003.
"Peru," *The CIA World Factbook*, last modified January 20, 2011, https://www.cia.gov/library/publications/the-world-factbook/geos/pe.html
Ramirez, Susan E. "To Serve God and King: The Origins of Public Schools for Native Children in Eighteenth-Century Northern Peru." *Colonial Latin American Review* 17, no. 1 (June 2008): 73–99.
Romero, Raúl R. "Andean Peru." *Music in Latin American Culture: Regional Tradition*. Edited by John M. Schecter. Schirmer Books, 1999.
Stevenson, Robert M. "Music Instruction in Inca Land." *Journal of Research in Music Education* 8, no. 2 (Autumn, 1960): 110–23.
Tomlinson, Gary. *Singing of the New World*. New York: Cambridge University Press, 2007.
Turino, Thomas. *Moving Away from Silence: Music of the Peruvian Altiplano and the Experience of Urban Migration*. Chicago, IL: University of Chicago Press, 1993.
Turino, Thomas. "Somos el Peru: 'Cumbia Andina' and the Children of Andean Migrants in Lima." *Studies in Latin American Popular Culture* 9 (1990): 15–38.
Wilson, Fiona. "Indians and Mestizos: Identity and Urban Popular Culture in Andean Peru." *Journal of Southern African Studies* 26, no. 2 (June 2000): 239–53.

Chapter Eighteen

Uruguay

Marita Fornaro Bordolli[1]

INTRODUCTION

The Eastern Republic of Uruguay—historically called the Eastern Strip—is located at the delta of the River Plate and the Atlantic Ocean, in the south of the continent, and stretching through an area of 176,215 km[2]. It has 3,240,000 people,[2] whereof 91.8 percent live in urban areas. It is a largely old population. Uruguayan capital's macrocephaly is very remarkable: as many as 1,400,000 people live there. Cultural composition is largely European—Spanish and Italian—with a remarkable African Uruguayan presence, although very low demographically speaking, and with very low aboriginal cultural participation.

Uruguay's political organization is a presidential republic, with nineteen departments as political-administrative units. Traditionally, Uruguay was a cattle ranching country. Uruguay's current economy is diversified, although with a strong farming base. In the late nineteenth century and early twentieth century, Uruguay attained a remarkable welfare status, which was impaired in the second half of that century. Consequently, the country was an important immigrant receiver during the eighteenth century and during the first half of the twentieth century. However, financial and political circumstances (military dictatorship between 1973 and 1985) spurred emigration in the last three decades of the twentieth century. In the last five years, this trend has been reversed, although the number of Uruguayans living abroad is still very large (approximately six hundred thousand Uruguayans, which is a relevant figure for a country of small population and a minimum population growth).

PRE-HISPANIC PERIOD

Aboriginal cultures at the Eastern Strip of the Uruguay River (a territory larger than the current republic, since it included part of the current Brazilian Rio Grande do Sul state) have been studied since prehistory, but from ethnohistory only since the second half of the twentieth century. Currently, there is exact information for specific areas of the country, such as the Littoral of the Uruguay River, one of the first areas studied for Lithic cultures and pottery cultures (Taddei, 1964, a pioneer work, among many others thereof; Díaz, 1975, 1977) and the Low Lands at the East (López Mazz, 2001, among others).

The hunting and fishing cultures—an incipient agriculture is revealed in findings in some deposits—and pottery ones have not been linked to cultures whose existence explorers, chroniclers, and priests have bared witness of. *Guaraní* culture is a different case, being clearly identifiable in the most recent strata from archaeological deposits in the Littoral of the Uruguay River, and on the River Plate coastline, and for which much documented information is available, especially for the Colony Period, which will be discussed later.

Archaeological excavations have not yielded any music-related material. According to ethnohistorical proofs, aboriginal cultures in the region did not use any musical instruments because the materials thereof could not survive the climate.

Confusion still reigns about the aboriginal cultures that used to live in the territory during the Conquests. Terms given by chroniclers are the core of this problem, adding the nomad lifestyle most of these groups had, and, in some cases, their probable fusion. A summary of the ethnohistorical testimonies can be consulted in Cavellini (1987).

The *Charrúa* ethnic group is the most renowned, and probably other groups are labeled as such too. Some authors have proposed the existence of a "*Charrúa* macro ethnic group." Renzo Pi Hugarte (2007) identifies, since the Conquests, "three totally different ethnicity groups: (a) *Charrúas*: made up by the *Charrúas* them-selves, the *Minuane*, the *Bohanes*, and the *Yaros*; (b) *Chanás*: called "Chaná-Timbú" by Eduardo Acosta y Lara (1955), which, by the time of the Conquests, was adopting farming, probably out of Guaraní influence; and (c) *Guaraníes*, in the region since the pre-Hispanic time, as said before, who were the inhabitants after the Jesuit Missions we will talk about during the Colony, and then present in Uruguayan territory after the missionary exodus. *Guaraníes* are involved in the miscegenation (*mestizaje*) where people of the Uruguayan countryside came from. The weight of miscegenation by the other cultures is impossible to determine.

This type of contact between aboriginal cultures and settlers, and then with Creoles, was of a varied type, from life in the so-called reductions (accepted by *Chaná*) and the *Guaraníes'* insertion into Uruguay's rural life, to the troubled contact with *Charrúas*, who were deemed a threat, and therefore exterminated by the first independent government after their participation in the freedom armies, having been previously deemed the rightful landowners by José Artigas, a hero of Uruguay's independence.

Ayestarán (1953) has collected ethnohistorical references related to aboriginal music: "grandes choros e cantigas muito tristes" ["sad chorus and songs"] (Pedro Lopes de Sousa, in 1535), "trumpets, horns, and drums" (Martín del Barco Centenera, in 1573), blowing trumpets as a signal instrument, accompanied by chants and women's war cries (Benito Silva, *Charrúas'* prisoner in 1825), a musical arch created in Paris by one of the aborigines taken to France for his exhibition in a circus and then studied by French scholars, Paul Rivet among them, in 1833.

During the last three decades, movements by aboriginal culture descendants demanding their rights have emerged and grown very strong, especially among *Charrúas*, who are considered the most representative ones, even in the national belief, where they have acquired a symbolic capital related to courage and libertarian attitudes. As for the *Guaraníes* present since prehistory, they lost their cultural identity and any visibility when integrating to a rural population. However, recent census information and genetic researches show data that question that said characterization of Uruguay as "the most Latin American European-like country." According to Mónica Sans, genetic analyses show that almost one-third of Uruguay's current population has an aboriginal ancestor on the mother's side (2009, 167). This is not to be confused with cultural presence.

COLONIAL PERIOD

During the colonial period, education, of a religious character, was in charge of the Jesuit, Franciscan, and Dominican orders, which arrived to the Eastern Strip of the Uruguay River by the first third of the seventeenth century. Schools in Montevideo were under their command. Jesuit missions in the Eastern Strip made up what were called "Misiones del Paraguay" (Paraguay Missions), outside the current Republic's territory. The six Jesuit missions in the then colonial territory were San Juan Bautista, Santo Angel, San Francisco de Borja, San Nicolas, San Luis Gonzaga, and San Miguel. The missioner exodus to the Eastern Strip has been studied, among others, by Padron Favre (2009). Information on musical life in these places is abundant.

Documentation has been analyzed by Lauro Ayestarán (1953, 9–10). Documents by explorers and priests allude to music performance, dances, composition, luthier, and, as in Jesuit music-related training activities in other South American regions, to the quality and willingness of aborigines in these activities. As for the current territory, a region's very ancient reference speaks of the efforts by Governor Francisco de Céspedes toward the foundation of *Charrúas* and *Chanáes* settlements in 1624. His efforts were supported by Franciscan Fray Juan de Vergara, who traveled to the Eastern Strip and founded two missions in the area of Soriano: San Francisco de Olivares, with *Charrúas* aborigines, and San Antonio de los Chaneces. He looked forward to evangelizing aborigines in the area, and even held sung masses,[3] with no results whatsoever, though. Although of a later date, there are references on the Jesuits' activities in the region. Documentation is available on the musical life in Santo Domingo de Soriano, such as for the celebration of the accession of Ferdinand VII to the Spanish throne. The celebration's description in the *Libro Copiador de Oficios del Cabildo de Soriano*[4] includes "aborigines' flutes and tabors" that participated in the parades (Ayestarán, 1953, 16).

During this period, the integration of African cultures begins under slavery by the 1750s. Luis Ferreira (1997, 29 and 32) analyzes the different African origins (Mozambique, Congo, Angola, Mina, Guinea, and others inferior in number, as per the 1812 census). As mentioned by Gustavo Goldman (2010, 163), participation of Africans and African descendants in colonial life was of compulsory traits—the work, and the Christian doctrine—as well as of volunteer participation, such as guilds, *sala de naciones*, clubs, and African associations, where a deep syncretism of several African cultures with European elements took place.

In Montevideo, colonial societies continued during the nineteenth and twentieth century in expressions related especially to these descendants' community life, with a strong presence in coastal towns near the ancient colonial city, Sur and Palermo. Currently, however, they have presence in different areas of the Uruguayan capital, and also in Uruguay's countryside. African-Uruguayan presence is low in demographic weight (10.2 percent as per data by the Instituto Nacional de Estadistica by the years 2006 and 2007) but culturally intense, and very musical.

From these colonial groups emerge manifestations that are later strongly related to the appearance of the Carnival, the most important being drum music, called *candombe*. The *candombe*'s polyrhythm is played on three instruments struck mainly on their membrane, but also on their wooden body, which are *chico*, *repique*, and *piano*. These instruments combined, and put in equal numbers, make up the so-called *cuerda de tambores*, which are the protagonists of the *llamadas*, street performances that have an institutionalized spot in Uruguay's Carnival. A deep analysis of these manifestations can be retrieved from Ferreira (1997, 2007). Goldman (2008) has investigated the weight of the African element in the origins of tango.

Along these African-Uruguayan manifestations, the European traditional music must be mentioned, whose origins go as far as the colonial period, and whose intense development starts in the nineteenth century. Ayestarán (1967, 1968) and Fornaro (1994, 1996 with Olarte, 1999), among others, have investigated the lyrical and choreographic expressions, where the deep Spanish root is evinced. In the north of the country, an area with a high Portuguese-Brazilian influence shapes up. The Italian immigration, very important in the second half of the nineteenth century and in the early twentieth century, had a lower influence, especially noticeable in tango.

NINETEENTH CENTURY

Cultural Activity

During the colonial period, music education was in charge of foreign teachers and their American students. Lauro Ayestarán has made efforts to identify a series of teachers of predominant Italian and French origins (1953, 745).

From the second half of the nineteenth century, philharmonic societies had a relevant role. Professionals and amateurs would create music there, especially chamber music and opera arias. While their function is not music education but interpretation, philharmonic societies are deemed to be the germinal location for the first systematic music education private institutions. The most remarkable one was the one organized and directed by Spanish musician Antonio Saenz, conductor of the Casa de Comedias orchestra. He performed between 1831 and 1835 in saloons in Montevideo, in theaters, and even during the celebrations of the third anniversary of the *Jura de la Constitución* (1833), when a *Misa Solemne* (High Mass) written by Saenz himself for this occasion was premiered (Ayestarán, 1953, 446).

Also in the 1830s two events occurred that would be pivotal to the evolution of the musical life in the newly declared republic: in 1837, *La Abeja del Plata* magazine publishes the first scores in the country (Ayestarán, 1953, 756); the "La Guirnalda Musical dedicada a las Bellas Americanas" collection by composer and professor Antonio Saenz is also published, as well as the edition of the first Montevideo music magazine, the *Ramillete Musical de las Damas Orientales* (Ayestarán, 1953). These first scores show the importance of piano in musical life, as well as the role of women as performers domestically and in family saloons. The music sheet industry will enter its golden age during the 1920s and 1930s through the edition of popular music (Fornaro and Sztern, 1997), and then will fade into its current near nonexistent status.

In the mid-nineteenth century, the first projects toward an official education shape up. In 1857, the newspaper *El Comercio del Plata* is published. A proposal by French maestro Pablo Faget does not flourish, but does attract enough students to lay the basis for the *La Lira* Philharmonic Society in 1866, which would be the origin of the first conservatory in the country, created in 1875. State funded, *La Lira* had composer León Ribeiro (1854–1931) as its most important director, and he would be kept in office until the early twentieth century. Programs of the 1920s reveal specifications regarding the musical theory and harmony methods used, and the mandatory singing, piano, organ, harmonium, violin, viola, violoncello, double bass, harp, guitar, mandoline, flute, oboe, clarinet and similar, bassoon, valve, horn, trombone, ophicleide, and euphonium repertoires. This offer reflects the main areas of the musical life during that time: family saloons, orchestras, churches, and bands.

In 1879, the *Escuela Nacional de Artes y Oficios* is created, including a music section, which will operate as a conservatory for the following two decades. Currently, this institution, integrated to the technician-professional education, keeps running music-related activities, since it is the sole official location where luthier is taught.

By the late nineteenth century, two outstanding figures in Uruguay's music, which are an example of the Italian influence in this activity, found conservatories. In 1890, Luis Sambucetti creates the *Instituto Verdi*, and in 1895, Camilo Giucci founds the *Liceo musical Franz Liszt*.

The Sambucetti family is a representative sample of the importance of Italian immigration in Uruguay's culture and of the convergence of the taste for romantic Italian music and its teaching by Italian teachers with the formation of French conservatories. His constant dedication to music education, the founding of a national orchestra and camera groups, and symphonic musical audience formation were important feats by Luis Sambucetti Jr. (the father, born in Liguria, was his first music teacher), a composer awarded in 1906 for his mystical poem *San Francisco de Asís*, and a performer of a renowned European career. At the *Instituto Verdi*, his brother Juan José and Luis's wife, Maria Verninck, a pianist educated at the Paris Music National Conservatory, ranked also among the teachers. The Institute's headquarters, currently *Sala Verdi* or Verdi Hall (acquired by Montevideo's municipal authorities), was also a tribute to the composer, who expressly authorized the use of his name thereon. In the hall, great oleo paintings would allude to the composer's biography as an extraordinary example regarding the reception of his work in Uruguay.

Activities by the *Instituto Verdi* and *La Lira Conservatory* have been described in two very important late-eighteenth-century music magazines: *Montevideo Musical*, Sambucetti directed, and *La Gaceta Musical*, with León Ribeiro among the editors. News on exams, incidents, and a hidden—and not so much at times—clash between institutions can give some idea on the reception this musical life had among Montevideo's audience.

A third institute is created in the late nineteenth century: the *Liceo Musical Franz Liszt* by the initiative of another Italian, Camilo Giucci, who was a student of Liszt himself. Giucci also founds the Santa Cecilia (1896), which was religious music oriented. This is another case of a musician family fully oriented toward education and the diffusion of academic music (his wife, Luisa Gallo, a pianist; and his sons, among them Carlos, a great composer).

Completing this period of founding activity, in 1898, oboe player Oseas Falleri founds a "School of Music" offering singing, piano, violin, and oboe lessons. Other disciplines are added as years pass, forming the *Instituto Musical Falleri*, directed by pianist Agar, the founder's daughter. From that moment on, the presence of this conservatory stretches throughout Uruguay's countryside, with a continuously operating work. The most outstanding student, pianist Hugo Balzo (1912–1982), after studying in Paris with Robert Casadesus, Noel Galon, Alfredo Casella, and Maurice Ravel, swears in as a director in 1945. From that year up to 2004, the Conservatory will be called *Falleri-Balzo*. From 2004 to present, it is called *Conservatorio Hugo Balzo*. It is the oldest continuously operating conservatory, still offering instrument, musical theory, and, with an unusual approach to Uruguay's private conservatories, the history of music.

As observed, the late eighteenth century was the second most significant moment in the history of Uruguay's music education with the creation of core education institutions in the 1870s and the 1890s. The training of directors and teachers, the intense diffusion activities, and community outreach are evidence of an enthusiasm and a confidence in arts development in a country whose economy was gaining a foothold and was already looking forward to a place in modernity. Within this job, orchestral entrepreneurship has a function of the utmost importance. The *Instituto Verdi* had a student orchestra and choir. The orchestra kicked off in 1893, directed by Luis and Juan José Sanbucetti. In addition, *La Lira* and the *Escuela Nacional de Artes y Oficios* had student orchestras. Many symphonic works from the baroque, classical, and romantic repertoire were first heard in the country through these activities (Salgado, 1980, 40).

Private conservatories kept growing in number, and throughout the country. For example, two from the different times and approaches are the *Conservatorio Musical Wilhelm Kolischer,* founded by musician Kolischer himself in 1916, and the *Nucleo de Educacion Musical* (NEMUS), where education will include popular music. Daniel Viglietti is among the founders.

Public Education

Origins of public and secular education were through José Artigas (a hero of the *1811 Revolucion Libertadora*), who founded in 1815 the first schools with those characteristics. During the other half of the century, religious and public schools will coexist. José Pedro Varela developed the great national education project, explained in his two core works, *La Educacion del Pueblo* (1874) and *La Legislación Escolar* (1877). Varela's theory places education as a public, political, and civic matter, as well as a State responsibility, through two main concerns: popular education and primary school, although he will deal with education from preschool to university. In the primary school's program, Vocal Music is a subject. In 1917, the Varelian ideal of a public and secular school concretes when that year's constitution sets forth the State-Catholic Church separation (Varela et al., 2007).

Education in Uruguay has historically followed European models, with a strong French influence in the eighteenth century and in early twentieth-century society.

Currently, the country has one of the lowest illiteracy rates in Latin America with 1.8 percent, and in a constant diminution in the long term. This characteristic and the very little rural population define a particular context for education if compared with other Latin American countries.

Uruguay's public education is free, secular, and, currently, compulsory for the first six years of elementary school. Currently, the basic middle school program is three years, offered by middle schools and technical schools with the same curriculum. The second middle school program is made up of three years, one being a transition into high school. This, following European tradition, offers two options: Diversified High School and Technical High School. Private education is organized following the same core curriculum.

TWENTIETH CENTURY

Studies on Music Education

There is barely any analytical bibliography on music education in Uruguay. Many documents are available, but no systematic research on the area is to be found. Coriún Aharonián, a composer, teacher, and journalist, has produced materials such as his book *Educación, Arte, Música* (2004a), a compilation of news articles and talks in congresses and theoretical reflections on music education and the role of popular music therein. They are, mostly, essays. He has also edited a *Cancionero Latinoamericano* of an international scope, produced by *Juventudes Musicales (Musical Youth)*, and is especially teacher oriented. Fornaro has drawn a historical panorama of musicology studies and research (2009e) and has analyzed some aspects of the studies on popular music (2011), but there are no systematic works on music education in elementary and middle schools, and, as can be seen, very little on high school education.

This analysis is, therefore, the first overview on music education in Uruguay, including both public and private education affairs.

PUBLIC MUSIC EDUCATION

Music in Early Education and Primary School

Music is included in the three-year program of early childhood education and the six-year program of elementary education.[5] The preschool program explores the basics of sounds, musical instruments, body postures, and the use of children's songs, distinguishing between three-, four-, and five-year-old children. Programs of the six elementary school years are extremely unstructured and generalist, with unclear yearly thematic focus[6] and unfocused themes throughout the six years. Training of teachers in music is minimal. There are no specific subjects on music, and those referred to as Arts Studies are of a theoretical approach, with no training and hard information on such an extensive and diverse topic included in the first six years of the elementary school programs, ranging from the basic elements of sound to aboriginal music and Western music history.

On the other hand, there are the elementary Education Schools of Music. There are eighteen of them in the country, and they are free to kids attending public school. Having passed the second year of common school and attending a public school are requirements for enrollment. Programs are broken down in four years, corresponding to the last four years of the school cycle. The model, although traditional in subjects, has a more innovative approach regarding in-class working methodology. Curricula include instrument, musical language, music appreciation, singing, rhythm studies, and folkloric dances. Piano, guitar, and recorder are the instruments taught. Trumpet is also included in Montevideo's programs.

Generally speaking, schools of music give a basic music education, enriching children who can have access to it. However, schools have not been included so far in projects and development lines in elementary school programs in Uruguay, working as "isles" within the system. This is evident, for example, in the discontinuity between general music education and the specific music education that these institutions offer, and in the trend of the public education system toward the extension of full-time schools, as children attending full-time schools cannot access the school of music. Lack of a mandatory teacher education and technical education for teachers and supervisors are also a problem. Free music programs are not stipulated in the public education system after schooling. This policy has created a vacuum, which the *Universidad de la República* is seeking to reduce through implementing a music preuniversity program, as explained later.

Music in Junior High School and Senior High School

The subject of Sound Education is included in the first two years of the Junior High School program.[7] The program in the freshman year is focused on sound basics; the sophomore year gets deeper in the subject and also works on the sound's production, diffusion, and storage systems, and even proposes the approach to composition through informatics. Music is focused on as a workshop in junior year. Deepening in the concept of "sound" and contextualizing thereof in contemporary life are the objectives of these programs. However, technical and musical requirements have been reduced if compared to previous curricula, especially in music history.

In the Senior High School program, music is only included in the subject Arts and Expression, although no propaedeutic nature for university education has been given to it. According to the 2006 program, this subject essentially aims to, on the one hand, favor musical sensibility, the aesthetic pleasure both musical audition and diffusion produce, and expression through music interpretation and creation; on the other hand, deepening knowledge in music from the artistic, communicative, scientific, technical, and social point of view. The curriculum sets a scenario that faces, practically, low professional training by teachers. According to the 2007 Teachers' Census,[8] in 1995 only 19.3 percent of high school music teachers had a professional teaching diploma. The tendency is negative, as 17.9 percent had the diploma in 2007. Officials at the Teachers' Training Council (TTC), a body in charge of this area in higher education, have announced that by early 2011, scholarships exist for education students in deficient courses, including music. The TTC's Improvement and University Education Institute (IPES) has worked between 2009 and 2010 on the creation of the first postgraduate program in Uruguay in Music Didactics.[9] The curriculum is under consideration by the Postgraduate Studies at the *Universidad de la República*, an official institution that gives the said degree as per current legislation (1958).

Music in Higher Education

Music in current Uruguay's Higher Education has two great core areas: the training of musicians, directors, composers, and musicologists in charge of the *Universidad de la República's Escuela Universitaria de Música* (EUM);[10] teachers' training takes place on-site at the *Instituto de Profesores "Artigas"* (IPA) in Montevideo; and at the Teachers' Training Institutes in the countryside, both on site and at semidistance.

The *Escuela Universitaria de Música* is the result of the unification of two institutions that emerged in mid-twentieth century: the National Music Conservatory and the Humanities and the Science Faculty's Musicology Institute. These institutions will be briefly described.

Two very different personalities mark the beginnings of musicology activities in Uruguay: Francisco (Franz) Curt Lang, of a broad Latin American scope, and Lauro Ayestarán, focused on research on Uruguay's music.

Franz Kurt Lange (1903–1997) was born in Germany and immigrated to South America twenty years later. Later, he would settle down in Montevideo. With an architecture and a musical background, he will be one of the founders of the field in Uruguay from the Higher Education Institute; the theorist of the composers' and researchers' movement called *Americanismo Musical*, and the creator of the *Boletín Latinoamericano de Música*, which was one of the main products of this movement, the promoter of the National Record Collection at the *Servicio Oficial de Difusión Radio Eléctrica* (SODRE, today the *Servicio Oficial de Difusión, Radiotelevisión y Espectáculo*), and the programs of CX6, the first radio station of this institution (Fornaro, 2009b).

Lauro Ayestarán (1913–1966) makes his way through music activity as a critic, and then dedicates himself to research, teaching, and management in the different teaching branches. His research work makes him the most important musicologist during the first half of the twentieth century in Uruguay (Fornaro, 2009e).

The Humanities and Sciences Faculty was founded in 1945 as a continuation to the Higher Education Institute's Musicological Research Section, under the *Universidad de la República*. Since its creation, it held music courses by Lauro Ayestarán. The Musicology Program was created there in 1951, being one of the earliest ones in Latin America, and then the Musicology Department in 1966. This department is named an institute in 1970. It is organized in three departments: Music Studies, in charge of Héctor Tosar, the most important Uruguayan composer of the second half of the twentieth century; the Music Historical Studies, in charge of the outstanding teacher and pianist Hugo Balzo; and the Ethnomusical Studies, in charge of researcher and composer Alberto Soriano.

Additionally, the National Music Conservatory is created in 1953 under what was then called the Ministry of Public Education and Social Care Affairs. Since 1954, courses are targeted toward the education of composers, instrumentalists, and music theory teachers. In 1957, the *Universidad de la República* (UdelaR) assumes its budget, one year ahead of what was stipulated by the 1958 UdelaR's Organic Law, which, in its Second Article, when addressing the "University's Scopes," gives great importance to culture and arts by establishing that "the University will be in charge of higher public education in all the areas of culture, arts education, as well the scientific professions and any exercise of other functions set forth by the law." Additionally, it is also its duty through all of its bodies with their relevant duties to promote, disseminate, and defend culture; to boost and protect scientific research and artistic activitie; to help with the study of the problems of general interest, aiming to their public understanding; and to defend moral values and the principles of justice, liberty, welfare, human rights, and the democratic and republican ways of the government.

During the 1970s, the fates of two music higher education institutions begin to intertwine, in some cases in a very convulsive way. In 1974, during the civil-military dictatorship in the country between 1972 and 1985, the conservatory was integrated with the Musicology Institution into what is called the University Music Conservatory. This integration, much criticized and disagreed with, remains in the return to democracy, and it is, since 1985, the *Escuela Universitaria de Música* (EUM).

The Musicology Institute/Department has educated all the generations of degrees in musicology in Uruguay. For years, its integration into the EUM was a waste of hierarchy and of resources, affecting the level of teaching and the production of critical thinking. This situation has been considerably reversed since 2003 by reorganizing it again into a department that is currently and actively involved in the education of all students in the institution, and which produces most of the research in Uruguay.

The current curricula, approved in 2004–2005, divides programs at the UEM into two major tracks of four years each: the Program in Music, with majors in Musicology, Composition, Orchestral Conducting, and Choral Conducting; and the Interpretation Program, where interpreters are educated with a focus on the academic repertoire. [11]

The main issues of higher education in music are the great lagging and the low number of graduated students. Labor insertion of graduated students is unequal, with better opportunities for performers. The nearly null insertion of musicologists has undergone a remarkable change in the last five years, especially through joint projects of the EUM with public and private institutions.

Since 1998, the EUM also has a unique preuniversity offer at the *Universidad de la República*, the Introduction Cycle to Music, which can be enrolled in upon completion of three years of high school, meaning that individuals will be fifteen or sixteen years of age as a minimum. This cycle's goal is to democratize music education by lowering the age for free access to a more comprehensive than at private conservatories, with courses of Sound Workshop, Scheduled Auditions, Body Sensitization, as well as instrument lessons and musicianship.

Also remarkable is the formation of teachers that the EUM is developing at the northern campus of the *Universidad de la República*. There, four-year-long technical degrees are offered, with majors in piano, guitar, choral direction, and singing. Professionals graduated from this program have a successful rate of employment in a labor market in need of teachers with higher education.

As for the *Instituto de Profesores "Artigas"* (IPA), it is the most important official office for middle school music teachers' training, complemented by the countryside's Teacher's Training Institutions. They are subordinated to the Teachers' Training and Improvement Office, as well as to the Public School Central Administration (ANEP)'s Central Directive Council (CODICEN). The IPA was created in 1949. It started operating two years later, chronologically coinciding with the bachelor in musicology degree and the National Conservatory.

The "Music Education" program tackles specific training, teachers' training (general and specific), and teachers' practice. [12] It includes courses on technical and musical training, history of music, voice education, and choir organization and direction, with emphasis on work training in the workshop modality.

The IPA was, previous to the 1970s, a center of quality education that brought outstanding teachers together, and that had students who would eventually become personalities in the cultural and scientific areas in the country. The changes in curriculum—including the program reduction—set forth during the dictatorship period wreaked havoc on the curriculum's level in a definite manner, a process still on reversion, within the project of the creation of a University Education Institute (IUDE), which is still under discussion by relevant education bodies.

Major shortcomings are evinced in the breakdown we just mentioned for higher education in music in Uruguay. As mentioned above, the music degree has the current lowest faculty ratio at secondary education. On the other hand, alumni from the University School of Music, with a deeper specific background, work as teachers at different education levels, but without the pedagogical or didactic training. An urgent review of the system is required. It is necessary therefore to strengthen ties, coordinate approaches and programs, as well as to draw closer the institutional cultures of the many bodies in charge of music education.

OTHER PUBLIC SPHERES

As an initiative by some municipal governments, called departments in Uruguay, there are conservatories or schools of music with a varied offer and level. Municipal Intendant's Municipal School of Music in Montevideo is the richest in this regard, with sixteen instrumental options, including the *bandoneón*. [13] Municipality-level conservatories operate in different regions in the country: in departments such as Salto, in the northwest;

in the littoral of the Uruguay River, in Tacuarembó, in the north center; Canelones in the South; and others. Music teaching in these institutions has no relation either in its structure or in its programs with the national system.

A National Lyrical Art School operates within the Ministry for Education and Cultural Affairs, connected with the tradition of the SODRE's defunct School of Supporting Actors.

NEW TRENDS: FOLK MUSIC AND CONTEMPORARY MUSIC

Education quality in current private institutions is extremely varied, as well as the offer of the instruments studied. Kids' and teens' specific offers are very important.

In the late twentieth century, some proposals of popular music–centered education have emerged, where the individual offer is very broad and includes many renowned professional performers and academic composers (at times, boundaries are very blurred, though). Here, there are often discrepancies between the teacher's artistic quality and pedagogical and didactic training occur.

On the private institutional level, the *Taller Uruguayo de Musica Popular* (TUMP) is very important. It is defined as "a non-profit cultural institution whose core goal is the development and research of a pedagogy based on Uruguayan popular music with a multicultural approach that includes therein all the knowledge of worldwide music." Created in 1983, the TUMP has developed alternative methodologies out of the mechanisms from folk music. Courses for different ages are offered with a variety of instruments, as well as workshops on specific, theoretical, and practical areas. An intense activity in community is conducted, funded by diverse state-level institutions such as the Montevideo's Municipal Intendant and the Youth National Institution. "Murga Joven"—the most popular and widespread one, based on the Spanish-Uruguayan street band, an important expression in music and folk theater—and the "Taller de Canto Colectivo" have been among these pioneer experiences in Uruguay, and in some cases on a massive scope. Editions are also important, especially the songbooks, where transcriptions of different Uruguay popular music expressions are included.

Attention must be paid to Uruguay's major insertion into an international experience that gathered teachers and students from different countries in the Americas and Europe: the *Cursos Latinoamericanos de Musica Contemporanea* (CLMC) The first, second, third, fourth, and fourteenth CLMC's sessions were held in Uruguay, with Uruguayan teachers and composers such as Héctor Tosar, Coriún Aharonián, and Miguel Marozzi; Graciela Paraskevaídis and Conrado Sílva were also part of the organizing team between 1971 and 1989.

OTHER AREAS WITH EDUCATIVE FUNCTIONS

Outside the education system, many state and private bodies help in the citizens' music education. A brief panorama will be hereinafter set out.

The *Servicio Oficial de Difusión, Radiotelevisión y Espectáculos* (SODRE) is the body attached to the Ministry of Education and Cultural Affairs in charge of music and performing arts at a national level. Its state bodies achieved high quality between the 1930s and the 1970s, with a frequent presence of foreign artists (see SODRE, 1963; Fornaro, 2009a). The countryside was included among its activities. This service underwent a strong fading process in which one of the important factors, was the burning of its emblematic building in 1971. While its operations continued in other halls, its new headquarters opened in December 2009: the "Adela Reta" National Auditorium. The Nelly Goitiño National Auditorium also operates in Montevideo. The OSSODRE and its choir, alongside the dance troupe, are among the SODRE's state bodies.

Official radio has been an important educative factor, especially regarding classical music. Actually, SODRE was born, as mentioned above, as the *Servicio Oficial de Difusión Radio Eléctrica*. When at the moment the country was celebrating its independence century, authorities looked forward to bolstering its insertion into modernity through the creation of new cultural bodies. Within this context, the *Servicio de Radiodifusión* was conceived to build up audiences and educate and disseminate music and word. The speech made when passing the 1929 bill for the creation of the first body's radio, CX6, stated that it conceives it "as an element that modern science has made available to bringing art and music, not only to urban centers incapable of bringing it by themselves, but to the most far away places in the country, being the only mean to bring to them the most beautiful of all the civilization expressions."

A National Record Collection is to be created alongside the foundation of the first SODRE's radio. Francisco Curt Lange is a key figure in this process. Its program combines musicological education and a teaching orientation, to such an extent that it even dedicates papers to his concept of "pedagogical phonography" (1938). As for CX6, he proposes a first season with a program based on the "variation," "free of aesthetic orientation," to which "special programs" are added "with the purpose of working pedagogically with the enormous mass of listeners commonly called an audience in programs of high quality that are beyond of the listeners' demands. This position, far from representing a program meant for minorities, enticed literate listeners to be curious while attracting new audiences." The criteria for music acquisition, the procedures to listen to every side of a record, and the analysis of a record's deterioration are evidence of its precise organization. It also conceives a Public Record Collection for record lending, which did not materialize.

In the following four decades, the SODRE's radios multiplied, including FM and shortwave. Currently, "Clásica" keeps the tradition of the old CX6. Besides that station, "Babel" and "Emisora del Sur" expanded the scope of Uruguayan and international popular music.

The major orchestras in the country are the OSSODRE, the national orchestra, and the Montevideo Philharmonic Orchestra, created in 1958 as the Symphonic Municipal Orchestra, reporting to the Montevideo government.

Orchestral and chamber offerings for kids and youth include the Youth Orchestra of the Ministry for Education and Cultural Affairs (created in 1992), the "José Artigas" National Youth Symphonic Orchestra (founded in 1996), following the Venezuelan *El Sistema*'s steps, and a growing student orchestra at the EUM, with the interesting position of a "composer in residence"—biannually, an advanced composition student must compose, adapting himself to the instruments available by the orchestra during that semester. The EUM is home to "Grupos Sonantes," the most important extended education project, which was born in 2000 at the university level, reopened in 2009, and is cofunded by the Ministry of Education and Cultural Affairs. Created by violinist Jorge Risi according to his Youth Music System and conceived as an alternative project for music education, it currently sponsors activities in several institutions in the countryside, which are the priority because of their deficiency in this regard. The project is strongly related to similar initiatives in Paraguay and Chile.

Theatrical institutions have had an important role in audience formation, since as far back as the "Casa de Comedias" in the colonial era (1793, then San Felipe Theater). This presence is even more relevant in the construction of major private theaters in the nineteenth century and twentieth century's first, such as the "Solis" in Montevideo (1856) and the Larrañaga in Salto (1882), among many others. These theaters became dependent on the municipal government in the 1930s.

There is a Uruguayan branch of *Juventudes Musicales*, and also an intense private and public choral movement with historical presence in the country. Many private institutions hold courses and artistic activities, among them the *Nucleo Música Nueva* and the *Fundación Mozarteum del Uruguay*, just to mention two very different profiles.

CONCLUSION

Music education activities mentioned in this chapter allow us to set some analytical considerations regarding the public and private areas:

1. Music is present throughout Uruguay's public education system from the inclusion of general programs at all levels to specific music education.
2. This system shows major deficiencies in coherence and continuity.
3. Higher education programs are relevant, and are almost half a century old. It covers a great variety of educational and labor options, although classical music education evidently prevails when compared with popular and traditional music.

4. There is no official field for the training of specialists on specific education, although a postgraduate program is under discussion.

5. University education diplomas are not appreciated enough in the job market. This is true for teachers at the national education system, as well as performers, musicologists, and composers in the relevant fields.

6. Private education is very varied regarding organization, thematic and pedagogical approaches, and quality of the program. This is not regulated or assessed by any official body.

7. During the last decade, there has been a major increase in the production of original knowledge on music created and/or played in the country. However, no major change in textbooks can be seen at preuniversity levels regarding the presence and the approach to these topics. Analytical bibliographies on music education are minimal.

8. There is an intense international exchange of Uruguayan teachers and a frequent presence of foreign experts in Uruguay's education field, especially at the university level.

9. Uruguay is a major exporter of music professionals. A systematic research has yet to be conducted on the causes of this emigration. As a temporary hypothesis, positive factors such as education level, and negative ones, such as those related with the salary and the extension of job opportunities, can be taken into consideration.

To conclude, with this panorama as a baseline, the following major events from a diachronic standpoint on music education in Uruguay are proposed:

- In the 1830s, when, alongside the country's independence, the first scores are edited, there are some first attempts toward a specialized press, and philharmonic societies start to be developed;
- From the 1870s to 1900, when the major private conservatories are founded;
- The 1930s, where the educative activity by SODRE, founded as the Official Radio Service, starts. In this decade, "Special Bodies" and its Internal Secretariat are created;
- The 1950s, where higher education starts;
- A period of major decline in music education, belonging to curriculum restructuring and modification conducted during the 1972 to 1985 dictatorship;
- The resurgence of democracy in 1985, when academic restructures are conducted according to the political context; and
- The first decade of the twenty-first century, where new curricula are set out for different levels, there are discussions on a music insertion into the project of an Arts Faculty and into a Education University Institution, and musicologist knowledge production is encouraged.

Therefore, we are in a moment for discussions on major changes in music education in Uruguay. Different music professionals look toward institutional insertion, and the institutions, at some levels, are conducting efforts toward a more coherent and related system establishment. On the other hand, projects of an Arts Faculty and of an Education University Institute require a new sort of partnership, at the university level, with other disciplines in the areas of arts and education. This new decade might, therefore, join the important moments that we have just described.

NOTES

1. This paper was cowritten with Cecilia Mauttoni, professor and researcher at the Music University School and a primary and high school teacher, and Alvin, a primary and high school teacher in the parts regarding the primary school music education and the music teacher's career.

2. Demographic information is retrieved from 2004 National Census, provided by the Instituto Nacional de Estadístic (INE), on www.ine.gub.uy/institucional/censo04.htm Retrieved on January 28, 2011.

3. Report by the Archdeacon at the Buenos Aires Cathedral, Francisco Caballero Bazán. The information is found in other documents (Ayestarán, 1953).

4. Nation's General Archive. Archive by Don Mariano Berro.

5. Programs are available on http://www.cep.edu.uy

6. The following is included in the first-year program: La música indígena en el Uruguay. Musical instruments: drums, blowing horns, and horns. Children's rounds in different countries. The accent sound quality in different sources (voice, body, and instruments). At www.cep.edu.uy. Retrieved on February 3, 2011.

7. Curricula and programs are available on www.ces.edu.uy. Retrieved on January 15, 2011.

8. Available on www.oei.es/pdf2/censo_nacional_docente_anep.pdf. Retrieved on January 15, 2001.

9. The author has worked as a representative at the Universidad de la República, and as an assessor in music for the said committee.

10. The Franciscan School in San Bernardino is the direct predecessor of higher education in Uruguay. This school, Jesuit in its origins, remains in charge of the Saint Francis Order in 1767 when Jesuits are expelled from the Americas by Carlos III's orders. In 1833, a law creating the university was passed, being proposed by Presbyterian Damaso Antonio Larrañaga. On July 18, 1849, the institution was opened as per decree by the then president, Joaquín Suárez.

11. The 2004 to 2005 Curricula are available on www.eumus.edu.uy. Retrieved on January 15th, 2011.

12. The 2008 curriculum available at: www.dfpd.edu.uy/cfe/estudiantes/planes_program/plan2008/programas_prof/ed_musical.html. Retrieved on January 15, 2011.

13. *Bandoneón*: a reedless air instrument blown through by activating bellows, and which is related to the concertina and accordion. Invented and perfected in Germany in the first half of the nineteenth century, it is named after Heinrich Band, one of the first traders. From that century to present, the *bandoneón* is a very popular instrument in Uruguay and Argentina, related to tango and other related genres. It is used in Uruguay, especially in central and north Uruguay, for the interpretation of traditional repertoire (especially polkas) along with accordion.

REFERENCES

Acosta y Lara, Eduardo. (1955). "Los Chaná Timbúes en la Banda Oriental." *Anales del Museo de Historia Natural*, 2nd Series VI, no. 5. Montevideo.

———. (1978). "Los guaraníes en el antiguo territorio de la República Oriental del Uruguay." *Revista de la Sociedad Amigos de la Arqueología*, XVII. Montevideo.

Aharonián, Coriún. (1990/1991). *Cancionero Latinoamericano* (2 vols., cassettes and booklets). Montevideo. Latin American Consultative Commission of Musical Youth.

———. (1992). *Conversaciones sobre música, cultura e identidad*. Montevideo. Ombú.

———. (2004a). *Educación, Arte, Música*. Montevideo. Tacuabé.

———. (2004b). "En procura de una cultura menos colonial: Educación musical para la creatividad." In Violeta Hemsy de Gainza y Carmen María Méndez Navas (orgs.), *Hacia una educación musical latinoamericana*. FLADEM: San Jose de Costa Rica.

———. (2007). "Resumen de los quince cursos latinoamericanos de música contemporánea." At: http://www.latinoamerica-musica.net/. Retrieved on February 5, 2011.

———. (2009). "La enseñanza institucional terciaria y las músicas populares." *Revista Musical Chilena* 63, no. 211.

Ardao, Arturo. (1968). *Etapas de la inteligencia uruguaya*. Montevideo. Universidad de la República.

Ayestarán, Lauro. (1953). *La música en el Uruguay, Vol. I*. Montevideo: SODRE.

———. (1967). *El folklore musical uruguayo*. Montevideo: Arca.

———. (1968). *Teoría y práctica del folklore*. Montevideo: Arca.

———. (1982). *Cinco canciones folklóricas infantiles*. Montevideo.

Bouret, Daniela, Gonzalo Vicci, Alexandra Nóvoa, and Carlos Correa de Paiva (2009). *Elementos para una historia de la Orquesta Filarmónica de Montevideo*. Montevideo. Intendencia Municipal de Montevideo (Orquesta Filarmónica de Montevideo/Teatro Solís).

Bralich, Jorge. (1996). *Una historia de la educación en el Uruguay. Del padre Astete a las computadoras*. Montevideo. Fondo de Cultura Universitaria.

Cavellini, Susana. (1987). "Síntesis etnohistórica." At: *Misión de Rescate Arqueológico Salto Grande*, Tomo I. Montevideo: Ministerio de Educación y Cultura.

Censo Nacional Docente. (2008). At: www.oei.es/pdf2/censo_nacional_docente_anep.pdf

Díaz, Antonio. (1975). "Perspectivas para el estudio de la cerámica del Río Uruguay Medio." *Anales del II Congreso Nacional de Arqueología* 2. Fray Bentos (Uruguay).

———. (1977). "Arqueología de Salto Grande: Secuencia cultural resusltante de las investigaciones realizadas en Isla de Arriba y del Medio (Uruguay)." *V Encuentro de Arqueología del Litoral*.

Errandonea Lennon, Gabriel (coord.) (2010). Anuario Estadístico de Educación 2009. Montevideo. MEC. Also available on: www.mec.gub.uy/innovaportal/.../anuario_estadistico_educacion_2009.pdf

Ferreira, Luis. (1997). Los tambores del candombe. Montevideo. Colihue Sepé.

———. (2007). " An Afrocentric Approach to Musical Performance in the Black South Atlantic: The Candombe Drumming in Uruguay." *Revista Transcultural de Música, 11*. At: http://www.sibetrans.com/trans/a129/an-afrocentric-approach-to-musical-performance-in-the-black-south-atlantic-the-candombe-drumming-in-uruguay

Figari, Pedro. (1965). *Educación y arte*. Montevideo. Clásicos Uruguayos.

———. (1994). El Cancionero Norteño. Música tradicional y popular de influencia brasileña en el Uruguay. Montevideo. Ediciones de la Banda Oriental.

———. (1999). "Los cantos inmigrantes se mezclaron. La murga uruguaya: encuentro de orígenes y lenguajes." *El Sonido de la Cultura. Textos de Antropología de la Música. Anthropology* 15–16, 139–70. Also at: http://www.sibetrans.com/trans/trans6/fornaro/htm

Fornaro, Marita. (2009a). "SODRE, un laboratorio de cultura," At: *SODRE. 80 años*. Montevideo. SODRE.

———. (2009b). "En el comienzo fue la radio." Exposition catalog. Montevideo. SODRE.

———. (2009c). "SODRE: las artes a escena." Exposition catalog. Montevideo. SODRE.

———. (2009d). "SODRE, 80 años: cierres y aperturas del tiempo." Exposition catalog. Montevideo. SODRE.

————. (2009e). "Musicología en Uruguay: el difícil arte de hacer ciencia." Trabajo presentado a las *Primeras Jornadas de Investigación del Archivo General de la Universidad.*

————. (2011). "Teoría y terminología en la música popular uruguaya: los primeros cincuenta años." At: *Actas del IX Congreso de la IASPM-AL.* Newspaper.

Fornaro, Marita, and M. Olarte. (1996). Entre rondas y juegos. Análisis comparativo del repertorio infantil tradicional de Castilla-León y Uruguay. Montevideo. Universidad de la República.

Fornaro, Marita, and Samuel Sztern. (1997). *Música popular e imagen gráfica en el Uruguay, 1920–1940.* Montevideo. Universidad de la República.

Goldman, Gustavo. (1997). *Salve Baltasar! La fiesta de Reyes en el barrio sur de Montevideo.* Montevideo. Escuela Universitaria de Música/CSIC.

————. (2008). *Lucamba. Herencia africana en el tango, 1870–1890.* Montevideo. Perro Andaluz.

————, (comp.). (2008). *Cultura y sociedad afro-rioplatense.* Montevideo. Perro Andaluz.

————. (2010). "Prácticas musicales afro en el Río de la Plata: continuidades y discontinuidades." *A tres bandas. Mestizaje, sincretismo e hibridación en el espacio sonoro iberoamericano.* Madrid: SEACEX.

Huertas, Julio César. (2003). *Raíces italianas en la música del Uruguay.* Montevideo. Ministry of Education and Cultural Affairs/Italian Embassy.

Lange, Francisco Curt. (1938). "Fonografía Pedagógica. II.—La Discoteca Nacional." *Boletín Latino-Americano de Música.* Year IV, Volume IV. Bogota.

Lopez Mazz, Jose Maria. (2001). "Las estructuras tumulares (cerritos) del Litoral Atlántico uruguayo." *Latin American Antiquity* 3.

Oddone, Juan Antonio, and Blanca Paris. (1963). *Historia de la Universidad de Montevideo. La Universidad Vieja 1849–1885.* Montevideo; Universidad de la República.

————. (1971). *La Universidad Uruguaya, del Militarismo a la Crisis, 1885–1958.* Volumes II and III. Montevideo. Universidad de la República.

Servicio Oficial de Difusión Radio Eléctrica (SODRE). (1963). *Servicio Oficial de Difusión Radio Eléctrica. Su organización y cometidos. Memoria de la labor realizada entre 1930–1962.* Montevideo. SODRE.

Padrón Favre, Oscar. (2009). *Ocaso de un pueblo indio: Historia del éxodo guaraní-misionero al Uruguay.* Durazno: Tierra Adentro.

Pi Hugarte, Renzo. (2007). *Los indios del Uruguay.* Montevideo. Ediciones de la Banda Oriental.

Salgado, Susana. (1980). *Breve historia de la música culta en el Uruguay.* Montevideo. Monteverde and others.

Sans, Mónica. (2009). "Raza: adscripción étnica y genética en Uruguay." *Runa* XXX, no. 2. Buenos Aires.

Scuro Somma, Lucía. (coord.). (2008). *Población afrodescendiente y desigualdades étnico-raciales en Uruguay.* Montevideo. PNUD Uruguay. Also available at: www.ine.gub.uy/biblioteca/Afrodescendientes.pdf. Retrieved on February 3, 2011.

Taddei, Antonio. (1964). "Un yacimiento precerámico en el Uruguay." *Baessler-Archiv, Neue Folge, Band XVII.* Berlin.

————. (1985). "El Río Negro Medio." *Estado actual de las investigaciones arqueológicas en el Uruguay,* Part I. Montevideo: Center for Archaeological Studies.

Universidad de la República. (1958). *Ley Orgánica de la Universidad de la República.* Available at: http://www.google.com/search?q=Ley+Org%C3%A1nica+Udelar&ie=utf-8&oe=utf-8&aq=t&rls=org.mozilla:es-ES:official&client=firefox-a

Varela, Daina et al. (2007). "Breve análisis histórico de la educación en el Uruguay." At: http://www.cep.edu.uy/index.php?option=com_content&view=article&id=664&Itemid=226. Retrieved on February 2, 2011.

Chapter Nineteen

Venezuela

Mariantonia Palacios

INTRODUCTION

The present chapter is dedicated to the study of the development of music education in Venezuela from the moment Christopher Columbus arrived on the shores of what he then called *La Tierra de Gracia* to our times. The information has been organized in five sections; each one of them corresponds to historical moments with fully differentiated cultural, social, and economic characteristics that brought about changes in the way music education was conceived.

The first section makes a reconstruction of the status of music created by the natives at the moment Europeans came to our lands, as well as the music they brought with them, based on the accounts by chroniclers and missioners that wrote about the Venezuela of that time. Among them we can highlight music education within the missions and reductions, where music was used as an effective tool for heathens' evangelization.

The second section is dedicated to the description of the development of music during Spanish colonial times. Emphasis is made on the organization of musical chapels' within city's cathedrals—where music education was taught according to the Spanish Church's model—and the inclusion of music studies in the *Real y Pontificia Universidad de Santiago de León de Caracas* (presently the *Universidad Central de Venezuela*).

In the section dedicated to the eighteenth century, the important music movement developed is centered around the character of Father Sojo and the so-called *Escuela de Chacao*. This is done without putting aside the news related to the hiring of music teachers in the private field.

During the nineteenth century, important changes took place in the country, leading to the establishment of the independent Republic of Venezuela. During this period the first institutions dedicated to the teaching of the fine arts were created, supported by the State. These, alongside the philharmonic societies, took care of the formation of professional musicians. Parallel to this specialized formation, the first attempts of including music as part of children's and young people's integral formation in some private and public primary schools and high schools were made.

The chapter concludes with the section dedicated to the twentieth century, describing the formation of professional musicians in conservatories, schools of music, and universities on the one hand and on the other hand music education as a signature within the basic school's curriculum. The revealing development of the choral and orchestral movement, which has been an important change in the paradigm of music education in Venezuela and the world, is also included.

SIXTEENTH CENTURY: MUSIC IN THIS *TIERRA DE GRACIA*

Pre-Hispanic and Hispanic Influences

The peninsula of Paria (Venezuelan northwest) was the first harbor on solid ground that Spanish caravels saw. Believing he had arrived in heaven and thus baptizing Venezuelan's shores as *Tierra de Gracia*,[1] Christopher Columbus did not dissimulate his amazement at the beauty of the landscape. In his letter to the Catholic monarchs relating his third voyage, Columbus highly praised this side of the ocean and its inhabitants. Being the first written document ever referring to this territory, Columbus's epistle marks the entrance of Venezuela into history. This is followed by a series of stories describing flora, fauna, geography, and the inhabitants; these are the work of chroniclers, cosmographers, and missionaries trying to give a full account of the events that happened from the moment Columbus explored the coasts of Venezuela in 1498.

Due to the absence of a written tradition among Venezuelan natives, we do not have a way to know about the music that was played in our land before Columbus's arrival. Therefore, chroniclers' texts give us the first music news of the country. It is through the eyes of those who came from Europe that we can imagine firsthand the music of the pre-Columbian province of Venezuela.[2]

Some of the chroniclers wrote from the place of the events (Christopher and Fernando Columbus, Amerigo Vespucci, Gonzalo Fernández de Oviedo, Nikolaus Federmann, Felippo Gilij, Bartolomé de Las Casas, José Gumilla, Matías Ruíz Blanco, Pedro Simón); others instead were based on oral stories or the revision of documents and files (López de Gomara, Antonio Herrera y Tordesillas, Pedro Mártir de Anglería). Most of them related historical events and soldiers' feats, always looking at the natives as, although free, inferior beings of barbaric and uncivilized acts. Missionaries' stories, instead, radically differ from this tendency. They show a bigger rapport with natives and a more genuine effort of understanding their culture, of speaking their language, of learning their customs, and of adapting to their world; it is clear, however, that missionaries did not tolerate any religion other than Christianity.

Needless to say, none of the chroniclers who wrote about the Province of Venezuela had the intention of describing the natives' music. However, reading between the lines the music information they contributed is of considerable interest. Their stories, in one way or another, describe dancing choreography, body painting for holidays, feathered decorations, musical instruments, lyrics and chants, and rites and myths. As an example, it is only necessary to mention the description made by fray Filippo Gilij about the beauty of natives' chants. He refers to the *Keyuvayé*, the dance of the tribe Pareca, as he describes it, comparing it with European canons:

> And although everything was very peculiar, as for the dancers' expressions as for the strange movements of their feet, nothing was more pleasant than the novelty of the nasal chant: dark and made with a Miserere pitch. The Spaniards wanted it to be repeated several times, arguing that had they heard in the distance, they would have believed it, not an aboriginal chant, but one of religious people of a cloistered life. (Filippo Gilij, Book Four, Chapter XVII, cited in Palacios, 2000a)

But those chroniclers' not only mention natives' music but also the music Christians brought to the New World: the one they played and sang in their daily routine and the one they used in their celebrations, feasts, and ceremonies.

The arrival of the missionaries, from many religious orders, to enlighten the heathens also brought to Venezuela a great quantity of elements belonging to Spanish culture. Music was favored in a remarkable way by members of religious orders; they used it as one of the most efficient tools for evangelizing. Since it helped to smooth the way for conversation, music could help the natives get acquainted with the knowledge of the faith. They preferred to soften them with this tool rather than making them believe in God's word by force.

Music was present in the daily routine of teaching the Christian doctrine and in solemn feasts such as the Twelfth Day, Corpus Christi, and Christmas. Franciscans, Dominicans, Augustans, and Jesuits later transformed the teaching of music as a main subject in every place they evangelized. Christian doctrine was taught through chanting, praying, and/or the singing of prayers for its better memorization, as referred in the detailed descriptions by Bishop Mariano Martí[3] during his pastoral visit to the diocese.

Furthermore, the teaching of the chanted Christian doctrine was a catalyst in the creation of a Venezuelan repertoire of liturgical music in native dialects. The chroniclers inform us about compound and chanted verses to celebrate the Nativity of Our Lord, the *auto sacramentales*, the life of the saints in the *Achagua* language, and carols in the Caribbean language. Jesuist Father José Gumilla[4] says it very clearly "shall the [Christian] doctrine be taught in the morning in their natural language, and in Spanish in the afternoon, for with the former God shall be served, and with the latter shall be our Lord the King" (cited in Palacios, 2000a, 48). The natives were taught to sing through papers; that is, to read and write music. They were educated on the *punto d'organo*, that is to say, on the art of the counterpoint; and they were also taught to strum and build musical instruments.

The easiness and the natural talent with which the natives learned music are mentioned constantly in the stories of the chroniclers. Chanting or playing an instrument at church was considered a privilege and a symbol of status for the natives. This had ancient and deep roots because in many pre-Hispanic cultures professionals with strict and long training made music. Since music was related to cult and rite, those who developed it were held in high esteem within society. Being selected as a chanter or as a player was a big reason for the head of a family to feel pride, thus establishing indissoluble bounds between family and church.

The African Influence

With the arrival of the African workforce to the shores of the American continent, new elements were introduced. Documental sources indicate that the first cargo of slaves transported from Africa landed in the mainland in 1518 (Strauss, 2004, 75). This trade lasted for approximately three hundred years, during which nine million Africans were brought to the mainland. These men, women, and children had different origins because they were from different ethnic groups with different cultural traits. The Spaniards always took care of keeping these differences as the order of the day to keep same origin groups from creating the possibility of cultural and social links that would eventually endanger their own condition as exploiters. Slaves were forced to give up their own values and to adopt completely different and strange new ones. However, the influence of such a big group eventually permeated American society. Many of the African values were smuggled and reshaped on the mainland, in spite of the clear intentions dominant classes had of uprooting the African culture in order to ease their exploitation as a working force. This event prevented the recognizing and establishment of links with tribal original customs. It is of value to also mention that documentary sources mention very little of the African culture in our country. This gap in the chronicles of the early centuries of the Spanish discovery and conquest does not allow us to have a perspective of the Africans' cultural manifestations, and to track down the way cultural values were passed down. There might be two main reasons for this lack of information. First, black slaves were not a novelty for Europeans; in 1441, a little before the arrival of Columbus to the continent, Portugal had already created a lucrative trade network of slaves with some of the biggest and more powerful countries of Western Africa, giving the Portugal Crown the monopoly of the trade of slaves in Europe. Second, black people were measured as the lowest kind of humans, even considering them as individuals with no soul at all, rendering thus the description of their barbaric customs simply a waste of time.

However, and in spite of the lack of information, undoubtedly dominated cultures, both the Indian and African ones, little by little penetrated into the dominant European culture. Many of their elements, preserved and re-created eagerly, merged in a definite way with elements imposed by the dominant class, which would eventually set the fundamental traits of Venezuelan music.

SEVENTEENTH CENTURY: CHURCH'S PRIMACY

The Church was one of the cornerstones for the Spanish monarchy during the conquest and colonization of the American continent: it was not only in charge of the natives' spiritual conversion and the care of the Christian souls but also had a role in the diverse fields of the economic, social, and cultural life. Throughout the whole Spanish Empire, the most important music activity was around this institution, and Venezuela was not an exception. Following the Spanish model established by the different religious orders settled in Venezuela, parish churches, cathedrals, missions, and natives' reductions were places to play and chant, to compose and teach.

Music Chapels' Organization

The cathedral of Santa Ana de Coro (the first one in Venezuelan territory) was founded in 1531. Following the model of Spanish cathedrals in Seville and Palencia, Bishop Rodrigo de Bastidas immediately organized his music chapel. In its *Constituciones* the same music charges as cathedrals were established, but poverty only permitted the resources for the chantry, a rector, and two canonists. The charge to provide an organist and chapel master would wait until the following century.

The *Actas del Cabildo Eclesiástico* (1943) bequeaths us the first professional musicians that held official posts. Juan Rodríguez de Robledo[5] is referred to in 1536 as a chantry that arrived in the northwestern city of Coro in 1528; he was a contralto chanter and versed on the plainchant. Teaching chant to the Church's ministers singing at the lectern and correcting the choir were among his duties. In 1581, Pedro Juárez[6] is appointed as cantor, giving him the responsibility of assisting the Church on an hourly basis, and of also teaching chanting to all the ordinands, with an annual salary of fifty silver pesos.

Thereafter we can find information on chantries, cantors, choir chanters, and chaplains, all of them related to the chapel music, with their respective payments and responsibilities. That denotes thus the concern of keeping the solemnity of the divine offices in the Venezuelan Church and of training people who would take care of music.

In 1591, an important data is mentioned: Luis Cárdenas Saavedra asks permission to establish an elementary school in Caracas for orphans' teaching, being the plainchant among the considered signatures. In 1593, the *Actas del Cabildo de Caracas* (1963) indicate that Pedro Arteaga was appointed as Saavedra's successor, with an assignation of thirty pesos a year.

In 1637, the official diocese of Venezuela is moved from Santa Ana de Coro to the city of Santiago de León de Caracas as part of a Royal Decree of Graces issued by King Phillip IV. Three years later, fifty pesos a year from the fabrica ecclesiæ (funds destined to the fabric) were assigned to pay the teacher in charge of the chant school, responsible for teaching a lesson every day at Church. However, since the bishop wrote to the king complaining about the lack of solemnity in the music taught, we assume that this school did not turn out that well. According to the *Actas del Cabildo Eclesiástico* of 1671, this lack was due to the nonexistence of someone who could teach chaplains, altar boys, clerics, and ministers. Therefore, Presbyter Gonzalo Cordero (c. 1620–1679, Caracas) is appointed as the first chapel master documented in Venezuela. Among the duties with which he was charged were the teaching of the plainchant and organ chant to ministers, and also in the assisting of ruling the music in the choir during feasts.

As for instruments and players, from 1583 the *Actas del Cabildo Eclesiástico* recorded the presence of an organ at the church of Santiago de León de Caracas acquired by the Caracas citizens; and in 1592 Melchor Quintella[7] is appointed as organist. From then on, one can make a more or less chronologic tracking of the musicians that held the charge at the Cathedral of Caracas until the early nineteenth century.

Besides organists, the *Actas del Cabildo* mention the paid charge of the bajón[8] player; among the most important ones are Juan de Zalaeta,[9] Francisco Pérez Camacho (1659, Valle del Totumo, 1720, Caracas), and José Ángel Lamas (1775–1814, Caracas). Harps and guitars are also mentioned as instruments used at church, alongside violins, cornettos, flutes, chirimias, trumpets, drums, bandurrias, oboes, and lute. By 1672, the authorities of the Cathedral of Caracas were informed about the existence of six choir chapelains, one chapel master, a sochantre with dinataries, six altar boys, one beadle, and one bell-ringer. This demonstrates that a more or less stable staff of musicians had been successfully formed.

In 1728, the *Regla de Coro de la Catedral de Caracas* was approved, thus giving organization and recurrence to music for liturgy inside and outside Church. One of the most important aspects we should highlight is that, as in Spain, the official posts would just be held by white people. Indians, Afro-descendants, or Mestizos would eventually be hired but could not apply for it. However, professional natives and black musicians are mentioned in the towns of the Venezuelan countryside, and in the missions, showing an insufficient number of European musicians *white and a pure-blood*[10] holding those posts.

As corresponded to the organization of Spanish music, chapels and the training of musicians, their teaching and their formation, at churches was systematic and was put in the hands of the chapel master.

Music at University

The Seminary of Santa Rosa[11] became a university under Royal mandate in 1721, when Philip V issued the Royal Decree of Graces that authorized the erection of the *Real y Pontificia Universidad de Santiago de León de Caracas*. From its foundation, it had a music chair, inherited from the ancient seminary. The chapel master of the Caracas Cathedral for that moment, Francisco Pérez Camacho, ran the seminary, and took office in 1687 with the obligation of teaching plainchant and figured chant to those who wanted to learn it. Pérez Camacho took the chair of music, giving classes of plainchant to seminarians and amateurs until 1720, when he was replaced by Silvestre Mediavilla. With the secularization of university studies in the nineteenth century, the chair of music went out of use until it disappeared from the curricula. It is not until the middle twentieth century that music studies came back to Venezuelan University (Cadenas, 2009, 1–7).

EIGHTEENTH CENTURY: MUSIC IN THE ENLIGHTENMENT

In 1728, the Royal Gipuzkoan Company of Navigation is set up in Venezuela in order to control and administer the booming exploitation of cocoa; in 1776 the Treasury Administration and Royal Financing[12] was created. A year later the Captaincy General of Venezuela was developed; in 1786 the Royal Audience is established, and so is the Royal Consulate in 1793. These institutions advanced Venezuela economically, in a fundamental way. They permitted the commercial exchange with Europe by providing political and administrative independence. This resulted in the modification of the social life of Venezuela's aristocratic class.

Well-off families as the Palacios, Sojo, Ustáriz, Toro, Ribas, Herrera, and the Tovar cultivated arts. The organization of literary-musical soirees was usual, which were recorded by the foreign visitors that were in Venezuela during the second half of the eighteenth century. Documents of a different kind also testify to the hiring of music and dance teachers for the training of Venezuelan *criollos*[13] in these arts, considered as fundamental for social development. To this exclusive group belongs one of the most important characters of the eighteenth century: Don Pedro Ramón Palacios y Sojo Gil de Arratia (1739, Guatire–1799, Caracas), best known as Father Sojo, Libertador Simón Bolívar's maternal grand-uncle.

The *Escuela de Chacao*

From 1770, the character of Father Sojo gains importance for the development of Venezuelan music. In 1771 he founded the Chapel of San Felipe Neri in Caracas, a secular friars' congregation of a great racial openness that had the particularity of allowing entrance to their congregation without requiring religious studies or special vows. Sojo thus surrounded himself with a group of musicians and learned people, constituting thus a real music chapel where the fact of not being *white and a pure blood* was not an exclusive condition.

This group of first-rate composers has been denominated in stylistic terms as *Escuela de Chacao*, referring to the place of *La Floresta*, one of Father Sojo's ranches, located in the surroundings of the town of Chacao. It was there and in Father José Antonio Mohedano's (1741, Talarrubias, Spain, 1804, Ciudad Bolívar, Venezuela) and Bartolomé Blandín's[14] properties where musicians met to play concerts and play ball day and night, annoying Bishop Mariano Martí, according to many reports sent by him to the king.

Around the *Escuela de Chacao*, two generations of remarkable composers met, many of them Pardoes.[15] The ones from the first generation were: Juan Manuel Olivares[16] (1760–1797), who, according to many sources, acted as *maestro*; José Francisco Velásquez (1755–1805); José Antonio Caro de Boesi (1758–1783); Bartolomé Bello (1758–1804); and Francisco Javier Ustáriz (1772–1814). And in the second generation, we have José Ángel Lamas (1775–1814), Lino Gallardo (1773–1837), Juan José Landaeta (1780–1814), Cayetano Carreño (1774–1836), Mateo Villalobos (1774–?), Juan Meserón[17] (1779–1845), Atanasio Bello Montero (1800–1876), and José Francisco Velásquez (el joven) (1781–1822). When Father Sojo died, these musicians kept meeting in many chapels; they were but a group of students around a master. The first chapel ever recorded is the Narciso Lauro[18] one, founded in 1795 on the corner of *La Faltriquera* (Calzavara, 1987, 109–21).

We might conclude then that music teaching during this period was made in a practical way, through the imitation of the masters, singing and playing church music, copying and studying scores, and reading different music theory books that could be found at the university.

NINETEENTH CENTURY: *¡ABAJO CADENAS!* THE ARISING OF AN INDEPENDENT REPUBLIC

Venezuela's nineteenth century was a particularly difficult time. It represents the final period toward independence; the arising of an autonomic country, whose beginnings were established in the 1830 Constitution. From that moment on, a new period begins for Venezuela; it emerges as a sovereign country that will not only look for political autonomy but also for cultural freedom.

Due to the general state of ruin in which the successive political revolts left the country, the great music genres characteristic of Europe's romanticism, such as opera and orchestral music, did not have a correct infrastructure for their development. Instead, manifestation of the music of the so-called *de salón* had an unusual increase. Among them, especially the dance (today called merengue) and the waltz, acquired national characteristics distinctive from their European's homonym.

Periodic publications of that time such as *El Cojo Ilustrado*, *La Lira Venezolana*, *El Zancudo*, and many others were the ideal way to spread this repertoire. Albums full of dances, polkas, mazurkas, contra dances, and waltzes were also published. Composers such as Salvador Narciso Llamozas (1854–1940), Heraclio Fernández (1851–1886), Federico Villena (1835–1899), Ramón Delgado Palacios (1863–1902), José Ángel (1832–1881), and Ramón Montero,[19] Jesús María Suárez (1845–1922), Federico Vollmer (1834–1901), and Sebastián Díaz-Peña (1844–1926) cultivated the *salón* music and took it to a high artistic level; besides, other composers such as Felipe Larrazábal (1818–1873), Redescal Uzcátegui (1871–1943), Manuel Leoncio Rodríguez (1870–1943), and Andrés Delgado Pardo (1870–1940) developed other music genres related to the sonata form. The piano was the king of the instruments in these spaces, and therefore most of the repertoire was made for this instrument. Since the learning of piano was part of the education they received, young ladies at home were the main public consumers of this music.

Hand in hand with the music cultivated in and for Venezuelan saloons, philharmonic societies appeared during the nineteenth century in Venezuela. These groups were orchestral groups created by outstanding teachers and students that held regular concerts. Most of them were civil organizations supported by their subscribers. There is a reference in 1811 about these subscription concerts for the first time in the Venezuelan press, and others from 1812, where subscription balls are promoted and mentioned. These events, to which previously only aristocrats had access, were now open to anyone who could afford them. This began the democratization of music customs in Venezuelan society.

Despite the important role played by philharmonic societies, the bands were the great music spreaders during this period of time. From Spanish colonial times there were already military bands, whose functions were mostly militaries during independence time (1811–1824). After the war was finished (1824), the bands kept working but with a more civilian orientation, holding public concerts known as *retretas* (open-air concerts). They were the major protagonists of music institutionalism during this period because many of the professional musicians were formed in their ranks.

As in most of Latin America, Italian opera ruled the music scene from the first decades: concerts, *sainetes*, *zarzuelas*, and *tonadillas escénicas* were the favorite shows of the public. Foreign opera companies visited many theaters in Venezuela and hired Venezuelan musicians and singers.

The second half of the nineteenth century saw the rising of remarkable composers, directors, and piano and violin virtuosos. Undoubtedly the most brilliant figure of this period of time is the exalted pianist, singer, composer, director, and teacher María Teresa Carreño García de Sena (1856, Caracas, 1917, New York), also known as Teresa Carreño. Born in a musical family, Teresa began her piano formation at an early age. First she was taught by her father, Manuel Antonio Carreño (1812–1874), author of, among many other works, the *Manual de Urbanidad y Buenas Costumbres*.[20] Soon she would shine as a prodigy girl, starting a brilliant career that would successfully take her to the most important concert halls in the American, European, and Oceania continents.

Musical Education

Musical education during this period was carried out in three ways: public and private schools of general education that provided music as another subject; philharmonic societies and specialized academies in the formation of music players; and private teachers specially hired to teach music.

Although the State did not support general or music education during the first decades of the nineteenth century, some private and primary schools were founded where music education was provided as part of the general education. The Colegio de la Paz, Colegio Roscio, and Colegio La Independencia (Milanca, 1993, 108–9) stand out in this category. In that time's press the services of these teachers in charge of music education in these schools were offered to the public; among them were remarkable composers and music players such as José María Montero (1782–1869), Juan Meserón, and Manuel María Larrazábal (1813–1881). Periodic publications also reviewed the public exams of these educative institutions where recitals of the most outstanding students were included, in addition to concerts of orchestral organizations that conformed with the participation of teachers and students.[21]

Along these private schools worked the Normal Schools; institutions specialized on the formation of teachers where one of the studied subjects was music. It should be added to this list of general educational establishments the *Colegios Nacionales de Niñas*, *Escuelas para Señoritas*, and *Colegios de Educandas*, institutions where girls and young ladies received music education as part of their formation for their future roles as good wives and excellent mothers.

A fact of great importance and significance is the decree issued by President Antonio Guzmán Blanco on June 27, 1870, by which education is democratized by declaring it as free and mandatory. This resolution establishes that the State has the obligation of encouraging, by all means possible, primary education, and creating and protecting public schools in villages and in the countryside in order to ensure the accessibility of compulsory knowledge to everyone (Fernández Heres, 1987). Educative authorities of those days gave great importance to music education as a special subject for other studies because they considered that it helped to create disciplines, to cultivate esthetic qualities, and to encourage intelligence. That is why at the pilot school *Guzmán Blanco*—which was a public school—they decided to set up a chair on *solfège* from 1871. Sources do not allow us to know what the outcome of this class was or if the experiment was reproduced in other public schools. Anyway, what is important to highlight here is the intention of the educative direction during those days.

As for the emergence of music education institutions in the nineteenth century, it is important to mention the role of the philharmonic societies; these groups had a double function: offering concert seasons and being in charge of the music education of their members. Lino Gallardo, Atanasio Bello Montero, José María Izaza, and Luis Jumel[22] are some of the musicians that were in charge of these special academies. In those days the press reviewed the regular activities of these societies, and parents were invited to educate their children in this artistic branch.

Diario de Avisos
Sábado 14 de octubre de 1854. (Mes 9° - N° 216. Serie 10ª - N° 77)
"Sociedad Filarmónica de Caracas"
Sabemos que se ha instalado una nueva sociedad filarmónica compuesta de mas de sesenta jóvenes aficionados y entusiastas por el arte divino de la música, que hoy está elevado al mas alto grado y supremacía sobre los demas, por la generosa proteccion de los gobiernos europeos y de todos los hombres de gusto, de génio y de influencias en el mundo. La Sociedad Filarmónica de Caracas, ha principiado ya sus trabajos de estudio y de organizacion: están á su cabeza hombres de teson y de interes por el progreso del arte, para sacarlo de la adyeccion y abatimiento en que ha permanecido tanto tiempo, tal vez por falta de entusiasmo y de recursos. Se ha hecho la sociedad de una famosa coleccion de instrumentos de arte y de cuerda, y cuenta con la proteccion de varios sugetos de gusto, de educacion esmerada y que conocen que la música es el mas poderoso auxiliar para las costumbres, para la civilizacion y para ligar los intereses morales de la sociedad. En efecto, ya han empezado varios padres de familia á incorporar á sus hijos en tan útil asociacion, y ya comienza el estimulo y el ardor juvenil á dar los resultados que son de esperarse. Cada cual ha ido á presentar á la sociedad sus ofrendas para ayudarle en la empresa de continuar en sus benéficos trabajos, y no hay que dudarlo, habrá un gran apoyo moral y material de todos, si la Sociedad Filarmónica continúa ardorosa, entusiasta y progresista. Todo el mundo se hace el deber de proteger el talento, las artes, lo útil, lo beneficioso; y en esta línea, nada

es mas importante en nuestro pais trabajado por las discordías civiles y gastados los ánimos con las personalidades ofendidas, que fomentar este divino arte, este embeleso del espiritu que nos trasporta á otro mundo adonde no se conocen pasiones sino fraternidad, union, amistad y amor.

Están abiertos dos registros: uno de socios filarmónicos activos y otro de socios honorarios protectores de la sociedad y del divino arte. En ambos, los socios contribuyen con una insignificante cuota mensual para el mobiliario, música é instrumentacion que se necesita.

Si, como es de esperarse, la Sociedad Filarmónica continúa como va, hay el pensamiento de establecer un Conservatorio de Música con clases dotadas adonde se enseñe gratis toda clase de instrumentos y el canto.

Quiera el cielo que se vean cumplidos los deseos de varios socios protectores.

Despite the important role played by these philharmonic societies, it was not until 1834 that the first music school, strictly speaking, was founded, with a semiofficial character. It worked under the authority of the *Sociedad Económica Amigos del País*,[23] organized and managed by Atanasio Bello Montero. To this initiative followed the installation of the Academy of Fine Arts in 1850, under the direction of the Provincial Council of Caracas with the authorization of the Superior Political Government of the Province. The academy had a school of music, also ran by Bello Montero (Rodríguez Legendre, 1999, 23).

In 1870, contemplating the free education of music, the Conservatory of Fine Arts is founded under the direction of Felipe Larrazábal. As an interesting fact, it is worth mentioning the rules contemplating that students could be sent to Europe as recognition to their academic merits. Financed by the government, they would continue their artistic studies during four years. Many Venezuelan musicians were deservers of these scholarships and awards, traveling to Italy and France; among others we find Narciso Salicrup (1869–1917), Redescal Uzcátegui, Ramón Delgado Palacios, and Andrés Delgado Pardo (Rodríguez Legendre, 1999, 28–29).

Undoubtedly these institutions played an important role in artistic education during the nineteenth century. However, the National Institute of Fine Arts, founded in 1877 by former president Francisco Linares Alcántara (1825–1878) would be the institution to become transcendent in the music education field. It had three academies: one for drawing and painting, one for sculpture, and one for music. In the latter, ruled by General Ramón de la Plaza, were established chairs on melody, *solfège*, singing, instrumental music, harmony, counterpoint, fugue, instrumentation, composition, art history, esthetic, and critical philosophy of music, taught by prominent teachers. Among them were Eduardo Calcaño, Salvador Narciso Llamozas, and José Ángel Montero y Jesús María Suárez.[24]

This Institute of Fine Arts had many transformations during its life, although more in form than in substance. It is worth noting the decree published in 1897 establishing the division of students according to their sexes, and the one from 1913 implicating the independence between the sections of Plastic Arts and the Conservatory of Music and Reciting (Milanca 1995, 183–84).

As for private education, periodic publications of those times are the best source, where ads appeared regularly offering the services of piano, singing, and *solfège* teachers, both Venezuelans and foreigners. As for these ads, it is worth mentioning the ones published by the pianist and composer Heraclio Fernández[25] in the newspaper *El Zancudo*,[26] offering his services as a piano tuner and restorer as well as for giving piano lessons and teaching accompaniments in the Venezuelan way for the dance genre in a usual fashion during those times, based on a method written by himself. In other cases, the lessons were offered as an aggregate for buying an instrument.

TWENTIETH CENTURY: MODERN TIMES

In the first half of the twentieth century, Venezuela's educational system began to be ruled by the official programs issued by the Public Education Ministry. It was organized as follows: Elemental or Primary School; High School, which instructed students for their entrance to university; Normal Schools, which were the ones that carried out the training of teachers; Superior Education (including the main branches: Medical, Political, Ecclesiastical, Mathematical, Physical, and Natural Sciences; Philosophy and Literature); and Special Education. Within the latter, artistic studies were included.

At that time, there was just one official music school in Caracas, the *Escuela de Música y Declamación*. Created according to the model of the French conservatories, its goal was the formation of virtuoso instrument players, chanters, and composers. The subjects taught there were music theory and *solfège*, harmony, composition and instrumentation, piano, singing, string, brass, and woodwind instruments.

This educational center would receive the decisive boost from Vicente Emilio Sojo,[27] who assumed its direction in 1936 and undertook, alongside Juan Bautista Plaza (1898–1965), Moisés Moleiro (1904–1979), José Antonio (1900–1978), and Miguel Ángel Calcaño (1904–1958), fundamental reforms for music education in Venezuela. He created new subjects; hired foreign teachers; and, from the chair of harmony, educated several generations of composers grouped according to an esthetic based on the valorization of the Venezuelan folkloric element and traditions known as the *Escuela Nacionalista de Santa Capilla*.[28] Under Sojo's direction, the Lamas Choir and the Venezuelan Symphonic Orchestra became the ideal means to promote the compositions of these novel composers. At the same time, those groups promoted the music of Venezuelan composers from the eighteenth and nineteenth centuries. Besides, they served as workplaces for the forging of many generations of directors.

In 1941, the National Education Ministry issued the policy that began to rule music studies in the school, rescinding thus the one the federal executive branch had issued in 1917. The name *Escuela de Música y Declamación* was changed into the *Escuela Nacional de Música*, and the objectives were established. These can be summarized as follows: teaching specialized music education to individuals who wanted to be composers, instrument players, or singers; providing the pedagogical training of teachers who would dedicate themselves to music teaching in the different branches; and encouraging the cultural diffusion in Venezuela. However, perhaps for lacking specialized teachers in this area, the second objective was never accomplished.

As for the school's syllabi, three subjects were established in them: the general subjects for all the courses (*solfège*, history of music, esthetics, and musical appreciation); specialized subjects (composition and instrument playing); and complementary subjects (harmony and piano playing). The courses had a three-level structure: basic, intermediate, and advanced; eight being the minimum age of entrance (Fernández Heres 1981–1984, Tomo V: 76–77).

This last requisite encouraged Juan Bautista Plaza[29] to establish a new official institution for the specialized teaching of music in 1945: the *Escuela Preparatoria de Música Juan Manuel Olivares*.[30] Initially, it was created for children and young men and women who would later enter into the *Escuela Nacional de Música* (called from then on *Escuela Superior de Música José Ángel Lamas*), and for the training of those students who wanted to serve as music teachers in the primary schools. According to the statutes, children from five years old could enter into this institution. As a consequence, this brought the need to apply new and more appropriate methodologies to the children, music innovations that Plaza encountered during his visits to conservatories and music schools in the United States and Europe.

Thirteen years after their foundation in 1958, both institutions were in the same academic ranks. Therefore, students would not continue their studies in the *Escuela Superior*. This brought a change in both institutions' names, which were now simply called *Escuela de Música José Ángel Lamas* and *Escuela de Música Juan Manuel Olivares*. In the second half of the twentieth century, these establishments became a model for conservatories and music schools that started to arise in Caracas and the countryside. Decree no. 530[31] established the policy that would regulate the way it worked, detailing the syllabi and the entrance requirements. In 1964,[32] Official Gazette no. 909, issued by the Ministry of Education, included the official syllabus for theoretical subjects, and for other tools, which, in general lines, are still in force.

Besides taking care of the specialized education taught in conservatories and music schools, Venezuela's State also cared for the inclusion of music as part of the integral education of children and youngsters. The Ministry of Education promulgated the 1940 Education Law, rescinding that of 1924. This new law demanded the professional degree for teaching in the different levels. It created the Pedagogic Institute or the Normal School, which had among its goals the formation of new professors and teachers. Since singing was compulsory in the primary school, music education was considered essential.

On the other hand, during this period several delegations of foreign teachers were officially invited to Venezuela, which allowed the implementation of new pedagogical methods and the renewing of programs for primary and high schools. In 1966 a department of music pedagogy and another of musical supervision were created, with the objective of watching over the compliance of the official programs and guaranteeing the training of teachers in the area of music. Professor Flor Roffé de Estévez (1921–c. 2006) was in charge of both institutions, and was in charge of teaching students about innovations in music education at that time.

The Organic Law of Education was promulgated in 1980, which proposed a reform to the educative system, establishing thus the levels of education: Preschool Education, Basic Education, Middle Education, High School Education, and Higher Education. It also included the implementation of several independent modalities of the system's levels, among which Esthetic Education and Education for the Arts can be found. This meant that specialized music education became a modality apart from the levels of Venezuela's educative system. Music also was considered in this law as a compulsory subject within the integral education of children and youngsters in the level of basic and middle school. [33]

The insertion of these specialized studies of music as a special modality apart from the levels of Venezuela's educative system produced some consequences and problems that are still unsolved. Before the 1980 Organic Law, music studies were considered within the category of technical education, on the third level of the educative system. Degrees acquired in conservatories and music schools (Instrumental Teacher, Composer Master, or Singer) were therefore equivalent to an associate degree.

At the moment music studies were set as an independent modality, degrees conferred stopped being equivalent to those obtained on the different levels of Venezuela's educative system. That is to say, their academic level was undefined. For that reason, in 1991 a last reform within official music education was proposed. This reform was made thanks to a joint effort by the Education Ministry and the National Council of Culture. The purpose of this reform was the reinsertion of Esthetic Education and Formation for the Arts on the levels of Venezuela's educative system in order to concede an academic level to artistic studies and standardize the curriculum. The general idea was to offer students the possibility of taking music studies parallel to the general studies, adding specific subjects corresponding to the specialty and thus making it possible to have a degree in music (high school) or with an associates degree in music. [34]

Since this proposal only took shape in pilot schools of the State, with no extension to the rest of educative institutions in Venezuela, conservatories and music schools are currently in charge of the training of professional musicians; degrees do not have an equivalent at different levels of the educative system.

At the End of Century: Airs of Renovation

From 1940 an important musical movement took place, encouraged by the creation of the concert societies, especially distinguishing the *Asociación Venezolana de Conciertos*[35] as the oldest group without commercial purposes; its goal was the stimulation of concerts in Venezuela. It is also worthwhile to highlight, as one of the most significant events during these years, the inauguration of the symphonic orchestras in the western cities of Maracaibo and Barquisimeto, and in the southern city of Ciudad Bolívar, alongside the creation of numerous music chamber groups and choir societies, distinguishing among them the *Orfeón Universitario de Caracas*, the *Coral Creole*, and the *Coral Venezuela*.

The favorable socioeconomic status of the second half of the twentieth century gave Venezuelan musicians a direct esthetic when facing other trends in other countries. The Latin-American Music Festivals of 1954, 1956, and 1966 organized by the businessman and art-lover Inocente Palacios (1908–1996, Caracas) allowed many Venezuelan composers to share experiences with their most important colleagues at a global scale for that moment, and with internationally renowned career directors and performers. Also in 1965, by the Palacios's initiative, the first electroacoustic music laboratory in Venezuela was created: the *Estudio de Fonología Musical* of the *Instituto Nacional de Cultura y Bellas Artes* (INCIBA) in the acoustic shell of Bello Monte, in the East of Caracas. This was the beginning of Venezuela's entry into musical modernity.

These airs of renovation coincide with the arrival and establishment in Venezuela of the Greek composer Yannis Ioannidis (1930, Athenas), who lived in Caracas between 1968 and 1976. Among many other activities, he founded the *Sociedad Venezolana de Música Contemporánea*, and, sponsored by the INCIBA, gave a course on modern and contemporary techniques of composition, very different from the nationalist esthetics proclaimed by Vicente Emilio Sojo as chair of composition at the *Escuela de Música José Ángel Lamas*.

At the end of the century we can see a proliferation of opportunities that allowed Venezuela's musicians testing themselves, and growing as artists in different disciplines. New conservatories and music schools, economically dependent of the central and regional governments, were created. There were also many musicians who had the opportunity of training themselves abroad with the help of scholarships and government aids.

From the 1970s on, the economic boom encouraged an unusual growth of a choral and orchestral movement of big dimensions throughout all the country, allowing the massification of musical practice in the different social stratas. The 1970s are especially considered as the golden times of Venezuela's choral movement. Public and private entities, educative institutions, banks, insurance companies, ministries, and universities encouraged choral chant, thus creating the possibility for a great number of people of embracing music (Rugeles et al., 1986, 36–60).

Following this direction of expansiveness and music spreading, it is worth mentioning the ambitious project of the National Network of Youth and Children Orchestras, begun in 1974, and led from that same year on by José Antonio Abreu.[36] In 1977, the Decree no. 3093[37] by the Ministry of the Youth Affairs created the Foundation of State for the support of the children and youth orchestras in Venezuela, which broke the paradigms of music education in the country. Within this network of orchestras (called "El Sistema" in Venezuela), collective education is preferred to individual, practical teaching rather than the theoretical one, and the students are directly introduced to the playing of the instrument without previous having *solfège*. The motto of the movement, *Aprender a tocar, tocando*,[38] perfectively describes the methodology followed: entering students instantly get in touch with music through singing and the recorder; almost immediately, however, they pick an orchestral instrument of their preference, provided by "El Sistema." The building up of the repertoire is made in a collective way through workshops given by specialist teachers.

The network of children and youth orchestras has had a growth of huge proportions, founding many headquarters all around the country and encouraging children and youngsters of all social classes to approach music. In the last decades, the movement has focused more directly on the social topics, more than the cultural aspect; working to rescue young people from the world of violence, drugs, prostitution, and crime; giving them an opportunity for a better quality of life and for learning a profession.

Its aim is the fomenting of the respect for life through esthetic education, as claimed by the great pedagogue Maurice Martenot. This aim not only benefits hundreds of young people playing in the orchestras of "El Sistema" but it also has an effect in their familiar and communal environments, making this an efficient tool for the formation of citizenship and spiritual growth. Its evident results have encouraged European and North American countries to imitate this model.

The 1970s also saw the arising of new academic music institutions of great importance for the country's development; among them, the School of Arts in the Humanities and Education Faculty at the Universidad Central de Venezuela (UCV). This school started its activities in April 1978 with five majors that nowadays are still working—plastic arts, scenic arts, cultural promotion, cinematography, and music—thus giving a space, for the first time in the century, to music studies at a university level in Venezuela. These latter are within the speculative tradition of the universities that seeks education in order to reach universal knowledge; this is the study of music from a strictly academic, scientific, research, and critical point of view.

The department of music at the school became, therefore, the first institution in charge of the formation of musicologists in Venezuela, basically focusing their studies on Venezuelan and Latin American music. The researches carried out here have been very important for knowing, analyzing, and spreading music in the American continent, and especially in Venezuela. Besides the publication of books and articles in specialized magazines, the outcomes have also been captured in several undergraduate theses and papers for professors' promotion. These papers are a very important database, and are, undoubtedly, a great contribution to the development of music in Latin America.[39]

Other important institutions created in the last decades of the twentieth century are the *Instituto Latinoamericano de Investigaciones Musicales Vicente Emilio Sojo* (nowadays called the Fundación Vicente Emilio Sojo, FUNVES); the current *Fundación de Etnomusicología y Folklore* (FUNDEF), whose purpose is the research, preservation, and spreading of traditional popular culture in Venezuela, Latin America, and the Caribbean area; the *Instituto Universitario de Estudios Musicales*, nowadays called the Faculty of Music at the University of Arts; the *Department of Music* at the *Universidad Pedagógica Experimental Libertador* (UPEL); and the degree in education with a major in music at the *Universidad Nacional Experimental Francisco de Miranda* (UNEFM), whose goal is the training of specialized teachers in that area; the degree in music education at the *Universidad Cecilio Acosta* (UNICA) in the Western state city of Maracaibo, Zulia; the degree in arts, major in music, at the *Universidad Arturo Michelena* (UAM) in Carabobo (Venezuela's central region); the degrees in music at the *Universidad de los Andes* (ULA), *Universidad Católica Cecilio Acosta* (UNICA), *Universidad del Zulia* (LUZ), and *Universidad Nacional Experimental del Táchira* (UNET); the master's degree in Latin American Musicology at the *Universidad Central de Venezuela* (UCV); and the master's degree in music at the *Universidad Simón Bolívar* (USB), also in Caracas, among others. Undoubtedly, this proliferation of institutions and orchestral and choral groups has contributed to the emerging of a public avid for concerts and festivals, and it is certainly what keeps an interesting permanent programming in boards and circuits all around the country. In this auspicious environment, a whole generation of new music creators and performers, some of them with a distinguished international career, such as the pianist Gabriela Montero (1970, Caracas), the director Gustavo Dudamel (1981, Barquisimeto), the bass player Ericsson Ruiz (c. 1992), the *Venezuelan Youth Orchestra Simón Bolívar*, and the *Schola Cantorum of Caracas*, among others, has emerged. All of them are worthy representatives of a country in which the musicality of its inhabitants have been recognized from the time of Christopher Columbus.

CONCLUSION

From the time when the missionaries used music as an evangelizing tool to the rise of the National Network of Youth and Children Orchestras of Venezuela as a social device for rescuing the poorest children and adolescents, music has been an important part of the country. This chapter has provided a look at the social, political, and cultural changes from the moment Columbus landed on the American mainland in 1498 to the arising of policies, institutions, and establishments in charge of music education. Whether with the support of the private sector field or the State, music has had a wide development. Venezuela then enters the twentieth-first century with a vigorous music movement reviewed in many countries of the world in present days; its model is being exported to other countries through multinational agreements.

Ironically, very little has been written about the development of music education in Venezuela. There are very few published papers focused on the critical study and evaluation of specific educative policies. On the other hand, the almost complete ignorance of the past results in the repetition of mistakes and the redoubling of efforts, thus producing a waste of energy and resources. This is why a book of this sort, where the current situation of music education in Latin America is presented, is so appropriate and necessary. Knowing the particularities of each one of the countries will allow us to discover the strengths and weaknesses of every educative system. Only in this way will we successfully establish the knowledge that will allow us to be a musical continent.

NOTES

1. "Here two lofty headlands appeared, one towards the east, and forming part of the land, which I have already called Gracia." "Carta del Almirante a los Reyes Católicos," in *Cristóbal Colón, diario de a bordo.* Los Libros de El Nacional, Caracas, 191.

2. For more information it is recommended to see my book, *Noticias musicales en los cronistas de la Venezuela de los siglos XVI–XVIII*, where I made an exhaustive study on the comments of the chroniclers about the natives' music in Venezuela.

3. Mariano Martí (circa 1721, Tarragona, Spain, 1792, Caracas, Venezuela) was a bishop in charge of the Caracas's Diocese from 1769 to his death. He compiled a great amount of information that he gathered during pastoral visits to more than 355 cities, towns, and villages in the west-central region of what is now Venezuela made between 1771 and 1784.

4. José Gumilla (circa 1687, Valencia, Spain, 1750, Los Llanos, Venezuela). He worked in the Venezuelan flat plains and in the Orinoco River (located in Venezuela's south), between 1716 and 1737 with the Salivas, Guahias, and Chricoas tribes. In 1741 he wrote the book *El Orinoco, historia natural, civil y geographica, de este gran río* with the intention of winning wills for these difficult and conflictive missions in the Orinoco. This book is an important organologic reference of the pre-Hispanic music because in there one can find valuable descriptions of aboriginal instruments.

5. Birthdate unknown; died in Coro, 1570.

6. Birth and death date unknown.

7. Birth and death date unknown.

8. Windy instrument like the modern bassoon.

9. Birth and death date unknown.

10. Pure blood means not being of Jewish, Indian, black, or Moorish descent.

11. The *Colegio Seminario de Santa Rosa de Lima* was founded in 1673 by Bishop Fray Antonio González de Acuña, and was officially inaugurated on 1696 by Bishop Diego Baños y Sotomayor. A *Real Cédula* of King Felipe V granted power to award degrees to the seminary, which was raised to the status of University. In 1722 Pope Innocent XIII granted pontifical status. In 1856 the *Real y Pontificia Universidad de Santiago de León de Caracas* became independent from the seminary moving their chairs, cabinets, and museums to the building of the Convent of San Francisco.

12. Intendencia de Hacienda y Real Ejercicio.

13. *Criollo* is a Spaniard's descendant born in Venezuela.

14. Birth and death date unknown.

15. The Pardoes were the result of the ethnic mixing between the different social groups, resulting thus in a heterogenic social class considered to be inferior to the white one in Venezuela Colony's times. From 1795 on, the Spanish Crown promulgated the Royal Decree of Graces of Equality (*Real Cédula de Gracias al Sacar*) in spite of whites' strong opposition. This document permitted Pardoes to enjoy a handful of benefits that were bound to the higher classes through the payment of a sum of money.

16. Juan Manual Olivares (1760, Caracas, 1797, El Valle), son of free Pardoes. He was an outstanding composer, violinist, harpsichord placer, and an organist. Also, according to many sources, master chapel of Church of the neristas in Caracas.

17. Juan Francisco Meserón (1779, circa 1845, Caracas) published the first text of music teaching ever printed in Venezuela, *Explicación y conocimiento de los principios generales de la música*, Caracas, Imprenta de Tomás Antero, 1824 (reprinted in 1852).

18. Dates are missing.

19. Dates are missing.

20. Manuel Antonio Carreño (1812, Caracas, 1874, Paris), son of Cayetano Carreño Rodríguez, one of the most important musicians in the seventeenth century, worked as an organist and chapel master of the Caracas Cathedral. In 1835 he wrote his *Manual de urbanidad y buenas maneras para uso de la juventud de ambos sexos en el cual se encuentran las principales reglas de civilidad y etiqueta que deben observarse en las diversas situaciones sociales, precedido de un breve tratado sobre los deberes morales del hombre*, a classic text about etiquette and good manners published in several issues in the Venezuelan press.

21. For additional information see Fidel Rodríguez Legendre (1999), *Caracas, la vida musical y sus sonidos (1830–1888)*, Fondo Editorial 60 años, Contraloría General de la República, Caracas, chapter II.

22. Birth and death date unknown.

23. Economic Society of Friends.

24. Jesús María Suárez (1845–1922, Caracas) was a pianist, pedagogue, and composer. He published several texts in Caracas for music teaching, used by many chairs of the Academy: *Rudimentos de la música* (1873), *Mecánica Musical* (1876), *La música al alcance de los niños* (1880), and *Compendio de historia musical desde la antigüedad hasta nuestros días* (1909).

25. Heraclio Fernández Noya (1851, Maracaibo, 1886, La Guaira) was one of the most versatile musicians in the nineteenth century. He was a composer and pianist; he was also teacher, editor, and journalist. As a performer he stood out as a distinguished improviser in Venezuelan music for ballroom dancing. Hence the success achieved by his book *Método para aprender a acompañar piezas de baile al estilo venezolano, sin necesidad de ningún otro estudio y á la altura de todas las capacidades*, published in 1876 and reedited in 1883.

26. The Mosquito.

27. Vicente Emilio Sojo (1887, Guatire, 1974, Caracas) was a composer, performer, compiler, musical arranger, and director. He was one of the most influential musicians in the first half of the nineteenth century.

28. Some of the composers formed by Vicente Emilio Sojo were Ángel Sauce, Antonio Estévez, Evencio Castellanos, Antonio José Ramos, Inocente Carreño, Antonio Lauro, Carlos Figueredo, Gonzalo Castellanos, Blanca Estrella de Méscoli, José Clemente Laya, Andrés Sandoval, Nazil Báez Finol, Raimundo Pereira, Leopoldo Billings, Nelly Mele Lara, José Luis Muñoz, Modesta Bor, José Antonio Abreu, Rogerio Pereira, Alba Quintanilla, Luis Morales Bance, Federico Ruíz, Francisco Rodrigo, and Juan Carlos Núñez.

29. Juan Bautista Plaza Alfonso (1898–1965, Caracas) was one of the most prominent Venezuelan musicians in the mid-twentieth century. He was the first person to publish colonial-period Venezuelan composers' works in conjunction with German musicologist Francisco Curt Lange. He was also a composer, chapel master at the Cathedral of Caracas, pianist, and organist.

30. Decree September 28th, 1945.

31. Decree by which is enacted the Reglamento para la Educación Artística emanado de la Presidencia de la República, Gazzete No. 25.362, year LXXXV, month VIII, May 23, 1957. Imprenta Nacional.

32. *Gazette of the Republic of Venezuela*, Year XCII, month VIII, May 29, 1965. Imprenta Nacional.

33. Decree 975. January 22th, 1986. Articules 16 and 36. *Reglamento General de la Ley Orgánica de Educación*, articules 36 and 37.

34. Resolution No. 751, June 17th, 1991.

35. Venezuelan Concert Society.

36. José Antonio Abreu (Trujillo, 1939) is a composer, an organist, a director, holds a PhD in petroleum economics, and is former Minister of Culture. He is the founder of the Sistema Nacional de Orquestas Juveniles e Infantiles de Venezuela (English: National Network of Youth and Children Orchestras of Venezuela), which has been a model to several countries and has deserved global recognition because of using of music as a tool to promote communal development, social integration, and solidarity.

37. National Executive Decree February 20, 1979. *Gazette of the Republic of Venezuela*, No. 31.681.

38. *Learning to play playing.*

39. For more details see to my article "El Departamento de Música de la Escuela de Artes de la UCV: un cuarto de siglo de producción intelectual," in *Revista Escritos en Arte y Cultura*, Fondo Editorial Facultad de Humanidades y Educación-Dirección de Cultura UCV, Año 16, III Etapa, No. 19-20, Caracas, 2004, 103–24.

REFERENCES

Actas del Cabildo de Caracas. Caracas: Editorial Elite, 1943.

Actas del Cabildo Eclesiástico de Caracas. (2 vols.). Caracas: Academia Nacional de la Historia, 1963.

Baños y Sotomayor, Diego. (1848). *Constituciones Synodales del obispado de Venezuela*. Reimpresiones Madrid: Joseph Rico, 1761; Caracas: Cármen Martel.

———. *Constituciones del Colegio Seminario de Nuestra Señora de S. María de la ciudad de Santiago de León de Caracas*. Madrid.

Cadenas, Viana. (2009). *La música en la Universidad Central de Venezuela*. EBUC, UCV, Caracas.

Calcaño, José Antonio. (1985). *La ciudad y su música*. Monteávila editores, Caracas.

———. (1939). *Contribución al estudio de la música en Venezuela*. Editorial Elite. Caracas.

Calzavara, Alberto. (1987). *Historia de la Música en Venezuela. Período hispánico con referencias al teatro y la danza*. Fundación Pampero, Caracas.

Colón, Cristóbal. (s/f). "El tercer viaje. Carta del Almirante a los Reyes Católicos." In *Cristóbal Colón. Diario de a bordo. Los cuatro viajes del Almirante y su testamento*. Caracas: Los libros de El Nacional, 183–206.

De Benedittis, Vincent. (2002). *Presencia de la música en los viajeros del siglo XIX en Venezuela*. Colección Fuentes para el estudio de la música en Venezuela, Fondo Editorial Humanidades, Universidad Central de Venezuela, Caracas.

De la Plaza, Ramón. (1895). *Primer libro venezolano de Literatura, ciencias y bellas artes*. Tipografía El Cojo, Caracas.

Diario de Avisos. Mes 9°, N° 216, Serie 10ª, N° 77, 1864.

Fernández Heres, Rafael. (1995). *La Educación Venezolana bajo el signo de la ilustración 1770–1870*. Colección Fuentes para la Historia Republicana de Venezuela, No. 65. Caracas: Biblioteca de la Academia Nacional de la Historia.

———. (1994). *La Educación Bajo el Signo del Positivismo*. Caracas: Academia Nacional de la Historia.

———. (1987). *La Instrucción Pública en el Proyecto Político de Guzmán Blanco*. Caracas: Academia Nacional de la Historia.

———. (1981). *La Instrucción de la generalidad. Historia de la educación en Venezuela, 1830–1980*. Tomos I y II. Caracas.

———. (1981–1984). *Memoria de 100 Años. Historia de la Educación en Venezuela*. 9 Volúmenes. Caracas: Ediciones del Ministerio de Educación.

———. (1965) (Intr. y Comp.). *Cedulario de la Universidad de Caracas*. Publicación del Instituto de Estudios Hispanoamericanos. Caracas: Universidad Central de Venezuela.

Gazette of the Republic of Venezuela No. 25.362, Year LXXXV, month VIII, May 23rd, 1957. Imprenta Nacional.

Gazette of the Republic of Venezuela, Year XCII, Month VIII, May 29th, 1965. Imprenta Nacional.

Gazette of the Republic of Venezuela. July 28th, 1980, Número 2.635 Extraordinario. Imprenta Nacional.

Gazette of the Republic of Venezuela. National Executive Decree February 20th 1979. No. 31.681.

Ley Orgánica de Educación. (1980). Imprenta Nacional.

Leyes y Decretos de Venezuela, 1861–1888. (1982). Academia de Ciencias Políticas y Sociales, Caracas, Vol. 4, 5 y 8.

Milanca, Mario. (1995). *La música en el tiempo histórico de Cipriano Castro*. Biblioteca de autores tachirenses, Caracas.

———. (1993). *La música venezolana. De la Colonia a la República*, Monte Ávila Latinoamericana, C.A., Caracas.

Palacios, Mariantonia. (2005). "La palabra cantada como herramienta evangelizadora en la América Colonial." In *Revista Extramuros*, No. 23, Nueva Serie, Octubre 2005, Fondo Editorial Facultad de Humanidades y Educación-ISSN: 1316-7480, Caracas, 49–62.

———. (2004). "El Departamento de Música de la Escuela de Artes de la UCV: un cuarto de siglo de producción intelectual." *Revista EscritoS en Arte y Cultura*, Fondo Editorial Facultad de Humanidades y Educación-Dirección de Cultura UCV, Año 16, III Etapa, No. 19–20, Caracas, 103–24.

———. (2003). "La visita pastoral del Obispo Mariano Martí a la Diócesis de Caracas y Venezuela, un documento fundamental para la historiografía musical venezolana," en *Extramuros*, No. 18, Nueva Serie, Mayo 2003, Fondo Editorial Facultad de Humanidades y Educación-ISSN: 1316-780, Caracas, 97–116.

———. (2000a). (Intr. y Comp.) *Encuentro Nacional de Educación Musical*. Fondo Editorial de la Facultad de Humanidades y Educación. Universidad Central de Venezuela, Caracas.

———. (2000b). *Noticias musicales en los cronistas de la Venezuela de los siglos XVI-XVIII*. Caracas: Fondo Editorial Humanidades y Educación-Fundación Vicente Emilio Sojo.

Rodríguez Legendre, Fidel (1999). *Caracas, la vida musical y sus sonidos (1830–1888)*. Fondo Editorial 60 años, Contraloría General de la República, Caracas.

Rugeles, Ana Mercedes, María Guinand, and Bolivia Bottome (1986). *Historia del Movimiento Coral y de las Orquestas Juveniles en Venezuela*. Cuadernos Lagoven, Caracas.

Strauss, Rafael A. (2004). "Aproximación a una demografía de la esclavitud negra en Venezuela, siglos XVI y XVII." In *Tierra Firme: Revista de Historia y Ciencias Sociales*, Vol. 22, No. 85, Universidad Central de Venezuela, Caracas, 75–106.

Index

About the Editor

Raymond Torres-Santos is a scholar, educator, administrator, composer, conductor, arranger, and pianist, equally at home in both classical and popular music. He has been described as the most versatile Puerto Rican composer active in the twenty-first century by Malena Kuss in her book *Music in Latin America and the Caribbean: An Encyclopedic History*. His works include orchestral, electronic, and vocal music for the concert hall, ballet, film, theater, television, and radio. In recent years his versatility and music has attracted audiences in Europe, Asia, Latin America, and the United States.

His works have been performed and/or commissioned by the American Composers Orchestra, Los Angeles Philharmonic, Pacific Symphony, North Massachusetts Philharmonic, the symphony orchestras of Reading, Queens, and Washington, DC, Opera, the Bronx Arts Ensemble, Continuum, New Jersey Chamber Music Society, West Point Woodwind Quintet, North Jersey Philharmonic Glee Club, North/South Consonance, Quintet of the Americas, Gabrieli Quintet, and Voix-Touche in the United States; the symphonies of Vancouver and Toronto as well as the Canadian Opera Orchestra in Canada, the Vienna Symphony, Prague Radio Symphony, Georgia Symphony, Soria Symphony, and Warsaw Conservatory of Music Chorus and Orchestra in Europe; the National Chinese Orchestra, Shanghai Symphony, Seoul Symphony, Kaohsiung Philharmonic, and Taipei Philharmonic Orchestras in Asia; the Buenos Aires, Chile, Colombia, and Mexico City Symphony Orchestras in Latin America; and the Puerto Rico and Dominican Republic Symphony and Philharmonic Orchestras in the Caribbean. Featured at the Casals Festival, World Fair in Seville, Venice Biennale, and Op Sail 2000, his music has been used for television and radio programs and choreographed by dance companies.

His compositions and arrangements have been recorded for Sony Music, OSPR, and SJP record labels; published by RTS Music and ANCO; and distributed by commercial retailers such as iTunes, Amazon, and CD Baby. His scholarly work focuses on music education, creativity, multiculturalism, music criticism, and interdisciplinary studies. His recent articles appear in peer-reviewed journals from City University of New York (CUNY) and Hofstra University as well as in a book published by Cambridge Scholar Publishing.

He is the recipient of awards given by ASCAP, BMI, Meet the Composer, American Composers Forum, American Music Center, California State University, and City University of New York. His music for film earned him a Henry Mancini Award, while his skills as a jazz composer earned him the Frank Sinatra Award, both given in Los Angeles.

Torres-Santos is an accomplished arranger, conductor, and pianist. As an arranger, he has worked with the best opera and pop performers, such as Plácido Domingo, Andrea Bocelli, Deborah Voigt, Angela Gheorghiu, Ana María Martínez, Nino Machaidze, Virginia Tola, Anita Rachvilishvili, Rafael Dávila, and Juan Luis Guerra. He has also served as orchestrator for film composers in Hollywood, such as Ralph Burns (*Phantom of the Opera*) and Ry Cooder (*Brewster's Millions*). As a studio jazz pianist, he worked with Maynard Ferguson, Freddie Hubbard, Bobby Shew, and Tito Puente.

As a conductor, he has led the London Session Orchestra, Taipei Philharmonic, Cosmopolitan Symphony, Puerto Rico Symphony and Philharmonic, Dominican Republic National Symphony, Queens Symphony, Adelphi Chamber Orchestra, Bronx Arts Ensemble Orchestra, and Hollywood studio orchestras in concerts and recordings. He has also conducted the symphony orchestras and choruses at UCLA, Manhattan School of Music, Northwestern University, South Carolina University, and California State University. In addition, he served as music director for pop singer Vikki Carr and Dianne Schuur.

Born in Puerto Rico, he studied at the Puerto Rico Conservatory of Music and the University of Puerto Rico. He holds a PhD and MA in composition from the University of California, Los Angeles (UCLA) and completed advanced educational studies at Stanford and Harvard University. He furthered his studies in Europe at the *Ferienkurse für Neue Musik* in Germany and at the University of Padua in Italy. His major professors were Henri Lazarof and David Raksin. He has taught at the City University of New York, California State University, University of Puerto Rico, UCLA, and Rutgers University.

In addition, his experience and skills have led him to administration posts as well as to develop programs for the community in general. He served as chancellor of the Puerto Rico Conservatory of Music; coordinator of the Music Technology Center and chair of the Music Department, both at the University of Puerto Rico; coordinator of the Commercial/Electronic Music Program at California State University, San Bernardino; and dean of the College of the Arts and Communication at William Paterson University as well as dean of the College of the Arts at California State University, Long Beach, where he currently teaches composition and theory.

Furthermore, he is a board member of the American Society of Music Arrangers and Composers (ASMAC) and a voting member of the National Academy of Recording Arts and Sciences (NARAS) for which he has acted as a judge. Recently, he has been nominated to be a board of directors member of the International Society of Music Education (ISME). He has also served as chair of the Diversity Committee, program coordinator, and member of the Professional Development Committee of the College Music Society (CMS).

About the Contributors

ARGENTINA

Claudia Dal Pino is a music professor with degrees in Piano and Music Education from the National Conservatory of Music "Carlos López Buchardo"; in Science of Education from the Argentine University "J. F. Kennedy"; and in Music Pedagogy and Music Instruction from the Instituto Superior del Profesorado "Dr. Joaquín V. González" (I:E.S. J. V. González).. She is a professor of Music Research Methodology at the IUN and teaches Pedagological Aspects at the National Conservatory of Music "Astor Piazzola." She has published research reports and articles in books and journals, such as: *Origins and Foundations of Music Education, The Bulletin of Historical Research in Music Education, Arts Education Policy Review, International Journal of Music Education,* and *Boletín de Investigación Educativo-Musical* (CIEM, Buenos Aires).

Alicia de Couve is a music professor with degrees in Piano from the National Conservatory of Music "Carlos López Buchardo"; in Science of Education from the Argentine Catholic University; in Professorship of Science of Education from the Argentine University "J. F. Kennedy"; in Music Education and Music Pedagogy from the University CAECE; and Music Research from the I:E.S. J. V. González. She is a professor of Music Research Methodology at the IUN and teaches Pedagological Aspects at the National Conservatory of Music "Astor Piazzola." She has published research reports and articles in books and journals, such as: *Origins and Foundations of Music Education, The Bulletin of Historical Research in Music Education, Arts Education Policy Review, International Journal of Music Education,* and *Boletín de Investigación Educativo-Musical* (CIEM, Buenos Aires).

BRAZIL

Sergio Figueiredo (Bachelor in Conducting and Composition, FAAM, Brazil; Master in Music Education, UFRGS, Brazil; PhD, RMIT, Australia; Postdoctoral Studies, IPP Porto, Portugal) is associate professor at the music department of the State University of Santa Catarina–UDESC, Brazil, working in the areas of Choral Singing, Conducting, and Music Education. Currently, Dr. Figueiredo is the coordinator of the Postgraduate Program in Music at UDESC. Accumulating experience as instrumentalist, conductor, and music educator in different contexts, Dr. Figueiredo also develops research in School Music Education, Foundations of Music Education, Initial and Continuing Teacher Education, Educational Policies, Assessment, and Choral Music Education. Dr. Figueiredo is a member of various national and international journals committees. He was a member of the Music Evaluation Commission at INEP (Brazilian Ministry of Education) and also a member of the National Commission for Cultural Incentive–CNIC (Brazilian Ministry of Culture). Dr. Figueiredo was president of the Brazilian Association of Music Education–ABEM (2005–2007 and 2007–2009), and also a member of the Directory of ANPPOM–The Brazilian Association for Research in Music (2011–2013 and

2013–2015). Dr. Figueiredo has been a member of the International Society for Music Education (ISME) for many years, acting as cochair of the ISME Research Commission (2012–2014) and as a member of the ISME Board (2012–2014 and 2014–2016).

CHILE

Ana Teresa Sepúlveda Cofré was born in Chillán, Chile. Between the years 1963 and 1968, she studied at the Saint Teresa Normal School, where she earned a Bachelor in Elementary Education with distinction in 1968. Between 1969 and 1970, she obtained the title of Professor of Elementary Education with a minor in music awarded by the Ministry of Education of Chile. Between 1972 and 1977, she studied Music Pedagogy at the University of Chile, obtaining a master's degree in Music Education. In 1988, she received a PhD degree in Pedagogy from the Pontifical University in Salamanca, Spain. Her dissertation is titled *La Presencia de la Música en el Sistema Educativo Secundario Chileno, a través de Cinco Reformas Educativas: 1873–1935–1945–1967–1981.* She pursued further studies in Dynamic Expression, Orff Music Pedagogy, Martenot Music Pedagogy, Psycho-Motorics, Music Therapy, Dalcroze Rhythm, Research Methodology, and Classical Guitar in Madrid, Salzburgo, Paris, Salamanca, and Santiago. Her teaching activities began in 1968 as a general teacher. Since then, she has taught at different levels in the Chilean school system and in different types of schools. From 1981 to 2010, she served as a professor of Music Education Methodology at the Metropolitan University of Educational Sciences in Santiago, Chile. Since 2014, she has been a professor of Didactic Music at Mayor University in Santiago, Chile.

COLOMBIA

Constanza Rincón holds a bachelor in Music Performance from the National University of Colombia, a master of Music from the University of Minnesota, United States, a master in Cultural Management from the University of Barcelona, Spain, and completed a PhD in Music Education at the University Computense in Madrid, Spain. She teaches Music Theory from beginner to advanced level at the Professional Music Conservatory "Padre Antonio Soler" in Madrid, Spain. Her musical career has included active performance, teaching, researching, and writing. She has twelve years of experience working and creating arts education programs in cooperation with public and private organizations aimed at helping children from several backgrounds overcome social circumstances through creative development using music as the central component of the projects. Her research interests include music making from early childhood to adolescence, its social functions, and its contributions to human development in a particular society. Among others, she has published book chapters and journal articles on issues related to the different aspects of music education in Latin America and the experience of attending musical performances at youth education programs. Aside from the academic world she has published several children's tales that have been used as pedagogical tools in the field of early music education.

COSTA RICA

Guillermo Rosabal-Coto teaches undergraduate courses in Music Education Foundations, Methods, and Research at the School of Music of the University of Costa Rica, where he also served as chair of the Music Education Department. Prior to his university tenure appointment, he taught at elementary and secondary schools, performed in orchestras and chamber ensembles, and served as arts manager to the National Symphony Orchestra and National Opera Company of Costa Rica. He has made presentations at seminars and conferences in Brazil, China, Costa Rica, Finland, Norway, and the United States. His articles have been published in *Action, Criticism and Theory in Music Education* (ACT), *Canadian Music Educator* (CME), *Gender, Education, Music and Society* (GEMS), *Finnish Journal of Music Education* (FJME), and journals in Spanish. He is on the editorial boards of ACT and *Epistemus*. In his native Costa Rica, Rosabal-Coto also works as arts and music education consultant to both the Ministry of Public Education and the Ministry of Culture, as well as to international nongovernment organizations such as UNDP, UNESCO, UNICEF, and OEI. He holds a doctorate in Music from the University of Helsinki-Sibelius Academy (Finland), a master's degree in Music Education from Brandon University (Canada), and a bachelor's degree in Bassoon Performance from the University of Costa Rica.

CUBA

Ricardo N. López-León has a doctorate in Education from the University of Granada (Spain) with a European mention from the University of Bologna (Italy), a master's degree in Music Education from Miami University (USA), and a bachelor's degree in Musical Arts from University of Puerto Rico. Conferences and workshops around the world are among the highlights of his musical and academic career. His book, *Evaluación en educación musical. ¿Técnica, arte o problema?* (2015), is widely used in music education programs as well as coauthored many others. Some of his articles have been published by prestigious reviews as the *International Journal of Music Education*. He currently serves as full professor at the University of Puerto Rico College of Education and the graduate program in music at the Inter-American University in Puerto Rico. He continues to undertake research into key areas of education, music, assessment, measurement, and evaluation in music education and history.

Oswaldo Lorenzo Quiles teaches Musical Education at the University of Granada (Spain) from 1995. He coordinates the Master/PhD postgraduate program "Music Education: A Multidisciplinary Perspective" at the University of Granada, Tamaulipas University, and Chihuahua University (Mexico); and directs several doctoral thesis in different countries. He holds a PhD in Philosophy and Sciences of Education with Extraordinary Prize of Doctorate from the National Distance Education University of Spain. He is the author of several research articles published in Journal Citation Reports and Arts and Humanities Citation Index journals, such as *Psychology of Music, Musicae Scientiae, Psicodidáctica*, and *International Review of the Aesthetics and Sociology of Music* (IRASM).

DOMINICAN REPUBLIC

Susana Acra-Brache began her musical training in Santo Domingo at the age of nine. She earned a bachelor's degree and a master's degree in Music Education and Conducting from the Hartt School at the University of Hartford. She studied conducting with Harold Farberman and Doreen Rao. She continued to pursue her passion for music education and earned a PhD at the Esther Boyer College of Music of Temple University. She founded the *Centro de Pedagogia Musical de la Republica Dominicana* and *Crescendo*. She has been a pioneer in the field of early childhood music education influenced by the teachings of Beth Bolton, John Feierabend, and Edwin Gordon. Dr. Acra-Brache has provided many workshops, seminars, and courses on music education in the Dominican Republic and taught Choral Conducting at the *Universidad Autónoma de Santo Domingo*. She is the first female Dominican orchestra conductor and was awarded by UNESCO the distinction of Artist for Peace.

ECUADOR

Ketty Wong-Cruz is an Ecuadorian musicologist and ethnomusicologist who joined the University of Kansas faculty in 2006, having taught previously at the University of Texas at Austin and in her home country of Ecuador. She received a master's and a PhD in Ethnomusicology from the University of Texas at Austin and a master's in Musicology from the Moscow Conservatory P. I. Tchaikovsky. Her research interests focus on Latin American art, folk, and traditional music, nationalism, identity, migration, popular music, and ballroom dancing in China. She has published articles in international musical encyclopedias and scholarly journals. Her book *La música nacional: Identidad, mestizaje y migración en Ecuador* won the Casa de las Americas Musicology Award in 2010. The English version of this book won the Latin American Studies Association–Ecuadorian

Section Book Award in 2013. A former Fulbright Senior Scholar in China, she is the author of the book *Luis Humberto Salgado: Un quijote de la música* and a member of Ecuador's National Academy of History.

EL SALVADOR

Cristian Daniel Guandique Araniva is a cellist born in El Salvador. He began his musical studies at the National Center for the Arts in El Salvador. In 2003 he attended the University of Costa Rica, where he earned a Bachelor in Music in 2009 with emphasis in cello under the tutelage of Elena Kharina Anatolievna. He is a member of the Contemporary Ensemble of the University, with which he recorded and sponsored Costa Rican music. He is also the principal cellist of the Municipal Orchestra of Heredia and the University Orchestra. In addition, he is a professor of cello and bass in the preparatory division of the Western campus of the University of Costa Rica and the School of Music of Pavas. Currently, he is a master's student at the University of Costa Rica.

GUATEMALA

Edgar Cajas, a native of Guatemala, holds a PhD in Music Education from the University of Oklahoma and a master's degree in Church Music and Piano Performance from Southwestern Baptist Theological Seminary in Fort Worth, Texas. He has completed additional studies at the Orff Institute in Salzburg, Austria; the Dalcroze Institute at Carnegie Mellon University; and Indiana University. He founded and served as the first director of the Christian School for Music Teachers "Alfredo Colom" and the first coordinator for the Music Education Department at Universidad del Valle both in Guatemala City. Currently, he is an associate professor of Music and coordinator of the Music Education Program at Houston Baptist University. Previously, he taught in the School of Music at Southwestern Baptist Theological Seminary in Fort Worth, Texas. He has published several articles on music education and church music and has been a writer for children's choir periodicals. Dr. Cajas has lectured on Music Education Methods, Piano Pedagogy, and Church Music in the United States, Latin America, and Spain. In October 2010 the government of Guatemala conferred him the Ambassador of Peace Award for his contributions to education and art in the country.

JAMAICA

Marilyn J. Anderson has been the dean of the College of Humanities, Behavioral and Social Sciences (HUBSS) at Northern Caribbean University. She is a licentiate of the Royal Schools of Music (LRSM), and during studies in America at Eastern Michigan University (EMU) she obtained a bachelor's degree in Business Administration and also a bachelor's degree in Music Education with emphasis in Choral Training and Directing. She also took private lessons in piano pedagogy and piano performance with one of the icons of the celebrated Mehta family, pianist Dada Mehta. Dr. Anderson taught music in the Detroit Public School System for five years and returned to Jamaica as lecturer and, eventually, chair of the Music Department of Northern Caribbean University (NCU), where she was a respected vocal and choral coach. She later attended Florida International University, where she pursued doctoral studies in Curriculum and Instruction (EdD). Her book, *Reading in Music Education: Philosophical and Educational Perspectives*, published in January 2008, was well received in the Jamaican school system. She has also written and published several articles on various aspects of music in Jamaican magazines and newspapers. Furthermore, she has been a member of the Assessment Team of the University Council of Jamaica.

MEXICO

Antonio Fermín has been published extensively on curriculum and audience development for the young. As manager of Elementary School Programs at Carnegie Hall, Dr. Fermín developed and implemented programs to motivate young audiences, including providing New York City public school teachers with pedagogical workshops to advance their teaching skills on cross-curricular music integration. For the past twenty-five years he has created comprehensive music curricula for grades pre-K–12 reflecting effective experimental and progressive approaches. He has developed programs for Scholastic, Inc., Carnegie Hall's Education Department, the Aspen Music Festival and School, and has served as project editor for nationwide curricula at McGraw-Hill Education. A graduate of the New England Conservatory and Juilliard School, he holds a PhD from New York University. A Visiting Fellow at Harvard University, Dr. Fermín has taught at Columbia Grammar School, New York University, and Juilliard School Pre-College Division.

NICARAGUA

Lylliam Meza de Roche is a music education professor with a higher education degree in Humanities with emphasis in Arts and Letters from the Central American University (UCA) in Nicaragua, and a master's degree in Music Technology from the University of Salamanca, Spain. Other studies include music education in the University of Chile (INTEM). She has vast experience in all levels of formal and informal education: from childhood, elementary, middle school to high school and university. In addition, she has served as an education consultant for international organization projects such as UNESCO and the Inter-American Development Bank.

PANAMA

Jaime Ingram Jaén was born in Panama. His first studies were realized at the La Salle College in Panama City. He began piano studies at home with his mother and later at the National Conservatory of Music and Oratory in Panama. After earning a Bachelor in Sciences and Letters from La Salle College in Panama City, he pursued studies at Juilliard School of Music in New York where he won a special prize to study with Mme. Olga Samarof. After earning the Diploma Course of Piano, he further studied in France at the National Conservatory of Music with the grand pianist Yves Nat, and later on in Vienna, Austria, with Prof. Brunno Seidlhofer. As a distinguished concertist, he has given many piano solo recitals in Europe and the Americas, as well as played concerti with orchestra and two-piano recitals with original repertoire with his wife, Nelly Hirsch, a distinguished pupil of Sousa Lima, in São Paulo, Brasil. He has been member of the jury in many prestigious international piano competitions, including Lisbon (*Vianna da Motta International Piano Competition*), Macao, Moscow (*Tchaikowsky International Piano Competition*), Valencia (*Jose Iturbi International Piano Competition*), as well as in Toledo (Spain) and La Habana (Cuba). He has been the creator of the *Asociación Nacional de Conciertos* (National Concert Association) as well as the creator of the *Panama International Piano Competition*. He has been honored with the University Prize and with an honorary doctor degree granted by the University of Panama. He has taught at the National Conservatory of Music of Panama, the São Paulo Academy of Music in Brasil, as well as in the music department of the National University of Panama. He is author of many articles and books on music and musicians. Furthermore, he has held various administrative and diplomatic positions as ambassador of the Republic of Panama in Spain, the Holy See in Rome, Morroco, and Argentina. He is currently the director general of the editorial of the Panamá National University.

Néstor Castillo was born in Santiago de Veraguas, Panama. He holds bachelor, master and doctorate degrees in orchestral conducting from universities in Brazil and the United States. His artistic and professional activities as a conductor, teacher, composer, poet, and author include conducting symphony orchestras and chamber ensembles in Panama, Brazil, and the United States, as well as presentations in Germany, Costa Rica, China, Japan, and Mexico. As a music professor at the University of Panama, he has served as Music Department Chair, coordinator of the Music Master's Program, director of the Graduate Studies and Research Program, dean of the College of the Fine Arts, and vice-chancellor of the Extension Program. Since 1998, he has also led the University Philharmonic Orchestra, which he founded.

PERU

Victoria Waxman is the director of Liberal Studies and a faculty member at Boston Architectural College. She received her PhD in World History at Northeastern University, and her research focuses on Cold War cultural exchange and its impact on American life in the first three decades of the war. In particular, her current research examines how the Moiseyev Dance Company's first tour of the United States in 1958 represents a cross-section of American views of gender, race, and ethnicity and cultural identity.

TRINIDAD AND TOBAGO

Hollis Liverpool is a professor of Calypso Art at the University of Trinidad and Tobago. He was educated at Patience Hill R. C. and Nelson Street Boys' R. C. primary schools, St. Mary's College, the Government Training College for Teachers (GTC), the University of the West Indies at St. Augustine, and the University of Michigan at Ann Arbor, Michigan. Besides O and A levels, he holds a Trained Teacher's Certificate, a postgraduate diploma in Education, a BA in History and Sociology, an MA in World History, an MA in African History, a certificate in Philosophy, and a PhD in History and Ethnomusicology. He taught primary and secondary schools over a period of thirty-five years, then served in the Ministry of Culture as Cultural Officer 111 and Director of Culture between the years 1993 to 1999, when he retired from the public service. He founded and served as the first director of the Carnival Institute and has carried out extensive research in all areas of culture pertaining to the Caribbean in general and Trinidad and Tobago in particular. He served as associate professor of History at the University of the Virgin Islands and was named an Honorary Distinguished Fellow of the University of Trinidad and Tobago in 2006. He is the current head of the Academy for Arts, Letters, Culture and Public Affairs. He has written many papers and several books, including *Rituals of Power and Rebellion* (2001), and has addressed several worldwide conferences on Carnival and culture generally. As Calypsonian Chalkdust, he has recorded over three hundred calypsoes. In terms of calypso performance, he has won the Buy Local Competition in Trinidad five times, the King of the World Calypso Contest in St. Thomas on eight occasions, the World Calypso Monarch on the two occasions it was held in New York, and the Calypso Monarch of Trinidad and Tobago seven times.

URUGUAY

Marita Fornaro Bordolli holds degrees in Musicology (1986), Anthropological Sciences (1983) and Historical Sciences (1978) from the University of the Republic, Uruguay. She holds master's degrees in Music and Anthropology from the University of Salamanca, Spain. She has been director of the Music School. She has done research on Music and Popular Culture, Music and Theatres, and Musical Education in Uruguay, Brazil, Cuba, Spain, and Portugal. Currently, she is the coordinator of the Department of Musicology at the School of Music and the Center for Research in Scenic-Musical Arts in the northwest campus of the University of the Republic. In addition, she was the secretary (2012–2014) of the Latin America section of the International Association for the Study of Popular Music (IASPM), and she was its president (2010–2012).

VENEZUELA

Mariantonia Palacios holds degrees as Performer Piano Professor from the *Juan Manuel Olivares Escuela de Música* (1982); Bachelor of Arts from the *Universidad Central de Venezuela* (UCV, 1984); *Maestro Compositor* from the *Juan José Landaeta Conservatorio* (1987); *Magíster Scientiarum* in Latin American Musicology from UCV (1998); and *Magister Artium* from the University of Costa Rica (2003). She is also a Titular Professor at the *Universidad Central de Venezuela* and Visiting Professor at the *Universidad Simón Bolívar, Universidad Metropolitana* (Caracas), and University of Costa Rica. In addition, she is the curator of the collection *Music in Colonial America* and cocurator of the collection *Clásicos de la Literatura Pianística Venezolana* and *Fuentes para el estudio de la música en Venezuela*. She was the former director of the School of Arts (UCV), the Choir of the Teresa Carreño Theater (Caracas), and the National Opera Company of Costa Rica, as well as coordinator of the Latin American Musicology Master. Currently, she coordinates the Digital Arts Center (UCV) and the Juan Meserón Musicological Digital Library. Awards and distinctions include, among others, the *Rházes Hernández López* National Research Award in Musicology, Caracas, 1998; *Premio de Musicología Casa de las Américas* Honourable Mention, Havana, 1999; *Samuel Claro Valdés* Honorable Mention Award, Chile, 2000; *José María Vargas* Award for academic merits, Caracas, 2004; CENAL Honorable Mention Award, Caracas, 2005; Municipal Music Award in Musical Research, Caracas, 2009; and CENAL Honorable Mention Award, Caracas, 2010.